DICTATORS
AND
TYRANTS

DICTATORS AND TYRANTS

Absolute Rulers and Would-Be Rulers in World History

Alan Axelrod
and
Charles Phillips

Facts On File®

AN INFOBASE HOLDINGS COMPANY

DICTATORS AND TYRANTS

Copyright © 1995 by Zenda, Inc.

Facts On File, Inc.
460 Park Avenue South
New York NY 10016

Library of Congress Cataloging-in-Publication Data

Axelrod, Alan, 1952–
    Dictators and tyrants / Alan Axelrod and Charles Phillips.
        p.   cm.
    Includes bibliographical references and index.
    ISBN 0-8160-2866-4
    1. Dictators—Biography.   2. Despotism—History.   I. Phillips,
Charles, 1948–   .   II. Title.
D107.A84   1994
920.02—dc20   94-6200

Facts On File books are available at special discounts when purchased in bulk quantities for businesses, associations, institutions or sales promotions. Please call our Special Sales Department in New York at 212/683-2244 or 800/322-8755.

Jacket design by Donald West
Printed in the United States of America

VB VC 10 9 8 7 6 5 4 3 2 1

This book is printed on acid-free paper.

Contents

Acknowledgments   vii
Introduction   ix
A–Z entries   1
Index   325

Acknowledgments

Although it was the ancient Greeks who first defined the concept of tyranny, absolute rulers—tyrants, dictators, and despots—have existed at least as long as history itself and, doubtless, much longer. We have had a great deal of help in conducting our survey of the vast field of tyranny.

We were assisted in research and writing by a remarkable team that includes Candace Floyd, John Kelly, Kurt Kemper, and Curtis Utz. Facts On File editors Kathy Ishizuka and Drew Silver treated the project with their customary skill and care. We are also very grateful to Michael G. Laraque for superb copyediting.

Introduction:
On Tyranny and Tyrants

For those of us living in 20th-century America, representative democracy, government based on "natural" rights and legitimated by a social contract (called a constitution) establishing government for, of, and by the people, appears to be quite typical a form of government, the only alternative to which is some form of tyranny. Authoritarian rule, whether it comes in the totalitarianism of the bureaucratized workers' states spawned by socialism or the romanticized terror fostered by modern fascism or the blunt and brutal machinations of mostly third-world, mostly military dictators, has been today largely discredited, at least in theory.

But throughout history, republics have been rare and democracies virtually nonexistent. There was Athens in the 4th century B.C., the 200-year Roman Republic, the early city-states of the Italian Renaissance, and the modern republics and democracies born during the Enlightenment's 18th-century revolutions. But, often, even these were (and, in many cases, are) representative governments in name only, plastering over with ideological theories the real struggle between a few elites and a mass of commoners. Ancient republics, like today's democracies, were frequently subject to civic strife between the rich and established and "the people"; as Machiavelli described the situation, "the former desiring to command, the latter unwilling to obey." Even today, such civic strife often leads to the longing for strong leadership, for the individual president or premier or prime minister who can "get things done."

The difference, of course, is that when we find such leaders, they rule in the name of the people, not by divine right or ancient privilege; we circumscribe their powers with elections and term limits and constitutions; and only when they overstep such boundaries do we call them tyrants. The 20th century is no stranger to such as these. Even in more ancient times, however, rulers were not considered tyrants or despots, regardless of the brutality of their rule or the absolute control of their subjects, unless they crossed the lines that defined their sovereignty.

This, then, is the major criterion by which we chose the tyrants, dictators, and despots included in this book: men—and a few women—whose lust for power, or ambition, or even love of country, people, or empire led them beyond the boundaries of their mandate, whether that mandate was provided by the people they ruled, by the god they served, or by traditional privileges they enjoyed. In other words, to some significant degree at least at some point in their careers, they ruled illegitimately by the terms of the society in which they originally came to power.

One did not qualify as a tyrant simply by wielding immense power and authority over human life and social destiny, since that would make almost every ancient king and emperor—not to mention a modern-day president or two, say an Abraham Lincoln or a Franklin D. Roosevelt—tyrants, and even to the most politically correct among us, such a notion is absurd.

Nor did exhibiting a lust for power and a penchant for arbitrary rule, what we might call the "tyrannical" personality, necessarily qualify a figure for inclusion here. During the mid-20th century, certain Populist governors in the American South—Huey Long, James K. Vardaman, and George Wallace, for example—and even a Northern mayor or two—such as Chicago's Richard J. Daley—clearly exhibited such personalities, and were often called tyrants and despots, without ever truly acquiring the authority needed to wield absolute power outside the bounds of their state or municipal governments.

Conversely, neither ability nor good intentions were enough by themselves to disqualify a ruler from being considered a despot. Many of the Greek tyrants were able men, and Augustus Caesar certainly worked in the long-term interest of the Roman Empire he more or less created, but they were tyrants nevertheless, who seized power illegitimately and exercised it for the most part absolutely and arbitrarily.

In addition, our notion of who is a tyrant or despot has much to do with the historical development of the forms of government. The Greeks called the rule of a man who took power by force a *monarchia*, or "sole rule," and the man himself a *tyrannus*, after a Lydian word for king or ruler that had just come into general use. A number of such tyrants, the first on record being Cypselus of Corinth, came to power suddenly in the 7th century B.C. Greek historian Thucydides, writing centuries later, thought that "in general, tyrannies were established in the city-states as revenues were increasing, when Greece was becoming more powerful and progressing in the acquisition of capital wealth."

Indeed, wealth—or the promise of wealth—seemed a prerequisite for the birth of tyranny. It was in the 7th century that money—invented most likely by the Lydian tyrant Gyges, who minted coins out of electrum, a natural alloy of gold and silver found throughout Asia Minor—first began to circulate in Greece. Not only portable wealth, but land, too, played a role in the rise of the tyrants, each of whom proposed land reforms that transferred wealth to citizen armies, the hoplites, on which their power rested. In fact, many have argued that it was the rise of the phalanx—a close-drill plebeian infantry formation—as a replacement for the aristocratic cavalry that provided the ideological fuel for tyrannical government.

Backed by an army of commoners, funded by new money, and promising the redistribution of land, the minor scions of aristocratic clans seized power throughout Greece and Asia Minor in the name of reform. Accompanied constantly by bodyguards, they were always on the alert for enemies: those among their own following who might be ambitious enough to do as *they* had done and those among the disgruntled ruling elites they had disenfranchised, deposed, and often banished. The popularly supported despots often undertook massive public works to justify their tyrannical rule, and they provided a measure of stability in a century of economic expansion. But the very nature of "sole rule" soon put the lie to its promise of reform. The last thing a tyrant wanted was others growing as strong as he, and in the long run he did little to distribute the growing wealth and thus failed to alter the social conditions that had produced him in the first place.

Since at least ancient Greece, then, the amassing of wealth, betrayed social reform, a military power-base, and rampant—if often justified—paranoia have been associated with tyranny. Even before that,

despotism proper seems inextricably bound to a huge bureaucracy, both religious and secular. Political historian Karl A. Wittfogel has argued that such bureaucracy is endemic to what he called "Oriental despotism," though the societies he so described were neither all in the East nor were they characteristic of all Eastern societies. The central notion of Oriental despotism is that our earliest civilizations grew up around water—the Nile, the Tigris and Euphrates, the Yangtze and Yellow Rivers. Such hydraulic civilizations required large-scale, government-managed waterworks for irrigation and flood control. Wherever the need for substantial and centralized government arose, its representatives soon monopolized political power and dominated the economy, creating an absolutist state based on a bureaucratic network that directed the forced labor required for the massive water-management projects. The bureaucrats became identified with the dominant religion, other centers of power atrophied, and the ruler, the despot, became a god.

Whether irrigation was the primary cause of the coercive political institution (as Wittfogel argued), or whether it merely helped to consolidate centralized political control (as Wittfogel's detractors argued), it is hard to deny that something like "Oriental despotism" characterized the hydraulic civilizations of ancient Egypt, Mesopotamia, China, and India, as well as pre-Columbian Central and South American cultures like those of the Olmecs, Mayans, and Aztecs.

Augustus Caesar, of course, also created a bureaucracy and made himself into a god as he created the Roman Empire. Religious bureaucracy also became associated with the Persian empires, whose Zoroastrian magi of the 3rd century A.D. merged church and state in the notion of *farr*—mystical majesty—emblematically represented by the *qurz*, the crown and scepter we have all come to associate with kings since the so-called new monarchs established their hereditary houses in Europe during the 17th century.

Russia became heir to both traditions, with a czar—like the German *kaiser*, a word derived from the Latin *caesar*—ruling through a rigid bureaucracy and by the divine grace of the Orthodox God. The 20th-century totalitarianisms that replaced czar, kaiser, and even caesar alike—Soviet, Nazi, and Italian Fascist—could do without neither the bureaucracy nor the quasi-religious ceremonial trappings.

Finally, tyrants seem traditionally to come to power during times of turmoil and strife. We know little about the "Oriental despots," since most of their history is based on obscure archaeological evidence rather than anything like detailed chronicles, though it is clear that Chinese dynasties always grew from the civil wars and years—sometimes centuries—of unrest that followed the decline of the previous dynasty. No less an authority than Aristotle claims that the birth of the Greek tyrants came about as a result of the chaos created by warring oligarchies. Augustus took power when the struggle between the hoary Roman Senate, the primary political body of the Republic, and the "dictators" who assumed control in declared states of emergency had degenerated into a program of public assassination. Italy's 14th-century *signoria* (rule of one man) replaced that region's republics after intrigue and assassination had led a number of cities to despair of finding a republican solution to civic strife. The *signori* (lords) themselves were the precursors of Europe's new monarchs—Spain's Charles V, England's Henry VII, Muscovy's Ivan III, to name a few—who first came to absolute power in the search for order that followed the absolute devastation of the Thirty Years' War. Napoléon became emperor of France after the Revolution had finally deconstructed itself. And in our own time, Stalin, Mussolini, Franco, and Hitler all took office as a result of World War I's destruction of Europe's ruling houses and the collapse of the world's capitalist economies.

The classical tyrant is a man (rarely a woman) backed by some sort of military loyal to him alone, who generally seizes power or exercises it illegitimately in times of turmoil, promising social reform while enriching himself and his friends, and who suppresses those in whose name he rules with brutal terror and arbitrary force through the auspices of a rigid bureaucracy and a ceremonial display of their own authority. Perhaps only one-third of the figures included in this book illustrate this classic definition, although most of the others partake of it in varying but recognizable degrees. This reflects the fact that the notion of tyranny itself has historically broadened to include all forms of absolute rule, dictatorship, and despotism. Moreover, it must be noted that by no means are all of the personalities in this book bad, evil, wicked, deluded, depraved, or even simply selfish. Absolute rulers have often acted from what can only be described as the best of intentions and the height of wisdom. It is also true that absolute rulers have sometimes brought economic and (though very rarely) even spiritual benefit to the people they govern. Yet, as Lord Acton observed, all power tends to corrupt, and absolute power corrupts absolutely. The "benevolent despots" comprise a distinct minority in the roster of tyranny, and vesting any individual with authority beyond challenge invites cruelty, persecution, and programs of physical death and moral devastation.

There have always been tyrants, dictators, and despots; there are tyrants, dictators, and despots today; and if we allow it, there will be tyrants, dictators, and despots in all the days to come.

A

Abbad I [Abbad ibn-Muhammad abu-'Amr] (d. 1042)
Exploiting the chaos of Spain during the early Middle Ages, Abbad I became king of Seville and founded the Abbadide dynasty.

Nothing is known about the birth, childhood, or early career of this Moorish ruler, who capitalized on some two decades of border warfare in central Spain in order to establish a dynastic state.

Abbad first appears in Spanish history as *qadi*—magistrate—of Seville some time before 1023, the year in which he became king of Seville. Abbad established himself in this position by uniting local aristocrats who feared the anarchy reigning during the period of the Córdoba caliphate. Following the death of Adbulmalik-al-Mozaffar in 1031, Abbad I was also recognized as suzerain by most of Muslim Spain.

During the period from 1023 until his death in 1042, Abbad successfully waged continual warfare against Ferdinand I of Castile, Ramiro I of Aragón, and various minor Muslim rulers. He not only held his power, but established the Abbadide dynasty, which endured until 1095.

Abbadid al-Mu'tadid (1042–69)
Helping to establish the Abbadid dynasty, Abbadid al-Mu'tadid was vigorous and cruel in the persecution of his enemies.

Abbadid al-Mu'tadid's father declared independence for Seville from the caliphate of Córdoba in 1023, leaving Abbadid al-Mu'tadid to maintain its independence, to consolidate his own power, and to expand his territory. Abbadid al-Mu'tadid was a gifted politician as well as a poet and patron of the arts, but he was above all else ruthless, his ambition matched only by his cruelty.

Some time around 1048, Abbadid al-Mu'tadid began a campaign of conquest in the frontier region, during which he subdued and annexed five principalities. In 1053, he invited a number of minor Berber princes from the south to his palace in Seville, suffocating them to death by treating them to a steam bath, having first sealed up all of the openings in the bathhouse. He then promptly seized their kingdoms of Arcos, Morón, and Ronda.

Abbadid al-Mu'tadid was executed by his own son, the crown prince Isma'il, who rebelled in an effort to create his own kingdom. Isma'il subsequently perished in the course of the rebellion, leaving Abbadid al-Mu'tadid's other son, Muhammad, as the last ruler of the Abbadid dynasty, which was destined to fall to encroaching Christians.

Abbas I [the Great] (1571–1629)
This warlike shah did much to strengthen the Persian Empire, in the process transforming the Persian army into a disciplined and formidable military force.

Abbas I became shah of Persia when his father, Mohammed Khudabanda, abdicated in 1587. Prior to this, since 1581, Abbas had been governor of the province of Khorasan. As shah, Abbas acted first to make peace with the Turks, ceding to them some western provinces of Persia in order to devote his forces to fighting the Uzbeks, who in 1590 threatened invasion. War against the Uzbeks lasted from 1590 to 1598. Abbas defeated an Uzbek force in the Battle of Herat in 1597, but he lost the decisive Battle of Balkh the next year. Nevertheless, his performance in the long war put him in a position to negotiate a very favorable peace.

Within four years, Abbas renewed warfare with the Ottoman Turks, storming Tabriz in 1602 and settling in for a long, cruel, and bitter siege that lasted until October 21, 1603, when the city at last fell to him. Abbas proved ruthless and unstoppable against the Ottomans. After the fall of Tabriz, he marched on Erevan, Kars, and Shirvan during 1603 to 1604. While the Turks prepared a counteroffensive during 1604 to 1605, Abbas set about modernizing his army. When the Ottoman army under Sultan Ahmed attacked at the Battle of Sis in 1606, the army of Abbas I won a decisive victory and was free to overrun Azerbaijan, Kurdistan, Mosul, and Baghdad. War between Persia and the Ottomans dragged on, however, until 1612, when Abbas concluded a peace agreement with Turkey.

From 1613 to 1615, Abbas invaded Georgia, which he compelled to acknowledge his sovereignty. This triggered a new war with the Turks, who repeatedly attacked Tabriz during 1616–18. Abbas not only held the Turks off, he won the Battle of Sultania in 1618 and, later that same year, concluded another peace with Turkey. The treaty of 1612 had required Persia to pay tribute to the Ottomans. The treaty of 1618 reduced this tribute.

1

In 1622, Abbas enlisted the aid of British ships in fighting the Portuguese and the Mongol Empire, capturing Kamdahar in 1623. This once again provoked war with Turkey and forced Abbas to lead an army to the relief of Baghdad during 1624–25. Abbas took the offensive during this period until a military mutiny forced the Turks to withdraw. Although border clashes continued intermittently during the balance of Abbas' reign, he had generally succeeded in expanding the Persian Empire and securing its sovereignty.

Further Reading: Iskandar Munshi. *The History of Shah Abbas the Great* (Boulder, Colo.: Westview Press, 1978).

Abd Allah   [Abdullahi] (d. 1899)

Successor to al-MAHDI as the leader of the Sudanese political and theological movement during the late 19th century, Abd Allah was the last native leader before British colonial rule.

Abd Allah, also called Abdullahi, was a fervent follower of the Mahdi and became his closest adviser. He was instrumental in the decisive defeat of the British General Lord Gordon at Khartoum in January 1885. Upon the Mahdi's death in June 1885, Abdullahi rose as the handpicked successor to lead the Mahdist state.

The fanatical nature of the power base within the Mahdist state sparked a war of succession in which Abdullahi emerged victorious by instilling in his followers the belief that he received divine instruction from the deceased Mahdi. He also maintained firm control over the military, most notably the vaunted Black Flag divisions stationed in the capital of Omdurman.

Once his power was secured, Abdullahi set about capitalizing on the expansionist momentum begun by the Mahdi. He embarked on a multi-front offensive against Ethiopia and Egypt in 1888. Having counted on more support from the Egyptian peasantry and less resistance from the remaining Anglo-Egyptian forces, Abdullahi was dealt a devastating defeat in Egypt in 1889. Yet he managed to survive both the expense of his military defeats and the effects of a famine, further consolidating his power. Inexorably, however, British forces, though still stunned by Gordon's defeat, began a systematic reconquest of the Sudan in 1896. Abdullahi could match neither the resources nor the firepower of the British.

He continued to resist for two more years, but was at length forced to evacuate Omdurman in 1898. Returning with the remnants of his army a year later, Abdullahi engaged the Anglo-Egyptians outside of Omdurman in November 1899 at the Battle of Karari. He was killed in the fighting, and the Mahdist state ceased to exist. The dawn of the 20th century found the Anglo-Egyptians firmly entrenched on Sudanese soil.

Further Reading: P. M. Holt. *A Modern History of the Sudan* (London: Wiedenfeld & Nicolson, 1961); P. M. Holt. *The Mahdist State in the Sudan, 1881–1898* (Oxford, Clarendon Press, 1958).

Abd al-Mu'min   (reigned 1130–63)

Caliph of the Almohad dynasty, Abd al-Mu'min unified the Berber peoples and ruled all of North Africa.

Born to a humble potter, Abd al-Mu'min was a scholarly youth who learned Arabic and studied religion. Moving to the east about 1117 to complete his studies, Abd al-Mu'min encountered Ibn Tumart, a self-styled Mahdi (messiah), en route. The Mahdi's teachings, his religious fervor, and his charisma persuaded Abd al-Mu'min to abandon his intellectual career and follow Ibn Tumart. From this time until the Mahdi's death in 1130, Abd al-Mu'min became one of the Mahdi's key lieutenants. When Ibn Tumart declared his opposition to the ruling Almoravid dynasty around 1119, he and his followers took to the mountainous High Atlas region, where they founded a small Almohad state and began guerrilla operations against the Almoravid regime. After the Mahdi's death in 1130, Abd al-Mu'min was declared the Almohad caliph.

Abd al-Mu'min's first task was to carry on the fight against the Almoravids. Like so many other successful guerrilla strategists in history, Abd al-Mu'min was patient, diligent, and ruthless. He waged guerrilla warfare on the Almoravids for 15 years, gaining control of the High Atlas, Middle Atlas, and Rif regions. By 1145, he had sufficiently damaged the Almoravids and built enough of a following to engage them in open battle, soundly defeating them that year.

The Almohads then began moving west through the coastal plain of Morocco, conquering as they went. After laying siege to Marrakesh, they stormed the city in 1147 and slaughtered the Almoravids inside. Abd al-Mu'min chose Marrakesh as his capital and began a relentless consolidation of his power by brutally purging all those whose loyalty he questioned or whose religious fervor he doubted. He spent the next 12 years wandering the North African plain, conquering all in his way: Constantine in 1151, Tunisia, in 1158, and Tripoli in 1159. By 1160, the Almohad regime ruled all of North Africa west of Egypt and a good part of Muslim Spain as well.

The dynasty began by Abd al-Mu'min endured long after his death in 1163. His two immediate successors were extremely capable and faithfully carried on his policies and beliefs. The Almohad regime maintained control over the North African coast for 500 years.

Abd ar-Rahman III (891–961)

The greatest ruler of Muslim Spain, Abd ar-Rahman extended his empire and became the first designated caliph in the region.

On the death of his grandfather, Abd Allah, in 912, Abd ar-Rahman ascended to the Muslim throne in a Spain that was racked by civil war and increasingly threatened by Christian encroachment. Abd ar-Rahman's first priority was to subdue the rebels who were rife in the mountainous regions of the southeast. Ten days after his accession, he exhibited the severed head of a rebel leader, and for the next two decades, he made annual expeditions to put down additional rebellions. In 917, the most powerful of the rebels, Hafsun, died, and by 928, Abd ar-Rahman had taken Bobastro, the center of the main rebellion. Hafsun's sons were executed, and the last embers of dissent extinguished.

While securing the southeastern edges of his kingdom, Abd ar-Rahman turned to the north in an effort to stem incursions by the Christians. The king of León, Ordono II, led an expedition into Muslim territory in 913, visiting wholesale slaughter there. Abd ar-Rahman began a campaign of revenge and soundly defeated the combined armies of León and Navarre at the Battle of Valdejunquera on July 26, 920. Having gained revenge, the caliph next sought submission, leading an army into Navarre during the spring of 924 and razing the capital of Pamplona.

Navarre's new king, Ramiro II, proved more formidable than his predecessors, and Rahman was not able to dominate him as he had Ordono. After enduring a series of minor defeats, Ramiro destroyed Abd ar-Rahman's army at the Battle of Simancas in 939. The caliph barely escaped with his life and vowed never again personally to lead troops into battle. Ramiro, however, proved unable to consolidate his gains, and when he died in 950, a Christian civil war broke out, making it possible for Abd ar-Rahman to regain everything he had lost.

With his military conquests, the caliph was able to build an empire, then secure it against political as well as religious foes. By the time of his death on October 15, 961, Abd ar-Rahman had built his capital of Cordova into a metropolis that rivaled Constantinople and surpassed in magnificence the capitals of Western Europe. His consolidation developed a Muslim Spain, the remnants of which are still in evidence today.

Further Reading: W. M. Walt. *A History of Islamic Spain* (Edinburgh: Edinburgh University Press, 1965); S. Lane-Poole. *The Moors in Spain* (New York: G. P. Putnam's Sons, 1897).

Abdul-Aziz (1830–1876)

The first Ottoman sultan to travel outside of the empire, Abdul-Aziz was undone by the failure of his program of modernizing reforms.

Born on February 9, 1830, into the empire's ruling family, Abdul-Aziz was fascinated with the advancements and material progress of the West. He succeeded his brother, who had been equally enamored of the West, on June 25, 1861, but he soon found that his own orthodox religious beliefs got in the way of modernization. Nevertheless, Abdul-Aziz did continue many of the reforms his brother had initiated. Education was broadened, and a new university was founded, the first Ottoman civil code was enacted, and Abdul-Aziz traveled to the West to establish good relations with Britain and France, the first Ottoman sultan to leave the empire.

By 1871, however, the capable ministers who had overseen the reforms were dead, and his European ideal, France, had suffered humiliating defeat at the hands of the Germans, who, following the Battle of Sedan, marched on Paris. With rebellion stirring in his own empire, Abdul-Aziz abruptly turned reactionary. He reaffirmed the Islamic basis of his empire and took upon himself the burden of absolute rule, without advisers. When rebellion in the Balkans spread from Bosnia-Hercegovina to Bulgaria, Abdul-Aziz blamed Russia, which, in fact, stood to gain territory if the Ottoman Empire at last collapsed.

The problems with the Balkans, the rise of the Young Turk movement in June 1865, the crop failure of 1873, and a mounting financial crisis rapidly eroded the stability of Abdul-Aziz's government. Finally, after the government officially declared itself bankrupt in 1876, Abdul-Aziz was deposed by his ministers on May 30. Five days later he committed suicide.

Further Reading: M. Philips Prince. *A History of Turkey from Empire to Republic* (London: Allen & Unwin, 1961); J. A. R. Marriot. *The Eastern Question* (New York: Oxford University Press, 1940).

Abdul-Hamid II (1842–1918)

One of the last Ottoman emperors, Abdul-Hamid would attempt to make pan-Islamism a reality, but succumbed to the Young Turk movement.

Abdul-Hamid II was born into the ruling family of the Ottoman Empire on September 21, 1842. His uncle, ABDUL-AZIZ, was deposed in 1876, and Abdul-Hamid's brother Murad V was installed in his place. However, after three months, the deranged Murad was himself deposed, and, on August 31, 1876, Abdul-Hamid II was installed as emperor.

To secure his position, he had to promise the grand vizier, Midhat Pasha—the leader of a reform movement—that he would establish a constitution. The first Ottoman constitution was promulgated on December 23, 1876, essentially Midhat's work. It provided for an elected legislature and guaranteed civil liberties and equality under the law. Abdul-Hamid soon tired of Midhat's progressive pseudo-regency and removed him from office, sending him into exile for good measure. Following this, Abdul-Hamid took steps to abrogate the constitution and reassert autocratic authority. On April 24, 1877, he declared war on Russia for intriguing with rebel elements in Ottoman possessions in the Balkans. He used the war as an excuse to suspend civil liberties at home, dismiss parliament, and essentially bypass the constitution for the next 31 years.

The Russo-Austro-Hungarian alliance, and its support of Serbia, was more than the Ottoman army could withstand. After marching within 10 miles of Constantinople, the Russians forced the humiliating Treaty of San Stefano (later the Treaty of Berlin, July 13, 1878) upon Abdul-Hamid, which essentially gave outright independence or regional autonomy to the Balkan provinces of Bosnia-Hercegovina, Serbia, Montenegro, Romania and Bulgaria, as well as reparations and territory to Czar ALEXANDER II.

Domestically, Abdul-Hamid maintained his despotism under the guise of pan-Islamism. Nevertheless the reform movement renewed its rebellion. In 1881, seeking to squelch the movement, Abdul-Hamid brought Midhat Pasha (returned from exile) to trial for the murder of Abdul-Aziz, found him guilty, banished him again, then had him murdered. This action, coupled with the effectiveness of Abdul-Hamid's brutal and universally feared secret police, temporarily derailed the reform movement.

In an attempt to shore up his regime both domestically and internationally, Abdul-Hamid renewed his appeal to all Muslims for pan-Islamism, citing Islam above all else, hoping to solidify his position as leader of the Islamic world. Instead of strengthening Abdul-Hamid's position, however, the appeal merely provoked the resentment of European colonial powers, whose Islamic possessions were stirred to Islamic-nationalist rebellion, but not to political solidarity with the Ottomans.

Internally, Abdul-Hamid's empire was increasingly racked with unrest. Various parts of the empire broke out in open rebellion, to which Abdul-Hamid responded violently, especially in Armenia, where 100,000 people were killed. He became known as "Abdul the Damned" and the "Red Sultan."

Protests were universal by 1907, and the leadership of the major reform movement fell to a liberal group, the Young Turks. In the summer of 1908, the III Army Corps threatened to march on Constantinople if Abdul-Hamid did not restore the constitution. He agreed, but on April 13, 1909, he sponsored a countercoup, ousting the liberals. Again the III Army Corps intervened. The liberals presented no further ultimatums, but summarily deposed Abdul-Hamid on April 27, 1909, replacing him with his brother Mohammed V. Abdul-Hamid died in Constantinople on February 10, 1918.

Further Reading: Sir Edwin Pears. *The Life of Abdul-Hamid* (New York: D. Appleton, 1917); Joan Haslip. *The Sultan: The Life of Abdul-Hamid* (New York: Holt, Rinehart & Winston, 1973).

Adrets, François de Beaumont, baron des (1512/13–1587)

A French military commander who became a Huguenot, François Adrets is remembered for his merciless butchery of Catholics during the Wars of Religion in 16th-century France.

Born in the Château of La Frette, Isère, France, François Adrets served in the royal army of French king HENRY II (1519–59). Adrets subsequently rose to the rank of colonel of the southeastern "legions" of Dauphiné, Languedoc, and Provence. Influenced by the Reformation, Adrets became a Huguenot in 1562.

His personality compounded of arrogance and ruthlessness, Adrets commanded several bloody campaigns against the Catholics. On one occasion, following the Battle of Montbrison, Adrets forced the suicides of 18 prisoners of war. This behavior alienated him from the Huguenots and eventually led to his arrest in 1563. Pardoned that same year by the terms of the Edict of Amboise, Adrets spent his remaining 23 years, as a Catholic, in retirement at his home in La Frette, where he died on February 2, 1587.

Afonso I [Nzinga Mbemba] (d. ca. 1550)

Afonso I was the first Portuguese vassal king of the Kongo and established the colonial relationship between his African kingdom and Portugal that was the basis of the slave trade.

The sixth lord (*manikongo*) of the Kongo (today Zaire and Angola), Nzinga Mbemba took the title of King Afonso I in 1507 or 1508, shortly after converting to Christianity. The Regimento, a 1512 treaty between Afonso I and MANUEL I of Portugal, established Portuguese imperial hegemony in the Kongo and initiated the slave trade.

Afonso I died about 1550, having instituted the European–African slave trade and having established a dynasty of vassal kings that would endure into the early 20th century.

Agathocles   (361–289 B.C.)

Agathocles became Hellenic king of Sicily through a series of bloody coups.

Born in Thermae Himeraeae, Sicily in 361 B.C., Agathocles soon moved to Syracuse (343) and enlisted in the army there. His relentless ambition led to several coup attempts against the oligarchical regime. By 317, after twice suffering exile, Agathocles conducted a successful coup, and banished or murdered the oligarchs as well as more than 10,000 citizens loyal to them. Agathocles next declared himself tyrant of Syracuse.

As self-proclaimed tyrant of the Sicilian region, Agathocles entered into conflict with Carthage about 312, thereby rekindling the long-smoldering animosity between the Greeks and Carthage. The larger and more highly skilled Carthaginian army blockaded Syracuse in 311, apparently trapping Agathocles, who, however, managed to escape and retaliate by means of guerrilla agitation in the heart of the Carthaginian homeland. Agathocles was finally defeated in 307, but the peace he concluded the following year preserved his rule, and in 304, Agathocles became king of Sicily, over which he reigned in peace until his death in 289.

Agha Mohammad Khan   (1742–1797)

First ruler of the Qajar dynasty of Iran (1794–1925), Agha Mohammad Khan forged a united kingdom of Iran through his aggressive despotism.

Born in Gorgan Qajar, Iran, in 1742, Agha Mohammad was castrated at age six by Adil Shah—a political rival of the Agha family. By the age of 15, Agha Mohammad was the de facto governor of the Iranian province of Azerbaijan, and at age 16 chief of the Qavavlu clan of the Qajars. Imprisoned in 1762 by a rival clan leader, Agha Mohammad spent the next 16 years as a political prisoner in Shiraz. He escaped in 1779 and reestablished his position as leader of northern Iran. Subsequent invasions of Georgia and Khorasan (whose blind ruler, Shah Rokh, Agha Mohammad tortured to death) in 1796 earned Agha Mohammad Khan the title of *shahan-shah* ("king of kings").

The political rivalry—amounting to civil war—that preceded Agha Mohammad Khan's assumption of power had been economically devastating for Iran. The king of kings coped with this through a combination of miserliness and extraordinary cruelty. Neither was conducive to loyalty, and Agha Mohammad Khan was assassinated by two of his servants while he was en route to a second Georgian invasion in 1797. He was succeeded by his nephew Fath Ali Shah.

Ahmad Grañ   (ca. 1506–1543)

Leader of the Muslim conquest of Abyssinia, Ahmad Grañ devoted his life to ravaging that country.

Apparently born a Somali, Ahmad's left-handedness earned him the epithet Grañ ("the left-handed"). He followed al-Djarad Abun, leader of the militant rebel party opposed to the pacific policy toward Christian Abyssinia. On Abun's death, Ahmad became leader of the rebel opposition, defeating and killing the sultan Abu Bakr Muhammad, before declaring himself imam.

In a deliberate gesture to provoke war, Ahmad refused to pay tribute to an Abyssinian governor. In a quick offensive executed sometime around 1527, Ahmad defeated the governor of Bali, then consolidated his forces for a concerted strike. Defeating the Abyssinians in 1529, Ahmad took the city of Shembera, and by 1531 he had taken the city of Shoa as well.

For six years, Ahmad kept up his offensive campaign, conquering most of Abyssinia. He ravaged everything in his path, pillaging churches and monasteries and forcing local populations to submit to Islam or die. The exiled Abyssinian emperor called for help from the Portuguese, and Ahmad, in turn, called for reinforcements from the Ottomans. With the aid of Turkish musketeers, Ahmad defeated Portuguese forces, but then—inexplicably—sent the mercenaries home. The new Abyssinian emperor, seeing his chance to expel Ahmad and his army, gathered the remnants of the Portuguese forces and engaged Ahmad in battle, defeating him at Zantera in 1543. Ahmad was killed in action, and the Muslim invasion immediately fell apart. The now leaderless Muslim forces were easily expelled from Abyssinia.

Ahmad ibn Tulun   (835–884)

The founder of the Tulunid dynasty, Ahmad was the first Muslim governor of Egypt to annex Syria.

Born into slavery to the Abbasid caliph of Baghdad, Ahmad ibn Tulun rose through the administrative ranks of the caliph's service, first becoming part of the caliph's guard, then lieutenant to the governor of Egypt in September 868. Once in Egypt, Ahmad recognized the power of the purse and spent the next four years attempting to wrest control of the treasury from the minister of finance. On account of the minister's greed, which had earned him the hatred of the Egyptians, and through his own cunning, Ahmad gained control of the ministry around 872.

After securing control of the finances of Egypt, Ahmad was named vice-governor and was invested with authority over Alexandria, Barka, and the Egyptian frontier areas. When the governor of Palestine rose in revolt, the caliph authorized Ahmad to purchase an army of slaves to put down the revolt. This army now provided Ahmad with a power base from which he might seek a measure of Egyptian independence from the caliph. This was the first time Egypt possessed a sizable army independent of the caliphate. The caliph, failing to recognize Ahmad for the threat he was to become, did not move against him or even attempt to neutralize his army.

Ahmad exploited a power struggle within the caliphate and a costly Zindia revolt against the caliph to make a bid for independence by stopping the payment of tribute. Then, in 878, under the pretext of fighting a holy war against the Byzantines, Ahmad marched his army into Syria and annexed it, without so much as a dispatch to the caliph, let alone his consent.

At his death in 884, Ahmad left a newly constructed Egyptian empire, essentially free from overlordship, complete with a tax base, a population satisfied with his rule (due to his military and agrarian reforms) and, most importantly, a proven army.

Ahmad Shah Durrani   (1722?–1772)

Architect of the state of Afghanistan, Ahmad Shah Durrani created the second largest Muslim empire of the mid-18th century.

Ahmad Shah, a member of the royal Sadozai clan, served as a bodyguard to Nader Shah of Persia. After the assassination of Nader, Ahmad was elected emir of Afghanistan, and assumed the title *durrani* ("pearl of pearls") in 1747. During his reign (1747–72), Ahmad Shah Durrani mounted nine invasions of India—not for the purpose of expanding his empire, but for plunder—and fought four largely unsuccessful wars with the Sikhs. Although his own empire was restive with incipient rebellion, Ahmad Shah Durrani was a popular leader, on whom was bestowed the title *baba* ("father," in the sense of father of his country).

Ahmad Shah Durrani died in October 1772. His mausoleum is in Ahmad Shahi, the capital city he founded.

Ahmed, Khandakar Mushtaque   (b. 1918)

Ahmed ruled Bangladesh for only three months. He was overthrown when he ordered the execution of former officials.

After receiving a law degree from Dacca University, Khandakar Mushtaque Ahmed entered politics in 1942 under the auspices of Mohandas Gandhi and his "Quit India" movement aimed at ending British colonial rule of the subcontinent. After stepping up his activities against the British, Ahmed was arrested in 1946. In 1947 the British withdrew from what then became the independent nations of India and Pakistan.

In 1949, Ahmed was one of four founders of the Awami League, which favored East Pakistani independence from West Pakistan. Arrested in 1952 for agitating against the Pakistani government, Ahmed was elected to the East Pakistan assembly in 1954. When martial law was declared in 1958 following continual clashes with India, Ahmed was again arrested and imprisoned until 1961. When martial law was lifted in 1961 and Pakistani political activity resumed, Ahmed joined Sheik Mujib in reorganizing the Awami League, only to be arrested and imprisoned until 1968.

Ahmed went into exile upon his release, but he returned in 1971 in the midst of the civil war in Pakistan that would lead to the declaration of East Pakistan's independence as Bangladesh in December. Under the Mujib regime, Ahmed served in varying cabinet posts, but it was rumored that a split had occurred between Ahmed and Mujib, his friend of 25 years. The rift (over corruption) became public on August 15, 1975, when Ahmed led a coup against Mujib in which Mujib was assassinated.

Ahmed's regime barely had a chance to swing Bangladesh from the Soviets toward the West when Ahmed was forced out on November 6, 1975. Apparently, this second coup in barely two and a half months was precipitated by the execution of at least four, possibly as many as eight, former high-ranking government officials in a Dacca jail. Ahmed apparently ordered the killings and then provided for the escape of the young army officers involved. Ahmed was allowed to step down peacefully, but he was arrested in November 1976 with 10 others for activities against the state, and again in May 1979 for corruption and violating martial law. He was sentenced to five years in prison.

Ahmose I   (d. 1525 B.C.)

First king of the 18th dynasty in Egypt, Ahmose I succeeded to the throne upon the death of his brother and ruled until his own death in 1525 B.C.

Although Ahmose I's reign in Egypt has been characterized as a time of peace, it was, in fact, a period of nearly constant warfare. Ahmose first completed the war begun by his father and brother to expel the Hyksos, the Asiatic rulers of Egypt.

During the war against the Hyksos, the Thebans revolted in Upper Egypt, and Ahmose was forced to leave the war to his commanders while he put down the internal rebellion. After the expulsion of the Hyksos, the Nubians revolted, and Ahmose sailed to that region, put down the rebellion, and established Ahmose Sitayet as viceroy of Nubia.

The later years of Ahmose's reign were, indeed, marked by peace, and he used the time to re-establish the government's authority, to rebuild canals, dikes, and irrigation systems, and to encourage trade, especially with the Greeks.

Further Reading: Margaret Bunson. *Encyclopedia of Ancient Egypt* (New York: Facts On File, 1991).

Ahuitzotl   (r. 1486–1503)
The Aztec king Ahuitzotl expanded the Aztec empire to its zenith in the late 15th century.

Succeeding his father, Tizoc, to the Aztec throne in 1486, Ahuitzotl proved himself a capable leader through his fearless military exploits. Immediately beginning a campaign of expansion and conquest, Ahuitzotl extended the empire's borders south into Central America to present-day Guatemala and west as far as the Gulf of California.

A brilliant tactician, Ahuitzotl commanded the discipline of his men because they feared him, and their respect because he shared their hardships in the field. Tactically, he used forced marches to cover large amounts of ground and launch surprise assaults and ambushes, all of which kept the enemy off-guard.

Ahuitzotl is primarily remembered for having commissioned perhaps the largest single orgy of human religious sacrifice in history. After building his enormous temple in the capital of Tenochtitlán (modern-day Mexico City), Ahuitzotl dedicated it in 1487 with a four-day ceremony that included sacrificial rites to the gods. For four days, prisoners of war forming four lines each over three miles long were led to the altar, where priests, nobles, and even Ahuitzotl himself, cut open their chests and ripped out their hearts. It is estimated that between 20,000 to 80,000 men perished while guests from the conquered provinces watched.

Ahuitzotl himself was killed in 1503 when he hit his head on a stone lintel while fleeing the great flood that swept Tenochtitlán that year.

Akbar   (1542–1605)
The greatest of the Mughal emperors of India, Akbar extended his rule over most of the Indian subcontinent.

Descended from GENGHIS KHAN and other Mongol conquerors, Akbar was born into the ruling class of northern India's Muslim invaders, the Mughals; however, his father Hemayun's hold on his kingdom was tenuous. Shortly after Akbar's birth on October 15, 1542, Hemayun had been driven from the capital of Delhi by the Afghan usurper Sher Shah

Sur and spent more than 10 years in exile in Afghanistan and Iran.

After gaining troops from the shah of Iran, Hemayun triumphantly returned, overthrowing Sher Shah Sur. Akbar was made governor of the Punjab, a role designed to groom him for the throne. Hemayun died less than a year later, and his empire, such as it was, now lay at the feet of his 13-year-old son. After a tumultuous five-year regency, Akbar forced out his chief minister Bairam Khan and the young ruler embarked on a savage conquest of the Indian subcontinent beginning in 1561. He showed no mercy to those tribes that resisted his forces and ruthlessly overran them, usually massacring any who opposed him. In the case of the Rajputs, however, he allowed them to submit to his overlordship with a yearly tribute and troops as needed in return for limited local autonomy and privileges within the civil government. In this way, he was able to maintain the loyalty of the Rajputs, whose troops would be instrumental in his other conquests. By the turn of the century, Akbar had firmly imposed his rule over the Indian subcontinent north of the Godavari River in central India and solidified his kingdom for future generations.

Perhaps Akbar's greatest accomplishment was his administrative reform. Akbar's conquest enabled him to centralize government, thereby minimizing the abuses of local administrators and tax collectors. He also reformed the military by decreeing that every promotion and appointment come from the emperor rather than local officials or lesser officers, a despotic measure that nevertheless eliminated corruption.

Akbar, although illiterate himself, encouraged all forms of cultural expression at his court, frequently hosting scholars, poets, painters, and musicians. He welcomed debate among Christians, Muslims, Hindus, and others, and his government, although ruthlessly established, came to be considered a model for future administrators of the region.

Further Reading: Vincent A. Smith. *Akbar the Great Mogul, 1542–1605* (Oxford: Clarendon Press, 1919).

Akhenaton   (r. 1379–62 B.C.)
Considered by some scholars the most remarkable of ancient Egyptian kings, Akhenaton wrought a religious revolution across Egypt, replacing the old gods with a new monotheistic deity, Aton.

Akhenaton was born Amenhotep, the son of AMENHOTEP III, a hunter of legendary prowess and a leader who brought to a climax the 18th dynasty's imperial gains in Asia and Africa. In contrast to his father and to the rulers, beginning with THUTMOSE III, who had preceded him, Akhenaton was physically frail and tended to pursue spiritual and intellectual interests. A sandstone pillar from the Aton temple Akhenaton built at Karnak depicts the pharaoh as awkward and thin, even gangling, with an overgrown jaw and receding forehead.

Scholars have been deeply divided over the reputation of Akhenaton, some seeing in him a social revolutionary, an early pacifist, a religious reformer, and a cultural pioneer. More recent scholars, however, have pointed out that Akhenaton's religious revolution was significantly reactionary, an effort to restore to the Egyptian monarchy the degree of absolute authority it had formerly enjoyed before the expansion of empire had spawned an extensive class of powerful bureaucrats, officials, landowners, and others who made the pharaohs, theoretically gods-on-earth, in fact virtual captives of the state.

It is not known whether Akhenaton succeeded to the throne after his father's death or whether he ruled alongside his father for a time. Whatever the case, within the first few years of his reign, young Amenhotep IV embraced a new monotheistic cult dedicated to the sun god Aton. In the sixth year of his reign, he changed his name to Akhenaton—He Who Serves the Aton—and built great new temples dedicated to this deity at Karnak, site of temples dedicated to the old gods. Next, he moved his capital from Thebes more than 200 miles north to a place now called Armana, on the east bank of the Nile. He built there a totally new city, which he called Akhetaton, erecting public buildings and more temples. Unlike the royal families of old, Akhenaton and his wife, Nefertiti (whose celebrated beauty is preserved in a graceful bust of the period), and their six daughters mingled with the people of their new city, worshiping Aton in a temple open to the sunlight. The worship of Aton was apparently a form of nature cult, and the art produced during Akhenaton's reign contrasts sharply with what had gone before. It is naturalistic, though the fleshy elements are exaggerated, even to the point of grotesqueness.

But while he lived among others and worshiped in a comparatively free-and-easy religious atmosphere, Akhenaton was no democrat. His program of building and patronage of the arts demanded huge amounts of capital. His political reforms effectually centralized Egypt's economy, appropriating vast tracts of land, levying heavy taxes, and stripping the old ruling class of much of its power. Moreover, Akhenaton was a ruthless iconoclast when it came to obliterating the artifacts, temples, and monuments of the old gods. He dispatched his agents of destruction to the four corners of his kingdom.

This ruler who arrogated so much power unto himself seems largely to have neglected affairs of state, preferring to practice his new religion and to commission works of art and architecture rather than regulate and defend the territories his father and those before him had accumulated. Internally, the poorly supervised Egyptian bureaucracy was plagued by corruption. The army, which previous rulers had built up, was now neglected, and, as a result, many of Egypt's holdings were quickly lost to various invaders. By the end of Akhenaton's reign, all that was left of territories acquired through conquest was the southwestern portion of Palestine.

Akhenaton's policies and religion produced a great deal of hostility among his subjects. On his death, he was succeeded briefly by Smenkhkare, then by a son-in-law, Tutankhaton. He, however, was soon compelled to change his name to Tutankhamon (popularly known in modern times as King Tut), signifying his public repudiation of his father-in-law's all-consuming god, Aton, and his embrace of Amon, the old god Aton had displaced.

Further Reading: James H. Breasted. *A History of Egypt* (New York: Scribner's, 1942); *Cambridge Ancient History,* vol. 2, part 2 (New York: Macmillan, 1975).

Alaric   (ca. 370–410)

Alaric was a ruthless Visigoth chieftain who ravaged much of Greece and Italy during the early Dark Ages.

Popularly characterized as a barbarian despoiler, Alaric was in fact an early Christian monarch—though nonetheless ruthless for that. He was raised in Moesia (northern Bulgaria) and quickly acquired a reputation as a charismatic leader. By 395, his influence was such that the Visigoths elected him their monarch. After this, he launched an invasion of Constantinople following the death of THEODOSIUS I the Great. Alaric justified the invasion on the grounds that the Roman Empire's subsidy to the Visigoths had not been paid and was overdue. The Roman prefect Rufinus diverted the invading force through skillful diplomacy, and Alaric marched on Thrace and Macedonia, ruthlessly ravaging the countryside. Alaric was met by a Roman army under Flavius Stilicho, but combat was averted, again through the diplomatic maneuverings of Rufinus and the eastern emperor Arcadius.

Alaric did not, however, return home. Instead, he led his army south, into Greece, where he ravaged Piraeus, Corinth, Argos, and, early in 397, Sparta. In spring of that year, Stilicho's army trapped him in Elis. Stilicho, however, scheming to enlist Alaric as an ally, allowed the Visigoth and his forces to escape from Elis. Arcadius then attempted to appease Alaric by naming him *magister militum* (commander in chief) in Illyricum about 398.

In October 401, Alaric proved himself a most unreliable ally when he staged a surprise invasion of Italy by way of the Julian Alps. He laid siege to Milan in the late winter and early spring of 402. Stilicho, stunned, was engaged in battle with Vandals under Radagasius in Rhaetia and Noricum (eastern Austria) and had to move quickly to the relief of Milan. With an army hastily assembled from Roman garrisons in the Rhineland and Britain, Stilicho fought Alaric to a draw at Asta probably in mid March. The Roman commander then pursued Alaric's forces to Pollentia and defeated them there on April 6, 402. Still bent on a policy of appeasement, Stilicho negotiated Alaric's departure from Italy.

Alaric returned to Italy in the summer of 403, but he was again met by Stilicho, who defeated him at Verona in June. This time, the Roman negotiated another settlement, and Emperor Honorius bestowed on Alaric the same office he had been granted by Arcadius, *magister militum* of Illyria. For his repeated efforts to appease Alaric, Stilicho was executed at Ravenna on August 22, 408 by order of Honorius. Immediately following the death of the Roman commander, Alaric was again on the move. He crossed the Alps in a march on Rome during 409. This time, the Roman Senate attempted to stop Alaric not by military force, but with a heavy bribe. The tribute was sufficient to persuade Alaric to halt for the winter in Tuscany, where he negotiated with Emperor Honorius from November 409 to April 410. After negotiations broke down, Alaric marched toward the capital. Honorius, having executed his most able general, was deposed, and Alaric replaced him with a puppet. Alaric then directed his attack on Ravenna. Turned back there, he laid siege against Rome, which quickly fell. Alaric sacked the capital for six terrible days, August 24–29, 410.

Had he chosen to do so, Stilicho could have defeated Alaric early on. After the Roman general's death, however, the Visigoth ruler visited on the waning Roman Empire devastation that was unchecked until, as he was preparing to invade Sicily, Alaric was felled by disease in December of 410.

Further Reading: Marcel Brion. *Alaric, the Goth* (New York: McBride, 1930).

Alboin   (r. 565–72)

At the head of a coalition of Germanic tribes, Alboin led the Lombard invasion of northern Italy.

Succeeding his father, Audoin, in 565, Alboin was in possession of the Drava River basin, present-day Austria and western Hungary. To the east were the Lombards' mortal enemies, the Gepidae, and to the east of them were the Mongolian Avars. Shortly after his accession, Alboin shrewdly allied himself

with the Avars, and in a classic pincer movement, annihilated the Gepidae, Alboin personally killing their king, Cunimund. As a trophy of war, Alboin took Cunimund's daughter, Rosamund, as his wife—a decision that would ultimately prove fatal.

Soon after this triumph, the Avars turned on Alboin, forcing him out of the Drava region. Alboin then concluded an alliance with other Germanic tribes, including several thousand Saxons, absorbed the remnants of the Gepidae, and prepared to move south through the Alps. The Lombards invaded Byzantine-held northern Italy in 568. The northern provinces, badly disorganized, were unprepared to repel the invasion, which proceeded against little resistance. Alboin swept his army south through Venice, Milan, Tuscany, Benevento, and finally reached the Po River Valley, establishing his new capital at Pavia in 572.

The Lombards became the first invaders to treat the Romans as subjects rather than allies. Shortly after the designation of Pavia as the capital, Rosamund had Alboin assassinated after he had compelled her to follow the Lombard custom of drinking from the skull of her murdered father.

Alcibiades   (ca. 450–404 B.C.)

One of the most colorful and unscrupulous of Athenian leaders, Alcibiades was afflicted with an overweening personal ambition that brought Athens' defeat at the hands of Sparta during the Peloponnesian War (431–404 B.C.)

Few men of state have been so gifted or so intellectually advantaged as Alcibiades. The son of a military commander, he was born to Athenian nobility and enjoyed a childhood of privilege. However, his father was killed at Coronea in 447 or 446 B.C., and Alcibiades was raised by the great statesman Pericles, a kinsman. As the biographer Plutarch relates, while Pericles must have provided an extraordinary example of statecraft, he was too preoccupied with matters of government to pay much attention to his ward. As a result, Alcibiades grew into a handsome and brilliant young man, but was supremely self-centered, selfish, and utterly without discipline. These deficiencies might have been corrected by his early association with Socrates, with whom Alcibiades served in a military capacity at Potidaea in 432 B.C. and at the Battle of Delium in 424. Yet this proved not to be the case, as Alcibiades went on to practice a most self-serving variety of unscrupulous politics diametrically opposed to any principles Socrates had taught.

During the 420s, Alcibiades acquired a reputation as a daring, brilliant, and personally reckless military commander and a persuasive political speaker. He also used his physical beauty and charm to great advantage. His early ambition was to make peace between the ever-warring states of Athens and Sparta by bringing to bear ancient family connections with the Spartans. However, when these plans failed because Sparta chose to negotiate through more established political channels, Alcibiades turned against the chief Athenian negotiator Nicias and, in 420, as general of an Athenian army, urged Athens into an alliance with Argos, Elis, and Mantineia against Sparta, therby wrecking any chance for peace between the two great powers. Two years later, at the Battle of Mantineia, the Spartans defeated Alcibiades and the three-state alliance. This defeat would have ended the political and military career of an ordinary man. Threatened with banishment, however, Alcibiades performed a rapid about-face and allied himself with the autocratic Nicias in opposition to the demagogue Hyperbolus. Having once again secured a position of power in the management of the state, Alcibiades redeemed himself in the eyes of the people by his spectacular performance in the Olympic chariot races of 416 (he took first, second, and fourth places).

With his reputation restored, Alcibiades persuaded Athens to send a military expedition against Syracuse in 415, with himself as co-commander. This enterprise was sabotaged by the discovery that the Hermae—ritual busts of Hermes, messenger of Zeus and patron of travelers—had been deliberately damaged, apparently to bring disaster on the Syracusan campaign. Alcibiades was accused not only of this sacrilege, but also of having profaned the Eleusinian Mysteries. He loudly demanded an inquiry to clear his name before embarking for Syracuse, but his enemies, including Androcles (demogogic successor to Hyperbolus) prevented the inquiry from going forward, and thus Alcibiades went to Sicily under a cloud of accusation.

In his absence, his enemies continued to conspire against him, and Alcibiades learned that he had been condemned to death. At this news, he defected to Sparta, to which he volunteered his military services, recommending fortifications in Decelea that seriously undermined the Athenian position. Alcibiades further improved his time at Decelea by seducing the wife of Spartan king Agis II.

Alcibiades continued his treachery against Athens in 412 B.C., when he incited a revolt in Ionia, but this time Sparta turned on him. Always agile, Alcibiades escaped to the Persian city of Sardis. From Sardis, he conspired with a cabal of Athenian oligarchs bent on overthrowing the democracy in Athens. Alcibiades believed that he could charm the Persians into financing the overthrow. This belief proved unfounded, and Alcibiades' coconspirators spurned him.

In the meantime, the Athenian fleet, which was loyal to the democracy Alcibiades had sought to overthrow, was being menaced by the fleet of Sparta. The Athenian commanders were willing to forgive Alcibiades' transgressions in return for his aid in this crisis, and from 411 to 408, he performed brilliantly against the Spartan forces. He led the Athenian fleet to victory in the Hellespont in 411 and at Cyzicus the following year. By 407, he was ready to return to Athens, where he was greeted tumultuously and given supreme command of the armed forces in the ongoing war against Sparta.

The adulation was not long lived. When his lieutenants suffered a trivial naval defeat late in 407, Alcibiades' many political enemies turned the populace against him. He retired to a Thracian stronghold, from which he continued to participate in Athenian politics. In 405, despite Alcibiades' warnings, the Athenians lost their entire fleet to a surprise Spartan attack. Alcibiades was forced to flee Thrace and took refuge with the Persian governor of Phrygia. Spartan intriguers induced the governor to order the assassination of his guest.

Thus ended the brilliant and crooked life of Alcibiades. His downfall continued to reverberate, however, when his example was used as evidence against Socrates during the philosopher's trial in 399 B.C. on charges of corrupting the youth of Athens.

Further Reading: Edward F. Benson. *The Life of Alcibiades* (London: E. Benn, 1928).

Alexander I [Aleksandr Pavlovich] (1777–1825)

This Russian czar was a ruler of contradictions: Motivated on the one hand by a desire to bring about reform, he was, when put to the test, a reactionary autocrat.

Alexander was born in Saint Petersburg, Russia, on December 23, 1777, the eldest son of Grand Duke Pavel Petrovich and Sophia Dorothea of Würtemburg. Alexander's marriage to Louise of Baden-Durlach on October 9, 1793, concluded without the consent of his father, provoked enmity, and it is possible that Alexander conspired in the March 24, 1801 murder of his father, who had become Czar Paul I. Following the death of Paul I, Alexander ascended the throne.

In the early years of his reign, Alexander was inspired by the reforms NAPOLÉON I was bringing to France, and he attempted to follow suit by liberalizing Russian government. In the face of resistance from an entrenched and reactionary aristocracy, however, Alexander readily abandoned the cause of reform, in which he seems never to have believed very deeply. Indeed, with each passing year of his reign, Alexander became increasingly authoritarian and repressive.

The czar began a long war against Persia in 1804, which was not ended until 1813. In 1805, he joined the Third Coalition against Napoléon and led his troops to terrible defeat at the Battle of Austerlitz on December 2 of that year. During 1806–1807, Alexander campaigned against Napoléon's forces in eastern Prussia before concluding a peace with the French emperor at Tilsit during July 7–9, 1807. Although Alexander waged sporadic war against French-allied Turkey from 1806 to 1812, he entered into a fitful period of friendly relations with Napoléon. The amity rapidly deteriorated, however, and came to an end early in 1811 when Alexander politely but firmly declined Napoléon's request for the hand of his youngest sister Anna. In 1812—from June 24 to December 2—Napoléon invaded Russia.

Following the failure of Napoléon's Russian campaign, Alexander accompanied his generals as nominal commander of armies fighting against the French in Germany. He was in nominal command at the Battle of Dresden, August 26–27, 1813, when Napoléon's army scored a costly victory against the Russian forces, but he was also present when the Russian army participated in the allied victory over the French leader at Leipzig during October 16–19.

Capitalizing on the expansion of power brought about by victories against Persia and Turkey and the prestige garnered from his part in the defeat of Napoléon, Alexander cast himself as the "peacemaker of Europe." The Congress of Vienna, convened during 1814–15, regarded his motives with suspicion, however, and little came of his efforts. Inspired by an increasingly religious, even mystical turn of mind and a growing fear of the forces of liberal reform active in the wake of the Napoleonic era, Alexander next tried to create a "Holy Alliance" intended to regulate all European affairs. A curious amalgam of farsighted international diplomacy and a desire to preserve pan-European aristocracy against the forces of change, the Holy Alliance failed to materialize.

Following these unsuccessful diplomatic projects, Alexander retired to the confines of his own country, becoming increasingly reactionary and repressive, yet other-worldly, engrossed in a religiosity that removed him from the day-to-day needs of his people.

He died at Taganrog, southern Russia, on December 1, 1825.

Further Reading: Leonid Ivan Strakhousky. *Alexander I of Russia: The Man Who Defeated Napoleon* (1947; reprint ed., Wesport, Conn.: Greenwood Press, 1970).

Alexander I   (1888–1934)

King of the Kingdom of Serbs, Croats, and Slovenes, Alexander I attempted to force unity on his diverse subjects by creating Yugoslavia, of which he served as absolute dictator until his assassination in 1934.

Born on December 16, 1888, in Cetinje, Montenegro, Alexander was the younger son of the Serbian king Peter Karageorgević. He spent much of his childhood and early youth in Geneva, Switzerland, while his father endured a period of exile from Serbia. In 1899 he moved to St. Petersburg, Russia, enrolling five years later in the Russian imperial corps of pages. Ten years later, in 1909, his elder brother renounced his right of succession, and Alexander, now heir-apparent, returned to Serbia.

During the Balkan Wars of 1912–13 Alexander proved himself a fine military commander. On the eve of World War I—June 24, 1914—King Peter, aged and infirm, appointed him regent, and with the beginning of the war, Alexander became commander in chief of Serbian armed forces. Immediately after the Armistice, in an effort to unify his diverse and fractious people, he proclaimed the creation of the Kingdom of Serbs, Croats, and Slovenes on December 1, 1918. A constitution was drafted, and, on June 28, 1921, Alexander participated in a ceremony in which he swore an oath to uphold the new document. An assassination attempt during the proceedings foreboded the violent dissension that would plague the fledgling state.

Alexander became king of the Kingdom of Serbs, Croats, and Slovenes on June 8, 1922, following the death of his father, and then made a politically advantageous marriage to Marie, daughter of Ferdinand I of Romania. Even as Alexander worked to consolidate diverse political parties and disparate ethnic and national groups into a single country, tensions mounted during the 1920s until, on June 20, 1928, a Montenegrin deputy to the Skupština (parliament) murdered a number of Croat deputies. The Croats promptly withdrew from the Skupština, and Alexander tried in vain to restructure the parliament. At length, he gave up, dissolved the Skupština, abolished the constitution he had sworn to uphold, and declared a royal dictatorship on January 6, 1929.

Singleminded in his efforts to enforce unity on his country, he renamed it Yugoslavia on October 3, 1929, then banned all political parties founded on principles of ethnicity, religion, or region. He reformed and standardized many cultural instutions, including the courts, the schools, and the calendar of national holidays. While Alexander's intentions were laudable, and while he showed particular concern for improving the economic lot of the peasantry (which was especially hard hit by the Great Depression then engulfing the world), the dictator created a police state based on a military presence to enforce unity and obedience to the new laws. With the constitution of September 3, 1931, his military dictatorship was formalized and given full legal status.

There were many in Yugoslavia who welcomed strong acts by a strong man, but soon other elements chafed under the tyrant's yoke. Alexander, who was also faced with a severe economic crisis, sought to forestall revolution by seriously considering the restoration of the parliament and moving back toward some form of democracy. He was apparently on the verge of just such actions when, while making a diplomatic visit to France, he was fatally shot by a Croation separatist on October 9, 1934.

Further Reading: Stephen Graham. *Alexander of Yugoslavia: The Story of the King Who Was Murdered* (Hamden, Conn.: Archon, 1972).

Alexander II (1818–1881)

Among the Russian czars, the greatest reformer since Peter the Great. Alexander II profoundly changed the social and economic structure of prerevolutionary Russia.

Born into the ruling Romanov family on April 17, 1881, Alexander Nikolayevich was given the traditional upbringing of a crown prince, studying Russian, German, and French, policy and law, and, of course, the military arts. After succeeding his father, NICHOLAS I, on February 19, 1855, Alexander's most pressing obligation was the prosecution of the Crimean War in which his father had plunged Russia, and in which he himself had perished. However, the fall of Sevastopol on September 11, 1855, reduced the Russian military to complete disarray. The war magnified the glaring ineptitudes of every aspect of the Russian government and military, especially compared with the industrialized countries of the West. Alexander negotiated the Peace of Paris in March 1856, which marked the nadir of imperial Russia's international standing.

From this inauspicious beginning, Alexander vowed to lead his country out of the social, economic, and military backwaters. He slowly parted with the conservative policies of his father and saw that reform at all levels must take place. The first Russian czar to surround himself with competent and qualified advisers to whom he allowed significant latitude, Alexander instituted reforms beginning with the local bureaucracy. The Zemstvo Law of January 11, 1864, created *zemstvos* (local assemblies), which removed the burden of direct local administration from the national government. The *zemstvos* were made up of peasants, townspeople,

and landowners, and went a long way toward improving practical government.

In reforming the Russian judicial system, Alexander showed how strongly he relied on his advisers, who produced and reviewed 446 drafts of a master plan, which was finally promulgated in 1864 and included trial by jury, due process, and the separation of the judiciary from the legislative branches of government. Perhaps the most liberal of Alexander's reforms, it received the least personal direction and inspiration from the emperor, but was the work of a trusted staff.

Longest in coming but most desperately needed was reform of the military in 1870 and 1874. Once again, most of the direction was provided by an advisor, Dmitrii Miliutin, the minister of war. The ministry and the general staff were reorganized and streamlined, and all military schooling was brought under the uniform control of the ministry. Social standing was put second to aptitude in promoting qualified officers, and elementary education was provided to all draftees and recruits.

By far, the most dramatic of Alexander's reforms was the liberation of the serfs in 1861. Realizing that true economic and social growth could not occur as long as serfdom prevailed, Alexander began studying the problem as early as 1856. After gathering all proposals from all levels, Alexander freed the serfs on February 19, 1861, giving them rights under the law and a small allotment of land to work.

Despite his reforms, Alexander was by no means a liberal. He firmly believed in the absolutism of autocracy, maintaining that his authority derived directly from God. Alexander also held that the people of Russia were simply incapable of living under a representative constitutional government.

As was the case with so many "enlightened despots" of the 19th century, Alexander's reforms were his undoing. The reform movement brought on a resurgence of revolutionary thought in a classic example of the theory of rising expectations. Having been given a small amount of social freedom, the Russian people now demanded more. Alexander was assassinated on March 9, 1881, by a terrorist group called the People's Will Party.

Further Reading: R. Charques. *The Twilight of Imperial Russia* (New York: Oxford University Press, 1959); Hugh Seton-Watson. *The Decline of Imperial Russia, 1855–1914* (London: Methuen, 1951).

Alexander III the Great (356 B.C.–323 B.C.)

King of Macedonia from 336 B.C. until his death, Alexander the Great conquered the Persian Empire, carried out military expeditions in India, and laid the foundations for the Hellenic Empire.

Alexander III the Great, as depicted on an ancient coin. (From Richard Delbruck, Antike Portrats, *1912)*

The son of PHILIP II of Macedon, Alexander was born in Pella, Macedonia. A student of Aristotle, he succeeded to the Macedonian throne in 336 B.C. First attending to matters of security at home, he liquidated many of his rivals and consolidated his political power.

In the spring of 334, he began the military expeditions that would occupy the rest of his life. Determined to liberate the Greek cities in Asia, he crossed the Hellespont with an army of about 40,000 men, conquered the Persian army, subdued his enemies in western Asia Minor, and in July 332 stormed the city of Tyre. Occupying Palestine and Phoenicia, he turned toward Egypt and subdued it between 332 and 331.

Returning to Tyre in 331, Alexander marched his army across Mesopotamia and occupied Babylon. The following year, he entered Media to the north and captured its capital. Facing Persian Emperor DARIUS III and his Grand Army, Alexander was victorious at the battle of Gaugamela in 331. On the death of the Persian emperor in 330, Alexander assumed the title Basileus (great king).

In midsummer 330, he set off for central Asia. Three long years of fighting were required to subdue the region. Here, Alexander adopted new measures to secure what he had gained. He married Roxane, a member of the Iranian nobility, and compelled 91 of his officers to marry Iranian women as well. In addition, he conscripted 30,000 Iranian boys into his army and encompassed the Iranian cavalry into his own. During his conquest of the area, his court was plagued by scandals and ugly incidents, but this was also the period in which the conqueror founded eight important cities named for himself: Alexandria.

Alexander's last great campaign was in India. He crossed the Indus River in 326, incorporating into his empire territories extending as far as the Hyphasis and lower Indus. The only real threat came from King Porus of Paurava. In the battle against Porus at the river Hydaspes in 326, Alexander's army scored a stunning victory—crossing the river in face of the advancing Paurava army, which included numerous elephants. Overrunning the Punjab, Alexander turned back only because his army refused to follow him farther. In 324, his officers, angered over the "mixed" army he had created of Macedonians and Iranians and also resenting the marriages they had been forced to make, nearly mutinied.

During the last year and a half of his life, Alexander increased his use of the Iranian troops and prepared for an Arabian campaign. While making preparations, he fell ill, probably of pernicious malaria, and died in Babylon on June 10, 323, at the age of 33.

A superb military leader with no peer among his countless opponents, Alexander was not equally proficient at administration. The task of overseeing and managing his vast conquests was for him secondary to the process of conquest itself. He was interested, however, in recognition for his military feats. Ancient historians wrote about Alexander's official request to the Greek city-states for deification. While the Greek religion allowed for the possibility of deifying a great benefactor, the request was politically inept. Nor could Alexander get past his political blunder of imposing the Iranians on his countrymen.

Further Reading: J. R. Hamilton. *Alexander the Great* (Pittsburgh: University of Pittsburgh Press, 1973); R. D. Milns. *Alexander the Great* (New York: Pegasus, 1969); D. Engels. *Alexander the Great and the Logistics of the Macedonian Army* (Berkeley: University of California Press, 1978).

Alexander III (1845–1894)

In sharp contrast to his reform-minded father, Czar ALEXANDER II, Alexander III was a reactionary ruler who opposed all attempts at liberalization and was intolerant of his father's policies.

Born the second son of Alexander II, the young Alexander was given only the perfunctory training of grand duke, limited to an acquaintance with foreign languages and basic military instruction. When the crown prince, Alexander's older brother Nicholas, suddenly died in 1865, Alexander became the heir-apparent.

Upon Alexander II's assassination on March 1, 1881, the younger Alexander wasted no time in reversing his father's policies. He quickly squelched a movement toward representative government, made loudly reactionary noises, and prompted his father's moderate ministers to resign, en masse, in disgust.

Alexander III believed his father's reforms had been responsible for his assassination and, consequently, lived in continual fear that he would meet the same fate. Fear, therefore, reinforced his ideological tendency toward repression, and he based his policies on the three immovable concepts of orthodoxy, autocracy, and a staunch Russian nationalism called *narodnost.* Anything that seemed to run contrary to these was rejected or purged.

Alexander's most reactionary policies were aimed at the revolutionary movement that had claimed his father's life. In the wake of the assassination, the new czar imposed a "temporary" state of martial law that in fact remained in place until the Bolshevik Revolution of 1917. The government had the option of subjecting certain areas to "reinforced security" or the even more stringent state of "extraordinary security." These conditions were enforced by an augmented, all-powerful, and greatly feared force of secret police who answered directly to the czar.

Along with secular reform, religious toleration was sacrificed during this period. Russia's Jews, perennial targets, were persecuted more harshly than ever, as were Russo-Germans, Poles, and Finns, whose crime was their failure to have been born 100 percent Russian. The authority of the *zemstvos* (local assemblies) was curtailed and a *nachalnuk* (land captain) was appointed to oversee administration of the freed serfs. The office of local justices of the peace was abolished, and the national government took a more direct and arbitrary role in dispensing justice. Whereas Alexander II had sought to decentralize authority in order to make it more responsive to the people, Alexander III reconstituted power in the central government and reasserted the absolute nature of autocracy.

Alexander's death on October 20, 1894, left Russia slightly better off economically, but greatly discontented socially. The Bolsheviks and Mensheviks were clearly on the horizon, and Russia was one step closer to revolution.

Further Reading: R. Charques. *The Twilight of Imperial Russia* (New York: Oxford University Press, 1959); Hugh Seton-Watson. *The Decline of Imperial Russia, 1855–1914* (London: Methuen, 1951).

Alexander IV (1199–1261)

The third pope from the Segni family, Alexander IV continued the militant policies of his predecessor by prosecuting wars and extending the Inquisition.

Born Rinaldo Dei Segni in Agnani, near Rome, Rinaldo was destined for the life of the cloth. His great grand uncle Innocent III and his uncle Gregory IX

had both been elected pope earlier in the 13th century. It was Gregory who appointed Rinaldo cardinal deacon in 1227 and then cardinal bishop of Ostia in 1231.

On the death of Innocent IV, the College of Cardinals nominated Rinaldo after two days of deliberation. Shortly before Innocent IV's death, the papal army had been routed by Manfred, the bastard son of Emperor FREDERICK II (1194–1250) of Germany, Italy, and Sicily. Alexander continued the war against Manfred by excommunicating him, but was otherwise unable to gain a military advantage. At the time of Alexander's death, Manfred was still securely in power in Sicily.

Alexander spent much of his pontificate outside Rome, traveling around Europe and extending the Inquisition in France. At the University of Paris, the secular professors adamantly opposed the influx of friars at the university. The professors denounced the Franciscans and the Dominicans, both favorites of Alexander; he confirmed the right of the friars to teach and gave them the full support of the papacy.

Alexander enjoyed more success than any other pope in unifying the Greek and Roman churches, but he died on May 25, 1261, in Viterbo, before he was able to finalize the union.

Alexander VI (1431–1503)

Thoroughly corrupt and worldly, Alexander VI was one of the most notorious of the so-called "bad popes," using his pontificate to further the interests of his family, the Borgias.

Alexander VI was born Rodrigo de Borja y Doms (in Italian, Rodrigo Borgia) in Játiva, Aragon in 1431. His was the relatively poor Spanish branch of Borgias, a family already powerful in Italy. Rodrigo's ambitious uncle, Alonso de Borgia, first bishop of Valencia and subsequently cardinal, directed the young man's education and heaped upon him ecclesiastical benefices. Alonso sent Rodrigo to Bologna to study law, then, after Alonso became Pope Calixtus III, he elevated Rodrigo, age 25, to cardinal, subsequently bestowing upon him the important papal office of vice-chancellor. Rodrigo would serve in this capacity for 36 years, under five popes, before he himself was elected pontiff on August 10–11, 1492.

During his 36 years in the *curia,* Rodrigo Borgia consolidated his power and influence, amassing enormous wealth, and living the life of a Renaissance prince with such flagrant disregard of his spiritual inheritance as to merit chastisement from Pope Pius II. Rodrigo fathered at least six children, four of them by a noblewoman of Rome, Vanozza Catanei. These were Juan, Cesare, Jofré, and Lucrezia Borgia.

Establishing their financial and political fortunes was Rodrigo's overriding concern, both before and after he was made pope.

The election of Rodrigo as Pope Alexander VI was deeply stained by charges—certainly true—of simony. Nevertheless, he was popular with the people of Rome, and he was a politically sound choice. Alexander VI instituted reforms of the papal finances and began a military campaign against the Ottomans. But he faced a significant threat from King Charles VIII of France, who invaded Italy during 1494–95 to make good his claims to Naples. Charles had the support of a rival cardinal—a member of the della Rovere family—and used this leverage to threaten Alexander with convocation of a council to depose him on grounds of simony. At this point, the pope temporarily acquiesced to Charles, but sought an alliance against him with the Turkish emperor Bayezid II. It was, however, the Holy League, and alliance Alexander engineered in March 1495 among Milan, Venice, Spain, Austria, and the Holy Roman Empire, that finally forced Charles to withdraw. The Holy League was a prime example of Alexander's mastery of diplomatic skills.

While Alexander dealt with external threats, he devoted most of his time and energy to creating a patrimony of wealth and influence for his children. In 1493, he made his teenaged son Cesare a cardinal—one of 47 cardinals (all friends, relatives, or political allies) he created during his pontificate. He also used his enormous influence to arrange connections for his children outside of the church. Juan Borgia became duke of Gandia and was married to the cousin of Ferdinand IV of Castile. Jofré was married to the granddaughter of the king of Naples. Lucrezia Borgia was first given in marriage to Giovanni Sforza of Milan, a union soon annulled by Alexander on grounds of impotence. Alexander next arranged a marriage with Alfonso of Aragon, who was subsequently assassinated, after which Lucrezia wed Alfonso I d'Este, the duke of Ferrara.

Alexander VI heedlessly pursued his program of family aggrandizement at the expense of church affairs until, on June 14, 1497, his favorite son, Juan, was murdered. The event propelled the pope into a frenzy of reform. He called for an end to papal luxury, to simony, to concubinage—all activities in which he was an accomplished master. He turned decisively at this point to dealing with the influential Dominican friar Savonarola, who had been preaching religious revolution in Florence, calling for widespread reform of the corrupt papacy. Alexander had spent some years in fruitless negotiation with the friar. In 1498, he finally excommunicated him and played upon the jealousy of the Franciscans, who challenged him to an ordeal by fire. When Savonarola declined the challenge, he lost popular support in Florence, and the city magistrates tried him for heresy. He was executed on May 23, 1498, and thus Alexander VI was rid of a persistent challenge to his power.

At about this time, CESARE BORGIA resigned his cardinalate in order to marry Charlotte d'Albret, a French princess, thereby forging a strong alliance between the Borgias and Louis XII of France. With Alexander's aid and complicity, Cesare brought northern Italy under the family's control with such ruthless efficiency that Niccolo Machiavelli used Cesare as the model for his treatise on political power, *The Prince*. On his own, Alexander effectively neutralized the power of Rome's Orsini and Colonna families. He also concluded a powerful alliance with Ferdinand and Isabella of Spain, dividing between them and Portugal, by means of the Treaty of Tordesillas (1494), the New World, which was then in process of being discovered by Europeans.

While alliances such as this undoubtedly strengthened the church politically, Alexander VI's general neglect of his role as a spiritual leader weakened the church morally, preparing the way for the development of the Protestant Reformation even as Alexander lavished huge sums on restoring the monuments of Roman Catholicism and building new ones, most significantly commissioning Michelangelo to draw up plans for the rebuilding of St. Peter's Basilica.

Alexander VI died in Rome on August 18, 1503, three years after he commissioned at extravagant expense a general celebration of 1500 as the Holy Year of the Jubilee.

Further Reading: Eric John, ed. *The Popes: A Concise Biographical History* (New York: George Rainbird, 1964).

Amenhotep III [the Magnificent] (r. 1417–1379 B.C.)

Pharaoh Amenhotep III's reign was marked by peace and architectural achievements.

Amenhotep III was the ninth king of the 18th dynasty of Egypt, grandson of King Amenhotep II and son of Thutmose IV. He married Tiy, a commoner, who gave birth to his son, the future King AKHENATEN. Once Amenhotep settled lingering disputes—chiefly in the area of Nubia (modern Sudan)—Egypt enjoyed a period of peace through the remainder of his reign. Subsequently, Amenhotep III focused his attention on expanding diplomatic relations and new construction.

Internationally, Amenhotep III negotiated trade agreements with Asia and fostered political alliances through marriages with foreign princesses. He also maintained relations with Cyprus, Assyria, and Babylon. The Amarna Letters, which record the diplomacy of Amenhotep III and his son, are a rich source of information about the political aspects of Amenhotep III's reign.

Domestically, Amenhotep III commissioned the building of the temple in Nubia and a mortuary in Thebes. Other projects included the temple to Amon in Luxor and a third pylon at Karnak. Only the remains of the Colossi of Memnon—which was part of his mortuary—survives today. In 1353 B.C., after a 38-year reign, Amenhotep III succumbed to a long illness said to have been associated with obesity.

Amin, Hafizollah (1929–1979)

President of Afghanistan (September 1979–December 1979) after overthrowing Noor Mohammed TAR-AKI in a bloody coup.

Hafizollah Amin was born on August 1, 1929, in Paghman, Afghanistan. He studied education as an undergraduate in Afghanistan, then came to New York City for graduate work at the Teachers' College of Columbia University. After receiving a master's degree—and, he said, having gained his "political consciousness" in the United States—he returned to Afghanistan and joined the People's Democratic Party. Elected to a four-year term in the parliament in 1969, Amin became chiefly responsible for garnering support among the military for the party's policies. He was so successful in this work that the press termed him the "commander of the revolution" after the April 1978 coup, in which Noor Mohammed Taraki came to power. Over the next year, Amin, named prime minister, earned a reputation as the regime's strongman, consolidated his own support, and, after a bloody coup, was elected president in September 1979.

His regime was brief. In December 1979, the Soviet Union invaded Afghanistan, overthrew the government, and assassinated Amin in the capital city of Kabul.

Further Reading: Ainslee T. Embree, ed. *Encyclopedia of Asian History* (New York: Scribner's/Asia Society, 1988).

Amin, Idi (b. 1924 or 1925)

An enigmatic and emotionally unbalanced individual, Idi Amin led a successful coup to become president-for-life of Uganda, ushering in a reign of terrorism and political assassination incongruously tinged with the dictator's tendency to buffoonery and outlandish behavior.

Born Idi Amin Dada Oumee to the Kakwa tribe of northwestern Uganda, Amin gained his military training as a member of the British colonial King's African Rifles during World War II. He served in the Burma theater of operations and, after the war, was part of the British effort to suppress the Mau Mau

revolt in Kenya during 1952–56. A colorful figure, Amin was heavyweight boxing champion of Uganda for nearly a decade, from 1951 to 1960, and was celebrated as a world-class rugby player.

When Uganda achieved independence in 1962, Amin became a close associate of President and Prime Minister Milton Obote. However, friction developed when Amin openly supported rebel forces in the Congo during 1965. He recovered from the resulting political scandal and served Obote as chief of the Ugandan army and air force from 1966 to 1970. Early in 1971, following increasing dissension with Obote, Amin staged a military coup, deposed Obote, and proclaimed himself president on January 25. He took the additional title of field marshal in 1975, affecting uniforms more befitting a member of a secret lodge than a national leader, and finally named himself president for life in 1976.

Amin alternately stunned, outraged, and puzzled much of the world with his actions. To many, he seemed on the verge of insanity—or even well beyond it. A fanatical nationalist, he expelled all Asians from his country in 1972, thereby precipitating widespread economic collapse. He repeatedly and gratuitously insulted such imperial powers as Great Britain and the United States, and he propelled his nation into an alliance with Libya under the similarly eccentric dictatorship of Muammar al-QADAFFI. He also voiced his support for the Palestine Liberation Organization, and in July 1976 sanctioned the hijacking to Entebbe of a French airliner bearing (among others) Jewish and Israeli passengers.

While incurring the wrath of most of the international community, which branded him a terrorist, Amin also conducted debilitating border warfare with Tanzania and Kenya and, within his own borders, authorized the persecution of various tribes. It is estimated that Amin's forces tortured and killed anywhere from 100,000 to 300,000 Ugandans.

In October 1978, nationalist Ugandan troops and their Tanzanian allies invaded Uganda, reaching the capital city of Kampala on April 13, 1979. They did not find Idi Amin there. He had fled, first to Libya an.' finally to Saudi Arabia.

Further Reading: Henry Kyemba. *A State of Blood: The Inside Story of Idi Amin* (New York: Grosset & Dunlap, 1977); David Martin. *General Amin* (London: Faber, 1974).

An Lushan (ca. 703–757)

An Lushan's rebellion against the Tang dynasty of China in 755 was the beginning of that dynasty's end.

An Lushan was born of Turkish-Iranian parentage in today's Manchuria. His ancestors were part of a foreign contingent who lived on China's frontiers.

An Lushan became a soldier early in life, and by the age of 33, he had attained the rank of general. Because the Tang rulers believed that foreigners made the best frontier commanders—they were less inclined to be influenced by internal politics—An Lushan quickly rose to become governor of three northeastern provinces. A favorite of the Tang court, he visited the capital often, and his charming buffoonery endeared him to the emperor and his administrators.

It was all an act. In 755, An Lushan and his followers rebelled against the Tang dynasty, and he proclaimed himself the new emperor, first of the Great Yen dynasty. An Lushan probably commanded significant popular support for his revolt. A recent series of natural disasters had visited China; since popular religion taught that the emperor was a mediator in all natural events, the recent drought, floods, and storms were widely viewed as evidence of the emperor's deficiency or evil.

In any event, An Lushan seized the Chinese government with an iron fist and soon had complete control of northern China. At the height of his powers, eye and skin disease—possibly the result of diabetes—caused him great pain and made him irascible to the point of madness, diminishing his ability to rule and ultimately driving him to a campaign of personal cruelty. Those closest to him came to fear his irrational temper. Soon, he lost popular support as well, and in January 757 he was assassinated by his second son, An Chinghsu.

Although the Tang dynasty recovered after An Lushan's coup d'état, it never regained its former strength and power. By 906, the last Tang emperor was gone, and the empire was ruled for more than 200 years by the Liao.

Further Reading: E. G. Pulleyblank, *The Background of the Rebellion of An Lushan* (London: Oxford University Press, 1955).

Andom, Aman Michael   (1924–1974)

Andom, who headed the Ethiopian armed forces that overthrew Emperor HAILE SELASSIE, became provisional head of state before he was killed by other members of the government.

Born in Khartoum, the Sudan, on July 21, 1924, Aman Andom attended Comboni College and later St. George's Military School in Khartoum. After Mussolini and the Italians invaded Ethiopia in 1935, Andom joined the Sudanese forces of Haile Selassie to fight the Italians, becoming a second lieutenant. At war's end, he traveled to Ethiopia and rose rapidly in the military establishment, becoming a major general in 1962.

In May 1964, Andom was assigned as military attaché to the Ethiopian Embassy in Washington, D.C. There, he received a bachelor's degree from Howard University. Upon his return to Ethiopia in July 1965, the general was named defense minister in Haile Selassie's cabinet. In August 1974, Andom was promoted to lieutenant general and made chief of staff of the armed forces. In September, following minor popular uprisings against Haile Selassie's regime, the military overthrew the emperor and named Andom as provisional head of government in addition to chief of staff and minister of defense.

Initial reports identified Andom as the strongman who had initiated the coup, but these were soon to be violently refuted as the bloodless coup turned bloody on the night of November 23, 1974. That night, a purge of the old aristocracy resulted in the executions of 59 former government officials. The same evening, at the direction of Mengistu Mariam, later revealed as "the true moving force" of the coup, military units were sent to Andom's home and, during a two-hour gun battle, the general was killed.

It was speculated that Andom, born to Eritrean parents, was killed because of his conciliatory attitude toward the continuing Eritrean struggle for independence from Ethiopia.

Antonescu, Ion   (1882–1946)

Dictator of Romania during World War II, Antonescu brought his country into a disastrous alliance with Nazi Germany.

Ion Antonescu was born in Piteşti, Romania, on June 15, 1882. After service in World War I, he was appointed to the diplomatically sensitive post of military attaché first in Paris, then in London. In 1934, he became chief of the general staff, and in 1937 he was named minister of defense. Shortly after King Carol II created a dictatorial government in 1938, he was dismissed as minister because of his association with the Iron Guard, a Romanian Fascist party.

But it was Antonescu and the Iron Guard who came into power in 1940, after Romania was partitioned among the Axis powers and the Soviet Union during June–September. Antonescu set himself up as an absolute dictator in the manner of Adolf HITLER and openly vowed allegiance to Germany. When his own Iron Guard instituted a reign of terror and corruption during 1940–41, Antonescu successfully suppressed the group, then recovered widespread public favor by instituting a program of domestic reform.

Antonescu entered World War II on the side of Germany, pouring large numbers of troops into the hopeless carnage of the Russian Front. Although he was a skillful leader during the war years—and far less repressive than his Fascist allies—support for Antonescu crumbled as Romanian war losses escalated. King Michael led a successful coup d'état against Antonescu in August of 1944. The dictator, deposed, was imprisoned and subsequently tried by the Romanian Communist People's Court for war crimes. He was executed near Jilava on June 1, 1946.

A-pao-chi   (d. 926)

A-pao-chi led the Mongolian Khitan clan into northwest China and helped establish the Liao dynasty.

Originally elected to a three-year term as Khitan khan, A-pao-chi refused to relinquish his power at the expiration of his term, proclaiming himself king of the Khitan nation. The collapse of the Tang dynasty in 907 created a power vacuum in northwest China, which A-pao-chi attempted to fill by setting himself up as emperor. By 916, A-pao-chi had established a Chinese-style dynasty, designating his son as heir apparent. In organizing the military, however, he stayed true to his people's nomadic heritage. He organized small, mobile fighting units called *ordos*, similar to the hordes of his ancestors. He then set up administrative districts with 12 *ordos* to a district for both defense and taxation purposes.

When in 926 the Chin rulers attempted to assert themselves in northern China, eventually establishing the Later Chin dynasty (936–947), A-pao-chi decided to aid the Chin ruler rather than oppose him and risk the loss of his fledgling dynasty. In return, A-pao-chi received what is now Beijing.

Upon A-pao-chi's death in 926, the Khitans proclaimed the Liao dynasty, acknowledging A-pao-chi as its founder and bestowing upon him the posthumous title of Grand Progenitor.

Arafat, Yasir   (b. 1929)

Chairman of the Palestine Liberation Organization (PLO) and president of the provisional government of Palestine, Arafat led the PLO campaign in the cause of Palestinian nationalism.

A native of Gaza, Palestine (now Israeli-occupied territory), one of seven children born to a wealthy merchant, Arafat emigrated to Egypt after the state of Israel was created. He attended the University of Cairo and became involved in the Muslim Brotherhood and the Union of Palestinian Students, serving as president of the latter from 1952 to 1956. Commissioned in the Egyptian army, he served in the Suez Campaign of 1956. While working as an engineer in Kuwait, Arafat co-founded al-Fatah, an anti-Israeli guerrilla group, of which he became the principal leader.

After, al-Fatah became the leading military component of the PLO and Arafat was named chairman of

the PLO in 1968. Setting as his uncompromising goal the replacement of Israel with a secular Palestinian state, Arafat directed a campaign of guerrilla action and out-and-out terrorism against Israel, becoming commander in chief of the Palestinian Revolutionary Forces in 1971. In 1973, however, after he was named to head the PLO's political department, Arafat's focus shifted from military and guerrilla tactics to political and diplomatic persuasion. By 1974, when he addressed the UN General Assembly, Arafat was widely recognized by the nations of the world as the chief spokesman for the Palestinian people.

Arafat's step away from direct violent confrontation with Israel was perceived by Syrian-supported factions within the PLO as weakness, and beginning in 1982 he found himself the target of criticism from his own organization. In a situation of civil war, political chaos and Israeli invasion in Lebanon, and fearful of military action from these factions, Arafat moved PLO headquarters from Beirut to Tunisia in August 1982, then to Baghdad, Iraq, in 1987.

After Palestinians in the Israeli-occupied territories launched an uprising in December 1987, Arafat persuaded the Palestine National Council to declare an independent Palestinian state in November 1988. At this time, he formally renounced terrorism and accepted United Nations resolution 242 and Israel's right to exist.

Arafat was named president of the Palestinian government-in-exile in 1989, and despite continued opposition from radicals and Syrian-backed rebels within the PLO, he carried on an extended dialogue with Israeli leaders in an effort to establish a Palestinian state and peaceful relations between Israelis and Palestinians. For the most part, however, Arafat's peace proposals were greeted with skepticism in Israel, and he became increasingly isolated diplomatically, particularly after the 1991 Persian Gulf War that followed Iraq's invasion of Kuwait. Despite this, Arafat has retained great power and influence among a majority of the Palestinians, and in 1993 he signed potentially epoch-making preliminary peace accords with Israel.

Further Reading: Allen Hart. *Arafat: A Political Biography* (Bloomington: Indiana University Press, 1989); Janet and John Wallach. *Arafat: In the Eyes of the Beholder* (New York: Carol Publishing Group, 1990).

Ardashir I   (r. 224–41)

This shadowy figure founded the Sasanian Empire of ancient Persia, building or rebuilding numerous cities, and making Zoroastrianism the official and dominant religion of his state.

Ardashir was the son of Babak, who was the son (or descendant) of one Sasan, a vassal of Gochihr, the king of Persis. Babak obtained for his son the military post of *argabad* in the settlement of Darabgerd (vicinity of modern Darab, Iran). Using this position, the young man soon extended his control over neighboring settlements. While his son was thus occupied, Babak murdered Gochihr and assumed the title of king. Babak sought permission from Artabanus V, king of Parthia, to name his eldest son, Shapur, as successor. Artabanus refused permission, but Shapur succeeded Babak anyway, touching off a struggle between him and his younger brother, Ardashir. Ardashir killed Shapur and was crowned king of Persis in 208.

The new king was immediately faced with a rebellion in Darabgerd, which he brutally suppressed, then went on to subjugate Kerman and territories along the Persian Gulf coast. He established as the capital of his enlarged empire the ancient city of Gur (Firuzabad, Iran), naming it in his own honor, Ardashir-Kwarrah.

Ardashir relentlessly extended his reach, conquering Isfahan, Kerman, Elymais and Mesene. In 224, he fought the Parthian army under King Artabanus V, winning a major victory and slaying the king. Following this, he marched on the Parthian capital of Ctesiphon and became "king of kings" of Iran. Naming his son, Shapur I, successor, Ardashir established the Sasanian Empire.

Further Reading: George Rawlinson. *The Five Great Monarchies of the Ancient Eastern World* (New York: Dodd, Mead, 1881).

Ashikaga Takauji (1305–1358)

First of the Ashikaga shoguns (military commanders) and founder of Muromachi shognate (or *bakufu* [military government]), Ashikaga Takauji commissioned the compilation of an important samurai warrior code.

Ashikaga Takauji came of age amid the turbulence of medieval Japan, which was racked by internal warfare between rival feudal lords and their coteries of warriors and warrior vassals. Takauji himself was the leader of a warrior family and became the vassal of the Hojo regents, the de facto rulers of Japan who controlled the country from their headquarters at Kamakura. The regents dispatched him in 1333 to western Japan to subdue a revolt against the Kamakura *bakufu* staged by Emperor Go-Daigo. Seizing the main chance, Takauji *joined* Go-Daigo and enlisted the alliance of other western warrior families to overthrow the Hojo regents.

The revolt was successful, and Go-Daigo, now restored to the imperial throne, rewarded Ashikaga

Takauji with numerous court titles. However, the wary emperor denied him real power by declining to make him shogun. In 1336, therefore, Takauji rebelled against Go-Daigo, driving him from the throne and installing another emperor, Komyo, in his place. Go-Daigo fled to the south, where he established a rival government known as the Southern Court, and for the next 56 years Japan was torn by redoubled civil strife among a bewildering array of factions.

Amid this chaos, Ashikaga Takauji assumed tight control over Kyoto, obtaining for himself at last, in 1338, the coveted title of shogun. He ordered the creation of *Kemmu shikimoku*, an important warrior code, and presided over the Ashikaga (or Muromachi) *bakufu*.

Ever ruthless, Takauji ended a rivalry with his brother Tadyoshi by poisoning him in 1352. He also participated in the endemic state of warfare his own actions against Go-Daigo had created. Paradoxically, this violent and ruthless warrior was a Buddhist poet and served as patron to the great Zen monk Muso Soseki.

Further Reading: H. Paul Varley. *Imperial Restoration in Medieval Japan* (New York: Columbia University Press, 1971).

Ashurbanipal (r. 668 B.C.–late 7th century B.C.)

The last of the great Assyrian kings, Ashurbanipal was one of the most learned rulers of the ancient Middle East. He is best known for the tremendous library he assembled in Nineveh, the first systematically organized library in the ancient Middle East.

Born in the 7th century B.C., Ashurbanipal was named crown prince of Assyria by his father, ESARHADDON, in May 672 to avert a power struggle between Ashurbanipal and his half-brother, Shumash-shum-ukin, who was made crown prince of Babylonia. Ashurbanipal's physical prowess and personal attractiveness, combined with the influence of the queen mother, virtually assured Ashurbanipal's selection as the royal successor even before Esarhaddon died.

During the period before his father's death, Ashurbanipal mastered scribal and priestly knowledge, learned to read various languages, and honed his considerable athletic talents. Upon Esarhaddon's death in 668, Ashurbanipal's first task was to deal with an insurrection in Egypt, where the Egyptian king, Taharqa, had managed to win popular support by invading the Nile Delta. Ashurbanipal quickly neutralized the threat from Taharqa and decided to invest local princes with Assyrian garrisons to oversee the administration of the Delta areas. After two failed attempts to find loyal local princes, he appointed a single ruler over all the Delta area. With this territory secured, Ashurbanipal turned to other military conquests—and to the growing tension between him and his half-brother.

While allowing his brother to maintain local control in Babylonia, Ashurbanipal ensured that garrisons and officials still reported directly to himself. Shumash-shum-ukin soon thirsted for power of his own and entered into secret alliances with some of the strongest of the outlying peoples in the Assyrian Empire. Had they risen together at once, Ashurbanipal surely would have been defeated. But he discovered the alliances and moved against Babylon. Shumash-shum-ukin committed suicide during the siege.

Not only was Ashurbanipal adept at dealing with military problems, he was also an able administrator. While financing his martial exploits and satisfying his appetite for learned works with which to stock his library, Ashurbanipal managed to operate in a fiscally sound manner. His legacy lives not in his conquests, policies, or administrative methods, but rather in his library. Many of the surviving works of the ancient Middle East come from his great library at Nineveh, which was impressive not only for its holdings—subjects ranged from astronomy to psychology to history—but for the systematic manner in which works were collected and catalogued. Ashurbanipal was one of the few enlightened rulers of the ancient Middle East.

Ashurnasirpal II   (d. 859 B.C.)

This Assyrian king greatly expanded his nation's holdings, forged the most powerful army the world had yet seen, and visited slaughter upon Mesopotamia, Kurdistan and Syria.

Nothing is known of Ashurnasirpal's birth or early life. He ascended the Assyrian throne after the death of his father, Tukulti-Ninurta, whose reign lasted only from 884 to 883 B.C. Immediately upon assuming power, Ashurnasirpal warred against and suppressed the hill tribes north of the Tigris River in what is now Kurdistan. He ruthlessly sacked the city of Nishtun in 883, then, the following year, put down a revolt begun in the city of Suru and backed by the Syrian kingdom of Bit-Adini. He next crushed the Aramaeans and, during 881–80, defeated an alliance of tribes located east of the Tigris.

After campaigning against Babylon, Ashurnasirpal captured Suhu, another rebellious city, in 878. He pushed into Syria, defeated Bit-Adini, and crossed the Orontes River, extorting tribute from the cities of Phoenicia during 875–74. His final campaign was a successful expedition against the Kashiari hill tribes, which were in rebellion on the northwest borderlands of Assyria during 866.

In an age of isolated city-states and loosely governed tribes, Ashurnasirpal greatly expanded the imperial reach of Assyria, molding his nation into a military society governed by institutionalized terror. An able military leader who equipped his well-trained army with the world's most advanced iron and bronze weaponry and made skillful tactical use of archers and apparently irresistible corps of combat charioteers, Ashurnasirpal showed his enemies no quarter. Military prisoners were routinely impaled and mutilated, and conquered populations were pressed into unconditional slavery.

Further Reading: Albert Ten Eyck Olmstead. *A History of Assyria* (New York: Scribner's, 1923).

Askia Muhammad   [Mohammad I Askia, Muhammad ibn abi Bakr Ture] (d. 1538)

The greatest emperor of the Songhai Empire of West Africa, Askia Muhammad founded the Askian dynasty.

Of obscure ancestry and birth, Askia Muhammad served as a military commander under Sonni Ali Ber, ruler of Songhai. On Sonni's death in 1492, the charismatic Askia Muhammad mustered an army and defeated the numerically superior forces of Sonni Baru, son of Sonni Ali Ber, in the spectacular Battle of Anfao on April 12, 1493.

Ascending the throne of Songhai, Askia Muhammad instituted a series of empire-wide reforms. He vigorously purged his land of the pagan practices that had characterized the dynasty of Sonni and instituted an orthodox form of Islam. He bureaucratized the government, establishing ministries responsible for finance, justice, the interior, and agriculture. Most important, he created a well-organized standing army and a navy consisting of war canoes plying the Niger River.

After making a pilgrimmage to Mecca in 1495–97, Askia Muhammad embarked on a series of ruthless military campaigns aimed at expanding his empire and, presumably, Islam. He conquered the Mossi of Yatenga (Upper Volta) during 1498–1502. He moved next against the Tuaregs of the Aïr Massif (vicinity of Agadez, Niger) during 1505–1506. For the next seven years, from 1507 to 1514, Askia pushed his armies toward Senegal and to the frontiers of modern-day Niger and Nigeria to fight the Fulani and the Borgu. These long and arduous campaigns did not result in the subjugation of the tribes. However, during this time, Askia's armies did defeat the Bornu of northeastern Nigeria.

In the wake of these campaigns of expansion, one of Askia's subordinates, the Karta of Kabi, staged a mutiny against him. During 1516–17, Askia suppressed the Karta's revolt, but it had become clear that the protracted spasm of Songhai expansion had come to an end. Soon, the children of Askia Muhammad fell to disputing over who should succeed their father. Amid these disputes, Askia grew increasingly bitter and physically infirm. Ill and nearly blind, he was deposed by his son Musa (who took the name Askia Musa) in 1528 and was sent into internal exile on a small island in the Niger River.

When another of Askia Muhammad's sons, Ismaïl, ascended the throne, he brought his father out of exile. The old ruler bestowed upon Ismaïl his turban and sword and died a short time later in the Songhai capital of Gao.

Further Reading: Sekene Mody Cissoko. *Tombouctou et l'empire Songhay* (Dakar, Senegal: Nouvelles Editions Africains, 1975).

Asoka [Ashoka] (273 B.C.?–232 B.C.? [also given as 238 B.C.])

King of Magadha and third and last effective emperor of the Mauryan dynasty, Asoka began his career as a ruthless conqueror, but then adopted a peaceful policy of "conquest by *dharma*."

Asoka was the grandson of CHANDRAGUPTA MAURYA and one of many sons of Bindusara. The Ceylonese Chronicles record that he fought a bloody war of succession with his brothers, killing 99 of them in order to ascend the throne. Other sources—most notably inscriptions left by Asoka himself—make no mention of this. Indisputable, however, are Asoka's early wars—fought in the eighth year of his reign—against the State of Kalinga on India's east coast. These bloody conflicts greatly expanded Asoka's realm to encompass all but the southern tip of India, but the carnage and suffering he himself wrought caused Asoka great remorse. The monarch turned to the teachings of Buddha, pledged to live and to govern by Buddha's teachings, and to spread the religion through his realm.

Asoka not only renounced war, he preached religious tolerance, advocated the ethical practice of government and commerce, built rest houses throughout his realm for the benefit of travelers, planted many trees, and established medical facilities for human beings as well as animals. He decreed an end to the slaughter of animals in the royal kitchens, and he is said to have ordered the construction of 84,000 *stupas* (reliquary mounds) throughout India. He is also credited with having established the basic sites of Buddhist pilgrimage and of providing a supreme example of Buddhist piety.

Asoka dedicated himself to the practice and dissemination of *dharma*—the practice of honesty, compassion, benevolence, non-violence, a selfless asceticism, and general civility toward all living things.

Asoka's remarkable policies seem to have been effective during his lifetime, but, following his death about 232 B.C. (or about 238 B.C.), the Mauryan empire quickly disintegrated. Thus Asoka is revered more for the ideals he exemplified than for having created an enduring state.

Further Reading: Sachchidananda Bhattacharyva. *A Dictionary of Indian History* (New York: Braziller, 1967); Ainslee T. Embree, ed. *Encyclopedia of Asian History* (New York: Scribner's, 1988).

Assad, Hafiz al- (b. 1928)

Assad has been president and absolute dictator of Syria since 1971—longer than any previous Syrian regime in modern history.

Assad was born in Qardaha, Syria, to a poor peasant family named Wahsh—"wild beast." In the process of remaking himself first into a military commander, then a national leader, the young man changed his name to Assad—"lion."

He attended the Hims Military Academy, graduating as an air force pilot in 1955. In 1958, he was sent to Syria's longtime ally, the Soviet Union, to study night warfare techniques and was promoted to squadron leader in the Syrian air force, only to be dismissed from the service in 1961 after he opposed Syria's secession from Egyptian president Nasser's United Arab Republic. Following this, Assad became a leader in the Ba'ath Party, which advocated pan-Arab unity under the banner of socialism. The Ba'ath Party assumed power in Syria in 1963, and on March 8, 1965, Assad was appointed chief of the air force, becoming minister of defense the following February.

In 1969–70, the civilian and military wings of the Ba'ath Party divided, and Assad, a member of the military wing, assumed control of the government in 1970, winning election as president the following year. Assad allied Syria with Egypt in the Yom Kippur War against Israel in October 1973. Defeated, he nevertheless emerged as a national hero and as a hero of the Arab world. In 1976, claiming Lebanon as part of "Greater Syria," he sent a large occupation force into that strife-torn nation. As part of his effort to create a union or alliance among Syria, Jordan, Lebanon, and the Palestine Liberation Organization (PLO), Assad both openly and covertly financed various terrorist groups, including Yasir ARAFAT's PLO.

Assad had also sought alliance with Iraq in 1979, but reasserted his nation's traditional animosity toward Iraq in 1983, when he closed his border. More dramatically, Assad joined the United States and other "coalition" nations in opposing Iraq during the Gulf War of 1991. Indeed, the Gulf War came at a most propitious time for Assad, who had long aligned his nation with the Soviet Union. With the breakup of that nation, he needed to seek some form of rapprochement with the United States and the West. Joining the coalition against Saddam HUSSEIN's Iraq provided just such an opportunity at a very critical time.

While Assad has shown remarkable political agility, his regime has come under severe attack from dissidents, particularly the Muslim Brotherhood. His response to those he considers rebels has been extremely harsh. In 1982, he virtually destroyed the city of Hamah, a stronghold of the Muslim Brotherhood, and killed some 20,000 dissidents. In addition to outright military measures, Assad has made extensive use of detention, torture, and execution as means of suppressing incipient rebellion. Like many other Arab leaders, he has deliberately fostered a personality cult, and his image is displayed prominently throughout Syria.

Further Reading: Europa Publications. *The Middle East and North Africa 1993* (London: Europa Publications, 1992); Bernard Reich, ed. *Political Leaders of the Continental Middle East and North Africa: A Biographical Dictionary* (New York: Greenwood Press, 1990).

Atahualpa   (1500–1533)

The last king of the Inca Empire in Peru, Atahualpa came to power after a devastating civil war against the forces of his half-brother. Upon winning power, however, he was captured by the invading Spanish conquistadores led by Francisco Pizarro and put to death.

Atahualpa, born in Quito, was the favorite son of Inca emperor Huayna Capac and the daughter of the king of Quito (Ecuador). When the emperor died in about 1527, Atahualpa was living in Quito and refused to return to the Incan capital of Cuzco. While his half-brother Huascar was crowned emperor, Atahualpa claimed his right to rule Quito as a sovereign nation. But Inca law specified that the emperor could be succeeded only by his son born of a lawful Inca wife, always his own sister. In addition, the law stated that no territory conquered by the emperor could be separated from the empire. Quito had been overrun by the late emperor, who then married the Quito king's daughter. Atahualpa was their son. Huascar was the son of the late emperor and his lawful Inca wife.

Even though the law was on his side, Huascar accepted Atahualpa's claims for a time, but as he grew more concerned about his half-brother's ambition, he demanded absolute fealty and ordered Atahualpa

to return to Cuzco. Atahualpa complied—secretly accompanied by 30,000 soldiers, dressed as ordinary citizens. Huascar was warned of impending trouble and began assembling his own soldiers.

The brothers met in battle near Quito, Atahualpa proving victorious. After imprisoning his half-brother, he summoned Huascar's supporters to a meeting ostensibly to discuss the government. Once they were all assembled—princes, governors, and officials from Huascar's court—Atahualpa ordered their slaughter, and they were beheaded, hanged, or drowned. Following this exertion, Atahualpa retired to the natural warm springs of Cajamarca, an Inca resort.

The bloody ruler's time of trouble was hardly over, however. While recuperating from the civil war, Atahualpa received word that the Spaniards had landed on the northern coast of Peru. The emperor sent messengers to invite them to Cajamarca, and Francisco PIZARRO led his small force into the town on November 15, 1532. Two of Pizarro's men then invited Atahualpa to attend a dinner with the Spanish leader the following day. The Inca king set out with a large entourage of unarmed men. Arriving at the city, Atahualpa was greeted by Friar Vicente de Valverde, Pizarro's chaplain. The friar proceeded to instruct his guests in Christian doctrine and then urged Atahualpa to accept Christianity and the sovereignty of Spain. He refused, politely offering to accept the Spanish king as his brother. On this, Friar Valverde gave a signal, and the conquistadores launched an ambush of Atahualpa and his entourage, killing thousands of the Indians. Atahualpa himself was taken prisoner. The following day, he offered as ransom a roomful of gold and two roomsful of silver. Pizarro agreed to free him upon receipt of the ransom. Atahualpa's retainers set about ravaging the countryside to obtain the requisite jewelry and ornaments, which were transported to Cajamarca, where the Spaniard ordered the treasure melted down into bullion and ingots—some 24 tons of gold and silver.

In the meantime, Huascar received word that his half-brother had been taken prisoner by the Spanish. He offered an even larger ransom for Atahualpa's release. Pizarro then ordered Huascar to present himself in Cajamarca so that the Spanish could evaluate his claim to the throne. En route to Cajamarca, Huascar and his entourage were ambushed—quite possibly on orders from Atahualpa, who feared that his half-brother would use the opportunity to regain the throne.

Once Pizarro received the full ransom offered by Atahualpa, he became concerned that, if freed, the Inca emperor would rally his people against him and his forces. Instead of releasing him as promised, Pizarro ordered him tried for usurping the Inca crown, ordering the assassination of Huascar, squandering the resources of the empire, committing idolatry and adultery, and inciting an insurrection against the Spaniards. Found guilty and sentenced to be burned at the stake, Atahualpa was given one last chance to convert to Christianity. Friar Valverde promised the emperor that if he converted, he would be garotted rather than burned alive. Atahualpa consented, was baptized, and was given the name Juan Atahualpa. His final request was for his children to be given the protection of Pizarro and that his remains be taken to Quito. The emperor was executed by strangulation on August 29, 1533.

Two months later, on October 30, the Spaniards exhumed his body and removed it to a church in San Francisco, where a Catholic funeral service was held. The ceremony was disrupted by Atahualpa's wives and sisters, who protested the violation of Inca funeral rites. The emperor's remains were buried in the churchyard nevertheless, but after the Spanish left, they were again exhumed and removed to Quito. It was a grim triumph for the Indians; for the death of Atahualpa marked the end of the Inca Empire.

Further Reading: Alan Axelrod. *Chronicle of the Indian Wars: From Colonial Times to Wounded Knee* (New York: Prentice Hall, 1993); Keith Irvine, ed. *Encyclopedia of Indians of the Americas* (St. Clair Shores, Michigan: Scholarly Press, 1979).

Atatürk, Mustafa Kemal (1881–1938)

The father of modern Turkey, Atatürk singlehandedly changed his nation from a backward Ottoman state to a reform-minded, modern country.

The son of a lower-middle-class customs clerk and his peasant wife, Mustafa Kemal was born in Salonika, Greece, which was then a part of Ottoman-controlled Macedonia. After a difficult and impoverished childhood resulting from the death of his father, the boy attended the state military school, then the Senior Military School, and, finally, in 1899, the Ottoman Military Academy in Istanbul. There, in addition to advanced military training, he read the likes of Rousseau, Voltaire, Hobbes, and other seminal social thinkers. At the age of 20, he was promoted to the General Staff College.

At the General Staff College, Kemal and his comrades founded the Vatan, a secret society with revolutionary leanings. Failing to expand the Vatan as he hoped, Kemal joined the Committee on Union and Progress, which was aligned with the Young Turk movement. While not directly associated with the Young Turks and their coup of 1908, Kemal worked closely with many of their key leaders.

With the outbreak of World War I, Kemal was shocked to see the sultan align the Ottoman Empire with the Germans, whom he despised. Regardless of his personal views, however, he led his troops with skill on every Ottoman front during the war. At Gallipoli, beginning in April 1915, he held off the British and ANZAC forces for more than a month, earning him the name of "Savior of Istanbul." From there, he took control of the 2nd and 3rd Armies, stopping the advance of the Russian forces south in the Caucasus in 1916. He was in command of the 7th Army against the British at Aleppo when the war ended in 1918.

The victorious Allies descended upon the Ottoman Empire like ravenous vultures. Long called the "Sick Man of Europe" because years of outmoded autocracy had led to internal decay, the Ottoman Empire appeared to have been dealt a death blow by the war, and every European nation, it seemed, wanted a piece of it. The terms of the armistice ending the war were harsh, and a secret agreement had been reached among the Allies about the partitioning of the Ottoman Empire. Accordingly, Britain wasted no time deploying her fleet to the harbor of Istanbul.

The Allies had hoped to maintain the sultanate nominally, as a pawn in southeastern Europe, and there were many within Turkey who wanted to see the sultanate survive under foreign regency. Kemal, however, wanted to create an independent state, sloughing off the old imperial holdings. Directed to Anatolia in 1919 to put down unrest there, he instead organized dissent and began a movement against the numerous "foreign interests." He set up a provisional government in Anatolia, of which he was elected president, and fostered unified resistance to foreigners. The sultan ordered a holy war against the nationalists and in particular called for Kemal's execution.

When the sultan signed the Treaty of Sèvres in August 1920, effectively giving the Ottoman Empire to the Allies in return for his continued power over its remnants, almost all public support went to Kemal. When the nationalist army moved on Istanbul, the Allies looked to Greece for help. After 18 months of costly combat, the Greeks were finally defeated in August 1922.

On November 1, 1922, the Grand National Assembly dissolved the sultanate of Mehmed VI, and on October 29, 1923, Mustafa Kemal was elected president of the new Republic of Turkey. The Sick Man of Europe had died, and Turkey arose. While he was called president, Kemal was, in fact, an unabashed dictator, outlawing any competing political parties, and engineering repeated reelection until his death.

Kemal reformed Turkey under six "isms," collectively referred to as Kemalism: republicanism, the adoption of democracy of the sultanate; secularism, removing Islam from official life and Turkish law; populism, emphasizing the common man and moving away from the favoritism of the sultanate; nationalism, building Turkish pride; statism, the revamping of the economy; and reformism, in hopes of keeping the movement from stagnating. His most notable reforms were in the areas of economy and society. He opened up the Turkish economy to the industrialized West, secularized the state, ended the Islamic suppression of women, and generally forced the Western way of life on his people, as PETER THE GREAT had done in Russia two centuries earlier.

After the declaration of the Turkish Republic, Kemal was given a new name, Atatürk, "father of the Turks." His unfailing energy and love of the republic gained him great popularity despite his despotism and his scandalous private life, which was marked by heavy drinking and generally unbridled behavior. Mustafa Kemal Atatürk died of cirrhosis of the liver on November 10, 1938.

Further Reading: Harold Armstrong. *Gray Wolf: The Life of Kemal Ataturk* (New York: Minton, Balch, 1933); John P. D. Balfour Kinross. *Atatürk* (New York: Morrow, 1965).

Attila the Hun (d. 453)

This aggressive and ambitious chief of the nomadic Huns was called in his own time the "Scourge of God" and bequeathed to history a name synonymous with ruthless conquest.

Attila and his brother Bleda became joint chieftains of the Huns, a warlike tribe of Germanic nomads, in 433, following the death of their uncle Ruas. Under Ruas, the Huns had grown to a major power in central Europe, and the Roman emperor Theodosius II concluded a treaty with Ruas in which he agreed to pay a tribute and to make the ruler a general in the Roman army, thereby effectively ceding to the Huns sovereignty over the province of Panonia (modern Hungary). On the death of Ruas, Attila and Bleda renewed the treaty with Theodosius, exacting from him a heavy tribute of 700 pounds of gold annually. This bought the Roman Empire a half-dozen years of peace, as Attila and Bleda turned their attention to wars of conquest against Scythia, Media, and Persia. Then, during 441–43, the Vandal king GAISERIC bribed Attila into invading Rome's Eastern Empire. The treaty with Theodosius notwithstanding, Attila advanced into Illyricum, leading his Huns into Moesia and Thrace and up to the walls of Constantinople itself. Attila destroyed the imperial army of Aspar and freely raided the Balkans. At last, in desperation, Theodosius concluded in August 443 another treaty, which levied an increased tribute payment.

A highly romanticized 19th-century vision of Attila the Hun. (From Charlotte M. Yonge, Pictorial History of the World's Great Nations, *1882)*

Two years later, Attila assassinated his brother, thereby making himself sole ruler of the Huns, whose empire now extended from southern Germany in the west to the Volga or Ural River in the east and from the Baltic in the north to the Danube, Black Sea, and Caucasus in the south.

In 447, Attila struck the Eastern Empire again. Constantinople was thrown into total panic because its walls, on which the defenders successfully relied during the first invasion, had been badly damaged by a recent earthquake. East Roman forces diverted Attila's advance, however, at the Battle of Utus. Although the imperial army was again defeated, the action did succeed in sending Attila's Huns toward Greece and away from Constantinople. In Greece, Attila reached, but failed to breach, the fortress city of Thermopylae. Yet Theodosius clearly had had enough of Attila's depredations and negotiated a peace that obligated him to pay three times the original tribute amount and included the cession of a 50-

mile-wide strip along the right bank of the Danube, from Singidunum (modern Belgrade) to Novae (Svistov, in modern Bulgaria).

Yet Attila was insatiable. In 450, he turned his attention toward the Western Empire of Rome. Pretexts for the invasion were readily forthcoming. Gaiseric of the Vandals wanted an ally in the West; one of two heirs to the Frankish throne asked Attila for an alliance; and, finally, Attila sought redress for the rebuff he had suffered from Valentinian III, ruler of the Western Empire, when he had sought the hand in marriage of his sister Honoria. In 451, then, Attila crossed the Rhine and attacked Gaul with a force reported to have numbered half a million (but which modern scholars believe was closer to 100,000).

Attila attempted to persuade the Visigoth THEODORIC I the Great to join the battle, but the Roman general Aetius convinced him to ally the Visigoths with Rome. Thus Aetius assembled a coalition of imperial forces, Visigoths, and others—principally the Alans, fickle kinsmen of the Huns—to confront Attila's horde.

During May and June of 451, Attila besieged Orléans, which was on the verge of surrender when Aetius arrived to relieve it, pursuing Attila's army as far as the Catalaunian Plains, near Châlons-sur-Marne. Aetius won a decisive victory at the ensuing Battle of Châlons during mid June 451. It was a contest of momentous consequences, for a Hun victory would have spelled the end of Roman and Christian civilization and perhaps would have signalled the commencement of the Asian domination of Europe. As it turned out, Attila, badly defeated, was permitted to retreat.

The following year, Attila again demanded the hand of Honoria and was again refused by Valentinian. He responded this time by invading Italy, destroying Aquileia and forcing the withdrawal of the people of Venetia (who, fleeing to islands off the Italian coast, contributed to the founding of Venice). Attila's hordes annihilated Padua and advanced on Minicio. Aetius had rushed back to Italy from Gaul, but could do relatively little with the small force with which he had been able to march. Fortunately for the Romans, Attila had just learned that forces under command of one of his underlings in Illyricum had suffered a bad defeat. With his own army in Italy being eroded by famine and pestilence, Attila consented to see Pope Leo I, who called on him in his camp.

What happened in Attila's tent is not known. Perhaps Leo made a new offer of tribute. Perhaps Attila feared the illness and starvation around him would destroy his army. Perhaps—as Catholic tradition has it—Attila was overawed by the holy majesty of the pontiff. For whatever reason or reasons, Attila sum-

marily withdrew from Italy. He died the next year, and his vast empire almost immediately shattered into fragments as his sons squabbled over the throne, and as tributary tribes, including the Ostrogoths and the Gepidae, rebelled.

Further Reading: Otto Maenchen-Helfen. *The World of the Huns* (Berkeley: University of California Press, 1973); E. A. Thompson. *A History of Attila and the Huns* (Oxford: Clarendon Press, 1948).

Augustus, Gaius Julius Caesar Octavianus (63 B.C.–A.D. 14)

The first emperor of Rome, Gaius Octavius (the honorary title "Augustus" was conferred by the Senate in 27 B.C.) stopped at nothing to achieve absolute imperial power but, having achieved it, ruled with moderation and wisdom.

Augustus—usually called Octavian before being honored by the Senate as Augustus—was born on September 23, 63 B.C., the son of Gaius Octavius, a senator, and Atia, niece of Julius CAESAR. The young

Portrait bust of Emperor Augustus. (From Richard Delbruck, Antike Portrats, 1912)

man became a favorite of Caesar's and accompanied him on his Spanish campaign in 44 B.C. By virtue of Caesar's will, acted upon after his assassination on March 15, 44 B.C., Octavian became the late dictator's adoptive son and thereafter styled himself Gaius Julius Caesar. The adoption conferred no official power, but it endowed the young man with a cachet of inestimable influence and helped him win the support of Caesar's loyal veterans, whom he formed into an illegal private army to oppose Mark Antony.

In January 43, the Senate, which distrusted Antony, made young Octavian a senator and legitimated his military command. In the spring of 43—probably April—Octavian met and defeated Antony at Mutina (modern-day Modena), then marched on Rome and promoted his own election as consul on August 19. With good reason, Cicero had originally proposed to the Senate that the young man be employed merely as a tool against Antony and, after he had served his purpose, that he be removed from power. It was now too late for such maneuvering, as Octavian deftly forged an alliance with Antony and Marcus Aemilius Lepidus. Thus united, they bullied the Senate into appointing them triumvirs—joint rulers—on November 27, 43 B.C. for a period of five years. Their ostensible mandate from the Senate was to reform and reorganize the republic. Acting under cover of this, they commenced their rule by relentlessly purging the government of enemies political and personal.

In September 42, Antony and Octavian invaded Greece to crush republican conspirators under the command of Brutus and Cassius, which they accomplished at the two battles of Philippi in Macedonia on October 26 and November 16, 42 B.C. Following this triumph, Antony remained in the East to rule that portion of the empire, and Octavian returned to Italy, where he put down a rebellion (41 B.C.) in Perusia (Perugia) led by Lucius Antonius, Mark Antony's brother. This nearly provoked a break with Antony, but the two came to an accord by means of the Treaty of Brundisium in 40 and through the marriage of Antony to Octavian's sister in 37. The triumvirate was extended for another five years.

From 40 to 36, Octavian campaigned against Sextus Pompeius. In the meantime, in 38, he wed Livia Drusilla, prominent daughter of the republican aristocracy, thereby signalling a desire to come to an accommodation with the republicans. He next caused the removal of Lepidus from power in 36 and assumed control of the African provinces himself. In 34, he led a military expedition to Dalmatia, Illyria, and Panonia in eastern Europe. When Antony's affair with the Egyptian monarch CLEOPATRA became known, Octavian seized the opportunity to turn political and popular opinion against his fellow triumvir, accusing him in 33 of despotic designs against the republic. The next year, Italy and all of the western provinces professed their allegiance to Octavian, but most of the Senate sided with Antony. On September 2, 31, Octavian met and defeated Mark Antony at the Battle of Actium, capturing most of Antony's army afterward and launching an invasion of Egypt, which he conquered by the summer of 30. A defeated Antony committed suicide, as did his paramour Cleopatra.

Octavian, now sole ruler of Rome, returned to the capital in triumph the next year. He proclaimed the restoration of the republic, and, with a grand sense of political theater, declared in 27 B.C. that he was placing "the republic at the disposal of the Senate and the Roman people." The Senate, beseeching him not to abandon the state, created him Augustus and Imperator—emperor. In 23 he was made tribune for life, in 12 he became pontifex maximus, head of Roman state religion, and in 2 B.C. he was endowed with the title "Father of His Country."

Having achieved great power through craft, intimidation, and utter ruthlessness, Augustus now proved himself a wise and skilled ruler. Instead of an absolute tyranny, he created the principate—the rule of the *princeps* ("first citizen"), a system in which the army and the people pledged allegiance to the *imperator* (emperor) and to a collaborative government of the emperor and the two ruling social classes, the senators and the equestrians.

Although Augustus was obliged to fight a series of wars on Rome's German frontier from 15 B.C. to A.D. 13 in an unsuccessful campaign to conquer Germany, his reign brought internal peace to the nation. He fostered literature, the arts, and learning generally; the historian Livy, the poet Virgil, and the master of the ode Horace were all products of the "Augustan age." While the principate was a lasting legacy to Roman government, Augustus produced no male heir to succeed him. His daughter, Julia, married three times, giving birth to two prospective heirs who, however, died prematurely. Augustus was compelled to adopt his daughter's third husband, Tiberius, whom he neither liked, trusted, nor respected. The principate, so promisingly established, survived a succession of poor emperors, and the Roman Empire would continue to expand for another century. Morally and culturally, the reign of Augustus was, however, the high point of the Roman Empire.

Augustus died in Rome on August 19, A.D. 14.

Further Reading: John Buchan. *Augustus* (Boston: Houghton Mifflin, 1937); Arnold H. Jones. *Augustus* (London: Chatto & Windus, 1970).

B

Babur (1483–1530)

Babur founded the great Mughal dynasty of northern India.

Babur, who was born near Fergana on February 14, 1483, claimed descent from TAMERLANE and GENGHIS KHAN. He was only 11 years old when he became ruler of Fergana following the death of his father in 1494. The youthful leader was immediately thrust into the ancient struggle for Transoxiana—Bukhara and Samarkand—a region hotly contested among the descendants of Tamerlane. Remarkably, the boy king was not only successful in thwarting attempts to seize the region, but he marched on and captured Samarkand in 1497 (when he was 14 years old) and repeated this during February-March of 1501. In April and May, however, he was defeated by an Uzbek-Turkoman chief named Shaibani Khan at the Battle of Sar-i-pul. Forced to withdraw from Fergana, Babur settled in Kabul by 1504, and during 1511–12 launched another invasion into Transoxiana. When this was repulsed, he turned toward India with greater success.

Babur periodically raided the Punjab during 1515–23. He occupied Qandahar in 1522 and launched a full-scale invasion of the Punjab the following year, occupying Lahore. Daulat Khan Lodi, governor of the region, pushed Babur out of Lahore, but invited him to attack Delhi. Babur invaded the Punjab again in 1525, then advanced on Delhi during March and April of 1526. At the Battle of Panipat, on April 20, he defeated and killed Daulat Khan's uncle, Ibrahim Lodi, the sultan of Delhi. Babur occupied Delhi on April 27, then attacked and took Agra. Engaging the vastly superior Rajput army led by Rana Sanga at the Battle of Kahnua on March 16, 1527, he emerged victorious and was free to invade Bihar, then Bengal, where he defeated the allied forces of Afghan chieftains at the Battle of the Gorga in May 1529.

Having thus expanded his empire, Babur seemed unstoppable. But, at the height of his military prowess, he fell ill and died at Agra on December 26, 1530.

Further Reading: John F. Richards. *The Mughal Empire* (New York: Cambridge University Press, 1993).

Bacon, Nathaniel (1647–1676)

A colonial American demagogue, Bacon exploited the tensions of the Virginia frontier to stage "Bacon's Rebellion" and foment war with the Indians in an attempt to seize power for himself.

Nathaniel Bacon was born in Suffolk, England, on January 2, 1647. A kinsman of Sir Francis Bacon, he had all the advantages of an English gentleman, including an education at Cambridge University and legal study. After Bacon became involved in a scheme to defraud a young man of his inheritance, his father sent him to Virginia in August 1647. There his cousins Colonel Nathaniel Bacon and Lady Frances Culpepper Berkeley—wife of Virginia governor William Berkeley—helped establish him as a planter on two properties, one about 40 miles upriver from Jamestown and the other at the site of modern Richmond. Governor Berkeley even appointed Bacon to a seat in the House of Burgesses.

The interests of the Virginia Tidewater and Piedmont were often at odds during the colonial period, those in the interior rightly feeling that they were poorly represented in the coastal centers of power. During the so-called Indian War of 1675–76, Governor Berkeley left the outlying settlements to fend for themselves, and the beleaguered frontier was ripe for rebellion.

Bacon, differing sharply with his in-law on the defense of the frontier, recruited a group of like-minded men and in May 1676 enlisted the aid of Occaneechi Indians (who lived along the Roanoke River) to fight the hostile Susquehannocks. Bacon accepted the Occaneechis' offer to do *all* of the fighting, but when the Occaneechi war party returned in triumph, bearing Susquehannock prisoners and a captured stock of fur, Bacon attempted to seize the pelts and proposed to enslave a band of Manikin Indians who had assisted the Occaneechis. When the Occaneechis protested, Bacon attacked his erstwhile allies.

Back in Jamestown, Nat Bacon and his "boys" were welcomed as heroes, but Berkeley branded the unauthorized warfare as treason on May 26, 1676. He arrested Bacon and took his seat in the House of Burgesses. The rebel apologized and was pardoned on June 5.

The atonement was short-lived. Bacon raised an army of 500, which he led into Jamestown on June 23, demanding that the Burgesses commission him commander of all forces fighting the Indians or his men would open fire on the Burgesses themselves.

Thoroughly intimidated, the Burgesses granted his commission. Bacon set out on another campaign— again against friendly Indians, the Pamunkeys of eastern Virginia, many of whom he killed or captured.

In the meantime, on July 29, Berkeley repealed Bacon's commission and again proclaimed him a traitor, but he failed to raise an army against him. Indeed, within a week of the declaration, a band of Virginia's most prominent planters took an oath to support Bacon, who continued his indiscriminate Indian war, breaking off long enough to return to Jamestown on September 13, where he seized the wives of Burgesses loyal to the governor and used them as human shields while his men constructed siege lines and forced Berkeley and his meager forces out of the capital and into exile on the Eastern Shore. On September 18, the rebels burned the town.

From his exile, Berkeley rallied a force against Bacon, who now spoke grandly of carving a free state out of portions of Maryland, Virginia, and North Carolina to be allied with the Dutch or the French. With his newly raised army, however, Berkeley retook Jamestown and forced Bacon to a stand at Yorktown, Virginia. There the rebel was cut down on October 18 or 26 (sources vary), not by Berkeley's musket balls, but by dysentery or typhoid. With its leader, so died "Bacon's Rebellion" and the Indian War of 1675–76.

Further Reading: Alan Axelrod. *Chronicle of the Indian Wars: From Colonial Times to Wounded Knee* (New York: Prentice Hall, 1992); Wilcomb Washburn. *The Governor and the Rebel: A History of Bacon's Rebellion in Virginia* (Chapel Hill: University of North Carolina Press, 1957).

Bajan (d. 609)

Bajan, a warrior-king, expanded and united the Avars, forging a nation from what had been a loose confederation of nomadic tribes related to the Huns.

Details of the birth and early life of Bajan are unknown, but he was elected *khagan* (great khan) of the Avars in 558. At the time of his election, the Avars had been pushed out of several lands in central Asia and were now precariously settled in the lower Danube region. To help secure their position, Bajan concluded a treaty with the Byzantine emperor JUSTINIAN I, who agreed to pay the Avars an annual tribute in exchange for their services as allies in defense of the Byzantines' northern frontiers. Bajan exploited this nominally defensive situation to lead offensive raids during 558–63 into the territory now encompassed by Romania and Hungary. He also moved against the Franks, who repelled him at Thuringia in 562. During one of his raids on the

Franks, however, Bajan captured King Siegebert I of Austrasia, releasing him in 566 only after the payment of a heavy ransom. Bajan allied the Avars with the Lombards to defeat the Gepidae nation under King Cunimund in 568.

When Justinian II ascended the Byzantine throne, he stopped the annual payment of tribute, and in retaliation Bajan turned against the Byzantine city of Sirmium (in the northern portion of modern Serbia). He met and defeated a Byzantine army sent to the relief of the city in 570, agreeing to return Sirmium only after Justinian II acceded to demands for increased tribute payments. These payments were continued by Tiberius II, when he became Byzantine emperor in 578.

Bajan proved as treacherous an ally as he was a ruthless adversary. In 581, Tiberius' forces were heavily engaged against the Persians when Slavs invaded Illyria. Tiberius called on his dearly bought Avar allies. Perceiving that the Byzantine forces were weak and overextended, Bajan came to the emperor's aid only after demanding and obtaining cession of Sirmium in 582. That same year, however, Maurice became Byzantine emperor and refused Bajan's demand for another increase in tribute. The Avar leader then marched on Singidunum (modern Belgrade) and Viminacium (at the confluence of the Morava and Danube rivers), occupying these places. Maurice backed down and settled with Bajan in 584, but, later that same year, again refused tribute; for Maurice believed that Bajan was behind renewed Slavic raids along the frontier.

Bajan now invaded the Byzantine Empire proper, penetrating as far as Adrianople in Thrace, but a strong army met him there and compelled his withdrawal in 587. Bajan was forced to conclude a tenuous truce with Maurice—one that would prove costly to the Avars. The truce bought the Byzantine emperor time to devote his full forces to defeating the Persians. With the Persian threat disposed of, he was able to turn his attention to the Balkans, and in 592 Maurice forged an alliance with the Franks to fight the Avars. By now of advanced age—he was perhaps 60 years old—Bajan nevertheless met the enemy head on. At Drizipera, he engaged and defeated a Byzantine army under Priscus, whose forces retreated from Drizipera to hole up in the fortress of Tzurulum in Thrace. Bajan, at the very threshold of the Byzantine capital of Constantinople itself, made a truce with the beleaguered Priscus and withdrew.

Once relieved of immediate danger, Priscus waged war anew in 595. He quickly retook Sirmium and Singidunum as well as other Danube River settlements that had earlier fallen to the Avars. In the meantime, Bajan viciously sacked the Dalmatian coast and invaded Moesia in 597. He laid cruel siege to the city of Tomi (modern Constanţa, Romania), defeating a Byzantine force sent to the relief of the city. After the fall of Tomi, Bajan retook Drizipera. These new Byzantine reversals brought Maurice to the bargaining table once again, and he concluded a treaty with Bajan in 599. The Avar ruler broke the agreement almost immediately by continuing to ravage Dalmatia. Maurice dispatched a large army commanded by Priscus and Comentiolus against Bajan, who was defeated in a series of battles that culminated in the 601 Battle of Viminacium, which pushed the Avars back to the Danube. The river now marked a relatively stable frontier separating the Byzantine empire from the Avars.

Following this defeat, the war-weary old Avar ruler retreated into his realm, which, thanks to his efforts, was now ample, stretching from the Julian Alps to the Volga River, and from the Baltic Sea to the Danube.

Further Reading: Alexander Avenarius. *Die Awaren in Europa* (Amsterdam: A. M. Hakkert; Bratislava: Veda, 1974).

Ballivián, José   (1805–1852)

Known as the Second Liberator of Bolivia, after Simon Bolívar, Ballivián prevented Bolivia's unification with Peru.

Born into a wealthy Spanish family in La Paz on November 30, 1805, José Ballivián entered the occupying Spanish army as a cadet. He quickly changed sides, however, and by 1820 was a lieutenant under Simon Bolívar, fighting for Bolivian independence. Bolívar won the war for independence in 1825, and Ballivián won respect as a hard fighter, reaching the rank of colonel. After the adoption of the first constitution in 1826, Ballivián was involved in the internal struggle over the presidency, which ended in the resignation of Antonio José de Sucre, and Ballivián did not reappear in Bolivian politics until the mid-1830s, after a confederation was formed to rule Peru and Bolivia under a single executive, effectively obliterating the national identity of the two countries. Ballivián led a rebellion against the confederation, but was defeated. The confederation itself was dissolved, however, in the subsequent war with Chile in 1839, which saw the overthrow of the Bolivian president, Andrés Santa Cruz.

With the defeat of the confederation, Ballivián saw a need for strong national leadership, and he again led a revolt, this time to attain the presidency himself. After a power struggle with President José Miguel Velasco, he was again defeated and fled to Peru.

Bolivia was invaded in 1841 by the Peruvian general Agustín Gamarra, who again attempted to unify the two countries. Ballivián returned to meet this new threat and assumed generalship of the army. He met Gamarra at the Battle of Ingavi on November 20, 1841, where he defeated the Peruvians, then turned on Velasco, ousting him to proclaim himself president. With the complete backing of the military and a resounding battlefield success, Ballivián faced little opposition.

The new president immediately set about shaping Bolivia into the modern country he envisioned. He had the remote sections of the country surveyed and incorporated, he improved the educational and transportation systems, and he opened a port on the Pacific. In 1843, he was formally named president by the Congress, and reelected in 1846. Opposition began to rise, however, and revolutions spread by 1847 when General Isidro Belzu led an army revolt. By December, it was evident that Ballivián had lost popular support. He resigned, fleeing to Peru in January.

José Ballivián died in Rio de Janeiro, Brazil, on October 16, 1852.

Further Reading: Robert Barton. *A Short History of the Republic of Bolivia* (La Paz: Editorial Los Amigos del Libro, 1968).

Barbarossa   [Khair ed-Din] (ca. 1483–1546)

A Greek-born Turk, Barbarossa (called such for his flaming red beard) captured Algiers from the Spanish and transformed it into the corsair capital of the Mediterranean—a base for politically motivated piracy.

Barbarossa was the youngest of four pirate brothers who operated from a base in Egypt. About 1504, following the death of Elias, the oldest of the brothers, Barbarossa and another brother, Aruj, left Egypt for the island of Jerba. From this new headquarters, they sided with the Berbers against the Spanish in a contest for Maghrib on the northwest coast of Africa. After changing their base of operation once again, to Djidjelli in 1512, Barbarossa and Aruj preyed on Spanish Algeria, taking Miliana, Médéa, Ténès, and Tlemçen by 1517. The following year, Aruj died, and Barbarossa, adopting the name Khair ed-Din, offered his allegiance to SELIM I, sultan of Turkey. The sultan named him *beglerbeg*—prince-governor—and sent him troops to use against the Spanish at Algiers. By 1519, Algiers had fallen to Barbarossa, who also tightened his grasp on much of Maghrib.

While he ruled with a warlike despotism, Barbarossa did much more for the economy of Algiers than the Spanish ever had. In the course of 1521 to 1534, he made the place a prosperous center of international brigandage, creating a thriving economy and a permanent naval force, both supported by institutionalized piracy principally in the service of the Turks.

He launched devastating raids against Malta in 1532, for which Suleiman II elevated him to the rank of *kapitan pasha*—admiral—the next year. Later in 1533, he took Coron and Patras. In 1534, returning to Africa, he captured Tunis, holding it only briefly before it fell in 1535 to an amphibious attack led by the Italian Andrea Doria in the service of CHARLES V.

As a Turkish admiral, Barbarossa forged that nation's navy into a formidable military force with which he visited devastating raids on the southeast coast of Italy from May to August of 1537. With Suleiman, he besieged Corfu on August 25, 1537, but was defeated by Andrea Doria and the Imperial Venetian fleet on September 15. This hardly stopped Barbarossa, however, who advanced on Napulia and Malvasia, capturing these Venetian fortress-ports. He next moved against Venice's Aegean possessions, Skíros, Pátmos, Aegina, Iós and Páros during 1537–38, taking all of them. Andrea Doria gave chase and offered battle off Préveza on September 27, 1538, but, this time, did not prevail against Barbarossa.

The brigand ruler fought Spain and its allies again during 1542 to 1544, when, sometimes in company with a French fleet under Francis, Prince of Enghien, he terrorized the western Mediterranean. Barbarossa attacked the Catalonian coast, then bombarded, besieged, took, and sacked Nice in 1543. Barbarossa wintered his fleet at Toulon, afterward making for the coast of northwest Italy, where he executed a series of savage raids. When Francis summarily concluded the Peace of Crépy on September 18, 1544, Barbarossa lost his western Mediterranean base of operations and withdrew to Constantinople. There he served in the sultan's court until his death two years later in May of 1546.

Further Reading: Ernle D. S. Bradford. *The Sultan's Admiral: The Life of Barbarossa* (New York: Harcourt, Brace & World, 1968).

Barrientos Ortuño, René (1919–1969)

Bolivian president from 1966 to 1969, Barrientos Ortuño clashed with miners, the military, and labor.

Born in Tunary, Cochabama, Bolivia, on May 30, 1919, Barrientos Ortuño attended school locally and then entered the Colegio Militar. His support of the government of Germân Busch earned him expulsion, but he was subsequently reinstated and graduated in 1943. He supported the coup of Gualberto Villarroel López in 1943 and was instrumental in organizing the 1944 peasant congress.

Barrientos was an officer in the Bolivian army at the time of the April 1952 revolution spearheaded by the Movimiento Nacionalista Revolucionario (MNR). He joined the MNR and served as a leader of the group's military cell. In 1964 the MNR selected Barrientos to run for the vice-presidency on the ticket with incumbent president Víctor Paz Estenssoro. Elected in June, Barrientos immediately began laying plans to overthrow the president. On November 5, Barrientos and General Alfredo Ovando Candia succeeded in their coup and were named co-presidents. Barrientos, however, resigned in order to run for president in 1966. Winning over several opponents, he adopted a flamboyant, populist style of leadership and forged strong ties with the peasantry, concluding the Military-Peasant Pact of 1966, which became the rationale for military rule in the 1970s. In fact, he merged his own Popular Christian Movement and Bolivian Revolutionary Front into a single official ruling party that was no more than a front for military dictatorship.

Favoring rule by a clique of mining and importing entrepreneurs and agrabusinessmen, Barrientos waged war against the mining unions during 1965 and 1967, effectively destroying the nation's labor movement. In 1967, his government was the target of guerrilla attacks led by the Cuban revolutionary Ernesto ("Che") Guevara. Barrientos' forces put down the uprising and captured and killed Guevara.

Barrientos himself was killed on April 27, 1969, when his helicopter went down near Tocopaya, Bolivia. The government reported that his craft had collided with power lines, but many believe that the helicopter was shot down.

Further Reading: Christopher Mitchell. *The Legacy of Populism in Bolivia: From the MNR to Military Rule* (New York: Prager, 1977).

Basil II Bulgaroctonos ["Bulgar-butcher"] (958–1025)

An aggressive expansionist, Byzantine emperor Basil II brought his nation to the height of its power.

Basil II, born in Constantinople, was the son of Emperor Romanus II and the Empress Theodora, and the great-great-grandson of Basil I. Upon the death of Romanus in 963, Basil became a child-king, nominally ruling with his brother Constantine under the "protection" first of Nicephorus II Phocas and then of John I Zimisces. When John died early in 976, Basil and Constantine became co-emperors, but the real power rested with yet another "protector," Basil Paracoemomenus, the young men's uncle.

The brothers' personalities differed sharply. Whereas Constantine was passive and self-indulgent, caring only for the perquisites and trappings of power, Basil was eager to prove his military prowess. In 981, he launched an invasion of Bulgaria, whose monarch, Czar Samuel, was making threatening expansionist moves. The young Basil met with defeat at his first engagement, the Battle of Sofia, but he continued to campaign within Bulgaria—for the most part, futilely, especially since his forces were subject to the same divisions and strife that were tearing at the Byzantine Empire itself during this period.

Facing rebellion among his troops, Basil returned to Constantinople and managed to engineer the overthrow of his uncle. Constantine offered no resistance to Basil's taking up the reins of leadership, and Basil assumed power in 985.

The Byzantine Empire was now in full crisis, however. Samuel of Bulgaria exploited Byzantine discord to extend his rule across all of eastern Bulgaria and well into Serbia. The Byzantine generals Bardas Phocas and Bardas Skleros, backed by an aristocratic faction opposed to Basil's assumption of the throne, rebelled, seizing much of Anatolia in 987 and marching on Constantinople itself. Basil appealed to Kiev for troops, which he led against the rebellious generals at the Battle of Chrysopolis in 988. Emerging victorious, he went on to fight the Battle of Abydos in 989. Bardas Phocas fell in this battle, apparently the victim of a heart attack, and Bardas Skleros thereafter settled with Basil. Basil cemented his alliance with Kiev by presenting its prince with the hand in marriage of his sister Anna, securing in the bargain the prince's pledge to convert to Christianity.

With the rebellion crushed, Basil turned once again to Bulgaria in 991 and campaigned until 995, when the Fatimids of Egypt attacked the empire's eastern frontier. Basil was forced to turn his attention to the Fatimids, whom he met in battle at the besieged city of Aleppo. Basil broke the siege and successfully warred against the Fatimids for the next year.

During this period, Samuel of Bulgaria invaded Greece, visiting havoc upon the country all the way to the Peloponnese. Basil hastened from the eastern frontier to return to the Balkans. He defeated Samuel at the Battle of Spercheios in 996 and went on to reconquer Greece and Macedonia. Basil took the forest surrounding the Bulgarian capital of Sofia, cutting off Samuel from Bulgarian lands along the Danube in 1001. When Samuel countered by reinvading Macedonia, capturing and sacking Adrianople in 1003, Basil took up an offensive that was as ruthless as it was unrelenting. He defeated Samuel at the Battle of Skopje in 1004, then set about ejecting the Bulgarians from Thrace and Macedonia,

an operation that was completed by 1007. In that year, Basil commenced an invasion of Bulgaria itself, advancing inexorably through seven long years until he met Samuel on the field at Balthista, July 29, 1014. Basil destroyed Samuel's army and in a terrorist gesture of extraordinary savagery, blinded the 15,000 Bulgarian prisoners he had taken, divided them into groups of 100, each led by a single prisoner whom he had allowed to retain one eye, and sent them marching back to Samuel. Appalled by the spectacle of his blinded army, the Bulgarian monarch instantly collapsed. He died within two days.

After Balthista, Bulgarian resistance crumbled rapidly. Basil, now called the Bulgar-butcher, swallowed up Bulgaria into the Byzantine Empire. This completed, he turned again to his realm's eastern frontier, annexing Armenia and establishing a defensive redoubt against the Seljuk Turks in 1020. His next operations were directed against the Arabs, whom he was planning to expel from Sicily when he died on December 15, 1025.

Further Reading: Michael McCormick. *Eternal Victory: Triumphal Rulership in Late Antiquity* (New York: Cambridge University Press, 1986).

Batista (y Zaldívar), Fulgencio (1901–1973)

From 1933 to 1944 and again from 1952 to 1959, Batista ruled Cuba as a corrupt dictator, often supported by American capital and business interests.

Born on January 16, 1901, Fulgencio Batista served as a sergeant in the Cuban army when he played a key role in the overthrow of the dictator Gerardo MACHADO Y MORALES and the establishment of a provisional government under Carlos Manuel de Cespedes. Shortly after this, in 1933, Batista led a coup d'état to oust Cespedes. In the manner of many Caribbean and Central American "strong man" leaders, Batista was elevated to high military command—he served as army chief of staff—rather than elective office. From his military position, he governed by means of a series of civilian puppet presidents until 1940, when he was finally elected to the office himself.

At the end of his first presidential term in 1944, Batista left Cuba to enjoy the fruits of his regime as a retiree in Florida. But, in 1952, he returned to Cuba, and, through a bloodless coup, once again became president. Popular elections were held two years later, and Batista was confirmed in office. He was reelected yet again in 1958.

If anything, Batista's second period of Cuban rule was marked by more repression, less tolerance of dissent, and a greater degree of corruption frankly aimed at self-enrichment. In this atmosphere, a number of dissident political organizations and individuals appeared on the scene, most notably Fidel CASTRO, who organized a guerrilla movement beginning in 1956 and attracted a large Cuban following as well as international attention, credibility, and prestige. The United States, which had very substantial economic interests in Cuba, long supported the Batista regime, but by the end of the 1950s, the mounting corruption and record of political excesses prompted President Dwight D. Eisenhower to cancel scheduled arms sales to Batista. In the meantime, Castro's guerrillas were steadily making gains against Batista, until his regime collapsed. On New Year's Day, 1959, Batista hurriedly fled Cuba. The dictator settled in Spain, which was led by the politically sympathetic right-wing dictator Francisco FRANCO. Batista died in comfortable exile on August 6, 1973.

Further Reading: Edmund A. Chester. *A Sergeant Named Batista* (New York: Holt, 1954).

Baybars I   (1223–1277)

Mamluk sultan of Egypt and Syria, Baybars I ruled from 1260 to 1277 after rising to preeminence through military exploits and assassinations of two Egyptian rulers.

Born on the northern shore of the Black Sea in 1223, Baybars, as a young man, was sold as a slave to the sultan of Egypt. Trained by his master in military science, he was freed and named head of the sultan's bodyguards. His first military exploit was against LOUIS IX of France and his Crusaders at al-Mansurah, where in February 1250 he captured the French king and held him for ransom. Baybars and a group of Mamluk officers then struck out against the Ayyubid dynasty, killing the sultan Turan Shah. Baybars next angered the first Mamluk sultan and fled to Syria, but was welcomed back in 1260 by the sultan Qutuz.

This proved a fatal mistake for Qutuz. After Baybars defeated a Mongol army in Palestine in September 1260, he expected the sultan to reward him with the town of Aleppo. When the sultan did not, Baybars and his officers assassinated Qutuz, and Baybars became the fourth Mamluk sultan in 1260.

His accomplishments were many. He united Syria and Egypt into one state, upgraded his military strength, carried out numerous raids against the Crusaders, decimated the Assassins (an Islamic sect in Syria), waged war successfully against the Christian Armenians, established diplomatic relations with the Byzantine Empire, Italy, and Sicily, and devised trade agreements with Aragón, León, and Cas-

tile. He died in Damascus, Syria, on July 1, 1277, after drinking a cup of poison apparently intended for someone else.

Further Reading: Syedah F. Sadeque, ed. *Baybars I of Egypt* (1956; reprint ed., Westport, Conn.: Greenwood Press, 1980); Abdul-Aziz Khowaiter. *Baibars the First: His Endeavours and Achievements* (London: Green Mountain Press, 1978).

Bayezid I   [The Thunderbolt] (ca. 1360–1403)

Ottoman sultan from 1389 to 1402, Bayezid I created the first centralized Ottoman state, which terrorized Europe with its expansionist activity.

Bayezid I's reign was a series of military campaigns aimed at building an empire based on Islamic fundamentalism. These campaigns ranged from the acquisition of territory in the Balkans and Anatolia, to a seven-year blockade of Constantinople (1391–98), to a landmark confrontation with the Hungarian-Venetian Crusade at Nicopolis (1396), in which Bayezid's forces demolished the Crusaders. By 1400, Bayezid's expansion had alarmed the central Asian conqueror TAMERLANE, who defeated Bayezid at Cubukovasi in 1402. Bayezid I was taken prisoner. He died in captivity a year later.

Bayezid II   [The Just] (1447/48–1512)

Ottoman sultan from 1481 to 1512, Bayezid II consolidated the Ottoman Empire through an extensive restructuring of administrative procedures.

The oldest son of sultan Mehmed II, conqueror of Constantinople, Bayezid II survived a power struggle with his brother Cem and ascended to the throne in 1481. He continued his father's tradition of economic and administrative reform, replacing the vassal system with a more centralized bureaucracy, initiating a budget process and creating a war-chest tax. On the international front, Bayezid acquired Hercegovina, Morea, and much of Asia Minor.

By 1511, Bayezid II became involved in another family power struggle, when his sons Selim and Ahmed fought over who would succeed him. Selim secured aid from the Tartar khan, but was defeated in battle by his father, who forced him into Crimean exile. However, fearing that Ahmed would make an alliance with the powerful Persian shah Isma'il and bowing to pressure from the independent-minded corps of Janissaries, partisans of Selim, Bayezid II recalled Selim from the Crimea and abdicated in his favor in April 1512. Bayezid II died the next month.

Further Reading: Halil Inalcik. *The Ottoman Empire: The Classical Age, 1300–1600* (London: Weidenfeld & Nicholson, 1973).

Bela III (d. 1196)

King of Hungary from 1173 to 1196, Bela III was an enlightened leader whose reign marked the emergence of Hungary as a leading power in Europe.

Aided by Byzantine emperor Manuel I Comnehus, Bela III was placed on the throne of Hungary through force of arms in 1173. He established sound diplomatic relations with both France and Rome, marrying the sister of PHILLIP II AUGUSTUS of France and, in a gesture to Rome, converting to Roman Catholicism. Bela III developed a court that came to be considered one of the most capable in Europe. He also established Hungary's hereditary monarchy.

Bela III enjoyed limited military success. He gained independence for Raskan Serbs from Greece, but, after two costly wars with Venice (1181–88 and 1190–91), he was unable to reclaim Dalmatia for Hungary. Bela III died in 1196.

Bela IV (1206–1270)

King of Hungary from 1235 to 1270, Bela IV rebuilt the nation following the devastating Mongolian invasion of 1241.

Bela IV was the son of Andrew II. Six years into his reign, the Mongols, led by Batu Khan, ravaged and occupied Hungary, killing more than half of the population in the course of a single terrible year. Bela IV, who was living as an exile in Dalmatia, returned after the Mongols withdrew in 1242. He set about restoring Hungary and was successful in defending Hungary against a second Mongol invasion in 1261.

Beyond the renewed struggle against the Mongols, Bela IV fought the Serbs and others who persistently nibbled away at his beleaguered realm.

Bela IV had seven daughters, the best known of whom was Margaret, subsequently canonized as Saint Margaret of Hungary. Bela IV died on May 3, 1270.

Belshazzar (d. ca. 539 B.C.)

A descendant of NEBUCHADNEZZAR, Belshazzar was co-regent of Babylon when Daniel foretold of the destruction of the city.

The oldest son of NABONIDUS, king of Babylon beginning in 555 B.C. until the destruction of the city in 539, and Nitocris, most likely Nebuchadnezzar's daughter, Belshazzar was named co-regent of the city in 550 when his father went into exile. Belshazzar, who controlled a large part of the army, was essentially king and is referred to as such in the Bible.

Belshazzar ably administered the government, despite continuous famine in the city as well as general economic difficulties resulting from military incursions by the Persians shortly before his father's return to the city around 540. In the fall of 539, Belshazzar invited many nobles to a banquet, where, according to the biblical Book of Daniel, a hand appeared and began to write on the wall. When Daniel was called upon to read the "handwriting on the wall," he said the Persians and the Medes were to destroy the city.

That same night or quite possibly shortly thereafter, the Persians, led by the general Gobryas, invaded Babylon, and the city fell without resistance. Belshazzar was killed by Gobryas on October 12, 539. He was succeeded by Darius the Mede.

Berengar (r. 915–924)

The king of Italy in 888, Berengar became Holy Roman Emperor after fierce power struggles.

When Emperor CHARLES III (839–888), the Fat, was deposed in 887, the breakup of CHARLEMAGNE's empire was complete. Berengar, marquess of Friuli, contended for the throne of Italy with Guy, duke of Spoleto, while local rulers throughout central Europe vied for supremacy elsewhere in the fragmented empire.

Berengar shrewdly aligned himself with Arnulf of Carinthia, one of the conspirators against Charles the Fat, and one of the last representatives of the Carolingian Empire. After acknowledging the suzerainty of Arnulf, Berengar was elected king of Italy in 888, but still faced opposition from Guy. In 898, the two gathered sizable armies and marched against each other. Some 7,000 men were engaged in battle on the banks of the Trebbia River. Guy defeated Berengar, but was unable to destroy him. Berengar managed to retreat beyond the Po River Valley, and Guy, content with his victory, failed to pursue. Instead, he marched on Rome, demanding that he be crowned emperor by Pope Stephen V in February 889.

When Guy died in 894, he was succeeded by his son Lambert, who renewed hostilities with Berengar. This conflict was resolved by a treaty returning to Berengar a portion of his former kingdom. When Lambert died in 898, Berengar was again recognized as king of Italy. However, before he could consolidate his power in the region, the Magyars invaded in 899 and Berengar wearily moved against them at the river Brenta, but was defeated on September 24.

With his position once again highly tenuous, Berengar was challenged by Louis of Provence, adopted son of Charles the Fat. Italian nobles, tired of Berengar's military defeats and wary of the lurking Magyars, invited Louis to rule in place of Berengar. After driving Berengar from Italy in March 901, Louis was crowned emperor by Pope Benedict IV. Berengar returned, however, and, in his turn, drove Louis out of Italy in 902. Louis subsequently returned in 905, but was surprised by Berengar at the Battle of Verona in July. Berengar took Louis prisoner, blinded him, and sent him back across the Alps.

Berengar was crowned king of Italy and Holy Roman Emperor by Pope John X in 915, but many of the Italian nobles were still dissatisfied with him and, once again, offered the crown to an outsider, Rudolph II, king of Burgundy. Rudolph accepted and marched into Lombardy in February 922, defeating Berengar at Fiorenzuola in July 923, killing over 1,500 of Berengar's troops. Berengar again escaped, but was finally murdered on April 7, 924, by one of his own vassals.

Berenice II (ca. 269 B.C.–221 B.C.)

Namesake of the constellation Como Berenices, Queen Berenice II was married to King Ptolemy III Euregetes of Egypt.

Berenice was the daughter of King Magas of Cyrene. Her arranged marriage to Ptolemy III (245 B.C.) reunited Cyrene with the Egyptian Empire. The constellation Como Berenices (Hair of Berenice) was named for her by the court astronomer to honor a gift of a lock of hair she had bestowed upon her husband to protect him in battle. The astronomer said that the gift had been translated into the heavens, where it appeared as the constellation.

Ptolemy and Berenice had four children. Her son Ptolemy IV Philopater ascended the throne of Egypt at her husband's death. Ptolemy IV accused his mother of plotting with her father, Magas, against him and had her poisoned in 221 B.C.

Berenice III (d. 80 B.C.)

Daughter of Ptolemy IX and either Cleopatra IV or Cleopatra Selene, Queen Berenice III married her uncle Ptolemy X and, later, PTOLEMY XI ALEXANDER II before assuming sole control over Egypt.

Berenice III was expelled from Egypt with her first husband Ptolemy X in 87 B.C. After his death, she married Ptolemy XI, who died in 80 B.C., after which Berenice III assumed control of Egypt.

The Roman dictator SULLA prevailed upon the son of Ptolemy X, Ptolemy XI Alexander II (a Roman political hostage) to marry his stepmother Queen Berenice. Berenice resisted the joint rule thus imposed and was murdered by her stepson-husband after 19 days of marriage in 80 B.C. Outraged by the death of their queen, an Alexandrian mob killed young Ptolemy XI Alexander II, thereby bringing to an end the line of Egypt's legitimate Ptolemaic rulers.

Bhutto, Zulfikar Ali (1928–1979)

President and prime minister of Pakistan from 1971 to 1977, Bhutto was an educator, author, lawyer and statesman who imposed martial law and a strict Islamic regime on his turbulent nation.

Zulfikar Ali Bhutto was born into a respected Islamic Rajput family in India, where his father was a politician in the colonial government. Educated in Bombay as well as at the University of California, Berkeley, and Oxford (from which he received a law degree), Bhutto began his career as a lecturer and lawyer at the University of Southampton, England, during 1952–53. He returned to Pakistan in 1953, where he set up a law practice. Four years later, Bhutto began his political career as a member of the Pakistan delegation to the United Nations. A series of subsequent appointments led him to the position of foreign minister during 1963–66.

In 1967, Bhutto resigned as foreign minister to form an opposition party, the Pakistan People's Party. Bhutto was imprisoned during 1968–69 for opposing the regime of Ayub Khan, but a 1970 coup freed Bhutto, who was subsequently elected president.

Berenice II, as depicted on an ancient coin. (Richard Delbruck, Antike Portrats, 1912)

At this time, Pakistan was plunged into a civil war, resulting in the breakaway of an independent Bangladesh. Bhutto remained president of Pakistan from 1971 to 1973, when a new constitution made him prime minister as well, effectively giving him dictatorial power. In an effort to impose order on his nation by force, Bhutto declared martial law, and instituted the mass Islamization of Pakistan.

Bhutto realized that the country was bridling under the yoke of martial rule and the Islamization program. Seeking a popular mandate, he decreed election in 1977, handily winning a majority. His powerful opposition accused him of election fraud, and he was deposed in a coup d'état led by Mohammad ZIA ul-Haq, army chief of staff. Tried for election fraud, Bhutto was found guilty and hanged on April 4, 1979. Bhutto's daughter, Benazir Bhutto, became Pakistan's prime minister following Zia's death in a suspicious plane crash in 1988. She was dismissed by the president of Pakistan in August 1990, over charges of corruption and malfeasance, and her party was decisively defeated in 1990 elections. She returned as prime minister after a narrow electoral victory in October 1993.

Birendra Bir Bikram Shah Dev (b. 1945)
Ruler of one of the last absolute monarchies, King Birendra struggles to keep his economically beleaguered country of Nepal afloat while resisting increasingly strident calls for democracy.

The first son of King Mahendra, Birendra was born December 28, 1945, only six years after his grandfather, King Tribhuvana, overthrew the Rana dynasty of India to rule Nepal independently. Birendra was given an education fit for a crown prince: schooled in India, England, the United States, and Japan. He also traveled extensively with his father and grandfather on official visits around the world. When King Mahendra died in 1972, Birendra became king of Nepal—though not without delaying his coronation for three years in accordance with the advice of royal astrologers.

Birendra maintained the absolute rule that his father had established, outlawing all that might oppose the crown, including political parties and freedom of speech. Obeisance to this monarch, whom his people regard as a reincarnation of the Hindu god Vishnu ("The Protector"), is required by law.

While Birendra has maintained his power through absolutism and the assertion of divine right, he has also sought to reform Nepal and bring it into the 20th century. The task has been a daunting one. Birendra inherited the throne of a nation with an illiteracy rate of 85 percent and an average per capita income of $75. There was no highway system, and the highland regions still relied on emergency airlifts in times of famine. The king has attacked such problems with vigor, surrounding himself with young, capable, Western-educated ministers. His efforts have been hampered by the inefficiency of an entrenched Nepalese bureaucracy and the almost total absence of infrastructure. Many in Nepal have, through the years, become discontent with Birendra's inability to bring about sweeping reform, and an anti-monarchist movement has been partially successful in exacting significant concessions from the palace. In 1980, a referendum was held on the existing constitution, which was barely reaffirmed. Heeding the handwriting on the wall, Birendra responded to the referendum by yielding his prerogative of appointing members of the National Assembly and instead putting their seats up for popular election. He also provided for the election of a prime minister by the Assembly.

Nepalese foreign policy has also caused many problems for the king. Sandwiched between India and China, Nepal has been forced to walk a fine line between these two countries, on which Nepal depends for commerce and aid, but which continually menace the nation's tenuous independence. While publicly stating that relations are good with the two neighbors, Birendra has expressed a desire to decrease dependence on India, which, having played a major part in the creation of Bangladesh and having taken over Sikkim in the early seventies, might well swallow up Nepal.

Further Reading: Rishikesh Shaha. *Three Decades and Two Kings (1960–1990)* (New Delhi: Sterling, 1990).

Bishop, Maurice (1944–1983)
Prime minister of Grenada from 1979 to 1983, Maurice Bishop led a bloodless coup against the regime of Eric Gairy. Despite his promises of a return to democracy, he assumed dictatorial powers and eradicated all political opposition.

Maurice Bishop, born in Aruba on May 29, 1944, to Grenadian parents, was a leader of the New Jewel Movement (Joint Endeavor for Welfare, Education, and Liberation). A lawyer by training, Bishop took part in the People's Revolutionary Government movement, whose members were brutally attacked by Prime Minister Eric Gairy's parapolice force known as the Mongoose Gang. After recovering in Barbados from a beating at the hands of the Gang, Bishop returned to Grenada to lead a movement to oust the prime minister and his government.

In 1976, Bishop was elected to Parliament, and in 1979 he exploited Gairy's absence from the country to seize a radio station and proclaim a revolutionary government, with himself as prime minister.

Bishop pledged a return to democracy, but took immediate steps to thwart all opposition to his policies by censoring the press and refusing to hold elections. During his pro-Marxist administration, Soviet and Cuban factions gained influence. Fearing that his alignment with the Communists would alienate the United States, Bishop began to adopt a more moderate stance, which angered supporters of his radical deputy, Bernard COARD.

Coard toppled Bishop in October 1983, but the army quickly stepped in and seized control from Coard, who disappeared. The army put Bishop under house arrest until October 19, when some 10,000 of his supporters freed him and took him to Fort Rupert. There Grenadian troops attacked, killing a hundred of Bishop's supporters and executing Bishop as well as three of his ministers. Six days later, U.S. President Ronald Reagan cited the assassination as well as what he called a Cuban military buildup on the island and ordered an American invasion of Grenada.

Further Reading: Phil Gunson, Greg Chamberlain, Andrew Thompson. *Dictionary of Contemporary Politics of Central America and the Carribean* (New York: Simon and Schuster, 1991).

Boabdil, Muhammad XI   (r. 1482–92)

The last Nasrid sultan of Granada, Muhammad XI Boabdil was never able to consolidate his rule and was eventually defeated by the Christian forces of Spain's Ferdinand and Isabella.

The son of the Nasrid sultan Abu al-Hasan, Muhammad Boabdil was goaded by his mother, al-Hasan's jealous wife, to overthrow his father and seize power for himself. Lacking strong character, Boabdil was easily persuaded into doing this and, with the aid of a powerful nobility, was able to seize the Alhambra in 1482. After a brief war, Abu al-Hasan recaptured the castle-capital, but failed to regain power, and in turn was deposed by his brother, az-Zaghall.

Now a three-way power struggle ensued between father, son, and uncle. In 1483, Boabdil, with the help of his father-in-law, marched against the forces of King FERDINAND II (1452–1516) and Queen ISABELLA I, who intended to force the Muslims out of Spain. At the town of Lucena, south of Córdoba, the Muslims were defeated on April 23, Boabdil was taken prisoner, and his father-in-law was killed. To obtain his release, Boabdil signed the Pact of Córdoba, promising Muslim aid in the defeat of az-

Zaghall in return for Castilian aid in the final defeat of al-Hasan.

With the death of al-Hasan in 1485, Boabdil was able to retake the Alhambra, and he was able to direct his full attention to his uncle. The Castilians forced az-Zaghall's defeat and emigration in 1491, but Boabdil was unable to defend the region against the Christians because the Muslim population resented him for his open patronage of the Christians. Thus deserted, Boabdil was easily defeated in the final siege of Granada that ended on January 2, 1492. This brought an end to Muslim rule in Spain and forced Boabdil's eventual exile to Morocco, where he died in 1527.

Bokassa, Eddine Ahmed [Jean-Bedel] (b. 1921–)

Chief of staff of the armed forces of the Central African Republic, Eddine Ahmed Bokassa overthrew the government of David Dacko and crowned himself emperor and president for life.

Born to a family of 12 children on February 22, 1921, in Bobangui, Oubangui-Chari in French Equatorial Africa, Jean-Bedel Bokassa was orphaned at the age of six. He was educated in missionary schools and in 1939 joined the French army as a private.

After World War II, Bokassa remained in the French army, serving in Indochina, then resigning in 1962 when he was appointed head of the Central African Republic army by President David Dacko. On December 31, 1965, Bokassa overthrew the Dacko government and declared himself president of the republic.

Soon infamous for his autocratic policies and his bloody administration of "justice" (for example, thieves had an ear cut off for the first two offenses, a hand for a third, and Bokassa personally supervised judicial beatings), Bokassa further secured his position by declaring himself emperor and renaming the country the Central African Empire in 1976. During his lavish December 4, 1977 coronation ceremony, costing some $30 million, Bokassa received a diamond-studded crown valued at $5 million. The total cost was only slightly less than the nation's entire revenue for the previous year.

Despite the elaborate coronation, Bokassa's empire was short-lived. On September 20, 1979, French paratroopers overthrew his government, and Dacko was reinstalled as president of the republic. The following year, Bokassa was charged with crimes that included embezzlement (he had plundered the treasury to buy châteaux and other properties in France), cannibalism, and the massacre of a hundred schoolchildren. He lived in exile in France until 1986, when he returned to the Central African Republic. President André Kolingba ordered him to stand trial again on the same charges. Acquitted of the charges of cannibalism, he was found guilty of the other offenses and sentenced to death. The sentence was subsequently commuted to life imprisonment in solitary confinement.

Further Reading: *Africa Contemporary Record: Annual Survey and Documents* (New York: Africana Publishing Company, 1979–80); Samuel Decalo. *Psychoses of Power: African Personal Dictatorships* (Boulder, Colo., and London: Westview Press, 1989); Alex Shoumatoff. *The African Madness* (New York: Knopf, 1988).

Boleslav I the Cruel   (d. 967)
Patriarch of a medieval ruling family of Bohemia, Boleslav I secured autonomy for the Czech state during the latter part of the first century.

Boleslav I assumed the Bohemian throne after arranging for the murder of his brother, Wenceslas (later canonized as St. Wenceslas). During his reign, he centralized the government in Prague and expanded the boundaries under Bohemian control. An early invasion by Germany's King OTTO I in 950 forced Bohemia into suzerainty under the German state, yet the country retained much autonomy. Boleslav I laid the foundation of Czech domination of Bohemia. He died on July 15, 967.

Boleslav II the Bold   (1039–1081)
King of Poland from 1058 to 1079. Boleslav II restored his turbulent nation to international prominence, but executed the bishop of Krakow, Saint Stanislav, on charges of treason, and finally was forced by rebellion into exile himself.

Boleslav II inherited the throne from his father, Kasimir I the Restorer. Despite perpetual conflict with Germany, Boleslav was able to establish Poland's position internationally through alliances with both Hungary and the papacy. Turmoil in the principality of Kiev sparked an internal revolt led by the Polish nobility. In 1079, while putting down this rebellion, Boleslav II ordered the execution of Stanislav, bishop of Krakow (later canonized as Saint Stanislav), and others for treason.

A second revolt deposed Boleslav, who fled the kingdom and died, in exile, at Ossiach in Carinthia or Wilten in Tirol, in 1081.

Boleslav II the Pious   (d. 999)
Prince of Bohemia from 967 to 999, Boleslav II continued the administrative reforms of his father Boleslav I.

A member of the Premyslid dynasty of Bohemia, Boleslav II secured his rule through a program of extermination directed against the rival political princes of Slavnikovci. During his reign, Boleslav II established the bishopric of Prague (973–74) and built several monasteries and churches. Initial cooperation with German emperors OTTO I, Otto II, and Otto III against Poland turned sour after Boleslav II aided Henry the Wrangler, duke of Bavaria. This resulted in several German retaliations between 975 and 978. Boleslav II died on February 7, 999.

Boleslav III the Blind   (d. 1035/37)
A third-generation Bohemian prince, who reigned from 999 to 1003, Boleslav III was imprisoned and blinded by rival Polish despot Boleslav I.

Struggles with Poland and Germany marked the reign of Boleslav III. The son of Boleslav II, Boleslav III was the last of the Premyslid princes of Bohemia. Internal strife sent the young ruler into exile, but he returned in 1003 with a vengeance, ruthlessly killing all political foes. The bloodletting was soon ended by Boleslav I the Brave of Poland, who took Boleslav III prisoner and blinded him. The Bohemian prince died in captivity sometime between 1035 and 1037.

Boleslav III the Wry-Mouthed   (1085–1138)
Prince of Poland from 1102 to 1138, Boleslav III converted the Pomeranians to Christianity and introduced the senioriate system to Poland.

Upon the death of their father, Vladyslav I Herman, in 1102, Boleslav and his half-brother Zbigniev battled for control of the country. By 1107, Boleslav III had won and sent Zbigniev into exile. He recalled his brother to Poland in 1112, only to accuse him of treason and order his blinding.

Boleslav's reign included a series of attempts to annex the former Polish province of Pomerania. An alliance with Holy Roman Emperor Lothair II at last accomplished this goal in 1135. Pursuant to the terms of his alliance, Boleslav set about converting the pagan Pomeranians to Christianity.

Boleslav's earlier struggles with Zbigniew led to his introduction of the senioriate system in Poland, whereby the eldest son was awarded the bulk of the royal inheritance. The senioriate system was to prove a dubious national legacy, serving to undermine the Polish state after the death of Boleslav III in 1138 because of the rabid jealousy it provoked among his own heirs.

Bonaparte, Joseph   (1768–1844)
Joseph Bonaparte was made king of Naples (1806) and later of Spain (1808) by his brother NAPOLÉON I.

Born on January 7, 1768, in Corte, Corsica, Joseph Bonaparte was the eldest surviving brother of Napoléon. Like Napoléon—and his other brothers—Joseph rallied to the French republican cause and, for this reason, was compelled to leave Corsica for France in 1796. He participated in Napoléon's early campaigns in Italy and was a part of the French expedition to recover Corsica for France. The legislative body of republican France, the Directory, made Bonaparte minister to the court of Parma in 1797. He subsequently became the Corsican representative to the Council of Five Hundred.

Joseph Bonaparte was instrumental in the diplomatic affairs of the Republic, and represented France in several key treaty negotiations. He came into disagreement with his brother in August 1802 when, after Napoléon was made consul for life, he laid claim to be recognized as heir to that title, whereas Napoléon wanted to nominate the son of Louis Bonaparte. The rift between Joseph and Napoléon deepened in March 1804, when the latter created himself emperor. Napoléon offered to make Joseph king of Lombardy in exchange for his renunciation of any claim to the French throne. Joseph, who had been named first prince of the blood upon Napoléon's proclamation of empire, declined.

Napoléon dispatched Joseph to Naples in 1806 to expel the Bourbons, and, that accomplished, proclaimed him king of Naples. In 1808, Napoléon called him away from Naples to become king of Spain, but he was almost immediately forced to flee by anti-French insurgents. Napoléon managed to reestablish Joseph on the throne, but saw to it that he served as nothing more than his puppet in prosecuting a repressive regime. Chafing under this arrangement, Joseph offered four times to abdicate.

Following Napoléon's fall in 1815, Joseph Bonaparte found asylum in the United States and sought fruitlessly to assert the claim of Napoléon's son, the duke of Reichstadt, to the French throne. Later in life, Joseph lived in Genoa and Florence, where he died on July 28, 1844.

Borgia, Cesare (1475–1507)

Cesare Borgia, the inspiration for Machiavelli's classic study in power, *The Prince*, was a member of an old Spanish family that moved to Italy and produced two popes and other prominent leaders of the church and body politic during the turbulent 15th century.

Born in Rome in September 1475, Cesare Borgia was the son of Rodrigo Borgia, a cardinal and later pope (ALEXANDER VI). His sister was Lucrezia Borgia—a ruthless wielder of power in her own right. Young Cesare studied at the universities of Perugia and Pisa, obtaining a degree in canon and civil law at the age of 15. In 1491, at the remarkably youthful age of 16, Cesare was made the bishop of Pamplona,

and the following year, when his father became pope, he was made the archbishop of Valencia. He became a cardinal in 1493 and was one of his father's closest advisers.

Despite his rapid rise in the church, young Borgia disliked the religious life and longed for a military career. In 1497 his brother Juan, who had earlier been made the commander of the papal army in preference to Cesare, was murdered under mysterious circumstances. Some historians believe that an extremely jealous Cesare instigated the crime, but there is no hard evidence of this beyond speculation and circumstance. Following the death of Juan, Cesare resigned his cardinalate in 1498 and traveled to France to make a politically strategic marriage to Charlotte d'Albret, the sister of the king of Navarre. This brought the French into Cesare Borgia's grandiose scheme to create a separate state for himself in Italy. Over the next two to three years, Cesare, now captain-general of the papal army, enlisted his French allies in a campaign to subdue many Italian towns that had strayed from the papal influence.

Cesare's father, Pope Alexander IV, died in August 1503, before his son could recapture all of the cities that he desired. With the ascension of a hostile pope, Julius II, Borgia was unable to complete his program for personal empire. At the behest of the new pope, he was arrested, then released, then fled to Naples, where he was arrested again. Removed to Spain for imprisonment there, he escaped, and enlisted in the service of his wife's brother, the king of Navarre. Borgia was killed in action at Viana, Spain, on March 12, 1507, six months short of his 32nd birthday.

Further Reading: Sarah Bradford. *Cesare Borgia: His Life and Times* (New York: Macmillan, 1976).

Boris III (1894–1943)

As king of Bulgaria, Boris III propelled his country into an alliance with the Axis powers in World War II, ruling as a royal dictator during his last five years in power.

The son of King Ferdinand I of Bulgaria, Boris III was born on January 30, 1894, in Sofia. He was raised in the Orthodox church and attended the military academy and university in Sofia. With the defeat of Bulgaria in World War I, his father was forced to abdicate, and Boris III was installed king in 1918.

On June 9, 1923, Boris III led conservative elements in a military coup and overthrew and executed the leftist prime minister Stambuliski. Boris III's hand-picked successor to the murdered prime minister was Professor Alexander Tsankov, a ruthless Fascist who dealt with rioting Communists,

Agrarians, Socialists, and peasants by mass slaughter. Most authorities believe that some 10,000 persons were executed without trial during a two-year period. ("Why so few dead?" Boris is said to have asked Tsankov. "You must give them a blood-letting they will never forget.")

A new prime minister briefly introduced mild democratic reforms in 1926, but these collapsed by 1930. Throughout the late 1920s and the 1930s, Boris III promoted friendly relations with Fascist governments in Europe. He married the Italian princess Giovanna in 1930 and 11 years later joined the Berlin-Rome-Tokyo alliance. Having established himself as dictator in Bulgaria, he allowed the Axis nations to use his country as a base for operations against Yugoslavia and Greece.

Boris III died on August 28, 1943, in Sofia. Some accounts report that he was shot by his own bodyguards. Others report that he was poisoned by the Nazis, who had failed to receive the degree of cooperation they wanted. Still other accounts attribute his death to a heart attack.

Bose, Subhas Chandra   (1897–1945)

With Mohandas Gandhi, Bose was one of the most important figures in securing Indian independence from Britain. He sought support from every quarter, regardless of cost or consequences.

Born in India on January 23, 1897, Subhas Chandra Bose, the son of a prominent lawyer, attended the European-style schools run by the British Baptist missionaries. Attending college in Calcutta, Bose became aware of the tensions between his countrymen and the British as well as the many problems brought by British colonial rule. He was continually outraged by colonial racism and was implicated in an incident involving a British professor, who had allegedly assaulted some students. Bose voluntarily left the college, subsequently matriculating at Oxford University.

Following graduation, Bose secured a civil service appointment, which he immediately resigned, declaring that "the best way to end a government is to withdraw from it." He joined a nationalist activist movement and became a follower of C. R. Das, an outspoken leader for Bengal nationalism. Bose went with Das when he was named mayor of Calcutta in 1924, and in 1925 was arrested in a roundup of terrorists.

After spending two years in a Mandalay prison (where he contracted tuberculosis), Bose was released to find that Das had died and the Bengal Provincial Congress had fallen into total disarray. Bose was named general secretary of the Congress, and

was again arrested. Upon his release, he was elected mayor of Calcutta. Traveling to Europe during the 1930s, Bose visited Indian students and observed the prominent politicians of the time, meeting with Adolf HITLER and studying both communism and fascism.

Returning to India in 1938, he was mentioned for the candidacy for the Indian National Congress. This proved to be a defining moment in the Indian independence movement; Bose stood for unconditional independence, including the use of violence if necessary. This meant a direct confrontation with the other leader of the INC, Mohandas Gandhi, who opposed Bose's candidacy, effectively splitting the Congress. When Bose was elected president of the INC, Gandhi advised Bose to form his own cabinet, excluding him. Bose was reelected in 1939, but continuing opposition from Gandhi prompted his resignation.

Declaring himself an "extremist," Bose formed the Forward Bloc with the intention of creating a new government that synthesized elements of communism and fascism. With the outbreak of World War II, British authorities again imprisoned Bose, but he escaped before he stood trial.

Bose embarked on a campaign of asking anyone for anything, feeling that Indian independence overrode any other concern. He met again with Hitler and Benito MUSSOLINI, seeking their help, and made pro-Axis propaganda broadcasts to England and India. Failing to receive the satisfaction he had hoped from these quarters, Bose turned to the Japanese embassy in Berlin, which arranged for him to fly to Tokyo in 1943. The Japanese high command organized the Indian National Army, comprised of British Indian Army POWs and Indian civilians, and named Bose—who had proclaimed an independent Indian government—commander. With three divisions and a battle strength of over 50,000, the INA engaged Allied forces in Rangoon and Burma, but was finally defeated at the Battle of Imphal in 1944, when promised Japanese air support failed to arrive. The INA was not disbanded, however, but maintained an identity as the Indian Liberation Army.

With the end of the war, Bose turned next to the Soviet Union, hoping that nations would pressure England to withdraw from India. He was on his way to the Soviet Union to enlist this support when his plane crashed on August 18, 1945 in Taipei; Bose burned to death. Despite their fundamental differences in philosophy, Mohandas Gandhi called him the "greatest patriot of patriots."

Further Reading: Leonard A. Gordon. *Brothers Against the Raj: A Biography of Indian Nationalists* (New York: Columbia University Press, 1990).

Boulanger, Georges Ernest   (1837–1891)

Briefly leader of an authoritarian reform movement in France, Boulanger failed to seize his moment of opportunity and was exiled.

Born April 29, 1837, Georges Boulanger became a career military man, graduating from the elite Ecole Saint-Cyr military academy and joining the French army in 1856, seeing action in the Franco-Prussian War of 1870–71. Appointed brigadier general in 1880 and director of infantry in 1882, Boulanger became commander of the French army in Tunisia, but was recalled because of differences with the political resident, Pierre-Paul Cambon. On his return to Paris, he took an interest in politics under the tutelage of Georges Clemenceau, leader of the Radical Party. In January 1886, he was named minister of war under President Charles-Louis de Saulses de Freycinet.

Boulanger's vigor and popularity, born in large measure of his pledge to avenge France's ignominious defeat in the 1870–71 war, drew comparisons with France's other famed military leader, NAPOLÉON. Many saw Boulanger as the figure capable of giving France the *revanche* it sought against Bismarck and the Germans. He soon gathered support from all the discontented and disenfranchised elements of the Third Republic. He remained minister of war through two administrations, but was dismissed in May 1887 by Prime Minister René Goblet and sent to command the XIII Corps.

Boulanger's ouster from the government gained him additional popularity verging on martyr status. His activism, including unauthorized visits to Paris and the exiled Prince Louis-Napoléon (later NAPOLÉON III) in Switzerland, caused him problems with the government. He was removed from active duty, but he quickly stood for election to the Chamber of Deputies in several districts simultaneously and won, taking his seat from the Nord department. As a deputy, he demanded sweeping authoritarian revisions to the constitution, including the creation of a stronger executive and the dissolution of the lower house. When the Chamber rejected his proposals, he resigned.

In January 1889, the citizens of Paris put Boulanger up for election as their own deputy and seated him with an overwhelming majority. When the election results were announced in Paris, the so-called Paris Mob took to the streets, shouting for Boulanger to seize control of the government immediately. Boulanger wavered, however, and when day broke on the Paris streets, the revolutionary fervor had dissipated under Boulanger's inaction.

Within two months, the government brought him up on charges of treason. On April 1, to the shock of his followers, Boulanger fled Paris. Shortly thereafter, he was tried in absentia, found guilty on August 14, 1889, and condemned to exile. In the subsequent elections, his partisans were trounced. Boulanger's moment had passed.

On September 30, 1891, Georges Boulanger committed suicide at the grave of his mistress in a cemetery near Brussels.

Brezhnev, Leonid Ilich   (1916–1982)

Leonid Brezhnev was leader of the Soviet Union and the Communist Party for 18 years, from 1964 to 1982.

Born in the Ukraine into a working-class family on December 19, 1916, Leonid Brezhnev worked briefly as a land surveyor before joining the Communist Party in 1931. After graduating from engineering school in 1935, Brezhnev became deputy chairman of the provincial Soviet Committee in Dnepropetrovsk. In 1941, he joined the Red Army and advanced to the rank of major general by 1943—a rapid rise spurred by the vacancies resulting from the wholesale purges of Josef STALIN.

By 1952, Brezhnev had become a member not only of the powerful Central Committee but also of its more influential inner circles. He became second secretary of the Kazakhstan Communist Party and a member of the Presidium of the Supreme Soviet. Brezhnev's friendship with Stalin's successor, Nikita KHRUSHCHEV, also advanced his career, bringing appointments in 1954 as first secretary of the Kazakhstan Communist Party and as effective head of Khrushchev's "Virgin Lands" agricultural plan. In 1956, Brezhnev returned to Moscow, where he was elevated to the Secretariat of the Central Committee, spearheading a victory over the "anti-party group" trying to unseat Khrushchev. In return for his services, Brezhnev was named chairman of the Presidium of the Supreme Soviet in 1960, followed by a stint as chief adviser to Khrushchev in 1964. This same year, however, Brezhnev joined the coalition that ultimately forced Khrushchev out, whereupon Leonid Brezhnev himself assumed a position in the collective leadership of the Soviet Union. After several years, Brezhnev emerged as the dominant figure in Russian politics and effective leader of the country.

As head of the Soviet Union, Brezhnev presided over a relaxation of Cold War tensions. Although this conservative Communist still advocated Soviet military buildup and maintenance of Soviet hegemony in the Warsaw Pact countries—as evidenced by his invasion of Prague in 1968 and of Afghanistan in the late 1970s, in addition to his hard-line domestic policies—Brezhnev did meet successively with U.S. presidents Nixon, Ford, and Carter, becoming the grandfather of détente. He signed numerous agreements with the United States promoting commerce and world peace, including the U.S.S.R.-U.S. Trade Agreement of 1972, the Helsinki Agreement of 1975, and Salt II in 1979.

Brezhnev died on November 10, 1982, in Moscow, after several years of poor health.

Further Reading: Leonid Brezhnev. *Leonid I. Brezhnev: His Life and Work* (New York: Sphinx, 1982).

C

Cabrera y Griñó, Ramón (1806–1887)

This Spanish Carlist general's ruthless attacks on the liberal supporters of Queen Isabella II sparked terror in early 19th-century Spain.

Under the leadership of General Cabrera, the Carlist Party (which supported the royal claims of Don Carlos against Isabella II) won several important military victories by 1838, when Cabrera was recognized as Conde de Morella. In 1840, however, Cabrera and his army of 10,000 were driven across the border into France. After several years of exile in France and England, Ramón Cabrera returned to Catalonia, where he led Carlist bands from 1846 to 1849.

Cabrera married an Englishwoman, Marriane Catherine Richards, in 1860, after which he settled in England and greatly moderated his radical views. As a result of his change of heart, he was expelled by the hard-line Carlist assembly in 1870. Cabrera finalized his break with the Carlists by recognizing the legitimist Spanish king, Alfonso XII, in 1875. Cabrera died in London on May 24, 1877.

Caesar, Gaius Julius (100 B.C.–44 B.C.)

Bearing the most famous name in Roman history, Julius Caesar was one of the greatest military commanders and most skillful politicians the world has ever known.

Gaius Julius Caesar was born on July 13, 100 B.C., to a venerable patrician family and claimed direct descent from Venus through Aeneas' son Iulus (Ascanius). Despite this pedigree, Caesar's family was not in the inner circles of power. Caesar's father was the brother-in-law of Gaius Marius and married to Aurelia, a member of the prominent Aurelii family. Despite these connections, he died, about 85 B.C., before attaining a consulship. In 84, his son Caesar entered the priesthood of Jupiter and married Cornelia, daughter of Marius' former partner, Lucius Cornelius Cinna. When Lucius Cornelius SULLA, the enemy of Marius, ordered Caesar to divorce her, the young man refused and was compelled to endure a brief period of exile.

Caesar served during this time in Asia, making himself conspicuous for bravery at the siege of Mytilene in 80 B.C. Returning to Rome after the death of Sulla in 78, he unsuccessfully attempted during 77–76 to prosecute two of his family's enemies, Gnaeus Cornelius Dolabella and Gaius Antonius Hibrida, both partisans of Sulla. Departing Rome for study in Rhodes, Caesar was captured en route by pirates, from whom he was ransomed. After assembling a small private army, he succeeded in capturing the pirates in turn and caused their execution in 75–74.

War with MITHRADATES VI EUPATOR of Pontus in 74 drew him away from Rhodes as he served under Lucullus against this ruler during 74–73. Caesar was made a pontiff at Rome in 73 B.C. and elected military tribune. He then saw service, possibly against the rebellious slave Spartacus in 72 or 71, and he supported Pompey, chief architect of the downfall of the Sullan political system.

Caesar was elected quaestor in 69 A.D., then earned popularity among the Transpadane Gauls by supporting their bid for Roman citizenship in 68. Following the death in 69 of his wife Cornelia, Caesar the following year married Pompeia, granddaughter of Sulla and relative of POMPEY. He apparently carried out high-level military assignments for Pompey in 67 and 66, then became aedile in 65, achieving great popularity by financing elaborate public games. During this year, he seems to have participated with Marcus Licinius Crassus in a scheme to annex Egypt. He also promoted the popular land-distribution bill of Publius Servilius Rullus. In 64 he presided over trials of persons who had committed murder during Sulla's proscriptions against the partisans of Marius, and in 63, Caesar employed bribery on a large scale to become pontifex maximus, head of Roman state religion.

Although Caesar did not participate in Catiline's conspiracy, he did oppose the execution of Catiline's accomplices, which gained him much public favor, leading to his election as praetor in 62. Shortly after this, he divorced Pompeia on suspicion of infidelity, and married Calpurnia in 58. In the meantime, he became governor of Further Spain in 61 and was elected in 60 to the consulate. That year, he formed with Pompey and Crassus the First Triumvirate in order to concentrate power and influence. Caesar became proconsul of Illyricum, Cisalpine Gaul and Transalpine Gaul. Using a large army that was put at his disposal, he fought the Gallic Wars from 58 to 51 B.C., subjugating the rebellious Gauls and thereby gaining tremendous political prestige and leverage.

Caesar's daughter, Julia, married Pompey in 59. Despite this, friction developed between Caesar and Pompey, which Crassus, jockeying for additional power, deliberately aggravated. The Triumvirate was renegotiated in 56, but the death of Julia in 54 and of Crassus the next year combined with Caesar's Gallic triumphs to destroy the relationship with Pompey once and for all. In 50 Pompey opposed Caesar's bid for a second consulate. On January 10, 49 B.C., Caesar initiated civil war when he committed the illegal act of leading his army across the Rubicon to oppose Pompey in Italy. Pompey's forces collapsed before Caesar's advance, and Pompey retreated to Greece.

In August 49, Caesar defeated Pompey's forces in Spain and was created dictator. He pursued Pompey into Greece, where he suffered a loss at Dyrrhachium, but quickly recovered by destroying Pompey's larger army at Pharsalus on August 9, 48. Pompey himself fled to Egypt, Caesar followed, and became involved in the civil war between Cleopatra and her brother Ptolemy XIII. Caesar took Cleopatra as his mistress and made her queen of Egypt.

The next year, Caesar went to Anatolia, where he crushed Pompey's ally Pharnaces, king of Bosporus, in a brief campaign at Zela. So swift was this victory that Caesar reported it in a single memorable phrase: "Veni, vidi, vici" ("I came, I saw, I conquered").

After returning briefly to Rome later in the year, Caesar had to travel to North Africa in December to head off another threat from forces loyal to Pompey. Following victory at Thapsus in April 46, he was made dictator for 10 more years. The sons of Pompey—whose father had been murdered in Egypt—now mounted a fresh resistance in Spain. Caesar met and defeated them at Munda on March 17, 45. The following year Julius Caesar was appointed dictator for life and deluged with additional honors.

As dictator, Caesar introduced many reforms, including the enlargement of the Senate, the revision of the system of taxation, and the extension of Roman citizenship to all subjects of the empire. Caesar sought to balance these popular measures with gestures meant to placate those who opposed him, granting unheard of clemency to his enemies. However, when this dictator for life compared himself to Alexander the Great and proposed, like him, to conquer Parthia, fear of his overweening ambition spread through an aristocratic clique that included those to whom he had extended pardons. A band of conspirators led by Marcus Junius Brutus and Gaius Cassius Longinus, approached him at a meeting of the Senate in Pompey's theater on the Ides of March—March 15, 44 B.C. Each conspirator stabbed him in turn, and Caesar, as he collapsed at the feet of Pompey's statue, spoke to Brutus not in Shakespeare's Latin—*Et tu, Brute*—but in Greek: "Even you, lad?"

Further Reading: John Fuller. *Julius Caesar: Man, Soldier and Tyrant* (New Brunswick, N.J.: Rutgers University Press, 1965); Julius Caesar. *Caesar's War Commentaries*, trans. by John Warrington (London: Oxford University Press, 1953).

Caligula [Gaius Julius Caesar Germanicus] (A.D. 12–A.D. 41)

Roman emperor from A.D. 37 to 41, Caligula, a psychopathic sadist, exemplified Roman tyranny at its worst and most perverse.

Gaius Julius Caesar Germanicus, born on August 31, A.D. 12, was the son of Germanicus Caesar and Agrippina I. He was raised in military cantonments in the Rhine region, where he became a favorite of his father's troops, who nicknamed him Caligula— Little Boots, Baby Boots, or Bootikins—after the child-size military footgear he wore in camp.

Caligula's father died in A.D. 19, and his mother and two elder brothers were killed at the behest of Emperor TIBERIUS in a political purge. Despite this, Caligula ingratiated himself to Tiberius, with whom he lived on Capri from 32 until the emperor died in 37.

Upon the death of Tiberius, the 25-year-old Caligula voided the emperor's will in which Tiberius' grandson Tiberius Gamellus was named heir. Thus supplanting Gamellus, Caligula was proclaimed emperor and lost little time in causing the execution of

The powerful Praetorian Guard could promote, protect, or destroy a Roman ruler. It was a Praetorian plot that resulted in the assassination of Caligula. (Richard Delbruck, Antike Portrats, *1912)*

his potential rival, as well as the praetorian prefect Macro. Caligula promised to cooperate with the Senate, but immediately assumed utter and arbitrary dictatorial authority. Sadistic and insane, he loudly broadcast his delusions of divinity, which bred revolutionary unrest among the Jews. The Senate circulated a story that Caligula had gone mad after an illness in October 37, to which the emperor contemptuously responded by bestowing the high office of first consul upon his horse.

Conceiving a vague plan to invade Britain, he conducted fruitless and foolish military operations on the Rhine during 39–40. In an atmosphere of murder, incest, and almost casual cruelty, Caligula himself was killed on January 24, 41, along with his fourth wife and his young daughter, in a plot masterminded by an officer of the Praetorian Guard.

Further Reading: John P. V. D. Balsdon. *The Emperor Gaius (Caligula)* (Oxford: Oxford University Press, 1964).

Camillus, Marcus Furius   (d. 365 B.C.)

Tribune and dictator, Marcus Furius Camillus led Rome to victory against the Gauls and became known as the "Second Founder of Rome."

Early exploits on the battlefield brought prominence to the young Marcus Furius Camillus. In wars against the Aequi and Volscians in 429 B.C., he led his troops to victory. In 396, he was called back to military service and appointed tribune and then dictator during the Roman war against the Etruscans, whose city of Veii he captured. When Rome was embroiled in war against the Falerii, he was again named tribune but was forced to resign amid charges of fraud. His troops, disappointed at being restrained from plundering the Falerian city, claimed that he had reserved the booty for himself. Camillus went into voluntary exile at Ardea in 389.

A few months later, Camillus recouped his power. The Gauls attacked Rome, plundered the city, and burned it to the ground. Camillus raised a force and attacked the barbarians near Ardea. He then marched to Rome, where the Gauls agreed to withdraw upon payment of a thousand pounds of gold. Camillus, named dictator again, refused to render the tribute, pushed the Gauls out of the city, and routed their forces.

Camillus was repeatedly named dictator and tribune, and he led the Romans against the Aequians, Volscians, Latins, and again, the Gauls. He was nearly 80 in 365 B.C. when he succumbed to the plague in Rome.

Further Reading: Catherine B. Avery, ed. *The New Century Classical Handbook* (New York: Appleton-Century-Crofts, 1962).

Canalejas y Méndez, José   (1854–1912)

Prime minister of Spain from 1910 to 1912, his anticlerical campaign resulted in a "Padlock Law" restricting new religious orders.

A career politician, José Canalejas held numerous positions in the government of Spain, including undersecretary to the presidency (1883), minister of public works and justice (1888), minister of finance (1894–95), co-minister of agriculture, industry, and commerce (1902), and, finally, prime minister (1910–12). Canalejas was a democrat with some radical policies, who took harsh stances against labor, in an effort to crush labor unrest, and the clergy. The "Padlock Law" rose out of his dispute with the Vatican (which had been conducting secret negotiations with the Spanish government) and prohibited the establishment of new religious orders in Spain.

Canalejas' policies alienated religious conservatives and liberal labor leaders alike. The universally unpopular prime minister was assassinated by Manuel Pardiñas, an anarchist, on November 12, 1912.

Canute IV   (ca. 1043–1086)

To assert Danish claims to the English throne, Canute was planning an invasion of England against WILLIAM I THE CONQUEROR when he was killed.

Succeeding his older brother Harold Hen as king in 1080, Canute opposed the Danish nobility and attempted to keep a tight rein on them. In an effort to combat the power of the aristocracy and create a strong centralized state, he closely aligned himself with the church. Although he was a pious man, Canute's policies beneficial to the church were the product of ulterior motives. For example, he established and enforced the tithe in large measure as a check against the power and wealth of the rural aristocracy.

Hoping to make good Danish claims to the English throne, Canute prepared an invasion against the Norman usurper William I the Conqueror. Canute stepped up his collection of the tithe to pay for his planned invasion and garnered the support of the count of Flanders and the king of Norway, Olaf III. Shortly before his departure for England, however, the aristocracy revolted over the increased taxation. Canute was forced to flee from the rebels and take refuge at St. Alban's Church, which he had founded. There the rebels discovered him, and, with his brother Prince Olaf, he was assassinated on July 10, 1086, while kneeling in prayer. He was subsequently canonized.

Caracalla   [Marcus Aurelius Antoninus] (188–217)

Roman emperor from 211 to 217, Caracalla is best remembered for his political ruthlessness, his financially ruinous program of grandiose building (which produced, among much else, the great Roman baths named after him), his success in defending the empire against barbarian threats, and his extension of Roman citizenship to residents of the provinces.

Caracalla was born on April 4, 188, at Lugdunum, modern-day Lyons, France. The son and successor of L. Septimus SEVERUS, his given name was Septimus Bassianus. In 198 the Senate made him Augustus and bestowed on him the name Marcus Aurelius Antoninus. When his father died in 211, he became co-emperor with his brother Geta, but the next year murdered him—as well as his many followers—and thus became sole emperor.

From the very beginning of his reign, Caracalla lavished huge expenditures on military expansion and on a program of building. In order to raise revenue for these projects, he depreciated the Roman

Cruel and brutal, Caracalla is best remembered today for the monumental baths he constructed in Rome. (Richard Delbruck, Antike Portrats, 1912)

currency and generally raised taxes, propelling the empire into a serious economic crisis. Probably in an effort to broaden the available tax base, he decreed the Constitutio Antoniniana in 212, whereby Roman citizenship was extended to all free inhabitants of the empire, including the farthest provinces.

Economic woes were not the only threats Caracalla faced. By 213, the Germanic tribes resumed their attacks on the empire's frontiers. Leaving the government in the hands of his mother, Julia Domna, Caracalla mounted a costly but successful campaign against the Alamanni on the Upper Rhine. It was in the course of this action that he received his nickname Caracalla, after the Gallic coat he habitually wore. The next year, he successfully repulsed a Goth invasion on the lower Danube.

Emboldened by his military successes against the Germanic tribes, he decided to take the offensive and, like ALEXANDER III THE GREAT, conquer Parthia in Mesopotamia and modern-day Iran. He captured the city of Edessa (Urfa) in 215 and reconquered from the Parthians the often-contested Armenia, Osrhoëne (modern Syria, east of the Euphrates River), and Roman Mesopotamia. As he was preparing to invade Parthia proper, this ruler who had assumed power through murder was himself assassinated on April 8, 217, by a cabal of his own officers. One of these, Macrinus, commander of the Praetorian Guard, succeeded him as emperor.

Further Reading: S. A. Cook *et al.*, eds. *Cambridge Ancient History*, vol. 12 (New York: Macmillan, 1939); William E. Mahoney, *Antoninus Bassianus Caraculla* (Salzburg: Institut fur Englische Spache und Literatur, Universitat Salzburg, 1976).

Carol II   (1893–1953)

King of Romania from 1930 to 1940, Carol II assumed dictatorial powers and mercilessly persecuted his political opponents.

Carol II was born to Romanian King Ferdinand I and Queen Marie (originally of England) on October 15, 1893, in Sinaia, Romania. As a young man, Carol married a commoner named Zizi Lambrino, but his parents had the marriage annulled. He then married Helen, the sister of the king of Greece, but continued his playboy life-style, supporting a mistress named Magda Lupescu, a scandal compounded in the eyes of Carol's countrymen by the fact that Magda was a Jew.

Although Carol had been excluded from the line of succession by an act of January 1926 and by his father's will, he returned to Romania in 1930 and took over the regency of his young son Michael. He himself took the royal oath on June 8, 1930.

As king, Carol II was plagued by opposition from the Iron Guard, a national Fascist group, and was squeezed in the power struggle between Russia and Germany. Although he himself greatly admired the policies and tactics of Benito MUSSOLINI, Carol saw the greatest danger to his rule in the Fascist Iron Guard and, in February 1938, declared a dictatorship largely with the object of suppressing them. However, as territories were stripped from Romania by Germany and the Soviet Union, Carol was forced to abdicate in favor of his son Michael on September 6, 1940. He sought exile in Spain and Portugal, married his mistress Lupescu (July 1947), and died in Estoril, Portugal, on April 4, 1953.

Carrera, José Miguel   (1785–1821)

The first president and self-proclaimed dictator of Chile, José Carrera battled to keep Chile independent from Spanish rule during the early 1800s.

After leading a successful coup against the Spanish colonial government of Chile in 1811, José Carrera proclaimed himself dictator of the South American nation. Internecine strife quickly escalated into civil war, however, and Carrera's rule was cut short in 1813 by a military junta that deposed him in favor of Bernardo O'Higgins.

Carrera returned to power the following year, but by 1815 Spanish forces defeated both Carrera and O'Higgins. In vain, Carrera sought aid from both the United States and Argentina. Failing to regain his former position, he threw in his lot with Argentine revolutionaries against the Buenos Aires government. Subsequently betrayed by his own men, José Carrera was captured and executed on September 4, 1821, in Mendoza, Argentina.

Casimir IV   (1427–1492)

As grand duke of Lithuania from 1440 to 1492, and king of Poland from 1442 to 1492, Casimir IV was instrumental in the defeat of the Teutonic Knights in 1466.

The son of Vladyslav II, Casimir IV was second in succession to the throne of Poland. At age 13, following the assassination of the grand duke of Lithuania, young Casimir was sent by his brother Vladyslav III—who had succeeded to the Polish throne in 1434—as governor of that country. Almost immediately a coup d'état was staged in Lithuania, severing ties with Poland. However, the rebels chose Casimir as grand duke, hoping to capitalize on the young man's lineage and use him as a tool. Inexperienced though he was, Casimir seized control from the boyars who had hoped to manipulate him.

In 1444, Vladyslav III was killed in battle, leaving Casimir the only candidate for the Polish throne. He was crowned in 1447, thereby reestablishing the bond between Lithuania and Poland. As king of Poland and grand duke of Lithuania, Casimir IV worked to establish a dual monarchy, while still preserving the independence of the two nations. Accordingly, his domestic achievements were mainly attempts at establishing a royal lineage, not much-needed social and political reform.

He married Elizabeth of Hapsburg in 1454, who brought with her claims to Bohemia and Hungary, and bore Casimir 13 children destined to make his name a familiar one in the noble houses of Germany.

As Casimir IV did little on the domestic scene, he also avoided most international conflicts. He did, however, render aid to the Prussians in their revolt against their overlords, the Teutonic Order, beginning in 1454. Although they were defeated almost immediately at Könitz, the Polish and Prussian armies held out for year after grueling year. Finally, in 1466, the Knights were forced to surrender at Touron, effectively ending the Teutonic Order. For the remainder of his reign Casimir IV resided in Lithuania. He died on June 7, 1492.

Castillo Armas, Carlos   (1914–1957)

Backed by the U.S. Central Intelligence Agency, Castillo Armas led a successful coup against Guatemalan president Jacobo Arbenz. Castillo Armas served as president from 1954 to 1957.

Born near Escuintla, Guatemala, on November 4, 1914, Castillo Armas was educated at the Guatemalan polytechnic (military) school and in the United States, where he studied military tactics and strategy during 1945–46. In 1950, Carlos Castillo Armas participated in the attempted coup against the government of Juan José Arévalo Bermejo. Captured and sentenced to death, Castillo escaped from prison and went into exile in Honduras. In 1954, the CIA and the United Fruit Company backed him as leader of a coup against the legally elected leftist president Jacobo Arbenz Guzman. Castillo Armas' forces invaded Guatemala from Honduras on June 18, 1954, while CIA-hired pilots dropped bombs on Guatemala City.

After the coup, Castillo Armas was named provisional president and later held an oral plebiscite—in preference to a more conventional secret ballot—in an effort to legalize his administration. His presidency was marked by a return to dictatorial rule and suspension of the 1945 constitution. Land that had been redistributed to Indian peasants during 1952 liberal agrarian reforms initiated by Arbenz was returned to its former owners. Political parties were outlawed, and Castillo ordered the execution of several hundred leaders of peasant and labor movements. He also caused the wholesale arrest of his opponents; some 9,000 individuals were imprisoned, and another 8,000–10,000 fled the country. The United States, in the meanwhile, eager to demonstrate that its support of the dictator had not been a mistake, flooded Guatemala with foreign aid.

Castillo Armas—"The Liberator," as he called himself—was assassinated on July 26, 1957, by a presidential guard (officially labeled a Communist), who then committed suicide.

Suggested Reading: Richard H. Immerman. *The CIA in Guatemala* (Austin: University of Texas Press, 1982); Stephen Schlesinger and Stephen Kinzer. *Bitter Fruit: The Untold Story of the American Coup in Guatemala* (Garden City, New York: Doubleday, 1982).

Castro Ruz, Fidel (b. 1926 or 1927–)

A leader of the Communist revolution in Cuba, Fidel Castro became prime minister, president, and de facto absolute dictator of the island nation.

Fidel Castro Ruz was born on August 13, 1926 (some sources report 1927), on a farm in Mayari municipality, Oriente province. Castro received a rigorous Catholic education, including training at Colegio de Belén, an austere Jesuit boarding school, which did much to instill in him a sense of spartan order and discipline. He subsequently attended the University of Havana, graduating in 1950 with a degree in law.

While he was at the university, Castro became active in the social-democratic Ortodoxo Party and gained notoriety as an early and eloquent opponent of the corrupt, American-backed dictatorship of Fulgencio BATISTA. Castro turned from words to deed on July 26, 1953, when he led an assault on the Moncada army barracks, a government armory. The attack failed, but it propelled the young radical into national prominence. Tried for the incident, Castro was sentenced to 15 years' imprisonment, but he was granted amnesty in 1955 after serving only two years. Upon his release, Castro went into self-exile in Mexico, where he founded the 26th of July Movement and prepared to carry out revolution in Cuba.

In Castro's absence, Cuba seethed with insurrection. An uprising at Matanzas was put down on April 29, 1956. In November of that year, Castro and 81 others, including the charismatic guerrilla leader Che Guevara, returned to Cuba, landing in Oriente province on November 30. Met by Batista's forces, the guerrillas were apparently routed, and, on December 2, Castro was reported to have been killed. Actually, he and his followers had set up a secret

base camp in the isolated Sierra Maestra Mountains. From here, they conducted a carefully planned and highly successful guerrilla war, applying constant pressure against Batista from 1957 through October 1958, when Castro and his followers emerged from hiding to take the offensive. Batista, having lost ground steadily, fled the country on New Year's Day, 1959, and Castro occupied Havana on January 8, the United States having declared its official recognition of his government the day before.

At this point, Fidel Castro was not an avowed Communist. He had conducted the revolution on a platform of anti-imperialism, nationalism, and general reform. Assuming the reins of government, he was initially careful to include in his inner circle moderates and democratic reformers. But, within a short time, the Castro government became increasingly radical and defiant, particularly of the United States. With the support of the masses, whose living conditions had indeed dramatically improved, Castro's forces summarily nationalized foreign-owned properties and industries—most of which were American—and waged quick and merciless war against all opposition, executing some and driving others into exile. Realizing that Castro was no mere reformer, but a full-blown Marxist, many of Cuba's professionals, technicians, and prosperous individuals fled the island, most of them coming to the United States.

On May 7, 1960, Castro announced the resumption of diplomatic relations with the Soviet Union (which had been broken off by Batista), and by the middle of the year, he explicitly aligned his nation with the U.S.S.R. At this point, Soviet premier Nikita KHRUSHCHEV warned the world that he would defend Cuba against American aggression, even to the point of thermonuclear war. Thus emboldened, Castro threatened the United States naval base at Guantánamo Bay. On November 1, 1960, President Dwight Eisenhower responded to the threats by declaring that the United States would take "whatever steps are necessary to defend" the base, and on January 3 of the next year he severed diplomatic relations with Cuba.

The new president of the United States, John F. Kennedy, responding to the perceived threat of a bellicose Communist regime a mere 90 miles from the U.S. mainland, authorized a covert invasion of Cuba by some 1,400 anti-Castro Cuban revolutionaries supported by the Central Intelligence Agency. The so-called Bay of Pigs Invasion, conducted during April 15–20, 1961, was a total failure, largely because the invaders did not receive the naval air support they had been promised. The Bay of Pigs fiasco was a tremendous blow to U.S. prestige and allowed Castro to consolidate his power further. In December 1961, he loudly and boldly declared his outright alliance with the Soviet Union, which, seizing an opportunity to gain a military and political toehold deep in the West, granted Cuba the extensive economic, technical, and military assistance it desperately needed, especially after so many of its most skilled people had fled.

Friction between Castro and Kennedy escalated during the balance of 1961 and came to a dangerous flash point on October 22, 1962, when the American president announced to the nation via television broadcast that U.S. surveillance had "established the fact that a series of offensive missile sites is now in preparation" in Cuba. In defiance of Soviet threats to commence, in effect, World War III, Kennedy ordered a naval blockade and "quarantine" of Cuba and prepared to invade the island. A tense showdown between the world's two great nuclear powers was resolved on November 2, when Khrushchev backed down and President Kennedy reported to the nation that the Soviet missile bases were being dismantled. Despite this victory over Cuba's Soviet allies, Castro remained characteristically defiant, and on February 6, 1964, he cut off the water supply to Guantánamo Naval Base. This was more a gesture of harassment than a serious threat, however, since the base was equipped with its own self-contained distillation plant. Castro's regime suffered another blow in July 1964, when the Organization of American States instituted sanctions against the island, finally prompting Castro to permit refugees to fly to the United States. These "freedom flights" continued from November 1965 until August 1971, during which time about a quarter of a million Cubans deserted the island.

While Castro remained closely tied to the Soviets, he broke with the Chinese Communists in 1966 because of their failure to deliver promised support.

From 1959 to 1976, Castro was prime minister of Cuba. In 1976, he officially became president—and also continues to serve as first secretary of the Cuban Communist Party as well as commander of the nation's armed forces. His election as chairman of the Nonaligned Nations movement in 1979 gained him a measure of international prestige. At home, he has been less successful as an economic reformer. His country remains poor, but, in the volatile world of Caribbean politics, it is a testament to his political skill and personal charisma that he has held power for so long—even in the shadow of a great ideological antagonist and in the wake of the collapse of his only significant economic and political ally, the Soviet Union.

Further Reading: Lee Lockwood. *Castro's Cuba, Cuba's Fidel* (New York: Macmillan, 1969); Herbert Matthews. *Fidel Castro* (New York: Simon & Schuster, 1969).

Catherine II the Great   (1729–1796)

Catherine II, known as Catherine the Great, built on the reforms of PETER I THE GREAT to transform Russia into a modern European country.

Born Sophie Fredericke Augusta in the Prussian town of Stettin (present-day Szczecin, Poland) on May 2, 1729, Catherine was the daughter of the prince of Anhalt-Zerbst. When she was 15, a marriage was arranged between her and Peter, the unattractive and dull-witted nephew and heir of the Russian empress Elizabeth. Catherine arrived in Moscow in 1744 and was wed, having been given the Russian name of Ekatarina—Catherine.

The new princess was popular in the Russian court, to which she brought an ample measure of cultivation and learning. She tolerated her loveless (indeed, repellent) marriage by taking a series of lovers, including Gregori Orlov, whose brother Aleksei was an influential army officer. When Empress Elizabeth died on December 25, 1761, Catherine's husband succeeded to the throne as Peter III. He quickly alienated his court, especially a cadre of senior officers, including Aleksei Orlov, who led a coup d'état in June 1762. Peter was deposed—and later assassinated—and the popular Catherine, 33-year-old daughter of an obscure Germanic prince, assumed the throne as absolute monarch of Europe's greatest empire.

Although she never succeeded in learning to speak the Russian language fluently, Catherine did have a genuine regard for her subjects, was anxious to institute good government, and was particularly determined to bring Russia out of its provincial backwardness and into the Age of Enlightenment that had already swept through Western Europe. Catherine was extraordinarily well read in an age when women were customarily little educated. She was also the most cultivated and Western-oriented Russian monarch since Peter I and was intent on continuing the work of modernization and Westernization he had begun. If anything, however, she was more concerned than Peter had been with efficient administration of the government, appointing 18-century Russia's most distinguished corps of advisers, including Nikita Panin, a progressive in foreign affairs, Aleksandr Suvorov, an extraordinary military commander, and Prince Gregori Potemkin, a remarkable statesman, administrator, and the architect of the Russian navy.

Catherine was also more liberal than Peter I—at least during the early years of her reign. Whereas Peter had sought to transform Russian society almost overnight by decree and by fiat, Catherine preferred to institute reforms by example and incentive, always encouraging individual initiative. In 1765, she established the Free Economic Society to foster the modernization of agriculture and industry. Rather than simply imposing her ideas on the nation, she sought an assessment of her people's needs, convening in 1767 an assembly of deputies representing all regions of the country to create a new code of laws. In this enterprise, Catherine did not relinquish all control; she herself drafted the *Nakaz* ("Instruction"), a set of guidelines.

Catherine also opened her traditionally insular nation to development by inviting foreign settlers and establishing new port cities, most notably Odessa on the Black Sea. She opened up an intellectual commerce with the world as well, encouraging a flowering of the arts, relaxing the country's strict censorship laws, and permitting the free and private establishment of printing presses. Catherine authorized many state and private schools and made the University of Moscow a genuinely international center of learning.

As with Peter's reforms, Catherine's—far-reaching as they were—met with only limited success. The court and the upper classes did indeed reach a new level of sophistication and enlightenment, but little changed in the rest of the country, and Catherine's innovations did absolutely nothing for the vast class of serfs that made up the majority of the Russian population. The work of the assembly of deputies had little practical effect, and in 1774–75, Catherine was faced with a full-blown insurrection led by Yemelian Pugachev, whose following consisted of Cossacks, peasants, and other disaffected minorities. With much of eastern Russia in rebellion, Catherine dispatched Suvorov with an army to crush the revolt. The work was carried out swiftly and without mercy. By 1775, Catherine was firmly in control again.

The empress realized that military action was insufficient to prevent further revolt. In 1775, she set about reforming local governmental administration and made the central government responsible for the administration and welfare of those serfs who had belonged to the Orthodox church. She also integrated the Cossacks into the regular army. A decade later, Catherine extended the reforms further, issuing royal charters to Russian towns and Russian nobility. The charters made the towns and nobles responsible for local administration while guarantee-ing to them the support and protection of the central government.

Toward the close of the 1780s, Catherine began to doubt the wisdom of her liberal policies. Schools, presses, and educational associations were developing rapidly and with complete independence from any official authority. They were, Catherine feared, spreading the seeds of change in an era that had seen first the American Revolution and, in 1789, was witnessing an even more sweeping revolution in France. In 1790, the Russian reformer Aleksandr Radishchev published his *Journey from St. Petersburg to Moscow,* a moving and detailed indictment of serfdom, as well as of the excesses of the ruling classes and the inequities of official government. Nothing like Radishchev's book had ever appeared in Russia before, and Catherine, feeling now that her liberal-minded policies had created a monster that would devour her and her empire alike, reinstituted many of the repressive measures she had earlier overthrown. Her government did not collapse, but her late wave of repression shocked and alienated many in the cultivated class she herself had fostered.

Catherine's reign not only brought internal changes, it continued the work Peter I had begun by further establishing Russia's position as a significant international power. Suvorov successfully prosecuted two wars against Turkey (in 1768–74 and 1787–92), which resulted in the establishment of Russian sovereignty over the Crimea, thereby giving the nation a militarily and economically strategic Black Sea port. The Ukraine and parts of Poland also came under Russian domination during Catherine's reign.

Catherine the Great died on November 17, 1796, having brought at least elements of her nation into the modern age and having made Russia a world power to be reckoned with.

Further Reading: John T. Alexander. *Catherine the Great: Life and Legend* (New York: Oxford University Press, 1989); Vincent Cronin. *Catherine, Empress of All the Russians* (New York: Morrow, 1978); Ian Grey. *Catherine the Great* (Philadelphia: Lippincott, 1961).

Catherine de' Medici   (1519–1589)

Queen of France, later queen mother to her three sons who would be king, Catherine was a dominant force in French politics for almost half a century.

Born to Lorenzo de' Medici, duke of Urbino, and Madeleine d'Auvergne, a Bourbon princess, on April 13, 1519, Catherine de' Medici was orphaned almost immediately. Her uncle, Pope Clement VII, supervised her upbringing and schooling at the hands of nuns. In 1533, at the age of 14, Catherine married Henry, duke of Orléans, whose father, Francis I, was king of France. Upon Francis' death in 1547, Henry, Duke of Orléans, was named HENRY II, king of France.

Catherine became an ideal figurehead queen of Reformationist Europe. She stoically endured Henry's open infidelities, made no attempt to interfere in his decisions, and avoided intrigue with anyone outside the government. Henry's sudden death in April 1559 from a jousting accident devastated Catherine emotionally—many say she never recovered from the loss—but also jolted her out of her wonted passivity and thrust her into the forefront of government.

Henry's death brought Francis II, the couple's 16-year-old first-born son, to the throne, and Catherine was named regent. On December 5, 1560, Francis II died suddenly, and his younger brother, Charles IX, assumed the throne. Charles was only 10, and Catherine retained the title regent—though she was essentially de facto queen of France.

Basically indifferent about religion herself, Catherine's primary task was keeping France's endemic religious animosity from turning to civil war. Her overriding concern was to preserve France, and her only enduring loyalty was to her dynasty.

Hoping to get the Catholics and the Protestant Huguenots to coexist peacefully, she attempted to legislate tolerance with the Edict of January in 1562, which gave the Huguenots specific religious rights. The Catholics rejected the Edict and demanded civil war. Catherine quickly and deftly ended that brief war by March 1563, by issuing the Edict of Amboise, a watered-down version of the earlier document. Hoping to consolidate the power of the dynasty, Catherine declared Charles of age in August 1563 at the Parliament of Rouen and took him on a whirlwind tour of the country to enforce the revised edict.

Catherine's efforts were not completely successful; two more civil wars followed as well as continued persecution of the Huguenots in the Catholic-dominated regions of France. With the Treaty of Saint-Germain in 1570, Catherine succeeded in ending the last civil war by granting generous concessions to the Huguenots as well as disgracing her Catholic enemies in the House of Guise who sought to control France by allying it with Spain.

Peace was not destined to last long, however. After the murder of several thousand Huguenots in the infamous St. Barthlomew's Day Massacre in Paris during August 23–24, 1572 (for which Catherine must bear at least some responsibility), the Huguenots now were ripe for full-blown insurrection.

Charles died in 1574, leaving Catherine's last son, Henry III, as king. Catherine did not dominate Henry as she had his two brothers, but rather put

herself at his service, working tirelessly to avoid subjugation by the Catholics and to avoid a war with Spain. Henry's ambitions drove his reckless statesmanship, which put these goals at risk. The labor of attempting to appease a host of violently jarring factions proved at last too much for Catherine, who died at Blois on January 5, 1589. She narrowly missed outliving all of the men in her life; Henry III was murdered just eight months after her own death.

Further Reading: Paul Van Dyke. *Catherine de Medicis* (2 vols.) (New York: Scribner's, 1922); N. M. Sutherland. *Catherine de' Medici and the Ancien Regime* (London: Historical Association, 1966).

Cavaignac, Louis-Eugène (1802–1857)

Governor-general and chief executive during the French revolution of 1848, Louis-Eugène Cavaignac was known as the "Butcher of June" for his suppression of a workers' revolt in June 1848.

Louis-Eugène Cavaignac was born in Paris on October 15, 1802, the son of Jean-Baptist Cavaignac, a Jacobin member of the Committee of General Security during the first French Revolution, 1789–1792. At his father's urging, Louis-Eugène attended military school at the Ecole Polytechnique, in 1820. Like his father, the young Cavaignac maintained strong republican principles, on account of which cause he was denied admission into the French army until his uncle, General Jacques Maria, intervened. In 1828, Cavaignac, an army officer, was sent to aid Greek revolutionary forces. His radical republicanism soon led to his reassignment in Algeria in 1832.

Cavaignac rose quickly through the ranks while in Algeria, his superiors willing to overlook his political philosophy in the face of his military ability. He proved himself a ruthless commander, at first opposing then zealously practicing the tactic of *razzia*—punitive raid—on Arab villages. In 1844, he ordered the asphyxiation by smoke of Arabs who had taken refuge in a cave. That year, Cavaignac was promoted to brigadier general and, four years later, became governor-general of Algeria. True to his convictions, Cavaignac renamed Algeria the Republic of Algeria.

Offered an appointment as minister of war, Cavaignac at first refused and instead successfully ran for election to the National Constituent Assembly. On his return to Paris, Cavaignac decided to accept the appointment previously offered and almost immediately, in June 1848, faced off against socialist workers who were protesting the removal of their leaders from the National Constituent Assembly. In a violent and decisive confrontation, Cavaignac, suppressed the protest and earned the nickname

"The Butcher of June." After the insurrection, Cavaignac was made president of the council of ministers, effectively assuming control of the French government.

Despite his brutality in Algeria and in the June uprising, Cavaignac's brief administration was characterized by a moderate republicanism. He extended universal suffrage and helped incorporate the first democratic constitution since the inactive constitution of 1793. Cavaignac was able to gain diplomatic recognition from Russia, and attempted to reconcile the crisis in Italy between Piedmont-Sardinia and Austria. In December 1848, however, he lost the election to Louis-Napoléon Bonaparte (subsequently NAPOLEON III). Cavaignac remained politically active as leader of the opposition to Louis-Napoléon, for which he was arrested in 1851. Soon released, he was elected to the Corps Législatif in 1852, but refused to take an oath of allegiance to Louis-Napoléon—now Emperor Napoléon III—and was denied his seat. Reelected in 1857, he again declined the oath and was again refused his seat, whereupon he resigned. On October 28, he died of a heart attack.

Suggested Reading: F. A. de Luna. *The French Republic under Cavaignac, 1848* (Princeton, New Jersey: Princeton University Press, 1969).

Ceauşescu, Nicolae (1918–1989)

A Communist hard-liner, Ceauşescu maintained independence from Soviet domination, but ruled Romania with heartless authority until he was executed by a revolutionary tribunal.

Born in Scorniceşti, Romania, on January 26, 1918, Nicolae Ceauşescu became an ardent Communist during the 1930s and was repeatedly imprisoned for his political activities. He married another Communist, Elena Petrescu, in 1939, and became the disciple of Gheorghe Gheorghiu-Dej, a Communist leader, while he and Ceauşescu were imprisoned together during the 1940s.

Ceauşescu escaped confinement in 1944, just before the Soviets occupied Romania. From 1944 to 1945, he served as secretary of the Union of Communist Youth, then, in 1947, after communism was fully established in Romania, he became head of the ministry of agriculture, serving from 1948 to 1950. From 1950 to 1954, he was deputy minister of the nation's armed forces, holding the rank of major general. When his mentor, Gheorghiu-Dej, became head of the Communist Party in 1952, Ceauşescu moved into the number-two party spot, heading up the politburo and secretariat. He was tapped as Gheorghiu-Dej's successor after the leader's death in 1965, becoming party head and, two years later, president of the State Council as well.

As president of the State Council and—from 1974—as president of Romania, he set his country on an orthodox Communist course, yet maintained a high degree of independence from the Soviet Union, pulling out of the Warsaw Pact alliance, condemning the pact's 1968 invasion of Czechoslovakia, and blasting the Soviet invasion of Afghanistan in 1979.

Ceauşescu's policy of independence did not translate into anything approaching domestic democracy. Quite the contrary, his regime was one of the most repressive of all European Communist governments. He relied heavily on a feared secret police force to maintain control over the press and media and to stamp out all incipient opposition. Like the Soviet Union's Stalin in the 1930s, Ceauşescu in the 1970s single-mindedly embarked on a crash program of industrialization, which succeeded only in amassing a large debt. To pay this off, Ceauşescu ordered the export of massive amounts of agricultural produce, even though his people were suffering from acute shortages of food, fuel, and other staples. As Ceauşescu drove his nation into poverty and want, he and his wife fostered a cult of personality about themselves. The dictator practiced a shameless form of nepotism, appointing his wife and many other family members to powerful and profitable posts.

As the Ceauşescu regime heaped outrage upon outrage—one scheme called for the leveling of thousands of Romanian peasant villages and the installation of the population in Stalinesque apartment blocks—opposition grew, even in the face of brutal repression. On December 17, 1989, Ceauşescu ordered his secret police forces to open fire on demonstrators in the town of Timisoara. Far from quelling the demonstrations, this action spread them to the capital, Bucharest. On December 22, the army deserted Ceauşescu en masse, joining the dissidents, and the dictator and his wife boarded a helicopter in a desperate escape attempt. They were captured and, on Christmas day, tried by a hurriedly convened military tribunal. Found guilty, Nicolae and Elena Ceauşescu were executed by firing squad that very day.

Further Reading: Mark Almond. *The Rise and Fall of Nicolae and Elena Ceausescu* (London: Chapmans, 1992); Edward Behr. *Kiss the Hand You Cannot Bite: The Rise and Fall of the Ceausescus* (New York: Villard, 1991); Nicolae Ceausescu. *Nicolae Ceausescu: The Builder of Modern Romania* (Oxford: University of Oxford Press, 1983).

Cetshwayo (c. 1826–1884)

The last great king of Zululand, Cetshwayo united his nation against the British and Afrikaners.

Born about 1826 near Eshowe, Zululand, Cetshwayo was one of many sons of the Zulu king

MPANDE. Cetshwayo secured his succession to the throne after killing his half-brother Mbulazi in a bloody civil war in 1856. He then spent the next 16 years consolidating his power and purging other rivals. When his father died in 1872, Cetshwayo emerged as the undisputed king.

Recognizing the threat posed by the British and the Afrikaners in South Africa, Cetshwayo increased his military force to 40,000 warriors. The British, too, recognized a threat, and in early 1879 they undertook a preemptive strike. At first the Zulu were victorious, but with the arrival of British reinforcements, they were unable to maintain the upper hand. Cetshwayo was captured and imprisoned at Cape Town, and Zululand was divided among 13 chiefs designated by the British.

In 1882, Cetshwayo persuaded his captors to release him. He traveled to London, presented his case to Queen Victoria, and made such a good impression that the queen did as he asked—returned him to power as Zulu king. Zulu unity had disintegrated during his imprisonment, however, and civil war broke out among the various factions. Cetshwayo died, possibly the victim of an assassin, on February 8, 1884, in Eshowe, Zululand.

Further Reading: Jeff Guy. *The Destruction of the Zulu Kingdom: The Civil War in Zululand* (London: Longman, 1979); Morris, D. R. *The Washing of the Spears* (New York: Simon & Schuster, 1965).

Chandragupta I (r./ca. 320–330 A.D.)

Founder of the imperial dynasty of the Guptas, Chandragupta I ruled a major portion of modern-day India from about 320 to 330, expanding his empire through marriage to a princess of a neighboring province.

Grandson of Sri Gupta, Chandragupta I was a chief of part of Magadha when he married a Lichchhavi princess named Kumara Devi. This marriage brought to him the territories of Bihar and perhaps Nepal. Chandragupta I built his capital in Pataliputra, and his kingdom spread beyond Magadha to Allahabad. Although he ruled for only about 10 years, he took the title *maharajadhiraja*, meaning "king of kings," and his successors, including his son SAMUDRAGUPTA, continued to expand the empire and rule over it until the 5th century.

Chandragupta II (r.c. 380–c. 413)

The second son of SAMUDRAGUPTA, Chandragupta II came to power in India in 375. He extended the vast empire he inherited largely though warfare and marriage.

According to Indian tradition, Chandragupta II seized power by killing his older brother, who had inherited a vast domain from their father. Chandragupta II ruled from 375 to 413. During his reign, he conquered Malwa, Gujarat, and Kathiawar and overthrew the Saka satraps of Ujjain. These lands he added to the already vast holdings of the Guptas. To the south, he acquired holdings by arranging the marriage of his daughter to Rudrasena II, king of the Vakatakas.

Assuming the title *Vikramaditya* ("Sun of Valor"), he was to become the central figure of a large body of Indian lore, still current in parts of the country. He was a great patron of the arts and architecture, and scholars attribute to his rule the climax of cultural development in India.

Despite the murderous beginnings of his rule, Chandragupta II was known to be a public benefactor. He maintained free hospitals for men and free rest-houses for travelers. His successors continued to rule India until the 5th century.

Chandragupta Maurya (r. c. 321–c. 297 B.C.)

The founder of the Maurya dynasty of India, Chandragupta Maurya usurped power from the last king of the Nanda dynasty and ruled from about 321 B.C. to 297 B.C., greatly expanding the Indian Empire during his reign.

Chandragupta Maurya is said to have been the illegitimate son of a Nanda king and a maid-servant. Early in life, he became an adventurer and traveled throughout India. One account has him meeting the Greek emperor ALEXANDER III THE GREAT at a camp in the Punjab and offending him "through boldness of speech." For this it is said that he was forced to flee for his life. While in hiding, Chandragupta Maurya met a Taxilian Brahman named Chanakya or Kautilya, who helped him raise an army of mercenaries in order to overthrow the last king of the Nanda dynasty. (Another account holds that Chandragupta Maurya was sold to Chanakya, who then educated the boy and compelled him to overthrow the king.)

Chandragupta Maurya won a decisive battle against the king and took control of the empire in Magadha. At this time, Alexander the Great died, and Chandragupta Maurya took advantage of the resulting disorder to attack the Macedonian outpost in the Punjab. Some time between 324 and 321 B.C., with a mighty army reputed to have comprised 600,000 infantry, 30,000 cavalry, and 9,000 elephants, he overran all of northern India.

About 20 years later, Chandragupta Maurya's supremacy was challenged by the Hellenic general Seleucus Nicator, who had inherited the eastern portion of Alexander the Great's empire. Chandragupta Maurya soundly defeated him and forced him to accept humiliating peace terms, including a forced marriage into the Maurya royal family. In return, Seleucus received the niggardly payment of 500 elephants. The treaty between Seleucus and Chandragupta Maurya, concluded about 303 B.C., brought to the Maurya dynasty all lands in northwest India as far as the Hindu Kush mountains.

During the closing years of his life, Chandragupta Maurya renounced the throne and became an ascetic devotee of the Jain sage Bhadrabahu. Prolonged drought had devastated his vast empire, and he became convinced that his own failings as king had brought about the disaster. Tradition records that he carried his self-abnegation to the point of death by starvation. He was succeeded by his son Bindusara, and the Maurya dynasty continued to rule India until 186 B.C.

Further Reading: P. L. Bhargava. *Candragupta Maurya* (Oxford: Clarendon Press, 1936).

Charlemagne   (742 or 743–814)

This Frankish ruler and Emperor of the West briefly but gloriously united much of Western Europe, creating a short-lived period of order and enlightenment at the end of the Dark Ages.

Born April 2, 742 (or 743) to the Frankish king Pepin the Short and his wife Berta, Charlemagne was annointed king with his brother Carloman by Pope Stephen III in 754. After Pepin died on September 24, 768, Charlemagne took possession of the western part—his portion—of the kingdom on October 9. Carloman died in December 771, and Charlemagne promptly annexed the eastern portion of the kingdom as well. The following year, he began the first of the approximately 40 campaigns that would chiefly occupy his 43-year reign. This was a punitive action against a Saxon tribe that had engaged in raiding. Invited by the pope to invade Italy and fight the Lombards under Desiderius, he prevailed in 773–74, then quashed a Lombard revolt the next year.

Charlemagne's next major campaign, against the Moors in Spain, met with defeat when he failed to breach the fortress of Saragossa in 778. Hroudland—better known to us as Roland—margrave of the Breton marchi, fought a rearguard action covering Charlemagne's withdrawal and was ambushed by Basques in the Pyrenees valley of Roncesvalles. The story of this defeat spread (and, with it, the further fame of Charlemagne), becoming a favorite subject of the troubadors. Some 300 years after the emperor's death, the story assumed its final form as the 12th-century chanson known as *The Song of Roland*.

Returning to the north, Charlemagne was again met with intractable resistance from barbarian Saxon tribes. He instituted a long series of brutal campaigns in Saxony, establishing the bishopric of Bremen in 781, then defeating the Saxons at Detmold and the Hase in 773 and triumphing over the Saxon leader Widukind in 785. Additional campaigns against the Saxons were fought through the 790s, including the suppression of the revolt of 793. During one of his Saxon campaigns, Charlemagne, who is traditionally hailed for having brought a measure of enlightenment to a Europe deep in the Dark Ages, beheaded 4,000 Saxons in a single day.

Simultaneously with his campaigning against the Saxons, Charlemagne expelled Duke Tossila III from Bavaria during 787–88 and annexed the region. Almost immediately, he turned to the Avars, who were raiding the Danube region. This resulted in expansion of Charlemagne's realm to Lake Balaton and northern Croatia during 791 to 803. He also invaded Spain for a second time during 796–801, this time succeeding in the capture of Barcelona in 801.

In 800, Pope LEO III recognized Charlemagne as the mightiest of European monarchs by crowning him emperor of the West. Some of the more enlightened and hopeful citizens of Europe thought this was the beginning of the restoration of the Roman Empire of classical times. And it is true that Charlemagne had unified much of western Europe. His campaigns against the Byzantines for control of Venice and the Dalmatian coast, during 802–812, were far less conclusive than what he had accomplished in the west; however, he did secure Byzantine recognition of his title.

Charlemagne was more than a conqueror. He introduced a degree of humanity into much of Europe, including an extensive system of justice administered by the *missi dominici*—a monk or bishop teamed with a count or military commander who traveled under royal commission through the provinces like circuit judges, hearing criminal and other cases. In this way, the petty tyrannies and corruption of local lords were counteracted. Charlemagne, semiliterate himself, brought scholars from all over Europe to his court at Aachen (Aix-la-Chappelle), including Alcuin and Theodulf, the foremost men of learning of their day. These efforts did much to keep the spark of classical learning alive in the closing years of the Dark Ages.

While the last years of the emperor's reign over his vast realm were fairly serene, his great reforms did not long endure after him, and nothing like a genuine revival of the Roman Empire took place. After Charlemagne sickened and died at Aachen on January 28, 814, his empire was divided among his heirs, and, throughout the Middle Ages, the continent was largely fragmented.

Further Reading: Donald A. Bullough. *The Age of Charlemagne* (New York: Putnam, 1966); James A. Cabaniss. *Charlemagne* (New York: Twayne, 1972); Einhard (770–ca. 840). *The Life of Charlemagne* (Ann Arbor: University of Michigan Press, 1960).

Charles   [King of Portugal] (1863–1908)

King of Portugal from 1889 to 1908, Charles inherited a politically troubled situation, which compelled him to compromise his own power by appointing the tyrannical and repressive João Franco prime minister.

Charles was the son of King Louis and Queen Maria of Portugal, and grandson of Emmanuel II of Italy. He married Marie Amélie of Orléans, a granddaughter of the French king Louis-Philippe, in 1886. An intellectual with a flair for the arts, Charles was unable to manage the growing dissension within his country. When he yielded to a British ultimatum of 1890 demanding withdrawal from certain African territories, popular indignation rose against him, leading to a republican revolt in 1891.

Faced with these internal difficulties. Charles appointed the autocratic João Franco prime minister in 1906, giving him unprecedented powers amounting to dictatorship. In the meantime, Charles proved himself insensitive to the economic plight of the Portuguese people, and, while Franco ruled, he busied himself with spending huge sums to finance his extravagant personal life. Discontent boiled over into assassination on February 1, 1908, when Charles was murdered, along with his eldest son Luis Felipe, while driving through the streets of Lisbon.

Charles I   (1600–1649)

The authoritarian rule of Charles I of England led to his execution, civil war, and a temporary end to the monarchy.

The second of the Stuart kings, Charles was born November 19, 1600, the second son of James I, previously James VI of Scotland. Charles' older brother, Henry, died in 1612, leaving Charles as Prince of Wales and next in the line of succession.

Immediately after he ascended the throne in 1625, Charles came into conflict with Parliament. His primary adviser, the Duke of Buckingham, was hated in Parliament and was, in fact, distrusted by everyone except the king. Moreover, the war with Spain, which James I had started, was going poorly, and the Puritans, who predominated in the House of Commons, were opposed to the king's High Church Party. Parliament rebelled against Charles by refusing to vote him the right to levy taxes, unless he increased its powers.

The Puritan "Rump Parliament" convicted King Charles I of treason and executed him on January 30, 1649, replacing the monarchy with the Commonwealth under Oliver Cromwell. (From Charlotte M. Yonge, Pictorial History of the World's Great Nations, *1882)*

When his second Parliament convened in February 1626, antagonism was renewed. Parliament blamed a failed naval expedition against Spain on Buckingham and attempted unsuccessfully to impeach him. In response, Charles dissolved Parliament in June of 1626; however, Buckingham's incompetence quickly embroiled Charles in a war with France as well as Spain. Now desperate to fund his military adventures, Charles ordered a tax that was declared illegal by his own judges. He promptly dismissed the chief justice and ordered the arrest and detention of more than 70 knights and gentlemen who refused to pay.

Charles reconvened Parliament in March 1628. In the meantime, Buckingham's mission to undermine the French king by aiding the French Protestants had failed miserably, further discrediting Charles' reign. Knowing Charles was desperate for funding, Parliament agreed to vote him the power to tax if he signed the Petition of Right. Charles balked at its sweeping provisions: no forced loans or taxes without Parliamentary consent, no quartering of troops in private homes, no imprisonment without specific charges being brought, and no martial law in peace time. Yet he signed the document in 1628.

By the time Charles convened his third Parliament in January 1629, Buckingham had been assassinated and the rift between the High Church Anglicans and the Puritans had deepened. The Puritan-dominated House of Commons decried the revival of "popish practices"; incensed, the king ordered the adjournment of Parliament in March. The speaker attempted to rise to declare the adjournment, but was physically restrained while three more resolutions were passed condemning the king's actions. Charles viewed this as treason and refused to convene Parliament for the next 11 years.

Charles turned next to his subjects in Presbyterian Scotland, on whom he tried to impose his ecclesiastical beliefs. Rebuked, he decided to make war on the Scots, reconvening Parliament in April 1640 for the approval of funds. Parliament declined, and instead gave voice to a host of grievances. In response, the king dissolved Parliament within a month. The king's forces were defeated by the Scots at Newburn. Charles then summoned in November 1640 what would become known as the Long Parliament.

The newly convened Parliament promptly ordered the arrest of Charles' ministers and condemned the king's conduct. Hoping to appease the legislative body, Charles signed the Triennial Act, ensuring that Parliament would be convened every three years. This failed to have the desired effect. Not only was Charles' most trusted adviser, the earl of Strafford, executed in May, but in November 1641, Parliament issued the Grand Remonstrance of the King, cataloguing everything that had gone awry since Charles' ascension.

At this juncture, news of a rebellion in Ireland reached Parliament, which feared that any army raised to combat the rebellion would be turned against them. Parliament moved to seize control of the military. In response, Charles ordered the arrest of six members of Parliament, but they escaped. Now it was Charles' turn to flee, as both sides scrambled to secure parties loyal to their cause.

In June 1642, Parliament sent the king the Nineteen Proposals, demanding among other things Parliamentary control of the military, Parliamentary approval of all ministers appointed by the king, and Parliamentary participation in the setting of church policy. The king refused to agree to the proposals and, in effect, began the English Civil War.

The war raged for three years before the king surrendered to the Scots, hoping they would be more lenient than Oliver CROMWELL and the forces of Parliament and that they might even be persuaded to back Charles' return to the throne. However, when the Scots came to terms with Parliament, they handed Charles I over to Parliamentary commissioners. In June, during a dispute between Cromwell's New Model Army and Parliament, a junior officer with 500 men absconded with the king to army headquarters at Newmarket. Charles was moved to Hampton Court and, in November, made good an escape, but was subsequently captured by forces loyal to Parliament.

Held under close surveillance, he continued to negotiate with the army, the Scots, and Parliament for his return to the throne. After he gained the support of the Scots in December 1647, their forces were defeated at the Battle of Preston, bringing the so-called Second Civil War to a close.

The New Model Army demanded that Charles be put on trial for treason as "the grand author of our troubles." He was accordingly charged with high treason and other crimes against the realm of England, but refused to recognize the legality of the proceedings, citing the divine right of kings and holding that "a king cannot be tried by any superior jurisdiction on earth." It was to no avail. Judged guilty, Charles I was executed January 30, 1649.

Further Reading: John Bowle. *Charles I: A Biography*, (Boston: Little, Brown and Co., 1975); G. Davies. *The Early Stuarts, 1603–1660* (Oxford: Clarendon, 1949); Pauline Gregg. *King Charles I* (London: J. M. Dent and Sons, 1981).

Charles III (1716–1788)

One of the greatest kings in Spanish history, Charles III led Spain in an economic revival.

The third son of King Philip of Spain, Charles was born on January 20, 1716, in Madrid. His education was excellent, and he was well versed in the arts and fluent in French by the age of four. His mother, Philip's second wife, realizing that Philip's two sons by his previous marriage were next in line for the Spanish throne, sought a kingdom for her son. She persuaded Philip to attack Austrian Italy in 1733; the resulting Austrian defeat forced the cession of Naples and Sicily, where Charles was proclaimed king in 1735. He was very successful and popular in Italy because he surrounded himself with capable advisers who accomplished much for the kingdom.

Philip died in 1746, and his two sons were both dead by 1759, making Charles king of Spain. He abdicated his Sicilian throne in favor of his son Ferdinand and quickly set about pursuing an active role in the rule of Spain. As in Sicily, he selected very competent ministers and allowed them the latitude to act. Charles offered challenge to England's colonial supremacy, entering into the Bourbon Compact with France to form an alliance. France's weakness brought about the dissolution of the pact, but not before Spain came to control Florida, Mobile, Minorca and Gibraltar.

As part of his plan to achieve and retain absolute power in Spain, Charles moved to subordinate the church to the state by ousting the Jesuits in 1767, removing them as well from all colonial possessions, where they had set up missions, and subjected all papal bulls or briefs to royal approval before allowing their publication in Spain. He formed a council of state, which acted as a cabinet to formulate policy on certain issues. He reformed the tax code and land policies to accommodate Spain's growing population. He also stimulated industry to encourage foreign commerce.

When Charles died on December 14, 1788, he left his nation more enlightened and more economically sound than when he had ascended the throne 30 years earlier.

Further Reading: Sir Charles Alexander Petrie. *King Charles III of Spain; An Enlightened Despot* (New York: J. Day, 1971).

Charles V   (1500–1558)

The last of the medieval rulers, Charles V struggled to hold together the anachronistic Holy Roman Empire that was facing social, political, and religious pressure from all sides.

The grandson of Emperor Maximilian I and FERDINAND and ISABELLA of Spain, and the son of Philip I of Castile who died when he was only six, Charles assumed the throne of the Netherlands at the age of 15. Upon Ferdinand's death in 1516, Charles was proclaimed king of Spain, landing there in 1517. Charles did not speak Spanish and knew none of the country's customs or traditions, factors that created deep resentment among the locals and led to a revolt.

Before Charles could deal with the problems in Spain, Maximilian died in 1519, leaving him the throne of Germany. In October 1520, Charles was crowned king of Germany and proclaimed Roman emperor-elect. As the political leader of Christendom, Charles now made war on Protestantism. He also sought hegemony in Western Europe, he hoped at the expense of his chief rival, Francis I of France.

After defeating Duke Maximilian Sforza in 1515, Francis secured the Duchy of Milan and prepared to war against Charles, who hurried back to Spain, where his agents had managed to contain the revolt against his rule. Although he granted amnesty to some who had perpetrated the revolt, Charles proved he could be ruthless as well, personally signing 270 death warrants. Remarkably, however, a period of rapprochement ensued between Charles and the Spanish people. He replaced his agents and ministers with local Spaniards and learned the language and customs of his new country.

With the resources and support of Spain behind him, Charles began his campaign to unite his universal Christian empire and defeat Protestantism. In 1522, Charles defeated Francis at the Battle of Pavia, taking Francis prisoner. Francis feigned agreement to the Treaty of Madrid, which assured Charles control of Italy, but promptly repudiated it as soon as he had been set free.

When SULEYMAN I THE MAGNIFICENT ascended to the sultanate of Turkey in 1520, Charles now faced pressure from France in the West and from Turkey in the East. While Suleyman made incursions into the West, however, Charles turned against the pope, who had betrayed him by forming the League of Cognac against him. With his German and Spanish troops, Charles marched on Rome in May 1527. The troops, their pay in arrears, mutinied against their leaders and sacked the defenseless city. Mutinous as they were, Charles' forces won the day for him, and the pope traveled to Bologna, where he crowned Charles Holy Roman Emperor—the last time an emperor would be crowned by a pope.

Charles now found himself trying to accomplish too much. Attempting to subdue Francis while trying to bring about the Holy Roman domination of Europe, he was forced to make concessions to the Protestants in order to gain their support for his mil-

Charles V, Holy Roman Emperor. (From Charlotte M. Yonge,
Pictorial History of the World's Great Nations, *1882)*

itary exploits and to postpone military campaigns against them. He was in a constant state of war and in the process of conducting campaigns of religious persecution.

After initial successes, Charles found himself facing too many enemies while trying to manage an empire grown too large to control with the limited resources available to him. Charles, ailing with gout, was driven from Germany in 1552. His military reversals forced him to make further concessions to the Protestant princes through the Treaty of Passau late in 1552. He returned to western Germany in an effort to regain some of what he had lost, but this campaign also failed and, in 1553, Charles handed over all responsibility for German affairs to his brother, Ferdinand. He then renounced his claims to the Netherlands in 1555. On September 12 of the same year, he abdicated the imperial crown and retired to a monastery in Spain, though not before renouncing his Spanish claims in favor of his son Philip. Charles died on September 21, 1558.

Charles' grand scheme to revive the Holy Roman Empire as a universal Christian empire, while genuine in purpose, was simply outdated. The rise of nationalism and the progress of the Protestant revolution had exceeded the ability of any one ruler to hold sway over vastly different peoples.

Further Reading: Karl Brandi. *The Emperor Charles V: The Growth and Destiny of a Man and a World Empire* (London: Cape, 1980); Royall Tyler, *The Emperor Charles the Fifth* (Fair Lawn, N.J.: Essential Books, 1956)

Charles VIII (1470–1498)

Charles VIII, king of France from 1483 to 1498, is remembered chiefly as the instigator of a largely unsuccessful 50-year campaign carried out by the French monarchy to invade and occupy Italy.

Born in Amboise, on June 30, 1470, Charles ascended to the throne when he was 13 years old. He was poorly qualified to rule, not only because of his youth and inexperience, but also because he was simple-minded. His older sister and her husband actually ruled France during the early years of Charles' reign, but, when he was about 21 years old, he took control himself.

Charles VIII accomplished virtually nothing during his reign, other than unsuccessfully prosecuting his grandiose scheme for the invasion of Italy. He ceded the provinces of Roussillon and Cerdagne back to Aragón in order to clear the way for the war he planned. Charles marched on Italy with an army of nearly 20,000 men. At first successful in his mission, he had himself crowned in the city of Naples, on February 22, 1495. But Charles soon found himself beating a hasty retreat to France. While prepar-

Charles VIII of France. (From Charlotte M. Yonge, Pictorial History of the World's Great Nations, *1882)*

ing for another Italian invasion, the hapless Charles was killed at Amboise on April 7, 1498, when he struck his head on a low doorframe.

Further Reading: Albert Guerardi. *France: A Modern History* (Ann Arbor: University of Michigan Press, 1959).

Charles X (1757–1836)

Charles X became the first member of the Bourbon royal family to go into exile after the French Revolution in 1789.

Charles X was born at Versailles on October 9, 1757, and ruled France from 1824 until 1830. He was a grandson of Louis XV and a brother of LOUIS XVI. His youth was spent in gambling, drinking, and womanizing, but in 1785, an alliance with Louise de Polastron added stability to his life and he took up an interest in politics and statecraft. When the Bastille fell in July 1789, Charles' brother, King Louis XVI, exiled Charles to Turin, where he was soon joined by another brother, the future King Louis XVIII.

When Louis XVIII became king, he made Charles lieutenant general of the kingdom. Charles himself ascended to the throne upon his brother's death and began a short rule of six years, during which time he worked to subvert the forces of republicanism and to return France to the *ancien régime*. His efforts resulted in the revolution of 1830 and Charles' overthrow, and he was exiled to Austria, where he died of cholera, at Gorizia, on November 6, 1836.

Further Reading: Albert Guerardi. *France: A Modern History* (Ann Arbor: University of Michigan Press, 1959).

Charles XI   (1655–1697)

Establishing an absolute monarchy that lasted into the next century, Charles reestablished the power of the Swedish crown at the expense of the parliament.

The only son and sole heir to King Charles X, Charles XI was born November 24, 1655 in Stockholm. His father died when he was only five, and Charles' first years as king passed under a regency of the nobility and the parliament. Charles began to rule on his own in 1672, but the nobility still had firm control over policy, and a treaty the nobles concluded with LOUIS XIV of France involved Sweden in the Dutch War of 1672–78. The Swedes were defeated by the Prussians at Fehrbellin in June 1675, and Charles took total control of both the army and the affairs of state after the disaster.

The Prussian victory gave the false impression that Sweden was vulnerable, and Denmark hoped to capitalize on this perceived vulnerability by invading the Swedish province of Skoane in 1676. Charles personally took the field and swiftly defeated the Danes at the Battle of Lund in 1676. His bravery gained him much needed respect and support at home, which allowed him to repossess the royal lands from the nobility, increasing the crown's holdings by some 3,000 percent. The revenues derived from these lands accounted for more than half the king's budget and enabled him to keep a standing army of professional soldiers, a navy that rivaled Denmark's, and a domestic government that effectively controlled the schools and churches. With the repossession of the royal lands, Charles forced the nobility into dependence on bureaucratic appointment.

By 1693 Charles extracted a declaration by the estates of the parliament proclaiming him an autocrat "responsible to no one on earth for his actions . . . to guide and govern his kingdom." When Charles died in Stockholm on April 5, 1697, he left Sweden with an ample treasury, solid international standing, and a stable internal administration that enabled the monarchy to rule with absolute authority until the death of his son, CHARLES XII in 1718.

Charles XII   (1682–1718)

This brilliant, daring, and warlike Swedish king gained and lost huge territories in Poland and Russia in the course of a remarkable but reckless campaign of expansion.

Charles XII was born in Stockholm on June 17, 1682, to CHARLES XI and Ulrika Eleonora. When his father died in 1697, Charles XII, aged 15, assumed the throne of one of the great powers of Europe, with territories encompassing all of present-day Sweden, Finland, the Gulf of Finland, Riga, Pomerania, and the vicinity of Bremen. Young Charles was subject to a regency prescribed by his late father, but the regents quickly decided that the youth's apparent exceptional abilities warranted the early termination of the regency, which was ended in November 1697. Three years later, an alliance of Russian, Polish, and Danish forces hoped to exploit the boy-king's inexperience by attacking Holstein, a duchy ruled by a duke who had married Charles' sister, and campaigning against Swedish possessions on the continent.

Charles took part in initial operations against the Danes, then led troops in the conquest of Zealand (Sjaelland), in the heart of Danish territory, in April 1700. The Danes quickly capitulated by the Treaty of Travendal on August 28, and Charles turned against his eastern enemies. He advanced into Livonia (modern Latvia) at the head of an army of 20,000 on October 16, marching to the relief of the Swedish outpost of Narva, which was besieged by the forces of Czar PETER I. Although he was greatly outnumbered, Charles had the element of surprise and commanded extraordinarily skilled troops. In a driving snowstorm, he attacked on November 30, 1700, routing the Russians in a quarter of an hour. He turned next to the Swedish port city of Riga, under siege by a Russian-Polish-Saxon army, which he defeated on June 27, 1701.

Flushed with these victories, Charles crossed the Dúna River and defeated another Russian-Polish-Saxon army at Dünamünde on June 18, 1701. He occupied Kurland and launched an invasion of Lithuania during August-December 1701. Next, he advanced on the Polish capital of Warsaw, occupying it on May 14, 1702, then continued westward. On July 19, 1702, he engaged Polish-Saxon forces at Kliszow, defeating them, and he captured Krakow shortly thereafter. These actions undermined the power of Augustus II, who was king of Poland and elector of Saxony. When Charles defeated a large Polish-Saxon force at Pultusk on May 1, 1703, Augustus II was forced off the throne, and the Swedish king put a puppet, Stanislas Leszczynski, in his place in 1704. Charles went on to further victories—

at Punitz and Wszawa in 1705—thereby wholly subduing Poland.

Returning to the Baltic, Charles drove the Russians out of Lithuania, pushing Peter's army as far as Pinsk during the late summer and early autumn of 1705, and, by the Treaty of Altranstädt, signed on October 4, 1706, compelling Augustus formally to abdicate the Polish throne and to renounce his nation's alliance with Russia.

With the collapse of his Polish ally, Czar Peter at last gave in and offered favorable terms. But Charles, who had begun to fight because he was forced to, was now driven by visions of greater glory and was not about to make peace. To demonstrate his contempt for Peter and his offer, he caused the Russian ambassador at Dresden to be arrested. Seizing on the fact that the ambassador had been born in Livonia, a Swedish possession, he branded the diplomat a traitor and had him publicly executed. Charles then raised additional troops and stockpiled supplies during 1707. On January 1, 1708, he began an invasion of Russia. Capturing Grodno on February 5—and very nearly taking the czar himself prisoner—he advanced on Minsk, where he awaited the spring thaw. On July 12, 1708, he crossed the River Berezina and defeated a large Russian army at Golovchin. He reached the Dnieper River at Mogilev on July 18, meeting with parties of skirmishers and enduring acute shortage of provisions because of the desperate Russians' scorched earth policy.

Still, Charles pushed his exhausted forces on toward Moscow, defeating a small body of troops at Dobroje on September 11 and striking up an alliance with Ivan Mazeppa and his Ukranian Cossacks, then in rebellion against Peter. To Charles' dismay, Mazeppa was ousted in late October 1708, and as the winter approached, it became apparent that the season was going to be extraordinarily harsh. It was only with great difficulty that the king kept his forces together during the terrible winter of November 1708 to April 1709. Impatient, he advanced on Voronezh, pausing to lay siege against Poltava. This proved disastrous. Charles' army suffered from an acute shortage of provisions, ammunition, and artillery from May 2 through July 7, 1709, and the king was painfully wounded in the foot during one skirmish against relief forces. On July 8, the Russians bore down with an army of 80,000 on the 23,000 Swedes remaining to Charles. The wounded king directed the desperate battle from a litter, then, painfully, on horseback. Although several mounts were shot from under him, his life was spared, and he saw his army virtually destroyed by July 9.

With the deposed Mazeppa and 1,500 cavalry troops, he slipped across the frontier to Turkish Moldavia, settling into a camp at Bendery. The Turks, seeing any enemy of the Russians as a friend, treated Charles royally from 1709 to 1714. At length, however, the Turks wearied of Charles' intrigues aimed at involving Turkey in an all-out war against Peter and arrested their guest—who submitted only after a fierce battle between Turkish Janissaries and his own corps of guards. In November 1714, Charles slipped out of Moldavia and made his way to Swedish Pomerania, reaching Stralsund on November 21. Almost immediately, allied forces laid a year-long siege against this town and Wismar. Charles fled to Sweden in December 1715.

The king set about rebuilding the Swedish army, and this time it was he who offered favorable peace terms to Peter, agreeing to cede all of his Baltic provinces. In the summer of 1716, he staved off an invasion of Sconia, then raised additional troops in preparation for an invasion of Norway, from which he planned, perhaps, to launch an invasion of Scotland or, at the very least, to strengthen the position from which he could negotiate the most advantageous terms with the many enemies still arrayed against his country. He attacked Norway and, by November 30, 1718, had penetrated as far as the fortified town of Fredrikshald (present-day Halden), near Oslo. During the siege of the town, he was struck in the head by a musketball and killed.

Further Reading: Michael Roberts. *From Oxenstierna to Charles XII: Four Studies* (Cambridge and New York: Cambridge University Press, 1991).

Charles the Bold (1433–1477)

As duke of Burgundy, Charles the Bold attempted to create an independent Burgundian kingdom through warfare and the capture of territory in France, Switzerland, and the Netherlands.

The son of Philip the Good and Isabella of Portugal, Charles the Bold was born on November 10, 1433, in Dijon, Burgundy.

Beginning about 1465, Charles was engaged in various wars and negotiations to achieve his goal of making Burgundy a kingdom independent from France. When France's King LOUIS XI acquired some Burgundian territory along the Somme River, Charles forced him to the negotiating table in October 1465, and through the Treaty of Conflans, wrested control of the territory. Subsequent to this, Louis XI encouraged towns under Charles' control to revolt against Burgundian rule and remain loyal to France. Dinant and Liège revolted, but in 1466 Charles sacked Dinant, and the following year subdued Liège. In the meantime, Charles' father died (June 15, 1467), and Charles was named duke of Burgundy.

In 1468, Louis XI and Charles met to negotiate at Peronne. During their meetings, Charles learned of a new revolt in Liège, again backed by the French king. Charles was able to intimidate Louis to remove Flanders, Ghent, and Bruges from the jurisdiction of the Parisian *parlement* (superior court) and to aid in the suppression of the revolt at Liège, which was largely destroyed and its population massacred.

The truce between Louis XI and Charles was short-lived. The French king ordered Charles to appear before the Parlement of Paris and seized some Burgundian towns along the Somme (1470–71). In retaliation, Charles invaded Normandy and the Île-de-France, sweeping across the country as far as Rouen. In November 1472, the king and the duke concluded another truce.

By September 1473, the stage was set for Charles to receive royal status. He had persuaded Holy Roman Emperor Frederick III to bestow on him the title king of Burgundy, but at the last moment, after the ceremony had been arranged and the royal insignia prepared, Frederick fled to avoid the coronation. This marked the beginning of the collapse of Charles' dreams of empire. Over the next three years, without a royal crown, he was forced to end his 11-month siege of Neuss, which he was trying to take from Cologne. He saw his friend Edward IV of England turn against him to ally himself with Louis XI. At last, during a battle with the Swiss at Nancy on January 5, 1477, Charles was killed.

Further Reading: A. G. Dickens, ed. *The Courts of Europe: Politics, Patronage, and Royalty, 1400–1800* (New York: Greenwich House, 1977); François Guizot. *A Popular History of France from the Earliest Times* (Boston: Dana Estes and Charles G. Lauriat, n.d.).

Cheng Ch'eng-kung [Koxinga] (1624–1662)

Cheng Ch'eng-kung, known in the West as Koxinga, was a pirate who attempted the restoration of the Ming dynasty and who established Chinese control over Taiwan.

Born to a Japanese mother and a Chinese father, Cheng lived in Japan until age seven, when he went to live with his father, a wealthy merchant whose piracy in the straits of Taiwan had earned him a position in the maritime defense forces of the Ming emperor. Cheng enrolled in the Imperial Academy of Learning at Nanking in 1644, but he and his father were forced the following year to retreat to Fukien after a Manchu invasion of the city. When Manchu forces next invaded Fukien, capturing and killing the prince of T'ang and leaving the Ming dynasty in disarray, Cheng's father accepted a Manchu bribe and joined forces with the invaders. Young Cheng, upon whom the slain prince had bestowed the title Kuo

Hsing (Chu)—"Lord of the Imperial Surname"—did not join his father in defection. Instead, he vowed to restore the Ming dynasty.

For the next 12 years, Cheng built up a formidable Ming opposition along the Fukien coast. Like his father, Cheng was an excellent naval tactician and, in 1659, led a maritime expedition of more than 100,000 men up the Yangtze River toward Nanking. Unbeatable at sea, Cheng was nevertheless turned back at the gates of Nanking and defeated the same year by the superior Manchu defenses.

Cheng next set his sights on the Dutch imperial presence in Taiwan. In 1661, after a nine-month siege, he captured the Dutch stronghold of Anping (near modern Tainan), Taiwan, and forced the Dutch off the island. His next objective was to oust the Spanish from the Philippines, but he died suddenly on June 23, 1662, before he could put his plans into motion.

Further Reading: W. Campbell. *Formosa Under the Dutch* (1903; reprint ed., Taipei: Ch'eng-Wen, 1967).

Cheng Chi-lung (1614–1661)

This Chinese pirate and political member of both the Ming and Manchu dynasties was the father of Chinese national hero CHENG CH'ENG-KUNG.

Born in the Fukien Province, China, Cheng Chi-lung spent his youth on the Portuguese colonial settlement of Macau, where, baptized a Catholic, he was given the Christian name Nicholas Gaspard. He left Macau to become a pirate, plundering Dutch and Chinese merchants in the Straits of Taiwan. Cheng jumped ship in 1628 and accepted a position with the Ming government to protect the waters he had formerly looted. Cheng attempted to restore Ming control of Fukien in 1644, but, unsuccessful, accepted a Manchu bribe to change allegiance in 1646. His own son, Cheng Ch'eng-kung, remained loyal to the Ming and became a leader of opposition to Manchu expansion. In consequence of his son's activities, the elder Cheng was stripped of rank by the Manchus, imprisoned in 1655, and executed in Peking (Beijing) on November 24, 1661.

Cheng-te [Chu Hou-chao] (1491–1521)

A Ming dynasty ruler, Cheng-te executed hundreds who opposed him.

Cheng-te ascended the throne in 1505 as the 10th emperor of the Ming dynasty and gave eunuchs such power that future governments were unable to expel them. The hedonistic Cheng-te left the actual running of the government to eunuch ministers while he devoted himself to a variety of pleasures. Corruption was rampant throughout the government, offices and government favors were bought and sold with regularity, and excessive taxation was the bane of the working class.

The southern provinces received harshest treatment under Cheng-te's government because the ruling eunuchs were all from the north, and accorded the south almost no representation. Frequent rebellions sprang up in the south, and many people turned to crime. The lawlessness in the region forced Cheng-te to take notice, and in 1510 he made a small attempt at halting the corruption by executing the chief eunuch, Liu Chin. After the execution, officials discovered that Liu's house was loaded with ill-gotten gold, silver, and jewels.

Despite this gesture toward reform, Cheng-te continued to ignore affairs of state and generally declined to crack down on corruption. Instead, he devoted himself to traveling about the country in disguise, learning several new languages. Anyone who criticized him or the government was immediately demoted, tortured, or executed. Cheng-te had hundreds killed in this manner.

The death of Cheng-te was a stroke of poetic justice. The emperor nearly drowned when his pleasure boat capsized, and he subsequently died of an illness related to the accident.

Chervenkov, Vulko (1900–1980)

Vulko Chervenkov was the premier of Bulgaria and leader of that country's Communist Party from 1950 until 1956.

Chervenkov was a hard-line Communist, who was dedicated to the philosophies and principles of Josef STALIN and was himself popularly dubbed "Little Stalin." Chervenkov lived in the Soviet Union between 1925 and 1944, when the Communist Party was outlawed in Bulgaria, and it was during this period that he was indoctrinated into the "Stalinist" faction of the party.

Returning to Bulgaria after World War II, when the Soviet Union was forging its bloc of Iron Curtain countries, Chervenkov rose rapidly in the party to the position of premier. He ruled his country with an iron grip, modeling his administration after Stalin's example of ruthlessness. After Soviet premier Nikita Khrushchev issued a general denunciation of Stalin's excesses, Chervenkov was toppled from power in 1956 and became minister of education and culture, before Nikita Khrushchev's ongoing anti-Stalin purge banned him from all government positions in 1961 and finally ousted him from the Communist Party itself. He lived in relative obscurity until his death in Sofia, Bulgaria, on October 21, 1980.

Chiang Kai-shek [Chiang Chung-cheng or Chiang Chieh-shih] (1887–1975)

Chiang Kai-shek headed the Nationalist government in China and, subsequently, on the island of Taiwan.

Chiang Kai-shek was born to a prosperous family in rural Chekiang Province on October 31, 1887. His father died when Chiang was young, and he was raised by his mother, who sent him to good schools, where he obtained a classical Chinese education. Chiang seemed destined for a career in the civil government, but when the civil service examination system was suspended in 1905, he enrolled in the Paoting Military Academy in northern China in 1906. The next year, he moved to the more prestigious Japanese Military Academy in Japan. Chiang first joined a Chinese revolutionary organization in 1908, but did not return to China from Japan until he deserted from the Japanese army in 1911. He reached Wuhan on October 11 of that year, the day after the revolution that would topple the Ch'ing (Manchu) dynasty had begun.

Chiang led a November 5 uprising in Chekiang, but found himself on the outside after revolutionary leader Sun Yat-sen allied himself with General Yüan Shi-k'ai. During July 12 through September 1913, he participated in a failed attempt to overthrow the general, whose regime had quickly become oppressively dictatorial. He escaped arrest by fleeing to Japan, but returned late in 1915, when he participated in the so-called Third Revolution, which blocked Yüan's bid to become emperor.

From this point until 1918, Chiang lived in Shanghai, in some obscurity, active during 1916–17 in the Green Gang, a secret society devoted to manipulating the volatile Chinese currency during this turbulent period. In 1918, Chiang Kai-shek resumed his association with Sun Yat-sen, who had briefly joined forces with Ch'en Chiung-ming before building up the Kuomintang or KMT (the Chinese Nationalist Party) with aid from Soviet Russia. In 1923, Chiang held the rank of major general in the KMT and the next year was made commandant of the party's Whampoa Military Academy. When Sun died in 1925, Chiang's prestige and power in the KMT rose rapidly. Having worked to consolidate the party's power in southern China during 1923–25, Chiang led the Northern Expedition during July 1926 through May 1927 to suppress the warlords in the north and unite the country under KMT rule. He backed his military gains by securing support from the Shanghai business community, moving to suppress the labor movement, breaking with the U.S.S.R., purging the KMT of Communist influence, and successfully fighting the Communists at Nanching and Hunan during August and September 1927. With the Russian advisers ousted, Chiang recruited many of China's contentious warlords into the KMT.

In 1927, Chiang briefly stepped down from leadership of the party in an effort to reconcile factionalism. In December 1927, he married Soong Mei-ling, who would prove a popular and influential leader in her own right and was especially effective later in helping to secure support for Chiang's Nationalist regime from the United States.

On January 6, 1928, Chiang Kai-shek returned to the KMT as military commander in chief and as chairman of the Central Executive Council. He took up the Northern Expedition once again, capturing Peking on June 4. With this, China was now unified under the Nationalist Party—or, at least in theory.

In fact, warlords and Communists ruled many areas, and from December 1930 to September 1934, Chiang led five Bandit Suppression Campaigns in southern China, directed primarily against the Communists. Except for the last campaign, which was carried out with assistance from Germany, these proved largely fruitless, as did Chiang's attempt to counter the Japanese occupation of Manchuria in 1931.

As chairman of the KMT executive council from 1935 to 1945, Chiang was the closest thing China had to a single ruler during this period. His difficult strategy was to tread a thin line between growing Japanese versus Communist domination of China. Before 1937, he tended to favor the Japanese, deeming the Communists a more serious threat. Then, in December 1936, he was kidnapped by Chang Hsüeh-liang (in the "Sian Incident") and was compelled to form a united front with the Communists against the Japanese. Shortly after this, on July 7, 1937, Japan invaded China, thereby commencing the Second Sino-Japanese War.

Chiang, as commander in chief, fought a losing battle against the invaders, progressively retreating with his command post southwest. As morale among his forces deteriorated, administrative corruption increased, and Chiang became increasingly dependent upon the United States, after its entry into World War II. Chiang never wholly committed his forces to military alliance with the United States, however, feeling that he needed to conserve his resources to fight the Communists after the war.

In October 1943, the Executive Council appointed Chiang Kai-shek president of China, and, as he had predicted, immediately following the Japanese surrender in 1945, the struggle between the KMT and CCP (Chinese Communist Party) bitterly recommenced. A civil war began, in which the National-

ists, riddled with corruption and lacking sufficient popular support, steadily lost ground, until, on December 7, 1949, Chiang was forced to flee to the island of Taiwan with the remnant of his party. There he set up a government in exile, in defiance of the People's Republic of China, which now controlled the vast mainland. Chiang presided in Taiwan until his death on April 5, 1975.

The temperament of Chiang Kai-shek was a conservative blend of Confucian authoritarianism and ideological pragmatism. Enemies and friends alike regarded Chiang as crafty, ready, and willing to strike an alliance with whoever could be of aid in a given situation. This resulted in short-term gains and often spelled the difference between immediate failure and temporary survival, but, ultimately, it contributed to the corruption, loss of morale, and erosion of popular support that plagued the KMT, thereby allowing the more ideologically committed Communists to gain the ascendancy.

Further Reading: Robert Berkov. *Strong Man of China* (Boston: Houghton Mifflin, 1938); Richard Curtis. *Chiang Kai-shek* (New York: Hawthorn Books, 1969).

Chilperic I (ca. 539–584)

The son of a Merovingian ruler, Chilperic sought to reunite his father's kingdom through whatever ruthless means were necessary.

One of four sons of Chlotar I, Merovingian emperor, Chilperic was frequently at odds with his brothers. When Chlotar died in 561, he apportioned his kingdom among his four sons, with Chilperic receiving Soissons, the least desirable of his father's lands. Vulture-like, however, Chilperic pounced on the lands of his brother Charibert, after he died in 567. This brought about a bitter standoff between Chilperic and his brother Sigebert, as the third brother, Guntram, attempted to maintain the balance of power.

When Sigebert married Brunhild, daughter of Athanagild, king of the Visigoths, he became the beneficiary not only of a large dowry, but was able to infuse into his court a measure of grandeur calculated to enflame the jealousy of Chilperic. He responded by marrying Brunhild's older sister, Galswintha, casting aside his first wife as well as his mistress, Fredegund. The marriage was short-lived, however; Chilperic quickly grew tired of Galswintha and returned to his mistress. He then ordered the murder of Galswintha as well as of his previous wife before marrying Fredegund.

The sibling war took on more savagery when the two wives—Brunhild and Fredegund—brought a new dimension of hatred to the fratricidal conflict. Brunhild swore revenge for her sister's murder and persuaded Sigebert to march against Chilperic, who was defeated at Tournai. Almost immediately, however, Fredegund engineered the assassination of Sigebert in 575, and Chilperic moved to seize Sigebert's lands, ruled by his son Childebert II, under the regency of Brunhild. Guntram now stepped in to oppose Chilperic, who responded by forming an alliance with Childebert in 581, offering to recognize the young king in return for his aid in opposing Guntram. This alliance quickly collapsed when Brunhild got wind of it and reconciled Guntram and Childebert in 583.

In 584, Chilperic was assassinated by an unknown man while he was returning from a hunting trip.

Ch'in Shih Huang-ti   (ca. 259–ca. 210 B.C.)

The first ruler of a unified China, Ch'in Shih Huang-ti founded the Ch'in dynasty, bringing China's feudal period to an end.

Born Chao Cheng and ascending to the throne of the feudal state of Ch'in at the age of 13 in 246 B.C., Chao Cheng took over Ch'in, the most powerful of the seven states that existed independently in pre-unified China. Chao Cheng's early reign was under the regency of Lü Pu-wei, who was also his prime minister. To consolidate his power, Chao Cheng had Lü exiled when he came of age in 236.

Through skillful diplomacy, outright bribery, espionage, and brutal military conquest, Chao Cheng consolidated all the rival feudal states, and China was now united for the first time under a single leader. Chao Cheng took the name Ch'in Shih Huang-ti, meaning First Emperor of Ch'in. He quickly set out to turn his domain into a centralized state, virtually abolishing feudalism and developing a civil service system based on merit. He set uniform standards for weights and measures, currency and axle width, codified laws and standardized the writing system. He forced all the wealthy families to live in the capital city, so he could closely monitor them. Huang-ti divided the country into 36 military districts, appointing a military governor for defense and a civilian governor for bureaucratic administration.

Fearful of divergence from current trends and hoping to avoid historical precedents, Huang-ti ordered the infamous Burning of the Books in 213, in which all books (save those dealing with medicine, agriculture, specific religions, and Ch'in history) were burned, in conformity with Ch'in's dominant Legalist philosophy. This outraged Confucian scholars, who condemned Huang-ti as a charlatan. Huang-ti was also obsessed with the Taoist concept of immortality, and he sent hundreds of magicians throughout Asia in search of the legendary islands of immortality ("Isles of the Blessed"); he employed hundreds more in an effort to develop an elixir of immortality. When all failed, Huang-ti ordered 460 of them executed.

Understandably, the tyrant feared for his own life and became increasingly reclusive, rarely appearing in public for fear of assassination or contact with evil spirits. By the time of his death, about 210 B.C., Huang-ti was so seldom seen that the precise date of his death cannot be determined. Within 15 years after his passing, the Ch'in dynasty itself was extinct—but the dynastic foundation he had laid for the nation of China was destined to endure for 20 centuries.

Further Reading: Derek Bodde. *China's First Unifier: A Study of the Ch'in Dynasty as Seen in the Life of Li Ssu, 280?–208 B.C.* (Leiden: E. J. Brill, 1938).

Chou En-lai   [Zhou Enlai] (1898–1976)

Chou En-lai was Communist China's premier for 25 years, personally directing the nation's affairs from 1949 until his death in 1976.

The son of a highly educated and wealthy family in Shaohsing (Shaoxing), Chekiang (Zhejiang), Chou attended schools in Mukden, Tientsin (Tianjin) and Japan. He became an ardent nationalist and a member of the May Fourth Movement in 1919 and was arrested and briefly imprisoned in 1920. After his release later that year, he traveled to France on a work-study program and joined the French branch of the Chinese Communist Party. Four years later, Chou returned to China and, in 1925, married Teng Ying-ch'ao (Deng Yingchao), another revolutionary.

In 1927, Chou En-lai made the first of numerous trips to the Soviet Union, where he developed his revolutionary specialty, military affairs. Chou frequently ran afoul of MAO TSE-TUNG, but following Mao's elevation to Communist Party chairman in 1935, Chou became a faithful and very able lieutenant, while remaining an advocate of moderation and surviving many purges.

Chou En-lai's special strength was his talent for negotiation and diplomacy. During 1937–45, the period of the Second Sino-Japanese War and World War II, Chou acted as the liaison between the Communist forces and those of CHIANG KAI-SHEK's anti-Communist Kuomintang (KMT) Nationalist party in what was intended to be the common struggle against the Japanese. Following the civil war and the triumph of the revolution, Chou negotiated the crucial Sino-Soviet friendship treaty of 1950 and organized the Geneva Conference on Indochina in 1954 as well as the Bandung Conference of nonaligned nations in 1955. It was Chou who drew up the momentous Shanghai Communiqué, signed with President Richard Nixon in 1972, which initiated the great thaw in what had been more than a quarter-century of highly dangerous and ideologically polarized relations between China and the United States.

Chou En-lai exercised strong personal leadership, but he was a dedicated moderate, performing the delicate and dangerous task of applying the brakes to extreme Maoism both in domestic affairs and, even more importantly, in foreign relations. He served continuously in the Politburo of the Chinese Communist Party from 1927 to 1976, and as premier from 1949 until his death on January 8, 1976.

Further Reading: Dick Wilson. *Zhou: The Story of Zhou Enlai, 1898–1976* (London: Hutchinson, 1984).

Christian III   (1503–1559)

Establishing the state Lutheran Church in Denmark, Christian III in effect founded the 17th-century Danish monarchy.

The oldest son of King Frederick I, Christian was born August 12, 1503, in the province of Schleswig. As crown prince he received Schleswig and Holstein, where he was educated by Lutheran tutors, and subsequently administered the provinces in accordance with Lutheran policies. When Frederick died in 1533, the Catholic-dominated state council rejected Christian as successor.

The Catholics, in an attempt to return the deposed Christian II, uncle of Christian III, to the throne, aligned themselves with Lübeck in northern Germany and held Copenhagen and Malmö. They invaded Holstein in 1533, thereby beginning civil war in Denmark. After laying siege to Copenhagen for a year, Christian finally wrested control of the city from the Catholics in 1536 and ended the civil war by establishing himself firmly on the throne. He vigorously persecuted the Catholic bishops who opposed him and organized the Diet of Copenhagen in October 1536 to force their conversion from Catholicism to Lutheranism.

Religious problems did not cease with the defeat of the Danish Catholics. CHARLES V, the Holy Roman Emperor, wanted to put the daughters of the imprisoned former Danish king Christian II on the various Scandinavian thrones. Christian III allied Denmark with the Protestant German rulers in a declaration of war on Charles in 1542. The allies blockaded the Baltic, with devastating effect on the Netherlands, forcing Charles to conclude the Peace of Speyer, whereby he promised to avoid further interference with the Scandinavian countries.

Christian III died January 1, 1559.

Christian IV   (1577–1648)

Although he entangled Denmark in two disastrous wars that cost him dearly, Christian IV did foster substantial internal economic growth.

The son of King Frederick II, Christian IV was born April 12, 1577, and succeeded to the throne only 11 years later on the death of his father in 1588. He ruled under a regency for eight years until his coronation in 1596. As king, he made an attempt to limit the powers of the Rigsrad, the parliament, by holding important offices vacant and gathering about himself a host of close advisers through whom he did his best to circumvent the Rigsrad.

After an inconclusive war with Sweden to reunite the two kingdoms in 1611–13, Christian made a stab at asserting himself as the Protestant Protector, as his father and grandfather had. He committed Denmark to action in the Thirty Years' War to protect Protestant interests in northern Germany and to counter the Swedish king's activities in European politics. In 1625, he advanced against the Catholic League in Germany, but was defeated in August. He managed to escape the Thirty Years' War without losing any territory, but his prestige and self-confidence were shattered.

Christian's war with Sweden and his involvement in the Thirty Years' War had cost Denmark financially as well, and he was compelled to raise the shipping tolls through The Sound (Øresund) into the Baltic. This angered his old allies in the Netherlands, who promptly allied with Sweden in a war on Christian. The two powers attacked Denmark in December 1643, and by the end of winter, Christian was on the run, having lost several important provinces. The entire Danish fleet was annihilated and the king was forced to accept a humiliating peace in 1645, yielding possessions all over Scandinavia

During this military turmoil, Christian did manage to found the East and West India companies to bring more revenue into Denmark. He also brought about the codification of Danish law, which administered justice more equitably to the lower classes, who had been locked in a perpetual struggle with the nobility. Hundreds of Christian's letters have survived, and their content, which encompasses religion to the brewing of beer, helped make him one of the most revered figures in Danish history. He died at Copenhagen on February 28, 1648.

Christophe, Henri   [King Henry I] (1767–1820)

A former slave and, afterward, a lieutenant under TOUSSAINT L'OUVERTURE, Christophe became ruler of northern Haiti.

Born on the British colonial island of St. Christopher (later St. Kitts) on October 6, 1767 (some authorities give his birthplace as Grenada), Henri (or Henry, as he preferred to spell his name) Christophe bought his freedom and traveled to Haiti. There he joined Toussaint L'Ouverture in his antislavery rebellion of 1791 and soon gained a reputation as an excellent fighter, becoming one of Toussaint's commanders.

French troops invaded Haiti in 1801 to put down the rebellion and soon captured Toussaint. Christophe surrendered in 1802 on condition that he retain his military rank in the French army. He then aligned himself with the military leader of Haiti, Jean-Jacques Dessalines, and helped him oust the French for good. In 1806, Christophe turned against Dessalines and helped engineer his assassination, whereupon he assumed the presidency of Haiti.

Although certain that autocracy was the only form of government suitable to his country, Christophe called a constituent assembly in December 1806. His chief rival for power, Alexandre Pétion, controlled large numbers of opposition constituents from the south and west and was accordingly named chairman of the assembly. The council then set up a constitution that significantly curtailed the power of the executive. Christophe, however, refused to accept the limitations and led his troops against Pétion, whose partisans defeated him on January 6, 1807. Christophe fled to the north, where he set up his own government.

Knowing he had to establish immediate financial legitimacy for his infant kingdom, Christophe opened up his ports to foreign investment and exacted forced field labor from all men, thereby rejuvenating the coffee and sugar industry. Through these expedients, his government amassed considerable wealth and Christophe had himself crowned King Henry I of Haiti. An admirer of Louis XIV, Christophe established courtly protocols and granted titles of nobility. In addition to a mountain citadel called La Ferrière, he built a palace at Sans Souci on the model of Versailles, and, like Louis, he encouraged the arts, literature, and philosophy.

King Henry's subjects tolerated his relatively benign excesses because he allowed them to keep three-fourths of their crops (collecting one-fourth as tax) and grow personal staples on private tracts of land. Although he nominally catered to the "nobility," he dispensed justice and favors equitably to all classes and was respected by all because of this. But, as he grew older, he became increasingly tyrannical and was soon forced to institute border patrols to keep discontented peasants from fleeing to the south.

After attending Mass in August 1820, Christophe suffered a paralytic stroke. When his invalid condition became known, revolts broke out and many of his supporters deserted him. Distraught over losing his kingdom and having been rendered too feeble to do anything about it, Henri Christophe committed suicide at Sans Souci by shooting himself with a silver bullet on October 8, 1820.

Further Reading: John W. Vandercook. *Black Majesty: The Life of Christophe, King of Haiti* (New York: Literary Guild of America, 1929).

Cimon (ca. 510–ca. 451 B.C.)

This Athenian statesman and general won brilliant military victories that expanded the Athenian empire, but his allegiance to the aristocracy was out of step with the ascendancy of democracy in Athens.

Cimon was the son of Miltiades, an Athenian aristocrat, and a Thracian princess. Although Miltiades had defeated the Persians at the Battle of Marathon in 490 B.C. he was disgraced for mishandling a subsequent operation, and he died, broken in spirit and wealth, in 489. Cimon engineered the marriage of his sister to the wealthiest man in Athens and was thereby able to discharge his father's massive debt. Having accomplished this, he distinguished himself in a sea battle against the Persians at Salamis in 480. The grateful Athenians annually elected him *strategos*, a post that combined the functions of war minister and general, from 480 to 461 B.C.

Cimon negotiated the transfer of the maritime states—newly won from Persia—from Spartan to Athenian control, thereby forming the Delian League, of which he became principal commander. In this capacity, he drove the Persians from much of the Thracian coast and defeated the pirates of Scyros, replacing them with Athenian settlers. Cimon also exhumed and transported back to Athens the supposed remains of Theseus, the state's ancient king.

But the greatest triumph of the *strategos* came about 466 B.C., when he led a fleet of 200 ships against the far superior Phoenician fleet near the mouth of the River Eurymedon. He followed this with a land victory that greatly undermined Persia's hold on the eastern Mediterranean. Next, he capped this victory with another on the Aegean, as he drove the Persians out of the Thracian Chersonese (modern Gallipoli). Shortly afterward, he was called on to put down a rebellion on the island of Thasos, which had seceded from the Delian League. After defeating a Thasian fleet, Cimon maintained a blockade of the island for some two years, until the populace surrendered in 463.

While Cimon was away winning victories, the forces of democracy were busy in Athens discrediting him. PERICLES and others charged Cimon with having accepted a bribe to refrain from attacking the King of Macedonia, who may have aided the rebellious Thasians. Cimon was at length acquitted, but it was clear that the aristocracy was on the wane and democracy on the rise. The hoplites, heavy infantry made up of wealthy Athenians, supported their popular aristocratic *strategos*, but the sailors in the fleets, poorer folk, voiced their support for Pericles and Ephialtes, democratic leaders.

Cimon's position was further eroded by his advocacy of military cooperation with Sparta. In 462 B.C., Sparta was faced with a rebellion of the helots—serf class—and asked Athens to assist in putting it down. Cimon urged compliance, arguing that, whatever their differences, Athens and Sparta were as oxen yoked, pulling together for the common good of Greece. Ephialtes argued that Sparta and Athens were rivals and that nothing was to be gained by lending aid. In the end, Cimon prevailed, but his assault against the rebels, using 4,000 hoplites, failed, and an ungrateful Sparta dismissed both Cimon and his troops. This gesture humiliated Cimon in the eyes of Athens, and the fickle populace ostracized him, sentencing him in 461 to 10 years of exile.

Broken-hearted, Cimon rendered his services to Athens when Sparta offered battle at Tanagra in Boeotia in 457. When he was rebuffed, he appealed to the generals to allow him to enlist in the ranks as a common soldier. This offer was likewise rejected. Nevertheless, Cimon urged his personal followers to fight bravely, which they did—to a man perishing in battle. Following this, a chastened Pericles supported curtailment of his adversary's exile, and Cimon returned to Athens to participate in peace negotiations with Sparta.

In 451, with peace between the two rival Greek states restored, Cimon was given command of a naval expedition against Persia. During this operation, he died of illness or of wounds.

Further Reading: Andrew R. Burn. *Pericles and Athens* (New York: Macmillan, 1949); Plutarch, *Life of Kimon* (London: Institute of Classical Studies, University of London, 1989).

Cincinnatus, Lucius Quinctius (b. 519 B.C.?)

Farmer-turned-dictator-turned-farmer, Cincinnatus became the archetype of the selfless and dutiful despot.

His life story compounded of history and mythology, this early Roman statesman was a farmer who (according to tradition) was appointed dictator of Rome in 458 in order to rescue a consular army surrounded by the Aequi on Mount Algidus. It is said that he defeated the invaders in a single day, then,

having done his duty, resigned immediately following the crisis and returned to his farm.

While little known of the historical basis of the story of Cincinnatus, the myth was revived in the late 18th century to describe George Washington (the "Cincinnatus of the West"), who left his plantation at Mount Vernon to answer the call of duty and, victorious, declined (unlike many another revolutionary leader) to become a dictator.

Claudius [Tiberius Claudius Germanicus] (10 B.C.–A.D. 54)

The Roman conqueror of Britain and North Africa, Claudius was plagued by indecisiveness and physical infirmities.

Born into the ruling Julio-Claudian dynasty at Lugdunum, Claudius succeeded CALIGULA as emperor when Roman society and government were at their most corrupt and degenerate. Claudius had been all but ignored by his predecessors because he was a singularly unattractive man burdened with a limp and a severe speech impediment that caused him to slobber and stammer to the point of total incoherence. Although physically unimposing, Claudius was by no means stupid. Left alone by the rest of his family, he read a great deal and became impressively learned, producing a biography of Augustus and histories of the Etruscans and the Carthaginians.

When the Praetorian Guard assassinated Caligula in A.D. 41, they found Claudius in the palace basement, cowering behind a curtain. Unpersuaded that they meant only to make him emperor, Claudius was forcefully hauled to his own installation. From this most inauspicious beginning, Claudius set about his new job with enthusiasm and energy.

Shunned by the Roman aristocracy before his accession, Claudius now snubbed them by surrounding himself with the lowborn companions of his youth: freedmen and slaves. This alienated most Romans, who felt the prestige of imperial power was thus degraded. Claudius earned the opposition of the Roman Senate because he refused to restore many of the privileges Caligula had taken away. By 42, many senators supported an abortive attempt to overthrow Claudius, and throughout the period of his rule, various senators and nobles were involved in attempts on his life. For his part, Claudius dealt with the conspirators harshly, executing many of them.

Claudius began the systematic conquest and colonization of North Africa in late 41, including the annexation of Macedonia in 42 and the inclusion of Thrace as a province in 46. In 43, Claudius launched his most successful endeavor, the attack on Britain.

When the Roman legions marched on London, Claudius crossed the Thames at the head of the columns, hoping thereby to curry favor at home.

Such hopes were in vain, and the plotting against Claudius became even more intense. His fourth wife—also his niece—Agrippina the Younger, poisoned Claudius in Rome on October 13, 54.

Further Reading: Arnaldo Momigliano. *Claudius: The Emperor and his Achievements:* (New York: Barnes & Noble, 1961); Vincent M. Scramuzza. *The Emperor Claudius* (Cambridge: Harvard University Press, 1940).

Cleisthenes of Sicyon (fl. early 6th century B.C.)

This tyrant of the Greek city of Sicyon made effective use of ridicule and censorship to suppress the Dorian family, his rivals.

Very little is known of Cleisthenes beyond the fact that he was of the family of Orthagoras, which had established tyranny over Sicyon. Cleisthenes eroded the preeminence of the rival Dorian family, which controlled numerous Greek cities, by popularizing ludicrous epithets to describe their tribes. Thus Hylleis became Hyatae (Swine men), Dymanes became Choireatae (Pig men), and Pamphyli became Oneatae (Ass men). He also acted to suppress the Homeric bards who sang the praises of Dorian heroes.

Cleisthenes rose to great prominence by espousing the cause of the Oracle at Delphi against Crisa in the Sacred War of 595–96 B.C. As a result of the war, Crisa was destroyed, and Delphi became a central meeting place of the Amphictyonic League, a religious confederation of adjacent states. Cleisthenes won great popularity and amassed prestige by reinstituting the Pythian games at Sicyon, winning himself the first chariot race in 582.

Further Reading: C. William J. Eliot. *Coastal Demes of Attika: A Study of the Policy of Kleisthenes* (Toronto: University of Toronto Press, 1962).

Clement IV (pope: 1265–68)

Having successfully countered antipapal opposition in Italy, Clement inadvertently succeeded in fostering a new threat to Rome.

Born Guy Foulques in St. Gilles, France, the future pope became a lawyer like his father and entered the service of the counts of Toulouse, also serving as a jurist to King LOUIS IX (later canonized as Saint Louis). Foulques joined the priesthood about 1256, following the death of his wife, and was ordained Bishop of Le Puy in 1257, archbishop of Narbonne in 1259, and cardinal in 1261.

Sent by Pope Urban IV to England in 1264–65 to help conciliate the troubles between Henry III and the barons, he was elected pope in absentia on February 5, 1265, on the death of Urban. Foulques attempted to decline the honor, but the College of Cardinals insisted on his elevation.

Guy took the name Clement IV and vowed to follow the policies of Urban IV in the prosecution of the century-old conflict between the papacy and the German Hohenstaufen family. Urban's plan, carried out by Clement, was to enlist the aid of Charles of Anjou against the Hohenstaufens. After much travail, including the necessity of circumventing a boom laid across the Tiber River, Charles entered Rome in May 1265. Clement raised an army and declared Charles king of Naples and Sicily on January 6, 1266. Charles immediately moved against Manfred, the Hohenstaufen leader, at Benevento, killing him.

The policies of Charles and his French ministers soon outraged many of the local rulers, who organized behind Conradin Hohenstaufen and the Ghibellines, an antipapal political party. Conradin captured Rome in 1268, but Charles defeated him at Tagliacozzo on August 23, 1268, took him captive, and had him beheaded. With that, the Hohenstaufen threat ended, but the papacy's troubles were not over. Clement's ally Charles now made designs on Rome, and by the time of Clement's death on November 29, 1268, he posed a grave threat.

Further Reading: Jean, sire de Joinville. *The History of Saint Louis* (London and New York: Oxford University Press, 1938).

Cleopatra VII [Thea Philopator] (69–30 B.C.)

One of the most famous women of all time, Cleopatra ruled Egypt and was notorious for trysts with Julius CAESAR and Marc Antony that not only shaped the fate of her kingdom, but changed the course of world history.

When Ptolemy XII died in 51 B.C., the Egyptian throne passed jointly to his son, Ptolemy XIII, and his daughter, Cleopatra. The two were married, as was the custom, but Ptolemy correctly feared that Cleopatra aimed to rule alone, and he ordered her exiled in 48. Shortly after, Julius Caesar arrived in Alexandria following his victory in the Battle of Pharsalus in October 48. Thereupon, Cleopatra returned from exile and, determined to win Caesar over and use his power to recover lost Ptolemaic territory, she arranged to be smuggled into his camp. Caesar, in turn, saw an opportunity to use Cleopatra to exploit Egypt in order to finance his military campaigns.

A civil war ensued in Egypt between Cleopatra and her brother-husband, but, with the help of Caesar, Cleopatra was victorious, and Ptolemy died in battle. Caesar apparently spent a brief period in

Cleopatra's company. The queen gave birth to a son a short time later, naming him Ptolemy Caesar and claiming Caesar as his father, but there is no other evidence that the relationship between Caesar and Cleopatra was anything other than a political one.

Cleopatra journeyed to Rome in 44 B.C. to conclude a treaty and was entertained as a guest in Caesar's home. The Roman dictator even dedicated a temple statue to her. On March 15, 44, Caesar was assassinated, and the Roman people turned against Cleopatra, who quickly returned to Alexandria, where she was prepared to wait out the ensuing Roman power struggle. While thus biding her time, she arranged the murder of her other brother in order to ensure her sole claim to the throne.

After Marc Antony routed Caesar's assassins at the Battle of Phillipi in 42, he summoned Cleopatra and other Eastern leaders to meet with him. Cleopatra now decided to ally herself with Marc Antony. He, in fact, was instantly captivated, and Cleopatra took full advantage of him. Marc Antony put off his proposed campaign against the Persians and returned to Alexandria smitten.

Compelled at last to return to Rome in 40 B.C. to combat the growing power of Octavian, Antony concluded an alliance with Octavian and married his sister. Despite this politically motivated marriage, he quickly left Rome to return to Cleopatra—a blatant insult both to Octavian and his sister. To compound the outrage, he married Cleopatra in Alexandria—a union that Roman law would not recognize. After acknowledging his two children by Cleopatra and ceding immense tracts of land to her, Antony made the most offensive gesture of all. He celebrated his military victory over Armenia not in Rome, to which he owed his allegiance, but in Alexandria.

The Roman Senate at last deprived Antony of his prospective consulship and generally stripped him of his standing in Roman society. With the blessing of the Senate, Octavian prepared to make war on Cleopatra. At the naval Battle of Actium on September 2, 31, as Octavian's forces gained the upper hand, Cleopatra suddenly broke off the battle and fled. This infuriated Marc Antony. Although they were eventually reconciled, Antony's defeat was assured, and the faithless Cleopatra now attempted to win the support of Octavian.

Cleopatra dispatched her messengers to tell Antony that she was dead, and she retired to her mausoleum. Antony committed suicide, pledging his undying love for her. When Octavian visited her, she was unable to seduce him. He regarded her as nothing more or less than a military prize, and she learned that she was to be paraded through the streets of Rome as a war trophy. Rather than suffer this ignominy, she returned to her mausoleum, and, according to possibly credible legend, induced a venomous asp (symbol of divine royalty) to bite her. She died on August 30, 30 B.C., and was buried beside Marc Antony.

Further Reading: Ernie Bradford. *Cleopatra* (New York: Harcourt Brace Jovanovich, 1972); Georg M. Ebers. *Cleopatra* (New York: D. Appleton, 1894); Grant Michael. *Cleopatra* (New York: Simon & Schuster, 1972); Oskar von Wertheimer. *Cleopatra: A Royal Voluptuary* (Philadelphia: J. B. Lippincott, 1931).

Clovis I   (ca. 466–511)

A Merovingian ruler, Clovis I established the Frankish kingdom that dominated much of Europe during the early Middle Ages. He was also the first of the barbarian kings to accept Roman Catholicism.

Born to the Salian Frank king Childeric I, Clovis succeeded his father in 481. Five years after assuming the throne, he fought and defeated the last of Gaul's Roman rulers, Syagrius, at the Battle of Soissons. This resulted in the fall of most of Gaul, although some individual cities resisted him, as did the Armoricans in western Gaul and various Rhenish groups. By 494, Clovis I was in control of the regions of the Somme and Seine.

Most of the history of Clovis I is known through the account of Bishop Gregory of Tours, who pictures him as having combined qualities of piety and religious intensity with pagan ruthlessness. For example, when one of Clovis' unruly Frankish followers appropriated a magnificent vase from a church, Clovis demanded that it be returned to the bishop. One of the Franks, incensed at this demand, smashed the precious object with his ax. Clovis restored the fragments to the bishop, saying nothing to the Frank. One year later, Clovis was reviewing his troops, when he recognized the warrior who had smashed the vase. He inspected the man's weapons and scolded him for maintaining them poorly. Clovis seized the man's axe and hurled it to the ground. When the Frank bent to retrieve it, the king split his skull with his own ax. "Thus," he declared, "you treated the vase at Soissons."

Raised a pagan, but having come to dominate a realm controlled on a local level by Catholic bishops, Clovis himself did not convert until about 493, when he married the Burgundian princess Clotilda. This was apparently a matter of mere convenience. But, three years later, at the Battle of Zülpich against the Alamanni in the middle Rhine region, Clovis converted in earnest. Facing imminent defeat, he prayed to Christ and managed to save the day. It was another two years before this battlefield conversion moved Clovis to accept baptism, but once he did, his interest in Catholicism and its theology became intense. In about 510, he convened an important church council at Orléans, in which he personally participated.

Clovis' reign was punctuated by frequent conflict with the Alamanni, Thuringians and the Visigoths. His 507 victory against the Visigoths at Vouillé he attributed to the intervention and patronage of St. Martin of Tours. Clovis penetrated into southern Gaul as far as Bordeaux. He did not, however, succeed in evicting the Goths from the region and ultimately withdrew from it, settling in Paris, from which he administered the vast Frankish empire he had succeeded in amassing. Clovis I died in Paris on November 27, 511.

Further Reading: O. M. Dalton. *The History of the Franks by Gregory of Tours* (Oxford: Clarendon Press, 1927).

Coard, Bernard   (b. 1944)

Socialist member of the ruling New Jewel movement in Grenada, Coard orchestrated an internal coup, which led to a United States invasion of Grenada in 1983.

Bernard Coard, born into a wealthy Grenadan family, was educated in England at the University of Sussex and also studied in the United States, on an economics scholarship, at Brandeis University. By the time Coard returned to Grenada, he had adopted a strict Marxist ideology. He formed the Organization for Revolutionary Education and Liberation, which merged with the revolutionary New Jewel (Joint Endeavor for Welfare, Education, and Liberation) movement in the 1970s. In 1979, the movement, led by Coard and Maurice BISHOP, gained control of the Grenadan government. Bishop became prime minister, and Coard deputy prime minister.

Dissension between Bishop and Coard soon developed over Coard's hard-line Marxism and alignment with the Soviet Union and Bishop's tendency toward moderation and conciliation with the United States. On October 14, 1983, a military coup ousted Bishop, who was placed under house arrest, and a military council was set up with Coard and Hudson Austin in nominal control. Five days later, Maurice Bishop was assassinated.

On October 25, 1983, six days after the coup, the forces of the United States invaded Grenada. Subsequently, Coard and 15 other leaders were arrested and tried for the murder of Maurice Bishop. The two-year trial resulted in Coard's conviction on December 4, 1986. His death sentence was commuted to life imprisonment in 1991.

Suggested Reading: Gordan Lewis. *Grenada: The Jewel Despoiled* (Baltimore: Johns Hopkins University Press, 1987)

Commodus   [Caesar Marcus Aurelius Commodus Antoninus Augustus] (161–192)

Son of the great MARCUS AURELIUS, Commodus ruled Rome as a brutish and arbitrary madman.

Commodus was born Lucius Aelius Aurelius Commodus in Lanuvium, Latium, on August 31, 161. His father, Marcus Aurelius, made him co-emperor with himself in 177, and Lucius participated in his father's campaigns against invading Germanic tribes. After his father's death, Lucius became sole emperor and adopted the name Caesar Marcus Aurelius Commodus Antoninus Augustus. Among his first actions was to bribe the Germans into peace by means of exorbitant tribute.

An assassination scheme plotted by Commodus' sister and a cabal of senators failed in 182, but seems to have unhinged the emperor. At least, from this year onward, his rule was marked by increasing cruelty and seemingly arbitrary viciousness. For the assassination plot, he took revenge on a number of the most prominent senators, executing them whether

Portrait bust of Emperor Commodus. (Richard Delbruck, Antike Portrats, *1912)*

they had been involved in the conspiracy or not. In 186, when the army took exception to his chief minister, Commodus had him summarily killed. His successor fared no better, as Commodus threw him to a rioting crowd in 189.

Upon the death of this second minister, Commodus' mistress and two close advisers assumed de facto rule of the empire. Commodus plunged into an ever-deepening psychosis, which manifested itself in the emperor's delusional belief that he was the god Hercules. He frequently fantasized that, as Hercules, he was about to enter the arena or venture into the woods to hunt wild animals with bow and arrow. Commodus even commissioned a marble bust of himself as Hercules. He also suddenly decreed a change in the name of Rome itself, calling it Colonia Commodiana.

The Roman populace and the Senate found Commodus' behavior increasingly intolerable. The proverbial last straw came at the end of 192, when the emperor announced his intention to assume the consulship in the garb of Hercules the gladiator. The public swelled with outrage, and on the eve of his investiture as consul, December 31, 192, Commodus' advisors commissioned a champion wrestler to strangle him. The Senate welcomed the event and acted quickly to proclaim a new emperor, Publius Helvius Pertinax. However, Commodus' misrule and neglect had already put the empire on the course of bloody civil war, which broke out shortly after the emperor's murder.

Further Reading: Anthony R. Birley. *Lives of the Later Caesars* (Harmondsworth: Penguin, 1976).

Conrad III (1093–1152)

King of Germany and founder of the Hohenstaufen dynasty, Conrad took part in the Second Crusade.

The son of Frederick I, duke of Swabia, Conrad was named duke of Franconia in 1115 by his uncle, Emperor Henry V. In 1116 Henry made Conrad and his brother, Frederick II, co-regents of Germany. However, when Henry died in 1125, the electors ignored both Frederick and Conrad and instead chose Lothair, duke of Saxony, as emperor. This incensed the two brothers, who rose in revolt. In December 1127, Conrad had himself elected anti-king by Lothair's opponents, and in June 1128, he was crowned king of Italy.

After returning to Germany in 1132, Conrad continued his struggle against Lothair until 1135 when the two signed a truce, with Conrad accepting Lothair's suzerainty in return for his lands. Lothair died in December 1137, and this time Conrad was elected emperor in March 1138. War broke out, how-

A fanciful depiction of the inauguration of the Second Crusade. (From M. Guizot, A Popular History of France from the Earliest Times, *n.d.)*

ever, when Lothair's son-in-law, Henry the Proud, refused to acknowledge Conrad. When Henry died in 1139, his brother Welf took up the standard but was defeated in December 1140 by Conrad.

After Conrad succeeded in having his son named as successor, he set out for the Holy Land in the fall of 1147 on the Second Crusade. He took Palestine in September 1148, then Conrad marched on Constantinople, where he concluded an alliance with the emperor Manuel Comnenus against Conrad's enemy Roger II, king of Sicily. Conrad was forced to abandon the crusade when he received word that Roger and Welf were in league together with Louis VII. Conrad returned to Europe to defend his realm, dying in Germany on February 15, 1152. He was succeeded by his nephew, FREDERICK I BARBAROSSA.

Constantine I the Great [Flavius Valerius Constantinus] (ca. 282–337)

This late Roman emperor completed the transformation of Rome into an absolute monarchy in the Asiatic manner, made Christianity the state religion of the empire, and moved the imperial capital from

Rome to Constantinople, a city he founded and built.

Constantine was born on February 17, about A.D. 282 at Naissus (Nis or Nish) in Illyria, a Balkan province. His father, Constantius I, was made Caesar in 293 after DIOCLETIAN and his fellow Augustus, Maximian, retired to private life. Constantine became military tribune in the East in 302 and joined his father, who was fighting in Britain during one of the declining empire's periods of civil war. When Constantius died on July 25, 306, at Eboracum (York), his legions elected Constantine *caesar et imperator*. It is not clear whether this meant his elevation to ruler of the entire Roman Empire or just Caesar of Britain and Gaul, but Constantine became involved in the conflict between Maximian and his son Maxentius during 307–310, then claimed the Roman throne toward the end of 310, after Maximian died. Constantine immediately invaded Italy and defeated Maxentius' forces at Turin and Verona early in 312. Later in the year, he defeated and killed Maxentius himself at the Milvian Bridge. After this, Constantine was universally recognized as emperor of the western empire.

A marble bust of Constantine the Great, who made Christianity the state religion of Rome. (From Richard Delbruck, Antike Portrats, *1912)*

The historian Eusebius created an enduring legend by writing that, at Milvian Bridge, a vision of a flaming cross appeared to Constantine bearing the legend, *In hoc signo vinces* ("By this sign conquer"), instantly converting the emperor to Christianity. In fact, Constantine did not convert until he was on his deathbed in 337, but he did champion Christianity and eventually made it the state religion of Rome. On June 15, 313, he issued the Edict of Milan, proclaiming toleration of all religions, including Christianity. Despite this gesture of liberality, Constantine was instrumental in mediating among rival Christian sects and expelling the Donatists—a sect of African puritans—in 314 as well as stamping out the so-called Arian heresy at the Council of Nicaea in 325. It was also at this council that the final link between the church and the state of Rome was forged.

Secure in his western holdings, Constantine turned next to the East, doing battle against Licinius, the eastern Augustus, at Cibalis and Mardia in southern Panonia (modern-day Hungary) during 314. He invaded Thrace in 323, defeating Licinius at Adrianople on July 3 and at Chrysopolis on September 18. The eastern Augustus surrendered, was taken captive, and, two years later, was executed on Constantine's orders.

Constantine realized that the empire, having endured a litany of bad or weak emperors prior to DIOCLETIAN, could no longer be effectively defended from the old western capital city of Rome. He decided that an eastern capital would offer a more strategically favorable position from which to defend and administer the beleaguered realm, and he accordingly moved the capital from Rome to Byzantium, renaming it Constantinople, after himself, in 330. He set about making this city on the Bosporus—meeting place of Europe and Asia—a magnificent center of learning and the capital not only of the Roman state, but of the Christian church.

Constantine continued to do battle with barbarian tribes, even as he struggled to assimilate them within the borders of the empire. He allied himself with the Sarmatians against the Goths during 332–34, but when his erstwhile allies indulged in an orgy of raids throughout the empire, he encouraged the Gothic king Gelimer to attack the Sarmatians, which he did with shattering effect. Constantine then granted asylum within the empire to the remnants of the conquered people.

Constantine was a ruler of great intelligence and far-sightedness. A brilliant military commander, he was also a skilled administrator. While he encouraged learning, improved the administration of justice, and decreed religious toleration, he was an

A 19th-century engraving of Constantine the Great in battle, presumably at Milvian Bridge, where he defeated Maxentius in 312, effectively becoming the most powerful ruler in the world. (From Charlotte M. Yonge, Pictorial History of the World's Great Nations, *1882)*

absolute monarch, who exacted unquestioning obedience. The Roman rulers who had succeeded Marcus Aurelius had all been de facto tyrants while claiming to share power with the Senate. Constantine simply relinquished all pretense of being anything less than an absolute ruler. Enlightened, he was nevertheless faced with the task of ruling an empire in decline and threatened on all sides by barbarians at the gate. As a consequence, he was ruthless in the application and preservation of power, ordering the murder of his own son Crispius when he became too popular with the people and the legions. He also directed the murder of at least one of his nephews and others whom he, increasingly paranoiac in his later years, suspected of plotting treachery against him. Historians believe that he even arranged the murder of his second wife, Fausta, mother of the son who succeeded him. Indeed, the later years of his court were marked by treachery. Constantine himself was said to have degenerated into a kind of decadent eastern potentate, loaded down with jewels and vestments of the most luxurious cloths and far removed from the ideal of the Roman soldier-king. Constantine died of an illness at Nicomedia on May 22, 337.

Further Reading: Timothy Barnes. *The New Empire of Diocletian and Constantine* (Cambridge: Harvard University Press, 1982); Paul Keresztes. *Constantine: A Great Christian Monarch and Apostle* (Amsterdam: J. C. Gieben, 1981).

Constantius II [Flavius Julianus Constantius] (317–361)

Using murder to secure his ascension to the throne, Constantius II was nevertheless forced into a power struggle with his brothers following the death of their father, CONSTANTINE THE GREAT.

The third son of Constantine the Great, Constantius II was heir apparent for 14 years before assuming the throne in 337 after Constantine's death. That emperor's vast realm was divided among his three sons, Constantius II, Constantine II, and Constans I. Upon his accession, Constantius probably ordered the murder of several family members to secure his position as sole emperor of the East. However, his two brothers split the West between them, and this arrangement made a power struggle inevitable. Constans I intrigued against his oldest brother, Constantine II, overthrowing and killing him in 340. Constans I was in turn killed by MAGNENTIUS, a usurper who had his own designs on the throne.

At first, the Danubian and Balkan legions did not know whom to support. Then Constantius' sister persuaded them to aid a third party, Ventranio, who, after initially allying himself with Magnentius, gave his allegiance to Constantius. Constantius then met Magnentius in battle at Mursa in 351, decisively defeating him and prompting Magnentius to commit suicide. This left Constantius unchallenged as emperor in both the East and West.

Expecting timidity and hesitancy in a new ruler exhausted by intrigues, the Persian king Shapur attacked Constantius almost immediately. Shapur retained the upper hand most of the time, yet he was never able to defeat Constantius' army. Forced to deal with more pressing threats to his empire, Shapur temporarily abandoned his campaign against Constantius in 353. Constantius named his younger cousin Gallus as heir and dispatched him to the east to deal with the continued Persian menace. Although Gallus succeeded, he proved so tyrannical and cruel that Constantius recalled him to account for his actions. He was tried and executed in 354.

After prosecuting successful campaigns against the Danubian tribes, Constantius was again called to the East to deal with Shapur. He sent word to his new heir, JULIAN (called Julian the Apostate), asking for reinforcements from Gaul. Julian's troops refused to answer the call, believing that it was a ploy to weaken their popular leader. Instead of coming to the aid of Constantius, they summarily proclaimed Julian emperor in 360. In response, Constantius marched his army west to meet this latest challenge. However, in the winter of 361, Constantius fell ill with a fever and died on November 3.

Further Reading: Michael Grant. *Roman Emperors*, (New York: Scribner's, 1985).

Cortés, Hernán   (1485–1547)

The most famous of the Spanish conquistadores, Cortés ruthlessly conquered the fabulous Mexican empire of the Aztecs.

Cortés was born into the minor nobility of Spain in Medellín, Extremadura, and was sent at age 14 to the University of Salamanca. An extremely bright student, he was also unruly, "much given to women," and, it was said, gratuitous cruelty. After two years, he abandoned his studies and spent the next several years drifting, until, excited by accounts of the early transoceanic voyages of exploration and colonial expansion, he sailed in 1504 to Santo Domingo to seek his fame and fortune in the New World.

Cortés served with Diego de Velázquez de Cuellar in the Spanish conquest of Cuba and became *alcalde* (mayor) of the colonial capital of Santiago. By 1519, Cortés was a figure of significant influence in the New World and wrested from Velázquez command

of an expedition to conquer Mexico from the Aztecs. He explored the Mexican coastal region as far as modern Veracruz, where he established a city. Carefully gathering intelligence concerning the political situation in the highlands, the conquistador marched inland, fought—then made alliance with—the Indians of Tlaxcala, traditional enemies of the Aztecs, and marched on the Aztec capital of Tenochtitlán (modern Mexico City). There, the Aztec ruler MOCTEZUMA II offered no resistance, probably believing Cortés to be an incarnation of the deity Quetzalcoatl, and the conquistadores entered the capital entirely unopposed in November 1519.

Hernán Cortés, one of the most successful—and one of the most ruthless—of the Spanish conquistadores, conquered and destroyed the Aztec Empire. (Library of Congress)

The invaders collected vast quantities of gold and other treasure for several months until Cortés was compelled to take an expedition to the coast in order to counter a threat from a rival Spanish army under Panfilo de Narváez. Easily defeating Narváez, he returned to Tenochtitlán only to discover that the Aztecs, who had been sadistically brutalized by his second-in-command, Pedro do Alvarado, were now in full revolt. After incurring heavy losses, Cortés and his men fled the capital during what they called the Noche Triste ("sad night") of June 30, 1520—but not before Moctezuma II had been killed, either by the Spanish (according to Aztec chroniclers) or by the outraged Aztecs themselves (according to the Spanish).

Evicted, the conquistador was not, however, defeated. After regrouping, he laid siege to Tenochtitlán in 1521. Three months of starvation and disease decimated the defenders, who surrendered to the Spanish on August 13, 1521.

Cortés thus acquired vast holdings throughout Mexico and became a fabulously wealthy and powerful man, virtually enslaving the Indians throughout the region. Of all the conquistadores, Cortés was the most successful; indeed, he was perhaps the only one who fully realized the Spanish dream of reaping boundless riches in the New World.

Cortés returned to Spain several times and also led expeditions to Honduras in 1524 and to Baja California in 1536. He participated in the unsuccessful Spanish attack on Algiers in 1541. He died near Seville on December 2, 1547.

Further Reading: Alan Axelrod. *Chronicle of the Indian Wars: From Colonial Times to Wounded Knee* (New York: Prentice Hall, 1993); Richard Lee Marks. *Cortés: The Great Adventurer and the Fate of Aztec Mexico* (New York: Knopf, 1993).

Crabb, Henry Alexander   (ca. 1823–1857)

With William WALKER, Henry Crabb was among the best-known filibusters of the 19th century.

Henry Crabb was born into an affluent Nashville family about 1823. His father, also Henry, was a justice on the Tennessee Supreme Court, and young Henry was trained in law. In 1845, he was admitted to the Mississippi bar, opening a practice at Vicksburg. In 1848, he became embroiled in a political dispute during which he killed a man. Although acquitted of murder, he left Vicksburg for California, where he was soon elected to the state legislature.

Crabb married a well-to-do Spanish woman in California and, after an unsuccessful race for the United States Senate, became engrossed in the filibustering activities of his fellow Nashvillian William Walker. Crabb decided to invade the volatile Mexi-can state of Sonora, upon the invitation of Ignacio Pesqueira, leader of one of two warring factions. The expedition was a logistical debacle, and by the time Crabb and the few men he had left with him reached the combat zone, the Americans were forced to surrender. Crabb was executed on April 7, 1857, his head cut off and placed on public display.

Further Reading: Robert H. Forbes. *Crabb's Filibustering Expedition into Sonora, 1857.* (Tucson, Arizona: Arizona Silhouettes, 1952).

Croesus   (d. ca. 546 B.C.)

The last king of Lydia, Croesus is widely remembered for his immense fortune and for the lessons the Athenian lawgiver SOLON taught him concerning wealth and happiness.

A member of the Mermnad dynasty founded by GYGES in 685 B.C., Croesus succeeded to the Lydian throne after the death of his father, Alyattes, and a power struggle with his half-brother. He immediately set out to complete the conquest of Ionia begun by his father and captured Ephesus and other cities in western Anatolia.

Croesus' wealth was enormous, and he donated funds to the city of Ephesus, to rebuild the Artemisium, and to the Greek shrines, including that of the Oracle at Delphi.

The historian Herodotus reported that Croesus was visited by the Athenian lawgiver Solon. Croesus, displaying his treasures to his guest, asked him who was the happiest man in the world, expecting Solon to reply that Croesus himself was the happiest because of his immense wealth. Solon responded with the names of two others and cautioned Croesus to "Account no man happy before his death."

Croesus would later have much cause for sorrow after (he claimed) the Oracle at Delphi led him astray. The Persians under Cyrus II the Great overthrew the Median Empire in 550 B.C., and Croesus consulted the Oracle, who predicted that a great empire would fall in the conflict between Persia and Lydia. To counter the growing Persian Empire, Croesus formed an alliance with Babylon. In 546 B.C., he invaded Cappadocia, in eastern Anatolia, fought an inconclusive batttle at Pteria, and then returned to his capital at Sardis. On his way to Sardis, he was captured by Cyrus II, and the Persian army sacked the city. Croesus later sent messengers to the oracle at Delphi and complained that he had been encouraged to go to war with the Persians. The Oracle explained that Croesus was being punished for the sins of his ancestor Gyges, who five generations earlier had killed the Lydian king and usurped the throne. In addition, the Oracle explained that, indeed, a great empire had fallen in the Persian-Lydian conflict; it had been Croesus' own.

There are differing accounts of Croesus' subsequent demise. The poet Bacchylides reported that Croesus attempted to burn himself on a funeral pyre. Herodotus wrote that Cyrus II condemned Croesus to be burned alive, but he was saved by the god Apollo. The Persian doctor Ctesias reported that Croesus was, in fact, spared, and that Cyrus gave him an advisory post and the governorship of Barene in Media.

Further Reading: Catherine B. Avery, ed. *The New Century Classical Handbook* (New York: Appleton-Century-Crofts, 1962); Diana Bowder. *Who Was Who in the Greek World* (Ithaca, New York: Cornell University Press, 1982).

Cromwell, Oliver (1599–1658)

Oliver Cromwell was one of the chief architects of the English civil wars of the 17th century, which overthrew the monarchy and instituted republican rule under the Commonwealth, with himself as Lord Protector.

Cromwell was born at Huntingdon on April 25, 1599, the second son in a family whose members had traditionally served in Parliament. Educated at Sidney Sussex College, Cambridge, during 1615–17, he married in 1620, and, within a few years, converted to Puritanism. In 1628, he successfully stood for election as the member of Parliament for Huntingdon and became well known for his unrelenting attacks on the bishops of the Church of England. In 1640, as the nation moved closer to civil war, Cromwell was chosen to represent Cambridge in the so-called Long Parliament. Again directing his fire against the bishops, this time calling for their total abolition and a general purification of the church, Cromwell aligned himself with those members of Parliament who advocated the overthrow of CHARLES I. As civil war became inevitable, Cromwell blocked the transfer of silver from Cambridge University to the king's coffers. He secured Cambridgeshire for Parliament and raised a troop of cavalry from his native Huntingdon. Late in October 1642, Parliament commissioned him commander of a military association of six counties, a double regiment of 14 troops later dubbed "the Ironsides."

Cromwell soon proved himself a great general. He defeated Loyalist forces at Grantham on May 13, 1643 and at Gainsborough on July 28. Appointed governor of Ely, he led his troops to victory at Winceby on October 11, 1643, then at Marston Moor on July 2, 1644. Unfavorable terrain prevented Cromwell from effectively employing his superior numbers in pursuit of Charles at the second Battle

Oliver Cromwell, mastermind of England's Puritan revolution and Lord Protector of the Commonwealth. (From J. N. Larned, A History of England for the Use of Schools and Academies, 1900)

of Newbury on October 27, 1644, and a brief truce ensued early in 1645 by virtue of the Treaty of Uxbridge. During this truce period, from January to March, Cromwell successfully argued in Parliament for vast military reforms. The "New Model Army" that resulted was a standing military force raised by conscription and supported by tax levy. Compared to the old militia system, it was an exceptionally stable and professional fighting force.

On June 14, 1645, Cromwell played a key role in the decisive victory at the Battle of Naseby, and, as second in command to Sir Thomas Fairfax, Cromwell helped take Oxford in 1646, which resulted in Charles' surrender and concluded the First Civil War.

Cromwell attempted without success to reach an accord with Charles I, and he also found himself embroiled in a schismatic dispute between Presbyterians in Parliament and Puritans in the New Model Army. Early in 1647, Parliament voted effectively to disband the army, which, however, resisted. Cromwell, siding with the soldiers, took command of the forces, seized Charles I, and occupied London. The king conducted secret negotiations with Scots Presbyterians during August through October of 1647, and in November fled to the Isle of Wight. He promised the Scots to impose Presbyterianism as the English state religion for a period of three years in return for military support of his effort to regain his kingdom. On January 15, 1648, Parliament formally renounced its allegiance to the king, and the Second Civil War commenced.

Cromwell besieged and captured Pembroke in south Wales during June and early July 1648, then met and defeated an invading Scots army at the Battle of Preston on August 17–19, 1648. With northern England secured, he returned to London on December 7, where, with his New Model Army backing him, he urged trial of King Charles. Late in January 1649, as one of 135 commissioners appointed to sit in judgment of the king, he successfully pushed for the monarch's execution, which was carried out on January 30.

Cromwell was chosen chairman of the republic's Council of State. He moved swiftly to put down a mutiny within the ranks of the army during the spring of 1649, then led his forces into Ireland, which, by virtue of a Royalist-Catholic alliance, defied the new Commonwealth's authority. The Irish campaign showed Cromwell at his most ruthless. Following the victory of a Puritan force led by Michael Jones at the Battle of Rathmines in September, Cromwell brought down upon the Irish countryside a reign of terror that spanned September 1649 to May of the next year. Systematically, he laid siege to one Royalist-Catholic stronghold after another, including Drogheda, Wexford, and Clonmel. At the fall of each of these fortresses, Cromwell slaughtered the defending garrisons, including women and children, creating the worst internal military atrocity in British history.

In 1650, Cromwell returned to London, leaving Henry Ireton, Edmond Ludlow, and Charles Fleetwood to complete the reduction of Irish resistance, which, despite the severity of the battles waged against the Irish, endured until the surrender of Galway in May 1652.

Cromwell's return virtually coincided with the commencement of a general uprising in Scotland, which is sometimes called the Third Civil War. Scottish Presbyterians proclaimed Charles II, son of the executed monarch, the new and rightful king of Great Britain. On January 1, 1651, Charles II was crowned in Scotland. In the meantime, during July through September 1650, Cromwell launched an invasion of Scotland. At first, the campaign went badly for the Puritans, who were hampered by disease and the Scottish people's scorched-earth policy, which resulted in the miserable deaths of some 5,000

of Cromwell's 16,000-man force. At Dunbar, a Scottish army of about 18,000 surrounded Cromwell's 11,000 remaining troops, but on September 3, 1650, the Puritan leader staged a surprise cavalry counterattack and scored a decisive victory that resulted in a rout of the Scots. Cromwell himself, however, was felled by malaria. This, combined with a dispute among the Scots, stalled the war for nearly a year.

In the early summer of 1651, Cromwell, having recovered his health, attempted to negotiate peace with the Scots. This proving unsuccessful, he led a lightning campaign in Scotland, taking Perth on August 2, 1651, and marching swiftly back down to England, where, at Worcester on September 3, he trapped and destroyed Royalist forces led by Charles II. The Scottish uprising—or Third Civil War—had ended.

Cromwell prosecuted another war, this time with the Dutch, largely over the East India trade, during 1652–54. His more immediate concern, however, was the "Rump Parliament"—what remained of the Long Parliament after the Royalists and Presbyterians had been purged from it—which continued to be antagonistic toward the army and which was failing to enact the sweeping reforms of church and state called for by the Puritan program. In April 1653, Cromwell forcibly dissolved the Rump Parliament, reportedly declaring, "You have sat long enough; let us have done with you. In the name of God, go!" He then established a new council, the Little, or Barebones, Parliament. Assigned no less a task than the remolding of English government and society, the Barebones Parliament acted too quickly and too radically for Cromwell, who compelled its dissolution in December 1653.

A group of New Model army officers then drew up the so-called Instrument of Government, a constitution that named Cromwell lord protector, empowering him to govern with the aid of a council of state and a single-chamber Parliament. But it was Cromwell and his council, not the new Parliament, that enacted the most significant governmental and legal reforms of the Protectorate. The lord protector dissolved his first Parliament on January 22, 1655, setting up a regionally based system of government led by his trusted generals. War with Spain, fought during 1656–59 in an attempt to reduce Spanish hegemony in the West Indies, nevertheless necessitated a new Parliament in order to raise funds. That body offered to make Cromwell king in 1657, which he angrily refused. From this point onward, he fell to disputing with Parliament again and dissolved it in February 1658. Later that year, his malarial infection flared, and on September 3, 1658, he died in London.

Oliver Cromwell held unbending political beliefs that he was willing to enforce even to the point of regicide and (in the case of the Irish) something approaching genocide, yet he was also capable of demonstrating great religious tolerance, allowing (for example) the Jews to settle in England for the first time since 1290. Contentious with king as well as Parliament, he nevertheless fashioned Great Britain into a formidable world power, creating a great army and navy, and acquiring the first of many imperial possessions in winning Jamaica and Dunkerque as a result of the war he fought in alliance with France against Spain. Cromwell's republican government was not destined to last. His son, Richard Cromwell, became Lord Protector on September 3, 1658, but quickly proved unable to control Parliament or the army. On May 7, 1659, Richard Cromwell resigned as Lord Protector, and in May 1660 Charles II was restored to the throne. Despite the failure of republicanism to endure, reform, tolerance, and the foundation of empire constituted the best part of Oliver Cromwell's legacy to England.

Further Reading: Robert S. Paul. *The Lord Protector: Religion and Politics in the Life of Oliver Cromwell* (London: Lutterworth Press, 1955); George Young. *Charles I and Cromwell* (London: P. Davies, 1936).

Cyaxares   (d. 585 B.C.)

As king of Media from 625 to 585 B.C., Cyaxares joined Nabopolassar of Babylonia to overcome Assyrian rule and expanded his empire into the largest the world had seen up to that time.

After his father, Phraortes, was killed in battle, Cyaxares inherited his struggle against the Assyrians. Phraortes had died while laying siege against Nineveh, when he was overwhelmed by a large army of Scythians, who dominated Media. After his father's death, in 625, Cyaxares caused the assassination of the Scythian chiefs at a banquet and thereby ended Scythian rule in Media. He then united the disparate tribes of ancient Iran and reformed the Median army, dividing it into efficient corps of spearmen, bowmen, and cavalry, and updating weaponry and clothing. At about the time of his father's death, he concluded an alliance with Nabopolassar of Babylon to overthrow Assyrian domination of the region.

Slowly and steadily, Cyaxares pushed the Assyrians back as he expanded his own frontiers. He took Ashur in 614 and invaded and ravaged Nineveh two years later. Simultaneously, he invaded and conquered Mannai (the region of modern Iranian Azerbaijan). By 609, Cyaxares had subjugated Urartu in the Armenian highlands. By about this time also, the Assyrians had been driven out of northern Mesopo-

tamia, and Cyaxares divided the spoils with his Babylonian allies, taking Assyria and Haran.

From 590 to 585 B.C., Cyaxares prosecuted a war with Lydia in Asia Minor, which fixed the Halys River as the boundary between the two empires.

At the time of Cyaxares' death in 585, Media stretched from Chaldea in the southwest, to the Halys in the west, and nearly to the Indus River in the east, making it the most extensive empire then extant and the largest the world had seen to that time. While he had acquired much territory, Cyaxares failed to establish the advanced administrative machinery necessary to sustain so vast a realm.

Further Reading: George Rawlinson. *The Five Great Monarchies of the Ancient Eastern World* (New York: Dodd, Mead, 1881).

Cypselus   (d. 625 B.C.)

Tyrant of Corinth, Cypselus came to power after overthrowing the Bacchiadae rulers who had attempted to kill him as an infant.

Cypselus was the son of Eetion and Labda, a member of the Bacchiadae line of Corinthian rulers. While Bacchiads had held power for years through intermarriage, Labda had been allowed to marry an outsider. After Labda bore a son, the Oracle at Delphi foretold that the child would bring about the fall of the Bacchiadae. Learning of the prophecy, the rulers ordered the infant killed. Labda hid the child in a corn bin—a *cypsele*—from which Cypselus got his name.

Reaching adulthood, Cypselus visited the Oracle at Delphi and learned of the prophecy that he would be king of Corinth. He overthrew the Bacchiads and established himself ruler of Corinth for 30 years and was so popular that he maintained no bodyguard. He was succeeded by his son Periander.

Further Reading: Catherine B. Avery, ed. *The New Century Classical Handbook* (New York: Appleton-Century-Crofts, 1962); Diana Bowder, ed. *Who Was Who in the Greek World* (Ithaca, New York: Cornell University Press, 1982).

Cyrus II the Great   (ca. 590–80 B.C.–ca. 529)

The founder of the Achaemenid (Persian) Empire— the largest empire known up to its time—Cyrus the Great looms large in Persian history much as ALEXANDER III THE GREAT figures in Greek culture or Moses in the Judeo-Christian tradition.

Cyrus was born in Media or Persis (in modern-day Iran). He was presumably one in a long line of ruling chiefs, but the kingdom he inherited, called Anshan, was small. By the end of his reign, he had extended it so that it encompassed much of the Near East, from the Aegean Sea to the Indus River. Most significantly, he conquered the Babylonian Empire and became master of the greatest city of his time, Babylon. As a conqueror in the ancient world, Cyrus would prove second only to Alexander the Great.

His childhood, known to us through accounts in Herodotus and Xenophon, is shrouded in myth, which testifies to the legendary, quasi-religious status Cyrus occupies in Persian culture as a founding figure. Astyages, king of the Medes, married his daughter to his vassal, a noble of Persis called Cambyses. The union produced Cyrus. Shortly after the birth, Astyages dreamed that the infant would grow up to overthrow him and immediately ordered the child's death. Astyages' chief adviser instead secretly gave the baby to a shepherd to raise. Ten years later, Cyrus' extraordinary abilities had already made him famous, and he became known to Astyages, who allowed himself to be persuaded to spare the boy. Grown to manhood, Cyrus did revolt against and overthrow his grandfather. In 550 B.C., Astyages attempted to suppress the rebellion, but such was the power of Cyrus' personality that his grandfather's army deserted and joined him.

Cyrus was a remarkably aggressive and energetic conqueror. He first subjugated the Iranian tribes in the vicinity of the Medes, then turned toward the west. CROESUS, powerful ruler of Lydia in Asia Minor, long an antagonist of the Medes, sought to capitalize on the overthrow of Astyages by carving out from the Medes a vaster empire for himself. Cyrus responded by attacking Lydia and capturing its capital city of Sardis in 547 or 546. Croesus was either killed in battle, committed suicide by self-immolation, or was taken captive by Cyrus. Accounts that claim the latter also note that Cyrus treated Croesus well. This seems to have been typical of the ruler, who was celebrated for the tolerance and generosity with which he treated those whom he conquered.

With the defeat of Croesus, the Greek cities of the Aegean fell to Cyrus, who periodically was called upon to suppress revolts, though, for the most part, the Ionian Greeks submitted peacefully.

After these conquests, Cyrus marched on Babylonia. That kingdom was in an unstable condition because of general dissatisfaction with the ruler Nabonidus. Indeed, much of the populace seems to have welcomed Cyrus, and the conquest was concluded quickly. Babylon fell in October 539. Cyrus' conquest of this mighty empire also occasioned the most celebrated instance of his tolerance. The Old Testament credits him with delivering the Jews from their long Babylonian captivity and permitting their return to their homeland. With equal tolerance, Cyrus permitted the Babylonians to retain their traditional gods and customs of worship. In this way, he avoided much of the resentment to be expected from a conquered people.

Having taken control of Babylonia, Cyrus acquired dominion over that nation's conquests, Syria and Palestine. Other kingdoms, most notably Cilicia, submitted to Cyrus out of diplomatic necessity, and the evidence is that Cyrus treated his allies well.

This most remarkable of conquerors, universally hailed by his people as their father and by generations ever afterward as the very ideal of the imperial ruler, is reported by Herodotus to have met his end at the hands of a woman. One of the nomadic tribes Cyrus conquered shortly after his overthrow of Astyages was the Massagetai, whose chieftain was female. Her son, whom Cyrus had taken prisoner, years later committed suicide while languishing in captivity. Vowing vengeance, his mother met Cyrus in battle and killed him.

Cyrus had two sons, Bardiya and Cambyses, the latter succeeding him. Soon after ascending the throne, Cambyses probably murdered Bardiya, a potential rival. Cambyses was married to his sister Atossa. Under Cambyses and the rulers of his line during the next two centuries, the empire Cyrus had created continued to expand and prosper.

Further Reading: *The Cambridge Ancient History*, vol. 6 (New York: Macmillan, 1939); Albert Ten Eyck Olmstead. *History of the Persian Empire* (Chicago: University of Chicago Press, 1959).

D

Danilo I [Danilo Nikola Petrović-Šćepčević] (ca. 1670–1735)
First of the Petrović-Njegoš dynasty of rulers of Montenegro, Danilo I persecuted and massacred the Muslims within his realm.

Danilo became *vladika*, bishop-prince, of the Montenegrin theocracy in 1696, empowered to name his relatives as successors. Since the Montenegrin bishop-princes were members of a monastic order and therefore celibate, succession generally devolved from uncle to nephew.

Danilo waged a campaign of persecution against the Muslims within his realm, perpetrating the 1702 Christmas Eve massacre of them known as the Montenegrin Vespers. Danilo defeated Turkish invaders in the 1712 Battle of Tzarevlatz, but suffered greatly from subsequent Turkish incursions, most notably the capture of Cetinje and the destruction of its monastery in 1714.

Danilo's struggle against the Turks prompted him to an alliance with Peter the Great of Russia in 1715, through which he was able to keep his small country from being overrun by the Ottomans.

Darius I (550 B.C.–486 B.C.)
Rising to power through ruthless guile, Darius became one of the great rulers of the ancient world.

The son of Hystaspes, satrap (governor) of Parthia, Darius attained the throne of the Persian empire through daring treachery. Herodotus records that CYRUS II THE GREAT suspected the youthful Darius of plotting against him. Nevertheless, Darius apparently served Cambyses II, the son of Cyrus, as a member of the royal bodyguard. When Cambyses died in Egypt during the summer of 522, Darius traveled to Media, where he and six conspirators successfully plotted the murder of Bardiya, another son of Cyrus, who had assumed the throne in March 522. According to Darius, the man he had killed was one Gaumata, a Magian *impersonating* Bardiya, who had actually been murdered by his brother Cambyses. This story may well have been true. Darius argued that he had acted to restore the Persian throne to the Achaemenid dynasty, but he met with a great deal of opposition in the form of widespread revolt in Susiana, Babylonia, Media, Sagartia, and Margiana. Even in Persia proper, one Vahyazdata, claiming to be Bardiya, staged a revolt. Darius vigor-

ously suppressed the uprisings one after the other in nineteen battles fought against nine rebel leaders.

Once Darius I secured control of his empire, he set about an ambitious program of fortifying his frontiers, then extending his borders. He triumphed over the Scythians in 519 and soon was in possession of the whole Indus Valley. He conquered eastern Thrace and the Getae, then, in 513, crossed the Danube into Europe, where he pursued bands of Scythian nomads. They adopted a scorched earth policy that effectively deprived Darius' forces of supplies and compelled the ruler to break off his campaign.

Darius' satraps in Asia Minor completed the subjugation of Thrace and Macedonia and secured the Aegean islands of Lemnos and Imbros. The way seemed clear to an invasion of Greece, but Darius proceeded with great caution and was prompted to take military action in 499 only after Athens and Eretria had supported an Ionian revolt against Persia. Darius suppressed the rebellion, then sent his son-in-law, Mardonius, against Athens and Eretria. His fleet was wrecked by a storm in 492, and the invasion was aborted. Two years later, Darius sent Datis of Media against Eretria, which he destroyed. He next engaged the Athenians at the Battle of Marathon, where he was defeated. Darius was planning a third attempt against Greece in 486, but died before the expedition got under way.

Despite his failure to conquer Greece, Darius must be counted among the major empire builders of the ancient world. Part of the great success he did enjoy was his policy—probably inspired by the example of Cyrus the Great—of tolerating the religion and customs of the peoples he subjugated. He was also a brilliant administrator, who organized a complex government of satrapies and a system of equitable and efficiently collected provincial tributes. Darius expanded trade and commerce, and he instituted the standardization of coinage, weights, and measures. An ambitious builder, he devoted much energy and resources to developing roads and canals, and he brought ancient Persian architecture to its earliest zenith in great public buildings and palaces.

Darius II Ochus (d. 404 B.C.)
A usurping Achaemenid king of Persia, Darius II Ochus presided over a corrupt court and a rebellious

realm, yet managed to prevail against the rival state of Athens.

In 423 B.C., Ochus, the illegitimate son of Artaxerxes I, seized power from his half-brother Secydianus (Sogdianus), whom he subsequently murdered. Ochus took the name Darius, though he was also known as Nothus—"bastard"—and while he had been bold enough in dispatching his half-brother, he allowed himself to be utterly dominated during his reign by scheming court eunuchs, his half-sister, and especially his wife, the sadistic Parysatis. The result was a court rotten with intrigue and corruption, which distracted Darius from the task of running his kingdom. When rebellion broke out among the disaffected populations of Hyrcania and Media, Darius, as if roused from a stupor, reacted swiftly and brutally.

When Athenian military fortunes faltered at Syracuse in 413 B.C., Darius decided to seize the opportunity to recover the coastal cities of Asia Minor, which had fallen to Athens in 448. Darius allied himself with Athens' arch-rival, Sparta, and he brought into the fold the satraps (governors) of Asia Minor, Tissaphernes and Pharnabazus. Through these alliances, Darius recovered a portion of Ionia, but Tissaphernes faltered in his support of Sparta and thereby retarded the progress of conquest. Darius removed Tissaphernes and replaced him with his own son, Cyrus the Younger, supplying him with funds to build a fleet to aid the Spartans in defeating Athens at Aegospotami in 405. Darius died the following year.

Further Reading: A. T. Olmstead. *History of the Persian Empire: Achaeminid Period* (Chicago: University of Chicago Press, 1959).

Darius III (r. 336 B.C.–330 B.C.)

Incompetent and cowardly, Darius twice fled the battlefield, abandoning his family, and sealing the fate of his empire.

A distant relative of the dead king of Armenia, Darius was born around 380 B.C. Because of his royal blood, he was placed on the throne of the Archaemenid Empire in 336 as the puppet of the eunuch Bagoas, who had murdered the previous two kings. When Darius began to rule on his own, Bagoas attempted to have Darius murdered as well, but was himself killed by Darius.

Darius immediately set about the reconquest of Egypt, which had declared its independence upon the death of the previous king, Artaxerxes, in 334. Meanwhile, PHILIP II OF MACEDON established the League of Corinth in 337 for the express purpose of defeating the Archaemenid Empire. He sent forces into Asia Minor in 336, but Darius engineered his

assassination in July. This did not, however, bring to an end Darius' problems with the League of Corinth, because Philip's son, ALEXANDER III THE GREAT, pursued Darius with renewed vigor.

After Alexander had conquered Asia Minor and moved into Syria, Darius engaged him at Issus in October 333 B.C. Alexander crushed Darius, forcing him to flee the battlefield, leaving his mother, wife, children, and substantial booty to the will and mercy of Alexander. Darius attempted to win back his family with letters of friendship to Alexander, but to no avail.

Alexander began moving down the Mediterranean coast, threatening more of Darius' holdings. Darius then offered all of his empire west of the Euphrates in exchange for his family, but again Alexander refused. Darius now prepared to do battle with Alexander. Although his forces outnumbered the conqueror's army, Darius was utterly defeated on the plain of Gaugamela, October 1, 331 B.C., and once again fled the field, even before the fighting had ended.

His empire all but gone, Darius was deposed by the Bactrian Bessus and murdered in July 330 B.C.

David (d. ca. 962 B.C.)

Second and greatest king of Israel, David united loosely constituted tribes into a genuine empire and transformed himself into the central and enduring symbol of the bond between God and the Jewish people.

Born in Bethlehem, Judah, David was the youngest son of Jesse and the grandson of Boaz and Ruth. Biblical tradition portrays David as a simple shepherd boy who became his people's champion in single combat against the "giant" Philistine warrior Goliath, slaying him with a slingshot stone. Whatever the historical basis of this story, young David began his political career proper as an aide in the court of Saul, who came to regard the youth as a second son. Indeed, David became as a brother to SAUL's son and heir, Jonathan, and he married Saul's daughter Michal.

The happy situation in Saul's court might have continued had not David's prowess as a warrior gained him a popularity that roused the aging king's fanatical jealousy. When Saul formulated a plot to kill David, the young warrior fled into southern Judah and Philistia, where he began to develop a popular following by taking up the life of a kind of biblical Robin Hood on the desert frontier of Judah. David gathered about him other bandits and refugees, forming them into an organized guerrilla force that defended the frontier populace against the depredations of various bands of raiders. In this way,

David won the loyalty of increasing numbers of people.

Yet, unlike most guerrilla leaders later in history, David was not a revolutionary and never designed the overthrow of King Saul. Instead, his actions and growing popularity won over influential Judahite elders, who invited him first to become king of Judah in Hebron and then to succeed Saul himself, after he and Jonathan were killed by Philistine warriors at the Battle of Mount Gilboa about 1000 B.C.

David did not hesitate in prosecuting a civil war with factions loyal to Saul's surviving son, Ishbaal. The struggle ended when Ishbaal was slain by his own courtiers, after which David was universally accepted as king of Israel, including the far-flung tribes beyond Judah. David turned his attention toward Jerusalem, besieging and taking it, expelling the Jebusites who had held it, and establishing it as the capital of the empire. David gave great spiritual significance to this secular victory by transporting the Ark of the Covenant, central symbol of the presence of Yahweh (God), into the new capital, thereby making Jerusalem a holy city.

Having secured and anointed his capital, King David campaigned vigorously against the Philistines, defeating them decisively. He went on to annex surrounding tribal kingdoms, including Edom, Moab and Ammon, creating a most substantial empire over which he ruled for about 40 years.

By any measure, David was a successful king. He neutralized the greatest threat against Israel, the Philistines; he united, as Saul had been unable to do, the disparate and often fractious tribes of Israel into a genuine nation; he expanded his territorial holdings; and he established his empire in both a temporal and a spiritual sense. Despite these successes, his reign was plagued by family dissension and rebellion. In order to unite the various groups from which he forged his nation, David took wives from diverse tribes, raising a family made up of strangers with little in common, who were often hostile to one another. The worst breach came when David's third son, Absalom, killed his half-brother Amnon, because the latter had raped Tamar, sister of Absalom and half-sister of Amnon. David exiled Absalom, then recalled him. However, during the period of exile, Absalom began to organize a rebellion against David. When Absalom returned to Jerusalem, he staged an organized revolt that sent David fleeing from the throne until the king could organize a force of his own to retake his empire. Absalom was killed in battle by Joab, one of David's loyal commanders.

Despite such strife, David passed down his empire intact to Solomon, his son by Bathsheba. After Solomon's death, the kingdom was divided. However, the religious aspects of the empire David created have endured through centuries of Judaism.

Further Reading: Walter Brueggemann. *David's Truth in Israel's Imagination and Memory* (Philadelphia: Fortress, 1985); David J. A. Clines. *Telling Queen Michal's Story* (Sheffield: Jsot Press, 1991); D. M. Gunn. *The Story of King David* (Sheffield: University of Sheffield, 1978); Eugene H. Maly. *The World of David and Solomon* (Englewood Cliffs, N.J.: Prentice-Hall, 1966).

Decius [Gaius Messius Quintus Trajanus Decius] (ca. 201–251)
Decius was the first Roman emperor to institutionalize persecution of the Christians.

Originally from the town of Budalia, Decius became a Roman senator, prefect of Rome, then consul, as well as adviser to the emperor Philip. Beset with widespread opposition, Philip proposed to abdicate in 248, but Decius convinced him that the usurpers would eventually lose support, which proved to be the case. Philip posted Decius to command Roman forces in Pannonia, where he was successful in restoring order and discipline. Decius was tremendously popular with his troops, who proclaimed him emperor in June 249, apparently against his wishes. Although he may have been reluctant at first, Decius did meet Philip in battle at Verona, killing the emperor and his son, then assuming the throne himself.

Decius felt he could unite the empire by affirming the pagan polytheism that Christianity was rapidly replacing. Toward this end, he began the first systematic persecution of the Christians, who, he believed, blocked Rome from reattaining its former glory. After executing Pope Fabianus, Decius is reported to have remarked, "I would far rather receive news of a rival to the throne than another bishop in Rome."

The Goths had crossed the Danube around 250, overrunning Moesia and Thrace. Decius set out after the Goths to meet this threat and initially enjoyed success against the invaders. The tide turned, however, at the Battle of Dobrudja in July 251, at which Decius and almost his entire army were exterminated by the Goths.

Further Reading: Michael Grant. *Roman Emperors,* (New York: Scribner's, 1985).

Demetrius (fl. 2nd century A.D.)
The conquests of this king of Bactria briefly reestablished the Mauryan Empire.

Succeeding to the throne some time between 180 and 190, Demetrius was able to make extensive conquests in northern India and briefly reestablish Mauryan control of the region. His reign is chiefly noted for his enlightened treatment of the peoples he conquered. In particular, he treated Indians and the Bactrian Greeks as equals and, later, as potential allies, rather than subjugated vassals. He was apparently murdered by Eucratides around 166, who then succeeded him as king of Bactria.

Demetrius I Soter (ca. 187 B.C.–150 B.C.)

Demetrius, one of the last rulers of the Seleucid dynasty, was king of Syria and given the byname Soter—Savior—for his efforts to restore the Seleucid dynasty.

The son of Seleucus IV, Demetrius spent much of his youth as a prisoner in Rome, his father sending him there as a hostage to be held as insurance against further insurrection. After Seleucus was murdered in 175 B.C., he was replaced by his brother Antiochus IV. When Antiochus died in 164 B.C., Demetrius requested permission from the Senate to return home and assume the throne. After the Senate refused, Demetrius escaped with the aid of Polybius, a Greek statesmen, and returned to Syria in 162 B.C.

Demetrius I unsuccessfully fought to preserve the Seleucid dynasty against the combined forces of much of the ancient world. (From Richard Delbruck, Antike Portrats, *1912)*

Upon his return, the Syrians rallied around Demetrius, executing his cousin Antiochus V, who had succeeded his father Antiochus IV upon the latter's death. Across the Euphrates, Timarchus, a favorite of Antiochus IV, declared himself king of Babylonia and independent of Demetrius and the rest of Syria. The Senate, hoping to maintain a weak puppet ruler in the region, partially supported Timarchus, but gave him no aid. Demetrius quickly marched against the usurper and defeated and executed him. After this victory, the Senate had no choice but formally to recognize Demetrius in 160 B.C.

Demetrius soon alienated Syria's three powerful neighbors, Egypt, Cappadocia, and Pergamum, by his threats to reassert Seleucid hegemony in Asia Minor. These powers, supported by the Roman Senate, turned against him. When Attalus II put forth Alexander Balas as the heir of Antiochus IV, all four supported Balas and aligned themselves against Demetrius. Demetrius next lost the support of the Jews, who aligned themselves with Alexander in retaliation for the defeat Demetrius had dealt them in 160 B.C.

Demetrius now found himself alone against every power in the region. In 150, Ptolemy invaded with a force from Egypt while Pergamum and Cappadocian forces attacked from the north in two separate advances. To make the dire situation even worse, several of Demetrius' generals defected just before battle. Demetrius fell to his enemies, and, with his death, the Seleucid Empire quickly crumbled.

Deng Xiaoping [Teng Hsiao-p'ing] (1904–   )

The most powerful political leader in China during the 1970s and 1980s, Deng Xiaoping liberalized the nation's hard-line Communist policies, but took a step back into orthodoxy by supporting the brutal suppression of pro-democratic 1989 demonstrations at Tiananmen Square, Beijing (Peking).

Deng Xiaoping was born on August 22, 1904, in China's Sichuan (Szechwan) Province. He was educated in France during 1921–24 and became active there in the Communist movement, visiting the Soviet Union during 1925–26. Returning to China, Deng became a key participant in the Jiangxi (Kiangsi) Soviet, the Communist enclave MAO TSE-TUNG had established in southeast China. Deng made the celebrated 6,000-mile Long March with Mao from the southeast to the northwest in 1934–35 and was instrumental in the resistance against the Japanese invasion of the country during World War II.

Deng Xiaoping became vice-premier of the People's Republic of China when it was formed in 1949. Two years later, he was appointed secretary-general of the Chinese Communist Party (CCP), and in 1955 was a full member of the ruling Politburo.

A close associate of Mao, Deng nevertheless came into conflict with him over economic policy. While Mao attempted inflexibly to impose his agrarian version of Marxism on China, Deng allied himself with more pragmatic leaders, most notably LIU SHAOQUI, (Liu Shao-ch'i), who advocated such quasi-capitalist economic expedients as material incentives and the formation of technical and managerial elites. Friction between Mao and Deng escalated during the 1960s, and during 1967–69 Deng was removed from his high party posts. He vanished from public view until 1973, when Premier ZHOU ENLAI (Chou En-lai) reinstated him, elevating him to the position of deputy premier. In 1975, he became vice-chairman of the Communist Party's Central Committee, a Politburo member, and chief of the general staff. With Zhou Enlai ailing, Deng was now effective head of the Chinese government.

Deng's career took a surprising turn in January 1976, however, when, following Zhou Enlai's death, the radical Maoist "Gang of Four" removed Deng from power. But times had changed for China, and radical Maoism was no longer in favor. With Mao's death in September 1976, the Gang of Four quickly fell from power, and Deng was recalled with the approval of Mao's handpicked successor, Hua Guofeng (Hua Kuo-feng). Beginning in July 1977, when Deng was restored to his high governmental posts, he wrestled with Hua Guofeng for ultimate control of the CCP and the nation. At last, in 1980–81, Hua yielded the premiership to Deng's candidate, Zhao Ziyang (Chao Tzu-Yang), and the party leadership to another of Deng's proteges, Hu Yaobang (Hu Yao-pang).

Firmly fixed at the head of the Chinese government, Deng instituted sweeping economic reforms, substantially liberalizing the Maoist policies that had guided the People's Republic since it was founded. Economic management was decentralized, peasant farmers were given an unprecedented degree of control over the lands they worked, individual initiative was encouraged and rewarded, and elite groups of skilled workers and technicians were formed. Deng chose to engineer these reforms not from the most conspicuous positions of power, but from less visible positions, including the CCP Central Military Commission and the Standing Committee of the Politburo. Nevertheless, he was clearly the principal power behind the nominal premier and party chairman and was instrumental in determining Chinese policy throughout most of the 1980s.

Deng retired from the CCP Central Committee and Politburo in 1987 and from the Military Commis-

sion late in 1989. These moves compelled other aged leaders to retire as well—most of them traditional Maoists. Thus Deng peacefully purged the Chinese government of its lingering hard-liners, while quietly, unofficially, retaining ultimate authority in the party himself.

In view of Deng's liberalism and his total avoidance of self-aggrandizement, observers in the West were shocked and dismayed by his approval of the brutal military suppression of pro-democratic student demonstrations in Beijing's Tiananmen Square during April-June 1989. Ironically, it was the very openness Deng had encouraged that resulted in worldwide television coverage of what came to be called the Tiananmen Square Massacre.

Further Reading: Katherine Forestier. "China: The Door Opens Still Wider," *Asian Business* 28, no. 8 (August 1992): 36–40; Horoshi Fukanaga. "Only a Matter of Time: The Torch Waits to Be Passed in Beijing," *Tokyo Business Today* 60, no. 9 (September 1992): 44–45; Carol Kennedy. "The China Connection," *Director* 45, no. 10 (May 1992): 62–66.

Díaz, Porfirio   (1830–1915)

This dictator came to power on the wings of a democratic revolution only to become the autocratic and repressive dictator of Mexico from 1876 to 1911.

Porfirio Díaz was born on September 15, 1830, to a humble mestizo family. Early on, he decided to become a priest and began studying for the priesthood, when he changed to the pursuit of law. But in 1854, he abandoned all studies to join the popular revolutionary movement that overthrew the dictator Antonio López de SANTA ANNA. He became a military commander in the new regime, coming to prominence during the Wars of the Reform (1858–61), by the end of which he had attained the rank of general. His performance in the wars also earned him political advancement, and in 1861 he was elected federal deputy (representative) from the state of Oaxaca.

With the conclusion of the Wars of the Reform in 1861, a coalition of Spain, France, and Britain sent a joint expeditionary force to Mexico in order to protect their interests and to obtain satisfaction of considerable debts. Louis-Napoléon (NAPOLÉON III) seized the occasion to intervene more aggressively in Mexican government and established a puppet empire under MAXIMILIAN. During the period of this intervention—from 1861 to 1867—Díaz sided with the liberal republican forces under Benito JUÁREZ. Díaz continued to rise in prominence and became a key figure in the eventual overthrow of the French-backed regime and the establishment of a republic headed by Juárez.

Within a short time, however, in 1871, Díaz staged a rebellion of his own, meant to block the reelection of Juárez. He failed, but in 1876 aggressively opposed the election of Juárez's handpicked successor, Sebastian Lerdo de Tejada. This time he prevailed, becoming president himself in 1877. Except for one term, in 1880–84, Díaz held office until 1911.

Like so many other popular revolutionaries of military bent, Díaz came to power on a liberal promise but assumed office as a harsh and reactionary dictator. Díaz was a consummate capitalist, who believed in economic growth literally at any price. He put himself, his government, and his nation's resources at the service of wealthy Mexicans and foreign investors, turning his back on Mexico's poor and failing to address the country's many social ills. Nor was the program of Porfirio Díaz simply one of benign neglect. He engineered the expropriation of land from Mexico's Indian peasant communities, and he took brutal measures to stamp out a struggling labor movement. In this repressive atmosphere, a class of quasi-revolutionary bandits grew up in the Mexican countryside, the precursors of Pancho Villa. Díaz responded by establishing a powerful state police force called the *rurales,* which did not eradicate banditry, but which did terrorize the nation's poor villages.

In 1909, Díaz pledged that he would reinstate democracy, but instead he attempted to fix the elections of 1910, touching off a revolution that year led by Francisco Madero, which drove Díaz from office in 1911, sending him into French exile. He died in Paris on July 2, 1915.

Further Reading: Carlton Beales. *Porfirio Díaz, Dictator of Mexico* (Philadelphia: Lippincott, 1932); Jose F. Godoy, *Porfirio Diaz* (New York: Putnam's, 1910).

Diem, Ngo Dinh *See* NGO DINH DIEM

Dimitry (II) Donskoy [Dimitry Ivanovich] (1350–1389)
This prince of Moscow and grand prince of Vladimir temporarily delivered Russia from domination by the Golden Horde.

Born on October 12, 1350, in Moscow, Dimitry was the son of Ivan II the Meek and succeeded his father as prince of Moscow at the age of nine. Just three years later, the ambitious boy persuaded the Great Khan of the Golden Horde to transfer to him the title grand prince of Vladimir, which had been held by Dimitry of Suzdal. His prestige and authority thus augmented, Dimitry went on to subdue the princes of Rostov and Ryazan and to depose outright the princes of Galich and Starodub. In this

way, the young man greatly expanded the territorial holdings of Muscovy.

After consolidating his power, Dimitry exploited internal dissension with the Golden Horde to make a move against them. He ceased payment of tribute to the Great Khan and rallied his fellow Russian princes to do the same and to resist Mongol invasion. In 1378, Dimitry and other princes met and defeated a Mongol army at the Vozha River.

Mamai, a Mongol general who effectively ruled the western portion of the Golden Horde, developed his own alliances to put down the rebellious Russians. Dimitry led a force to the Don River, and defeated Mamai at the Battle of Kulikovo Pole, taking the name Donskoy ("of the Don") in commemoration of the victory.

Dimitry's triumph was short-lived, however, as the renegade Mongol leader Tokhtamysh overthrew Mamai in 1381 and, the following year, marched on Moscow, which he sacked, thereby reinstating Mongol suzerainty over the Russian lands.

Dingane [Dingaan] (d. 1843)
Half brother and successor to the famed SHAKA, this Zulu king of Natal struggled unsuccessfully against the Boers.

Dingane conspired to murder his half-brother, the famed Zulu warrior king Shaka, and assumed rule of Natal in 1828. In November 1837, Dingane offered the Boer leader Piet Retief a vast portion of Natal in return for his aid in recovering a stolen Zulu cattle herd. Once the animals were recovered, Dingane turned on Retief, killing him and about 600 Boer immigrants in February 1838. The Boer commander Andries Pretorius conducted a vengeance expedition against Dingane and his Zulus, killing some 3,000 of them in the Battle of Blood River on December 16, 1838. This disaster greatly undermined Dingane's power, and his brother MPANDE ousted him in January 1840. Dingane fled to Swaziland, only to be murdered there three years later.

Diocletian [Gaius Aurelius Valerius Diocletianus] (ca. 250–ca. 313)
A common soldier who rose to become the greatest of the late Roman emperors, Diocletian was merciless with rebels and Christians, but introduced administrative and military reforms that staved off dissolution of the Roman Empire for at least a century.

Diocletian was born in Dalmatia to humble parents. He enlisted in the Roman army and rose quickly through the ranks to become commander of the personal bodyguard of Emperor Numerian in 283. When Numerian was murdered on November

20, 284, Diocletian acted with dispatch to seize and execute the supposed assassin, the praetorian prefect Aper, who was also Diocletian's archrival. Diocletian was elected emperor after Numerian's death, whereupon he led an army against Numerian's brother Carinus, who ruled the Western Empire. He engaged Carinus in battle on the Margus River in Illyricum in the spring of 285. There Diocletian not only defeated Carinus' army, but killed Carinus himself.

Diocletian did not rule long as sole emperor. Faced with a crumbling empire, he realized that a single ruler could not successfully defend the nation against the numerous threats now rife. He elevated his trusted friend Maximian to the office of Caesar—assistant emperor—in the summer of 285. Subsequently, he made Maximian augustus—co-emperor. Then, as part of a series of sweeping administrative reforms designed to rescue the empire from disintegration, Diocletian appointed two additional Caesars, Gaius Valerius GALERIUS and Flavius Valerius CONSTANTIUS. Thus Rome came to be ruled by the Tetrarchy.

Diocletian's many reforms included attempts at centralized wage and price controls to curb runaway inflation and a general restructuring of the imperial administration. Diocletian decreed the separation of military from civil authority, and he apportioned the empire into smaller, more manageable provinces, gathered in groups of 12 to form larger administrative units or *dioceses*. His most profound reforms came in the military. Diocletian roughly doubled the size of the Roman army, and he totally reorganized it. He recognized that, faced with increasingly sophisticated military threats along the wide frontiers, the army needed a combination of strong standing forces in place on the frontier and large, highly mobile forces available for rapid reinforcement of frontiers that were particularly menaced. While Diocletian increased the size of the army, he reduced the size of each legion in order to facilitate strategic and tactical flexibility.

Diocletian's reformed army was put to the test in 294–96, when a Roman usurper named Domitius Domitianus—or Achilleus—established himself as emperor in Alexandria, Egypt. Diocletian himself led an army to Alexandria, which he besieged brutally for eight months before the city fell. He ordered the execution of Achilleus in 296. Diocletian next provided aid to the Upper Egyptians and Nubians in repelling incursions by a barbarian tribe known as the Blemmyes. Closer to the heart of the empire, Diocletian unleashed the last mass persecution of Christians during 303–304, believing that the cults were eroding the empire from the inside.

Shortly after this spasm of persecution, in 305, Diocletian abdicated, as did Maximian, leaving the empire to the two Caesars. He retired to his palace in Spalatum—modern Split—on the Dalmatian coast and died some seven years later.

Dionysius I   (ca. 430 B.C.–367 B.C.)

Tyrant of Syracuse, Dionysius I led three wars against Carthage and made Syracuse the strongest Greek city west of the mainland.

Dionysius was a public official when war broke out in 409 B.C. between Syracuse and Carthage. Maneuvering himself into a position of power, he became *strategos autokrator* (military dictator) in 405. Over the next several years, he consolidated his power and built a huge private fortress on Ortygia, a Syracusan island. One by one, he overthrew the governments of the major cities in eastern Sicily, transferred and sometimes enslaved their populations, and then in 397 was ready to take on the Carthaginians again. Although he was unable to push them out of Sicily, he did confine them to the western part of the island by 392.

Dionysius then looked to the Italian mainland for further conquests. He defeated Croton in 388 and Rhegium in 386 and looted Pyrgi in about 384. He fought in the Adriatic and in Greece, where the brutality of his conquests provoked popular outrage. In 383 or 382, he began another war with Carthage and was defeated at Cronium in about 375. More determined than ever to defeat the Carthaginians, he attacked again in 368 but died the following year, not in battle but of overindulgence during a victory celebration at the Lenaean tragic festival in Athens.

Further Reading: Brian Caven. *Dionysius I: War Lord of Sicily* (New Haven: Yale University Press, 1990); L. J. Sanders. *Dionysius I of Syracuse and Greek Tyranny* (London & New York: Croom Helm, 1987).

Doe, Samuel K.   (ca. 1951–1990)

Military ruler of Liberia from 1980 until his assassination in 1990, Samuel K. Doe was declared winner in the highly dubious 1985 presidential election and spent the last years of his administration fighting off attempts by two rebel leaders to overthrow the government.

According to the best available information, Doe was born on May 6, 1951, in Tuzon, Liberia. He quit high school in the 11th grade and joined the Liberian army, receiving training at a U.S. Special Forces camp and becoming a master sergeant in 1979. On April 12, 1980, Doe and 17 other soldiers staged a pre-dawn attack on the executive mansion in Monrovia, killing 30 government officials and President William R. Tolbert, Jr. Doe seized control of the government as commander in chief and head of the People's Redemption Council, pledging a rapid return to civilian government.

The pledge came to nothing, as Doe ordered the summary execution of 13 of the president's associates and suspended Liberia's 133-year-old constitution.

In October 1985, Doe allowed free elections to be held, despite an attempted coup six months earlier. Amid charges of election rigging and intimidation at the polls, a special election committee nevertheless determined that Doe had won 51 percent of the vote. On November 12, Doe survived a coup attempt, led by former military commander General Thomas Quiwonkpa. Doe retaliated by unleashing the army on a rampage of looting. Over the next few years, reports of human rights violations increased, and added to them were charges that his government had mismanaged millions of dollars in aid from the United States. Opposition, organized primarily by two rebel leaders—Charles Taylor, a former government official, and Prince Yormie Johnson—continued to mount. By the beginning of January 1990, the country was torn by a full-scale civil war.

In an attempt to end the hostilities, Doe announced that he would not seek re-election and that he would consider holding elections before the end of his term. Rebel leader Charles Taylor, however, demanded Doe's immediate resignation. Peace negotiations, first under the auspices of the United States government and the Liberian Council of Churches and later under a multinational peacekeeping team, failed. Finally, five West African nations sent troops to Liberia. On September 9, 1990, rebel forces led by Prince Johnson captured Doe outside the headquarters of the peacekeeping force. Wounded in both legs during a gunfight, Doe was taken into custody by the rebels and tortured to death that day or the next. While the rebels announced a cease-fire later in the month, fighting and retaliations against followers of Doe continued until November, when the West African peacekeeping force installed an interim government.

Dollfuss, Engelbert (1892–1934)

Opposed to the impending Nazi takeover of his native Austria, Dollfuss aligned himself with Benito MUSSOLINI in the hopes of remaining independent of Adolf HITLER's Nazi regime.

Born in Lower Austria on October 4, 1892, Engelbert Dollfuss studied law at the University of Vienna and economics at the University of Berlin. With the

outbreak of World War I, he served as an officer in the Austrian army, and, after the war, as a conservative Roman Catholic, he became active in the Christian Socialist Party. Dollfuss served as secretary of the Lower Austrian Peasant Federation and, in 1927, as director of the Lower Austria Chamber of Agriculture. After a brief stint as president of the railways system in 1930, he became secretary of agriculture in 1931.

With the Christian Socialists maintaining a one-vote majority in the Austrian lower house, Dollfuss was named chancellor of Austria on May 20, 1932. His major concern was the economic depression. Drawn by the promise of $9 million in loans from the League of Nations and fearful of Allied pressure, Dollfuss declined to join Germany in a customs union. This alienated him from the German and Austrian Nazis, as well as from pan-German opinion generally. Amid a public outcry against him, the three presidents of the Austrian parliament resigned, whereupon Dollfuss suspended parliament and ruled by decree.

In desperate need of foreign support and increasingly concerned over the threat posed by Hitler, Dollfuss turned to Benito Mussolini. At Riccione in 1933, he secured from the Italian dictator a guarantee of Austrian independence in return for the abolition of political parties in Austria and the restructuring of the constitution along Fascist guidelines. Finally abolishing parliament altogether in September 1933, Dollfuss went about establishing a Fascist Austria with his "Fatherland Front," which replaced political parties; his secret police, which he used indiscriminately; and increasing subjugation to Italy. At the behest of Mussolini, Dollfuss deliberately instigated social unrest in Austria to give him an excuse for the bloody suppression of the Austrian Socialists in February 1934. On May 1, 1934, Dollfuss proclaimed a new constitution in Austria, which effectively made Austria an Italian satellite.

In delivering Austria to Mussolini, Dollfuss cut himself off from all domestic support, and Hitler rapidly made strides among Austrians, who jealously watched the revitalization of postwar Germany. A failed Austrian Nazi coup attempt on July 25, 1934, resulted in the assassination of Dollfuss. For the next four years, Austrian fascism reigned, until March 1938, when Hitler's army marched into Vienna and peacefully made a willing Austria the first tributary country in a projected German-dominated Europe.

Further Reading: Paul R. Sweet. "Mussolini and Dollfuss: An Episode in Fascist Diplomacy," in Julius Braunthal, *The Tragedy of Austria* (London: Gollancz, 1948).

Domitian [Titus Flavius Domitianus] (51–96)
Emperor of the Roman Empire from A.D. 81 to 96,
Domitian exercised absolute control over the Roman
Senate and instituted a reign of terror, while under-
taking campaigns to expand and strengthen the
empire.

The second son of VESPASIAN and Flavia Domitilla
and brother to TITUS (Titus Flavius Vespasianus),
Domitian was born on October 24, 51. When he was
18 years old, his father rebelled against Vitellius (in
69), and Domitian remained in Rome. When Vitellius died, Domitian was hailed as Caesar and temporarily took control of the city. His authority was
brief, however, since his father soon arrived to take
over.

Emperor Vespasian died in June 79, and Titus succeeded to the throne. It is thought that Domitian expected Titus to grant him the same titles and
responsibility Titus had held under their father, but
the new emperor withheld any real power from his
brother. Titus died childless on September 13, 81,
and Domitian succeeded to the throne, eager to exert his authority.

The aristocracy hated Domitian for several reasons. He was cruel and ostentatious—wearing the
dress of a triumphant general in the Senate and insisting on being addressed as *dominus et deus* ("master and god"). He maintained absolute control over
the magistrates in Rome and the provinces and required meticulous records to be kept on army personnel for his review. In 85, he claimed the title
Perpetual Censor, gaining absolute control over the
membership and behavior of the Senate. While he
was himself sexually promiscuous, he ordered the
execution of three Vestal Virgins on grounds of immorality in 83 and had the Chief Vestal, Cornelia,
buried alive in 90.

A military revolt in Upper Germany broke out on
January 1, 89, under the command of Lucius Antonius Saturninus. Proclaiming himself emperor, Saturninus rallied two legions at Moguntiacum and
some German auxiliaries to the rebellion. Lappius
Maximus, commander in Lower Germany, remained
loyal to Domitian, however, and put down the rebellion. Saturninus was killed in battle near Castellum.

After Saturninus' revolt, Domitian became even
more autocratic. Seeing conspiracies everywhere, he
cracked down on all perceived threats. He strengthened the policy his father had begun against the
Jews in Judaea by tracking down and killing all who
claimed descent from the royal house of DAVID. In
Rome, Jews faced heavy taxes and were condemned
for "godlessness." This persecution extended to Jewish sympathizers as well, notably the Consul Flavius

Clemens and his wife, Flavia Domitilla (a relative of
Domitian). In 95, the emperor ordered Clemens's execution and his wife's banishment. Their two sons,
who stood to inherit the throne, were probably
killed.

Treason trials, imperial spies and informants, and
executions of ex-consuls (Suetonius estimated that
12 were killed) proliferated at Domitian's court. The
emperor hastened his own demise by dismissing his
joint preatorian prefects and replacing them with Petronius Secundus and Norbanus. These men, worried that their tenure under Domitian would be
brief, conspired with leaders in the provinces, Domitian's court chamberlain, a state secretary, Domitian's wife (Domitia Longina), and others to
assassinate the emperor. They recruited Stephanus,
a former slave of Flavia Domitilla—Clemens's banished widow—to do the job, and in a hand-to-hand
struggle, both the assassin and the emperor died on
September 18, 96, in Rome.

Further Reading: M. P. Charlesworth and Ronald Syme.
The Cambridge Ancient History, vol. 11, chapters 1 and 4
(1936; reprint ed., New York: Macmillan, 1954); Tenney
Frank, ed. *An Economic Survey of Ancient Rome,* vol. 5 (New
York: Octagon, 1975).

Draco (fl. 7th century B.C.)
An Athenian lawgiver, Draco formulated a code that
punished serious and comparatively trivial crimes
alike with death.

Virtually nothing is known of the person of Draco,
whose name is also sometimes spelled Dracon. He
was an Athenian lawgiver empowered to revise the
body of Athenian law into a comprehensive code.
The date of this revision is traditionally assigned to
621 B.C. and the action was presumably prompted
by some political crisis.

Judged by the standards of later times, Draco's
laws, which apparently prescribed capital punishment for a wide spectrum of offenses, were considered too severe and were repealed and replaced by
the code of SOLON in 594 B.C. Solon did not, however, repeal Draco's laws concerning homicide,
which were meant to address the serious problem of
blood feuding, a destabilizing force in Athenian government.

The word *draconian,* signifying laws or regulations
that are excessively harsh, is derived from Draco.

Duong Van Minh (b. 1916–)
Duong Van Minh ousted President NGO DINH DIEM
of the Republic of Vietnam (South Vietnam), later
served briefly as president, and surrendered unconditionally to the North Vietnamese Army in 1975.

Duong Van Minh was born on February 19, 1916, in the Mekong Delta of the French colony of Cochin China (Vietnam). Educated in France, he returned to Vietnam and, in 1955, was named ranking military officer in the army of the newly proclaimed Republic of Vietnam. After scoring several military successes, Minh became immensely popular among the people of South Vietnam. President Ngo Dinh Diem, recognizing a threat to his power, "promoted" Minh to an advisery position—largely honorific in nature.

In November 1963, with the backing of the United States' Central Intelligence Agency, Minh and a group of generals seized power from Diem, assassinated him, and replaced the government with a Military Revolutionary Council. This group's tenure was short; in January 1964, Minh and the council were ousted, and he fled into exile.

Four years later, Minh returned to Vietnam, and in 1971 entered the presidential race. Realizing that he could not possibly win, however, he withdrew. But on April 21, 1975, he reentered the political spotlight when President Nguyen Van Thieu resigned and Minh was named president.

His administration lasted only a few days. North Vietnamese troops converged on Saigon, occupied the presidential palace, and accepted Minh's unconditional surrender of the Republic of Vietnam on April 29, 1975. Minh was captured by the North Vietnamese but was later released and allowed to immigrate to France in 1983.

Further Reading: Frances FitzGerald. *Fire in the Lake: The Vietnamese and the Americans in Vietnam* (Boston: Little, Brown, 1972); Stanley Karnow. *Vietnam: A History* (New York: Viking, 1983).

Duvalier, François   ["Papa Doc"] (1907–1971)

President of Haiti from 1957 to 1971, "Papa Doc" Duvalier employed a voodoo-inspired grassroots terrorism to maintain his repressive regime in chronically strife-torn Haiti.

François Duvalier, born to a middle-class Haitian family on April 14, 1907, was trained as a physician specializing in rural medicine. During the 1940s, he gained great popularity through his tireless work as director of Haitian efforts to eradicate such primarily rural diseases as yaws and malaria, which had reached epidemic proportions in the country. During this period, Duvalier became involved in Haitian nationalist movements, including Le Groupe des Griots, a writers' group dedicated to the promotion of voodoo, Haiti's powerful grassroots religion derived from African origins. Along with this religious expression of nationalism, the Griots generally expressed and supported cultural nationalism and political self-determination.

Duvalier used his considerable popular prestige to support the election of President Dumarsais Estimé in the 1940s, serving in his administration as director of public health during 1946 to 1948, then, at the cabinet level, as secretary of labor from 1949 to 1950. When Paul E. Magloire displaced Estimé in 1950, Duvalier was at first vocal in his opposition, then, from 1954 to 1956, worked underground, quietly directing forces opposed to Magloire's government.

Under pressure, Magloire resigned, and Duvalier emerged with an announcement of his candidacy for the presidency. He was elected in 1957, the rigged election giving him the greatest majority in Haiti's history (in some districts the Duvalier vote exceeded the total population). Realizing that even genuine popularity is volatile in Haiti, Duvalier consolidated his power through a widespread program of fear and terror carried out by a far-flung palace army called the Tontons Macoutes, who combined brutality with the more intimidating aspects of voodoo to enforce obedience to the Duvalier regime in every village of the country. By 1964, Duvalier was able easily to push through a constitutional revision making him president for life.

Papa Doc Duvalier was one of history's most frightening and fascinating dictators, deliberately combining in himself imagery reminiscent of such medical humanitarians as Albert Schweitzer even as he skillfully exploited the darkest aspects of the popular voodoo religion and used the strongarm methods of a gangster. His trademark pearl-handled revolver was always kept, loaded, on his desk in the presidential palace.

Upon Duvalier's death on April 21, 1971, the dictator's 19-year-old son, JEAN CLAUDE ("BABY DOC") DUVALIER, incongruously rotund and baby-faced, used the Tontons Macoutes to rule Haiti before a popular revolt sent him into exile in 1986.

Further Reading: Elizabeth Abbott. *Haiti: The Duvaliers and Their Legacy* (New York: McGraw-Hill, 1988); Jean-Pierre O. Gingras. *Duvalier: Caribbean Cyclone* (New York: Exposition Press, 1967).

Duvalier, Jean-Claude   ["Baby Doc"] (1951–   )

Son of and successor to his father, FRANÇOIS ("PAPA DOC") DUVALIER, this Haitian dictator attempted to continue a repressive, terror-enforced regime.

Jean Claude ("Baby Doc") Duvalier was born on July 3, 1951. On the death of his father in April 1971, the 19-year-old was proclaimed, like François Duvalier, president of Haiti for life.

Rotund and infantile in appearance, Baby Doc pledged extensive economic reform and a general easing of his father's harshest excesses. Such promises were sufficient to attract much-needed foreign investment capital, but it soon became apparent that little was going to change in this nation ruled through terror enforced by the paramilitary, voodoo-inspired palace guards known as the Tontons Macoutes. Baby Doc, however, lacked the absolute grip on government that his father had enjoyed, and even the Tontons Macoutes were unable to enforce obedience. Baby Doc's personal and administrative corruption sparked widespread protests, which swelled to rebellion in November 1985.

By the beginning of the next year, the United States drastically cut foreign aid to Haiti because of the Duvalier regime's blatant human rights abuses. Without the economic support of the United States, Baby Doc's government was doomed, and, on February 7, 1986, Jean-Claude Duvalier turned the government over to an interim ruling council. The United States, which had bargained for his peaceful ouster, furnished an Air Force jet to evacuate him to France, where he had secured political asylum.

Further Reading: Elizabeth Abbott. *Haiti: The Duvaliers and Their Legacy* (New York: McGraw-Hill, 1988).

E

Edward I Longshanks (1239–1307)

Earning the name the "English Justinian" because of his legislative reform, Edward I established Parliament as a permanent aspect of English law.

The first of more than a dozen children of King Henry III, Edward was born on June 17, 1239, and was given enormous tracts of land under the English system of primacy, including ireland, Wales, the duchy of Gascony, and the earldom of Chester.

After 1255, Edward became aligned with a group of barons, led by Simon de Montfort, who attempted to overthrow Henry and rule England themselves. After a period during which Edward first supported Montfort, then his father, and back to Montfort again, he finally deserted the usurpers by late 1260 and sought and received the forgiveness of his father. When civil war broke out in 1263, Edward stood by his father, but his reckless conduct at the Battle of Lewes on May 14, 1264, brought about his defeat. Edward was taken prisoner by Montfort, but escaped a year later.

Immediately upon his escape, Edward took command of the royalist forces and trapped Montfort's baronial forces behind the Severn River. On August 1, Edward devastated Montfort's reserve forces at Kenilworth, and on August 4, he killed Montfort himself at Evesham, rescuing his father, whose troops had been penned in by the baronial army.

After Edward had subdued the English countryside, he attempted to join Louis IX of France in the Crusades of 1271, but learned upon his arrival that Louis had died. During his journey home, he received news that Henry had died on November 16, 1272. After Edward's ministers received assurances of loyalty from the barons, Edward took his time journeying back to England, finally reaching Westminster Abbey for his coronation on August 19, 1274.

Edward, having matured and finding himself in control of his temper, dedicated himself to organized, efficient, strong government. He institutionalized the practice of calling borough and shire leaders together and thereby made Parliament the dominating force of English politics, a force that remains potent eight centuries later.

He used Parliament as an effective tool of policy. Through Parliament Edward was able to enact measures of reform at all levels, specifically in the areas of land and trade.

Although he had largely mastered himself, Edward was still bellicose by nature, and when the Prince of Wales shirked his feudal responsibilities, Edward attacked, destroying the prince's forces and subjugating all his land. When a popular rebellion arose, Edward marched through Wales, ruthlessly putting down the revolt, killing both the prince and his brother, leaving no independent heir. Hoping to avoid further problems with Wales, Edward installed his first son, and heir apparent, as prince of Wales, establishing another English tradition whereby the crown prince assumes the title Prince of Wales.

The end of Edward's reign saw a deterioration of government, as his best advisers died and he resorted to the war-mongering ways of his youth. He provoked war with Scotland, the effects of which would be felt for the next 250 years. Although victorious on the field, he could not completely subdue the Scots, and he gave up trying after eight years. After making concessions both at home and abroad in an effort to raise more money, he again took after the Scots, defeating them in 1305 and executing the rebel leaders. But the rebellion soon revived, and, en route to battle with the Scots yet again, Edward succumbed to dysentery and died near Carlisle on July 7, 1307.

Further Reading: Michael Prestwich. *Edward I* (Berkeley: University of California Press, 1988).

Edward III (of Windsor) (1312–1377)

Edward III's reign (1327–77) marked the beginning of England's Hundred Years' War with France.

The son of King Edward II of England and Isabella of France, 15-year-old Edward III ascended to the English throne after his mother and her lover, Mortimer, succeeded in deposing his father in 1327. At first, Edward was no more than a figurehead, a puppet controlled by Isabella and Mortimer, but in 1330 he moved against Mortimer, had him executed, and assumed the reins of government in earnest.

Increasing hostilities between England and France led to his invading France in 1339 and 1340. Although relatively successful, the invasions strained the treasury, and Edward finally had to withdraw,

The pious Edward III, depicted in an engraving copied from a medieval painting. (From J. N. Larned, A History of England for the Use of Schools and Academies, *1900)*

but not without declaring himself king of France in 1340, initiating a tradition (which endured until 1801) of English monarchs claiming rule over France. These invasions marked the beginning of the mutually ruinous Hundred Years' War between France and England.

At home, Edward III created the Order of the Garter, Britain's highest order of knighthood, and expanded Windsor Castle. Married to Philippa of York in 1328, Edward had seven sons and five daughters. His future grandchildren would be involved in the royal dispute known as the Wars of the Roses (1455–85).

After the death of Queen Philippa, Edward fell under the spell of his avaricious mistress Alice Perrers, whose affiliation with John of Gaunt alienated both Parliament and the people. Edward III died during this period of estrangement, on June 21, 1377, in Sheen, Surrey.

Further Reading: William Warburton. *Edward III* (New York: Scribner's, 1888).

Elagabalus [Caesar Marcus Aurelius Antoninus Augustus] (204–222)

Elagabalus was a mentally unbalanced Roman emperor whose blatant favoritism toward his lovers—

most of whom were lowborn aliens—and his unseemly behavior alienated Roman public opinion.

Elagabalus was born Varius Avitus Bassianus in Emesa, Syria, to a family of high priests of the sun god Baal. In Syria, the deity was called Elah-Gabal, and it is from this that the future emperor's byname derived.

In 217, the emperor CARACALLA, Bassianus' cousin, was murdered and replaced by the praetorian prefect Macrinus. Bassianus' grandmother and mother (Julia Soaemias) convinced local troops that Bassianus was the illegitimate son of Caracalla, and by 218, Rome's eastern armies had deserted Macrinus and thrown their support behind Caracalla's "son." The Senate acknowledged the young man as emperor later that year, and thenceforth he was generally known as Elagabalus.

No sooner did he assume the throne than he embarked on an eccentric and offensive course of tyranny. He began by imposing the worship of his god, Baal, upon a most unwilling Rome. Next, he summarily executed numerous dissident generals, then thrust into high office a legion of his lovers, who were distinguished exclusively by their good looks; they not only lacked qualification for office, but, mostly lowborn and of non-Roman origin, they were destined to be unpopular at best and despised at worst.

In an empire that had known many erratic leaders and had witnessed every form of sensual extravagance, Elagabalus managed to scandalize the public and the powerful alike with elaborate homosexual orgies. The young man's mother, who was the true force behind the throne, persuaded Elagabalus to

The Hundred Years' War between France and England was inaugurated by a great English naval victory at Sluys Harbor in 1340, overture to Edward III's invasion of France. (From Charlotte M. Yonge, Pictorial History of the World's Great Nations, *1882)*

adopt his cousin Alexander as his son and successor, which he did in 221, only to change his mind almost immediately. At this, the Praetorian Guard mutinied against Elagabalus, killing him—as well as his mother—and elevating Alexander to emperor.

Elizabeth   [Yelizaveta Petrovna] (1709–1762)

Coming to power through a coup d'etat, Elizabeth introduced elements of Western culture into Russia, but also fostered tyrannical privilege among the gentry.

Elizabeth was born on December 18, 1709, at Kolomenskoye, near Moscow. The daughter of PETER I THE GREAT, she was a favorite at court, but she was content to stay out of politics during the reigns of Peter II and the empress Anna. However, when Anna assumed the regency for her infant son Ivan VI, threatening to banish Elizabeth to a convent, the princess listened to the French ambassador and disaffected members of the court who, eager to depose the pro-Austrian, anti-French Anna, counseled a coup.

Elizabeth made her move on the night of December 5–6, 1741, arresting the child, his mother, and their advisers. She immediately summoned to court the chief civil and ecclesatical authorities of St. Petersburg and caused herself to be proclaimed empress of Russia.

Ostensibly, Elizabeth restored to Russia the government of her father, most visibly by abolishing the cabinet council and reestablishing the senate. In reality, however, Elizabeth's government was even more autocratic than that of Peter II or Anna; for the real power resided with her private chancery. Moreover, Elizabeth personally cared little for affairs of state, but immersed herself instead in the luxurious trappings of power and in such cultural activities as the founding of Moscow University and the Academy of Arts (in St. Petersburg). The actual running of the country was left to the chancery and to a coterie of backbiting court favorites and advisers, under whom intrigue and corruption flourished, the gentry grew wealthier, and the peasantry fared increasingly poorly.

While most of the Russian people languished under the rule of Elizabeth, her country's international visibility and prestige as a world power grew. She allowed her chief counselor, Aleksei Bestuzhev-Ryumin, to align the country with Austria and against Prussia, a move that ultimately resulted in Russia's entry into the Seven Years' War against Prussia. A portion of Finland was annexed to Russia following a successful war with Sweden during 1741–43, and relations with the West, especially Great Britain, were generally expanded and improved.

Elizabeth I   (1533–1603)

Along with Catherine the Great, one of the greatest women in history, Elizabeth I was able to keep England relatively free from the continuing religious strife that dominated the times.

The daughter of King HENRY VIII and his second wife, Anne Boleyn, Elizabeth was born September 7, 1533, at Greenwich Palace. Due to the failure of either of Henry's first two wives to produce male children, he divorced the first and had the second, Ann, executed, in order to marry a third, Jane Seymour, in hopes of producing a male heir. When Jane bore Henry Edward VI, Parliament declared Elizabeth and Mary (her older sister by Henry's first marriage) illegitimate.

Elizabeth's early years were filled with uncertainty and danger. Because she was deemed illegitimate, and because she was female, many in court considered her expendable, yet, since she was of the blood, she could still be considered a danger to any potential pretenders to the throne. She was made a virtual prisoner during the short reign of Edward when, in 1549, it was falsely alleged that Elizabeth was in league with a potential schemer against the English throne. When Edward died without any

Elizabeth I—"Good Queen Bess"—depicted in an engraving reproduced above her royal signature. (From J. N. Larned, A History of England for the Use of Schools and Academies, *1900)*

An illustration from a 1589 book depicts Elizabeth I saluting her people from a royal chariot. A strong, even merciless monarch, Elizabeth was nevertheless tremendously popular with her subjects. (British Museum)

children in 1553, MARY I became queen. An ardent Catholic, Mary became the object of several Protestant plots aimed—without Elizabeth's knowledge or complicity—at replacing Mary with Elizabeth. Mary had Elizabeth imprisoned in the Tower of London, and would have had her executed if she could have gotten away with it.

With Mary's death on November 17, 1558, Elizabeth was proclaimed Elizabeth I, Queen of England. Immediately, she made it clear that England would return to the ways of the Protestant Reformation begun by Edward. Parliament passed the Second Act of Supremacy in 1559, which did away with Catholicism as the state religion and installed Elizabeth as head of the Church of England. This did not quell the controversy, however. Elizabeth's rival claimant to the throne, Mary, Queen of Scots, who continued to harp on the illegitimacy charge, was a fervent Catholic who had many supporters in France.

The situation worsened in 1570, when Pope PIUS V excommunicated Elizabeth and deposed her in the eyes of God, creating a dilemma for her subjects, who were compelled to choose between her and the papacy. Mary's extreme popularity with her own subjects helped ease this crisis, and Elizabeth used it to her advantage by playing to English nationalism, saying that to support her and the Church of England was to uphold England itself.

Elizabeth most effectively consolidated her reign with her foreign policy, particularly in successfully challenging Spain's domination of the seas. In an act of deliberate defiance of Spain's monopoly in the New World, Elizabeth financed the global circumnavigation of Sir Francis Drake and the colonization efforts of Sir Walter Raleigh. She also supported

Dutch independence from Spain, winning an ally that would stand by England for the next 400 years. The army reached a fighting efficiency previously unknown, and Elizabeth demanded that the navy likewise be upgraded. The confrontation, as momentous as it was unavoidable, came in 1588, when England defeated the mighty Spanish Armada, achieving new status among the nations of Europe and assuming sovereignty of the seas from that point ever after.

Perhaps the only cloud over Elizabeth's reign was the matter of succession. Yet again, she used circumstances to her advantage. Many men, including the czar of Russia, King PHILIP II of Spain, and Eric of Sweden, proposed to her, and she played them off against one another masterfully, getting what she wanted from each without compromising either the crown or England. She once told Parliament "that a marble stone shall declare that a Queen, having reigned such a time died a virgin." Indeed, Elizabeth never married, and, on her death on March 24, 1603, she left no successor.

Further Reading: John E. Neale. *Queen Elizabeth*, (New York: Harcourt, Brace & Co., 1934); Neville Williams. *Elizabeth, Queen of England*, (New York: Dutton, 1967); J. B. Black. *The Reign of Elizabeth 1558–1603*, (Oxford: Clarendon Press, 1959).

Erik I Bloodax (ca. 905–954)

Erik reunified Norway after the death of his father and also attempted to reassert Norse control of Northumbria.

The son of HARALD I FAIRHAIR, king of Norway, Erik succeeded his father upon his death around 930. Harald had divided his kingdom among three of his sons, with Erik receiving the largest parcel as well as the designation of king. Erik wanted more, however, and sought to reunify the Norwegian lands under his sole rule. He went to war against his brothers, quickly defeating both of them, then ordering their deaths, thereby reunifying the Norwegian crown.

Erik's brothers were not alone in suffering the king's cruelty. Erik abused his subjects, who at length rose up in rebellion. The Norwegian nobles called on Haakon, another of Erik's brothers, who had been raised in England, to overthrow Erik and rule in his own right. Haakon handily deposed Erik, who fled to a decade-long exile beginning in 935.

In 948, Erik was invited to Northumbria by Aethelstan, a friend of Harald's, and was given charge of the region, ruling from York. He immediately imposed a cruel tyranny and was quickly driven out before he had governed a year.

Returning to Northumbria in 952, Erik again established himself as king. King Eadred of England, determined to wrest control of Northumbria from the Norse, opposed Erik. In 954, Eadred invaded Northumbria and deposed Erik, seizing the region for the English crown. Eadred then killed Erik at the Battle of Stainmore the same year, forever ending Norse rule in Northumbria.

Erik VII   [Erik of Pomerania, Erik of Denmark] (ca. 1381–ca. 1459)

King of the dominions of Denmark, Norway, and Sweden from 1397 to 1439, Erik VII attempted to establish a Scandanavian Baltic empire through a series of wars against the Holstein counts.

The son of Duke Vratislav VII of Pomerania, Erik was adopted by his great-aunt Margeret, queen of the three Scandinavian realms. In 1397, Erik ascended to Margeret's throne, but his ambitions soon outweighed his finances. Two wars with the counts of Holstein over the territory of Schleswig (1416–22 and 1426–35) strained the loyalty of his subjects, who were obliged to bear heavy war taxes. To make matters worse, Erik levied the bulk of these taxes on Norway and Sweden, thereby provoking protests of favoritism toward Denmark. A Hanseatic blockade in 1434 sparked a revolt among Swedish miners and brought about a call for a constitutional government. Erik steadfastly refused to yield power in a constiutional monarchy and was deposed, first in Denmark and Sweden (1439), and then in Norway (1442). Exiled to the tiny island of Gotland, the unbending former monarch made repeated attempts to restore himself to the throne. Finally, in 1449, he retired to Pomerania, where he died a decade later.

Erik XIV   (1533–1577)

King of Sweden from 1560 to 1568, Erik XIV sought to liberate the Swedish Baltic Sea trade from Denmark.

Born in Stockholm, Erik XIV was the son of King Gustav I Vasa. In 1560, Erik succeeded his father, and, the next year, instituted the Articles of Arboga, which limited the powers of his brothers and consolidated his own rule. Erik's expansionist reign focused on obtaining the port of Reval (Tallinn) and others on the Baltic. His success in Estonia immediately alarmed Denmark and Norway, which allied with Poland against Erik, thereby sparking the Seven Years' War of the North (1563–70).

The war was destined to outlast Erik. The monarch developed a paranoid fear of treason, which drove him to order the preemptive murder of leading members of the politically influential Sture family in 1567. Erik's adviser, Joran Persson, bore the blame for this crime and was imprisoned. After a short time, however, Erik freed Persson and restored him to power. The king further outraged the nobility by elevating his commoner mistress, Karin Mansdotter, to the status of queen.

In 1568, Duke John (later King John III) and his brother (who would subsequently reign as Charles IX) led a revolt against Erik and deposed him. The former king died in prison at Orbyhus, Sweden, nine years later.

Ermaneric   (r. ca. 350–ca. 375)

As ruler of the Ostrogothic Empire, Ermaneric extended his vast borders throughout the Ukraine, but he could not withstand the onslaught of the Huns.

The reputation of Ermaneric as a strong, courageous leader spread to neighboring peoples and caused him to be feared by all whom he opposed. This reputation helped him greatly in extending the Ostrogothic Empire, which, by the time of his death, stretched south from the headwaters of the Volga and Dnieper rivers and the Pripet marshes; west from the Don; east from the Dniester River; and north from the Black Sea, encompassing all of what is now the Ukraine.

Ermaneric's reputation was built not only on his strength and courage, but also his cruelty, which was awakened in the face of opposition or betrayal. For example, when, early in his reign, one of his vassals crossed him, Ermaneric had the man's wife quartered—tying her between two horses, then driving them in opposite directions, tearing her to pieces.

Neither the fearsome reputation nor the military might of Ermaneric was enough to suppress the great invasion of the Huns from the East in 370. After conquering eastern Europe, the Huns moved against the Ostrogoths, who, after holding the horde off for a time, were overrun. Distraught over his inability to defeat the Huns, Ermaneric took his own life about 375.

Esarhaddon   (r. 680–669 B.C.)

King of Assyria, Esarhaddon conquered Egypt in 671 B.C.

Descended from SARGON II, Esarhaddon was the younger son of the mighty SENNACHERIB. Although he was a second son, he was proclaimed successor to the throne even before Sennacherib died. The king appointed Esarhaddon to the post of governor of Babylon after that city fell to Sennacherib. While Esarhaddon was serving there, word reached him that his father had been murdered by one or more of his other sons, presumably as the first step in a rebellion. Esarhaddon hurriedly marched back from

Ezzelino III da Romano   95

Babylon and faced down the rebels at Hanigalbat in western Assyria. There most of the rebellious soldiers defected to him, whereupon their leaders fled. Esarhaddon marched on to Nineveh and claimed the throne of his father unopposed.

His kingdom was not quiet for long, however. A Chaldean tribe exploited the destabilizing effect of the revolt to attack the Assyrian governor at Ur. Esarhaddon dispatched a force to capture the offending Chaldean chief, who fled in search of asylum with the king of Elam. That ruler responded by executing the rebel. The chief's brother journeyed to Esarhaddon in Assyria and pledged his loyalty to the Assyrian ruler. The mercy Esarhaddon showed this man was likewise extended to all the cities of northern Babylonia, which had been ravaged by Sennacherib. Esarhaddon granted them special favors and was careful to restore to their rightful owners any lands that Sennacherib had appropriated.

When Scythians menaced his northern boundaries, Esarhaddon made a marriage alliance with that people. He did not fare so well against another northern tribe, the Cimmerians, and finally lost to them the provinces of Cilicia and Tabal.

At first, his campaign against Egypt was also prosecuted with disappointing results. Esarhaddon moved against Egypt in 675 when that nation incited the revolt of Tyre. It was not until 671 B.C., however, that he was able to capture the important city of Memphis, forcing King Taharqa to flee. Esarhaddon then declared himself king of Egypt.

Taharqa was not completely out of the picture, however. He gathered about him a large following and rebelled against Assyrian domination. Esarhaddon marched to meet the new revolt, but died enroute in 669.

Ethelred II the Unready   [Aethelred Unraed] (968?–1016)

Ethelred II was a vicious and incompetent ruler who brought great misery upon the English.

Ethelred's epithet—"the Unready"—is a corruption of the original late Old English *unraed*, meaning "evil counsel." However, either meaning aptly describes this feeble and inept king.

The son of King Edgar, Ethelred came to the throne following the assassination of his half-brother King Edward the Martyr in March 978. It was widely believed that Ethelred was complicitous in the murder, and, therefore, he began his reign under a very dark cloud. During this period, England was periodically ravaged by invading Danes. Ethelred proved wholly incapable of mounting an effective defense against the especially devastating invasion of 980. Having failed militarily, the king clumsily attempted

A 19th-century conception of the kind of troops Ethelred II and other Anglo-Saxon leaders commanded in the 10th century. (From Charlotte M. Yonge, Pictorial History of the World's Great Nations, *1882)*

to buy off the invaders, a display of weakness that only served to whet their appetite for further destruction.

By the opening of the 11th century, it was apparent that the Danes, who had begun to settle in towns, had come to England to stay. The wise course would have been to accept and to assimilate them, but Ethelred instead launched a massacre against the Danish settlers on November 13, 1002. This touched off additional invasions year after year until 1013, when the Danish monarch Sweyn I was accepted as king of England and Ethelred was sent scurrying to exile in Normandy.

Sweyn's reign lasted less than a year. He died in February 1014, and Ethelred's advisers beckoned the erstwhile king back to the English throne on condition that he promise to address the people's many grievances. No sooner did he return to England than the invasions from the north resumed, led by Sweyn's son Canute. Ethelred II died in London on April 23, 1016, leaving his son Edmund II Ironside to rule briefly during the balance of 1016 and another, more famous son to assume the throne as Edward the Confessor from 1042 to 1066.

Ezzelino III da Romano   (1194–1259)

The feudal mayor of Verona and other Italian states, Ezzelino allied himself with Holy Roman Emperor FREDERICK II (1194–1250) and eventually controlled much of northeast Italy.

Born into the Italian nobility on April 25, 1194, Ezzelino would not begin gathering his vast Italian holdings until he was almost 30. In 1223, his father gave him the city of Trevignano, and Ezzelino quickly garnered the support of other nobles, who helped him seize Verona in 1225. By 1226, he had amassed enough power to become the *podestà*, feudal mayor, of Verona.

That same year, Ezzelino joined the Lombard League in its struggle against Holy Roman Emperor Frederick II. He soon separated from the League, however, and resigned as *podesta* of Verona in 1230. After a short time, Ezzelino became allied with Frederick and retook Verona in 1232. League allies in Mantua, Padua, and Brescia, all of which bordered Verona, furious over Ezzelino's withdrawal and subsequent alliance with Frederick, threatened Ezzelino's position in Verona. Frederick was forced to send troops into the city in May 1236 to assure Ezzelino's continued presence in the area.

With the full backing of Frederick, Ezzelino now expanded rapidly into northern Italy and earned himself a much-deserved reputation for ruthless cruelty. In November 1236, he led imperial troops on a raid of Vicenza and sacked the town. Within a few months, he took Padua and visited similar devastation on it. In 1237, Frederick and the League met at the Battle of Cortenuova, and the Lombards were defeated. As a reward for his support, Ezzelino was given Frederick's daughter in marriage. Armed with this final measure of support from the emperor, Ez-

zelino began a purge of all his enemies, savagely murdering all who had ever opposed him. In the process of this purge, he continued to acquire territory: In 1247 he took Cremona, and in 1250 he conquered Belluno.

The death of Frederick in 1250 left Ezzelino without his most powerful ally, and he was now exposed to the retribution of the many enemies he had made. Freed of Frederick's imperial yoke, Pope Innocent IV quickly excommunicated Ezzelino as a vicious heretic and called for a crusade against him. Innocent was succeeded by Alexander IV, who went a step further in December 1255 by calling on Philip of Ravenna to lead an army against Ezzelino.

Philip's army retook Padua from Ezzelino in June 1256 while Ezzelino was away wreaking havoc in Mantua. Ezzelino retaliated by taking Brescia in 1258, savaging the town, and taking Philip himself prisoner at the Battle of Gambara. Hoping to break the alliance against him, Ezzelino went on the offensive, invading Milan in 1259. However, he was met at Cassano by a great army, defeated, wounded, and captured. Offered food and medical aid by his captors, he refused and died within four days, on October 1, 1259.

F

Fabius Maximus Cunctator Quintus (d. 203 B.C.)

This Roman dictator effectively employed a cautious strategy of delaying tactics against Hannibal's invasion of Rome. In his own time, he was given the epithet "Cunctator"—delayer—and in later ages the term "Fabianism" came to denote a policy of cautious change.

Fabius served Rome in various capacities as a statesman and a military commander. He was consul in 233 and 228 B.C. and censor in 230. He was elected dictator in 217 after Hannibal's devastating victory over Roman forces at Lake Trasimene. Fabius' strategy was to wage a war of attrition against the invaders rather than attempt to annihilate them by direct military action. Such a strategy exacted a heavy price in Roman pride and in the devastation suffered in the occupied territories. Fabius managed to draw Hannibal's forces into hill country, where cavalry attack was impossible. He cut off the invaders' lines of supply and sniped at Hannibal's army piecemeal.

Despite the painstaking success of Fabius' strategy, the people voted to divide command of the Roman forces between the more conventionally aggressive general Minucius and Fabius. Fabius allowed Hannibal to wreak havoc on Campania, believing that a scorched-earth policy would eventually exhaust him. However, impatient, even outraged by the fate of this region, the Romans allowed Fabius' term as dictator to lapse and then staged an all-out attack against Hannibal, who dealt the legions a disastrous defeat at Cannae in 216. After this, Rome adopted the Fabian approach once again, and Fabius was elected consul for a third and fourth term, in 215 and 214. By 209, Fabius succeeded in retaking Tarentum (Taranto) from Hannibal, whose forces had held it for three years.

Always an advocate of conservative and defense-oriented military policy, Fabius unsuccessfully opposed the plan of Publius Cornelius Scipio to take the war to Hannibal by aggressively invading Africa.

Ferdinand I (1861–1948)

The first ruler of fully independent Bulgaria, Ferdinand legitimated the small Balkan country through several political alliances, a royal marriage alliance, and the birth of an heir.

Born the youngest son of Prince Augustus I of Saxe-Coburg on February 26, 1861, Ferdinand succeeded Alexander I—who had abdicated the previous year—as prince of Bulgaria on July 7, 1887. As prince of Bulgaria, Ferdinand was early on subject to overbearing influence from his brutally repressive prime minister, Stefan Stambolov, but after Stambolov fell from power in 1894, Ferdinand mastered national affairs on his own.

Ferdinand's immediate goal was to gain greater international recognition for Bulgaria. In April 1893, he married the Bourbon princess Maria Louisa of Parma, who bore him a son and heir, Boris. Allied by marriage with one of Europe's leading families and possessing a legitimate heir, Bulgaria had taken an important step toward recognition by the international community. Complete acceptance came in 1896, when Boris was received into the Greek Orthodox Church, thereby prompting Russia to seek immediate rapprochement with Bulgaria.

Now that he had strengthened Bulgaria's position internationally, Ferdinand declared the nation fully independent from the Ottoman Empire on October 5, 1908, on the eve of Austria-Hungary's annexation of Bosnia-Hercegovina, and assumed an imperial title. Hoping to get a piece of the crumbling Ottoman Empire and assert his country's supremacy in the Balkans, Ferdinand urged the formation of the Balkan League in 1912 among Serbia, Greece, and Montenegro. This sparked the First Balkan War, from October 1912–May 1913. The League emerged victorious, but the ensuing quarrel over Macedonia led to its dissolution and Bulgaria's invasion of Serbia and Greece in the Second Balkan War, June–July 1913, which resulted in Bulgaria's abject defeat.

The breakup of the Balkan coalition largely dictated Ferdinand's alliances leading up to World War I. Hoping to gain control of Macedonia and revenge over Serbia and Greece, Ferdinand entered the war on the side of Germany and Austria-Hungary in October 1915. With the defeat of the Central Powers in 1918, Ferdinand was forced to abdicate in favor of his son Boris in October 1918. He retired to Coburg, where he died September 10, 1948.

Ferdinand I (1423–1494)

This Neapolitan monarch, continually under fire from all sides during his reign, ruthlessly suppressed internal dissent by arrests and executions.

Ferdinand was the illegitimate son of Alfonso V of Aragon, who became king of Naples in 1442. Upon his accession, Alfonso legitimated Ferdinand, designating him heir. Accordingly, on Alfonso's death in 1458, Ferdinand assumed the throne of Naples.

He was faced with trouble almost immediately. The Neapolitan barons opposed Ferdinand from the outset and attempted to replace him. They frequently curried favor with the French, and in 1458 they supported René of Anjou, and later his son John, in a bid to overthrow Ferdinand. This revolt lasted until 1464, when Ferdinand finally succeeded in putting down the rebellion. Once he was victorious over the barons, he exacted a ruthless revenge against them, confiscating property, arresting and imprisoning many, and executing many more. Ferdinand's efforts to suppress the barons led to another revolt in 1485; this time, the barons sought to replace Ferdinand with either René II of Lorraine or Frederick, Ferdinand's own son. Again, the king suppressed the revolt, and again he resorted to brutal retaliation.

In addition to internal threats, Ferdinand was also faced with the expansionist program of the Italian princes and the Ottoman Empire. In 1480, Lorenzo de' Medici allied Florence with the papacy and moved against Ferdinand, but Ferdinand defeated the two that same year, granting generous peace terms to Florence. Also in 1480, the Turks invaded the southern Italian port of Otranto. With financial assistance from Florence—in accordance with the peace agreement—Ferdinand pushed the Turks out of Otranto in 1481.

Faced with repeated incursions against his rule, Ferdinand was never able to consolidate his power. Only his death on January 25, 1494, saved him from witnessing the alliance of Ludovico SFORZA and King CHARLES VIII and the French invasion of Naples in 1495.

Ferdinand II the Catholic (1452–1516)

Regarded by some as the monarch who brought unity to Spain, Ferdinand has also been condemned for policies of oppression and for his vigorous support of the Inquisition.

Ferdinand II was born on March 10, 1452, in Sos, Aragón, the son of John II of Aragón and Juana Enriquez. To quell internecine strife, John II named Ferdinand heir apparent in 1461, making him governor of all his realms. In 1466, John—like his wife, of Castilian origin—made Ferdinand king of Sicily in an effort to groom him for placement in the court of Castile. A spirited youth, Ferdinand exhibited his military prowess in 1468 during the Catalonian Wars and in the same year revealed his romantic prowess

as well, fathering two children out of wedlock, Alfonso of Aragón (who became archbishop of Zaragoza) and Juana of Aragón, who became insane at an early age, earning the epithet La Loca, "The Mad." The next year, he married ISABELLA of Castile, thereby making possible the long-cherished union of the kingdoms of Aragón and Castile.

The process of unifying the two kingdoms was not an easy one, however, and Ferdinand was often compelled to play the interests of one side against the other, nimbly garnering support in one court then in the other, while also traveling widely throughout Castile and Aragón. During this period, he fathered John, his heir apparent, in 1478, Catalina, who as Catherine of Aragón became the first wife of England's Henry VIII, and Maria. He also fathered at least two more illegitimate daughters in the course of his travels.

During the middle to late 1470s, Ferdinand worked to consolidate his hold over both Aragón and Castile, remaking the Castilian political structure along the lines of that in force in Aragón. Most sweeping of the king's reforms was a ban on all religions except Catholicism and the establishment of the Spanish Inquisition in 1478 to ensure compliance with religious uniformity. The Inquisition reached a climax in 1492 with the expulsion of the Jews from Spain. This policy of intolerance, which sanctioned gross injustice, persecution, torture, and killing in the name of orthodoxy, was not the product of Ferdinand's religious zeal alone. Rather, by making the Catholic church more powerful and securing its full support, Ferdinand successfully sought to solidify his own power base.

He needed all the support he could get; for, from 1482 to 1492, he was engaged in an ultimately successful but time-consuming and arduous campaign to subdue and conquer Granada, the last remaining Moorish stronghold in Spain. During this period, he continued to travel widely throughout his realms, ascertaining directly the issues and concerns that occupied his people. In a spirit of triumph following the capitulation of Granada in 1492, Ferdinand was persuaded to grant his support of the first of Christopher Columbus' voyages to the New World. He secured a papal treaty that in effect divided the New World between Spain and Portugal, thereby establishing the foundation of his nation's colonial empire.

The conquest of Granada and the launching of a colonial empire marked the high point of Ferdinand's reign. In 1493, he suffered a painful wound in battle at Barcelona. During this period as well, his heir apparent and his eldest daughter both died, even as the first signs of madness began to appear in Juana. Finally, in 1504, his powerful and beloved consort, Isabella, died. Ferdinand had little choice other than to make another politically advantageous marriage, and he wed Germaine de Foix, niece of the king of France, in October 1505. He continued to pursue a policy of expansion, both with regard to colonies and by annexing to Castile the kingdom of Navarre in 1512.

From 1513 to the beginning of 1516, Ferdinand's health steadily deteriorated, and he finally succumbed during a trip to Granada on January 23, 1516.

Further Reading: William Hickling Prescott. *History of the Reign of Ferdinand and Isabella, the Catholic, of Spain* (Philadelphia: Lippincott, 1872).

Ferdinand II (1578–1637)

As Holy Roman Emperor, Ferdinand was fanatical in his promotion of the Catholic Counter-Reformation and thereby incited the Thirty Years' War.

Born in Graz, Austria, to Archduke Charles on July 9, 1578, Ferdinand II was raised and educated during the Protestant Reformation by Jesuit priests, who groomed him to be the zealous Catholic ruler he did indeed become. By 1596, Ferdinand had taken over his hereditary lands and began his ruthless persecution of the Protestants. In Styria, he expelled all Protestant preachers and lay people, ordering all others to convert to Catholicism or suffer exile.

The Bohemian Diet recognized Ferdinand as king of Bohemia in 1617 and, the following year, he was elected king of Hungary as well. Fearing now that holding sway over the two realms would enable Ferdinand essentially to outlaw Protestantism, the mostly Protestant Diet of Bohemia deposed Ferdinand in Bohemia and named Frederick V, Elector of the Palatinate, as king. Partisans of Ferdinand rioted in the so-called Defenestration of Prague on May 23, 1618, hurling two Protestant governors to their deaths from a 70-foot-high palace window. In response, Protestant rebels prepared for war against Ferdinand, and the stage was set for the Thirty Years' War.

After the death of his two cousins, Ferdinand was named Holy Roman Emperor in 1619 and became the dominant political leader of Catholicism. He now fully intended to use his position to expunge Protestantism from Europe.

With support from various Catholic heads of state, especially in Spain and Poland, Ferdinand unleashed his army on the Protestants under Frederick V of the Palatinate at the Battle of the White Mountain on November 8, 1620. The rebels were annihilated, and Bohemia lay at Ferdinand's feet. He

forcibly Catholicized the nation, confiscating all Protestant land and stripping the Diet of all power. Subjects were offered the option of converting or facing exile or execution.

With continued successes in the field under the direction of his general Albrecht von Wallenstein, Ferdinand and his forces soon occupied the Palatinate, Saxony, Silesia, Schleswig, Holstein, and Moravia. The emperor was now in a position to dictate a lasting peace that would devastate the Protestants. Accordingly, in 1629, Ferdinand issued the Edict of Restitution by which he confiscated all lands secularized since 1552 and returned them to the Catholic church.

Ferdinand's greed on behalf of the church was insatiable and cost his cause heavily. Twice he might have ended the war on terms crippling to the Protestants, but he chose to fight on in the hope of more and more gains. When the Swedes scored victories against him in 1630, Ferdinand was forced by the electors—now wary of his power and weary of continual combat—to dismiss Wallenstein, who had become the virtual mainstay of his power. Ferdinand consented to a second dismissal in 1634 and acquiesced in Wallenstein's assassination.

In 1635, with the alliance of France and Sweden as protectors of the Protestants, Ferdinand's chance for domination ended. His son Ferdinand III succeeded him after his death on Februrary 15, 1637. The war he had created would last another 11 bloody and ruinous years.

Further Reading: Cicely V. Wedgwood. *The Thirty Years' War,* (Garden City, New York: Doubleday, 1961); H. G. Koenigsberger. *The Habsburgs and Europe, 1516–1660,* (Ithaca, New York: Cornell University Press, 1971).

Fonseca, Manuel Deodoro da (1827–1892)

The first president of Brazil, Fonseca was also the leader of the military junta that overthrew Emperor Dom Pedro II.

A career military man, Manuel Deodoro da Fonseca was born August 5, 1827, in Alagoas, Brazil, which he left to attend the Brazilian military academy. When war with Paraguay broke out in 1864, Fonseca distinguished himself through the war's end in 1870. In 1887, he became president of the Military Club, which meant that he was virtual leader of the entire Brazilian military establishment. Although conservative in nature and both professionally and personally loyal to Brazil's emperor Pedro II, Fonseca felt obligated as a professional soldier to oppose the ruthless acts of despotism and upheld the right of his officers to express their political opinions.

When King Pedro denounced Fonseca and declared him insubordinate, Fonseca formally withdrew his loyalty and led a revolt against him on November 15, 1889, toppling the emperor and establishing the Republic of Brazil. Fonseca served as provisional head of state, separating church and state and convening and presiding over a constituent assembly in 1891. The assembly, largely controlled by the generals, elected him president in February. He then dismissed the newly convened Congress, which prompted a naval revolt. Fonseca resigned on November 23, 1891, after only nine months in office. He died exactly nine months later in Rio de Janeiro.

Foscari, Francesco   (ca. 1373–1457)

Foscari, doge of Venice, kept the city-state at war with Milan, finally ruining the Venetian economy and the army.

Born to a wealthy family, Francesco Foscari was named head of the ruling body of Venice, the Council of Forty, in 1401, at the height of Venice's wars for territorial expansion. Four years later, he was named head of the Council of Ten, which replaced the Council of Forty in an effort to maintain tighter control over the city. In 1423, Foscari was elected doge of the city and promptly made an alliance with Florence against the duke of Milan, Filippo Maria Visconti.

The Venetian armies marched into Brescia and conquered it in 1426, concluding a peace shortly thereafter. Foscari again attacked Milan in 1431, but this war was inconclusive and ended with the Peace of Ferrara in 1433. Hoping to gain an advantage over Milan before again renewing hostilities, Foscari invaded Bologna in 1441, taking Ravenna in the process and tipping the balance of Italian power in his favor.

Zealot-like, Foscari again attacked Milan in 1443. By 1446, the Venetians crossed the Adda River and were in sight of Milan, having taken much territory. Foscari continued to prosecute the war even after Filippo Maria died in 1447. He had essentially razed northern Italy, yet had not emerged as the clear victor. In 1454, the Peace of Lodi ended the hostilities and formed the Italian League of Venice, Florence and Milan to establish a balance of power.

Because he was so intent on punishing Milan, Foscari had neglected Venice's eastern territory, and Constantinople had fallen to the Turks in 1453. This devastated what was left of Venetian trade by cutting off access to the East. Foscari's opponents now sought to depose him, accusing him of murdering the Admiral Piero Loredan and unjustly banishing his son for treason. These accusations forced him to resign from the Council of Ten in October 1457. He died eight days later.

Francis I (of the Two Sicilies)   (1777–1830)

King of the Two Sicilies from 1825 to 1830, Francis I led a reactionary regime that brutally restrained an internal revolution of 1828 in Cilento.

Francis I was the son of Ferdinand I and Maria Carolina of Austria. Of a liberal mind in his youth, Francis renounced his idealism after ascending the throne in 1825. Indeed, his reign was virulently reactionary. Francis dissolved the National Guard and enlisted Austria's support in a campaign of extermination directed against the revolutionary opposition, chiefly in Cilento. Francis I died in Arco, Italy, on December 27, 1894.

Francis Joseph   [Franz Josef] (1830–1916)

Francis Joseph's 68-year reign as Hapsburg emperor of Austria (1848–1916) and king of the dual monarchy of Austria-Hungary (1867–1916) was overshadowed by his 1914 ultimatum to Serbia, which sparked World War I.

Born on August 18, 1830, Francis Joseph was the son of Archduke Francis Charles and grandson of Holy Roman Emperor—and emperor of Austria—Francis II. Following the abdication of his childless uncle, the Austrian emperor Ferdinand I, in the revolution-torn year of 1848, Francis Joseph was crowned on December 2, 1848, at Olmütz. He married Duchess Elizabeth of Bavaria in 1854.

Francis Joseph's reign was characterized by its formality and rigidness. A firm believer in divine right and the traditions of the monarchy, Francis Joseph considered himself—in later years—the last monarch of the old school.

During the first decade of his reign, Francis Joseph commanded one of the largest empires in continental Europe. By 1859, however, Austria was becoming overshadowed by Prussia under the leadership of Otto von Bismarck, and its status as a German power was diminished, as was its influence in Italy. As nationalist feeling swept Europe, Francis Joseph compromised with Hungary in 1867, agreeing to a dual monarchy in which the nations of Austria and Hungary were to be considered equal partners.

In 1873, Francis Joseph participated in the League of Three Emperors, which sought to deal with the troubles in the strife-torn Balkans. Francis Joseph was committed to a peaceful solution in the Balkans, rightly fearing conflict with the Russians, but he was operating according to the outworn principles of autocratic diplomacy—the notion that the fate of nations was determined by royal heads of state bound in friendship and familial relationships. Despite the league, the Balkan situation remained unresolved. Inclined toward peace, Francis Joseph, backed by a so-called "blank check" from the bellicose German

Kaiser WILHELM II, nevertheless yielded to the counsel of his sinister foreign minister, Count Leopold Berchtold, and issued a war ultimatum to Serbia following the assassination of his heir, Archduke Francis Ferdinand, on June 28, 1914, in Sarajevo. It was this ultimatum that ignited World War I.

As historians have frequently pointed out, World War I effectively marked the end of the old order in Europe. Perhaps fittingly, the old emperor died on November 21, 1916, in the third year of the war.

Suggested Reading: Joseph Redlich. *Emperor Francis Joseph of Austria* (New York: Macmillan, 1929)

Franco (-Bahamonde), Francisco (Paulino Hermenegildo Teódulo)   (1892–1975)

Generalissimo Francisco Franco led the Nationalist forces in the Spanish Civil War (1936–39), ruling Spain as dictator until his death in 1975.

Born on December 4, 1892, in El Ferrol, Franco enrolled in the Toledo Academia de Infantería in 1907 and was commissioned second lieutenant in 1910. His service in a 1912 war against Morocco earned him a reputation as an able and courageous young officer and led to very rapid promotion. By 1920 he was deputy commander of the Spanish Foreign Legion in Morocco and served with these forces during the Riff Rebellion of Abd-el-Krim (1921–26). In 1923, he was promoted to full commander of the Foreign Legion, and in 1925 led a brilliant assault on Alhucemas Bay, which eventually brought Spanish victory in the Riff conflict.

Franco's spectacular performance garnered a promotion in 1926 as Spain's youngest brigadier general. Two years later, he was given the influential post of director of the Academia General Militar at Saragossa during the dictatorship of General José Antonio PRIMO DE RIVERA. Franco served in this capacity until 1931, when Republican forces, having overthrown the monarchy, accused him of monarchist sympathies.

There followed a confused and turbulent period on the eve of the Spanish Civil War, during which Franco, transferred to duty in the Balearic Islands from 1931 to 1934, managed to steer clear of the military's many conspiracies against the new republic. After returning to suppress a 1934 miners' revolt in Asturias, Franco earned the respect of the conservative right wing and the hatred of the left. With the conservatives in ascendency, he was named chief of the general staff in 1935. But the following year, the left-wing Popular Front gained a majority in the elections, and Franco was effectively exiled to a command in the Canary Islands. From this position, however, he participated in a military and conserva-

tive conspiracy that erupted, on July 18, 1936, into the Spanish Civil War.

Franco flew to Morocco, took over the Spanish Foreign Legion garrison there, and airlifted a large contingent of it to Spain later in the month. During July and August, Franco led a motorized advance on Madrid, where government forces repulsed him during September and October. By this time, the country was divided between Loyalist and Nationalist territories. On September 29, 1936, the Nationalists established their own government, with Franco as head of state. In April 1937, Franco became head of the Falange Party as, slowly and inexorably, with other aid of Fascist Italy and Nazi Germany, the Nationalists defeated the Loyalists. After the fall of Madrid on March 28, 1939, the Spanish Civil War ended, and Franco became de facto dictator of Spain.

As a politician and a military strategist, Franco was cautious and methodical. Following victory in the civil war, he now proved himself ruthless as he outlawed political parties and ordered the execution or imprisonment of many thousands of Loyalists. During World War II, Franco did not repay the support he had received from Germany by joining the Axis. Instead, he kept Spain officially neutral, although it was always clear where his allegiance lay, and he not only sent workers to Germany, but created a volunteer Blue Division to fight for the Germans on the Russian front. As the tide of the war clearly turned against Germany, the pragmatic Franco enforced a more genuine neutrality. He also deemed it prudent to back down somewhat from absolute dictatorship, promulgating the Fuero de los Españoles (a kind of bill of rights) in July 1945. By referendum in 1947, he agreed to reorganize the government as a monarchy, with himself as regent endowed with the power to choose the next king.

In the postwar years, Franco generally moderated his brutal Fascist image into an anti-Communist stance more palatable to western Europe and the United States. In 1953, at the height of the Cold War, he concluded an agreement permitting the United States to establish and maintain certain military bases in Spain. Franco's trend toward moderation increased his nation's economic and political contacts with other countries of the West, and this, in turn, encouraged further liberalization. In 1955, Spain joined the United Nations and pulled out of northern Morocco the next year.

The 1960s brought renewed unrest in Spain, from students, workers, clergymen, and Basque and Catalan separatists, to which Franco responded by somewhat reversing his drift toward greater liberalism. In July 1969, he chose Juan Carlos de Bourbon, grandson of Alfonso XIII, as heir to the throne. After a long illness, Franco died on November 20, 1975.

Further Reading: Brian Crozier. *Franco: A Biographical History* (Boston: Little, Brown, 1967); Alan Lloyd. *Franco* (Garden City, N.Y.: Doubleday, 1969); J. W. D. Trythall. *El Caudillo: A Political Biography of Franco* (New York: McGraw-Hill, 1970).

Frederick I   [Frederick Barbarossa] (ca. 1123– 1190)

Called Barbarossa because of his red beard and considered the most important German emperor after CHARLEMAGNE, Frederick I did much to unite under central imperial rule the fractious collection of dukedoms and principalities that made up early medieval Germany.

Frederick was the eldest son of the duke of Swabia, Frederick II of Hohenstaufen. The Germany into which he had been born was far less a nation than it was a loose agglomeration of competitive, often warring realms ruled by dukes and princes who did elect in common an emperor, but invested in him little real authority. After his father's death in 1147, Frederick became duke of Swabia and followed his uncle, Emperor Conrad III, on the Second Crusade, 1148–49, which proved an abortive failure. Conrad died in 1152, and Frederick, whom his uncle had anointed his successor, was elected emperor at Frankfurt-am-Main on March 4, 1152.

The choice of Frederick was, from the start, a momentous one. Many of the dukes and princes of Germany realized that, disunited, they were at the mercy of threats posed by Danes, Norsemen, Poles, Magyars, and others. The Hohenstaufens—also known as the Waiblingen—and the Welfs were the most powerful families in Germany, and they were perpetually at war with one another. Frederick was a Hohenstaufen, but he was related on his mother's side to the Welfs. His election brought to the imperial throne a union of the two hostile bloodlines.

But Frederick resolved to do far more than bring two rival families together. Germany was plagued not only by internecine disputes, but by a continual conflict between the papal and the German thrones. Since the time of Charlemagne, whom the pope had crowned emperor of the West, a succession of popes asserted their domination over the German monarchs. Frederick sought to end this situation by cleaving to the doctrine of rule by divine right. It was not, he declared, the pope who *conferred* imperial power, but God himself directly; the pope merely *confirmed* God's will.

Armed with this doctrine and at least partial German unity, Frederick sought to strengthen German imperial power further by expanding it into Italy and Burgundy. Accordingly, he invaded Italy in 1144, the first of six such incursions by which he subjugated many of the northern Italian cities by assigning his royal governors *(podestas)* to preside over them. In 1155, he rescued Pope Eugenius from a mob stirred to riot by the religious fanatic Arnold of Brescia. Frederick caused Arnold's execution, but he also aroused the pope's suspicions by refusing to perform the traditional act of submission—holding the pope's stirrup as he dismounted his horse. Tension between emperor and pope intensified after Hadrian (Adrian) IV succeeded to the papacy and asserted that it was the pontiff who had conferred the crown upon Frederick. The German responded by publishing a circular in which he claimed rule by divine right and election of the princes.

Before making the second of his six invasions of Italy in 1158, Frederick bolstered his position at home in Germany by mending fences with his powerful Welf kinsman, Duke Henry the Lion, restoring to him Bavaria, which his uncle Conrad had seized. At the same time, to keep Henry from becoming too strong, he reinforced the power of Henry's rival, Albert the Bear, margrave of Brandenberg. Frederick also set about ruthlessly suppressing feuds among lesser rival lords throughout the German realm, usually by capturing the offending warlord and causing his execution. On June 9, 1156, he also married Beatrice of Burgundy, thereby positioning himself to claim the Burgundian throne.

In June of 1158, Frederick took Milan and other northern Italian cities. He convened the diet of Roncaglia in November, effectively asserting his royal authority over Italy and appointing a host of royal officers to administer the country. The troublesome Pope Hadrian IV died in 1159, and Alexander III replaced him. Frederick, mistrusting Alexander, opposed him by securing the election of an anti-pope, Victor IV, whereupon Alexander excommunicated Frederick in March 1160, Milan rebelled against German rule, and Frederick responded by virtually destroying the city.

The emperor returned to Germany in 1162, but Alexander III, having taken refuge in France, encouraged the Lombards to rebel against the German administration and the anti-pope. Victor IV died in 1164, and Frederick secured the election of another anti-pope, Paschel III. He entered Italy again in October 1166, this time attacking Rome itself, to which Alexander had returned. When the city fell, Alexander fled to Sicily, and Frederick enthroned his elected anti-pope. At the moment of this triumph, however, Frederick's army was visited by retribution in the form of the plague. The oppressed cities of Lombardy exploited Frederick's present weakness by forming the Lombard League, and Frederick, much of his army sick, dying, or dead, was forced to beat a retreat to Germany in the spring of 1168.

During the next half-dozen years, Frederick concentrated operations in Germany and on the eastern frontiers, installing German governments in Bohemia, Hungary, and part of Poland, subduing there the rebellious Duke Boleslav, known as Curly-Hair. Frederick also made diplomatic advances, solidifying cordial relations with the Byzantine Empire, France, and England. By 1174, he was ready for another invasion of Italy, intending to defeat the Lombard League. He sought aid from Henry the Lion, who refused, but he mounted the expedition nevertheless, meeting armies of the League at Legnano on May 29, 1176. Here Frederick suffered a disastrous defeat, as Italian spearmen successfully defended against his advancing cavalry and enabled a devastating counterattack.

Frederick realized that it was time to make peace with Alexander, concluding a treaty with him in June 1177 and a six-year truce with the Lombard League shortly afterward. Now he was free to return to Germany, where he exacted vengeance upon Henry the Lion by stripping him of all of his fiefdoms in 1179, giving the whole of Bavaria to Otto of Wittelsbach. In 1183, Frederick concluded a lasting peace with the Lombard League, relinquishing certain of his Italian gains. He then betrothed his eldest son, Henry, to Constance, heiress to the Norman kingdom of Sicily, in 1184. The resulting alliance alarmed the papacy, and a growing dispute over the Tuscan lands of Countess Matilda created additional friction. But, reigning over a Germany united to a degree hitherto unknown, Frederick was clearly a Holy Roman Emperor to be reckoned with. Instead of pushing for war against him, Pope Clement III prevailed upon the aging monarch to lead a new Crusade to Palestine. This Frederick did willingly, and, almost 70 years old, embarked on his last great military adventure.

In May 1189, he assembled an army at Regensburg and advanced into Byzantine territory. Although Byzantine emperor Isaac II Angelus had granted his army safe conduct, his camp was repeatedly harassed by guerrillas, and the population fled before his advance, taking all food and provisions with them. Frederick managed at length to negotiate the remainder of his passage through this territory and reached the empire of the Seljuk Turks in May of 1190. The sultan, Kilidsh Arslan, pledged his support, but promptly reneged and attacked. It was a greatly reduced force of only some 600 nearly starving knights that reached the Seljuk capital of Iconium. Despite their condition and inferiority of numbers, Frederick's small force took the capital in June, forced the sultan's surrender, and secured supplies from him. On June 10, 1190, however, while he either crossed the River Saleph or sought in it relief from the intense heat, Frederick Barbarossa drowned. The ill-fated Crusade quickly dissolved, and the emperor's disheartened knights returned to Germany.

Further Reading: Peter Munz. *Frederick Barbarossa* (Ithaca, New York: Cornell University Press, 1969); Otto of Freising. *The Deeds of Frederick Barbarossa,* translated by C. C. Mierow (New York: Columbia University Press, 1953).

Frederick II (1194–1250)

As Holy Roman Emperor, king of Sicily, Jerusalem, and Germany, Frederick II dominated his age through his expansionist policies and his epochal struggles with the papacy.

A Hohenstaufen, grandson of FREDERICK I BARBAROSSA, Frederick II was elected king at the age of two by the German princes at Frankfurt in 1196. His father, Henry, died the following year, and Frederick was crowned king of Sicily in May 1198. With Frederick placed under the regency of Pope INNOCENT III, Sicily languished for many years in near-anarchy until Frederick was declared of age in December of 1208 and began to reign in his own right. The following year he married Constance of Aragón, whose dowry consisted of an order of knights whom Frederick used to gain control of his chaotic kingdom.

As king of Sicily, Frederick II managed to regain territories lost during his youth. In 1211, a series of events in Germany deposed the reigning King Otto IV. Leaving his year-old son Henry VII as king of Sicily, Frederick left for Germany, which he quickly conquered, gaining election as king in December 1212. Concluding an alliance with France, he defeated Otto once and for all at the Battle of Bouvines in July 1214.

In 1220, Henry VII, then nine years old, was elected king by the German princes. This abrogated Frederick's promise to the pope that Sicily and Germany would remain separate kingdoms. Frederick exonerated himself with Pope Honorius III in part by pledging to lead future crusades into the Holy Land, and on November 20, 1220, Honorius crowned Frederick II Holy Roman Emperor at St. Peter's in Rome.

As emperor, Frederick II established a civil service and founded the first European state university in Naples. He consolidated rule in Sicily and successfully asserted imperial authority over warring baronial interests. Frederick built a great chain of castles and border fortresses, and he expanded his kingdom's navy and merchant fleet. Under Frederick, much trade and commerce were brought under state control.

In 1227, Frederick prepared for a crusade to the Holy Land, but an epidemic broke out, and he was forced to abort the expedition. The new pope, Gregory IX, deemed this a breach of Frederick's promise and excommunicated him. Despite this, Frederick did set sail for the Holy Land the following year and, after several weeks of campaigning, forced Sultan al-Kamil of Egypt to the negotiating table. Frederick wrested from him Jerusalem, Bethlehem, and Nazareth. In 1229, Frederick II—although excommunicated—crowned himself king of Jerusalem at the Church of the Holy Sepulchre. Frederick now saw himself as a new David, a messiah even, and issued a manifesto comparing himself to Jesus Christ.

While Frederick was in the Holy Land, papal forces invaded Sicily. Frederick managed to reconquer the lost territory, but, in a demonstration of diplomatic restraint, he did not attack the Papal States and was subsequently absolved from excommunication in 1230.

In 1231, Frederick II issued his codes of law for the Kingdom of Sicily—the *Liber augustalis*—which were the first attempts at such legal codification since the sixth century. In response, the former Sicilian opposition party reformed itself as the Lombard League to oppose him. The emperor defeated the League at the Battle of Cortenuova in 1239, after which Pope Gregory IX, likening Frederick to the anti-Christ, excommunicated him a second time and joined in battle against him. Frederick II, still imbued with a messianic sense of destiny, now set aside diplomacy and plunged into all-out war against that papacy. The conflict continued into the reign of Innocent IV, with Frederick steadily losing ground because most of the German princes remained neutral. Worse, in 1247, a revolt broke out in Parma, and much of central Italy and Romagna were lost to Frederick.

Despite these and other setbacks—including accusations of treason against Pietro della Vigna, Frederick's most trusted adviser, and the capture of Frederick's favorite son, King Enzio of Sardinia—Frederick began to regain lost territories. Nevertheless, warfare abruptly ended with Frederick's sudden death on December 13, 1250, in Sicily.

Further Reading: Thomas Curtis Van Cleve. *The Emperor Frederick II of Hohenstaufen, Immutator Mundi* (Oxford: Clarendon Press, 1972).

Frederick II the Great (1712–1786)
Frederick the Great, king of Prussia from 1740 until 1786, forged the modern state of Germany and forever changed European politics and history.

Born in Berlin on January 24, 1712, Frederick was the son of the Prussian King FREDERICK WILLIAM I and Sophia Dorothea of Hanover, the daughter of England's King George I. From an early age, Frederick loved art and music and the high-style cultural influence of the French. However, his stern father imposed on the young man an austere military discipline. When he was 18 years old, Frederick unsuccessfully attempted to flee from his father's domination by going to England. For this, his father had him arrested and imprisoned, even threatening him with death. Yielding at last to the king's will, Frederick managed to ingratiate himself with his father and, for the next few years, lived a reasonably happy life in Rheinsberg, where he studied and pursued his literary and artistic interests.

Frederick inherited the crown on May 21, 1740, following the death of his father. Observers across Europe had little hope for the new king, believing him to be the antithesis of an assertive, powerful ruler. The Austrian ambassador wrote that Frederick had confided in him that he was "a poet and can

The performance of Frederick II the Great at the 1757 Battle of Leuthen, which Napoleon called a "masterpiece of maneuver and resolution," demonstrated the Prussian emperor's consummate skill as a tactician. (From Charlotte M. Yonge, Pictorial History of the World's Great Nations, *1882)*

write a hundred lines in two hours. He could also be a musician, a philosopher, a physicist, or a mechanician. What he never will be is a general or warrior."

To say that Frederick's critics grossly underestimated the new king is a profound understatement. Within seven months of his accession to the throne, Frederick marched on Silesia, thus firing the opening round of the War of the Austrian Succession. Although his army was routed, he acquired Silesia by treaty in 1742, and the kingdom of Prussia grew in size.

Frederick would not only prove himself an impressive military commander, he became the very model of the "benevolent despot." Among the first domestic directives Frederick issued as king were the lifting of censorship of the press and the abolition of penal torture. He also announced a new era of religious toleration. Frederick's reforms extended to economic policy, and his early years as king were marked by a balanced budget, the production of a surplus, and improvements in agriculture and manufacturing. The modern army he established was second to none in Europe.

When Russia, France and Austria became allies in 1756, Frederick invaded Saxony and started the Seven Years' War, the European phase of the French and Indian War in North America. The death of Russia's czarina, Elizabeth, took that country out of the war and thus allowed Frederick to make peace with the other powers. The result of the long and expensive war was a fruitless reversion to the *status quo ante bellum*, but Frederick had demonstrated to the world that he was a military genius and that Prussia was a power to be reckoned with.

After fighting many battles, Frederick settled in as a strong, autocratic, yet enlightened, monarch. In 1772, part of Poland was divided among Russia, Austria and Prussia, thereby further enlarging Frederick's holdings. He immersed himself in the arts and literature once again, wrote music of considerable merit, and seems to have enjoyed his later years as an accomplished man of the Enlightenment. Frederick spoke German poorly, preferring to speak and write in French. Although married, he sired no children and looked to his nephew as heir-apparent.

During the early days of August 1786, Frederick reviewed his troops in Potsdam during a downpour. Drenched, he caught a chill, sickened, and died several days later on August 17. In later centuries, the likes of NAPOLÉON I and Adolf HITLER would pay homage at his gravesite.

Further Reading: Edith Simon. *The Making of Frederick the Great* (Boston: Little, Brown, 1963).

Frederick III   (1609–1670)

Desperate for relief from the financial burden of wars with Sweden, the Danish clergy and bourgeoisie handed Frederick an absolute hereditary monarchy.

The son of King CHRISTIAN IV, Frederick was born March 18, 1609. Before succeeding to the throne, Frederick served in a number of church positions, including bishop coadjutor of the German dioceses. He also received a commission in the Danish military and led troops against Sweden in the disastrous war of 1643–45.

By the time of Christian's death, the Rigsrad—parliament—had tired of incessant warfare and the constant strain on state finances. Frederick had to agree to limited royal prerogatives before his ascension in 1648. This, however, did not limit his desire for revenge against Sweden or for warfare in general. When the Swedish king Charles X Gustav invaded Poland, Frederick invaded Sweden in 1657, hoping to regain lost territories. Charles, however, shattered the Danish army and seized the province of Jutland. Frederick conceded much territory in the ensuing peace. Five months later, Charles again invaded Denmark, laying siege to Copenhagen itself. The Swedes were finally defeated, though, when the siege failed. The Danish fleet, aided by the Dutch navy, drove the Swedes out of The Sound. Frederick was able to recover some of the recently lost territory through the Treaty of Copenhagen.

In 1660, Frederick called a meeting of the estates to deal with the postwar financial crisis that now gripped Denmark. The clergy and bourgeoisie, weary of the ineffectual Rigsrad, which was dominated by the nobility, backed the king in a power struggle for greater royal prerogatives—specifically the power of the purse. In January 1661, a charter was issued declaring Frederick absolute sovereign, and on November 14, 1665, a hereditary monarchy was established. With the help of his chief adviser, he introduced reform that reorganized the government, creating a central administration giving more authority to the king. Frederick died in Copenhagen on February 9, 1670, having established an absolute monarchy for Denmark.

Frederick William I   (1688–1740)

Frederick William I laid the foundation of the modern militarist Prussian state, building up the Prussian army into one of the finest on the Continent.

The son of the elector of Brandenburg, Frederick III (later Frederick I, king of Prussia), Frederick William was born August 15, 1688, in Berlin. He was active in his father's government near the end of

Frederick's reign, and he opposed his father's extravagant spending and maintenance of a lavish court far beyond the financial means of the small kingdom. When Frederick died in 1713, Frederick William began transforming his little kingdom into a dominant Continental power.

The primary achievement of Frederick William's reign was his development of the Prussian army. Having a passion for tall soldiers, Frederick William instituted the Potsdam Guard, his personal palace grenadiers. All of them were over six feet and they came from all over the world. If one of the king's ministers offered a man a commission and he refused, he was often taken forcibly to Berlin to join the Guard. By the time of Frederick William's death in 1740, he had more than doubled the size of the standing regular army to over 83,000 professional soldiers, more than two-thirds of them foreign born.

The need of funds to support his new military machine caused Frederick William to reform the Prussian economy. First and foremost, he dissolved the costly court that his father had kept, he resettled with exiled Protestants areas depopulated from the plague, thereby increasing the tax base, freed the serfs in 1719, and abolished hereditary leases. He replaced the feudal levy with a direct property tax on land held by the nobility. Thus Frederick William increased the income of the Prussian treasury by 250 percent.

Frederick William's immense administrative success did not carry over to his personal life. He treated his family as he did his army, with rigid discipline, often beating anyone who angered him. His particular disappointment was his son and heir, Frederick, who took no interest in the affairs of state or the military, and attempted to flee Prussia in 1730. Frederick William wanted to have him executed but was talked out of it by several heads of state.

Frederick William never unleashed his army in a major war. Some speculate that he loved it too much to risk it in combat. He had achieved his goal, however; Prussia was no longer financially dependent on or at the mercy of the other Continental armies. By then reconciled with his father, Frederick succeeded Frederick William on his death in 1740 and promptly unleashed his father's toy, invading Silesia on December 16, 1740, devastating the Austrians. The Prussian military was never reduced, and its offspring would destroy the French in 1870, bring the Continent to its knees before being defeated in 1918, and take the world to the edge of the abyss in 1939–45.

Further Reading: Robert Ergang. *The Potsdam Fuhrer* (New York: Columbia University Press, 1941); Sidney B. Fay. *The Rise of Brandenburg-Prussia to 1786* (New York: Holt, 1937).

Frontenac, Louis de Buade de [Count de Frontenac et Palluau] (1622–1698)

Despite his tyrannical misgovernment during two stints as governor of New France, North America, Frontenac, employing what he called *la petite guerre* (guerrilla warfare), managed to defeat the British in 1689 and save the French colony in the New World.

Frontenac was born into the "nobility of the sword" (feudal nobility) on May 22, 1622, just outside of Paris. He joined the French army in his teens and fought in the Thirty Years' War. By the age of 21, he had risen to the rank of colonel, commanding the Normandy Regiment. In 1646, he was brigadier general, but, through extravagant living, had amassed a staggering personal debt. In desperate need of a job to pay his debts, he was posted as lieutenant general to assist Venetian forces defending Crete against the Turks in 1669. Always contentious, he was dismissed after three months because of disputes with his superior officers.

Using his considerable influence in the court of Louis XIV, he was sent to New France and named governor of the colony in 1672. On his arrival, he immediately realized that tremendous profits were to be made in the fur trade, and he promptly founded a trading post on Lake Ontario called Fort Frontenac. The new governor and his associates were constantly seeking ways—lawful or otherwise—to expand the western fur trade. His activities brought him into frequent conflict with the established Montreal fur traders as well as the Indians. Frontenac also made himself unpopular by arguing incessantly with local officials and the clergy. More seriously, however, was the revival of the militancy of the Iroquois Confederacy, a powerful league of five northeastern Indian tribes. Rather than fortify the defenses of the colony and prepare for conflict, Frontenac chose to appease the Indians. However, this was perceived as a sign of weakness and only served to strengthen the Iroquois' resolve. In the meantime, the English founded trading posts in James Bay, directly challenging the French Canadian monopoly of the fur trade.

Frontenac responded to both of these threats with inaction. At last, in 1682, LOUIS XIV recalled his governor.

After England declared war on France in May 1689, Frontenac returned to New France in command of an expedition to take New York. He was also reappointed as governor. Bad weather delayed his attack, and when the Iroquois beat him to the punch, attacking Quebec and inflicting heavy casualties, Frontenac was forced to abandon the attack on New York and take the defensive instead.

The governor realized that he lacked the forces to engage the English and their Indian allies head on. Instead, he deployed his troops, together with a growing body of Indian allies, in what he dubbed *la petite guerre*—the phrase from which "guerrilla warfare" is derived. Frontenac's policy became one of systematically terrorizing settlers and soldiers alike through small, sharp raids.

Sporadic fighting continued in this manner for the next few years, during which time Frontenac continued to push westward to expand the fur trade, blatantly ignoring Louis XIV's policy of halting expansion in order to consolidate the central colony. Frontenac's expansionism soon created a pelt sur-

plus of one million pounds in Montreal, which contributed to a glut in the European market, temporarily wrecked the Canadian fur trade, and nearly drove the North American beaver into extinction.

Forced to curtail his fur trading activity, Frontenac turned his full attention to *la petite guerre*, destroying two major Iroquois villages in 1696. As he aged, he grew increasingly despotic, and Louis XIV was about to recall him again when, on November 28, 1698, Frontenac died.

Further Reading: Alan Axelrod. *Chronicle of the Indian Wars: From Colonial Times to Wounded Knee* (New York: Prentice Hall, 1992); Francis Parkman. *Count Frontenac and New France under Lousi XIV* (Boston: Little, Brown, 1909).

G

Gaiseric [Genseric] (389–477)
King of the Vandals from 428 to 477, Gaiseric conquered a large portion of Roman Africa, built up an effective naval force, and sacked Rome in 455.

Born in 389, Gaiseric became king of the Vandals in 428. By that time, the Vandals had migrated from Germany, through Gaul, and into Spain, where they had settled in Andalusía. A year after Gaiseric became king, he led his people into North Africa.

In 430, Gaiseric turned against the African governor Count Bonifacius and set out to overturn Roman rule in northern Africa. Five years later, the first treaty between the Vandals and Rome was signed, resulting in a peace that lasted only four years. On October 19, 439, Gaiseric captured Carthage and three years later signed a treaty with Roman emperor Valentinianus III by which the Vandals were given control of proconsular Africa, Byzacena and part of Numidia.

In June 455, Gaiseric sailed for Rome, sacked the city, and captured the empress Eudoxia—Valentinianus's widow—and her daughters. He subsequently

The exploits of the Vandal leader Gaiseric fired the romantic imagination, as evidenced in this 19th-century engraving. (From Charlotte M. Yonge, Pictorial History of the World's Great Nations, *1882)*

repelled the attempts of the Roman emperors Majorianus (in 460) and Basiliscus (in 468) to overthrow him. Gaiseric died in 477 and was succeeded by his son Huneric.

Galerius [Gaius Galerius Valerius Maximianus] (ca. 250–311)
Famous for his organized and ruthless persecution of the Christians, Galerius recanted and repented his deeds on his deathbed, feeling his illness was an act of retribution.

Beginning life as a shepherd boy, Galerius enlisted in the Roman army and served under both Aurelian and Probus, becoming a senior officer under DIOCLETIAN, emperor of the East. After Galerius showed substantial military promise, Diocletian named him his heir on March 1, 293, and he was immediately posted to the Danubian frontier as commander of defensive operations there. Galerius grew impatient with this duty because he saw others advancing faster than he and with far less effort. At last in 296, Diocletian sent him east to fight the Sassanians in Persia. When the Sassanians invaded Syria in 297, Galerius crossed the Euphrates in haste and with insufficient forces. He was severely beaten, losing all of Mesopotamia for the empire. In an effort to regain standing with the emperor, he conducted a brilliant rout of the Persians in Armenia in 298, capturing huge amounts of booty, including King Narses' harem, and taking the capital city. Galerius' victory not only won back Mesopotamia, but regained Armenia for the empire as well.

It was at this time, with his favor restored, that Galerius pushed Diocletian to begin a program of persecuting the Christians. Citing some Christian acts of civil disobedience and calling them terrorism, Galerius pushed the feeble Diocletian to move against the sect. Diocletian imposed compulsory acts of pagan sacrifice on all Christians. Those who refused to perform the rites were brutally exterminated.

Diocletian abdicated in 305—essentially entering a self-imposed retirement—and Galerius became emperor of the East. The emperor of the West, Constantius I, was technically his superior, but since Galerius controlled both the heirs in the West and the East, he held, in fact, the greater power. After several pretenders were bloodily suppressed by 307, his position was secure. However, Galerius fell gravely ill in 311 with what was probably cancer of the groin. Fearing that the Christian god was punishing him for his treatment of the Christians, he recanted and repented on his deathbed, granting the sect religious freedom and recognition. He died three days later.

Further Reading: Michael Grant. *Roman Emperors* (New York: Scribner's, 1985).

Gallienus [Publius Licinius Egantius Gallienus] (ca. 218–268)

Emperor during the time of the Thirty Tyrants, Gallienus presided over a shrinking and disintegrating Roman Empire.

When Gallienus' father, VALERIAN, was proclaimed emperor by his troops in 253, the Roman Senate, aware of intense external military pressures, named Gallienus co-emperor in hopes that the two could restore order to the far-flung empire. The two split the empire between them, with Valerian fighting in the East and Gallienus fighting in the West.

Gallienus enjoyed several initial successes in the West, moving against the Goths on the Rhine frontier and smashing the Alemanni in 258. When Ingenuus, governor of Pannonia, declared himself emperor, Gallienus quickly moved against him before he could gain any popular support, defeating and killing him in 260. His troops, however, remained opposed to Gallienus, and they immediately proclaimed Regalianus—governor of Upper Pannonia—emperor. Gallienus returned within a few weeks, easily crushed Regalianus, and put him to death.

In the East, Valerian was taken prisoner by the Persians, and Gallienus made no effort to save him. After Valerian was executed in 260, Gallienus emerged as the sole emperor of Rome. With Valerian dead, the Persians roamed the East with impunity for a time, taking Antioch, Tarsus and all of Mesotamia. In the West, the Goths renewed their activity on the Rhine, and soon Gallienus was in control only of Italy and the Balkan provinces.

When yet another general rose to claim the purple for himself, Gallienus quickly moved against him, but was assassinated in 268.

Further Reading: Michael Grant. *Roman Emperors* (New York: Scribner's, 1985).

Galtieri, Leopoldo Fortunato (b. 1926–)

An Argentine army officer, Leopoldo Fortunato Galtieri was a member of the military junta that seized power in 1976 and served as president of Argentina

A marble bust of Gallienus. (From Richard Delbruck, Antike Portrats, *1912)*

from 1981 to 1982, when he was arrested and later convicted of negligence in fomenting—and losing—the Falkland Islands (Malvinas) War.

The son of Italian immigrants to Argentina, Leopoldo Fortunato Galtieri was born in Caseros, Buenos Aires, on July 15, 1926. He entered the military academy in 1943 and, after graduation, rose steadily through the ranks. By 1980, he was military commander in chief.

In 1979 Galtieri became a member of the military junta that ousted President Isabel Martinez de Perón in March 1976. Galtieri became leader of the government on December 22, 1981, when President Roberto Viola resigned due to ill health and opposition by the army. Throughout the 1970s and early 1980s, Argentina's economy had declined steadily, with inflation out of control and monetary reserves dwindling. Opposition to the military government became increasingly vocal. At the end of March

1982, Buenos Aires and other large cities erupted in massive anti-government demonstrations. Then, on April 2, 1982, Galtieri and his government advisers ordered the invasion of the Falkland Islands.

The invasion was immensely popular with the Argentines, who long considered the islands to be part of their country and resented Great Britain's control of them. Clearly, the invasion was an attempt by the government to quell civil unrest by drawing public attention from its economic failures. The ploy almost worked. The Argentine people rallied behind the war effort. But British forces prevailed in the Falklands (Malvinas) War, and Galtieri surrendered on June 15, 1982. Public support for his regime instantly collapsed.

Two days after the surrender, Galtieri resigned as president and commander in chief, and was replaced by retired General Reynaldo Bignone. Galtieri was arrested and court martialed in 1983 for his actions during the Falklands War. He was also tried for human rights violations, but was acquitted in December 1985. In 1986 he was convicted of negligence for starting and losing the war and was sentenced to imprisonment for 12 years. In October 1989, President Carlos Saul Menem pardoned Galtieri along with nearly 280 other military men and so-called "leftist subversives."

Garcia Meza Tejada, Luis   (b. ca. 1930–   )

Coming to power in Bolivia through the 188th coup in 100 years, General Garcia Meza established himself as a ruthless military dictator who patterned himself after Chilean strongman Augusto PINOCHET.

The son of an army colonel, Luis Garcia Meza was educated at the elite La Salle School in La Paz, and later at the Military College. At the age of 14, he began to talk of someday becoming president of Bolivia—a reasonable ambition in a country that averaged just under two coups a year during the course of its modern history.

Garcia Meza apparently failed to graduate from the academy, having been suspended in 1950 or 1951 for excessively cruel hazing of cadets.

Rejoining the army after its reformation following its dissolution in a revolution of 1952, the conservative Garcia Meza rapidly rose in the Bolivian military. In November 1979, during another military coup, he was named army commander by Colonel Alberto NATUSCH BUSCH. When Natusch Busch's regime tottered after only 16 days, his successor, Lydia Gueiler Tejada, Garcia Meza's cousin, ordered the general to relinquish control of the military. Garcia Meza refused and led a military revolt against the new president.

On July 17, 1980, Garcia Meza overthrew his cousin and seized power in the bloody Latin American tradition by executing several people who opposed his fledgling regime, including old army colleagues. Once he consolidated his power, Garcia Meza showed no signs of letting up on his persecution of political enemies, declaring a "war on domestic extremists," killing and imprisoning hundreds.

His regime, however, could not withstand the fickle tenor of Bolivian politics, and within a year it was on the verge of collapse. Pressured to resign in June 1981, he finally agreed on condition that he could pick a successor friendly to the military.

After setting a date of August 6 to resign, two failed coup attempts were made, throwing Garcia Meza's plans into confusion. After a third semi-successful coup attempt was made on August 4, the rebels seized Santa Cruz, and Garcia Meza immediately resigned. After four days out of power, he attempted to oust the rebels and take control of the military again. The military refused to follow him, and Garcia Meza went into exile.

In November 1982, Garcia Meza was charged with complicity in drug trafficking that brought him multimillion-dollar payments with which he bribed public officials to support his government. At the end of December, he and 14 others were dismissed from the army for "destroying the prestige of the armed forces." In what quickly became a witch hunt, Garcia Meza was arrested on May 25, 1983, with 29 others from his administration and charged with corruption and the misuse of over $50 million in federal funds. Attempting to escape prosecution, he fled to Argentina, but was expelled from that nation in February 1984 and sent back to Bolivia. In April 1993, an Argentine tribunal sentenced him to 30 years' imprisonment.

García Moreno, Gabriel   (1821–1875)

Political writer, president and virtual dictator of Ecuador, Gabriel García Moreno seized power from President Juan José Flores, imposed his orthodox Catholic morality on his country, and centralized the government.

Born in Guayaquil, Ecuador, on December 24, 1821, Gabriel García Moreno was raised in a staunch Catholic family. He was educated at the Colegio Nacional de la Universidad, became a seminarian—receiving tonsure and taking minor orders—studied law and science, and received his doctorate in law (October 26, 1844).

As a student at the university, García Moreno led a group of young rebels in abortive conspiracies to overthrow President Juan José Flores. Forced to leave the country for a time, García Moreno published a revolutionary newspaper and garnered support for his political beliefs. In 1847, he was elected city councillor of Quito.

Between 1853 and 1859, García Moreno was twice more exiled for his political writings. He returned to Guayaquil in May 1859 as leader of one of four factions laying claim to the presidency. By 1861 he had established himself as leader of the revolution and was elected president by the Assembly.

At the end of his term as president, García Moreno accepted a diplomatic post in Chile, but he was recalled to Ecuador and again elected president in 1869. He then had legislation passed to extend the presidential term to six years and to allow for reelection. His enemies feared that García Moreno was trying to become president for life, and on August 6, 1875, he was assassinated.

García Moreno instituted many reforms in Ecuador, especially in education (he increased the number of schools from 200 to 500 and opened some of them to women and Indians), road building and general modernization. However, he was stern and narrowly autocratic, suppressing liberal dissent swiftly and absolutely. Nevertheless, he was sufficiently well remembered in Ecuador that the archbishop of Quito proposed him in 1939 for canonization.

Further Reading: A. S. Tibesar. "García Moreno, Gabriel," in *New Catholic Encyclopedia* (New York: McGraw-Hill, 1967).

Gelon (ca. 540–478 B.C.)

This tyrant built Syracuse into an important power and cruelly conquered most of Sicily.

Gelon had served Hippocrates, tyrant of the city of Gela, as a commander of cavalry. When Hippocrates died in 491, Gelon succeeded him. He fought sporadically with Carthage, then, in 485, he seized on an appeal by the *gamoroi*—the landowners—of Syracuse to aid them in regaining the properties from which the people had evicted them. Gelon took over rule of Syracuse and concentrated on developing its navy and, using mercenary troops, its land forces as well. With these, he conquered the Sicilian cities of Euboea and Megara Hyblaea about 483. The common folk, of whom he was contemptuous, Gelon sold into slavery. The rulers he brought back to Syracuse.

Gelon soon came to control Syracuse and most of eastern Sicily. He also forged an alliance with Theron, the tyrant of Acragas (modern-day Agrigento) through marriage. Gelon came to the aid of his ally in 480 when Carthage invaded Sicily. He led the Greek forces to a spectacular victory against the Carthaginians at the Battle of Himera.

Genghis Khan (1155–67–1227)

With ALEXANDER III THE GREAT, perhaps the greatest conqueror in history, Genghis Khan rose from being an outcast to unify the Mongol state and elevate it to dominance in central Asia.

Born into the Borjigin clan in the middle of the 12th century—the dates assigned vary from 1155 to 1167—he was given the name Temujin. When Temujin was eight or nine, his father, Yesukai the Strong, a ranking member of the royal clan, was poisoned by the rival Tatars, another nomadic band, in the course of an old feud. With his father dead, a rival family took over the clan, casting Temujin and his mother out. Temujin's mother responded by determining to raise her son to be a Mongol chief. The first lesson she taught him was to surround himself with a loyal network of men, a precept he followed unfailingly.

By developing early prowess in hunting and warfare, Temujin inspired awe in those around him and began to win a following. His first opportunity to exercise power came when his new bride was taken and ravished by the Merkit clan. Through a crafty alliance with an acquaintance of his father's, Temujin was able literally to borrow an army and lead it against the Merkit in 1180. He not only won his bride back, but utterly destroyed the Merkit in the process, acquiring a larger following and an army of 20,000, while setting a grim example for the many conquests to follow.

While Temujin was away fighting the Merkit, the Jurkin clan took advantage of his absence to plunder his property. Temujin returned and summarily exterminated the clan nobility. In his conquest of both the Merkit and the Jurkin, Temujin developed a very sound military policy: Always keep your rear free. Taking on enemies one at a time, he was able to destroy one foe without having to worry about a resurgence of his previous enemy; he saw to it that the first enemy no longer existed.

Finally able to risk a showdown with the formidable Tatars, who had become allied with the eastern Mongols, and seek revenge for the murder of his father, Temujin routed them in battle in 1201 and then systematically slaughtered every Tatar taller than the height of a cart axle. Having killed the adults, he prevented their hatreds and prejudices from being passed on to the children and thereby assured a second generation loyal to himself. Conquests of the Naiman and Karait tribes followed in 1203, and by 1204, establishing his capital at Karakorum, Temujin was master of Mongolia. The only other Mongolian clan leader who offered a challenge to him, Jamuka, a childhood friend and tenuous ally who had helped Temujin defeat both the Merkit and Tatars, quickly lost adherents, who flocked to the far more charismatic Temujin. At this time, during a great assembly by the River Onon, Temujin took a new name—Genghis Khan, meaning universal ruler.

With all the clans now unified under Genghis Khan, the Mongols could now look even beyond the steppe regions. It is at this stage that Genghis Khan's true military genius became evident. In prosecuting tribal warfare, he used cavalry exclusively, riding the tough Mongolian ponies against the nomads. But in assaulting cities, he soon mastered the art of siege works, catapults, ladders, burning oil, and even such engineering feats as diverting rivers. Genghis Khan used such tactics in his invasion of the Western Hsia Empire in 1205, 1207, and 1209, enlisting Chinese engineers to help him breach city walls. In April 1211 he crossed the Great Wall to begin his conquest of the Mongols' traditionally richer, more powerful neighbor, the Chin Dynasty of northern China. By 1215, Beijing (Peking) had fallen and within two more years the last Chin resistance was neutralized.

Insatiable, Genghis Khan turned next to the south, to Khwarezm, where a local official had massacred a Mongol trading envoy. This was ample pretext for battle, and Genghis Khan promptly made war on Khwarezm, bringing 200,000 troops who consumed everything in their path. Transoxiana (Bukhara and Samarkand), Khorasan, Afghanistan, and northwestern India fell in succession, culminating in the defeat of Shah Mohammed's son Jellaluddin on the Indus River in a battle of November 24, 1221.

Genghis Khan sent his generals into southern Russia during 1221–23 and invaded northwestern China in 1225 to put down a rebellion of the Chin and His-Hsia, winning a great battle on the Yellow River in December 1226. He had to confront more rebellious Chins in 1227, but fell ill and died on August 18. He was secretly buried on Mount Burkan-Kaldan, the place to which he and his mother had been exiled.

Genghis Khan was a fine strategist, a great organizer, and a ruler of tremendous personal magnetism. His military successes were due not so much to his abilities as a field commander—which were considerable—as to the skill of his subordinate field commanders, who were totally committed to him and to his obsession of conquest. His corps of commanders was made up of his sons and closest longtime allies, whom he could trust above all else. With Genghis Khan they forged an enduring legend of ruthless conquest and domination. Yet it must also be noted that Genghis Khan, while he gave no quarter and stopped at nothing, was no mere plunderer, but endeavored to provide for the efficient and just government of all the peoples he conquered.

Further Reading: René Grousset. *The Conqueror of the World* (New York: Orion, 1966); Richard P. Lister. *Genghis Khan* (New York: Stein & Day, 1969).

Geoffrey II Martel   (1006–1060)

Although he expanded the Angevin holdings, Geoffrey, in so doing, defied his father and eventually ran afoul of William the Conqueror.

The son of the duke of Anjou, Fulk III Nerra, Geoffrey was born October 14, 1006. Early on, he sought—against the duke's wishes—to expand his father's lands and thereby increase his own holdings. In 1032, Geoffrey married Agnes, widow of William V of Aquitaine, hoping thereby to seize Aquitaine for himself by claiming the duchy in the name of William's children by Agnes. However, William the Fat, William V's son from a previous marriage and the current duke of Aquitaine, offered opposition. Geoffrey attacked William, an act that left Fulk, as William's vassal, in a most awkward position. Fulk had no choice but to join William in fighting his son. Now in open conflict with his father, Geoffrey attempted to seize his lands as well, when Fulk was on a pilgrimage to the Holy Land in 1039. William defeated Geoffrey, and, upon his return, Fulk subjected his son to great humiliation, but finally pardoned him.

Upon Fulk's death in 1040, Geoffrey rightfully assumed control of Anjou. For the next 20 years, Geoffrey made attempts to expand the Angevin domains in all directions. After a war with HENRY I (1008-1060) of France, he annexed Touraine. By 1051, Geoffrey had defeated Herbert, count of Maine, driving him from the province and claiming it for himself. In Maine, however, Geoffrey impinged upon the domains of William I, duke of Normandy, who had designs on extending Norman control into the region. Before William could move against Geoffrey however, Geoffrey died on November 14, 1060.

Geoffrey IV Plantagenet   (1158–1186)

The son of HENRY II (1333–89) of England, Geoffrey turned against both his father and his brother, RICHARD I THE LIONHEARTED, in an attempt to gain possession of Anjou.

The son of Henry II and Eleanor of Aquitaine, Geoffrey was born September 23, 1158. As part of his father's attempt to consolidate and extend the power of the Angevins, eight-year-old Geoffrey was betrothed to Constance, the daughter of Conan IV, duke of Brittany, in 1166. In return for the engagement, Conan gave Henry the duchy of Brittany as Geoffrey's domain.

As Geoffrey grew older, however, he became embroiled in the chronic conflict between his brothers and his father, in which alliances and enmities shifted until, eventually, each opposed the other. When Henry attempted to seize Aquitaine from his son Richard I the Lionhearted in 1173, he was opposed by all four sons. Geoffrey, hoping Henry's defeat might mean a greater share for himself, stood by his brothers, twice turning back Henry's invading forces in Aquitaine. Henry, however, finally emerged victorious, pardoning all his sons in 1174.

After pardoning him, Henry sent Geoffrey back to Brittany to act as a watchdog in the region, subduing rebellious nobles and recovering lost Angevin estates. He again became involved in familial conflict, however, when the Aquitaine nobility called on him and his brother Henry III, the heir apparent, to overthrow their brother Richard I and rule Aquitaine in their own right. The rebellion collapsed when Henry III died in 1183, making Richard heir to the English throne as well as those of Anjou and Aquitaine, and leaving Geoffrey with nothing but Brittany. Geoffrey died in Paris in mid-August 1186.

George of Podebrady   (1420–1471)

The last native king of Bohemia, George incurred the wrath of the papacy and Hapsburg emperor Frederick III, which ultimately led to his downfall.

Born to the baronial family of Podebrady in central Bohemia on April 23, 1420, George became leader of the moderate Utraquist party, a faction of the Hussite Protestants. George captured Prague in 1448 while the Roman Catholic Hapsburg candidate, Ladislav, was still a minor. Realizing that George had the support of the local nobility, Emperor Frederick III—Ladislav's guardian—made George regent in 1451 until Ladislav reached his majority.

Two years later, Ladislav began to rule in his own right, and George was limited to ministerial duties. However, Ladislav died in 1457, leaving George to be crowned king on March 2, 1458.

George was a successful king, creating a strong government that was relatively tolerant. Hoping to advance Bohemia's international prestige, he proposed the League of Princes, an anti-Turkish compact of Christian states that aimed to maintain peace on the Continent without papal interference. Pope Pius II, wary of any moderate religious movement, now demanded George disavow his relationship with the Utraquist party, which Pius saw as a threat to Catholicism in south-central Europe. George refused, and the pope prepared to mount a crusade against Bohemia. Pius died before he could move against George, but his successor, Pope Paul II, excommunicated George on October 23, 1466, and pro-

nounced him deposed, forbidding all Catholics to support him. The emperor Frederick now opposed George, and Mathias Corvinus of Hungary rose as a rival. George gained Polish support by naming the son of King CASIMIR IV heir to the Bohemian throne—but this was not enough. Mathias established himself as rival king of Bohemia in 1469 and demanded George's abdication. George refused, but was unable to regain control and died on March 22, 1471.

George III   (1738–1820)

Reigning over England during the Seven Years' War, the American Revolution, the French Revolution, the Napoleonic Wars, and the War of 1812, George III sank steadily into the depths of mental derangement.

The son of Frederick, Prince of Wales, George was born June 4, 1738, in London. When Frederick died in 1751, George became heir to his grandfather, George II, and the Hanoverian crown of England. George studied diligently as a youth and wanted desperately to be a good king. Yet his native intellectual abilities were mediocre at best, and many regarded him as slow-witted. He did understand English law and accepted—indeed, embraced—the constitutional limits of the monarchy.

George was the first Hanoverian king to be born in England, and he was well liked, both on account of his moral fortitude and his claim that he gloried "in the name of England." Lamentably, he seemed incapable of choosing a prime minister satisfactory both to himself and the needs of the nation. His chief adviser, Lord Bute, was detested by many because he was a Scot and because he made a questionable peace with the hated French. Bute had neither the savvy nor the experience to be an effective adviser and was a hinderance to George in his search for a prime minister. The king went through seven of them in the space of 19 years.

The incredible expense of the Seven Years' War in Europe and the concommitant French and Indian War in North America put a dangerous strain on the treasury. Parliament was in complete agreement with George, who wanted to make the colonies pay for their own defense. One tax after another was enacted, repealed, and replaced. Within a few years of the conclusion of the French and Indian War, the colonies, taxed but denied sovereignty and self-determination, rebelled against "taxation without representation," and the American Revolution was born.

Still suffering the financial consequences of the Seven Years' War and the French and Indian War, the British people were never very enthusiastic in

England's King George III, earnest but thoroughly mediocre, was plagued by a neurological disease that brought debility and madness. (From J. N. Larned, A History of England for the Use of Schools and Academies, *1900)*

their support of the fight against the American Revolution. George successfully argued, however, that to let the colonies go without a struggle would be to unravel the entire empire by encouraging other colonies to declare independence. Only after years of stalemate and defeat in North America did English subjects begin to oppose the war in earnest, turning against their once-popular king.

It was at the end of the American Revolution that George finally found a prime minister he could trust and whose competence was matched only by his consummate ability to deal with Parliament. In 1783, George named William Pitt the Younger as prime minister and dramatically turned public opinion in his favor. While he was not in total agreement with all of Pitt's policies, George recognized that he desperately needed Pitt's competence.

And George's needs would become increasingly desperate. During the era of the Napoleonic Wars, the king suffered a severe mental decline. By 1810, George had three times exhibited lapses that lasted several months, with symptoms including great pain, delirium, and temporary paralysis. Most

thought he was completely insane, but, based on the symptoms, it is more probable that he was suffering from a hereditary metabolic disorder called porphyria. Near the end of his life, he became blind and deaf, and his son was named regent for the last decade of George's reign. The king died in Windsor Castle on January 29, 1820.

Further Reading: John Brooke. *King George III* (Chicago: University of Chicago Press, 1972); Richard Pares. *King George III and the Politicians* (Oxford: Oxford University Press, 1988).

Ghazan, Mahmud   (1271–1304)

The most prominent ruler of Iran under the Mongol dynasty, Ghazan is most famous for having converted the nation to Islam.

Raised a Buddhist in Iran, Mahmud Ghazan was born November 5, 1271, and became viceroy of the northeastern Persian provinces under the reign of his father, beginning in 1284. Ghazan remained in Persia for 10 years, defending the provinces against the raiding Mongols from central Asia and, in particular, from Nawruz, his former lieutenant, who had joined the Mongols. After Ghazan turned back the incursions, Nawruz and Ghazan were reconciled, and Nawruz became Ghazan's chief adviser.

When Ghazan waged open warfare against the new khan, Baydu, Ghazan was forced into the mountains north of Tehran in 1295. Hoping to gain the support of his own troops as well as of the surrounding peoples, Ghazan converted to Islam and led a unified Muslim force against Baydu. Ghazan crushed Baydu, executing him and seizing the throne for himself in 1295. Wary of his timely conversion to Islam, however, many questioned Ghazan's faith and revolted. Ghazan ruthlessly suppressed any who rose against him, executing all who were implicated. He eventually executed five princes of the blood, who were involved in various plots. He also ordered the death of Nawruz, who had helped Ghazan to the throne in the first place.

Ghazan invaded Syria in 1299 and occupied Aleppo, defeating the Egyptians at Homs and seized Damascus shortly thereafter. Upon his return to Persia in February 1300, Ghazan discovered that the region had been overrun by the Mamluks. He made preparations to move against them, but bad weather forced him to abandon the campaign temporarily. Hoping to rout the Mamluks when he resumed the offensive, he sought an alliance with Pope Boniface VIII in 1302. The pope rebuffed him, and Ghazan resumed the campaign on his own in 1303, moving through Syria, but suffering a heavy defeat at Damascus. Before he could resume the attack against the infidels, Ghazan died on May 11, 1304.

Godunov, Boris (ca. 1551–1605)

The chief adviser to IVAN IV THE TERRIBLE, Boris was elected czar after the death of Fyodor, the czarevich, but his short reign ended in the Time of Troubles.

A member of the Tatar tribe that had migrated to Muscovy in the 14th century, Boris Godunov was close to the royal court in Moscow and soon became adviser to Ivan IV. Boris was not a member of the Muscovite nobility, but he married into it when he wed the daughter of the most highly placed Muscovite noble. His place in court was further cemented when his sister married the czarevich Fyodor in 1580, and Ivan named him a boyar, an aristocratic rank below that of prince.

After serving as Ivan's most trusted minister, Boris was named co-regent for the mentally incompetent Fyodor upon Ivan's death. Fyodor succeeded his father in 1584, and Boris became sole regent in 1586 on the death of the other co-regent, Fyodor's uncle. When a group of boyars, resentful of Boris, conspired against him, Boris, using his own secret police force, swiftly crushed the uprising and banished the leaders. Thus Boris Godunov came to rule Moscow without opposition.

Boris quickly engaged Muscovy in a war with Sweden in 1590, recovering lost territories on the Gulf of Finland in 1595. Boris was unable to recover the port of Narva, however, which was his real goal. When Fyodor died in 1598, the Russian Church offered the throne to Boris, who refused, demanding the convention and approval of a national assembly before he would ascend the throne. When the Zemski Sobor convened in February 1598, it quickly elected Boris czar, and he accepted.

The new czar undertook a vigorous program of reform, especially of the judicial and educational systems, sending students to study in the West and attempting to establish a university in Moscow. He also made efforts to reduce the influence of the nobility, especially the boyars who had opposed his regency. He banished the entire Romanov family and set up an extensive spy network, savagely persecuting those who were suspected of opposing him.

Boris Godunov's reform efforts were suspended in 1601 when a severe famine struck Moscow and lasted through 1603. His government made earnest efforts to feed as many people as possible, but chaos soon reigned. More than 100,000 of Boris' subjects starved to death, and people fled Moscow to join the Cossacks in the steppes.

Coupled with the crackdown on the boyars, the famine turned popular opinion against Boris. A rumor soon circulated that Fyodor's younger brother Dmitry was alive and was coming to seize the throne from the usurper. In 1603, a pretender arose claiming to be Dmitry (who had actually died in 1591) and gathered supporters in Poland. He crossed the border with a thousand men in 1604, quickly attracting more supporters as he marched toward Moscow. Boris' troops were able to defeat Dmitry, but they did not wipe him out. Before he could discredit the pretender, Boris Godunov died on April 23, 1605, and Moscovy fell into anarchy. Boris was succeeded by his son, who was soon murdered, and all of Russia was now plunged into the "Time of Troubles," which would not end until 1613.

Further Reading: Stephen Graham. *Boris Godunof* (New Haven: Yale University Press, 1933).

Gómez Castro, Laureano Eleuterio (1889–1965)

Laureano Gómez was the hard-line Fascist president of Colombia from 1950 to 1953.

Born in Bogotá in 1889, Gómez was educated as an engineer, but he soon turned to politics and by 1932 he was leader of the Conservative Party. An enthusiastic supporter of both Adolf HITLER and Francisco FRANCO, Gómez was repeatedly exiled. But, in 1946, conservatives regained control of the Colombian government and Gómez accepted the position as foreign minister—only to be exiled once again, on suspicion of having participated in the assassination of the Liberal political leader Jorge Gaitán.

Gómez returned to Colombia in 1950, at which time an election—held under martial law—gave him the presidency. His iron-fisted tenure was characterized by censorship of the press, violent persecution of Protestants, and a rigged judiciary system. All of this provoked widespread rural rebellion, which led to his ouster by a bipartisan coalition in 1953. Gómez fled to Franco's Spain.

Remarkably enough, the regime of Gómez's successor, Gustavo Rojas Pinilla, proved even more brutal than his own, and in 1957 Gómez returned, this time cooperating with the Liberals, to appoint Alberto Camargo president. Gómez died in Bogotá, July 13, 1965.

Gowon, Yakubu (1934–)

Leader of the victorious forces during the Nigerian Civil War of 1967–70, Gowon headed his country's government until 1975.

Yakubu Gowon was born on October 19, 1934, a member of a small northern tribe called the Angas. He received military training in England at the Royal Military Academy, Sandhurst—the British equivalent of West Point. He received further training in British-held Ghana and twice fought in conflicts that beset the Congo. Following the bloody Nigerian coup d'état of January 1966, Gowon emerged as the senior surviving army officer and was therefore named chief of staff. From this post, he participated in a countercoup during July 1966 and became head of the new government that resulted.

Gowon's compromise government was maintained by the military, but he consistently pledged to return the nation to civilian rule as soon as possible. Tribal dissension, however, made this impossible. In particular, the Ibos of eastern Nigeria were driven to rebellion by widespread massacres against them and by Gowon's refusal to name their leader, Odumegwu Ojukwu, military commander of the east. In response to the growing unrest and general violence, Gowon declared a state of emergency, assumed absolute martial authority, and divided his country into 12 small states, which cut the Ibos off from their port. Instead of crushing the rebellion, however, this move prompted the former eastern region of Nigeria to declare its independence as Biafra on May 30, 1967.

After the loss of Biafra, the civil war dragged on until the beginning of 1970, when the conflict ended with a remarkable lack of malice on any of the several sides. Gowon had prosecuted the war almost indirectly, giving his top three commanders virtual autonomy in the field. When his government emerged victorious, Gowon not only healed Nigeria's wounds, but seemed destined for a leadership position of preeminence across the entire continent. However, fearing his growing influence and his developing liberalism, the army removed Gowon from office on July 29, 1975, while he was on state business in Uganda. Unable to return to Nigeria, Gowon sought refuge in England.

Gregory VII   (ca. 1020–1085)

One of the most important figures in the history of the papacy, Gregory VII instituted vigorous reforms and forced a showdown with the Holy Roman Emperor Henry IV.

Born Hildebrand in Tuscany, Gregory spent his early years in Rome studying at the Monastery of Saint Mary. Some time during this period he became a monk and entered the School of Musicians for clergy. Here he met the future Pope Gregory VI, who, after he assumed the papacy in 1045, assigned Hildebrand the task of bringing law and order to the chaotic streets of Rome. Hildebrand formed a police force and was successful in bringing a modicum of order to the city's streets. When Gregory VI was deposed by the Holy Roman Emperor Henry III in 1046, he retired to Germany, taking Hildebrand with him.

Pope Gregory VII. (From Charlotte M. Yonge, Pictorial History of the World's Great Nations, *1882)*

Pope Leo IX, recognizing the piety and virtue of Hildebrand, recalled him to Rome in 1049 to head the reform groups Leo was organizing. When Leo was succeeded by Alexander II in 1061, Hildebrand became known as "the man behind the throne," wielding considerable influence over the reform groups. Upon Alexander's death on 1073, Hildebrand was the obvious choice to lead the reform movement. A mob gathered and proclaimed him pope even before the College of Cardinals could vote on the matter. The cardinals readily accepted Hildebrand, who took the name of Gregory VII in honor of his mentor.

Gregory inherited a Catholic church rife with corruption, and he realized that, at best, he would be able to address only the most serious problems: the morality and sanctity of the church itself. These two issues were compromised by the large number of priests who were married in open defiance of the Vatican; the buying and selling of church offices (simony); and lay investiture, the process whereby political rulers installed favorites in church offices.

Gregory held a synod in Rome each Lent to address these issues, denouncing the immorality and depravity of married clergy and of simony. By far, his most famous and most public struggle was with Holy Roman Emperor Henry IV over lay investiture. Gregory issued a bull outlawing lay investiture in the eyes of God. Henry rebuked this by appointing a host of bishops in Italy in 1075. At Gregory's Lenten Synod, he excommunicated five of Henry's advisers who had been instrumental in the appointments, hoping to send a message to Henry. But the reform movement did not fare well in Milan, and, seizing upon this, Henry openly defied the papacy by naming an anti-reform bishop in that city in place of the legitimate bishop. Henry and the bishops he had appointed renounced obedience to Gregory and bade him to step down. The pope responded by excommunicating Henry in 1076 and moving to depose him by relieving Henry's subjects of their allegiance. When Saxony rose up to defend the pope, Henry's supporters backed down.

Gregory sent representatives to the meeting of nobles in Germany and persuaded them to give Henry a chance to repent before officially ousting him. Then he made his way to Augsburg to deal with the situation personally. On his way, he was met by Henry, dressed in penitential garb, and asking for absolution, having stood barefoot in the cold for three days straight.

The priest in Gregory triumphed over the politician. He granted the absolution and restored Henry to the throne. The nobles at Augsburg were, however, outraged and proceeded to elect a new emperor, thereby precipitating a bloody civil war. Henry's willful and despotic abuses during the civil war caused Gregory to excommunicate him again, to which Henry responded by setting up Clement III as antipope. Henry's troops stormed Rome on March 21, 1084, and Gregory was forced to watch the coronation of Clement from the castle of St. Angelo, where he had taken refuge. Clement, in turn, crowned Henry emperor.

Gregory would surely have been doomed had it not been for Robert GUISCARD, who fought through Henry's army to rescue the deposed pontiff. Fighting in the course of the rescue resulted in the burning of a large section of the city, for which the populace blamed Gregory. He left Rome with Guiscard and died in Salerno on May 25, 1085.

Further Reading: Allen J. Macdonald. *Hildebrand: A Life of Gregory VII* (New York: Richwood Publishers, 1977).

Gustav II Adolf (1594–1632)

King of Sweden from 1611 until his death in 1632, Gustav II Adolf, known as the "Lion of the North," waged three wars started by his father and entered the Thirty Years' War on the side of the German Protestant princes.

Born on December 9, 1594, in Stockholm, Gustav was the son of Charles IX and Christina of Holstein. In 1611, he succeeded to the throne after masterful

political maneuverings by Axel Oxenstierna, who, as a member of the ruling council, led the aristocracy to accept Gustav as king in exchange for concessions from the crown.

The throne Gustav inherited was far from secure. In 1599, his father had usurped power from Sigismund III Vasa, who was also king of Poland. The dynastic struggle that followed erupted in intermittent warfare between Sweden and Poland over the next 50 years. In addition, Gustav inherited wars with Denmark and Russia. The war with Denmark ended with the Peace of Knäred (1613) by which Sweden relinquished control of Älvsborg, its only port on the North Sea, to Denmark as security for the payment of a war indemnity. The Russian conflict had begun when Charles IX attempted to fill the vacant Russian throne with a Swedish nobleman,

King Gustav II Adolf of Sweden. (From M. Guizot, A Popular History of France from the Earliest Times, *n.d.)*

and war between the two countries continued until 1617. With the Peace of Stolbova, Gustav secured Ingria and Kexholm for Sweden and cut Russia off from the Baltic.

While continuing the conflict with Poland, Gustav set out to secure his hold over his own country. His throne had been won primarily through the work of Oxenstierna, who had asked the council to draw up a list of grievances and had advised Gustav to sign a charter of guarantees—which was potent enough to have stripped the monarchy of all power, but Gustav's charismatic personality swayed the nobility to his side, and he was able to institute sweeping governmental reforms while retaining full authority.

In 1621, Gustav took advantage of a Turkish attack on Poland to renew his war with Sigismund. Capturing Riga and Livonia, he transferred his war headquarters to Prussia. In 1629, peace was achieved with the Truce of Altmark, whereby Sigismund renounced his claim to the Swedish throne. Now Gustav was free to enter the Thirty Years' War (1618–1648) in Germany between the Hapsburgs and the Protestant princes. The Hapsburgs were ably served by Generals Johann Tilly and Albrecht von Wallenstein. Fearful that a Catholic victory in Germany would lead to the reinstatement of Catholicism in Sweden, Gustav sailed for Germany in May 1630 with 13,000 troops, soon reinforced by an additional 27,000. Despite this formidable array, he was defeated at Mecklenburg, but then went on to victories that swept him through Germany. Gustav defeated the Hapsburg army at Breitenfeld on September 7, 1631, and at the Lech River in Bavaria in April 1632.

With much of central and northern Germany under his control, Gustav laid the foundation for a Protestant League, but was unable to win the loyalty of all the Protestant princes, who were wary of Gustav's ambitions and resentful of his imposition of Swedish administration in conquered territories. Then, on November 6, 1632, Gustav's army attacked Wallenstein's troops at Lützen, Saxony, and the Lion of the North was killed in battle.

Despite the failure of his plan for a Protestant League and his own death in battle, Gustav's entry into the Thirty Years' War ensured the survival of Germany's Protestant princes during the Counter-Reformation. The inability of the Hapsburgs and the Catholic League to sustain their earlier victories in the face of opposition from Gustav delayed the emergence of a unified Germany until the 19th century.

Gyges (d. 657 B.C.)

Founder of the Mermnad dynasty in Lydia, Gyges came to power after murdering King Candaules and ruled from about 685 B.C. to 657 B.C.

Gyges was a humble shepherd in service to the king of Lydia, Candaules, when, according to Plato, he found a bronze horse and a corpse in a chasm. Taking a ring from the corpse, he became invisible and killed the king, thereby becoming king himself.

Herodotus tells a different story: Gyges was the trusted friend of the king, who boasted to Gyges that his wife was the most beautiful woman in the world. Eager to prove his point, the king persuaded Gyges to hide in the queen's bedroom and spy on her as she went to bed. Gyges did so, but the queen saw him. The next day she called Gyges to her and offered two choices: he could be killed for breaking the law, or he could kill the king and marry her. Gyges chose the latter. The Lydians rose against Gyges, but were appeased by a favorable pronouncement from the Oracle at Delphi.

As king, Gyges began the Lydian conquest of Ionia and died during the Cimmerian invasion in 657 B.C.

Further Reading: Catherine B. Avery, ed. *The New Century Classical Handbook* (New York: Appleton-Century-Crofts, 1962).

H

Hadrian [Publius Aelius Hadrianus] (76–138)
In many ways an able ruler, though unpopular, Hadrian clumsily incited a Jewish revolt, which he crushed mercilessly.

Hadrian was born on January 24, 76, in the Iberian town of Italica, near present-day Seville. Orphaned at an early age in 85, he was raised by his cousin Marcus Ulpius Trajanus, who became the emperor TRAJAN. Under Trajan, Hadrian served well in the Dacian Wars and became governor of Lower Panonia (modern-day Hungary) in 107. By 114, he had been appointed governor of Syria. Although Trajan assumed the imperial throne in 98 and Hadrian had long been a favorite with Trajan's wife, Plotina, the emperor did not formally adopt his ward until he lay on his deathbed on August 8, 117, at which time he also designated him his successor. On August 11, despite internal opposition, Hadrian became emperor.

Hadrian's imperial vision was considerably more modest than Trajan's had been, and while he retained the province of Dacia (modern Romania), he forsook the inroads Trajan had made in Parthia. In Dacia, during 117–18, Hadrian suppressed a rebellion headed by four of Trajan's generals and executed the conspirators. Having secured the internal empire from rebellion, he embarked on several tours of inspection through the provinces during roughly 121 to 132. Whereas Trajan and earlier rulers had advocated a strategy of aggressive expansion, Hadrian concluded from his tour that what the empire now required was a strategy of containment and defense. He ordered the construction of great defensive works on the German frontiers and in northern England, where large stretches of "Hadrian's Wall," begun in 121 or 122, still stand.

In other provinces—especially Greece—he sought to impose the imperial imprint through massive building projects. In Palestine, he decreed the construction of a new city, Aelia Capitolina, on the site of Jerusalem. Its central shrine, a temple dedicated to Jupiter Capitolinus, was planned to displace the Temple of Jerusalem. Adding insult to injury, Hadrian further decreed a prohibition against circumcision. In 132, the Jewish leader Bar Kochba led a bloody revolt that lasted until 135, proving costly to Hadrian and brutally devastating to the Jews. Much of Palestine was laid waste.

Following the wars in Palestine, Hadrian retreated to his villa at Tivoli, outside of Rome. He groomed his aging brother-in-law, L. Julius Ursus Servianus, as his successor, but then adopted L. Ceionius Commodus, giving him the name L. Aelius Caesar and nominating him as his heir in 136. Aelius died, and Hadrian adopted T. Aurelius Antoninus in January 138. After Hadrian's death on July 10, 138, Aurelius assumed the throne as Antoninus Pius.

Further Reading: Stewart Perowne, *Hadrian* (1960; reprint ed., London and Dover, N.H.: Croom Helm, 1987).

Haile Selassie (1892–1975)
Haile Selassie was emperor of Ethiopia from 1930 to 1974 and, though a confirmed autocrat who suppressed stories concerning the starvation of his people, is best remembered for his desperate resistance against Mussolini's 1935 invasion.

Emperor Hadrian, as depicted in a bust in the Vatican collection. (From Richard Delbruck, Antike Portrats, *1912)*

Haile Selassie was born Tafari Makonnen on July 23, 1892, the grandnephew of Emperor MENELIK II. Menelik was succeeded in 1913 by his grandson Lij Yasu, who had been converted to Islam and was now a zealous Muslim. In 1916, when he attempted to change the state religion of Ethiopia from Coptic Christianity to Islam, Tafari Makonnen succeeded in driving him from the throne, installing Lij Yasu's aunt as Empress Zauditu. As Ras ("Prince") Tafari, Makonnen assumed the regency. He also declared himself heir to the throne, but, in fact, virtually ruled the country as regent even before he was crowned king in 1928. Two years after this, Zauditu died under mysterious circumstances, and Ras Tafari became Emperor Haile Selassie I.

As absolute monarch, Haile Selassie aggressively centralized Ethiopian government and instituted various reforms, most significantly the abolition of slavery. A noble and dignified figure, he came to be regarded as an early anti-Fascist hero when he appeared before the League of Nations to seek aid against the Italian invasion of Benito MUSSOLINI. Powerful and moving, Haile Selassie's plea for assistance proved fruitless, since the League lacked the military authority to intervene in the Italian aggression. After Italy annexed Ethiopia, the emperor was forced into exile.

Ethiopia was liberated very early in World War II, so that Haile Selassie was restored to his throne by 1941. His record after the war can best be characterized as enlightened despotism. Haile Selassie refused to relinquish any authority, but he did formulate and put into operation long-range plans to modernize his nation. Yet as Ethiopia emerged more fully into the modern world, resistance against the emperor's arbitrary autocracy grew. By the 1960s, a number of attempted coups d'état were directed against his rule, and he responded to each attempt with redoubled despotism.

Aging and ill, Haile Selassie was finally deposed by the army in 1974. Initially, he was merely stripped of his authority, but before year's end he was removed from the throne and confined under house arrest. He died in the Ethiopian capital of Addis Ababa on August 27, 1975.

Further Reading: Haile Selassie I. *The Autobiography of Emperor Haile Selassie I*, trans. by E. Ullendorff (Oxford: Oxford University Press, 1976); Leonard Mosley. *Haile Selassie: The Conquering Lion* (Englewood Cliffs, N.J.: Prentice-Hall, 1964).

Hamilcar Barca   (ca. 285–ca. 229 B.C.)

The father of Hannibal and a great Carthaginian general in his own right, Hamilcar Barca firmly established Carthaginian rule in Spain.

Appointed general late in the First Punic War, Hamilcar took charge of the Carthaginian forces in Sicily in 247 B.C., after Carthage had already lost almost all of its Sicilian possessions. He immediately began offensive operations by decimating the coastline of Lucania and Bruttium, seizing Mt. Pellegrino near Palermo. He fortified the site, building a harbor for the fleet and continuing to raid the Italian coastline.

Hamilcar left Mt. Pellegrino suddenly in 250 B.C. and swiftly captured Mt. Eryx, splitting the Roman army in two. Having gained the strategic advantage, he ravaged the Italian and Sicilian coastlines.

In 241 B.C., the Carthaginian fleet was finally defeated, and Hamilcar was cut off from his lines of supply and communication. He was empowered to negotiate the best possible peace with the Romans, which he did.

After returning to Carthage, Hamilcar's mercenary troops revolted because they had not been paid. Hamilcar proceeded to destroy the rebel mercenaries in successive battles, taking the prisoners in as soldiers of his own army. He altered this policy of clemency, however, after the penultimate battle of the rebellion, during which the rebel leaders hideously mutilated and murdered their Carthaginian prisoners. Even though Hamilcar's forces killed over 10,000 mercenaries, the rebels managed to regroup and laid siege to Carthage itself. Again, Hamilcar's superior generalship prevailed. He drove the besiegers into a gorge and annihilated them.

Following his victories against the mercenaries, Hamilcar took charge of the army on an expedition to Spain in 237 B.C. to recover territory lost in the First Punic War. He took back all of southern Spain and established the city of Akra Leuke on the hills of Alicante to defend the newly conquered area. Before he could continue his conquests, however, Hamilcar drowned in the River Alebos while withdrawing from a siege against the Spanish town of Helice.

Further Reading: Brian H. Warmington. *Carthage* (London: Hale, 1960).

Hammurabi   (d. 1750 B.C.)

The sixth and best-known ruler of the 1st Dynasty of Babylon, Hammurabi is remembered for the code of laws he produced, one of the oldest such promulgations in human history.

Hammurabi, of the Amorite tribe, was born in Babylon, the son of the ruler Sin-muballit, whom he succeeded in 1792 B.C. In the year of Hammurabi's accession to the throne, Rim-Sin of Larsa, ruler of southern Babylonia, conquered Isin, a traditional buffer zone between Babylon and Larsa. From this point forward, Rim-Sin became Hammurabi's principal rival.

The focus of the ongoing struggle between the two leaders was control of the waters of the Euphrates River. In 1787 B.C., Hammurabi conquered the city of Uruk and took it from Rim-Sin Isin, whom he fought a second time in 1786 B.C. After this, however, an interval of perhaps two decades of relative peace prevailed, during which Hammurabi built temples and other public works. Presumably, it was also during this period that Hammurabi developed his code of laws, 282 case laws governing economic rules (prices, tariffs, and the like), marriage and divorce, and criminal as well as civil matters. While the code embodies many features one would consider typical of tribal custom—such as trial by ordeal and *lex talionis* (an eye for an eye), it also strikes the modern student as forward-looking in its abrogation of such "primitive" customs as the blood feud, private retribution, and marriage by capture.

Despite the long interval of peace and the establishment of the Code of Hammurabi, the last 14 years of this ruler's reign were absorbed in continuous and ruinous warfare. In 1764, Hammurabi moved against an alliance among Ashur, Eshunna, and Elam—principal powers along the Tigris—who blocked access to the all-important metal-producing regions of the territory corresponding to modern-day Iran. The next year, he fought Rim-Sin again, employing the particularly inventive and ruthless stratagem of damming up a principal watercourse, probably a canal flowing out of the Euphrates, either with the object of flooding Larsa or of withholding all water from it. After a long siege of several months, Larsa fell.

In 1762 B.C., Hammurabi fought his eastern neighbors, and the following year he turned against a longtime ally, King Zimrilim of Mari. The reasons for this enmity are not known. During 1755–57, Hammurabi turned to the east once again, this time destroying Eshunna, again by damming the waters. Historians believe this was, however, a pyrrhic victory because it actually exposed Babylon directly to aggression from the east, especially from the Kassites. Hammurabi seems to have directed all of his energies to these battles, spending much of the last two years of his reign constructing elaborate fortifications.

Further Reading: Cyril J. Gadd. "Hammurabi and the End of His Dynasty," in *Cambridge Ancient History,* vol 2 (Cambridge: Cambridge University Press, 1965).

Harald I Fairhair [Finehair] (ca 860–ca. 940)

One of Scandinavia's great warrior chiefs, Harald I was the first king to claim sovereignty over all of Norway.

Son of Halvdan the Black, Harald assumed rule of a portion of southeastern Norway at the age of 10.

Early in his reign, he directed the suppression of a revolt in the Uplands, then made a pact with Haakon, earl of Lade, which freed him to conduct a campaign of conquest throughout western Norway. The decisive Battle of Hafrsfjord, dated in contemporary sources to 872, but placed by most modern historians some 10 to 20 years later, gave Harald direct control of Norway's western coastal districts and, through a network of semi-tributary chieftains, indirect dominion over other parts of the country as well. Those chieftains who did not submit to Harald either perished in conquest or fled to Britain or Iceland, which was discovered during Harald's reign.

Although Harald was aggressive and ruthless, he sought to establish his authority on the basis of more than intimidation alone. Using local chieftains, he established a system of provincial administrations called *lagtings* by which he was able to introduce some degree of central authority over a most unruly realm.

Most of what is known of Harald I Fairhair comes from legendary and literary sources, most notably the *Heimskringla,* a history of Norway's kings by the Icelandic poet and author of the great *Prose Edda,* Snorri Sturlison (1179–1241).

Harald II Eiriksson (ca. 935–ca. 970)

After overthrowing King Haakon I, Harald II Eiriksson oppressively ruled Norway and established the first Christian missions there.

The son of ERIK I BLOODAX, king of Norway from 930 to 935, Harald Eiriksson fled to Denmark following his father's death in 954 in Northumbria at the hands of King Eadred of England. Haakon had deposed Harald's half-brother Eric as king of Norway, and now Harald and his brothers, with the aid of their uncle, Harald Bluetooth, began to launch raids against Haakon in retribution. They managed to kill Haakon around 961, and Harald assumed the throne.

Harald ruled savagely, violently suppressing all dissent. Shortly after his ascension, he killed the kings in the Oslo region and the earl of Lade. He instituted Christian missions in Norway, the first king to do so, but was unable to force adherence to Christian doctrine. Indeed, his ban on pagan worship, combined with other elements of his harsh reign, brought only opposition and rebellion from the people.

After securing the throne, Harald appropriated lands from the nobles, including his uncle, Harald Bluetooth. This infuriated Bluetooth, who aided the son of the earl of Lade, Haakon the Great, and, together, they killed Harald around 970. Haakon the Great succeeded him as king of Norway.

Harald III Sigurdson [Harald the Ruthless]
(1015–1066)
This warlike king consolidated his hegemony in Norway by viciously suppressing lesser chieftains, but thereby lost support for his unsuccessful bid to conquer Denmark.

Harald III was the son of Sigurd Sow (Syr), a Norwegian chieftain, and Estrid, the mother of Norwegian king Olaf II Haraldsson (later canonized as St. Olaf, Norway's patron saint). Harald was only 15 years old when he was given his first taste of combat at the disastrous Battle of Stiklestad against the Danes in 1030. Olaf II perished in the slaughter, and Harald was forced to flee for his life to Russia, where he enlisted in the service of Yaroslav I the Wise, grand prince of Kiev. While in Yaroslav's service, Harald met the grand prince's daughter Elizabeth, whom he subsequently married.

Before Harald returned to Norway in 1045, he left Yaroslav and served with the forces of Byzantine emperor Michael IV, fighting in Sicily and Bulgaria. He may also have made a pilgrimage to Jerusalem during this period.

After his arrival in Norway, Harald shared the throne with his nephew Magnus I Olafsson, becoming sole ruler in 1047 when Magnus was killed in battle against the Danes. Between 1047 and 1062, Harald waged war against the Danish king Sweyn II while he engaged in a continual and bloody power struggle with Norway's many jealous chieftains. The culminating Battle of Niz against Sweyn in 1062 resulted in both monarchs recognizing each other as sovereign over their countries and brought a measure of peace between Denmark and Norway.

No sooner was the enmity with Sweyn II resolved than Harald began a bitter dispute with Pope Alexander II and Adalbert, archbishop of Bremen (the pope's vicar for Scandinavia) over the independence of Norway's church. Harald also expanded Norway's colonial holdings during this time, claiming portions of the Orkney, Shetland, and Hebrides islands. In 1066, he joined forces with Tostig against England's king HAROLD II GODWINESON in a bid to conquer England. King Harold routed the Norwegian army at the Battle of Stamford Bridge in Yorkshire on September 25, 1066, killing Harald the Ruthless. The Norwegian king was succeeded by two sons, Magnus and Olaf III, who ruled jointly until Magnus died in 1069.

Harald IV Gille [Harald Gilchrist]
(ca. 1103–1136)
Harald IV, a cruel and craven monarch, plunged Norway into a century of sporadic and bitter civil war.

Born in Ireland, Harald came to Norway in 1128, claiming to be the son of Magnus III Barefoot, who had reigned as Norway's king from 1093 to 1103. Harald consented to undergo a trial by ordeal to legitimate his claim to the Norwegian throne and successfully walked over red-hot ploughshares. Following this display, Sigurd I Jerusalemfarer—son of Magnus III and king of Norway—acknowledged Harald as his brother, securing a promise that Harald would not claim sovereignty during his lifetime or that of his son Magnus. Immediately following Sigurd's death in 1130, however, Harald violated his pledge and managed to gain acceptance as monarch over half of Norway.

He and Magnus ruled their respective portions of the country until 1134, when the two went to war with one another. Magnus prevailed against Harald at the Battle of Fyrileif, and forced his opponent to flee to Denmark. There, however, Harald gathered reinforcements, renewed hostilities, and captured Magnus in 1135. He tortured, maimed, and blinded the monarch—who became known thereafter as Magnus the Blind—and exiled him to a monastery.

Harald IV became sole ruler of a Norway that was now racked with dissension. The next year, he himself was killed by Sigurd Slembi, a pretender to the throne claiming, as Harald had done, to be the son of Magnus III Barefoot.

Harold I Barefoot (d. 1040)
Bastard son of King Canute, Harold seized the English throne after murdering Alfred the Aetheling, son of ETHELRED II THE UNREADY.

Illegitimate son of Canute of Denmark, who ruled England from 1017 to 1035, Harold became regent in England following Canute's death because Hardecanute, the legitimate son and heir, was absent attending to matters in Denmark.

In 1036, Harold commissioned the murder of another royal claimant, Alfred the Aetheling, son of Ethelred II the Unready, and banished the mother of Hardecanute from England.

Harold assumed the English throne himself, devoting most of his energies to fighting off invaders from Wales and Scotland. Harold I Barefoot died on March 17, 1040, after which Hardecanute returned to England to ascend the throne.

Harold II Godwineson (ca. 1020–1066)
Harold, the last Anglo-Saxon king of England, ruled for only nine months.

With the return of Edward the Confessor to the English throne in 1042 came the restoration of the house of Wessex to English politics. Harold's father, Godwine, earl of Wessex and Kent, was the most powerful baron in the country. On his death in 1053, Harold assumed his lands and prerogatives, gradually becoming Edward's most trusted adviser as well as one of his ablest generals.

Harold commanded the English forces from 1055 to 1063 in a number of campaigns against the Welsh king Lewelyn. Not satisfied with merely defeating the Welsh, Harold totally and brutally subjugated them, laying waste to the Welsh countryside and killing Llewelyn himself. This enhanced his political standing in England and endeared him to Edward. With Edward's only living relative a distant Hungarian cousin, the king named Harold as his heir.

In 1064, Harold, on an unknown mission for Edward, was shipwrecked in Normandy and captured by William, duke of Normandy. As a condition of his release, William compelled Harold to renounce his claim to the throne in favor of William. But when Edward died in January 1066, Harold was nevertheless named king. His military resolve was quickly put to the test, however.

Harold's younger brother, Tostig, disgruntled over Harold's treatment of himself, made an alliance with yet another rival for the throne, KING HARALD III of Norway, and prepared to invade England. The two landed near Yorkshire with more than 300 ships in September 1066. Harold, who was awaiting William's anticipated invasion in the south, was forced to march north immediately. He crushed the invaders at the Battle of Stamford Bridge on September 25, killing both Tostig and the Norwegian king and inflicting greater than 80 percent casualties on their troops.

Two days after the triumph at Stamford Bridge, William landed in Sussex. Harold marched south again, and the two met at the momentous Battle of Hastings on October 15, 1066, where William earned the sobriquet WILLIAM I THE CONQUEROR by destroying Harold's army and killing the king, thereby bringing to an end the Anglo-Saxon hegemony in England and initiating the Norman phase of English history.

Further Reading: George N. Garmonsway, ed. *The Anglo-Saxon Chronicle* (London: Dent, 1953); F. M. Stenton. *Anglo-Saxon England* (Oxford and New York: Oxford University Press, 1989).

Harsha [Harshavardhana] (ca. 590–ca. 647)

A ruthless conqueror but a benevolent ruler, Harsha amassed a large empire in northern India, which did not, however, outlast his lifetime.

Harsha was the second son of Prabhakaravardhana, who was king of Thaneswar (Sthanvisvara, in the Punjab). Harsha succeeded his elder brother Rajayavardhana to the throne in 606 when the latter was assassinated by Sasanka, king of Bengal. At this time as well, Grahavarman, the husband of Harsha's sister Rajyasri, was defeated and killed in battle by the king of Malwa, prompting Rajyasri to flee to parts unknown. One of Harsha's first acts, therefore, was to locate and recover his sister and to form an alliance with King Kumara Bhaskarvarman of Karmarupa in order to send an army against Sasanka. Harsha failed to unseat Sasanka, but he waged incessant war against him from 606 to 612, conquering what the Chinese pilgrim Hsüang-tsang calls the "five Indies" (probably Valabhi, Magadha, Kashmir, Gujarat, and Sind). In 620, he also moved against the Deccan, but was pushed back by King Pulakeshin II of Chaluyka. Apparently, Harsha conducted sporadic warfare throughout his entire reign.

The empire he amassed was more of a realm of influence and control than a centralized nation. The kings he conquered were permitted to remain on their thrones in return for tribute and homage. Nevertheless, in this way, Harsha came to dominate a very large area, stretching from the snow-covered hills of the subcontinent's northern reaches to the Narmada in the south, and from Ganjam in the east to Valabhi in the west.

Except that he was continually at war, Harsha appears in Indian chronicles as a model ruler not unlike Asoka. A Hindu turned Mahayana Buddhist, Harsha practiced benevolence and established institutions to care for travelers, the poor, and the sick. At quinquennial assemblies convened at the confluence of the Ganges and the Jumna, he distributed treasure accumulated during the previous four years. His court supported learning and literature, including Bana (author of the *Kadambari* and the *Harshacharita*), Mayura (lyric poet who wrote the *Subhasitabali*), and the Chinese pilgrim-scholar Hsüang-tsang. Harsha's own Sanskrit poems, *Nagananda, Ratnavali,* and *Priyadarsika* are described by scholars as "literary gems."

Despite his aggression as a conqueror, benevolence as a ruler, and the force of his personality, Harsha left no enduring political legacy. When he died about 647, his realm instantly shattered into anarchic and warring factionalism.

Further Reading: Sachchidananda Bhattacharya. *A Dictionary of Indian History* (New York: Braziller, 1967).

Harun ar-Rashid (ca. 763–809)

The fifth caliph of the Arab Abbasid dynasty, Harun mercilessly suppressed those who opposed him.

The second son of the caliph al-Mahdi, Harun was raised by his mother, a former slave girl, and Yahya the Barmakid, a Persian and Harun's tutor. Harun and his brother, Hadi, were educated as nobles, reading the Koran extensively. In 780, Harun was sent as nominal commander against the Byzantine Empire. While it is doubtful that he made any substantive military decisions, the success of the campaign added to Harun's growing popularity. In 782, he was again sent as nominal commander of an expedition, this time to the Bosphorus, and again the campaign was successful.

For his efforts, his father gave him the title "ar-Rashid," meaning the "one following the right path,"and appointed Harun governor of Tunisia, Egypt, Syria, Armenia, and Azerbaijan. Yahya joined him as chief administrator and adviser. Apparently, all of this was engineered by Harun's mother and Yahya himself, who had gained considerable influence at court. Harun's mother unsuccessfully tried to persuade the caliph to name Harun his successor. But al-Mahdi died in August 786 and Hadi died just a month later—possibly the victim of a plot hatched by Harun's mother. In any case, the throne was now Harun's, and he was named caliph on September 14, 786.

Harun named Yahya his chief minister, who in turn named his two sons Fadl and Jafar as his advisers. Harun's mother continued to exercise considerable influence over her son and the government until her death in 789, after which the Barmakids essentially controlled the caliph, though they did not abuse the privilege, governing wisely. The Abbasid dynasty having been inaugurated only 40 years earlier, there was still much internal dissent, and Harun was soon faced with rebellion in Egypt, Syria, Yemen, and several provinces in the east. Harun managed to squash each rebellion before it gained a substantial following.

Once installed, Harun began to show a vicious side of his personality that had not been apparent previously. He took fanatical pleasure in watching cock and dog fighting, which soon replaced his love for music and the arts in a royal court so elaborate that it was celebrated in *The Thousand and One Nights*. A notorious insomniac, he wandered about the city at night in disguise, taking with him Jafar and an executioner, should he feel inclined to exercise his authority to order the immediate death of anyone he chose.

This violent and degenerate streak reached a climax in 803 with the Barmakid fall from grace. It was precipitated by either homosexual jealousy between Jafar and Harun, an illicit affair between Jafar and Harun's sister, or Harun's fear of Barmakid power. Perhaps it was a combination of these causes. In any case, Harun had Jafar decapitated and the head brought to him. The caliph addressed the severed head, charging it with the crimes for which Jafar had already been executed.

Harun ordered further executions—including those of his own sister and her two children by Jafar. He then imprisoned Fadl and Yahya and confiscated all Barmakid property.

After further successful operations against the Byzantine Empire, Harun personally marched against a revolt in Iran in the fall of 808. During operations there, he fell ill and was expected to die very shortly. Before his death, however, the brother of the rebel leader was captured and taken before Harun. Reportedly, Harun's last words before his death were, "If I had no more breath left but to say a single word, it would be, 'slay him.' "

Further Reading: André Clot. *Harun al-Rashid and the World of the Thousand and One Nights* (New York: New Amsterdam Books, 1989); Philip Hitti. *History of the Arabs.* (London: Macmillan, 1937).

Hasan-e-Sabbah   (ca. 1055–1124)

A leader of the Islamic sect of Nizari Ismailis, Hasan is believed to be the founder of the Nizari order of the Assassins.

As a youth, Hasan-e-Sabbah studied religion at the Persian city of Rayy. There, about the age of 17, Hasan converted to Ismail, becoming a devout believer, quickly rising in the Ismaili organization, and becoming deputy to the chief of the Seljuk regions in 1071. Around 1076 he was sent to Egypt for additional studies, staying there for three years. After returning to Persia, he traveled about the country, spreading word of the Ismaili faith.

In his travels, Hasan attracted a number of converts, including many inside the rock fortress of Alamut at Daylam, a province of the Seljuk Turks. In 1090, with the aid of these converts inside as well as many outside, Hasan successfully stormed Alamut, using the technique of assassinating key strategic personnel. The Seljuk Turks attempted to retake the fortress, but were defeated at the second battle of Alamut in 1118.

Hasan, now recognized as the leader of the Nizari movement—called such because the movement supported Nizar's claim to the imamate—got down to the difficult business of governing his far-flung, non-contiguous lands. Personally, he led a spartan life under the strict doctrines of his radical Islamic faith. In the course of his reign, he caused the execution of both of his sons, one for alleged murder and the other for drunkenness. By the time of his death in 1124, he was looked upon not only as a political leader, but as a religious symbol and worthy successor to Imam Nizar.

Further Reading: Marshall G. S. Hodgson. *The Order of Assassins: The Struggle of the Early Nizari Ismailis Against the Islamic World* (The Hague: Mouton, 1955)

Hatshepsut   (r. 1503–1482 B.C.)

One of the first great female rulers in history, Hatshepsut reigned over Egypt in the days of the pharoahs.

The daughter of King THUTMOSE I and Queen Ahmose, Hatshepsut was married to her half-brother, THUTMOSE II. When Hatshepsut's older brothers died, Thutmose II became heir and then king on the death of their father around 1512. He and Hatshepsut ruled jointly. When Thutmose II died in 1503, Hatsheput's stepson and nephew, THUTMOSE III, should have been proclaimed king, but Hatshepsut declared herself regent for the young heir.

The regency charade did not content her for long, and she soon had herself crowned as a pharaoh, adopting male royal dress, including the traditional false beard. Although Hatshepsut did manage to maintain her office in the male-dominated society of Egypt, she either was not permitted—or judiciously chose not—to make war. Instead, she busied herself with other undertakings, such as a trading expedition to Punt, in Sudan or Ethiopia near the Red Sea, from which she brought home precious metals and hides as well as animals and scents. She also supervised the moving of two 100-foot-high red granite obelisks to her father's temple at Karnak.

In the meantime, Thutmose III became commander of the army and amassed considerable power. He marshaled his supporters and assumed the throne on the death of Hatshepsut in 1482 B.C. It is unclear whether she was murdered or died from other causes. Thutmose III caused her tomb to be defiled and removed her name from monuments on which it could be found.

Further Reading: James H. Breasted. *A History of Egypt from the Earliest Times to the Persian Conquest* (London: Hodder & Stoughton, 1906); William F. Edgerton. *The Thutmosid Succession* (Oxford: Clarendon Press, 1933).

Hayashi Senjuro   (1876–1943)

This Japanese general purged his opponents from the military and attempted to form a one-party state, but was crushed in elections.

A career army officer, Hayashi Senjuro was born February 23, 1876, in Kanazawa, Japan. Stationed on the Korean frontier, he was given command of the entire Japanese force in that region by 1931. Without authorization from Tokyo, Senjuro marched into Manchuria that same year and precipitated the first Japanese aggression that became World War II in the Pacific. In spite of the fact that his move into Manchuria had been unauthorized, Senjuro was promoted to full general in 1932, and named minister of war in 1934, succeeding his opponent, Araki Sadao.

As war minister, Senjuro attempted to purge all of Sadao's supporters, who were reported to have Fascist leanings, and he did succeed in forcing out more than 5,000 high-ranking officers.

In 1935, Senjuro stepped down as war minister and took a position on the Japanese Supreme Court, but resigned the following year. Inactive in politics for over a year, Senjuro was named prime minister when his party took control of the government in 1937. In an attempt to create an administration that would avoid the political infighting of the past, Senjuro demanded that all cabinet members renounce any party affiliations or obligations.

When it was apparent he would not be able to force his non-partisan absolutist system on Japanese politics, Senjuro threw his government's support behind the pro-military Showakai Party. He dissolved the assembly and called for general elections, which, he hoped, would give him a mandate and a one-party government. He received neither. His electors were crushed at the ballot box, and he was forced to resign. Senjuro died on February 4, 1943.

Henry I   (ca. 1008–1060)

Continually at war with his vassals, King Henry I of France was unable to consolidate his power, and, eventually defeated, conceded something to all who rose against him.

The son of Robert II and grandson of Hugh Capet, the first king of France and founder of the Capetian dynasty, Henry I rose to the French throne in 1026, during his father's lifetime. His mother, Constance of Provence, favored Henry's younger brother, Robert, and civil war broke out when Robert II died in 1031. Constance and Robert were supported by Eudes, count of Blois, while Henry gained the support of Robert, duke of Normandy. Henry managed to subdue his brother in 1032 by giving him Burgundy, and he defeated Eudes two years later. Eudes' sons, Stephen and Theobald, renewed the conflict in 1037. Henry was able to defeat Stephen on his own, but he had to rely on Geoffrey of Anjou to defeat Theobald.

Although he emerged nominally victorious from these initial power struggles, Henry was, in fact, nearly devastated by them. He had given Burgundy to his brother, and, for their support, he had relinquished French Vexin and Tours to Robert, duke of Normandy, and Geoffrey of Anjou, respectively. When Robert, duke of Normandy, died in 1047, he was succeeded by William (later WILLIAM I THE CONQUEROR, of England). Henry saw a possible ally and helped William at the Battle of Val-aux-Dunes, but the two soon split and warred frequently with each other, climaxing in the 1058 Battle of Varaville, at which Henry was routed.

Henry's attempt at absolute sovereignty fell short in every respect, including in matters of the church. He attempted to resist papal authority in France, but he proved unable to stop Pope Leo IX from holding a council at Reims, and eventually he was forced to concede to Leo as well. France lost territory during Henry's beleaguered reign, but the king did secure the throne for his infant son Philip shortly before his death on August 2, 1060.

Henry I Beauclerc   (1069–1135)

Ascending to the English throne under questionable circumstances, Henry struggled to pacify contentious parties and maintain his position.

The third son of WILLIAM I THE CONQUEROR, Henry, who could read and write Latin, once told his illiterate father that "an illiterate king is a crowned ass." After William's death on September 9, 1087, his oldest son, Robert (Robert Curthose), received the duchy of Normandy and his second son, William II, ascended to the English throne under the law of primogeniture. Henry received £5,000 silver and used it to buy land in Normandy.

When a group of English barons tired of William's rule, Henry craftily allied himself with them. In August 1100, while on a hunting trip with a notable baronial family and Henry, William was killed in a hunting "accident." With his other brother, Robert, off fighting the Crusades, Henry rushed to Westchester to seize the treasury and claim his throne. He was crowned king in Westminster Abbey on August 5, 1100. To gain baronial support for his reign, Henry issued a reform charter beneficial to the landowners and the church, and he dismissed the unpopular ministers from his brother's regime.

Robert returned from the Crusade in 1101 and promptly invaded England. Henry bought off his brother with a generous pension and lands in Normandy, but he still found it necessary to move against the barons who had supported Robert. They, in turn, looked to Robert to defend them. Despite the pension, Robert led a rebellion, which only served to give Henry an excuse to invade Normandy and depose his brother there on grounds of misgovernment. In October 1106, Henry defeated Robert at the Battle of Tinchebrai and subsequently annexed Normandy.

With his power secured, Henry's problem was now one of succession. He had more than 20 children, only two of whom were legitimate. His son drowned in 1120, and his daughter, Matilda, was already married to Henry V of Germany, which dis-

qualified her as heir to the throne. This problem was apparently solved in 1125, when her husband died. Henry quickly secured from the barons oaths of fealty to Matilda and felt secure in the knowledge that he had established a legitimate successor.

In 1135, Henry gorged on a meal of lampreys. He developed indigestion, which turned into a fever. On December 1, 1135, he died at Lyons-la-forêt, Normandy. His nephew, Stephen of Blois, brushed aside Matilda's claim and seized the throne for himself, thereby precipitating a civil war that dragged on until Stephen's death and the accession of Henry II in 1154.

Further Reading: Richard William Southern. *Medieval Humanism and Other Studies* (New York: Harper & Row, 1970).

Henry I the Fowler   (ca. 876–936)

Henry I the Fowler, first monarch of the Saxon dynasty, led a loose German confederation allied for defense against the Danes and Hungarians.

The son of Otto of Erlauchten, duke of Saxony, Henry received an education designed expressly to train him as heir. He gained a reputation for great intelligence and for physical strength. When Otto died in 912, Henry became duke of Saxony.

He immediately found himself at war with Conrad I, duke of Franconia, over the territory of Thuringia, which lay between Saxony and Franconia. Henry temporarily lost control of the contested region, but in 918 persuaded Conrad, on his deathbed, to name him heir not only to the throne of Thuringia, but of Franconia as well. Having gained control of two of the four most powerful duchies in Germany, Henry was elected king of Germany in May 919. After two brief military campaigns, he also brought the other two duchies, Swabia and Bavaria, into the fold. Next, in 925, he reconquered Lorraine, adding it to the German confederation.

Henry did not make himself a ruler of a truly unified Germany. His policy was to grant to the dukes at least nominal control of their duchies, and he always looked first to the interests of Saxony. His goal was not to forge a nation so much as to create and maintain a united effort against the Danes and Hungarians, who had pillaged a fragmented Germany for decades.

In 926, the Hungarians invaded again, but Henry was able to capture a Magyar chieftain and use him for ransom. He reached an accord with the Hungarians, agreeing to ransom the chieftain and pay an indemnity for nine years in return for cessation of hostilities. Henry used the long armistice to fortify his towns, augment his army, and build defensive fortifications along the border. He also used the respite from Hungarian attacks to exact revenge on the marauding Slavs, capturing from them Brandenburg and Meissen. In 929, Henry invaded Bohemia, capturing King Wenceslas and exacting tribute from him. When the Hungarians resumed hostilities in 933, Henry was ready and destroyed their army at the Battle of the Unstrut River.

Henry the Fowler died on July 2, 936, leaving the Saxon dynasty to his son, OTTO I THE GREAT.

Further Reading: Geoffrey Barraclough. *The Origins of Modern Germany* (Oxford: B. Blackwell, 1952).

Henry II   (1133–1189)

One of the greatest of English monarchs and, for a time, the most powerful man in Europe, Henry II did much to establish the central power of the English crown.

Born March 5, 1133, at Le Mans, Henry was the son of Geoffrey Plantagenet, count of Anjou, and Matilda, the daughter of King Henry I of England. Henry I was an able monarch, who had taken the first steps in forging for his kingdom an English, as opposed to Anglo-Saxon or Norman, identity. He granted royal charters to many English towns, thereby delivering the emerging merchant classes from domination by capricious and rapacious barons. He also promoted learning in his realm. Henry I failed, however, to establish an enduring legacy of reform and good government. The only son of Henry I, William the Atheling, died before his father. The nobles pledged to accept Henry's daughter, Matilda, as their queen, but when Henry I died in 1135, Stephen, count of Blois, claimed the throne.

Stephen did not enjoy universal acceptance, and Matilda invaded England to claim her right of rule. A period of civil war resulted, during which Henry was taken to England to be educated, then in 1144 went to Normandy, which Geoffrey Plantagenet had just captured from Stephen. In 1147, Henry campaigned against Stephen in England with disastrous lack of success. Two years later, allied with King David of Scotland, he attacked Stephen again, but was defeated and barely escaped with his life.

Henry became duke of Normandy in 1150 and succeeded his father as count of Anjou the next year. He married Eleanor of Aquitaine, former wife of France's Louis VII, in 1152, and thereby came to control vast realms in southern France. Now operating from a much stronger base of power, he invaded England yet again in January 1153. Although his military confrontation with Stephen at the Battle of Wallingford in July 1153 was essentially inconclusive, Henry had garnered popular support and, with the aid of Theobald, archbishop of Canterbury, hammered out an uneasy but favorable peace. It was agreed that Stephen would rule until his death, at which time Henry would succeed him.

Henry did not have long to wait. Stephen died in October 1154, and Henry was crowned on December 19. England was only one part of Henry's realm—called the Angevin Empire—which included much of present-day France and, in size, was second only to the Holy Roman Empire among European states. But it was upon England proper that Henry's rule left its most enduring legacy. He began by recovering the northern regions of Northumberland, Cumberland, and Westmoreland from Scottish domination during 1157. From 1159 to 1165, he campaigned in Wales, for a time (at least) subjugating it, and in 1171 he annexed Ireland to the English crown. All during this period, from 1159 through 1174, he also fought with his continental rival, Louis VII of France.

On the civil front, he replaced feudal service with a system of scutage, "shield money" paid to the crown in lieu of service. He vastly reformed the system of English justice, concentrating all authority in the hands of royal circuit judges, thereby making the administration of law solely the responsibility of the crown. He established the primacy of English common law traditions, enriched by Norman refinements, thereby guaranteeing that the administration of justice would be governed by enduring principles rather than be subject to the whim of this or that monarch. Henry introduced trial by jury and the right of appeal.

Henry's judicial reforms brought him into sharp conflict with his close friend Thomas à Becket, archbishop of Canterbury, over the authority of church courts versus that of royal justice. The conflict escalated, with brief periods of reconciliation, during 1162–70. In 1164, at the Council of Clarendon, Henry II summoned the bishops to sign an agreement essentially pledging their allegiance and obedience to the king. Refusing to sign, Becket went into exile for six years, and many of the bishops sided with him. Moreover, many among the English populace felt greater allegiance to the church than to the king, seeing in the church an alternative to royal tyranny. When Becket returned to England in 1170, he enflamed a Christmas Day audience with a sermon in which he excommunicated certain knights loyal to Henry. He also predicted his own martyrdom. Henry, who was in France at this time, exasperately declared to his knights, "Will no one rid me of this turbulent priest?" Four knights took this as an injunction to assassinate Becket, which they did in 1171. Henry took upon himself the responsibility for his former friend's murder, made a public act of contrition, and performed various other acts of penance as prescribed by the pope.

While Henry retained his power following the death of Becket, parts of England, which simmered with revolt, boiled over in simultaneous war with France, the Scots, and rebellious English barons in 1173. Henry was compelled to rush to France, where he successfully fought off attacks on Normandy and Anjou during the summer and fall. He then had to hurry back to England, to counter the threat of a Scots invasion. At the Battle of Alnwick, July 13, 1174, he captured the Scots king William the Lion.

While Henry struggled with great energy, skill, and efficiency to impose and maintain order in his realms, he neglected the anarchy and rebellion that was brewing within his own family. He endowed his sons Richard (later RICHARD I, called the Lion-Hearted), Geoffrey, and John (later King JOHN) with lands and titles, but withheld funds from them. To avoid the kind of strife that had followed the death of Henry I, he crowned his eldest son, Henry, king. Young Henry repaid this act by rebelling against his father in 1183. The revolt was put down, and young Henry died of a fever soon afterward.

Following his son's death, Henry II stirred further family discord by formally recognizing the right of his next son, Richard, to succeed him, but openly favoring sons Geoffrey and John. Eleanor of Aquitaine encouraged Richard and Geoffrey to act against their father, and Richard allied himself with the new king of France, PHILIP II AUGUSTUS. The two began a war of rebellion against Henry II, which was secretly joined by John. In 1189, Henry II was forced to retreat at the Battle of Le Mans, fell ill, and called for a truce. He agreed to generally unfavorable peace terms and retired to his castle in Chinon, where his illness worsened. On his deathbed, he was informed that John—his favorite son—had participated in the rebellion against him. He died, on July 6, 1189, in the arms of his youngest son Geoffrey, muttering his last words: "Shame, shame on a conquered king."

Henry II   (1333–1379)

The founder of the Castilian House of Trastamara, Henry was engaged in a power struggle with his half-brother and brutally suppressed all opposition.

· The illegitimate son of Alfonso XI, Henry labored in the shadow of his half-brother, PETER I THE CRUEL, who was king of Castile and León beginning in 1350. After enduring two years of exile during Peter's brutal reign, Henry began a popular uprising in Asturias against his brother. Failing at first, Henry continued to wage intermittent civil war against Peter for the next 17 years.

In 1366, Henry's followers proclaimed him king and, aided by the French, invaded Castile. Henry was crowned at Burgos, but Peter turned back the invaders, routing Henry at Nájera on April 3, 1367, with the aid of the Englishman, Edward the Black Prince. In his turn, Henry was not discouraged, and, with additional French support, marched on Peter again, capturing and murdering him on March 23, 1369.

Nevertheless, Henry's crown was not secure. Castile was caught up in the Hundred Years' War in 1369, facing attack from all sides. Henry moved against Portugal, Navarre, and Aragón and then was forced to confront John of Gaunt, Peter's son-in-law and a pretender to the throne. In the midst of grave external pressures, Henry defeated John and others who opposed him from within. He forestalled further foreign incursions by a host of dynastic marriages and treaties. Henry died on May 29, 1379.

Henry II   (1519–1559)

Henry was king of France from 1547 to 1559, a reign characterized by his merciless persecution of French Protestants.

The second son of Francis I and Claude of France, Henry II spent four years as a hostage in Spain before returning to France in 1530. Henry quarreled incessantly with his father, particularly over the rivalry between his mistress, Diane de Poitiers, and his father's, Anne, duchess d'Etampes. The death of Henry's brother, the Dauphin, in 1536 made Henry heir, and he ascended the throne in 1547.

Once in power, Henry II made attempts to reform the French administrative system by establishing an efficient royal bureaucracy. Also on his domestic agenda was the repression of French Protestants. In the very year of his ascension, Henry II set up the Chambre Ardente in the Parliament of Paris for the sole purpose of trying heretics. The body proceeded with ruthless zeal.

Internationally, Henry II continued the French war with Holy Roman Emperor CHARLES V in 1552, but, preoccupied with purging France of Protestants, Henry II broke off the war and initiated the Peace of Cateau-Cambrésis with Charles V in 1559.

Henry was married to CATHERINE DE' MEDICI, with whom he produced his greatest legacy to France and Europe—an extended family that included his sons, the future kings Francis II, Charles IX, and Henry III, and his sons-in-law Henry of Navarre and Charles III the Great, duke of Lorraine.

Henry's life and reign were cut short by a grotesque accident suffered while participating in a tournament in Paris. He was struck in the head by a misguided lance and died 10 days later on July 10, 1559.

Henry III   (1551–1589)

Last Valois king of France, Henry III maintained an extravagant court, prosecuted the ruinous Wars of Religion, and revoked the edicts that had granted toleration to the Protestant Huguenots.

The third son of HENRY II and CATHERINE DE' MEDICI, Henry III was known as the duke of Anjou during the reign of his brother Charles IX. He was elected king of Poland in 1573, but summarily abandoned that kingdom in June 1574 after the sudden death of his brother left the French throne vacant.

Henry III was a ruler given to great extremes of behavior, practicing ascetic piety one day and indulging in extravagant luxury and licentiousness the next. He demonstrated considerable ability to govern, yet his court was undisciplined and, in particular, plagued by numerous deadly duels among the *mignons* (court favorites). When he attempted to renew war against the Huguenots in 1576, the Estates General, disgusted with his extravagance, refused to grant the necessary funds. Accordingly, Henry concluded a peace with the Huguenots in 1577, which provoked the Roman Catholic radicals to form the Catholic League, led by the house of Guise. By 1585, the League had forced Henry to rescind the edicts of toleration and once again ban Protestantism in France. Pressured by the Catholic League, Henry also acted to bar the Protestant Henry of Navarre—later HENRY IV—from succession to the French throne.

The king's actions finally failed to placate the League, which, in May 1588, incited a popular uprising that sent Henry fleeing from Paris. The monarch took his revenge in December of that year by arranging for the murders of Henry, duke of Guise, and his brother, the cardinal of Guise. In response, the Catholic League and the pope declared Henry deposed, driving him to ally himself with Henry of Navarre. The two allies were marching on Paris on August 2, 1589, when a Catholic fanatic named Jacques Clement assassinated Henry III at St. Cloud.

Henry III   (1017–1056)

One of the greatest rulers of the Holy Roman Empire, Henry was an uncompromising advocate of church reform.

The only son of Holy Roman Emperor Conrad II, Henry was born October 28, 1017, in the Netherlands. His mother, Gisela, took responsibility for his upbringing and raised one of the most highly qualified crown princes in history. Henry was instructed by a number of tutors in several subjects, and was imbued with a sense of piety and a love of the arts, especially literature.

Conrad named Henry co-king of Germany (emperor designate) in 1026. After his father's death in 1039, Henry assumed the throne as sole ruler. He amassed power and territory at a remarkable rate, winning control of Poland, Bohemia, Hungary, and Lorraine, while maintaining his powerful German duchies of Bavaria, Swabia, Franconia, and Carinthia. He also controlled the north of Italy and the regions around Rome.

One object of his march on Rome was to install a pope who could properly crown him Holy Roman Emperor. He deposed three papal pretenders, whom he did not feel morally worthy of the office, and installed Clement II, who in turn crowned him emperor in 1046. That year marked the zenith of power for the Holy Roman Empire of the Middle Ages.

Henry felt that his title as emperor entitled him to reform the church as he saw fit. He attacked the practice of simony (the selling of church offices and indulgences) and lay investiture (the right of secular leaders to appoint church officials). That Henry was himself guilty of both of the practices he sought to reform alienated much of the clergy, which began to undermine his foreign policy as well. Many of the provinces he had conquered rose up in rebellion until, by the time of his death on October 5, 1056, he had lost almost all the territory he had gained—though one of the popes Henry appointed, Leo IX, did surround himself with reformers and began to free the papacy from secular control.

Further Reading: Geoffrey Barraclough. *Origins of Modern Germany* (Oxford: B. Blackwell, 1952). Jeffery Russell. *Dissent and Reform in the Early Middle Ages* (Berkeley: University of California Press, 1965).

Henry III the Sufferer   (1379–1406)

As king of Castile, Henry III, though sickly, resolved his kingdom's long struggle with Portugal and suppressed fanatical anti-Jewish rioting.

Henry III was born in Burgos, Castile, on October 4, 1379, the son of John I. He assumed the throne at age 11, during which time his regents encouraged the fanatical Catholic preaching that resulted in a reign of terror against Castile's Jews. When Henry assumed power in his own right at age 14, he did not stop the persecution of the Jews, but he did act to restore order in the land and to reinvigorate the royal council and courts.

Although he was chronically ill and therefore never led an army in the field, Henry established a strongly autocratic rule through his royal council, the Audencia (equivalent to a supreme court), and a network of loyal *corregidores*, or magistrates. He made a politically strategic marriage to Catherine of Lancaster, which ended a dynastic rift that had long plagued Castile, and he appointed his younger brother Ferdinand to campaign against the Moorish Kingdom of Granada. From 1396 to 1398, he directed an ongoing war with Portugal, forcing that nation to a favorable truce. He also commissioned the Norman Jean de Béthencourt to conquer and colonize the Canary Islands, thereby securing a rich prize for his kingdom.

Henry IV of Bourbon-Navarre   (1553–1610)

The first Bourbon king of France, Henry IV ended nearly 40 years of civil war.

Henry was born December 4, 1553, to Antoine of Bourbon and Jeanne d'Albret of Navarre. Through his father, Henry was descended from the Capetian kings of France. Nevertheless, his chances of ascending the French throne were slim, since Catherine de' Medici was to bear the reigning king, Henry II, four sons. Henry's parents, particularly his mother, were liberal-minded people, who raised their son as a Huguenot. Indeed, Jeanne, a morally strong individual, was also fiercely independent, proclaiming her Protestant faith on Christmas Day, 1560. These qualities of high-mindedness and independent thinking were passed on to her son.

The religious climate in France during the 16th and 17th centuries was volcanic, with mutual hatred between the Catholics and the Huguenots. When Antoine was killed in battle in 1562, Henry became king of Navarre (Henry III of Navarre). Hoping to avoid further bloodshed and preserve the kingdom for her children, CATHERINE DE' MÉDICI arranged for Henry's marriage to her daughter, Margaret of Valois. However, the French court was fearful of Huguenot influence and instigated the St. Bartholomew's Day Massacre of August 24, 1572, only six days after the wedding. Who, precisely, had ordered the slaughter is unclear, but it appears that both Catherine and Henry, duke of Guise, had a hand in it. In its wake, panic swept Paris, and Henry of Navarre was taken virtual prisoner by Catherine's second son, Charles IX, king of France, who demanded that he renounce his faith and convert to Catholicism. Henry did so, but no one was convinced of the sincerity of his conversion, and his imprisonment endured into the reign of Charles' brother, Henry III. After three and a half years of confinement, Henry, through the secret cooperation of Catherine de' Medici, escaped, renounced his conversion, and assumed command of the Huguenot forces.

The ensuing struggle revealed Henry to be a military genius, who dealt the Catholics one defeat after

King Henry IV of Navarre. (From M. Guizot, A Popular History of France from the Earliest Times, *n.d.)*

another. His troops even stormed towns under cover of darkness—this in an age when nighttime battle was unheard of. When the duke of Anjou, Catherine's last son, died in 1584, Henry of Navarre emerged as undisputed heir to the French throne—undisputed, but vehemently opposed by most of the Catholics in France as well as Spain.

Henry, duke of Guise, formed the Holy League to oppose Henry of Navarre's claim to the throne. Navarre was also excommunicated by the pope, who decreed that no non-Catholic could ever be king of France. The Holy League, backed by PHILIP II (1577–98) of Spain, now became the dominant political force in France, even stronger than the king, Henry III.

Henry III, knowing that further war would destroy France, allied himself with Henry of Navarre; he also engineered the assassination of Henry, duke of Guise. When Henry III was himself assassinated on August 1, 1589, France found itself with a Protestant king who was denied his kingdom by ousted Catholics backed by the king of Spain. He battled both the Holy League and Philip II of Spain for five years before he could enter Paris, and, even then, it required his reconversion to Catholicism ("Paris is worth a Mass," Henry observed). He was crowned on February 27, 1594.

But the fighting did not end with Henry's coronation. Henry battled Philip for four more years, finally forcing the Spanish king to surrender after the Battle of Amiens on September 19, 1597, and concluding the Treaty of Vervins on May 2, 1598. On April 13 of that year, Henry issued the Edict of Nantes, which established limited religious freedom for the Huguenots in France—the first such decree of tolerance in the history of Europe.

It was one thing to decree tolerance and quite another actually to institute it. On May 14, 1610, while riding through the streets of Paris, Henry was stabbed to death by a religious fanatic named François Ravaillac.

Further Reading: Desmond Seward. *The First Bourbon* (Boston: Gambit, 1971); Henry Sedgwick. *Henry of Navarre*, (Indianapolis: Bobbs-Merrill, 1930); Heinrich Mann. *Henry, King of France* (New York: Overlook Press, 1985).

Henry V (1387–1422)

Perhaps England's most beloved king, Henry V brought stability to the nation and expanded England's French domains, very nearly uniting England and France under a single crown.

Henry was born at Monmouth on or about September 16, 1387, the first son of King Henry IV, who was then embroiled in quelling rebellion in England, Wales, and Ireland, while fending off invasion from Scotland. During the exile of Henry IV, Henry V was raised in the household of RICHARD II. He was knighted for his services during his father's Irish campaign during the spring of 1399 and was made Prince of Wales on October 15, upon the coronation of his father. From 1402 to 1409, Henry V fought against Welsh rebel followers of Owen Glendower.

Henry V was no slavish adherent to his father's policies, and after 1408, he began increasingly to assert himself, often in opposition to Henry IV and his ministers. On the death of his father, March 20, 1413, Henry V assumed the throne and promptly turned his attention to suppressing a rebellion of radical Christians known as the Lollards. Preaching the supremacy of individual conscience, the Lollards collaborated with others in a political revolt and were feared as agents of anarchy. Henry IV had actively persecuted them, and Henry V intensified the campaign against them, ruthlessly crushing armed revolts conducted from December 1413 to January 1414 and executing the Lollard leader, Sir John Oldcastle. No sooner were the Lollards suppressed than Henry was faced with a revolt among nobles who wanted to place Edmund Mortimer, earl of Monmouth, on the throne. This rebellion was quelled—again, without quarter—in July 1415.

In the meantime, taking advantage of a chaotic political situation in France, Henry declared war on that country. Claiming that Normandy was, by absolute right, an English possession, he set sail for the continent on August 10, 1415, and laid siege against the formidable fortress of Harfleur from August 13 to September 22. The army he commanded consisted of professional soldiers rather than the usual conglomeration yielded by medieval levies. It was, however, made up of men of mixed background and loyalties, including Welshmen, Irishmen, Gascons, and others. Accordingly, Henry enforced iron discipline among them.

Harfleur surrendered on September 22, and Henry installed an English garrison, allowing most of the town's inhabitants to remain—though he exacted a ransom from the well-to-do and exiled the aged, infirm, and very young, all of whom were deemed useless mouths to feed. This act of brutality was judged, in its time, a necessity of conquest. From Harfleur, Henry marched with 900 men-at-arms and some 5,000 archers to Calais in an effort to enlarge the area under his control. By October 1515, Henry's force was just south of the River Somme. Constable Charles d'Albret assembled a vastly superior army of 35,000 and engaged Henry's 5,900 in battle at Agincourt on October 25.

The situation seemed hopeless, but the French managed their forces with disastrous ineptitude. Henry used his long-bowmen with great skill, taking a heavy toll on the slow-moving French artillery and on mounted knights, who were arrayed in ranks so tightly packed that they had little room in which to maneuver and do battle effectively. Estimates of French killed at Agincourt vary from some 3,000 to as many as 8,000, with English losses put at a mere 250. The battle not only marked the high point of Henry's reign, but spelled the end of the heavily armored medieval knight as an effective agent of warfare. It also seemed to mark the ascendency of the common soldier—in the person of the long-bowman—over the noble.

The French had lost two of the three cavalry waves at their disposal when a band of raiders attacked the English baggage train at Henry's rear. The king realized that, thus distracted, his forces were now vulnerable to attack by the third wave of French cavalry, which might act in concert with the many French prisoners that had been taken and in this way snatch victory from the proverbial jaws of defeat. Henry acted with terrible decisiveness, ordering that all prisoners be put to death, whereupon the remainder of the French forces withdrew from the field.

Henry went on to conquer all of Normandy during 1417–19, capturing Rouen after a siege that lasted from September 1418 to January 1419, marching on Paris in May 1420, and concluding an alliance with the Burgundian faction that ultimately resulted in the Treaty of Troyes. By this agreement, the feeble French king, Charles VI, acknowledged Henry V heir to the throne of France, making him, for the present, regent. Thus empowered, Henry went onto subdue northern France, laying siege to and capturing Meaux during October 1421 to May 1422.

At this culminating point, Henry's great plan and ambition was to unite and lead all of western Europe in one mammoth Crusade against the heathen. He was, in the words of Sir Winston Churchill, "the supreme figure in Europe."

But Henry V did not long remain on the heights. Exhausted by his campaigning in northern France, he fell ill with dysentery and died at Bois de Vincennes on August 31, 1422. The king's successors proved unable to hold France for long, and England failed to capitalize on most of Henry's gains.

Henry VII (1457–1509)

By ending the long and bloody Wars of the Roses, Henry VII brought peace to England after 30 years and installed the house of Tudor as the reigning dynasty.

Henry was born on January 28, 1457. His father, Edmund Tudor, died three months before Henry's birth, making the boy earl of Richmond.

The English struggle for succession between the houses of Lancaster and York, known as the Wars of the Roses, raged on and off for 30 years because neither party could lay absolute claim to the throne, and no one side held a sustained military advantage

King Henry VII of England. (From J. N. Larned, A History of England for the Use of Schools and Academies, *1900)*

long enough to support a tenuous claim. In May 1471, the Yorkists defeated the Lancastrians at the Battle of Tewkesbury, and Edward IV recovered the throne for the House of York. This sent Henry into exile—presumably for life. However, Edward IV died in 1483, and his two sons were murdered in the Tower of London, most likely by RICHARD III, who had succeeded Edward. Richard was not a favorite of the Yorks, and he created dissension within the house. Henry seized this opportunity to return from exile in Brittany in order to join the renewed rebellion.

He landed at Milford Haven, Wales, in August 1484 and was victorious at the Battle of Bosworth Field, Richard having been killed in the fighting. According to legend, Lord Stanley, finding the fallen Richard's crown in a thornbush, placed it upon Henry's head, proclaiming him king of England.

Henry was officially crowned on October 30, 1484, installing the House of Tudor. In an effort to unite the two warring factions, Henry married Elizabeth of York on January 18, 1486. The new king's crown was far from secure, however. Henry had no financial resources, no military support, and his mother's family were barred by Parliament law from succession to the throne. Nevertheless, he would successfully defeat three attempts by the Yorkists to reclaim the throne.

The first plot, hatched by Lord Lovell, was put down without much difficulty. The second, involving one Lambert Simnel and supported by Margaret, dowager duchess of Burgundy, sister of Edward IV, was almost as easily put down. Henry, realizing that Simnel, who pretended to be the earl of Warwick, son of Edward IV's brother George, was just a pawn of the Yorkists, offered him a job in the royal kitchens, and Simnel happily agreed. The third plot was by far the most serious, and required the harshest measures to quell.

In 1491, a man first claiming to be the earl of Warwick, Edward IV's nephew, surfaced in Ireland. Henry knew that the real earl of Warwick had been imprisoned in the Tower since the Battle of Bosworth Field, but in 1495 King James IV of Scotland supported the pretender, who now claimed to be Richard, duke of York, son of Edward IV. Popular support was never sustained, however, and the impersonator, Perkin Warbeck, as well as the author of the whole scheme, Sir William Stanley, were both executed—along with the real earl of Warwick.

Henry helped ensure the legitimacy of his reign and his family's claim through matrimonial alliances. His first son, Arthur, married Princess Catherine of Aragón, daughter of FERDINAND and ISABELLA of Spain. When Arthur died in 1502, Catherine married his brother, later HENRY VIII; Henry's daughter married King James IV of Scotland. By making connections with other European heads of state, Henry ensured the continuance of the House of Tudor upon his death on April 21, 1509.

Further Reading: Michael Van Cleave. *The First of the Tudors: A Study of Henry VII and His Reign* (Totowa, New Jersey: Rowman and Littlefield, 1980); Eric N. Simons. *Henry VII: The First Tudor King* (New York: Barnes and Noble Books, 1968).

Henry VIII (1491–1547)

England's most celebrated, accomplished, colorful, and terrifying king, Henry VIII instigated the reformation of the English church and did much to establish the supremacy of the throne over a welter of feudal authorities and to fashion his nation into a world power.

Henry was born at Greenwich on June 28, 1491, the son of the first Tudor king, HENRY VII. He was given an excellent Renaissance education and became enthusiastically adept at philosophical discourse, languages, and literature. He was a musician and composer of some merit and, as a young man, was an accomplished athelete, particularly skilled in the hunt and the joust. Henry might well have lived the carefree life of a courtier had his older brother, Prince Arthur, not died prematurely in 1502, making Henry the heir apparent.

Henry succeeded to the throne on the death of his father on April 22, 1509. Prior to his coronation, Henry married Arthur's widow, Catherine of Aragón, daughter of FERDINAND II and ISABELLA I of Spain. By all accounts, the marriage was a happy one for almost two decades, during which time Henry personally commanded several moderately successful military expeditions against the French. By 1527, however, Henry had become obsessed with Catherine's apparent inability to produce a male heir. He had by this time become enamored of Anne Boleyn, a lady of the royal court, and was anxious to divorce Catherine in order to marry her. Seizing on a text from Leviticus 20:21, which proscribes marriage to a dead brother's widow, Henry argued that God would never permit male "issue" from such an unlawful union. He commanded his chief minister, Cardinal Wolsey, to petition Pope Clement VII for a decree of proclaiming the marriage invalid and permitting Henry to remarry.

Catherine vehemently opposed the annulment, as did her nephew CHARLES V, Holy Roman Emperor and king of Spain. The pope relied heavily on the protection of Charles, who dominated Italy during this period, and, while inclined to grant Henry's petition on scriptural grounds, was politically unwill-

King Henry VIII, legendary for his girth and his six wives, broke away from the Catholic church to establish the Church of England. (From J. N. Larned, A History of England for the Use of Schools and Academies, *1900)*

ing to do so. A divorce trial was conducted in London in 1529, but in the absence of a papal decree was adjourned without a decision. Henry, enraged, dismissed Wolsey, and replaced him in 1532 with the crafty Thomas Cromwell. It was he who proposed the radical solution to Henry's marital dilemma, advising the king to break with the Roman church, thereby empowering the archbishop of Canterbury, as head of the English church, to grant the divorce unimpeded. Henry pushed the necessary legislation through Parliament in 1533. He divorced Catherine, married Anne Boleyn, and—almost incidentally, as far as he was concerned—established the Church of England as an independent national church, answerable neither to the Roman Catholic church nor to the person of the pope.

Having secured what he most wanted—the freedom to remarry—Henry at first proceeded moderately with a program of reformation, but he soon moved at an accelerated pace. Between 1536 and 1540, Henry ordered the dissolution of the monasteries and nunneries in England. Their considerable wealth and property were confiscated by the government. To enforce these actions, Henry commanded his subjects to swear an oath of supremacy, pledging loyalty to the king as head of the church. The penalty for refusing the oath was death, and the theologian and philosopher Sir Thomas More became an early martyr to the Catholic cause in England when he was executed for refusing the oath. Despite the absoluteness and vehemence of Henry's break with the pope, the king—who had in 1521 written a treatise against Martin Luther, in recognition of which Pope Leo X had named him "Defender of the Faith"—embraced neither Protestant ideology nor Protestant church ritual. During Henry's reign, the Latin Mass remained unchanged, as did the central tenets and practices of theology.

In September 1533, Anne Boleyn bore Henry a daughter, Elizabeth (subsequently ELIZABETH I), who was declared heir to the throne in place of Catherine's daughter, Mary. That union having been decreed illegal, Mary was declared illegitimate. But Anne, like Catherine, failed to bear a son. She was also unfaithful to Henry—in a queen, an act of treason punishable by death. For her infidelity (and, doubtless, also for the failure to bear a son), Anne was executed in 1536.

The union of Henry and a third wife, Jane Seymour, did produce a son, Edward, a sickly and frail child who did not seem destined for a long life. Jane also fell ill and died shortly after Edward's birth, and Henry took as his fourth wife Anne of Cleves in 1540. This marriage, negotiated by Thomas Cromwell, had a sound political basis. Fearing that the Catholic nations would align against England, Cromwell sought through the union of Henry and the Lutheran Anne to garner diplomatic support from continental Lutherans. Henry, whose legendary girth attested to his passion for the pleasures of the flesh, found the plain woman intolerably unattractive and almost immediately divorced her. He charged the hapless Cromwell with treason, for which he was tried and executed.

Henry next wed the young and beautiful Catherine Howard, niece of Cromwell's ambitious enemy Thomas Howard, duke of Norfolk. Headstrong and impressionable—and doubtless physically repelled by her aging and obese royal spouse—she was discovered in a liaison with a courtier and was beheaded in 1542. Henry's last wife, who survived him, was Catherine Parr. None of his last three wives bore Henry children.

As a military commander, Henry was, on balance, successful, earning his most significant victory at the Battle of the Spurs (so called because of the haste with which the French cavalry beat their retreat) on August 16, 1513. In 1520, Henry met the French king

Francis I in a ceremonial demonstration of friendship on the Field of the Cloth of Gold, near Calais, but from 1522 to 1527 he allied with Charles V against Francis. Henry fought the French a third time in 1544–46. Closer to home, Henry successfully waged war against the Scots at Flodden (1513) and Solway Moss (1542).

Despite a reasonable degree of success in prosecuting foreign wars, these activities greatly strained English coffers, although it can be argued that, while the wars resulted in no tangible territorial gains, they did earn England a significant measure of prestige, which helped position the small island nation for the role it would play in world affairs during the reign of Henry's second daughter, Elizabeth.

Henry was a tyrant, intolerant, despotic, choleric, and vengeful, who held his court—not to mention the majority of his wives—in a chronic state of fear. However, he did keep his kingdom together and fostered a sense of national identity. He also transformed the royal court of England from a backwater to a center of sophistication, art, and learning.

Henry died on January 28, 1547, and was succeeded by the short-lived Edward VI, followed by Mary I (though he had declared her illegitimate, Henry specified in his will that she was to succeed to the throne after Edward), and finally Elizabeth I.

Further Reading: Edward Hall. *Henry VIII* (London: T. C. & E. C. Jack, 1904); A. F. Pollard. *Henry VIII* (London: Longmans, Green, 1905); Jasper Ridley. *Henry VIII* (New York: Viking, 1985); J. J. Scarisbrick. *Henry VIII* (London: Penguin, 1971).

Heraclius   (ca. 575–641)

Heraclius deposed Phocas to become emperor of the rapidly disintegrating Eastern Roman Empire.

Heraclius was born of Armenian lineage in eastern Anatolia. While his father was serving as governor of the Roman province of Africa during the reign of Emperor Phocas, influential elements in Constantinople appealed to him to rescue the empire from misrule. Accordingly, he dispatched Heraclius with an army to effect the emperor's overthrow. Heraclius landed in Constantinople in October 610, deposed Phocas, and was crowned emperor.

The realm over which he now presided was torn by civil strife from within and menaced by Slavic, Persian, and Turkish raiders from without. Not only were the frontiers harried, the exorbitant tributes demanded by various invaders critically and chronically undermined the economy.

Heraclius set about reorganizing the imperial bureaucracy, strengthening the armies, and generally reforming the administration of government in an effort to stave off the collapse of the Eastern Empire. Despite his efforts, however, the Persians took Syria and Palestine in 614, even capturing Jerusalem and appropriating the holiest of holy Christian relics, what was believed to be Christ's cross. Five years later, Egypt and Libya fell to a Persian army of occupation. In the meantime, Heraclius did his best to bring about peace with the Avars, parleying with them at Thracian Heraclea in 617 or 619. Breaking the truce, the tribesmen attempted to capture Heraclius, who managed to outride them all the way back to Constantinople.

It was not until 622 that Heraclius was able to come to terms with the Avars, and, having done so, direct his resources against the Persians. His expedition against invading armies of that empire, aimed at recovering Jerusalem and the Cross, was, in effect, the first Crusade. He fought brilliantly, pushing the Persians out of Anatolia, whereupon he offered a truce to the emperor Khosrow II. The Persian ruler loudly rejected Heraclius' terms and publicly denigrated Christ and Christianity. This served as ample motivation for an extended two-year campaign—beginning in Armenia, to secure the manpower necessary for an invasion of Persia proper—which proved highly successful.

Heraclius commanded his troops personally. In 625, while camped on the west bank of the Sarus River in Anatolia, his men, catching sight of Persian forces on the east bank, made an unauthorized charge across the bridge. Persians emerged from ambush and were on the verge of annihilating Heraclius' forces when the emperor took up his sword, advanced to the bridge, struck down the leader of the Persian troops, and rallied his men in a well-organized and devastating assault. The next year, the Persians counterattacked at the Bosporus, intending to join the Avars in an assault on Constantinople itself. Heraclius' forces sank the Persian fleet, leaving the Persian troops without transport. Unsupported, the Avar assault failed.

Late in 627, Heraclius finally penetrated Persia. In a grand battle near Nineveh, he met the Persians, killing three generals in one-on-one combat, then leading his troops into the thick of the Persian lines. There he personally slew the chief commander of the Persian forces, which rapidly scattered. Early in 628, Heraclius entered the capital city of Dastagird. At his approach, Khosrow II was overthrown by his son, who willingly reached terms with Heraclius. The emperor demanded the redemption of all captives, the return of captured Roman lands, and the return of the Holy Cross, which, in 630, he bore to Jerusalem and reinstalled in the Church of the Holy Sepulcher.

Heraclius believed that the key to retaining the gains he had made was to unite the diverse Christian world by conciliating the diverse theologies of Egypt, Syria, and Armenia, which had long been subject to persecution at the hands of Christianized Roman emperors. Heraclius failed in this effort and was in a state of exhaustion and near collapse in 634 when Arab forces invaded Syria. Unable to take personal command of his army, the emperor entrusted the Byzantine forces to other commanders, who suffered a decisive defeat at the Battle of Yarmuk in 636. The result was the loss of all Heraclius had won in Syria and Egypt. The emperor had to remove the hard-won Cross from the Church of the Holy Sepulcher and evacuate it northward.

Fearless in battle, Heraclius greatly feared water. As a result, he tarried an entire year on the Asian side of the Bosporus. His men fashioned a pontoon bridge screened with leaves that hid the water from view. This Heraclius crossed into Constantinople, where he grew increasingly ill. He died, apparently of a condition related to an enlargement of the prostate, on February 11, 641.

Herod Antipas   (21 B.C.–A.D. 39)
Roman tetrarch of Galilee from 4 B.C. to about A.D. 37, Herod Antipas is most famous for having yielded to his step-daughter/niece Salome in beheading John the Baptist.

The son of HEROD I the Great, Herod Antipas inherited the kingdom of Judaea in 4 B.C. After divorcing his first wife, daughter of the Nabataean king Aretas, Herod Antipas married Herodias, the former wife of his half-brother. The quasi-incestuous marriage drew the ire of Herod's Jewish subjects, including John the Baptist, whom Herod subsequently arrested. Herodias' daughter Salome made a birthday request that Herod behead the radical religious leader. Herod complied—and the entire episode has become the substance of numerous works of art and literature, most famously a play by Oscar Wilde and an opera by Richard Strauss.

When Pontius Pilate, procurator of Judaea, arrested Jesus Christ, he sent him first to Herod Antipas, who refused to pass judgment on him. In A.D. 36, Herod Antipas mediated the Roman-Parthian peace talks. The following year, he fell into a dispute with the new Roman emperor CALIGULA and was banished to Gaul, where he died in 39.

Further Reading: Harold Hoehner. *Herod Antipas* (Cambridge: Cambridge University Press, 1972).

Herod Archelaus   (22 B.C.–ca. A.D. 18)
The son of HEROD I THE GREAT, Archelaus was sent to receive his father's vast kingdom, but his brutal

treatment of the Jews forced AUGUSTUS Caesar to abrogate Herod's will.

Named as the principal beneficiary of the kingdom of Herod I the Great, Herod Archelaus was to receive Judaea, Idumaea, and Samaria. However, his brothers, Philip and HEROD ANTIPAS, challenged their father's will, and in 4 B.C. Herod Archelaus went to Rome to argue his case before the Emperor Augustus. Before his departure, the Jewish leaders of Judaea went to Archelaus to demand reduction of taxes imposed by Herod I the Great. They also demanded leniency for two condemned men who were charged with vandalism. Wary of a revolt, Archelaus sent a company of troops into the area to keep order. When they were stoned, Archelaus ordered them to attack. They did so, killing some 3,000 Jews. Believing that he had enforced relative peace in Judaea, Archelaus set off for Rome.

When he reached the imperial capital, news of the massacre had preceded him, and the Jews of Rome petitioned Augustus to supplant Herod Archelaus in Judaea. This, in addition to his brothers' demand for equal partitioning of the lands, moved Augustus to abolish Herod's monarchy and name Herod Archelaus ethnarch—essentially a regent for the lands, conditional on his ability to rule effectively, at which point he would be named king. His brothers received the land allotted them in the will and were named tetrarchs.

Returned to Judaea, Archelaus ruled with an iron hand, suppressing any hint of Jewish rebelliousness. The Jews, in turn, saw Archelaus as they had seen his father, an alien oppressor. To make matters worse, Herod Archelaus married his step-brother's widow, an abomination in Jewish law. In A.D. 6, another delegation was sent to Augustus to complain about Herod Archelaus' rule. The ethnarch was summoned to the capital and tried for his misrule. Although he was defended by the future emperor Tiberius, Herod Archelaus was convicted. Augustus relieved him of his ethnarchy, confiscated his property, and exiled him to Gaul, where he died around A.D. 18.

Herod I the Great (73–4 B.C.)

Roman-appointed king of Judaea from 37 to 4 B.C., Herod was the despot in whose kingdom Jesus of Nazareth was born.

The son of a wealthy and prominent Edomite, Antipater, Herod was born in southern Palestine. His father was named procurator of Judaea by Julius CAESAR in 47 B.C., whereupon the family received Roman citizenship. Herod was subsequently appointed governor of Galilee by his father, and in 41 B.C., Marc Antony gave Herod the position of tet-

This Gustave Doré book illustration depicts the Massacre of the Innocents—the murder of all male infants in Jerusalem ordered by Herod the Great. (From Gustave Doré, The Doré Bible Gallery, *1879)*

rarch of Galilee. An anti-Roman insurrection in Palestine forced Herod to flee to Rome in 40 B.C. While he was there, the Roman Senate elected him king of Judaea and furnished him with an army to retake the Palestinian capital in 37 B.C. The following year, Herod rode unchallenged into Judaea, over which he ruled for the next 32 years.

Herod married a Hasmonean princess named Mariamne (who became one of nine wives), and he supported his friend Marc Antony in his struggle with AUGUSTUS for the Roman throne—even though Antony's mistress, CLEOPATRA, persuaded Antony to annex part of Herod's kingdom. Upon Antony's defeat in 31 B.C., Herod was forced to face Augustus, but, instead of suffering reprisals, he received Augustus' reaffirmation of Rome's support for his rule in Judaea.

Herod undertook many construction projects during his reign, including the great temple still standing today at Al-Haram ash-Sharif in Jerusalem.

Like many emperors of Rome proper, Herod the Great was personally unstable, even insane. Fearing conspiracy, he murdered his wife Mariamne and her whole family. He also disowned and killed his first-born son Antipater. Then, plagued by internal rebellion, a dispute with his Nabataean neighbors, and racked by diseases mental and physical, he ordered the infamous Massacre of the Innocents, the murder of all male infants in Bethlehem.

He attempted unsuccessfully to commit suicide, and finally died in 4 B.C.

Further Reading: Michael Avi-Yonah. *The Herodian Period* (New Brunswick, N.J.: Rutgers University Press, 1975).

Heureaux, Ulíses   (1845–1899)

President and absolute dictator of the Dominican Republic, Heureaux maintained his brutal regime by executing anyone who dared to oppose him and by making his country an economic vassal of the United States.

Heureaux was born on October 21, 1845, in Puerto Plata, Dominican Republic, and was schooled at a Methodist mission. During the 1860s, he distinguished himself in the rebellion that secured independence from Spain but that plunged the nation into virtual anarchy. Heureaux stepped in to fill the leadership vacuum, becoming president in 1882. Forbidden by law from succeeding himself in office, Heureaux handpicked the next two presidents in 1884 and 1886, while effectively continuing to run the government himself. In 1887, he overturned the constitutional injunction against reelection and assumed the presidency officially. To those who protested his high-handed abuse of the nation's fledgling democracy, Heureaux dealt swift and summary execution.

Heureaux bolstered his regime by building the Dominican Republic's agriculture and trade, especially the production and export of sugar, which became the basis of the nation's economy. To accelerate the influx of revenue, Heureaux granted a monopoly to the San Domingo Improvement Company of New York, which made large loans to the regime, built railroads, and generally developed the country—at the price of acquiring virtual ownership of national assets. Before Heureaux was assassinated on July 26, 1899, the San Domingo Improvement Company had even begun collecting the nation's customs revenue.

Heureaux brought short-term economic gains to some of his countrymen, but he made the Dominican Republic an economic vassal of the United States, which sent troops to restore order and protect extensive American financial interests after Heureaux's death.

Hippias   (490 B.C.)

This tyrant of Athens ruled well, fostering prosperity and the arts, until the assassination of his brother HIPPARCHUS set him on a cruelly repressive course.

Hippias was the eldest son of PEISISTRATUS, tyrant of Athens. On the death of the father, rule passed to Hippias and his brother Hipparchus in 527 B.C. The two brothers had inherited a peaceful realm guided by a policy of neutrality. The tyrants patronized such poets as Anacreon and Simonides of Ceos and the musical innovator Lasus of Hermione as well as the Orphic bard Onomacritus.

These halcyon days did not long endure, however, since Hippias and his brother found it increasingly difficult to maintain peaceful neutrality, especially as the power of their closest ally, Thessaly, declined, and Sparta emerged as a menacing threat, organizing alliances that weakened Athens' position. In 519 B.C., the Spartans managed to foment conflict between Athens and Thebes, which resulted in territorial gains for Athens, but also in an enduring and debilitating enmity between Athens and Thebes that proportionately improved Sparta's standing.

In 514, Athens was rocked by another crisis as Harmodius and Aristogeiton, members of the Gephyrean clan, plotted the assassination of the brothers in a general revolt against the reign of Athenian tyranny. The conspirators attacked at the Great Panathenaic Festival, but the operation miscarried. Hipparchus was slain, but Hippias escaped, quickly took command of the situation, killed or exiled all of the conspirators, and disarmed the Athenian populace.

The enlightened tenor of the tyrant's rule quickly changed to a spirit of suspicion and repression. Worse, by disarming the Athenians, Hippias exposed his state to foreign invasion and had to rely for defense on mercenaries and Thessalian allies. Cleisthenes, leader of the Alcmaeonidae, a noble family who had been exiled from Athens, rushed in to invade Attica, but he received little support from inside Athens itself, and his invasion ended in failure. The Alcmaeonidae now turned to Sparta for help, persuading the Spartans—who were also influenced in this action by the Oracle at Delphi—to help overthrow the Athenian tyranny. In 511 B.C., Sparta dispatched a small force under Anchimolius, which landed at the Bay of Phalerum. Hippias met this force and dealt it a sound defeat.

To his credit, Hippias was not lulled into complacency by his triumph. He fortified the hill of Munychia at the Piraeus and prepared a stout defense against the full-scale invasion he knew would come. In 510 B.C., Cleomenes I, ruler of Sparta, personally led a large army against Athens. Hippias boldly advanced to meet him, but his Thessalian cavalry, effective against Anchimolius, failed against this much greater force. Hippias was driven back into Athens and was finally besieged on the Acropolis itself. The historian Herodotus records that the Acropolis, well fortified and amply stocked with provisions, could have withstood the Spartan siege. However, Hippias' children fell into the hands of the Spartans and, in order to save them, Hippias surrendered, agreeing to leave Athens within five days.

The tyrant and his kin evacuated, eventually securing refuge with the Persian governor at Sardis. Years later, in 490, Hippias crossed the Aegean with a Persian army. The force landed at Marathon, where it was badly defeated by the Athenian army. Hippias died at Lemnos during the retreat of his forces, and the reign of the house of Peisistratus ended.

Hitler, Adolf   (1889–1945)

Absolute dictator of Germany from 1933 to 1945, Adolf Hitler established nazism, instituted policies of racial supremacy and genocide, and plunged the world into the second great war of the century.

The man who, for a dark time, dominated not only Germany but much of Europe, intimidating and terrorizing the world, came from an undistinguished and squalid background. Born on April 20, 1889, in the Austrian town of Braunau am Inn, but raised mainly in Linz, he was the son of a minor customs official. Alois Hilter, an illegitimate child, had used his mother's maiden name, Schicklgruber, until 1876, when he took his step-father's name, Hitler. Alois was a brutal father, contemptuous of what he saw as Adolf's dreaminess. The boy fared poorly in his studies, leaving secondary school in 1905 without a graduation certificate. He decided to become an artist, but his uninspired drawings and watercolors twice failed to gain him admission to the Academy of Fine Arts in Vienna. After the death of his mother, whom he idolized, Hitler went to Vienna, hoping to make a living as an artist. From 1907 to 1913, he eked out a meager existence by painting advertisements, postcards, and the like, falling into an aimless depression given direction only by a growing racial hatred focused primarily on the Jews, whom Hitler began to see as a threat to the Germanic—or "Aryan"—race.

Hitler moved to Munich in 1913, presumably to evade conscription into the Austrian army. He was nevertheless recalled to Austria in February 1914 for examination for military service, but was rejected as unfit. Yet, in August 1914, with the outbreak of World War I, Hitler eagerly enlisted in the 16th Bavarian Reserve Infantry (List) Regiment.

War service transformed the lackluster youth into a passionately militaristic nationalist. He served in the front lines as a runner, was promoted to corpo-

ral, and was decorated four times, receiving the Iron Cross 1st Class on August 4, 1918. He was seriously wounded in October 1916 and was gassed at the end of the war. Having apparently found a home in the army, Hitler remained with his regiment until April 1920. He served as an army political agent, joining the German Worker's Party in Munich in September 1919. In April 1920, he left the army to go to work full-time for the party's propaganda section.

This was a time of terrific ferment and crisis in Germany. The Treaty of Versailles, which ended World War I, was heavily punitive, and Germany was also rocked by an abortive Communist revolution. Seizing on the unrest, Hitler was instrumental in transforming the German Worker's Party by August 1920 into the Nazionalsozialistische Deutsche Arbeiterpartei, commonly shortened to NSDAP or Nazi Party. Forming an alliance with Ernst Roehm, an army staff officer, he was elected president of the party in July 1921. Hitler became a streetcorner orator, loudly assaulting Germany's enemies—principally Communists and Jews, as well as the nations that had forced upon the German people an ignominious peace—and during November 8–9, 1923, he led the Munich Beer Hall Putsch, a bold attempt to seize control of the Bavarian government.

The rebellion was quickly suppressed, and Hitler was arrested, tried, and convicted of treason, for which he was sentenced to five years in prison. While incarcerated at Landesberg prison, near Munich, he wrote his political autobiography, *Mein Kampf* ("My Struggle"), in which he crystallized the political philosophy of nazism, proclaiming eternal opposition to Jews, Communists, effete liberals, and exploitive capitalists the world over, and extolling a reborn Germany of racial purity and unstoppable national will. He wrote of a Germany that would rise again to become the dominant power in the world, a Germany that would claim and obtain *Lebensraum*—living space—in central Europe and in Russia.

Adolf Hitler was released from prison after serving only nine months of his sentence, and he set about strengthening his party, especially in the industrial German north. During this period, he recruited the men who would lead the country into mass atrocity and all-consuming war: Hermann Goering, popular World War I air ace; Josef Goebbels, master propagandist; Heinrich Himmler, skilled in strongarm, terror, and police tactics; and Julius Streicher, a popular anti-Semitic journalist. The party's greatest boon came with the worldwide economic collapse of 1929 and the depression that followed. Forging an alliance with the Nationalist Party headed by industrialist Alfred Hugenberg, the Nazis increased the number of Reichstag seats they held from 12 to 107, becoming the second largest party in Germany. Hitler did not confine his party's activities to the Reichstag, but developed the SA (*Sturmabeteilung*, or Brownshirts) into an effective paramilitary arm that quite literally beat down the opposition in the streets of Germany.

Hitler ran for president of the German republic in 1932, narrowly losing to Paul von HINDENBERG, the superannuated incumbent hero of World War I. But the July elections gained the Nazis 230 Reichstag seats, 37 percent of the vote, making it the largest party represented, and eventually Hindenberg was compelled to appoint Hitler *Reichskanzler* (Reich chancellor, or prime minister) on January 30, 1933.

Hitler now worked vigorously to consolidate his power, building himself into a formidable dictator. When fire destroyed the Reichstag on February 27, 1933, Hitler found a pretext for legally abolishing the Communist Party and imprisoning its leaders. On March 23, 1933, he engineered passage of the Enabling Act, which granted him four years of unalloyed dictatorial powers. He began systematically dismantling all German parties, save for the NSDAP, purged Jews from all government institutions, and brought all government offices under the direct control of the party. He then purged his own ranks during the Night of the Long Knives, June 30, 1934, murdering Ernst Roehm and hundreds of other Nazis whose radicalism posed a threat to Hitler's absolute domination. Shortly after this, in August 1934, Hindenberg died and Hitler assumed the functions of the presidency, but adopted the title of *Führer*—Supreme Leader—of the Third Reich.

The Führer replaced the SA—Brownshirts—with the SS—*Schutzstaffel*, or Blackshirts—under Himmler. Together with a secret police organization called the Gestapo, the SS created a system of concentration camps to which political enemies, Jews, and others "undesirables" were "deported." In 1935, Hitler enacted the Nuremberg Racial Laws, which deprived Jews of citizenship. Such policies of terror were carefully orchestrated by propaganda minister Goebbels with programs of economic recovery as, in defiance of the Versailles treaty, Hitler put his nation on a war footing by creating the *Luftwaffe* (air force) under Goering, remilitarizing the Rhineland (in 1936), and rearming generally.

In October 1936, Hitler made an alliance with Benito MUSSOLINI, Fascist dictator of Italy. In March 1938, Hitler invaded and annexed Austria in the *Anschluss*, then pressured Czechoslovakia into relinquishing the Sudetenland, a border region Germany long coveted.

In the face of this aggression, the two major western European military powers seemed paralyzed into a policy of craven and cowering appeasement. In 1935, England agreed to an Anglo-German Naval Pact, then, at the Munich Conference of September 29–30, 1938, France and England agreed to the dismemberment of Czechoslovakia, feeling that this would appease the Führer. Hitler quickly annexed not only the Sudetenland, but the remainder of western Czechoslovakia as well, then went on to claim the "Memel strip" from Lithuania in March 1939. After concluding a nonagression pact with Josef STALIN of the Soviet Union on August 23, 1939, Hitler invaded Poland on September 1.

Thus World War II began. Hitler quickly overran Poland and Scandinavia during April 9–June 9, 1940. France and England, having foolishly appeased Hitler, belatedly responded to the Polish invasion. France fell quickly, during May 25–June 5, 1940, but Great Britain held out. Instead of mounting a mass invasion of England, Hitler sought air supremacy over its skies, and during July–October 1940, the Luftwaffe and the Royal Air Force fought the Battle of Britain. Suffering their first reversal of the war, the Germans were forced to back down from their British invasion plans.

But such Allied victories were rare. Hitler's armies controlled territory from North Africa to the Arctic and from France to central Europe. In April 1941, the German army invaded the Balkans, occupying Yugoslavia and Greece. Then, on June 22, abrogating the Nazi-Soviet nonaggression pact, Hitler executed "Operation Barbarossa," the invasion of the Soviet Union. Victories were quickly forthcoming in this vast country until, as with Napoleon before him, the Russian winter, combined with the dogged resistance of the Russian people and their army, stalled Hitler's forces, first outside Moscow in December 1941, then, during the winter of 1942–43, at Stalingrad. The Russians began to exact a tremendous toll on the German army, draining Hitler's resources.

In the meantime, following the Japanese attack on Pearl Harbor on December 7, 1941, the United States declared war on Japan and Germany—a contingency for which Hitler had not planned. At home, the Führer became increasingly obsessed with consummating the "Final Solution" to the "Jewish Question" and instituted the Holocaust: genocide of some 6 million Jews, mostly in concentration camps now transformed into death camps designed for mass murder.

By 1943, the tide of the war was turning hopelessly against Adolf Hitler's Germany. The ruinous retreat from Russia was under way, North Africa was lost, and Mussolini had fallen to the Allied invasion of Italy. American and British bombers pummeled German cities, and in June 1944, the Allied D-Day operation commenced, troops were landed on the coast of France, and the invasion of western Europe had begun. In the face of these defeats, the Führer made increasingly desperate, reckless, and irrational military decisions, which turned many in his high command against him. On July 20, 1944, a cabal of officers attempted to assassinate him with a bomb hidden in a briefcase. Miraculously, Hitler survived, but was seriously injured and emotionally devastated.

From December 16, 1944, to January 1945, Hitler committed his last reserves to a final offensive in the Ardennes, hoping to arrest the Allied advance and retake Antwerp. After the hard-fought Battle of the Bulge, the offensive was crushed, and Hitler retreated to the *Führerbunker*, a hardened underground command shelter in Berlin. From this headquarters, he attempted to direct the fight to the last man. Finally, on April 29, 1945, as American, British, and Free French forces closed in from the west and the Russian army approached from the east, Hitler hastily married his long-time mistress, Eva Braun. The next day, the couple committed suicide. Admiral Karl Dönitz, whom Hitler had appointed as his successor, sued for peace, and the Third Reich—which Hitler had called the Thousand-Year Reich—crumbled.

Further Reading: Alan Bullock. *Hitler: A Study in Tyranny*, rev. ed. (New York: Harper, 1962); Bullock. *Hitler and Stalin: Parallel Lives* (New York: Knopf, 1992); John Toland. *Adolf Hitler* (Garden City, N.Y.: Doubleday, 1976).

Ho Chi Minh [Nguyen That Thanh] (1890–1969)

A dynamic anti-colonial leader, Ho Chi Minh was the first president of the Democratic Republic of Vietnam (North Vietnam), from 1945 to 1969.

Born Nguyen That Thanh (and also called Nguyen Al Quoc), Ho was the son of an impoverished rural scholar in the village of Kim Lien. Growing up in great want, he nevertheless managed to receive an education at the grammar school in Hue, became a schoolmaster for a time, then was apprenticed at a technical institute in Saigon.

Ho left Vietnam (at the time part of French Indochina) in 1911 to work as a cook on a French ocean liner and then at a London hotel. As World War I came to an end, he moved to France, where he became active in the Socialist Party, and, at the 1919 Paris Peace Conference, unsuccessfully lobbied and petitioned on behalf of civil rights in Indochina. Increasingly radicalized after this experience, Ho became a founding member of the French Communist Party and traveled to the Soviet Union to study revolutionary methods. Inducted into the Comintern—

the international Communist organization controlled from Moscow—he was given the task of installing communism throughout East Asia. Ho founded the Indochinese Communist party in 1930, and for the balance of that decade he lived in the Soviet Union and China.

When World War II erupted, Ho returned to Vietnam, where, in 1941, he organized the Communist-controlled League for the Independence of Vietnam, or Viet Minh, which led the resistance against the occupying forces of Japan. At war's end, on September 2, 1945, Ho Chi Minh proclaimed the independence of the Democratic Republic of Vietnam and became its first president. The French, however, were determined to reclaim Vietnam for their empire.

For the next 24 years, Ho served as president of a divided and perpetually embattled people. He led the Viet Minh in eight years of brutal guerrilla warfare against French colonial forces from 1946 to 1954, and he vigorously supported the Viet Cong, successor to the Viet Minh, in another 15 years of costly battle against the anti-Communist regime of the South Vietnamese state, which had been established on what was to have been a temporary basis in 1954 at an international peace conference in Geneva.

From 1959 to 1975, the United States became increasingly involved in the war on the side of the South Vietnamese government, committing more than half a million men to the effort by the end of the 1960s. Throughout the bitter struggle, Ho Chi Minh served as a symbol of unity for Vietnam, no matter what the cost—although his active role in the war was steadily reduced beginning in 1959, when he began to suffer from ill health.

Ho Chi Minh did not live to see the Communist victory in 1975, following the U.S. withdrawal from South Vietnam, which resulted in the unification of the country. Although Ho died on September 2, 1969, his death is officially remembered on September 3 so that it does not coincide with the celebration of Vietnam's National Day. His remains are enshrined in a mausoleum in Hanoi.

Further Reading: Jean Lacouture. *Ho Chi Minh: A Political Biography* (New York: Random House, 1968); Jean Sainteny. *Ho Chi Minh and His Vietnam: A Personal Memoir* (Chicago: Cowles, 1972).

Hojo Masako (1157–1225)

Hojo Masako, wife of the first shogun (military leader) of Japan and daughter of the first of the Hojo regents, who exercised de facto power over feudal Japan until 1333, wielded great power after her husband died.

When the last leader of the powerful Minamoto family, Yoritomo, who established the feudal order in Japan, died in 1199, the Hojo family of his wife was installed at first as advisers, then as regents, over the shogun designates. While the shoguns continued to be the nominal military rulers of Japan, the Hojo family retained the real power, establishing a hereditary control that would last more than 130 years. Masako engineered the creation of her father Tokimasa as regent for her sons by Minamoto no Yoritomo in 1203.

After Masako's first son was assassinated in 1204, he was succeeded by her second son, Sanetomo, who was also soon the subject of an assassination plot. Masako's father, the regent, was implicated in both assassination plots against her sons. With the help of her brother Yoshitoki, Masako deposed her father and retained the regency for herself and Yoshitoki. As she had taken vows as a Buddhist nun after the death of her husband, she became known as *ama shogun* ("nun shogun").

When Sanetomo was finally assassinated in 1219, Masako ruled indirectly as the regent for the new shogun designate, an infant great-grandson of Yoritomo. Masako continued to rule indirectly with her brother until her death on August 16, 1225.

Further Reading: Carl Steenstrup. *Hojo Shigetoki, 1198–1261* (London: Curzon, 1979).

Hojo Tokimasa   (1138–1215)

The first of nine Hojo regents to govern medieval Japan, Tokimasa established the Hojo regency.

A member of the Japanese warrior (samurai) class, Hojo Tokimasa became attached to Minamoto no Yoritomo during Yoritomo's exile after his father was killed in a power struggle in 1160. Yoritomo married Tokimasa's daughter and in 1181, Tokimasa aided Yoritomo in defeating his father's killer and establishing the Kamakura shogunate, or military regime. When Yoritomo died in 1199, Tokimasa became head of an advisory council set up to limit the powers of Yoritomo's unreliable son and successor, Yoriie.

In 1204, Tokimasa had Yoriie killed, and rule passed to Yoriie's brother, Sanetomo, who had not attained his majority. Tokimasa was installed as regent for his grandson, thereby establishing the Hojo regency that would last until 1333.

After attempts on the young Sanetomo's life in 1205, Tokimasa was forced by his son Yoshitoki and daughter Masako to resign the regency. Yoshitoki then succeeded his father as regent, and set the precedent for a hereditary regency.

After being removed as regent, Tokimasa entered the priesthood and remained in a monastery until his death on February 6, 1216.

Further reading: Carl Steenstrup. *Hojo Shigetoki, 1198–1261* (London: Curzon, 1979).

Hojo Tokimune   (1251–1284)

One of nine hereditary regents, all members of the Hojo family, who controlled the government of the military ruler (shogun) of feudal Japan, Tokimune successfully fought off two Mongol invasions, though at terrific cost to the nation.

In 1199, the Hojo family became advisers, then formal regents over the shogun designates. While the shogun could never assume the imperial throne, he was the nominal head of the de facto military regime over which the Hojo family exercised real power, establishing a hereditary regency that would last more than 130 years. Assuming the regency at the age of 17 in 1268, Hojo Tokimune was immediately faced with a Mongol invasion dispatched by Kublai Khan. Khan sent envoys to Japan demanding tribute, which Tokimune steadfastly refused, preparing instead to resist the inevitable invasion.

In 1274, upwards of 25,000 (some sources put the figure at 40,000) Mongol and Korean troops under Kublai invaded the northern islands of Japan. The small outer islands were quickly taken, but the main Japanese force held firmly on the big island. They were saved from further attack by a tremendous storm (the so-called *kamikaze*, or "divine wind) that forced the Mongol fleet to turn back. Hoping to stave off further invasion, Tokimune quickly set about fortifying the outer islands, including the building of a huge seawall to prevent any landings.

The Mongols nevertheless returned in the summer of 1281 with as many as 140,000 Chinese, Mongol, and Korean troops. Fighting from behind the newly built fortifications, the Japanese held off the onslaught for more than two months in what was not so much a siege as it was an unremitting two-month battle. Again the Japanese were saved by a storm when a typhoon destroyed the Mongol fleet, rendering the survivors easy targets. Possibly as many as 100,000 of Kublai Khan's men were killed.

Despite their effectiveness, the massive fortifications and the general cost of war had drained the government coffers, bringing on the slow decline of Hojo authority. The Hojo regency would disappear within 50 years of Tokimune's death on April 20, 1284.

Further Reading: Carl Steenstrup. *Hojo Shigetoki, 1198–1261* (London: Curzon, 1979).

Hojo Yasutoki   (1183–1242)

The third of nine shogunal regents of the Hojo family to rule medieval Japan, Yasutoki reformed the administration of the regency and generally consolidated Hojo hegemony over the military feudal regime that controlled Japan.

First as advisers and then as regents over the shogun (the nominal head of the military government), the Hojo family retained real power, establishing a hereditary regency that would last more than 130 years. When the retired emperor (the imperial family, because of its divine character, could not be replaced) launched a revolt against the shogunate (military regime) in an attempt to restore imperial rule in 1221, Yasutoki was given command of the shogunal forces and quickly suppressed the rebels, marching on the imperial capital at Kyoto and establishing military headquarters to ensure Hojo supremacy in the region and keep a close watch on imperial actions.

After his father, Yoshitoki, died in 1224, Yasutoki became regent and immediately set about improving the administration of government. He established a policy of co-regents to increase administrative productivity and, in 1225, established the Council of State, an advisory council comprised of prominent warriors and government officials. Yasutoki firmly established his authority in 1226 by ruthlessly suppressing a rebellion led by warrior monks, who believed they possessed the spiritual authority to assume the reins of government.

One of Yasutoki's greatest accomplishments was his promulgation of the *Joei Shikimoku* in 1232, a legal code that effectively codified feudalism and provided for a reformed judicial process, and that defined the various duties of civil administrators. Yasutoki died on July 14, 1242.

Further reading: Carl Steenstrup. *Hojo Shigetoki, 1198–1261* (London: Curzon, 1979).

Hojo Yoshitoki (1163–1224)

Yoshitoki was able to consolidate the power of the Hojo family over the shogunate, or military regime, and make the regency a hereditary office.

Yoshitoki deposed his father, Tokimasa, the first Hojo regent, around 1208, making the regency a hereditary post within the Hojo family. Yoshitoki governed as regent with his sister, Masako, and the two ensured their dominance over the feudal military regime in 1219 by replacing the assassinated shogun with an infant great-grandson of the original shogun, Minamoto no Yoritomo, almost guaranteeing there would be no challenges to succession. The imperial court was highly resentful of this usurpation, as traditionally it had been an imperial prerogative to appoint the shogun, and in 1221 the retired emperor Go-Toba raised a rebellion in an attempt to overthrow Yoshitoki and reassert imperial authority.

Yoshitoki uncompromisingly crushed the revolt, exiling the former emperor and his two sons, executing almost all of the generals who had taken part in the uprising, and establishing a military command post just south of Kyoto to check any future rebellions. He also confiscated most of the imperial estates and parcelled them out to loyal supporters of the Hojo family in an attempt to maintain favor in the region.

His measures to suppress imperial authority were wholly successful, and Yoshitoki continued to rule with an iron fist until his death on July 1, 1224.

Further reading: Carl Steenstrup. *Hojo Shigetoki, 1198–1261* (London: Curzon, 1979).

Horemhab [Horemheb] (d. 1307 b.c.)

Last king of the 18th dynasty of Egypt, Horemhab reigned from 1319 to 1307 b.c.

When King Aya died without an heir, Horemhab, chief of the army since Tutankhamun's reign and a member of the provincial aristocracy, assumed the throne and married Queen Mutnodjmet in 1319 b.c.

His rule was characterized by a return to the old religion of Amon, supplanted by the sun god Aton by AKHENATON. He destroyed temples and symbols of the worship of the god Aton and rebuilt temples to honor the earlier deity. In addition, he removed from the list of kings those who had worshiped Aton, an act that dates the beginning of his reign at 1353 b.c. While he produced no heir to the throne before his death in 1307 b.c., he arranged for a military aide, Rameses I, to succeed him.

Further Reading: Bunson, Margaret. *Encyclopedia of Ancient Egypt* (New York: Facts On File, 1991).

Horthy de Nagybányai, Miklós (1868–1957)

A conservative aristocrat and military leader, Admiral Horthy instituted a repressive right-wing government in Hungary aimed at opposing Bolshevism.

Miklós Horthy was born into a privileged and aristocratic Hungarian family. At the age of 14 he entered the Austro-Hungarian naval academy at Fiume and became aide-de-camp to Archduke Francis Ferdinand from 1909 until that figure's fateful assassination at Sarajevo in August 1914. Propelled with his nation into World War I, Horthy proved himself an able and courageous naval commander, successfully running the Allies' blockade of the Adriatic. Promoted to admiral, it was Horthy who supervised the transfer of the Austro-Hungarian fleet to Yugoslavia in October 1918.

The end of the world war hardly brought peace to Hungary, which was restive under the brutal Communist regime of Béla KUN. Counterrevolutionary forces based at Szeged, Hungary, asked Horthy to organize an army to march on Budapest and depose Kun once and for all. Horthy advanced into the capital in November 1919, after Kun, perceiving his situation as hopeless, had fled. In January 1920, a conservative-dominated Hungarian parliament voted to restore the monarchy and named Horthy regent on March 1.

To the astonishment of the parliament, Horthy thwarted Charles IV in his bid to regain the throne and, serving as de facto head of government himself, entrusted the day-to-day conduct of the administration to Count István Bethlen. This situation endured from 1921 to 1931, when Hungary was again menaced by Bolshevism and the effects of worldwide economic depression. Horthy assumed increasingly personal control of the Hungarian government and persuaded parliament to vote him dictatorial powers in 1937. He distrusted and personally disliked Adolf HITLER, but he saw an alliance with that dictator as necessary to ward off a Communist takeover. Thus, at the outbreak of World War II, Hungary entered the hostilities on the side of Germany. Almost immediately, however, Horthy regretted his alliance, and he began a campaign to extricate his nation from involvement in the war. These efforts not only failed, they resulted in his forced abdication and his kidnapping by German agents in 1944.

Horthy was liberated by Allied troops in May 1945. Unable to return to what was now Communist-dominated Hungary, he was permitted to seek refuge in neutral Portugal. He lived at Estoril, Portugal, until his death on February 9, 1957.

Hoxha, Enver (1908–1985)

One of the founders of Communist Albania and its ruler for four decades, Hoxha was a hard-line Stalinist who opposed the policies of Yugoslavia, the Soviet Union, and, finally, China.

Enver Hoxha was born October 16, 1908, to a poor Muslim merchant from Korçë, in southern Albania. Hoxha was sent to the liberal French-language lycée to study on scholarship. In 1930, he traveled to France, where he studied engineering at the University of Montpellier on a state scholarship. After he become involved with Socialists and Communists in France, Albania rescinded his grant, and Hoxha went to Paris to look for work. There he met Paul Vaillant-Couturier, editor of the Communist newspaper L'Humanité. Hoxha wrote numerous articles on Albania for the paper, many critical of the current regime. He secured, in 1934, an appointment as secretary to the Albanian consulate general in Brussels, where he also began studying law. However, when the Albanian government discovered his critical

writings for L'Humanité, he was sent home and never earned a law degree.

In 1936 he returned to Korçë and began teaching at the lycée, also becoming active in an Albanian Communist group. His domestic political activities soon attracted official attention, and Hoxha was arrested in January 1939 on conspiracy charges. He served a short prison term.

When the Italians invaded Albania on April 7, 1939, Hoxha was working against his own government, but was nevertheless dismissed from the lycée by the Italians for his anti-Fascist views. He then moved to the capital, Tirana, and set up a tobacco shop as a front for resistance against the Fascists.

The several Communist groups in prewar Albania were fragmented and quarreled frequently, but the German invasion of the Soviet Union in 1941 unified the Communists. With organizational help from Yugoslavian Communists, the Communist Party of Albania was formed on November 8, 1941, and Enver Hoxha was elected general secretary.

Within a year, the CPA was contributing trained brigades to the resistance movement. By 1944, Hoxha announced proudly that the Germans and Italians had been pushed out of Albania without any aid from the Allies.

In November 1945, Hoxha's provisional government was recognized by the Big Four, and he began to solidify his power in Albania. Hoxha ordered trials for all those suspected of subversive behavior or collaboration with the enemy. Several persons were executed. Hoxha successfully resisted attempts by Tito's Yugoslavia to seize control of Albanian Communists. When TITO broke with Josef STALIN in 1948 and was expelled from the Comintern, Albania was one of the first satellites to endorse the decision. This allowed Hoxha and his supporters publicly to denounce the Yugoslavs and their efforts. Hoxha ordered the execution of many pro-Tito Communists in Albania, including their leader, Koci Xoxe, in May 1949.

Hoxha wholeheartedly supported the Soviet Union and Stalin, crushing all attempts at anti-Communist rebellion and "Titoist" reform both at home and abroad. The Soviet Union, in return, funneled into Albania tremendous amounts of aid to continue the "socialization" process. This honeymoon did not long endure, however. Hoxha became increasingly discontent with the policies of Stalin's successor, Nikita Khrushchev, and he particularly resented Khruschev's efforts to bring Yugoslavia back into the international Communist fold and his program of purging Soviet Communism of its lingering Stalinism. Hoxha's attacks on Khrushchev became more pointed, and by 1961 Soviet economic aid to Albania was cut and, eventually, all diplomatic ties were severed.

Hoxha now aligned Albania with MAO TSE-TUNG, who was also disillusioned with the Soviets. The vacuum created by the withdrawal of Soviet aid was filled by Chinese aid and technical assistance. Hoxha continued to criticize the Soviets, particularly the 1968 invasion of Afghanistan. In that year, Albania officially withdrew from the Warsaw Pact. Then, by the mid-1970s, Hoxha was becoming critical of China's opening of relations with the United States and its rapprochement with Yugoslavia. In 1978, China suspended aid to Albania, leaving that nation in virtual diplomatic isolation at the time of Enver Hoxha's death on April 11, 1985.

Further Reading: Nicholas Pano. *The People's Republic of Albania* (Baltimore: Johns Hopkins University Press, 1968); Peter R. Prifti. *Socialist Albania Since 1944: Domestic and Foreign Developments* (Cambridge, Mass.: MIT Press, 1978).

Huerta, Victoriano (1854–1916)

President of Mexico for little more than a year (February 1913 to July 1914), Victoriano Huerta came to power after a military revolt in Mexico City and resigned amid increasing opposition, both domestic and foreign.

Born of Indian parents on December 23, 1854, in Colotlán, Jalisco, Victoriano Huerta studied at the Colegio Militar and became an army officer. Demonstrating great contempt for and revulsion from his Indian origins, Huerta was responsible for the slaughter of dozens of Maya in the 1880 uprising in the Yucatán. Later, in 1911, determined to defeat the guerrilla forces of Emiliano Zapata, he terrorized all of Mexico with indiscriminate raids on civilians and guerrillas alike.

Despite his brutality and an avowed admiration for the dictator PORFIRIO DÍAZ, Huerta was appointed chief of staff in 1912 by liberal President Francisco Madero. Huerta soon turned against the president, joining a military revolt against the government and ordering Madera's imprisonment. On February 22, 1913, Huerta managed to see to it that Madero was shot in the back "while trying to escape." He then proclaimed himself president.

Huerta's first act as provisional president was to dissolve the legislature and assume dictatorial powers. Although he generally tried simply to crush opposition, Huerta did permit the enactment of two moderate agrarian reforms. Despite this concession, the country remained in a state of revolution as the likes of Venustiano Carranza, Alvaro Obregón, Pancho Villa, and Emiliano Zapata fought against government forces. The United States refused to recognize Huerta as president, and President Woodrow

Wilson authorized the seizure of Veracruz and permitted arms to reach anti-government forces. In the face of such pressures, Huerta resigned on July 15, 1914, fleeing first to Spain, then moving to the United States. In 1915, American authorities arrested him near the Mexican border, under charges of gun running and fomenting a revolution in Mexico. He was incarcerated at Fort Bliss, Texas, and died while in custody on January 13, 1916.

Suggested Reading: Kenneth J. Brieb. *The United States and Huerta* (Lincoln: University of Nebraska Press, 1969).

Hung Hsiu-ch'uan (1812–1864)

Leader of the Taiping rebellion, an anti-Manchu (Ch'ing) dynasty revolt with quasi-Christian underpinnings, begun in South China (1850–1864).

Hung Hsiu-Chu'an was born into an impoverished family of Hakka, an ethnic minority of southeastern China. After recovering from a long illness (which came after his failing for the second time the rigorous civil service examination, almost the only means of upward mobility for a poor Chinese), Hung claimed he had met with God. His subsequent reading of Protestant missionary works convinced him that his visions were of the Christian God, who, Hung believed, had set for him a mission to expel the "demons"—Manchu rulers—from China. He joined "The Society of God Worshipers" led by his cousin Feng Yun-shan. Hung's anti-Manchu ideology rallied the oppressed Hakka minority, who began to challenge local Buddhist and Taoist officials. In 1851, the Society of God Worshipers captured the Kwangsi city of Yung-an. There Hung assumed the title of Heavenly King and declared a new dynasty. Hung established a utopian community he called Taiping tien kuo—the Heavenly Kingdom of Perfect Peace. From Yung-an, the Taiping movement advanced northward, where followers captured Nanking in 1853, renaming it "Heavenly Capital."

Hung's Taiping revolt quickly spread across the central and lower Yangtze region of China. His advance northward to Beijing (Peking) met with a combination of heavy Manchu resistance and floods along the Yellow River. In the meantime, dissension within the movement and ineffective rule of conquered territories combined to depose Hung. He died on June 30, 1864, shortly before the fall of Nanking, which occurred on July 19.

Although it was ultimately suppressed, the Taiping revolt exposed the rapidly growing vulnerability of the once invincible Manchu dynasty.

Further Reading: Jacques Gernet. *A History of Chinese Civilization* (Cambridge & New York: Cambridge University Press, 1982); Brian Hook, ed. *Cambridge Encyclopedia of China* (New York: Cambridge University Press, 1982).

Husák, Gustav (1913–1991)

President of Czechoslovakia from 1975 until December 1989, Gustav Husák oversaw the purge of thousands of intellectuals and the general suppression of independent thought and culture.

Gustav Husák was born on January 10, 1913, in Pressburg, Austria-Hungary. As a young man he joined the Slovakian Communist Party and by the end of World War II had risen through its ranks, becoming chairman of the Board of Commissioners in 1946. Removed from office in 1950 in a purge of "national communists," he was arrested for treason and sabotage on February 6, 1951, expelled from the party, and sentenced to life in prison.

Nine years later, he was released from prison and reinstated into the Communist Party. When Alexander Dubček became party chief, Husák served as a deputy premier and assisted in formulating a reform program. By the summer of 1968, however, he warned against liberalization. After the Soviet invasion of August 20, 1968, Husák curried favor with the Soviets. On April 17, 1969, he was named First Secretary of the Communist Party, and in 1975 became president. During his administration, he oversaw the destruction of books, newspapers, and films and purged Czechoslovakia of thousands of intellectuals.

The 1980s saw the economic disintegration and general collapse of communism in the Soviet Union and the Eastern bloc. In December 1989, a democratic government won control of Czechoslovakia, and Husák resigned as president. In February 1990, he was expelled from the Communist Party and died on November 18, 1991, in Bratislava.

Hussein, Saddam (Takriti) (b. 1937–)

President of Iraq since 1979, Saddam Hussein warred for eight years with neighboring Iran and, in 1990, invaded and attempted to annex Kuwait, thereby triggering the brief, destructive Persian Gulf War (January 17, 1991–April 10, 1991).

Orphaned at nine months, Saddam (Takriti) Hussein was raised by an uncle, Khairallah Talfah, an anticolonialist who led an unsuccessful coup and bid for independence in 1941. Without advantageous family connections, young Saddam was refused enrollment in the Baghdad Military Academy and turned instead to membership in the radical Ba'ath (Arab Socialist Renaissance) Party, which had been founded by Michel Aflaq. The party first supported Abdul Karim Kassim's overthrow of the Iraqi monarchy in 1958, then turned against Kassim. Saddam, having already killed a Communist politician who ran against his uncle in a parliamentary election, volunteered to assassinate Kassim. The attempt failed, and Saddam, wounded in the leg, fled to Syria. From there he went to Cairo, where he studied law.

Saddam remained in exile for three years and, in an effort to confound police, dropped the name Takriti, by which he was known at the time, taking as his last name his father's first, Hussein. He returned to Baghdad and organized a secret Ba'ath militia, which in February 1963 deposed and executed Kassim. One of Saddam's relatives, Ahmed Hassan Bakr, became premier; five years later (July 17, 1968), Bakr overthrew President Aref (who had installed him), and a decade after that, in July 1979, stepped down himself in favor of Saddam Hussein.

Domestically, Saddam's rule has been marked by police-state terror. He has struggled particularly with the rebellious Kurds, against whom he used nerve gas on March 16, 1988. Internationally, he has shown himself to be bellicose, blustering and, many have suggested, wholly irrational. Controlling the world's fifth-largest army, he began in September 1980 an eight-year war against Iran so costly that it nearly led to a military coup in Iraq. In 1990, he invaded and attempted to annex the small, oil-rich nation of Kuwait. His army, air force and navy were quickly defeated by a United Nations–sanctioned coalition of 28 countries led by the United States (January 17, 1991–April 10, 1991), and Saddam was compelled to withdraw from Kuwait. During the brief Persian Gulf War, Iraqi armed forces inflicted minimal damage against military targets. Against civilian targets in noncombatant Israel, however, Saddam launched numerous small-missile attacks. In Kuwait, Iraqi forces terrorized citizens and laid waste some 300 oil fields. Through 1991 and into 1992, oil-field fires and massive, deliberate oil spills in the Persian Gulf continued to pose a grave ecological threat. Iraqi military losses were estimated in excess of 80,000 men, with overwhelming loss of matériel and severe damage to the civilian infrastructure. Varying degrees of civil unrest followed the ruinous war, especially in outlying provinces (particularly Kurdistan), but Saddam Hussein managed to maintain power. Throughout 1991 and 1992, he exhibited bouts of defiance against sanctions levied by the United Nations.

Suggested Reading: Efraim Karsh and Inari Rautsi. *Saddam Hussein: A Political Biography* (New York: Free Press, 1991); Elaine Sciolino. *The Outlaw State: Saddam Hussein's Quest for Power and the War in the Gulf* (New York: Wiley, 1991).

I

Innocent III (1160/61–1216)

Innocent III brought the medieval church to a high point of prestige and power, but political circumstances prompted him to such tyrannical acts as the annulment of the English Magna Carta and the authorization of the Albigensian Crusade, which resulted in widespread persecution, death, and devastation.

Related on his mother's side to Roman nobility, Innocent III was born Lothair of Segni (Lotario de Segni) in Gaviganano Castle, Campagna di Roma. Lothair studied theology in Paris and canon law in Bologna, imbibing there the moderate teachings of Huguccio of Pisa. Pope Clement III created Lothair cardinal deacon of St. Sergius and St. Bacchus in 1190, and during the pontificate of Celestine III, Lothair rose in the hierarchy of church government. He also acquired a reputation as a theologian of ascetic stamp, writing two important works, "On the Miserable Condition of Man" and "On the Mysteries of the Mass."

Immediately upon the death of Celestine III, on January 8, 1198, Lothair was unanimously elected pope. He reigned until his death in 1216.

Through his writings and sermons, Innocent greatly elevated the spiritual power and prestige of the papacy in the Christian world. At the same time, he declared his intention to limit the temporal power of the papacy, except with regard to the Papal States, to kingdoms that voluntarily recognized the feudal suzerainty of the pope, and Germany, whose king was also Holy Roman Emperor. Despite these moderate views with regard to the papacy's role in temporal affairs, Innocent III did have to exert military force to maintain control of the Papal States and was confronted by a crisis in Germany when the nobility there split over the selection of a successor to Henry VI, electing two rivals, Philip of Hohenstaufen and the duke of Brunswick, Otto IV. Innocent favored Otto, but Philip prevailed against him, so that the pope had to shift his allegiance. In 1208, however, Philip was murdered, and Innocent crowned Otto IV emperor. To the pope's chagrin, Otto immediately worked to undermine the sovereignty of the Papal States and, against the pope's wishes, sought to unify the Holy Roman Empire and Sicily. Innocent excommunicated Otto and backed the election of Frederick II as emperor.

The German crisis became linked to the Capetian-Angevin War between France and England, and Innocent III had to navigate a difficult course between PHILIP AUGUSTUS of France and King JOHN of England. In 1213, in order to prevent a French invasion of England, Innocent declared England a fief of the Holy See. While he thus opposed Philip Augustus in this way, he encouraged the French king to provide military assistance to his German protégé Frederick II, thereby alarming King John by apparently helping to forge an alliance between France and Germany. Perhaps to assuage the English monarch, Innocent responded to John's protest that he had been forced to sign the Magna Carta (1215) by declaring it null and void. For this, later ages have seen Innocent III as upholding tyranny—though he most probably regarded his action as no more than an attempt to quell a feudal insurrection against royal authority.

Posterity has also looked harshly on Innocent's conduct of a crusade against the Albigensian heretics during 1208–09. Typical of the bloodshed this crusade engendered was the slaughter at Béziers, an Albigensian stronghold, on July 21, 1209. As an army sent at the behest of Innocent III and commanded by northern French barons approached, the Albigensian leader Raymond of Toulouse submitted to the papal legate and promised to do penance. Despite this, the city of Béziers was sacked, and more than 7,000 persons who had taken refuge in the Church of the Madeleine were slain. The example of Béziers prompted other Albigensian strongholds to surrender. The pope had put down the heretics, but at a tremendous price, as what had begun as a holy crusade degenerated into a war of conquest conducted by the French barons.

Innocent also called for the Fourth Crusade (1202–04), which, financed by Venice, was diverted to serve the purposes of that state. On July 17, 1203, the Crusaders took Constantinople and restored to the throne Isaac Angelos. In February 1204, the city rebelled, deposing Isaac Angelos, killing his son, and putting the usurper Alexis Dukas in Isaac's place. In April, the Crusaders returned and viciously sacked the city in what has been called one of the great crimes of the Middle Ages. Although the sack resulted in the temporary unification of the Eastern and Western churches, Innocent protested the slaughter of so many in the city—though he believed to the end of his life that he had accomplished a lasting union of the two churches.

In principle and intention, Innocent III was one of the great popes. Nevertheless, much that was commissioned by him or carried out in his name proved destructive, ruinous, and tyrannical.

Further Reading: Joseph Clayton. *Pope Innocent III and His Times* (Milwaukee: Bruce, 1941); Eric John, ed. *The Popes: A Concise Bio-History* (New York: George Rainbird, 1964).

Isabella I   [Isabella the Catholic] (1451–1504)

Co-ruler of Castile and Aragón with her husband FERDINAND II, Isabella was instrumental in effecting the union of Spain and in creating its colonial empire by sponsoring the voyage of Christopher Columbus to the New World.

Isabella was born on April 22, 1451, at Madrigal de las Atlas Torres, Castile. The daughter of John II of Castile and his second wife, Isabella of Portugal, Isabella was introduced early on to the complex politics of Castile. Her half-brother, Henry IV, assumed the Castilian throne when Isabella was only three, and at age 13, she was brought from her quiet childhood home of Arevalo to the court of Castile. Rebellious elements in the court gathered round Isabella's younger brother Alfonso, intending to put him on the throne in place of HENRY IV. When Alfonso died prematurely in July 1468, the courtiers turned their attention on Isabella. She remained loyal to Henry, however, and, by means of the Accord of Toros de Guisando of September 19, 1468, Henry recognized her as his heir apparent.

Immediately, suitors from Portugal, France, and Aragón presented themselves as marriage partners for Isabella. Henry favored the Portuguese contender, King Afonso V, but she chose Ferdinand of Aragón, whom she married, without Henry's approval, in October 1469.

The union brought dissension in some quarters, and a rival party supported Henry's daughter Joan as heiress to the Castilian throne. Henry, for a time, supported this claim, but was eventually reconciled with Isabella. Nevertheless, civil war broke out in 1474 when Henry died and Isabella assumed the throne. Warfare lasted four years, but Isabella's faction at last prevailed, and, in 1479, with the death of King John II of Aragón, the kingdoms of Castile and Aragón were united by virtue of the marriage of Ferdinand and Isabella. In effect, the foundation of modern Spain had been laid.

The two sovereigns now addressed themselves to the conquest of the last stronghold of Muslim rule in Spain, initiating a campaign against Granada. The epic struggle consumed a decade, and both rulers took a personal interest in its conduct. For her part, Isabella developed new and more efficient methods of supplying her army, and she founded a military hospital for care of the sick and wounded.

Isabella was at Santa Fe, the royal headquarters throughout the long campaign against Granada, when she and Ferdinand were approached by the Italian-born mariner Christopher Columbus with his project of an expedition to the Indies. Although she did not provide the extensive financial support popular legend suggests (unfounded myth has the queen selling her jewels to fund the expedition), she did sponsor and approve it, thereby enabling Columbus to go forward. The resulting discoveries were annexed to the crown of Castile and were the foundation of Spain's vast New World empire.

Isabella's role in Columbus' project revealed her as a monarch of considerable vision. She also showed herself as surprisingly liberal when it came to the question of the rights of the "Indians" Columbus had discovered. While Columbus did not scruple to claim the native peoples of the New World as slaves of Spain, Isabella disputed this move and even ordered the release of those few Indians the Great Navigator had brought back to Spain with him.

If she was liberal in this regard, however, she did participate with her husband in authorizing the notorious Spanish Inquisition, begun in 1480 in Andalusia and aimed at ferreting out non-Catholics and doubtful converts, who were destined for expulsion from the empire. In 1492, the very year of Columbus' first voyage, the Jews of Spain were summarily ordered into exile.

The Inquisition was one of several steps Ferdinand and Isabella took to strengthen the Catholic church in Spain, thereby securing their own hold on an empire they were struggling to unify. Isabella also sponsored general reforms of the Catholic church and supported scholarship and learning in her kingdom.

While the Inquisition was a manifest and infamous evil on moral grounds, it was also a serious blow to the Spanish economy, as the Jews represented an exceptionally productive and prosperous element of Spanish society. This infamous and financially crippling action notwithstanding, Isabella and her husband did create the foundation of a modern, unified Spain and initiated a worldwide empire of tremendous power and influence.

Further Reading: William Hickling Prescott. *History of the Reign of Ferdinand and Isabella, the Catholic* (Boston: Little, Brown, 1838).

Ivan III the Great [Ivan Vasilievich] (1440–1505)

Through numerous military conquests and skillful diplomacy, Ivan was able to throw off the yoke of feudal overlordship of the Tatars of the Golden Horde and unite the Russian principalities and appanages into one kingdom.

Born on January 22, 1440, in Moscow at the height of the power struggle between his father, Vasily II, and his uncles, Ivan endured an early life of constant danger. After his father was captured and blinded by Mongols in 1446, Ivan was hidden in a monastery, then betrayed to his father's enemies. Through a bizarre series of circumstances, his father's captors suddenly repented of their act and renewed their allegiance to Vasily, releasing him, blinded as he was, to rule again.

As heir, Ivan was given nominal command of a military unit and was present when his father made policy decisions. At the age of 18, Ivan led a successful campaign against the Tatars in 1458. When his father died in 1462, Ivan succeeded Vasily as grand prince of Moscow. In the wake of his traumatic childhood, Ivan resolved to get free of the welter of feudal obligations that bound him and to unite the Russian lands under his sole control.

Beginning with successful campaigns against the Golden Horde during 1467–69, Ivan managed to free Russia of subservience to the Tatars in the east. Next, he turned to the powerful city-state of Novgorod. After numerous, costly attempts, Ivan finally took Novgorod through siege in 1478. Upon entering the city, he stripped it of all political autonomy, annexed its possessions, and colonized it with people loyal to him. The lands of Yaroslavl and Rostov were diplomatically acquired by 1474, and finally the city of Tver, after one last attempt at intrigue with the Lithuanians, gave in to Ivan in 1485. Only two cities retained any independence by this time.

Ivan masterfully played the different tribes that were allied against him against one another. For example, when Khan Ahmed of the Golden Horde allied himself with Poland-Lithuania, Ivan concluded an alliance with Khan Girei of the Crimea, then led troops against Ahmed and crushed him, now completely freeing Moscow from any Tatar influence.

Ivan's thirst for unification did not come without conflict. Following his territorial conquests, Ivan failed to distribute any land to his brothers. Worse, when his brother Yurii died, Ivan promptly seized all his possessions without apportioning any to his surviving brothers. Yet another brother voluntarily ceded all his lands to Ivan, which left two disaffected brothers, Boris and Andrei, aligned against Ivan. They approached King Casimir IV of Poland with a proposal for an alliance, but were rebuffed and the two returned to the fold. However, Andrei continued to dispute with his brother and was finally arrested in 1491, Ivan seizing all his land. After the death of Boris in 1494, half of his land was ceded to Ivan, the other going to one of Boris' sons. By the turn of the century, Ivan had successfully acquired and united almost all of the Russian lands.

Ivan was not as successful, however, in designating an heir to his new-formed kingdom. He had a son, Dmitry, by his first wife, Maria, who died in 1467. Ivan's second marriage produced a son, Vasily; however, his second wife Zoë (or Sophia) was from Byzantium, niece of the last emperor, and her religious orthodoxy—as well as her son's—was called into question. Perhaps even worse, Sophia was an ugly woman much disliked in the Kremlin court. Accordingly, Ivan designated Dmitry as his heir, which prompted Vasily and his mother to plot a revolt in 1497. Ivan acted swiftly and bloodily to put down the rebellion, and Vasily as well as his mother was imprisoned.

Dmitry, however, presented his own problems. He had become associated with a heretical religious party, which not only distressed Ivan, but provoked the metropolitan (bishop) of Moscow, who was touting Moscow as "The Third Rome," based in part on Zoë's Byzantine connections. In an about-face, Ivan designated Vasily as heir and imprisoned Dmitry.

When Ivan III died on October 27, 1505, Vasily succeeded—unopposed—to the throne of a Russia that would dominate eastern European politics into the 20th century. He ranks among the greatest Russian rulers.

Further Reading: John Lister Fennell. *Ivan the Great of Moscow* (London: Macmillan 1961); Ian Grey. *Ivan III and the Unification of Russia* (London: English Universities Press, 1964); G. V. Vernadsky. *Russia at the Dawn of the Modern Age* (New Haven: Yale University Press, 1959).

Ivan IV the Terrible (1530–1584)

Grand prince of Moscow and the first formally crowned czar of all the Russias, Ivan IV centralized Russian government in an absolute monarchy, unleashing upon his people a reign of torture and execution that earned him a reputation as a madman and the epithet "the Terrible."

Despite the consolidation of power under IVAN III and Vasily II, Russia, at the time of Ivan's birth, was still a collection of disparate principalities and fiefdoms loosely governed by a class of noblemen called the boyars, of which Ivan's father, the Muscovite Vasily III, was one. When Vasily died in 1533, the three-year-old Ivan ascended the Muscovite throne. Ivan's mother, Helen, and a group of boyars governed Muscovy in his name while various boyar factions waged brutal war upon one another. Young Ivan was frequently witness to acts of cruelty and torture.

After the death of his mother in 1538 (possibly by poisoning), Ivan was variously abused by his boyar mentors and advisers. An intelligent, strong-willed youth, he gradually freed himself from their domination and, in January 1547, was crowned czar of all the Russias. The title was significant: *czar* is derived from the Roman *caesar* (emperor), and, under the tutelage of Macarius (1542–63), metropolitan of the Orthodox church, Ivan subscribed to the doctrine asserting Moscow to be the "Third Rome," the successor of Constantinople, which had fallen to the Turks in 1453. Ivan was determined to become the absolute ruler of a unified and greatly expanded Russian empire, with Moscow at its center.

Shortly after he became czar, a mysterious fire destroyed much of Moscow. Rivals of the Glinskys—the family of Ivan's mother—blamed the fire on them and incited a mob against the family. With their elimination, the boyar aristocracy rapidly weakened, and Ivan appointed in their place a "selected council" *(Zemsky Sobor)* of non-aristocrats whose advice he closely followed for the next decade. During this period he initiated a program of reforms that served to centralize Russian government in Moscow even as the territories of Muscovy expanded. He waged war against the Tatars and annexed Kazan and Astrakhan as well as vast regions beyond the Urals, but he failed to defeat the Crimean Tatars, who raided Moscow itself in 1571. His plans for westward expansion into Lithuania and the Baltic region were likewise checked by defeats during the Livonian War (1558–83).

In 1560, fearing treason, Ivan summarily dissolved the "selected council" and embarked upon a regime of political terror that has become the subject of legend, literature, art, opera and film. The czar tortured and killed thousands. He kept a list of his victims—

the documents that survive include some 4,000 names—and donated money to churches and monasteries to pray for their souls. Ivan was married at least five times, perhaps seven; his wives either died (Ivan claimed they were poisoned) or became nuns.

In an atmosphere of dread and revolt, the czar and his family left Moscow and settled in nearby Aleksandrovskaia Sloboda (which became his official residence), where Ivan announced his intention to abdicate. The people of Muscovy, however, preferred the rule of a mad czar to that of the boyars and beseeched Ivan to reconsider. He agreed to remain on the throne provided that a large indemnity be paid to him, that the principal boyars be executed, and that he be granted an *oprichnina*, a royal domain under his direct and exclusive control.

The *oprichnina* was ruthlessly regulated by *oprichniki*—in effect, a secret police force—and Ivan evicted from the territory all the landed aristocracy. He ruled his domain with absolute authority and redoubled cruelty. Ivan fortified his residence, ran it like a bizarre parody of a monastery, and reveled alternately in Church ritual and the sadistic torture of his enemies, real and imagined. Inexplicably, in 1574, Ivan assumed the title of prince of Moscow and installed Simeon Bekbulatovich, a Christianized Tatar prince, as a puppet czar, only later to deport him to Tver.

Ivan's final years were marked by increasing melancholy, morbidity and madness. In 1581, during a fit of rage, he struck his son and heir, Ivan V, killing him. This act of murder or manslaughter haunted the remaining three years of the monarch's life, and (probably credible) legend has it that Ivan took monastic vows on his deathbed.

Further Reading: Andrei Kurbskii. *Prince A. M. Kurbsky's History of Ivan IV* (Cambridge: Cambridge University Press, 1965); Sergei Fedorovich Platonov. *Ivan the Terrible* (Gulf Breeze, Florida: Academic International Press, 1974); Hans von Eckardt. *Ivan the Terrible* (New York: Knopf, 1949).

J

Jaruzelski, Wojciech [Witold] (b. 1923–)
During his tenure as Polish chief of state and president from 1981 to 1990, Jaruzelski's clashes with the popular labor movement Solidarity ended with the breakdown of the Polish Communist regime in 1990.

Born in Kurow, Poland, on July 6, 1923, into a middle-class family—his father was an officer in the Polish cavalry—Jaruzelski was educated in Jesuit schools. His family was captured during the Russian invasion of 1939 and presumably died in Stalinist labor camps. Young Jaruzelski, however, was sent to a Soviet officer training school, was commissioned in the Polish army in 1943, and fought with distinction against the armies of Adolf HITLER. In 1956, at age 33, Jaruzelski became the youngest brigadier general in the Polish army.

In 1961, Jaruzelski was elected to the Sejm (Polish parliament), and seven years later was appointed minister of defense. In this post he strengthened the military while maintaining close ties with Moscow. In 1971 he became a member of Poland's ruling politburo, and, on February 11, 1981, was elected premier, also becoming secretary of the Communist Party on October 18, 1981.

As chief of state and supreme commander of the military, Jaruzelski faced off with Solidarity, Poland's rising labor movement. Early in 1981, he tried to reach a compromise with the movement and its leader Lech Walesa, but, by December, talks had broken down, and Wojciech declared martial law. Backed by the Soviet Union, which stationed 265 army divisions outside the Polish border, Jaruzelski dispatched Polish troops to more than 1,000 towns throughout the country. This action outraged leaders in the West, including U.S. president Ronald Reagan and Pope John Paul II, himself an anti-Communist Pole. By 1983, after suppressing Solidarity through mass arrests, Jaruzelski yielded to international moral and economic sanctions and lifted martial law.

As in virtually all of the Communist nations during the 1980s, Poland's economy was on the brink of collapse. An economic crisis in 1988 rekindled Solidarity—despite the arrests of many key members—and Jaruzelski was compelled to begin negotiations anew. Chief among Jaruzelski's concessions was the legalization of Solidarity as a political party and the authorization of free elections. The Polish parliament elected Jaruzelski president in July 1989, but in December 1990 Lech Walesa was made president by popular election and Jaruzelski resigned. With his resignation, Poland's long Communist regime came to an end.

On December 12, 1990, Jaruzelski, in his farewell address, apologized for the injustices of his regime: "The word *sorry* may sound all too casual, but I cannot find another."

John [John Lackland] (1167–1216)
Succeeding to the throne of England in the midst of feudal upheaval on the continent, John lost the Angevin Empire to PHILIP II AUGUSTUS of France and, more importantly, was forced to sign the Magna Carta in 1215.

The fourth and youngest son of King Henry II, John was born on Christmas Eve 1167 in Oxford. He quickly became his father's favorite son, having been assigned the lands of Ireland and the earldom of Gloucester, which caused friction with the Queen Mother and John's three older brothers. Two of John's older brothers died the same year as their father, 1189, and RICHARD I LIONHEART ascended to the throne.

Richard made peace with his brother, confirming the details of John's agreement with their father and conferring on him a hefty annual payment from the English coffers. In return, John pledged not to enter England while Richard was away fighting the Crusades. However, before his departure, Richard designated his nephew Arthur, son of his younger brother Geoffrey, as heir to the throne in preference to John. Enraged, John promptly broke his oath to his brother and entered England to challenge Richard's chancellor. John failed in this power struggle and was banished from the kingdom and deprived of all his possessions when Richard returned. Despite this, John was finally reconciled with Richard before the king's death, and Richard designated John, rather than Arthur, as his heir. Following his brother's death in 1199, John became king of England.

King John's first priority was to consolidate his grasp on the French possessions that were part of the Angevin Empire, which extended from Spain to Scotland. After a political marriage to Isabella of Angoulême, John failed to compensate the previously

King John of England signed the Magna Carta under duress—not in the ceremonial hall depicted in this 19th-century engraving, but in a tent at Runnymede.

betrothed, Hugh de Luisgnan, as was the custom, thereby igniting a war through which he lost the provinces of Normandy and Anjou. In the process, however, John captured Arthur—whose claim to the throne was backed by Philip II Augustus of France—and he disappeared into one of John's dungeons, never to be seen again.

John's next political disaster was his feud with Pope INNOCENT III over the archbishop of Canterbury. John's refusal to accept the pope's candidate for archbishop led to his excommunication, an interdict against England, and an eight-year feud that provoked the pope to makes plans to depose John and support Philip Augustus of France as ruler of England. Realizing his peril, John at last surrendered to the pope, accepting the archbishop, and making himself a papal vassal.

John's failures on the continent prompted him to consolidate authority in England by promoting members of his family to key offices and by instituting a ruthless program of heavy taxation, which included especially heavy burdens assessed against England's Jews. Moreover, John increasingly usurped the prerogatives of the country's feudal barons, who came to resent his interference in their affairs. The barons were further incensed at having to bear so much of the financial burden for John's numerous military misadventures, which had gained England nothing.

John was faced with increasing opposition from the united barons, for whom the new—and most unwelcome—archbishop of Canterbury proved to be an able spokesmen. Accused of tyranny and threatened with rebellion, John at last agreed to make formal concessions to the barons. In the meadow of

Runnymede, on June 19, 1215, he was compelled to sign the Magna Carta. Intended by the feudal lords to secure their rights, this document, which stated that the king was not above the law of the land and that the law reigned supreme in England, became a cornerstone of English common law and of human rights generally.

John did not readily accept the Magna Carta. No sooner had he, under duress, signed the document than he appealed to Pope Innocent III to annul the charter. In the meantime, he gathered military forces to oppose the barons, who, in turn, sought support from the French. Hostilities commenced, as John captured Rochester Castle and attacked the counties bordering Scotland. A full-scale civil war appeared inevitable. However, while preparing to repel French invaders under Prince Louis, John died of dysentery on October 18, 1216.

John's death made compromise between the barons and the new king, Henry III, possible. Louis withdrew, and full-scale war was averted. The barons—and, eventually, the English people—had secured important rights, but the loss of the Angevin Empire meant that England would never again have substantial territory on the European continent.

Further Reading: Kate Norgate. *John Lackland* (London: Macmillan, 1970); Wilfred Lewis Warren. *King John* (New York: W. W. Norton, 1961); James Clark Holt. *The Northerners: A Study in the Reign of King John* (Oxford: Oxford University Press, 1961).

John I Zimisces   (924–976)

In his ruthlessness, political skill, consummate craftiness, and military prowess, John I Zimisces embodied the qualities that distinguish the ablest Byzantine emperors.

John I Zimisces was descended from Armenian nobility and was related to the Kurkuas and Phocas families, who were highly influential in Byzantine affairs. He built his early reputation on military accomplishments, fighting in the service of Romanus II and NICEPHORUS II PHOCAS, emerging as the hero of the Battle of Samosata, northern Mesopotamia, in 958. Following this victory, Zimisces earned more than the praise of his countrymen when Theophano, the wife of Nicephorus, became his mistress. In a stroke of treachery not unusual in any number of imperial political situations, but especially characteristic of Byzantine politics, Theophano conspired with Zimisces and his friends to eliminate Emperor Nicephorus II. He was murdered on December 10 or 11, 969, whereupon Zimisces ascended the throne. In order to legitimate his power, Zimisces needed to secure the sanction and support of the patriarch of the Orthodox Church, Polyeuktos of Constantino-

ple. The patriarch considered the relationship between Zimisces and Theophano sinful and made his
support of the new emperor conditional on his exiling the unfaithful widow of Nicephorus. This Zimisces did.

Zimisces was forced to respond to pressure from
outside as well, when Russian prince Sviatoslav and
his Bulgarian allies made increasing demands for territory. From 969 to 972, Zimisces did battle with Sviatoslav and his allies, scoring a major land victory at
Arcadiopolis in 970 and an equally significant triumph at sea when he drove off the Russian fleet and
blockaded the Danube. In April of the following
year, Zimisces turned his attention to the Bulgarians, attacking the capital city of Great Preslav. He
then took up the pursuit of Sviatoslav's forces, pushing them northward to the Danube River fortress of
Dorostorum. There Sviatoslav holed up under siege
for two months, surrendering at last in July 971 and
yielding all of Bulgaria to the Byzantines.

Flushed with victory, Zimisces moved next against
the Muslims, pushing them back beyond the middle
Euphrates River and extending the Byzantine Empire well into Syria. In May 975, Zimisces took Damascus and advanced on Jerusalem itself. Near this
objective, his forces were stalled by stiff resistance
from the Fatimids. Zimisces himself was felled, not
by Fatimid weapons, but by typhoid fever. Desperately ill, he returned to Constantinople, where he
died on January 10, 976.

Juárez, Benito (Pablo)   (1806–1872)

President of Mexico from 1861 to 1872 and leader of
the resistance movement against French occupation
(1864–1867), Benito Juárez is venerated as a national
hero of Mexico.

Born on March 21, 1806, to Zapotec Indian parents
in the mountains of Oaxaca, Juárez was unable to
speak Spanish until the age of 12, when he moved
to the city of Oaxaca to work as a household servant.
His employer, perhaps recognizing the intellectual
ability of his servant, sent him to school as a full-
time student. Originally intent on becoming a priest,
Juárez decided in 1828 to study law instead, enrolling in the Oaxaca Institute of Arts and Sciences,
from which he received his law degree in 1831. After
practicing law in Oaxaca City and Mexico City for a
time, Juárez entered politics, winning a seat on the
municipal council.

For the next decade, Juárez served with honesty
and integrity in the state and national legislatures,
securing an appointment as judge in 1841, then becoming governor of Oaxaca in 1846. In this office he
proved to be an able and talented administrator. The
state was nearly bankrupt when he took office, but

by the end of his term, it had a surplus for the first
time since 1821.

During his early political life, Juárez began developing his liberal views on government and social reform. The church and the landed aristocracy held
too much power, he believed, and the economy
would improve only with the development of a
strong middle class. For the national government, he
supported a strong federal system.

The 1853 elections returned the Conservative
Party of General Antonio López de SANTA ANNA to
power, and Juárez found himself exiled to New Orleans, where the distinguished Mexican politician
and jurist earned a living rolling cigarettes. When
the Liberals under Juan Alvarez were elected in
1855, however, Juárez returned to Mexico City,
where he was given the post of minister of justice
and public instruction. During this time, he wrote
and saw through to passage a landmark law that
abolished special courts for the military and clergy.
Traditionally, these groups had been assured trials
with juries composed of their colleagues, but Juárez
believed that judicial equality was necessary to promote social equality.

In 1857 Mexico adopted a new liberal constitution
and elected Ignacio Comonfort president. Congress
selected Juárez to preside over the Supreme Court,
which meant that he was also ex-officio vice president. When, in 1858, the Conservatives rebelled and
ousted Comonfort from office. Juárez had a constitutional claim to the presidency but lacked the support
necessary to make good on it. He withdrew to Veracruz, where he set up an opposition government.
The task of raising an army to defeat the Conservatives and enforce the new constitution were daunting, but Juárez persevered. He began by securing
passage of a law that nationalized all church property—except those buildings actually used for worship—and put under civil service control the
registration of births and deaths. He decreed the
permanent separation of church and state, and guaranteed religious freedom to all Mexicans.

In 1861, the Conservatives at last began to lose
their grip on the country. Juárez was able to return
to Mexico City, and was elected president. Again,
however, he immediately faced overwhelming difficulties, most pressing of which was an empty treasury. He sought financial relief by suspending
repayment of the national debt for two years. England, Spain, and France took alarm at this order
and, largely at the direction of NAPOLEON III, sent an
invasion force to Veracruz. When England and
Spain realized that Napoleon III intended not only to
secure Mexico's debts, but in fact intended to make
Mexico a colony of France, they quickly withdrew

from the expedition. Napoleon III continued to increase his forces, however, and by June 1863 the French captured Mexico City. Napoleon then installed Archduke MAXIMILIAN of Austria as emperor of Mexico.

Juárez and his government retreated to the United States border, setting up their headquarters at the city now named Ciudad Juárez. With the American Civil War drawing to a close, President Abraham Lincoln sent supplies and aid to Juárez, and when the war ended, President Andrew Johnson invoked the Monroe Doctrine, warning the French to leave the continent. General Ulysses S. Grant raised troops for the Mexican war against the French. At this, the French withdrew, and Juárez's forces captured, tried and—despite pleas on his behalf from such notable European democrats as Victor Hugo and Garibaldi—executed Maximilian.

Juárez returned to the capital city in 1867. He ran for reelection and proposed a series of five constitutional amendments, which would strengthen the office of chief executive. While Juárez was reelected, the issue of the amendments ignited bitter controversy and brought about a popular crisis of confidence. Assailed by the doubts of his countrymen and afflicted by illness (he suffered a stroke in October 1870) and loss (his wife died in January 1871), Juárez nevertheless ran for reelection, securing victory even as he lost more of his popular support. He died, harried and broken in spirit as well as health in 1872.

Further Reading: Ralph Roeder. *Juarez and His Mexico* (New York: Viking, 1947); Charles A. Smart. *Viva Juárez* (Philadelphia: Lippincott, 1963).

Julian the Apostate [Flavius Claudius Julianus] (331/332–363)

Rising to power in the chaos of the late Roman empire, Julian became an avowed enemy of Christianity, instituting a policy of persecution and advocating a return to pagan belief.

Julian was born Flavius Claudius Julianus in Constantinople, the younger son of Julius Constantius, who was the half-brother of CONSTANTINE I THE GREAT. Julius Constantius' nephew, also called Constantius, became emperor of the Eastern Empire, then, on the death of his brother Constantine II, became sole emperor of Rome as CONSTANTIUS II. Julian was nine years old at this time and witnessed, at this tender age, a bloodbath wrought by the army, which wanted to ensure that none but the sons of Constantine I would succeed to the throne. All of Constantine I's half-brothers (and some others) were murdered. Constantius II ordered the death of Julian's father and, later, that of Julian's elder brother.

Since his mother, Basalina, had died shortly after his birth, Julian, at age 10 or 11, was left an orphan.

To save his life, Julian and his half-brother Gallus were taken into virtual hiding and raised first by Eusebius, bishop of Nicomedia, then by a noble Roman named Macellum in his remote estate at Cappadocia. At the age of 19, Julian found a protector in Eusebia, wife of Constantius II. She sponsored his education in Como and then in Greece—at Pergamum, Ephesus, and Athens—where he developed a keen interest in philosophy and pagan Neoplatonism.

In 351, Constantius II appointed Gallus caesar, in effect his co-emperor and designated successor. Gallus proved a dismal failure and was executed in 354, whereupon Constantius turned to Gallus' half-brother, Julian. He arrived from Greece and in November 355 was proclaimed caesar. Julian married Constantius' sister Helena, who died five years later. As to Julian, he was dispatched to the ever-rebellious Gaul, where he proved himself a superb commander, defeating the Alemanni and the Franks.

As was often the case in the Roman Empire, too great success could be as undesirable as failure, and a jealous Constantius deliberately kept Julian short of funds and set spies upon him. In 360 he went even further, demanding that Julian relinquish his best troops for service in the East. At this, Julian's

At the behest of Constantius, Julian led Roman legions to Gaul, where he defeated the Franks and Alemanni. Later, as emperor, Julian instituted the vigorous and single-minded persecution of Roman Christians. (From Charlotte M. Yonge, Pictorial History of the World's Great Nations, *1882)*

army rebelled and proclaimed Julian augustus. War between Julian and Constantius seemed inevitable, but the emperor sickened late in 361, and, near death, named Julian his successor.

With the passing of Constantius II in November 361, Julian became sole augustus of Rome. Having imbibed a philosophical asceticism, he reformed palace life, proclaimed his intention to rule as a philosopher-king in the manner of Marcus Aurelius, and promulgated freedom of worship open to all religions.

Despite his avowed tolerance, Julian's own religion was pagan, and he was determined to overturn Christianity as Rome's state religion, replacing it with his own version of a well-ordered paganism. Julian's advocacy of pagan worship soon spawned intolerance and fanaticism as well as a round of persecution of Christians that ranged from legally sanctioned acts of prejudice (Christians were purged from the army, and they were prohibited from teaching) to torture and murder. Christian iconography was replaced by pagan images in churches throughout the empire, Christian cities were fined and generally penalized, and some churches were destroyed. Ironically, though they enjoyed favored treatment, many pagans rejected Julian on account of his asceticism.

Julian was not content to reform Roman religion. Like many Roman rulers before and after him, he set his sights on conquering Persia. Toward this end, he assembled the greatest Roman army ever to venture against Persia—65,000 men—and, acting against the advice of Roman counselors, commenced the invasion. He was quickly defeated while attempting an assault on Ctesiphon (near modern Baghdad) and was retreating with his routed troops when a hurled spear pierced his liver. He died June 26 or 27, 363.

Further Reading: G. W. Bowersock. *Julian the Apostate* (Cambridge, Mass.: Harvard University Press, 1978).

Julianus [Marcus Didius Julianus] (133–193)

Julianus bought the office of emperor from the Praetorian Guard and reigned 64 days before he was assassinated.

Born into one of the most prominent and wealthy families of Milan, Julianus dedicated his life to public service. An officer in the army in 162, he commanded a legion, then became governor of Gallia Belgica about 170. He assumed the consulship in 175 with the future emperor Pertinax, then was governor of Illyricum from 167 to 177 and Lower Germany in 178. After becoming director of child welfare of Italy, he was accused of taking part in a conspiracy against the life of COMMODUS in 182, but was acquitted and appointed proconsul, serving until 190.

In 190, Julianus came to Rome, where his former co-consul, Pertinax, had succeeded Commodus as emperor. Upon Pertinax's assassination by the Praetorian Guard on March 28, 193, Julianus made his way to their camp to see if the empire could be bought. Unfortunately for Julianus, Titus Flavius Sulpicianus had the same idea, and the two engaged in a bidding war over the title of Roman emperor. Julianus won out in one of the more shameful incidents in the history of the empire.

After seeing to the execution of various persons involved in the murders of Commodus and Pertinax, Julianus took the title Pater Patriae, "Father of the Country." But the manner of his ascension to the throne offended many people, and Julianus could not appear in the streets of Rome without surrounding himself with a substantial guard. Then, he failed to pay the Praetorian Guard the amount he had promised them, and they abandoned him. With Septimius Severus and his Danubian legions advancing on Rome, the Senate rescinded Julianus' confirmation and sentenced him to death. He retreated to his palace, where he was executed on June 1, 193.

Further Reading: Michael Grant. *Roman Emperors* (New York: Scribner's, 1985).

Justinian I [Flavius Petrus Sabbatius] (b. ca. 482–565)

Byzantine emperor from 527 to 565, Justinian I codified Roman law and attempted to bring an end to the discord that plagued the Christian religion.

Justinian I was born Flavius Petrus Sabbatius in the Macedonian Balkans to Latin-speaking parents of peasant background. As a child, he accompanied his uncle Justin, head of the imperial guard, to Constantinople where he received a thorough education. To honor his uncle, he took the name Justinian.

In 518, on the death of Byzantine emperor Anastasius I, Justin was made emperor. Justinian was awarded increasingly important positions and on April 1, 527, was named co-emperor. (During this period, he married the actress Theodora.) Justin I died on August 1, 527, and Justinian succeeded to the throne.

Warfare with Persia had depleted much of the empire's resources, and the first years of Justinian's rule were condemned by the Senate as autocratic and oppressive. On January 13–18, 532, Justinian faced a real threat to his throne in the Nika riots. The turmoil began as brawling among the circus factions of the Hippodrome, escalated into cries for governmental reform, and ended as an attempt by the aristocracy to oust Justinian. The emperor suppressed the revolt by ordering his troops to massacre the rioters.

That same year, Justinian seized on a chance for peace in the East. The new Persian king, Chosroes I, signed a "Perpetual Peace" with Justinian, thereby freeing Roman resources for the liberation of territories in the West taken by the barbarians. Justinian aimed first at North Africa, where the Vandals were defeated by Justinian's general Belisarius in 533–534. Next, the emperor turned to Italy, and by 540 Belisarius had negotiated a settlement with the Ostrogoths. The peace in Italy was short-lived, however, as the Ostrogoths rebelled again, only to be put down by the Narses in 552. The region had been ravaged by war for so long, however, that its prosperity was broken, and Justinian could not afford to keep up the massive defenses needed to repel future invasions—notably by the Lombards a few years after the emperor's death.

In 540, Chosroes broke his treaty with Justinian and invaded Syria-Palestine. For years, Justinian had to shuffle his resources between two distant theaters of war. Peace was finally secured 22 years later by means of Justinian's payment of larger tributes to Persia.

The most enduring act of Justinian's reign was the codification of Roman law. Begun in 528 by the lawyer Tribonian, the work included all valid laws, opinions by Roman jurists, a textbook for students, and new laws. While Justinian's codification and strict enforcement of laws—especially those against tax evasion and illegal use of power—angered the aristocracy, the work had enormous influence on the future development of European law.

Religious affairs required much of the emperor's attention. Dissident groups within the Christian church fought over the divinity of Christ, the separation of religious and secular authority, and other matters. Justinian sought to reconcile these differences and convened the fifth ecumenical council (Second Council of Constantinople). The differences were not resolved, however, and eventually the Eastern dissidents—the Monophysites—transformed themselves into a separate church, dominant in Syria and Egypt.

The last years of Justinian's reign were burdened by increasing economic difficulties, continuing religious differences, and a pandemic of bubonic plague (542–543) throughout the empire. Opposition to the emperor mounted, and repeated barbarian attacks from the Balkans came dangerously close to the capital. Thus, when Justinian died on November 14, 565, the people of Constantinople rejoiced.

Further Reading: Robert Browning. *Justinian and Theodora* (New York: Praeger, 1971); John B. Bury. *History of the Later Roman Empire from the Death of Theodosius I to the Death of Justinian I*, vol 1. (New York: Dover, 1958); Percy N. Ure. *Justinian and His Age* (Harmondsworth, Middlesex: Penguin, 1951).

K

Kamehameha I the Great (1758?–1819)
The most famous of Hawaiian rulers, Kamehameha I united the Hawaiian islands and established a dynasty that endured until 1872.

Kamehameha was born in the Kohala district on the island of Hawaii probably in November 1758. His given name was Paiea—"Soft-Shelled Crab"—and he was the son of Keoua, a tribal chief, and his wife, Kekuiapoiwa, daughter of a former Hawaiian king named Alapai. Hawaiian tradition relates that the birth and infancy of Paiea were accompanied by signs of great portent. It is said that Koloiki, a brilliant star, appeared in the heavens just prior to the boy's birth. Later scholars have pointed out that Halley's Comet appeared in November 1758. When he was an infant, various Hawaiian priests and mystics predicted that Paiea would become a fearless conqueror who would defeat all rivals. Hearing this, his grandfather Alapai ordered the infant killed, but others spirited him away, and he grew to manhood in seclusion, for which reason he took the name Kamehameha, "The Very Lonely One" or "The One Set Apart."

In the period of Kamehameha's coming of age, the Hawaiian islands were not unified, but the principal island of Hawaii itself was ruled by a single king, Kalaniopuu. On his death in 1782, the island was divided between his son, Kiwalao, and his nephew, Kamehameha. For a few months, this arrangement was peaceful enough, but in July 1782, conflict broke out between chiefs loyal to Kiwalao and those whose allegiance was to Kamehameha. The dispute developed into a brief full-scale war, and in a battle at Mokuohai, Kiwalao was killed. Thus Kamehameha emerged as sole ruler of the island of Hawaii. In 1795, he set about subduing the other islands of the Hawaiian group, conquering all but Kauai and Niihau. These were peacefully ceded to him by a treaty of 1810, and from this point forward, Kamehameha ruled a unified Hawaii.

The king was certainly no democrat, but he did carefully select governors to administer each of the islands and look after the needs of his subjects. While he perpetuated the *kapu*, Hawaii's traditional strict code of tribal laws, he also introduced the *mamalahoe kanawai*—"The Splintered Paddle"—which substantially mitigated the absolute and often arbitrary authority of tribal chieftains to punish offend-ers at will. Kamehameha I also brought to an end the ages-old practice of human sacrifice.

The king brought a measure of humanity to the conduct of government in Hawaii, and he ushered in an era of limited intercourse with the world at large, bringing substantial revenues from the trade in sandalwood and by charging vessels a port duty. Despite these reforms, he managed to preserve the islands' independence during a period of intense European activity in the Pacific. However, following his death (on May 8, 1819, at Kailua), subsequent rulers of his dynasty failed to maintain Hawaii's independence, which steadily eroded throughout the 19th century.

Further Reading: Richard W. Tregaskis. *Kamehameha the Great* (New York: Macmillan, 1973).

Kanishka [Kanişka] (fl. 1st century A.D.)
Greatest of the Kushan kings, Kanishka reigned over a vast region encompassing the northern Indian subcontinent, Afghanistan, and (probably) much of central Asia. He was a major patron of Buddhism.

Very little is known about this monarch. Estimates as to the year of his ascension to the throne vary from A.D. 78 to 225, with 78 to 144 being most plausible. Since the year 78 marks the beginning of the Saka era, a dating system some scholars believe Kanishka introduced, that date may also mark the beginning of his reign. It is believed that Kanishka ruled for about 23 years.

Kanishka's realm extended from Bukhara (in modern Uzbekistan) in the west to Patna in the east, and from the Pamirs (in modern Tadzhikistan) in the north to central India in the south. There is evidence that he also subjugated the city-states of Khotan, Kashgar, and Yarkand (all in modern Chinese Turkestan).

Kanishka convened a great Buddhist council—the fourth such of its kind—at Kashmir, which resulted in the codification of Mahayana Buddhism and the production of learned religious texts and commentaries. Despite his advocacy of Buddhism, Kanishka apparently tolerated within his realm Zoroastrian, Brahamanic, and other beliefs. He also fostered trade with the Roman Empire, resulting in many instances of cross-cultural fertilization as evidenced in the Gandhara school of art, which incorporates

Greek and Roman classicism into Buddhist religious imagery.

Further Reading: Alistair Embree. *Encyclopedia of Asian History* (New York: Scribner's, 1988).

Kao Tsu, Han   *See* LIU PANG

Kao Tsu, T'ang   [Li Yuan] (566–635)
Instrumental in overthrowing the Sui dynasty, Kao Tsu became the founder and first emperor of the T'ang dynasty.

Li Yuan was from an aristocratic family intermarried with the nomadic tribes that invaded North China. He served as a regional defense minister, under the two emperors who constituted the Sui dynasty. His mission was to protect the region from incursions by nomads and from internal peasant revolts. He gained a popular following around 609 when he put down a rebellion in Shansi province and also turned back Turkic raiders.

With the Sui dynasty on the verge of collapse from its enormous military and public works expenditures and at the urging of his son, Li Shih-min, Li proclaimed the "Righteous Army" in 611 and attempted to take over the government. With the aid of the East Turkic khan—leader of the very Turks he had defeated—Li was able to take the Sui capital of Ch'ang-an and the strategic Wei valley in 617. In the south, the Sui emperor was murdered, and Li Yuan proclaimed the T'ang dynasty June 18, 618. As emperor, he took the name T'ang Kao Tsu.

Kao Tsu reformed the tax structure to make it more equitable and regularized coinage. His son, Shih-min, was in charge of the military and worked to eliminate all opponents and rival claimants to the throne. Largely through the efforts of Shih-min, the T'ang Dynasty was able to achieve supremacy in northern China. After the last of the revolts was suppressed in 626, Kao Tsu abdicated in favor of Li Shih-min, who had murdered his rival brothers and raised an army to oust his father.

Karmal, Babrak   (b. 1929–   )
Leader of the pro-communist party in Afghanistan, Karmal seized power in the wake of the 1979 Soviet invasion of Afghanistan.

The son of a high-ranking Afghan army official, Babrak Karmal was born in Kabul, where he attended a German-language school before entering Kabul University to study law and politics. At the university, Karmal was first exposed to Marxist philosophy and became interested in Marxist politics. His radical activities led to his arrest in 1949, where he was imprisoned for five years. Upon his release, he returned to school to complete his law degree.

After graduation, and a one-year stint in the Afghan army, Karmal worked in the Ministry of Planning for 12 years under the constitutional monarch, Muhammad Zahir Shah.

In 1965, Karmal joined the nascent pro-Communist party PDPA and was elected to the lower house of the national assembly. He soon clashed with the party founder, Noor Mohammad TARAKI, and by the mid-1970s, the party had split, Taraki leading the radical Khalq faction and Karmal the pro-Soviet Parcham faction. Deteriorating social conditions led to a military coup against King Zahir in 1973, leading to the installation of former prime minister Prince Daoud as president.

Daoud outlawed all forms of political opposition and abolished the legislature in 1977. This prompted the PDPA to reunite, and when Taraki and Karmal demonstrated against the killing of a PDPA official, Daoud had them imprisoned in April 1978. The following day, in retaliation, a military junta seized power and executed Daoud and his ministers. Taraki was named president and Karmal vice president. The coalition within the party soon collapsed, and Taraki led a purge of Parcham members of the government, beginning with Karmal, who had been sent to Czechoslovakia as ambassador in July, but was then recalled in September to stand trial for treason.

Instead of returning to Afghanistan, Karmal went into hiding in eastern Europe. In the meantime, Taraki was overthrown by chief adviser Hafizullah Amin. Apparently without invitation from anyone within the government, the Soviet Union launched an invasion of Afghanistan on Christmas Day, 1979, and within 48 hours had seized Kabul and arrested, tried, and executed Amin for crimes against the state. Karmal was named president, prime minister, secretary general of the PDPA, and commander in chief of the armed forces.

Most Afghan citizens saw Karmal as a puppet of the Soviets and resented him deeply, especially the devout Muslims, who regarded Karmal as an atheist. In January 1980, he abolished the hated secret police, but then installed a Soviet-style intelligence agency in its place. He also freed about 2,000 political prisoners, all Parchamists, then rounded up some 1,700 Khalq sympathizers.

Opposition to the Soviet occupation and Karmal's government grew exponentially both domestically and internationally. From the United States, the CIA funneled millions of dollars to the Afghan freedom fighters in the hills surrounding Kabul and in the Khyber Pass. Within Afghanistan, fewer than 10 percent of the people supported Karmal. In July 1980, the Soviets were forced to check Karmal's own troops, who planned to assassinate the leader. The rebellion against Karmal wore on, and only the presence of Soviet troops kept him in power. Finally in 1985, faced with increasing revolt in Afghanistan and the weakening of Soviet resolve, Karmal resigned.

Kassem [Qassim], Abdul Karim   (1914–1963)

The premier of Iraq who overthrew the monarchy, Kassem was wary of both the Communists and the Pan-Arab supporters of Gamal Abdel NASSER.

Raised by his grandfather in Baghdad, Abdul Karim Kassem was born on November 21, 1914. At 17 he enrolled in the Iraqi Military College in Baghdad. He graduated in 1936 and was commissioned a second lieutenant in the infantry. Ascending through the Iraqi military hierarchy, Kassem acquired a strong disdain for the pro-Western advocates of the regime of King Faisal II. Likewise, however, he detested the Communist elements hoping to gain a foothold in the Middle East of the late fifties.

By 1955, he was made a brigadier in the army, and in 1957 was given command of a brigade stationed in Jordan. At this time, he formed the Free Officer's Movement, searching for loyal officers opposed to the current regime and who would support a change. When the king ordered Kassem and his brigade to march through Baghdad on their way to Lebanon, Kassem and his loyal officers seized a golden opportunity. On the night of July 13, 1958, Kassem and his military junta assassinated King Faisal, his son the crown prince, and the prime minister, proclaiming a republic. Kassem declared himself prime minister as well as minister of defense.

The fledgling republic was pressured by Egypt's premier, Gamal Abdel Nasser, to join Egypt and Syria in the United Arab Republic. But Kassem was wary of joining such a union without first consolidating his power at home. Nasser responded to Kassem's resistance by fomenting a rebellion in Iraq. In March 1959, pro-Nasserists rose in Mosul—with a little help from the army—in support of the UAR. Kassem quickly crushed the rebellion and purged some 200 officers in the process.

After initially relying on support from the pro-Communist factions in Iraq, Kassem subsequently rebuffed Communist overtures and demands during the later 1950s, and by mid-1959, purged his government of all Communists.

Repeated purges and the largely unsettled question of Arab unity progressively narrowed Kassem's support. By the end of 1960, he found himself having to suppress a fast-growing opposition. By the spring of 1961, a revolt of the Kurds had broken out in the north, and Kassem was unable to muster the support needed to put down the rebellion. In February 1961, a military junta overthrew Kassem and executed him on February 9.

Khanh, Nguyen   (b. 1927–   )

One of several military leaders of South Vietnam during the tumultuous 1960s, Nguyen Khanh was involved in no fewer than three coups, all of which had the backing of the U.S. government.

Born to a family of modest means in northern Vietnam, Khanh was an incorrigible schemer, willing, it seemed, to sell anyone out for his own best interests. In 1943, he quit school to join the Viet Minh in their efforts to rid the country of both the imperialist Japanese and French forces. However, due to his craftiness and apparent lack of loyalty, the Viet Minh expelled Khanh, who promptly joined the French forces shortly before their decisive defeat at Dien Bien Phu in 1954.

At the Geneva Conference in 1954, Khanh came to the aid of Ngo Dinh DIEM and eventually rose to become Diem's deputy chief of staff. When it became apparent that Diem, an American-educated Catholic, was losing support in Buddhist-controlled South Vietnam, Khanh and a group of senior military officials under General Duong Van Minh staged a successful coup d'état, deposing Diem in November 1963. The coup was conducted with the support of the Kennedy and Johnson administrations, acting on the advice of U.S. Ambassador to South Vietnam Henry Cabot Lodge, who was tiring of Diem's obstinacy, corruption, and incompetent conduct of the war.

General Minh was set up as chief of state, and, for his efforts in the coup, Khanh was named as Minh's chief of staff. This union lasted only three months before Khanh led "young Turks" in a coup against Minh in January 1964. Again, the Johnson administration backed the coup, since backing Minh would have been perceived as bolstering what had become a military dictatorship. Acting in accordance with U.S. instructions, Khanh set up a civilian government centered on a Supreme National Council. This created a convoluted body at the center of government and was essentially worthless. The Viet Cong took advantage of this attenuated government to advance its incursions into the south. Added to Khanh's problems was destructive factionalism between Buddhist and Christian elements.

Nguyen Khanh's government was ripe for a coup, and Generals Nguyen Cao Ky and Nguyen Van Thieu, who had participated in the coups against both Diem and Minh, now led one against Khanh, ousting him in February 1965, but confering upon him the post of "roving ambassador" to France. In effect, this meant exile to France. Later, Khanh moved to the United States, where he set up residence in luxurious Palm Beach, Florida.

In one of the turnabouts that marked his career, Nguyen Khanh returned to Vietnam some time after the war had ended and, in the mid-1980s, was named general secretary to the Council of Ministers in the Communist Party.

Further Reading: Stanley Karnow. *Vietnam: A History* (New York: Viking, 1983); Frances FitzGerald. *Fire in the Lake: The Vietnamese and the Americans in Vietnam* (Boston: Little, Brown, 1972).

Khomeini, Ayatollah Ruhollah [Sayyid Ruhollah Moussavi] (1900–1989)

Ayatollah Ruhollah Khomeini led the movement that overthrew the U.S.–allied Muhammad Reza Shah PAHLAVI of Iran and that resulted in the capture of 90 American embassy staffmembers in the Iran hostage crisis.

Born in Khomein, Iran, in 1900, the son of an ayatollah (literally, "reflection of Allah," a learned priest) of the orthodox Shiite Muslim sect, Khomeini devoted himself to the study of theology. By 1962, he had become one of the six grand ayatollahs of Iran's Shiite Muslims. As a Shiite, Khomeini was also a nationalist who opposed the shah, not only for his repressiveness and corruption, but for his alliance with such Western powers as the United States. He was exiled in 1963 for leading religious demonstrations against the shah, and in 1978 moved to France. There, far from his country, he organized and led a rapidly growing anti-shah movement, which finally resulted in the ouster of Muhammad Reza Shah Pahlavi. In January 1979, after the shah had left Iran, Khomeini returned to Iran as its secular and religious head of state, becoming in December 1979 *faqih* ("supreme religious guide") of the Islamic Republic of Iran.

Elevated to his position as absolute ruler for life, Khomeini quickly became the focus of a personality cult that seemed fanatical to Western observers. Unalterably opposed to the West—and to the United States in particular—Khomeini supported the November 4, 1979, takeover of the United States embassy by some 500 militant students. Sixty-three Americans were taken hostage and imprisoned for more than a year.

Although Khomeini and his fundamentalist regime were opposed by Western-educated moderates and other minorities, the regime rapidly consolidated its control, fostering the virtual idolatry of the person of Khomeini, imposing stringent controls on the press, legislating the elimination of all Western customs and practices, and freely executing members of the opposition. Protracted war with neighboring Iraq (led by Saddam HUSSEIN) gave Khomeini leverage to quell dissent and unify his country, although, with his economy battered after eight years of hostilities, Khomeini was compelled to conclude a cease-fire in 1988.

The Ayatollah Khomeini succeeded in maintaining control over Iran until his death on June 3, 1989, which, if anything, provoked a renewal of fundamentalist fervor. Khomeini had clearly bequeathed to Iran a stern theocracy—mitigated only somewhat by constitutional revisions granting greater power to a secular president—but he had fallen far short of his goal of achieving a fundamentalist unity among Islamic nations in strict opposition to the West.

Further Reading: Robin Wright. *In the Name of God: The Khomeini Decade* (New York: Simon & Schuster, 1989).

Kieft, Willem (1597–1647)

Governor of New Netherland, Kieft is principally known for his senseless massacre of Wappinger Indians in 1643.

Born in Amsterdam in September 1597, Willem Kieft became a merchant before moving to La Rochelle, France, around 1630. His business soon failed, however, and he journeyed to the Ottoman Empire to ransom Christian prisoners—presumably for a profit—but, lacking the funds to free all of them, he redeemed only the cheapest.

In May 1637, the Dutch West India Company received permission to dismiss Wouter Van Twiller as governor of New Netherland and appoint Kieft as the fifth governor of the colony. He sailed for the New World in September 1637, but did not reach New Netherland until March 28, 1638. Arriving in New Amsterdam (present-day New York City), he found the city in terrible condition. Defenses were practically useless, and only one ship was seaworthy. He promptly assumed dictatorial powers and ordered reforms in the civil and military administration as well as reform of the police.

In his dealing with the Indians, Kieft was gratuitously brutal. In 1641, he forced the Raritan Indians, who lived near New Amsterdam, to pay a tribute to the city. The Raritans refused and retaliated by destroying an outlying colony, thereby sparking a war with the white settlers. During the next four years, there would be only five months of relative peace.

Kieft still preserved an active trading relationship with the powerful Mohawk tribe, which sought to exact tribute from the Wappinger Indians, who lived along the Hudson River above Manhattan. Terrified by the Mohawk onslaught, the Wappingers fled to

Pavonia (present-day Jersey City, New Jersey) and New Amsterdam proper, appealing to Kieft for aid.

They had come to the wrong man.

Kieft not only refused to help the Wappingers, he turned the Mohawks loose against them in Pavonia, then sent in Dutch troops to finish off the refugees. During the terrible night of February 25–26, 1643, the troops perpetrated the infamous "Slaughter of the Innocents," killing men, women, and children indiscriminately. The heads of 80 slain Indians were brought back to New Amsterdam, where soldiers and citizens used them as footballs. Some 30 prisoners were publicly tortured to death. The atrocity greatly increased the intensity of the chronic Dutch-Indian war.

Under the economic and military pressures brought by the war, the population of New Netherland became rebellious, and Kieft, who had dismissed the administrative council in 1642, now forbade any public meetings without his consent. When the colonists blamed the Indian troubles on him, Kieft convened a meeting at which he was charged with hypocrisy, impudence, and self-aggrandizement. He was then reported to the States-General in Holland and replaced by Governor Peter STUYVESANT in 1645. In August 1647, Willem Kieft sailed for Holland, but died when the ship was wrecked off the coast of the British Isles on September 27, 1647.

Kim Il-sung   (b. 1912–1994)

Kim Il-sung was the premier of the Democratic People's Republic of Korea (North Korea) from 1948 to 1972 and president from 1972 until his death.

Born Kim Song Ju on April 15, 1912, near P'yongyang, Korea, Kim Il-sung fled with his parents to Manchuria in order to escape the harsh Japanese occupation. Kim soon returned, however, and joined the Korean Communist Party in 1927 or 1931 (sources differ), participating in anti-Japanese activities. Rising rapidly in the party, Kim was sent to the Soviet Union for military training and political indoctrination. In the USSR, Kim changed his name to Kim Il-sung in honor of a much celebrated anti-Japanese guerrilla.

Kim Il-sung spent World War II as leader of a Korean unit of the Soviet Red Army, returning to Korea after the war to establish a provisional Communist government in the north. This became the Democratic People's Republic of Korea, and in 1948 Kim was named premier. Two years later, he invaded South Korea with the intention of reunifying the nation under communism.

The invasion went well at first until the United Nations, led chiefly by U.S. forces, intervened.

Kim's forces were pushed far back into the North. The timely entry of Chinese forces on the side of North Korea expelled the U.N. forces and brought the war to a stalemate. With the cease-fire of 1953, Korea remained divided, and Kim turned his attention to eliminating all opposition in the north against his regime. He created a monolithic state directed toward two goals: industrialization and reunification. Toward these ends, he forged strong ties with the Soviet Union and China, often playing the two against one another. Like other Communist strongmen, he encouraged a cult of personality about himself and insured that he would be succeeded by his son, Kim Chong Il.

The collapse of the Soviet Union and China's increasingly cordial relations with the West brought severe economic hardship on North Korea during the 1980s and early 1990s. His country facing financial ruin, Kim Il-sung was forced to back off from his uncompromising hard line and make overtures to Western investors. Decades of isolation, human rights violations and an apparent nuclear arms program have posed formidable barriers to recovery. His death on July 8, 1994 has given some cause to hope for change.

Kittikachorn, Thanom,   (1911–)

As a division commander in the army, Kittikachorn helped overthrow the Phibunsongkhram regime and served twice as Thai prime minister.

Born in northwestern Thailand on August 11, 1911, Thanom Kittikachorn was destined for military service from early childhood. He was sent to Bangkok at the age of nine to attend the Royal Thai Military Academy, graduating in 1929. After being commissioned a second lieutenant, Kittikachorn rose through the Thai military hierarchy without particular distinction, serving in a variety of instructor posts. In 1941, he was sent into the field for active duty against the Shan States and was promoted to major in 1943 and lieutenant colonel the following year.

By 1951, he was made major general and appointed deputy commanding general of the vaunted Thai First Army. In September 1954, he was made commanding general of the First, controlling all military operations around Bangkok. He was also elected to the House of Representatives in 1951 and named deputy minister of defense in 1957. In August, he was named assistant commander in chief under his mentor, Sarit Thanarat. With Kittikachorn's control of the First Army, Thanarat was able to seize power from Field Marshal Phibunsongkhram. Kittikachorn was made minister of defense in the new regime.

After the elections of December 1957, Thanarat's party won a plurality, and, with former supporters of Phibunsongkhram, they formed the National Socialist Party to control the legislature. On January 1, 1958, Kittikachorn was installed as prime minister. From the outset, he stated that the goal of his administration would be to halt the spread of Chinese communism and to continue support of the United Nations and the United States.

Kittikachorn's government collapsed in October 1958 because of internal strife. Thanarat again seized power, again naming Kittikachorn as minister of defense. When Thanarat died in December 1963, Kittikachorn was named prime minister.

During his second stint as prime minister, Kittikachorn waged a war against corruption. He demanded that all his cabinet members, as well as himself, resign their posts in commercial firms; he cracked down on corruption in government contracts; and he gave the press more freedom to expose such corruption. He also continued to align Thailand with the United States.

With the help of China, Communist guerrillas in Thailand stepped up their activities in 1965, but Kittikachorn swiftly squashed the uprising.

Keeping his promise upon his second appointment as prime minister, Kittikachorn restored parliamentary democracy to Thailand in 1968 with a new constitution and free elections in 1969. After security concerns in the region brought on by American involvement in Vietnam caused unrest in Thailand, Kittikachorn dissolved parliament and the cabinet and suspended the constitution in 1971. He was forced to resign in 1973, however, after student riots over the dissolution of the government became uncontrollable. He returned in August 1976 to aid in the return of authoritarian rule, but was not again directly involved in government.

Kuang Wu Ti   [Liu Hsiu] (4 B.C.–A.D. 57)

The first emperor of the Later Han dynasty of China, Kuang Wu Ti defeated a usurper and restored peace to China.

Originally named Liu Hsiu, Kuang Wu Ti was posthumously given the name meaning Shining Martial Emperor by which he is known to history. Liu Hsiu was descended from the ruling family of the earlier Han dynasty and was part of the powerful landed aristocracy of China. Although sent to the capital of Ch'ang-an to study, he preferred the day-to-day running of his estate and left school to return home. Liu Hsiu and his brother Po-sheng joined the rebellion against the regime of Wang Mang, who had usurped the throne from the Han. Many of the rebels were peasants, however, and were wary of the aristocratic Liu Hsiu and his brother.

When Wang Mang was overthrown in A.D. 23 by the rebels, who now called themselves the Han army, a non-aristocrat was named emperor. Fearing that Po-sheng might try to gain power, the new emperor had him murdered, but the emperor himself was killed two years later when the capital was sacked by a marauding terrorist group called the Red Eyebrows. This opened the way for Liu Hsiu to seize power and restore the Han dynasty officially in A.D 25.

A power struggle ensued among no fewer than 12 pretenders. Liu Hsiu prevailed, finally securing his throne by A.D. 37. He relocated the capital to Lo-yang, east of the site of the Former Han capital and structured his government according to Han practice, except that he approached the task more economically, eliminating over 400 local-level government posts. He also abolished military posts in the local provinces, not only to save money, but to make certain that no local army would ever rise against him.

Aware of the strain that the recent civil wars had put on his people and in accordance with his own distaste for war, Hsiu attempted to make peace on China's borders, which he accomplished through skilled generals and deft diplomacy. While the Later Han dynasty was never as powerful as the Former Han, it did survive for two centuries.

Further Reading: Demetrius Boulger. *The History of China* (Freeport, N.Y: Books for Libraries, 1972).

Kublai Khan   [Yuan Shih Tsu] (1215–1294)

Grandson of GENGHIS KHAN and founder of the Yuan (Mongol) dynasty of China, Kublai Khan became well known to the West through the writings of Venetian explorer Marco Polo.

The fourth son of Tolou—whose father was Genghis Khan—Kublai Khan exhibited little ambition until 1251, when he took over the civil and military administration of China from his brother Hulegu. In 1260, Kublai arranged a truce with other Mongolian leaders, and, on May 5, was elected khan in succession to his deceased brother Mongke. During this year, he established his residence of Kaiping or Shangtu, which Samuel Taylor Coleridge celebrated as Xanadu in his famous 19th-century poem.

Kublai Khan established Mongol rule over North China from his capital in Ta-tu (modern-day Peking). From there he initiated a conquest of the Sung dynasty of southern China in 1267, and by 1279 Kublai had conquered all of China, the first non-Chinese to become emperor of the entire country.

As emperor Kublai befriended Venetian traveler Marco Polo, whose accounts of the ruler became for Renaissance Europeans the chief source of information on the East. The Mongols were notorious for their inability to govern conquered territory, but Kublai proved to be an exception. A ruthless conqueror as well as competent administrator, he surrounded himself with a court of Confucian advisers and kept traditional Chinese institutions but put them under Mongol control, establishing a regime that was not overly oppressive. Kublai Khan introduced paper money and granted extensive religious freedom to the Chinese Buddhist and Tibetan monks.

The main obstacles to Kublai's rule lay in the complex nature of Chinese society. It became difficult for Kublai to avoid assimilation into Chinese culture; therefore, his political and territorial gains in China came at the expense of his Mongolian heritage. His 1274 and 1281 attempts to invade Japan both ended in disaster. Kublai also badly strained Mongol coffers by his many extravagant building projects, including the repair and extension of the Grand Canal. Following his death in 1294, his Mongolian successors became increasingly isolated from Chinese culture and, effectively cut off, the Mongolian regime ultimately collapsed in 1367.

Further Reading: John Joseph Saunders. *The History of the Mongol Conquests* (New York: Barnes & Noble, 1971).

Kun, Béla   (1886–1939)

One of the founders of the Hungarian Communist Party, Béla Kun was dictator of a short-lived Communist government established in Hungary following World War I.

Born February 20, 1886, Béla Kun fought in World War I until 1916, when he was taken to Russia as a prisoner of war. While there, he witnessed the Russian revolution and became converted to Bolshevist thought. Following the end of the war in 1918, Hungary was declared a republic on November 16 after a brief revolution led by Count Mihaly Károlyi, who served as its first president. In the meantime, Kun had come to the attention of Soviet leader V. I. LENIN, who returned him to Hungary as a Communist agitator. In part through Kun's efforts, the republic collapsed, and Károlyi stepped down as president in March 1919. Kun became commissar for war and foreign affairs in the new Communist regime established on March 22, 1919. He was, in effect, dictatorial head of state.

At the behest of Lenin and acting largely as his puppet, Kun instituted radical Communist reforms and moved swiftly and brutally to crush dissent. Kun's repressive policies provoked internal rebellion as well as opposition from the outside. On March 28, 1919, Kun declared war on Czechoslovakia and his troops invaded the Slovakian region. When it became apparent that Kun intended next to reconquer Transylvania, which Romania had occupied after World War I, Romanian forces invaded Hungary on April 10, 1919. The nation was in the throes of an anti-Communist revolution, and this, combined with the invasion, brought about the downfall of Kun's regime.

On August 1, 1919, as Romanian troops approached Budapest, Kun fled to Vienna. Later, he went to Moscow, where he became a leading figure in the Comintern, the governing body of international communism. Like many others, however, Kun fell victim to one of STALIN's great purges. He was arrested in 1936 and died in prison on November 30, 1939.

Further Reading: Rudolf L. Toakes. *Bela Kun and the Hungarian Soviet Republic* (Stanford, Conn.: Praeger, 1967).

L

Ladislas (1377–1414)

Involving himself in such matters as the papal succession, Ladislas was able to expand greatly his Neapolitan kingdom.

Ladislas was born February 11, 1377, the son of Charles III of Naples. Succeeding his father at the age of nine in 1386, Ladislas ruled under the regency of his mother until 1387, when he was expelled from Naples by Louis II of Anjou, who claimed the throne for himself and took advantage of the young king's age. With the help of his mother and his advisers, Ladislas mastered politics and diplomacy at an early age. By 1399, he had subdued the rebellious barons loyal to Louis, and next drove the usurper out of Naples.

Now wary of being taken advantage of, Ladislas took the offensive, invading Dalmatia in Hungary and declaring himself king in August 1404, even though he did not actually control much of the country. He was forced to return to Naples, however, to again subjugate the nobles, freshly risen against him.

When Pope Boniface IX died in 1404, he was succeeded by Innocent VII; however, the antipope, Benedict XIII, received the support of Louis of Anjou. Ladislas immediately declared his support of Innocent and occupied Rome, for which Innocent named him protector of the church as well as governor of Campagna and Maritima. When the prince of Taranto died around 1405, Ladislas quickly married his widow and added Taranto to his holdings as well. Ladislas now controlled much of central Italy.

With the death of Innocent in 1406, who was succeeded officially by Gregory XII, another antipope, Alexander V, arose to claim the papacy. Alexander V was named pope by the Council of Pisa, but he soon died, being succeeded by John XXIII, who was also supported by Louis of Anjou. Ladislas took up the cause of Gregory, and John promptly crowned Louis king of Naples in 1411. Louis then defeated Ladislas at the Battle of Roccasecca. After reorganizing his forces, making peace with Florence and receiving aid from Muzio Sforza, Ladislas substantially intimidated John into giving him money and territory in return for renouncing Gregory in 1412.

Ladislas' plans were upset, however, when Sigismund was elected king of Germany, and a proposed pact between him and John was announced. Ladis-

las quickly marched against John, sacking Rome on June 6, 1413. He then followed the retreating John to Bologna to prevent his forces from uniting with those of Sigismund's. But in this he failed. After again invading Rome in March 1414 and then moving north, where he reached a new accord with Florence and Siena, he fell ill, was carried back to Naples, and died on August 6, 1414.

Laud, William (1573–1645)

As archbishop of Canterbury and religious adviser to King Charles I, Laud relentlessly persecuted the Puritans, for which he ultimately suffered execution.

Born in Reading to a prominent clothier on October 7, 1573, William Laud attended St. Johns College, Oxford. There, he fell in with anti-Puritan Arminians, who opposed the doctrine of predestination and any form of Presbyterianism. Laud subscribed to the Arminian theories wholeheartedly, and they would dominate his thought and actions for the rest of his life. Inspired by his theological discussions at St. Johns, Laud entered the service of the Church of England in 1601. With the help of Richard Neile, bishop of Rochester, he received successive ecclesiastical appointments and at last came to the attention of King James I. In 1616, he was appointed dean of Gloucester Cathedral, and in 1621 was bishop of St. David's in Wales.

Through the patronage of the duke of Buckingham, Laud became Buckingham's chaplain, an office that gave him an important voice in church policies and appointments. By 1627, he was privy councillor, and in 1628 he was named bishop of London. There he made it his personal struggle to eradicate Puritanism wherever he found it, enforcing absolute adherence to the Book of Common Prayer. He also redecorated, remodeled, and repaired churches, from the most magnificent cathedrals to the smallest village chapels. In 1633, Laud was named Archbishop of Canterbury. Many saw him moving toward the establishment of an Anglican papacy.

Beginning in 1634, Laud visited every diocese in England and was appalled by the extent to which Puritanism had supplanted the Anglican Church. He forbade the practice of local governments financially supporting Puritan clergy, he strongly opposed the Puritan manner of preaching, and he quickly moved to crush those who opposed him. He mutilated, whipped, and imprisoned Puritan sympathizers. He also sought to restore the Anglican church as a major landholder in post-feudal England, alienating many private landowners who might otherwise have supported him.

With the help of Thomas Wentworth, earl of Strafford, Laud developed a policy that included the reintroduction of church officials to government office. The two called the plan the "Thorough"; it called for a strong central government founded on the church. Laud sought to implement the Thorough first in Presbyterian Scotland, but it failed miserably.

With the rise of Parliamentary power and the concomitant friction with King CHARLES I, the end was in sight for William Laud. After Charles fled north to raise an army to battle Parliament, that body, eager to avenge the 11-year hiatus the king had imposed on it, acted vigorously to reverse Laud's policies. Laud had made himself sufficiently unpopular, especially with the landed interests, that supporters of varied persuasions were attracted to Parliament's cause. In the absence of the king, Parliament ordered Laud's arrest on charges of high treason and had him imprisoned in the Tower of London in 1641. He was not tried until 1644, and was found guilty by the House of Commons. On January 10, 1645, William Laud was beheaded.

Further Reading: H. R. Trevor-Roper. *Archbishop Laud, 1573–1645* (London: Macmillan, 1940); Henry Bell. *Archbishop Laud and Priestly Government* (London: Constable, 1905); Charles Carlton. *Archbishop William Laud* (London & New York: Routledge & Kegan Paul, 1987).

Lauderdale, John Maitland, duke of (1616–1682)

One of CHARLES II's chief advisers after the Restoration, Lauderdale was known for his repression of Presbyterians in Scotland.

John Maitland was born May 24, 1616, to a Scottish lord. He was one of the signers of the Solemn League and Covenant, which pledged to protect Scottish Presbyterianism against any encroachments by CHARLES I. When civil war broke out between Charles I and Parliament in 1642, Lauderdale quickly aligned the Scots with the Parliamentarians. Hoping to secure better treatment from the Scots than the Parliamentarians, Charles surrendered to the former in 1646, but was turned over to the Parliamentarians anyway. In an attempt to gain support, Charles secured an agreement with Lauderdale, called the Engagement, which provided for Scottish aid against the rebels in return for the imposition of Presbyterianism on England.

Under Lauderdale's direction, the Scottish invasion was planned for 1648, but failed miserably.

Once he had plotted with the king, he could not go back, and began fighting for the restoration of the crown—his only hope for avoiding execution. After Charles I's execution in January 1649, Lauderdale threw his support to the slain king's son, Charles II. Lauderdale was captured with Charles II's forces while fighting against Oliver CROMWELL's New Model Army at the Battle of Worcester in 1650. Lauderdale was imprisoned, and finally released in 1660 after the restoration of Charles II as king of England.

In return for his loyalty during the interregnum, Lauderdale was made Charles' chief minister in Scotland and a member of the famed Cabal, the king's private cabinet. Charles soon reneged on the Engagement and signed the Treaty of Dover with France, by which he pledged to restore Catholicism to England in return for French funds. At the same time, he set about restoring Episcopacy to Scotland, and placed Lauderdale in charge. Lauderdale soon made himself the most hated man in Scotland for the ruthlessness with which he carried out the task of stamping out Presbyterianism.

The Presbyterians grew rebellious against this oppression and rose up in revolt against Lauderdale in 1679. Fearful that Lauderdale was trying to help the king justify a standing army, the English Parliament discredited Lauderdale, who resigned in 1680. He died two years later in England on August 24, 1682.

Laurel, José Paciano (1891–1959)

A lawyer and senator, Laurel became president of the Philippines under Japanese occupation during World War II, governing amid allegations of collaboration with the invaders.

Born to a peasant family on March 9, 1891, José Laurel was soon recognized as an exceptional individual and became a brilliant student. After joining the civil service in 1909, working for the Bureau of Forestry, he began studying law at the University of the Philippines. He received his law degree in 1915 and was appointed clerk at the Executive Bureau, then chief clerk in 1921. He also undertook graduate work at Yale University.

Laurel was appointed under-secretary of the interior in 1922 and the following year was named secretary of the interior. His ascendancy in public service was abruptly halted in 1922, by what became known as the "Conley incident." Conley was the American chief of the vice squad in Manila, who reported to Secretary of the Interior Laurel. For reasons that are not clear, Laurel wished to oust Conley and brought charges of bribery against him. When the charges were dismissed and Laurel was ordered by Governor General Leonard Wood to reinstate him, Laurel resigned and persuaded other cabinet members to do the same.

Laurel returned to his law practice, nursing a growing bitterness toward the Americans while learning to admire the Japanese. Returning to politics in 1925, Laurel was elected senator and served as floor leader until 1931, when he returned to academia to earn his Ph.D. In 1934, he served as a delegate to the constitutional convention and temporary chairman of the convention. In 1936, he was named associate justice of the Philippine Supreme Court.

After the Japanese attacked Pearl Harbor in December 1941, Philippine president Manuel Quezon fled, and Laurel became acting chief justice of the Supreme Court. When Japan occupied the Philippines in early January 1942, Laurel offered them his services. After the war, he insisted that he was acting on Quezon's orders, who, having died in 1944, was unable to confirm or refute Laurel's statement.

Under the occupation, Laurel was made commissioner of justice and interior. In 1943, he was shot twice by local guerrillas active in the resistance to the occupation forces.

On October 14, 1943, the Philippine Republic was declared, with Laurel as its first president. He gave amnesty to all guerrillas and was granted dictatorial powers by the assembly. In September, he declared war on the United States and Great Britain, but refused to order conscription, thereby making the declaration essentially worthless. Toward the end of the war, Laurel was captured by American forces and imprisoned, pending trial on 132 counts of treason. After a flurry of countercharges blaming the United States for his actions, he and all other accused traitors were pardoned by Manuel Roxas, first president of the independent Philippine Republic.

Laurel ran for president in 1949 and was narrowly defeated by the Liberal Party. In 1951, he was elected to the senate but lost the speakership by one vote. In 1955, Laurel headed an economic commission charged with improving relations with the United States and bolstering the Philippine economy. He retired from public life in 1957 and died on November 6, 1959.

Leguía y Salcedo, Augusto Bernardino (1863–1932)

Twice elected president of Peru, Leguía y Salcedo made tremendous improvements in Peru's infrastructure and settled boundary disputes with his country's neighbors.

Born on February 19, 1863, Leguía y Salcedo served against Chile in the War of the Pacific, which ended in 1881. After the war, he became a highly successful executive with the New York Life Insurance Company, amassing a large personal fortune. In 1903, he was named Peru's minister of finance, serving until 1907, when he resigned to run for the presidency in 1908.

During his first term as president, Leguía y Salcedo began his extensive reform of the Peruvian infrastructure by building hospitals and improving primitive sewage systems. Based on his experience as finance minister, he fostered extensive fiscal reform. Most important, though, he settled once and for all in 1909 the long-troublesome border dispute among Peru, Bolivia, and Brazil.

During a revolutionary uprising later in 1909, Leguía y Salcedo was deposed and fled to London, where he became president of the Latin American Chamber of Commerce. He returned to Peru in 1919 to run for president again and was easily elected, but he feared that his opposition would not allow him to take office. Accordingly, his supporters staged a coup in July 1919 and installed him as president.

His second term saw the continuation of reform, backed by $90 million worth of loans from Wall Street. He built railroads, roads, irrigation works, and sewage systems. He increased the national budget by almost 300 percent, more than quadrupling the national debt within 10 years.

Leguía y Salcedo also implemented constitutional reform, including direct election of the president and congress and extending suffrage to all adult males. The president failed, however, to abide by the very constitution that he was reforming. In the course of his second term, he assumed dictatorial powers. His now financially overextended country was particularly hard hit by the Great Depression, which immediately cut off the flow of loan money late in 1929.

Leguía y Salcedo was deposed in a coup on August 24, 1930, and held prisoner in the Lima penitentiary. He sickened and was transferred to the naval hospital at Bellavista, where he died on February 6, 1932.

Further Reading: Frederick B. Pike. *The Modern History of Peru* (New York: Praeger, 1967).

Lenin, Vladimir Ilich   [Vladimir Ilich Ulyanov] (1870–1924)

Vladimir Ilich Lenin was the founder of the Russian Communist Party, leader of the Bolshevik Revolution of 1917, and the first head of state of the Union of Soviet Socialist Republics.

Lenin was born Vladimir Ilich Ulyanov on April 22, 1870, in Simbirsk (later renamed Ulyanovsk after him). In sharp contrast to such mass-movement leaders as Adolf HITLER, Benito MUSSOLINI, and Josef STALIN, Lenin enjoyed a prosperous middle-class upbringing by educated parents (both were teachers by profession) who treated their children well. From his parents, Lenin absorbed a zealous concern for the welfare of the Russian people, which soon translated itself into revolutionary sympathies. In 1887, young Lenin's older brother Aleksandr was convicted of plotting against the czar and was hanged. Traumatized, Lenin immersed himself in the works of Karl Marx and other radical political philosophers. He did not, however, turn immediately to revolutionary activity, but completed his secondary school education and enrolled at the University of Kazan. There his radicalism did develop further, and he was expelled. Undaunted, Lenin earned a law degree from the University of St. Petersburg in 1891 and started a law practice in Samara (present-day Kuibyshev).

By 1893, Lenin abandoned the law for the full-time pursuit of revolutionary activity. An intense intellectual, he methodically reshaped Marxist theory to fit the conditions he perceived in czarist Russia. Marx had theorized that the seeds of the radical transformation of government lay in emerging industrial capitalism, that industrial workers—unlike agricultural peasants—would spontaneously and inevitably develop a radical group consciousness that would energize a popular political movement. Lenin agreed with Marx that the key to revolution was the radical consciousness of the industrial proletariat, but he observed that the requisite radical consciousness was failing to develop in Russian workers, who still perceived themselves as, in effect, peasants. The essence of what came to be called Leninism—Lenin's reformulation of Marxist theory—was the creation of political programs through which radical consciousness might be deliberately cultivated among workers. This required the creation of a thoroughly organized revolutionary party, which would inform, persuade, generally agitate, and then direct the proletariat.

At this time, the revolutionary thinker adopted the pseudonym "Lenin," which did not, however, save him from arrest and Siberian exile in 1895. Five years later, he left Russia and published, with Georgy Valentinovich Plekhanov, an underground newspaper called *Iskra* ("The Spark"). In the pages of *Iskra*, Lenin argued for an extreme radicalism that spurned common cause with moderates, liberals, or other members of what he identified as the bourgeoisie, who (Lenin argued) would ultimately attempt to assert dominance over workers and peasants. He also developed and promulgated the conviction that the basis for individual liberty would be found not in mere political democracy, but in a social democracy that rendered society entirely classless. In 1902, he expressed these ideas in their final form in his influential pamphlet *What Is To Be Done?* and created within the Russian Social Democratic Labor Party the radical Bolshevik wing during 1903.

From the Bolsheviks Lenin sought to create a revolutionary vanguard, which he forged over the long period from 1903 to the revolutionary year of 1917. Although he briefly returned to Russia during 1905–07, these years of most intense revolutionary activity were lived in exile, with Lenin conducting the affairs of his party from London, Paris, Geneva, and other European cities.

Lenin was ruthless in his condemnation of Social Democratic revolutionaries who did not share his radicalism, calling them the minority—the "Mensheviks"—in contrast to his own majority faction—"Bolsheviks"—even though the Mensheviks actually outnumbered the Bolsheviks. Lenin's successful attempt to polarize the Social Democrats glossed over the fact that many Mensheviks held radical ideas akin to Lenin's but feared that Lenin's Bolshevism would result not in equality for the masses but in a dictatorship of the revolutionary elite—the party vanguard. Brushing aside such fears, Lenin pushed on, waiting in exile for his moment to come.

The advent of World War I and the Russian revolutions of 1917 provided that moment. Lenin published *Imperialism: The Highest Stage of Capitalism*, analyzing World War I as a fight among the imperialist powers for control of the markets, raw materials, and cheap labor of the underdeveloped world. Lenin declared that none of the combatant nations offered any benefit to the working classes, so he enjoined all Socialists to withhold support from the war effort. The provisional government that had been installed after the overthrow of Czar NICHOLAS II continued to support the Allies, but, following the publication of Lenin's book, the Russian Bolsheviks withdrew support for the war. In the meantime, the Germans, seeing a chance to close the war's eastern front so that they could concentrate on the west, permitted Lenin to return to Russia from Swiss exile. He was enthusiastically greeted in Petrograd (the post-revolutionary name for Saint Petersburg, which later became Leningrad, and is now once again Saint Petersburg) on April 16, 1917. Immediately, he published the so-called "April Theses" in *Pravda*, the Bolshevik newspaper. In these, he denounced the liberal provisional government and called for a full-scale socialist revolution. With the support of the influential radical Leon Trotsky, a Bolshevik uprising was staged in July, but quickly collapsed, resulting in the arrest of Trotsky and the self-exile of Lenin, this time to Finland.

In September of 1917, Lenin sent a widely publicized letter to the Bolshevik central committee calling for armed insurrection against the provisional government. Seizing on his country's prevailing mood of radical reform, he ventured back into Russia and overthrew the government of Aleksandr Kerensky, thereby bringing the Bolsheviks to power during the so-called October Revolution. (According to the "New Style" [Gregorian] calendar used by most of the world, this was during the first week of November; by Russia's "Old Style" [Julian] calendar, the revolution took place at the end of October.) When the first Bolshevik government was officially formed on November 7, Lenin was named as chairman.

The new head of government moved swiftly and decisively, cementing the various Communist splinter groups into a single state political organization, the Russian Communist Party. The need for absolute power at this juncture prompted the creation of a secret police force, the Cheka, which soon became more powerful and more feared than the czar's secret police had been. Lenin tried by mere fiat to reshape the Russian economy according to strict Marxist principles. To facilitate this, he needed to pull out of World War I as expeditiously as possible, and he concluded a separate peace with Germany by means of the Armistice (December 15, 1917) and subsequent Treaty of Brest-Litovsk (March 3, 1918), which granted autonomy to the former Russian territories of Poland, Finland, Estonia, Latvia, Lithuania, and the Ukraine—all of which were in revolt against the Bolshevik government. Throughout the balance of the war, the Ukraine was occupied by German troops.

Beginning in 1917, civil war raged in Communist Russia from the Black Sea to the Caspian, with the dissident groups—the so-called Whites—gaining support from the nations that had allied against the Germans in the course of World War I. The bitter and destructive war lasted until 1921, when the Whites were finally defeated, leaving the Russian economy in a worse condition than ever and putting the new nation on a very precarious political footing. Lenin had no choice but to retreat from Marxist absolutism, and he granted economic concessions to foreign capitalists in order to spur trade. He also returned some industrial and many retail concerns to private ownership. Even more significantly, he permitted peasant farmers to sell their produce on the open market. At the same time, Lenin worked to extend the Communist revolution to the rest of the world. In 1919, he created the Comintern, designed to ensure that Russian Marxism would coordinate and dominate international Marxist movements.

Even though, by the end of the Russian Civil War, Lenin was installed as absolute dictator of the new Soviet Union, his control of the Communist Party itself was less certain. Rivalries and disputes were continual, and a great struggle for control of the party was developing between Josef Stalin and Leon Trotsky. Beset with political and economic problems, and plagued by complications that developed after he was wounded by a would-be assassin's bullet in 1918, Lenin suffered a severe stroke on May 25, 1922. Weakened and partially paralyzed, he never fully recovered, suffering in 1924 further strokes, to which he finally succumbed on January 21, 1924.

Lenin was virtually deified by the Communist world. Petrograd became Leningrad, and the leader's body was preserved under glass in a specially built mausoleum in Moscow's Red Square. With the erosion of Soviet communism in the 1980s and the breakup of the Soviet Union itself, Lenin's role in Russian history has been subjected to extensive reassessment by Russian historians. His early agricultural policies have been criticized for having brought about a famine during 1921–23, which caused almost 6 million Russians to starve to death. Others have seen in Leninist Marxism the seeds of the enormities committed during the regime of Josef STALIN. On June 12, 1991, by popular referendum, the city of Leningrad restored to itself the name of Saint Petersburg.

Further Reading: Ronald Clark. *Lenin: The Man Behind the Mask* (London: Faber & Faber, 1988); Louis Fischer. *The Life of Lenin* (New York: Harper & Row, 1964); Vladimir I. Lenin. *The Collected Works* (New York: International Publishers, 1942); Robert Service. *Lenin: A Political Life* (Bloomington: Indiana University Press, 1985).

Leo III the Isaurian   [Isauricus] (b. ca. 680–741)

The founder of the Isaurian—or Syrian—dynasty, Leo III repelled repeated Arab invasions and banned the display and worship of religious icons.

Originally from Germanica, northern Syria, Leo III and his family moved to Thrace during the great migrations orchestrated by the Emperor Justinian II. During Justinian's attempt to recover the throne in 705, Leo, who by this time had amassed considerable wealth, attracted the emperor's favor, receiving a military commission. About 713, Justinian's successor, Anastasius II, named Leo as head of the Anatolikon Theme, the largest of the military provinces of Asia Minor.

Anastasius' control over the military was weak, and he was deposed in 715, only to be replaced by the equally weak Theodosius III. Leo aligned himself with Artavasdos, the commander of the Armeniakon

Theme, the second largest in Asia Minor, and, with his support, marched on Constantinople. After Anastasius abdicated without a fight, Leo was crowned emperor on March 25, 717.

The first task that confronted him was the immediate defense of Constantinople from invading Arabs, who threatened the very existence of the Byzantine Empire by their numerous incursions into Asia Minor. They laid siege to Constantinople for exactly one year, from August 717 to August 718, but Leo proved a capable military commander and, with the help of a severe winter that halted the Arab advance into southeastern Europe, was able to defeat the Arabs.

After crushing a movement among some of his officers to restore Anastasius, Leo consolidated his alliance with Artavasdos by giving him his daughter in marriage. Artavasdos remained the second most powerful man in the empire, controlling much of the strategic military posts. In 740, the Arabs made another half-hearted attempt to invade Asia Minor, but Leo soundly defeated them at Akroinos. This victory essentially ended the Arab threat in Asia Minor for the duration of Leo's reign.

Leo reorganized the army, downsizing the themes so that no one leader could gain too much power. This also stabilized the military to a great degree. The emperor earned tremendous popularity with his military successes, and he hoped to capitalize on this approbation to promote a program of religious reform. In 722, he personally ordered the compulsory baptism of Jews and other "heretical" adherents. His most controversial attempt at reform was the destruction and outlawing of religious symbols, pictures, and icons—the so-called Iconoclast movement. By 730, he proclaimed Iconoclastic Christianity the official religion of the empire. When the patriarch of the Eastern church refused to implement this new policy, Leo quickly replaced him. The pope also vehemently opposed Iconoclasm. Leo responded by promptly calling a halt to all financial aid to the papacy. The debate over Iconoclasm continued for the next century before the movement was finally defeated.

When death ended his reign in 741, Leo left a stable army that was a proven fighting force; he had developed a uniform code of law—the Ecloga—which was a revision of Roman law; and he had solidified support from the military for the succession of his son, Constantine V, to continue the rule of the Isaurian dynasty until 802.

Further Reading: J. B. Bury. *A History of the Later Roman Empire: Arcadius to Irene* (London: Macmillan, 1889); George Ostrogorsky. *History of the Byzantine State* (Oxford: B. Blackwell, 1968).

Leo V (r. 813–20)

Leo rose from obscurity to become the Byzantine emperor who inaugurated the Second Iconoclastic Period.

Apparently from the lower classes, Leo V joined the army at a young age. After distinguishing himself in combat on several occasions, he rose in command, finally reaching the rank of general. In 803, a power struggle over the throne occurred between Bardanes Turcus and NICEPHOROUS I. Leo first sided with Bardanes, but then joined Nicephorous, who was eventually crowned emperor. In return for his support, Nicephorous named Leo military commander of the Anatolikon province. But Nicephorous soon replaced Leo in Anatolikon and banished him from the empire on charges of having neglected his duty. When Nicephorous was succeeded by Michael I, Leo was recalled and again named commander of Anatolikon. In 813, Michael made war on the Bulgars, and Leo led troops in the campaign to defeat Krum, the Bulgar khan. The Byzantines were defeated, but Michael refused the peace terms offered, and Leo's troops deserted *en masse* at the Battle of Versinikia, near Adrianople. Leo now seized his opportunity and overthrew Michael, declaring himself emperor in July 813.

Leo immediately set about restoring order to the empire. Krum was at the walls of Constantinople and threatening to overrun the city. Fortunately for Leo, the Bulgar khan died before the attack commenced, and Leo was able to negotiate a peace with his successor, calling for a 30-year truce.

Hoping to restore Iconoclasm, the outlawing of symbols and icons in religion, Leo deposed the Orthodox patriarch Nicephorous in March 815 and called for a synod in April. Dominating the synod, he reimposed the decrees of Iconoclasm for the first time since 754. Leo was assassinated on Christmas Day, 820, while attending Christmas services.

Leo X (1475–1521)

Raising the papacy to a great political power in Europe, Leo X was slow in responding to the Reformation, begun in part by Martin Luther, whom Leo excommunicated.

Giovanni de' Medici was born December 11, 1475, in Florence to Lorenzo the Magnificent, ruler of that city. Through his father's influence, after receiving a classical humanist education, 13-year-old Giovanni was made cardinal by Pope Innocent VIII. In 1492, Giovanni moved to Rome as a member of the College of Cardinals, but he returned to Florence that same year when his father died. With the death of Lorenzo, the Medici's enemies were able to exile the

Pope Leo X was the worldly Giovanni de' Medici. (From Charlotte Yonge, Pictorial History of the World's Great Nations, *1882)*

family on a trumped up charge of treason against the Republic of Florence. Giovanni spent the next six years traveling around Europe.

In 1512, Pope Julius II offered to Giovanni the papal army to lead against the family's enemies in Florence. The expedition was a disaster; Giovanni's forces were crushed, and he was taken prisoner. After his release, he continued to court the interests of Julius, and, with his support, the Medici were reestablished in Florence. When Julius died in 1513, the College of Cardinals met to choose a less bellicose pope and settled on Giovanni de' Medici, who chose the name Leo X. Interestingly, Giovanni de' Medici, though he was a cardinal, had never been formally ordained a priest. Accordingly, he was elected on March 11, 1513, ordained on the 15th, and consecrated a bishop on the 17th, before being crowned on the 19th.

Having grown up in his father's lavish court, Pope Leo X reestablished Rome as an expansive, and expensive, center of European culture, enlarging the Vatican Library, authorizing the construction of St. Peter's Basilica, and lending much support to the arts. This attention to things other than theology was precisely what the Protestant Reformation

sought to change. Leo inherited the Fifth Lateran Council, called by Julius, to discuss matters of reform within the church. It was opposed both by the Holy Roman Emperor Maximilian I and the king of France, Louis XII, and was poorly attended. Given little guidance, the council essentially achieved nothing and was dissolved on March 16, 1517, one day before Martin Luther nailed his 95 Theses on the door of the Wittenberg Castle Church.

Martin Luther was not Leo's only problem, however. The French still occupied northern Italy, and Leo formed the League of Mechlin with the Emperor MAXIMILIAN I, King FERDINAND II of Aragón and HENRY VIII of England to rout the French at Novara in 1515. When the French again invaded, Leo signed the Concordat of Bologna, which gave the French king power to select all high-ranking church officials in France, an agreement that would endure until the French Revolution. Leo further stabilized his political standing by naming his relatives to several important positions throughout Italy. When a plot to assassinate him was discovered in the College, Leo had several cardinals arrested and executed.

The subject of Martin Luther's 95 Theses, among other things, was the church practice of selling indulgences for papal profit. Luther received popular support because many resented the large sums of money going to Rome, and many also felt the practice of buying absolution was morally wrong. After extensive negotiations, Leo issued a papal bull in 1520 condemning Martin Luther and his teachings; Luther promptly burned it. Leo had no other choice but to excommunicate Martin Luther on January 3, 1521. When Leo died suddenly a year later, on December 1, 1521, he had yet to take seriously the Protestant Reformation, which was nevertheless in full swing.

Further Reading: William Roscoe. *The Life and Pontificate of Leo the Tenth* (Philadelphia: Lorenzo Press of E. Bronson, 1805–1806); Joseph Gobineau. *The Golden Flower* (Freeport, N.Y.: Books for Libraries, 1968).

Leopold I (1640–1705)

After securing Hapsburg domination of Hungary, Leopold established Austria as a major European military and diplomatic power.

The second son of Emperor Ferdinand III, Leopold was born on June 9, 1640, and, as a second son, was destined for a career in the church. He received an excellent education, studying Latin, French, Italian, and Spanish. (He despised French and later forbade its use at court, the first of his numerous Francophobic policies.) Leopold became well-versed in ancient studies, history, literature, the sciences, and had a special interest in music.

When his older brother Ferdinand IV died in July 1654, Leopold became heir to one of the largest family holdings in all of Europe. In rapid succession, Leopold assumed the lower offices of the Hapsburg family, becoming king of Hungary in 1655 and of Bohemia in 1656. After a brief contestation by France, Leopold succeeded his father to the imperial throne in 1658, following the latter's death the previous year.

As Holy Roman Emperor, Leopold was faced with an increasingly hostile France as well as encroachments in the east from the Turks. He moved quickly against the Turks, declaring war in 1663. The contest proved indecisive, and it was not until 1683, when they moved through Hungary and laid siege to Vienna, that the Turks were soundly defeated by a joint force under Charles of Lorraine and John III Sobieski of Poland. Hoping to exact a measure of revenge for the siege of the capital, Leopold ordered an offensive against Ottoman-controlled Hungary. Evicting the Turks from much of Hungary by 1687, Austria would control Hungary until the end of World War I, and would eventually become known as Austria-Hungary (1867). After the Turks were again defeated, at Zenta in 1697 by Prince Eugene of Savoy, Austria gained nearly all of Hungary through the Treaty of Karlowitz of 1699. Austria's possession of Hungary was no simple matter, however. The Hungarian nobles, mostly Calvinists, feared a Counter-Reformation under Catholic Hapsburg rule, and revolted. Leopold swiftly crushed the rebellion and ordered the execution of the most prominent noble leaders.

The imperialist tendencies of LOUIS XIV of France led much of western and central Europe to oppose him in the League of Augsburg. When war broke out in 1688, Leopold was unable to play more than a minor part against France. Although France was eventually defeated, the League allies were unable to mount a full-scale invasion. The Peace of Ryswick in 1697 ended the War of the League of Augsburg, but forced Leopold to cede Strasbourg to Louis.

In 1666, Leopold's first marriage to Margarita Theresa of Spain had given him a claim to the Spanish throne, which was ruled by the Spanish Hapsburgs. Leopold hoped to unite the Hapsburg houses and claim the Spanish possessions. When Charles II of Spain died childless in 1700, the kingdom passed to the duke of Anjou, a grandson of Louis XIV, and Leopold called for war. France stood against a nearly unified Europe, with only the aid of Spain and Bavaria. The coalition quickly had Louis on the defensive and scored a major victory at the Battle of Blenheim in 1704. Before he would see his forces to-

tally victorious, however, Leopold died on May 5, 1705.

Further Reading: John P. Spielman. *Leopold I of Austria* (London: Thames & Hudson, 1977).

Leopold II   (1747–1792)

An enlightened despot in the Age of Enlightenment, Leopold II, Holy Roman Emperor, used his diplomatic talents to quell possible universal European revolt in the wake of the French Revolution.

Born the third son of MARIA THERESA and Emperor Francis I in Vienna on May 5, 1747, Leopold received an education typical of the times, tolerant of religious differences and mindful of reform. Upon his father's death in 1765, he became duke of Tuscany and governed as a true believer of Montesquieu's doctrine of separation of powers, reducing state expenditures, lessening the power and influence of the church, and lessening the power of the landed aristocracy over the peasant.

When Leopold's older brother Joseph II died in 1790, Leopold became Holy Roman Emperor. Although Joseph had thought highly of his brother, Leopold had disliked him and quickly moved to distance himself from his policies. Indeed, when Joseph had summoned him to his deathbed, Leopold made excuses and did not come.

Leopold used his highly developed diplomatic skills to quell a revolt brewing in Belgium with the Peace of the Hague in December 1790; to maintain Prussian neutrality in any upcoming wars against the Hapsburgs; and to extract Austria from a war with Turkey in August 1791. But Leopold grew increasingly concerned over the French Revolution and the safety of LOUIS XVI and Marie Antoinette. Not only was Marie Antoinette Leopold's sister, but the execution of the French monarchs would set a dangerous precedent for regicide throughout Europe. Leopold hoped a peaceful solution could be arrived at, but he joined Frederick William III of Prussia in signing the Declaration of Pillnitz, essentially pledging to go to war if the revolution got out of hand. Before Leopold could act against France, however, he died suddenly in Vienna on March 1, 1792.

Leopold II   (1835–1909)

Leopold II governed Belgium as a constitutional monarch, but he ruled and exploited the nation's African colonial possession, the Congo, as a personal domain.

Born Léopold-Louis-Phillipe-Marie-Victor (in Dutch, Leopold Lodewijk Filips Maria Victor) on April 9, tne long run would require a strong Belgian military presence. Leopold obtained funding for the fortification of the strategic towns of Liège and Namur and, throughout his reign, advocated a universal conscription law, which was enacted only when he was on his deathbed.

Liliuokalani   (1838–1917)

Hawaii's last and only female sovereign, she was deposed in the campaign of American missionaries to destroy native Hawaiian culture and to promote the annexation of the islands by the United States.

Born into the Hawaiian royal family on September 2, 1838, Liliuokalani received a thorough education, traveling to Europe and meeting with Queen Victoria of England in 1887. When her younger brother Leleiohoku died in 1877, she was named heir, and when her oldest brother King Kalakaua died in 1891, she became the only woman ever to ascend the Hawaiian throne.

Liliuokalani regretted the diminution of monarchical power under Kalakaua and tried desperately to reassert royal authority. She opposed the Treaty of Reciprocity of 1887, which granted favorable trading rights to the United States and ceded Pearl Harbor. Her attempts at royal assertion and particularly the opposition to the treaty earned her the undying enmity of American business interests and the American missionaries, who found Hawaii's polytheistic culture unacceptable.

In January 1893, Liliuokalani attempted to issue a new constitution guaranteeing greater royal control. The Missionary Party, led by pineapple magnate Sanford Dole, immediately demanded her abdication and announced the establishment of a provisional government. The American minister to Hawaii called in U.S. troops, stating ingenuously that they were present only to protect American life and property. To avoid wholesale bloodshed, Liliuokalani surrendered, but sent an appeal to President Grover Cleveland, who, while ordering her restoration, refused to enforce the order when Dole arrogantly and simply ignored it.

A royalist insurrection, led by Robert Wilcox in the queen's name, erupted in 1895, but was bloodily put down by the Missionaries. On January 24, 1895, Liliuokalani was forced to sign her abdication in order to gain the release of those jailed by the Missionaries during the revolt. The United States annexed Hawaii in 1898, but did not proclaim it a state for another 61 years. When Liliuokalani died on November 11, 1917, she was given a traditional royal state funeral—one of the last remaining vestiges of native Hawaiian culture.

King Leopold II of the Belgians (Courtesy Institut Belge d'Information et de Documentation)

1835, Leopold II succeeded his father, Leopold I, to the Belgian throne in 1865 and is best known for his ruthless colonial ambitions. As king, he sponsored Sir Henry Stanley's famous 1879–84 Congo expedition, which was instrumental in gaining Leopold recognition from the United States and the nations of Europe as *personal* sovereign of the Congo Free State in 1885.

Leopold sought to develop and reap the economic potential of the Congo, in particular its vast rubber crop, which became enormously lucrative for Belgium—and for himself—by the 1890s. However, in 1904, the international community was outraged by widespread and graphic reports of abuse of the native people of the Congo in what were called the "rubber atrocities." Under pressure from a worldwide protest movement, in 1908, the Belgian parliament forced Leopold to give up personal control of the region and cede the Congo Free State to Belgium as a colonial possession.

On the domestic front, Leopold maintained Belgian neutrality during the Franco-Prussian War of 1870–71, but realized that sustaining neutrality in

Further Reading: Liliuokalani. *Hawaii's Story of Hawaii's Queen* (Boston: Lee and Shepard, 1898); Aldyth Morris. *Lili'uokalani* (Honolulu: University of Hawaii Press, 1993).

Liu Pang [posthumously, Han Kao Tsu] (256–195 B.C.)

The founder and first emperor of the Han dynasty, Liu put in place the Chinese imperial system that was to last until 1911.

Born a peasant, Liu Pang began as a military officer in the state of Ch'u which had been integrated by CH'IN SHIH HUANG-TI into a unified China. Around 200 B.C., Liu became a rebel and fought in the savage civil wars that racked China following Shih Huang-ti's death. The Ch'in forces were defeated by an aristocratic warlord and colleague of Liu's named Hsiang Yü, who tried to reinstate the feudalism of pre-Ch'in China.

Liu, now in control of the areas known as Han for the Han River, resented his ally's efforts to restore the nobility and enslave the peasants again. He rose up against Hsiang in 202 B.C. and defeated him, establishing the Han dynasty. His first efforts were to force the dependence of the generals and the nobles upon himself in an effort to consolidate power. He did this by granting them principalities, but declared all social classes his vassals. Whenever anyone got too powerful, he would simply reduce their holdings and social standing.

Liu showed his continuing concern for the peasant by his efforts to revitalize the rural economy, particularly by lowering taxes. He was a fair ruler, but he harshly suppressed all attempts from within China to supplant him. The Han dynasty would last almost 400 years and is regarded as the classical period of China's history.

Liu Shaoqi [Liu Shao-ch'i] (1898–1969)

Liu Shaoqi was MAO TSE-TUNG's second in command and eventual chairman of the People's Republic of China; he was purged in the Great Proletarian Cultural Revolution.

The son of a relatively prosperous peasant landowner, Liu attended normal school in 1916, where he first met Mao Tse-tung. The normal school was a hotbed of young radical activity, and Liu became interested in political action and agitation, helping Mao edit the radical magazine *Hsiang River Review*. In 1920, he joined the Socialist Youth League, but was arrested for radical activities. On his release, he went to Shanghai and then to Russia in 1921, for training at the University for the Toilers of the East.

After he returned from his Russian sojourn, Liu began his monumental work with labor organizations that would result in his rapid rise up the Chinese Communist hierarchy. He organized successful strikes and worked underground to organize labor unions, becoming general secretary of the All-China Federation of Labor in May 1927. When war with Japan broke out in 1937, he spent most of the Japanese occupation behind enemy lines, organizing partisans in north and central China. It was during this time that Liu managed to win over many Chinese students to the Communist movement, a step essential to the eventual success of the revolution.

In 1939, Liu emerged as a major party figure with publication of his landmark *How to Be a Good Communist*, which outlined orthodox Socialist values and promoted them among the Chinese peasant and student population. Liu continued his ascendancy in the party, and when the People's Republic was formally declared in 1949, he was named Mao's second vice-deputy.

The zenith of Liu's power came in 1958 and 1959, when he was elected to the number-two spot in the Politburo and named to replace Mao as chairman of the People's Republic—though Mao still retained the more powerful Communist Party chairmanship. In the mid-1960s, however, a break occurred between Liu and Mao over the direction of the revolution. Mao felt the revolution needed to build continually, always on the verge of spiralling out of control, or it would lose momentum. In contrast, Liu believed that the revolutionary efforts should be confined and carefully controlled. Liu wanted slow, steadily increased economic growth and tighter central policy control, while Mao demanded rapid economic growth and less centralized structure for the masses.

In 1965, Mao instituted the Great Proletarian Cultural Revolution, which signaled the end for Liu. Liu was derided in party meetings, his rank in the party fell from number two to number eight, and Red Guard publications publicly denounced him. In 1967, the official press called him "top person in authority taking the capitalist road" and "China's Khrushchev." Finally, in 1968, he was dismissed from the party altogether and disappeared completely. Rumors of his death circulated in 1974 and were confirmed by the party without specifying the date. Not until 1980 was it revealed that Liu had been imprisoned and died in captivity on November 12, 1969.

Further Reading: Liu Shaoqi. *The Collected Works of Liu Shaoqi* (Kwoloon: Union Research Institute, 1969); Donald Klein and Anne B. Clark. *Biographic Dictionary of Chinese Communism, 1921–1965* (Cambridge, Mass.: Harvard University Press, 1971).

López, Carlos Antonio (1790–1862)

The second dictator of Paraguay, López looted his country shamelessly, but also sought to modernize it and establish its place in the international arena.

López was born of poor parents in Asunción, Paraguay, on November 4, 1790. He secured an education at the Seminary of San Carlos in his hometown, where he subsequently became a teacher until the institution was closed down by López's uncle, Paraguay's first dictator, José Gaspar Rodriguez de Francia. In the meantime, López had made an excellent marriage into one of the nation's most important families, but Rodriguez de Francia forced his exile to the ranch López had purchased with his new-found wealth. He reemerged after Rodriguez de Francia's death, and by 1841 had risen to prominence as the more powerful of two "consuls" who ruled Paraguay according to a newly drawn up constitution.

López maintained constitutional rule until 1844, when he summarily suspended the constitution and ousted his fellow consul. From this time until his death almost 20 years later, he ruled Paraguay as absolute dictator, freely pillaging the nation in order to amass greater and greater wealth for himself and his family.

Intensely corrupt, López did not relish foreign interference in his nation's affairs. However, he recognized the necessity of ending Paraguay's long isolation in order to develop the country's economy. He encouraged the immigration of skilled Europeans in an effort to develop industry and put his army on a par with those of Europe. He established diplomatic relations with many nations, including the United States, although these relations were frequently strained nearly to the point of war.

López gave lip service to extensive programs of reform, including the liberalization of government, the release of political prisoners, the abolition of slavery, an end to judicial torture, and the introduction of public elementary education. In fact, relatively few political prisoners were released during the López administration; slavery, though it was made illegal, continued to flourish; officials still routinely practiced torture; and most Paraguayans remained uneducated and wholly illiterate.

López's son FRANCISCO SOLANO LÓPEZ assumed the dictatorship immediately after his father's death on September 10, 1862, in Asunción, and maneuvered Paraguay into eight years of ruinous and largely pointless warfare.

López, Francisco Solano   (1827–1870)

The son and successor of a corrupt dictator, López blindly blundered Paraguay into a disastrous war with Brazil, Argentina, and Uruguay.

Francisco Solano López was born on July 24, 1827, in Asunción, Paraguay, to the dictator CARLOS ANTONIO LÓPEZ. Immediately upon his father's death, on September 10, 1862, López seized power and used the army to neutralize all opposition.

For reasons that are not entirely clear—perhaps seeing an opportunity to become in the world's eyes the leading ruler of Latin America—he intervened in warfare between Brazil and Argentina, and simultaneously in a civil war raging in Uruguay, in which Brazil and Argentina also played a part. Instead of emerging from these complex struggles as a distinguished mediator, López entangled his nation in a war with Brazil beginning in December 1864. To make matters worse, he demanded of Argentina the right to station troops in the Argentine province of Corrientes. On May 1, 1865, Brazil, Argentina, and Uruguay were indeed reconciled with one another—*against* Paraguay.

Having invaded the Brazilian Mato Grosso during 1864, López moved against Uruguay in 1865. The allies responded by crushing his army and driving its remnants deep into northern Paraguay. There, in Concepción province, López was killed in 1870, having been forced to yield some 55,000 square miles of territory with a population of approximately one million.

López Arellano, Oswaldo   (b. 1921–   )

Participant in three coups and twice president of Honduras, Oswaldo López Arellano was at first repressive and dictatorial, but subsequently brought sweeping reform to his country before he was at last forced to resign amid charges of corruption.

Born on June 30, 1921, Oswaldo López Arellano joined the Honduran military in 1939 and was trained at the U.S. School of Military Aviation and Flight Training. By October 21, 1956, he was a colonel in the Honduran army and participated in the coup that ousted the administration of Julio Lozano Díaz. Beginning on November 16, 1957, he served as minister of defense in a three-man military junta, and he continued in that position after the December 1957 inauguration of President Ramón Villeda Morales.

After participating in a right-wing coup that overthrew Villeda's liberal administration on October 3, 1963, López served as head of the military government charged with supervising the February 1965 national elections. López easily won the elections he "supervised" and immediately set about reversing the liberal reforms initiated by Villeda. He also suppressed activities of trade unions and the Liberal (PL) Party. However, López subsequently reversed himself, reviving and even strengthening land reforms as well as promoting the formation of peasant cooperatives.

In 1971, López allowed elections to be held, and Ramón Ernesto Cruz of the National Party was elected. Cruz served only until December 4, 1972, when López engineered a coup, this time with the support of business groups and reformist unions.

On April 22, 1975, López was himself forced to resign the presidency amid charges that he and his minister of the economy had accepted a $1.25 million bribe from United Brands Company to permit evasion of export taxes. López continues to live in Honduras, where he is engaged in several business activities.

Further Reading: James A. Morris. *Honduras: Caudillo Politics and Military Rulers* (Boulder: University of Colorado Press, 1984).

Lothair I (795–855)

Aspiring to unify the Frankish Empire as CHARLE-MAGNE had done, Lothair instead fought continually with his brothers over possession of the throne.

The oldest son of Louis I the Pious and grandson of Charlemagne, Lothair I was named king of Bavaria in 814 when his father became emperor of the west following Charlemagne's death. Louis made Lothair co-emperor in 817 and provided for Lothair to receive the bulk of the empire on his death. Louis gave small parcels to his other two sons, Pepin and Louis the German, who were to remain suzerains under Lothair.

Lothair ascended to the Italian throne in 822, and journeyed to Rome to be crowned, this time by Pope Paschal I on April 5, 823. In 824, he promulgated the Constitutio Romana, which effectively gave him control over Roman affairs and demanded that the pope declare an oath of fealty to him.

In 829, Louis I revised the 817 agreement granting the empire to Lothair to account for the subsequent birth of a fourth son, Charles the Bald, who received a portion of Lothair's realm. Lothair broke with his father, who deposed him, but he was restored by loyal followers the next year, only to be deposed again in the ensuing power struggle among all the brothers in 830.

In 833, Pepin, and Louis the German, all discontent with Louis I's rule, joined Lothair in a rebellion that overthrew Louis. Louis, however, was restored in 834, in turn deposing Lothair, whose authority was now limited to Italy. From this point, the four brothers and their father repeatedly shifted allegiance and enmity, sometimes fighting with each other, sometimes against each other. When Pepin died in 838, Louis I promulgated a new partitioning of the realms, splitting the empire between Charles the Bald and Lothair, while granting Bavaria to Louis the German. But when Louis I died in 840, Lothair claimed everything that had been promised him in the original 817 agreement. Louis the German

and Charles the Bald responded by allying themselves and marching against Lothair, crushing him at the Battle of Fontenoy on June 25, 841. The Treaty of Verdun dictated an equal partitioning of the empire in thirds.

Lothair continued to hope to gain supremacy over his brothers, but failed to do so. He divided his lands between his two sons in 855, abdicated in disgust, and became a monk. Lothair died in the abbey of Prum on September 29, 855.

Louis IV the Bavarian (b. ca.1283–1347)

Louis IV was the first member of the German Wittelsbach family to become Holy Roman Emperor. He defended the right to elect an emperor independently of the papacy.

The younger son of Louis von Wittelsbach, duke of Upper Bavaria, Louis IV became the ward of his older brother Rudolf and his mother, Mechtild, after his father's death in 1294. In a regional power struggle, Rudolf, against the wishes of his mother, threw his support to Adolf of Nassau, who was defeated. His credibility badly damaged, Rudolf was forced to allow young Louis to assume his share of the government, which Rudolf had withheld. Next, in 1313, after successfully repelling the Hapsburg invasion at the Battle of Gammelsdorf on November 9, Louis was in a position to rule all of Bavaria.

The death of German emperor Henry VII in August 1313 brought confusion over the succession, which Louis exploited, persuading the German electors to make him emperor in 1314. The Hapsburgs, however, nominated Frederick III, and the two contested the crown for eight years before Louis defeated Frederick at the Battle of Muhldorf in September 1322.

Louis' power seemed secure. However, Pope John XXII, citing papal precedent, stepped in to claim the right to nominate the emperor. In 1323, he invited Louis to step down without any further consequence from the papacy, but Louis steadfastly refused. When Louis proceeded to attack Pope John in dispatches, he was excommunicated in March 1324. Louis answered by charging the pope with heresy and stepped up his diplomatic assault, nominating a pope. John decreed Louis' deposal, stripping him irrevocably of all land and titles. (Louis was henceforth called simply Louis the Bavarian.) Papal troops forced Louis to retreat in 1330, and the two were never reconciled.

While Louis received a vote of confidence in July 1338 from the German electors, he was faced with a rival claimant, Charles of Bohemia, in the 1340s. As he was preparing to meet Charles in battle, he died suddenly in Munich on October 11, 1347.

Louis VII (b. ca. 1120–1180)

Louis successfully allied the French and Germans for the first time in history to fight the Second Crusade.

The son of Louis VI, king of France, Louis VII was named as his father's successor in 1131 and was crowned king on his father's death in 1137. Shortly before he assumed the throne, Louis married Eleanor of Aquitaine, daughter of William X, and acquired Aquitaine as part of Eleanor's dowry, thereby extending Capetian influence to the Pyrenees.

When the Christian city of Edessa (present-day Urfa in southeast Turkey) fell in 1144, Pope Eugenius III implored Louis to lead a crusade against the infidels. After securing the support of Conrad III of Germany—the first time the French and the Germans were ever aligned—the allies set out for Palestine in the fall of 1147 and took Constantinople the following spring. They were defeated later in 1148, however, in an attempt to take Damascus.

Returning to France, Louis found that his marriage had disintegrated. It was annulled in March 1152, and Eleanor wasted no more than two months before marrying Henry Plantagenet of Anjou and Normandy, taking Aquitaine with her. That same year, Louis attacked Normandy and suffered a heavy defeat that left him in a vulnerable position. Only internal dissension in Normandy saved Louis from a concerted attack and probable invasion.

In 1154, Henry was crowned HENRY II of England, inaugurating an enmity between himself and Louis that would endure until Louis' death on September 18, 1180 in Paris.

Louis IX [Saint Louis] (1214–1270)

Considered one of the greatest of the French kings, Louis IX consolidated royal power and established enduring moral and ethical standards.

The fourth son of King Louis VIII and Blanche of Castille, Louis was born on April 25, 1214. His education was supervised directly by Blanche, who exposed him to many fields of interest. She personally attended to his religious training, instilling in him her piety and philosophy of toleration. After his three older brothers died, Louis became heir. On the death of Louis VIII in November 1226, the youthful Louis IX ascended to the French throne.

Louis IX of France was canonized Saint Louis. (From M. Guizot, A Popular History of France from the Earliest Times, *n.d.)*

Blanche acted as regent for her minor son and, in fact, dominated French politics for several years. The feudal lords, hoping to take advantage of the regency, revolted almost immediately, but enjoyed little support, and their revolt soon collapsed. As other sparks of rebellion flared up in France, Blanche stamped them out in turn and proved quite capable. When HENRY III, king of England, invaded France in 1229, it was 15-year-old Louis IX who personally led an army against him, compelling his withdrawal without a battle. The dukes who supported Henry now submitted to Louis.

Louis ruled in his own right beginning in 1234. A staunch advocate of justice for all, he was also very pious, founding an abbey and protecting holy orders. He defended his church against unreasonable papal demands and protected his clergy as if they were his children. He outlawed prostitution, gambling, and blasphemy.

In 1242, Henry III made another attempt at conquest on the continent, and again Louis beat him back, this time at the Battle of the Bridge of Taillebourg. Following this victory, Louis fell seriously ill with malaria. He pledged that if he ever recovered, he would go on a crusade. On his recovery, he made good his word to God and sailed to Egypt in August 1248 to "liberate" the Holy Land. Jerusalem had fallen to the Muslims in August 1244 and Damascus had been overrun as well. Louis hoped to save the East from collapse. After several successes, the army began to wear down and was forced to retreat. Egyptians took many captives in April 1250, including King Louis. At length gaining his release, Louis returned to France and to the news of the death of his mother in 1254.

Henry's reputation as a fair and impartial man spread throughout Europe, and he was well loved by many outside of France. He was frequently called upon to arbitrate disputes between rival kingdoms. He took advantage of his popularity to reorganize the kingdom and reform the nobles, enacting ordinances governing the ethical conduct of royal officials and stabilizing currency by cracking down on counterfeiting. But as Louis grew older, he became increasingly obsessed with ousting the Muslims from the Holy Land. He made plans to embark on another crusade, and in July 1270 landed at Tunis. Again, he enjoyed initial success, but this time plague overtook his army, and Louis—with many of his troops—died in Tunis in August 1270. He was canonized by Pope Boniface VIII in 1297.

Further Reading: Maureen Slattery. *Myth, Man, and Sovereign Saint* (New York: P. Lang, 1985); Margaret Wade Labarge. *Saint Louis: Louis IX: Most Christian King of France* (Boston: Little, Brown, 1968).

Louis XI (1423–1483)

Louis XI ruled France from 1461 until 1483, a reign that saw a unification of the country in the wake of the disastrous Hundred Years' War.

Born in Bourges, France, on July 3, 1423, Louis XI was the son of King Charles VII and Mary of Anjou. Fat and ugly, he was reclusive as a child, but ruthless and superstitious as an adult. He was intelligent, however, and by the time he was 17, he was proving an able assistant to his father in his campaigns against the English.

Louis was unhappily married to Margaret, daughter of Scotland's James I, in 1436. Three years later, Charles sent Louis to superintend the defense in Languedoc and to become royal lieutenant in Poitou. Discontented in these roles, Louis assumed leadership of the Praguerie, a rebellion of local lords against his father. The king pardoned his son, however, and Louis was made ruler of Dauphiné. He participated in his father's ceaseless prosecution of the Hundred Years' War, which he expanded by attacking Basel, Switzerland, and the Hapsburg possessions in the Alsace. During this period as well, he founded the University of Valence and introduced sweeping reforms that curbed the autonomy of the nobles.

When Charles died in 1461, Louis became king of France as Louis XI. He was quick to shuffle his father's administrative staff, replacing most of them with men from his own inner circle of advisers. Louis acted quickly to neutralize vassal lords who did not support him and who sought strength through alliances with each other and with England. In 1465, the disaffected vassals formed the League of Public Weal against Louis, and France teetered on anarchy. Louis ceded substantial territory to the rebels and concluded treaties with them. When he violated these accords, he was attacked by an alliance among Charles the Bold of Burgundy, Francis, duke of Brittany, and Edward IV of England, and others. Through a complex series of bribes and truces, Louis managed to avoid political disaster.

As he worked to unify France politically, Louis introduced economic and other reforms that helped forge a modern kingdom. He developed the silk industry in Lyons and Tours, encouraged commerce with England, raised taxes, created a network of messengers to bring him news from all over France, and did much to centralize the age-old fragmented government.

The last few years of Louis' life were lived reclusively in the province of Touraine. Yet he had transformed a weak kingdom of jarring factions into a genuine nation. When he died at Plessis-les-Tours on August 30, 1483, he was perhaps the most powerful man in Europe.

Further Reading: Albert Guerardi. *France: A Modern History* (Ann Arbor: University of Michigan Press, 1959).

Louis XIV (1638–1715)

Louis XIV of France was the longest-reigning monarch in European history (1643–1715) and his reign was the apotheosis of absolute monarchy. The dazzling brilliance of his Versailles court earned him the epithet the "Sun King."

Louis, eldest child of Louis XIII and Anne of Austria, was born late in his parents' lives, on September 5, 1638. His father died when Louis was only four years old, and his mother served as regent during his minority. This was a period of great turbulence, as the Parlement of Paris and the nobility staged menacing though inadequately coordinated rebellions known as the Wars of the Fronde (political opposition) during 1648–53 in protest over the policies of Louis XIII's minister Cardinal RICHELIEU and his successor Cardinal Giulio Mazarin to secure royal authority and financial autonomy. Twice the royal family was driven out of Paris, and young Louis and his mother were held for a time under house arrest in the royal palace.

When Mazarin at last suppressed the Fronde, thereby avoiding outright revolution, France was moving toward becoming the dominant European power. In 1648, it had emerged from the Thirty Years' War having gained Alsace and most of Lorraine. War with Spain continued until the signing of the Peace of the Pyrenees in 1659, which was in effect sealed by Louis XIV's marriage in 1660 to MARIA THERESA, the daughter of Spain's King Philip IV. France acquired Rousillion, Artois and fortifications in the Spanish Netherlands.

Cardinal Mazarin, like Richelieu before him, virtually ran the government of Louis XIV. Following Mazarin's death in 1661, Louis announced that, henceforth, he would serve as his own chief minister. Nicholas Fouquet, who had served as the royal finance minister and who was next in line for the post of chief minister, was sentenced to life imprisonment for corruption. After this, there was never any further question about finding a chief minister for the king. Louis did rely on a select coterie of ministers, including Jean-Baptiste Colbert (domestic affairs) and the marquis de Louvois (military affairs), but other ministers were appointed and relieved at royal pleasure. Louis also retained the *conseil d'en haut* (high council), but, in a sharp break with tradition, he excluded members of his immediate family, great princes, and others of the *noblesse d'epée* (old military nobility). In place of these traditional wielders of power, Louis relied on the newer, younger, and more progressive *noblesse de robe* (judicial nobility). Moreover, he put the administration of local government in the hands of *intendants,* who could be removed and replaced, depending on royal assessment of their performance.

The longest-reigning of all European monarchs, Louis XIV created a court so brilliant that he became known as Le Roi Soleil—The Sun King. (From M. Guizot, A Popular History of France from the Earliest Times, *n.d.)*

The reforms of Louis' "personal reign" were remarkably successful, ameliorating many of the administrative and social ills earlier monarchs, including Louis' father, had failed to address. The obstructionism of the old *parlements* was eliminated, and the system of criminal justice vastly improved. Commerce, industry, and colonial development and administration were improved, and the national debt appreciably reduced. To some extent, French tax laws, grossly inequitable, were made more just, and the collection of taxes due was rendered more efficient.

Louis also regarded the arts as a means of celebrating the monarchy, and the Sun King became patron to the greatest French literary and artistic figures of the age, including the playwright Jean-Baptiste Molière, the composer Jean-Baptiste Lully, and many other notables. Under Louis, great academies of art and learning were founded, and the Académie française, founded by Cardinal Richelieu, came under formal royal patronage and control in

1671. Like the great emperors of the classical age, Louis was anxious to leave behind a legacy of monumental structures and completed the Louvre in Paris and the incomparable palace at Versailles, which had been Louis XIII's hunting lodge. A remarkably elaborate subculture, governed by ritual, developed among the courtiers within this palace after Louis officially moved his court there in 1682.

Louis proved to be almost as prodigal with his war making as he was with the development of high civilization and architecture. He launched the War of Devolution during 1667–68 against the Spanish Netherlands on the grounds that these provinces had "devolved" by succession to his Spanish wife rather than to her half-brother Charles II. Louis next opened hostilities against the United Provinces of the Netherlands in the third Anglo-Dutch War of 1672–78, seeking retribution for Dutch intervention in the War of Devolution and aiming to cripple Dutch trade. Through both of these wars, Louis gained territory in Flanders. Having also acquired the formerly Spanish Franche Comté, Louis commissioned military architect Sébastien Le Prestre de Vauban to design an impregnable fortress for this outpost of what was now France's eastern frontier. With unparalleled arrogance, Louis established "courts of reunion," which provided legal rationales for annexing various towns along the Franco-German border. In the Alsace, Louis seized the great city of Strasbourg, and in Italy, Casale. These events marked the high-water mark of Louis' reign.

In 1685, Louis made the catastrophic move of revoking the Protestant (Huguenot) minority's right to worship as guaranteed by his own Edict of Nantes (also called the Edict of Fontainebleu). The revocation of the Edict of Nantes had three grave effects: It revealed Louis' religious intolerance; it sent many of the Huguenots, a most productive and valuable segment of French society, out of the country; and it united many of the Protestant powers of Europe against France.

In September 1688, Louis found himself in a military confrontation with the member states of the League of Augsburg. This was the commencement of nine years of costly and inconclusive warfare known as the War of the Grand Alliance (War of the League of Augsburg). Although France emerged from it still in possession of Strasbourg and other "reunion" acquisitions, this war was no sooner concluded than another, the War of the Spanish Succession, commenced in 1701. This war to enforce the succession of Louis' grandson, Philip V, to the Spanish throne following the death of Charles II dragged on for 14 years. The struggle took a terrible toll on the French economy, but ended with most of Louis'

former conquests intact. Philip V did, indeed, inherit Spain and its overseas colonies, while the Holy Roman Emperor Charles VI, who had been backed by France's opponents, acquired the Spanish Netherlands and Spain's Italian possessions. Louis agreed that the crowns of France and Spain would remain separate, notwithstanding their connection through the Bourbon dynasty.

Toward the end of his reign, Louis also waged a bitter battle to supress the theologically radical followers of Cornelis Jansen. In this struggle he was able to enlist the aid of the pope in return for renouncing his claim to the semi-independence of the French Catholic church. By the time of Louis' death on September 1, 1715, the French economy was badly strained. Even worse, the aging and exhausted monarch had gradually let slip the personal control he had exercised earlier in his reign. His administration became an entrenched bureaucracy, arrogant and out of touch with the needs of the people. Before the end of the century, this situation would erupt into violent revolution.

Further Reading: Oliver Bernier. *Louis XIV: A Royal Life* (New York: Doubleday, 1987); David Ogg. *Louis Fourteenth*, 2d ed. (London: Oxford University Press, 1967); Paul Sonnino, ed. *The Reign of Louis XIV* (Cambridge and New York: Cambridge University Press, 1990).

Louis XVI   (1754–1793)

King of France from 1774 to 1793, Louis XVI—together with his celebrated wife, Marie-Antoinette—fell victim to the French Revolution.

Born at Versailles, France, on August 23, 1754, Louis became heir to the throne of his grandfather Louis XV after his father died in 1765. Given a liberal education, Louis was exposed to the Enlightenment ideals then circulating throughout Europe. In 1770, Louis was married to the daughter of Holy Roman Emperor Francis I and MARIA THERESA, the Archduchess Marie-Antoinette. Four years later, on May 10, 1774, he ascended to the throne after the death of his grandfather. Louis inherited the financial difficulties that had plagued France for more than a century.

King Louis XVI was at first highly popular, and his appointment of Jacques Turgot as finance minister indicated that he was earnest about modernizing the French economy. Never able to complete his reforms, however, Louis XVI struggled between two economic worlds: the old peasant/mercantile system, and the emerging market economy/capitalist system. Worse, while the French people struggled in poverty and want, Louis and Marie-Antoinette lived in notorious extravagance. In addition, the perennial struggles between the king and the Parlement (court of

A stubborn aristocrat, Louis XVI was swept away on the tide of the French Revolution. (From M. Guizot, A Popular History of France from the Earliest Times, *n.d.*

justice) of Paris became increasingly acrimonious. In an effort to curb the growing radicalism in Paris, Louis XVI and his finance minister of the period, Charles-Alexandre de Calonne, decided to call a meeting of the Estates-General—the first such assembly in 175 years—to be held at Versailles in May 1789. Louis XVI, indifferent and condescending, refused to address the Third Estate—the bourgeoisie (the other two estates were composed of the nobility and the clergy)—at Versailles. This would prove fatal for the monarchy and, ultimately, for Louis personally.

After a prolonged session, which saw the fusion of all three estates into a single National Assembly, a group of Parisians on July 14, 1789, stormed the Bastille—a fortress-prison that symbolized Bourbon oppression, and even today symbolizes the French Revolution itself. Three months later, on October 6, Louis XVI and his family were forced from Versailles and detained at the Tuileries in Paris. The king and queen escaped in June 1791, only to be apprehended just short of the border in Varennes. They were returned to Paris.

Now powerless, Louis XVI was forced to recognize the constitution of 1791, which created a limited monarchy. But, yielding to the imperious advice of Marie-Antoinette, Louis did not administer the new constitution in good faith. Subsequently, revelations came to light that Louis had been secretly working

against the Revolution. This at last prompted a mob to storm the Tuileries on August 10, 1792. Louis and Marie-Antoinette were tried for treason, convicted, and guillotined at the Place de la Revolution (now Place de la Concorde) on January 21, 1793.

Further Reading: Vincent Cronin. *Louis and Antoinette* (New York: Morrow, 1974); Andrew Freeman. *The Compromising of Louis XVI* (Exeter: University of Exeter, 1989); David P. Jordan. *The King's Trial: The French Revolution vs. Louis XVI* (Berkeley: University of California Press, 1979).

Louis-Philippe (1773–1850)

Louis-Philippe was king of France from 1830 until 1848, when a popular revolution ousted him.

The son of Louis-Philippe Joseph de Bourbon-Orléans, duke of Chartres, and Adélaïde de Bourbon-Penthièvre, Louis-Philippe became duke of Chartres after his father inherited the title duke of Orléans in 1785. During the French Revolution, young Louis-Philippe joined the Jacobin Club in 1790 and fought in the war with Austria in 1792. The following year he left France, living under an assumed name in Switzerland and then in the United States.

Like her husband, Louis XVI, Marie-Antoinette fell victim to the French Revolution. (From M. Guizot, A Popular History of France from the Earliest Times, *n.d.)*

Louis-Philippe returned to Europe in 1800, residing in England for a while until his marriage to Marie-Amélie, the daughter of King Ferdinand IV of Naples, in 1809. Following his marriage, he moved to Sicily. The abdication of CHARLES X of France led to Louis-Philippe's ascension in 1830.

As king, Louis-Philippe was a moderate who managed to maintain a precarious balance between right- and left-wing extremes in France. As the threat of rebellion grew, however, Louis-Philippe conducted a purge of the opposition, succeeding by 1830 in temporarily silencing it. During the late 1840s, however, a rising middle-class and proletariat movement mounted irresistible opposition, finally forcing Louis-Philippe to abdicate on February 24, 1848.

An exile in Surrey, England, Louis-Philippe died on August 26, 1850.

Louis (Ludwig) II [Mad King Ludwig] (1845–1886)

Wary of German nationalism and loss of regional autonomy, Bavaria's Louis II, the eccentric and extravagant patron of composer Richard Wagner and builder of a fabulous fairytale castle, became increasingly opposed to a unified Germany—and increasingly insane.

The oldest son of King Maximilian II of Bavaria, Louis was born August 25, 1845, and was given a thorough education, becoming a confirmed conservative. When Maximilian died in 1864, Louis assumed the throne at the age of 18. In the Austro-Prussian War of 1866, Otto von Bismarck proposed a German confederation minus the Hapsburg domains in Austria, but inclusive of Schleswig-Holstein. Both the Prussians and the Austrians immediately mobilized, and Louis sided with the Austrians, who were decimated at the Battle of Sadowa on July 3, 1866.

After Sadowa, Louis signed an alliance with Prussia, working toward reconciliation between Prussia and Austria. When NAPOLÉON III suggested a Franco-Austro-Bavarian alliance against Prussia, Louis, a staunch patriot, adamantly refused, joining Prussian forces in the Franco-Prussian War of 1870, contributing troops to the crushing French defeat at Sedan. When Bismarck again clamored for a unified Germany in 1870, Louis was wary of a diminished Bavarian role in the proposed confederation. He proposed several special clauses favorable to Bavaria, but they were rejected.

Increasingly disturbed by his loss of prestige and by the nationalist fervor sweeping Bavaria, he gradually withdrew from politics. By the 1880s, Louis had withdrawn from royal society altogether and indulged himself in building and expanding extrava-

gant castles and in patronizing the arts, most importantly the composer Richard Wagner. On June 10, 1886, he was declared insane, placed under psychiatric custody, and the conduct of the nation entrusted to a regency. On June 13, 1886, the king went for a walk accompanied, as usual, by Dr. Bernhard von Gudden, a psychiatrist. When the two failed to return, searchers were sent out and discovered the bodies of Louis and Gudden in shallow Lake Starnberg. Although the matter has never been completely settled, the king apparently shot his hated doctor, then drowned himself. Louis' diaries and letters reveal a lifelong struggle not only with his mental illness but homosexuality as well.

Further Reading: Wilfrid Blunt. *The Dream King: Ludwig II of Bavaria* (London: Penguin, 1970).

Lysander (d. 395 B.C.)

Admiral of the Peloponnesian fleet, Lysander defeated the Athenians, installed his friends in positions of power in former Athenian possessions, and led the Spartans in war against Thebes.

An ambitious, ruthless war commander, Lysander had been raised in poverty in an atmosphere of strict Spartan discipline. He came to power in 408 B.C. as *navarch* (admiral) of the Peloponnesian fleet. Setting up a base at Ephesus, he established friendly relations with Cyrus the Younger and the Persian satrap at Sardis. The following year, he defeated an Athenian fleet at Notium, but despite his victory, he was compelled to relinquish the title of *navarch*, because Spartan law limited the term to one year. In 406, the new *navarch*, Callicratidas, was defeated, and Lysander's friends called for his reappointment. Again, Spartan law intervened: no man could serve as *navarch* twice.

Nevertheless, though he held no official title, Lysander remained powerful.

With funds from Cyrus the Younger's satrapy, Lysander sailed out of Ephesus to engage the Athenians in battle once more. First he attacked Lampsacus on the eastern shore of the Hellespont and allowed his men to plunder the city. Then he met the Athenians at Aegospotami. Three or four thousand Athenians were taken prisoner and killed by the Spartans, and only twenty Athenian ships survived. The total defeat of the Athenian fleet marked the end of the Peloponnesian War. Lysander then sailed to Athens and blockaded it, so that the starving Athenians soon sued for peace. Lysander set up the Tyranny of Thirty in 404 as the government of Athens and installed Spartan governors over former Athenian cities in Greece and Asia Minor.

Lysander continued to pillage the coasts of Asia and to send booty to his friends in Sparta. He executed the enemies of his friends without compunction and promised amnesty to exiles—only to kill them upon their return. At length, his brutality provoked outrage among the Persians, who complained to Sparta. Lysander was ordered to appear before the Spartan *ephors*, who chastised him. With difficulty, he wrangled from them permission to visit the temple of Zeus Ammon in Libya.

Upon his return from Libya, he was welcomed by the Spartan masses as a hero. Using his popular influence, he helped Agesilaus II secure the throne and then persuaded the king to wage war on the Persians. Lysander accompanied Agesilaus to Asia, expecting to be named commander. Instead, the king named Lysander official Carver-of-Meats, an insult that precipitated his return to Sparta.

Lysander returned to military service in 395, when the Spartans attacked Thebes at the start of the Co-rinthian War. Leading a force that attacked Haliartus in Boeotia, Lysander was slain in a surprise preemptive raid against his troops.

An arrogant and brutal military commander, Lysander was not greedy for material wealth. He never took booty for himself, sending all captured prizes to his friends and to the treasury of Sparta. Traditionally, Sparta had never been wealthy; its currency consisted of iron coins. With the influx of treasure from Lysander's campaigns, not only did the city-state's coffers swell, but the strict discipline and morality characteristic of the Spartans were undermined, and the character of Sparta was forever changed.

Further Reading: Catherine B. Avery, ed. *The New Century Classical Handbook* (New York: Appleton-Century-Crofts, 1962); Diana Bowder. *Who Was Who in the Greek World* (Ithaca, New York: Cornell University Press, 1982).

M

Macbeth (b. ca. 1005–1057)

Chiefly known as the great dramatic invention of William Shakespeare, the historical Macbeth was an ambitious Scots governor who contended for and attained the Scottish throne.

Because of his portrayal in William Shakespeare's great play (probably composed during 1605–06), the name of Macbeth is virtually synonymous with the word tyrant in its most pejorative contemporary sense as one who rules by wielding absolute power with ruthless cruelty. Indeed, Macbeth seems to have figured in Scottish history and legend as a tyrant, but, even in Shakespeare's day, it was impossible to separate the historical from the legendary figure. Shakespeare's principal source for his dramatic character was the famous *Chronicles* of Raphael Holinshed (1587), a compendium of British history that makes little effort to distinguish fact from legend. Shakespeare also deliberately fictionalized Macbeth by attributing to him not only the murdering ruthlessness found in Holinshed, but also the evil deeds of another Scots chieftain, Donwald, who killed King Duff.

All that is known with any certainty about Macbeth is that he was born about 1005 and about 1031 succeeded his father, known only as Finlay, to the post of *moarmaer*—in effect, governor—of the Scottish province of Moray. Macbeth seems to have had some claim to the Scottish throne through actual royal descent. This he augmented by marrying one Gruoch, granddaughter of King Kenneth III, who had reigned from 997 to 1005.

That Macbeth sought to make good his claim to the crown is certain. He was also responsible for King Duncan's death—but not, as Shakespeare has it, through a treacherous act of assassination. Rather, he killed the king in battle near Elgin in 1040. Tradition has it that Duncan had been a good and a popular sovereign, while Macbeth was covetous, cruel, and unpopular with the Scottish chieftains and nobility. However accurate this tradition may or may not be, Macbeth did have to defend himself against a 1046 attempt to depose him in favor of Malcolm Canmore, the son of the slain King Duncan. Although Macbeth prevailed, he was compelled in 1054 to cede to Malcolm the southern portion of his kingdom. Three years later, on August 15, 1057, Malcolm met, defeated, and killed Macbeth

on the field of battle at Lumphanan. Although Malcolm ascended the throne in 1058 as Malcolm III, Macbeth was buried at Iona with all honors due a legitimate monarch.

Further Reading: William C. Dickinson. *A New History of Scotland* (London and New York: Nelson, 1965); Gordon Donaldson. *Scottish Kings* (New York: Wiley, 1967).

Machado y Morales, Gerardo (1871–1939)

One of the heroes in Cuba's war for independence from Spain, Machado was elected president, but became a corrupt despot.

Born on a cattle ranch on September 28, 1871, in Santa Clara, Gerardo Machado y Morales received a private education before going into the tobacco business. When Spain renewed the ongoing war against Cuba in 1895, Machado left his tobacco business and enlisted in the rebel army. By war's end in 1898, Machado had risen to brigadier general and emerged from the war a hero.

He returned to his tobacco business and was elected mayor of Santa Clara. President José Miguel Gómez next appointed him inspector of the armed forces in 1909 and, subsequently, secretary of the interior. Later, Machado returned to farming and business, amassing a great personal fortune and making intimate connections with American businessmen, whom he persuaded to invest in Cuban public works. In 1920, Machado won control of the Liberal Party, and in 1924, using the slogan, "Water, roads, and schools," he was elected president.

Machado immediately set about industrializing his country while attempting to reduce Cuban dependence on the United States. He expanded sugar production and embarked on a prodigious program of internal improvements, building the Central Highway, constructing a national capitol, enlarging the University of Havana, and modernizing and expanding health care facilities. He also protected fledgling Cuban industry with a tariff in 1927. Despite these measures, Cuba remained largely dependent on U.S. investment—especially the mainstay sugar industry.

Declaring that he needed more time for his economic programs to work, Machado pushed through a constitutional amendment in 1928 extending the presidential term from four years to five, then reneged on a promise not to run again. After clamping down on the opposition by gaining control of the other two parties and using bribes and coercion, he was reelected later in the year. Worse, Machado had set a precedent of bribery and threat, not only for his own administration, but for Cuban government generally.

With the onset of the worldwide depression in 1929, Cuba's frail economy faltered, money stopped coming from the United States, and resistance to Machado increased. In 1931, a popular uprising of the secret ABC Society, led by former president Mario García Menocal, was put down in Pinar del Rio, and another uprising was crushed by the army in Oriente. The ABC Society now began an underground campaign against Machado. U.S. president Franklin D. Roosevelt sent special envoy Sumner Welles to Cuba to mediate a solution to the crisis, but opposition continued to increase. A general strike was called, and the army deserted Machado, who was forced into exile on August 12, 1933, dying in Miami Beach, Florida, on March 29, 1939.

Further Reading: Wyatt MacGaffey and Clifford R. Barnett. *Twentieth Century Cuba* (Garden City, N.Y.: Anchor Books, 1965).

Magnentius [Flavius Magnus Magnentius] (r. 350–353)

Attempting to reunite the Roman Empire, divided since the death of CONSTANTINE THE GREAT in 337, Magnentius briefly usurped the throne of the Roman Empire of the West, but was defeated by Constans II, emperor of the East.

Originally a soldier in the barbarian ranks of Constantine's army, Magnentius rose to become a staff officer, a field commander, and finally commander of the elite legions. In 350, he appeared at a private party dressed in purple robes and was acclaimed emperor. Constans I, fearing the pretender, fled, only to be killed by Magnentius' supporters. In June 350, Nepotianus refused to accept Magnentius and declared himself emperor, but was deposed by Magnentius' lieutenants after nominally ruling for 28 days. Magnentius was now secure as emperor of the West.

Magnentius next faced rigid opposition in the East from Constans II. Magnentius was able to repulse Constans II's advances on the Italian border, inflicting heavy losses. Magnentius next rejected Constans II's proposal of compromise, confident that he could destroy Constans uttterly, thereby unifying the East and West for the first time since Constantine. Magnentius was on the verge of dealing Constans a deathblow when the tables were suddenly turned. On September 28, 351, Constans II's cavalry forces met and devastated Magnentius'

troops at the Battle of Mursa in a military first—an unprecedented defeat inflicted by cavalry on Roman legionaries. Indeed, Mursa was the bloodiest battle of the century, with combined casualties of more that 54,000.

Magnentius was now on the run. Unable to halt the advance of Constans II, he was beaten out of Italy, then lost control of the Rhine. Seeing that his position was hopeless, he committed suicide on August 11, 353, rather than submit to capture.

Further Reading: Michael Grant. *Roman Emperors* (New York: Scribner's, 1985).

Mahdi, al- [Muhammad Ahmad Ibn As-Sayyid 'Abd Allah] (1844–1885)

Leader of an Islamic movement that freed the Sudan from Egyptian rule, al-Mahdi created a theocratic state and a religious movement that lasted for nearly a century.

Born on August 12, 1844, to a shipbuilder in the Dongola District of Nubia, Muhammad Ahmad Ibn As-Sayyid 'Abd Allah moved with his family to Karari, a village near Khartoum. As a child, Muhammad Ahmad exhibited a propensity for religious study and was especially attracted to a mystic interpretation of Islam. He joined the Sammaniyah order and began developing a circle of disciples. In 1870, his group of followers moved with him to Aba Island in the While Nile, 175 miles south of Khartoum.

During this time, the Sudan was a dependency of Egypt, a province of the Ottoman Empire. Many Sudanese were disaffected. The governing class— multiracial, Turkish-speaking officials—had little connection to local life. Moreover, the Sudanese were oppressed by heavy taxation and were outraged that decadent "Europeans" served as their provinical governors. It fell to Muhammad Ahmad to organize this growing group of discontented individuals into an armed religious movement.

In the spring of 1881, Muhammad Ahmad disclosed to his followers that his divine mission was to purify Islam and destroy the non-Muslim government. On June 29, he assumed the title of al-Mahdi, a messianic figure who the Islamic faithful believed was God's anointed leader who would restore and purify Islam. Over the next four years, the movement spread wildly.

At first armed only with sticks and spears, the Mahdists set out from Aba Island. By the end of 1883, they had annihilated three Egyptian armies. Both El Obeid and Bara fell to the Mahdists after long sieges, and on January 26, 1885, al-Mahdi captured Khartoum and massacred many of its citizens, including the great British general Charles George "Chinese" Gordon, who had been sent to relieve the

Egyptian defenders. Al-Mahdi entered the city in triumph, but did not remain there to administer his new government. Instead he moved to Omdurman, a village of mud houses across the White Nile from Khartoum.

From Omdurman, al-Madhi directed every aspect of Islamic life. Leaving the administration of his government to appointed officials, he issued proclamations, delivered sermons and warnings, and wrote letters, all dealing with the principles of Islam. The government itself was based on ancient Islamic forms, with four caliphs, or deputies, selected by al-Mahdi to direct governmental affairs.

Only six months after al-Mahdi's triumphal entry into Khartoum, he fell ill, possibly of typhus, and died on June 22, 1885. The Sudanese government was then headed by his trusted adviser 'Abd Allah ibn Muhammad, who ordered the construction of a domed tomb in Omdurman for al-Mahdi's remains.

At the Battle of Omdurman on September 2, 1898, a combined English and Egyptian force nearly destroyed the Mahdists. However, Mahdism remained a powerful presence in the Sudan for nearly a century after al-Mahdi's death. When 'Abd Allah died, leadership of the movement passed to al-Mahdi's son, 'Abd ar-Rahman, who, along with his son and other members of the family, kept the movement alive. In 1970, the leftist revolutionary government of the Sudan forced the family into exile.

Further Reading: Sir Francis R. Wingate. *Mahdiism and the Egyptian Sudan* (1891; reprint ed., London: Cass, 1968); Peter Holt. *The Mahdist State in the Sudan* (Oxford: Clarendon Press, 1950).

Mahmud of Ghazna   (971–1030)

Mahmud extended the sultanate of Ghazna into a vast empire, transforming his capital into the cultural center of central Asia, and, in the course of 17 invasions, carrying Islam deep into India.

Mahmud was the son of Amir Sabuktigin, a Turkish slave who became ruler of the small sultanate of Ghazna in 977. Mahmud was 27 years old in 998 when he succeeded his father. With diplomatic skill and military boldness, Mahmud vastly expanded Ghazna until it included Kashmir, Punjab, and most of Iran.

He began by striking an alliance with the mighty Abasid caliph in Baghdad, whose recognition would legitimate many of Mahmud's conquests. Early in his reign, Mahmud vowed to invade India annually, and did, in fact, lead no fewer than 17 expeditions there between 1001 and 1026. On his first invasion, Mahmud rode at the head of 15,000 cavalry troops. At Peshawar, he was met by 12,000 cavalrymen, 30,000 infantry soldiers, and 300 elephants commanded by Jaipal, ruler of the Punjab. Although he was vastly outnumbered, Mahmud routed Jaipal's forces, killing some 15,000 of his men and capturing Jaipal himself, together with 15 of his relatives and commanders. While Mahmud was an aggressive and relentless conqueror, he was not ruthless, and he released Jaipal. The raja, however, promptly abdicated in favor of his son, Anandpal, ascended his own funeral pyre, and immolated himself.

In the meantime, Anandpal gathered an alliance of rajas from all over India and gradually assembled a huge army to counter the annual assaults against the subcontinent. By 1008, Anandpal fielded a huge force against Mahmud at a place between Und and Peshawar. For 40 days and nights the rival armies faced one another. At last, Anandpal attacked, making extensive use of 30,000 fierce Khokar tribesmen, who fought Mahmud's army to the point of retreat. On the verge of defeat, however, the tide turned when Anandpal's elephant became frightened and fled from the battlefield. Seeing their leader in apparent full retreat, the Indian forces panicked, broke ranks, and fled. Mahmud, now victorious, advanced deep into India, annexing the Punjab, and looting its riches.

With the bounty gained from his many invasions, Mahmud transformed the capital city of Ghazna into a wealthy metropolis of magnificent buildings. He fostered the development of the arts and learning, and soon his city rivaled Baghdad itself as a cultural center.

Although Mahmud subjugated a huge area of India, he treated the people he conquered with considerable respect. It is true that, in 1024, when he sacked the city of Somnath, he defiled the Hindu temple there, breaking its sacred *lingam;* however, he was generally tolerant of non-Islamic faiths. While he attempted to spread Islam into India, he also maintained a large unit of Hindu troops under the command of Indians, and he did not practice religious persecution.

Mahmud Nedim Pasha   (ca. 1818–1883)

As grand vizier to Ottoman sultan ABDÜLAZIZ, Mahmud Nedim exerted a conservative influence over the sultanate that had a direct effect on the revival of the Young Turk movement.

The son of a former governor of Baghdad, Mahmud Nedim Pasha quickly rose in the Ottoman bureaucracy. When Grand Vizier Ali Pasha died in 1871, Sultan Abdülaziz named Mahmud Nedim to succeed him, remarking that he was the first of his ministers to do exactly what he wanted. Mahmud Nedim soon added to the chaos surrounding the administration by constantly rotating or removing altogether any official whose position might come to rival his or compromise his influence with the sultan.

Mahmud was removed the following year under the direction of the reform-minded Midhat Pasha, after widespread demonstrations against the grand vizier forced the sultan to take action. Mahmud returned as grand vizier in 1875, after Midhat Pasha's death, and gained even greater influence in the government.

Mahmud fell under the anti-Western influence of the Russian ambassador to the Ottoman Empire, Nicolai Ignatyev, who persuaded Mahmud Nedim and, subsequently, the sultan to default on loans from both France and England. Ignatyev, aided and abetted by Mahmud Nedim, also precipitated a revolt in Bulgaria.

Mahmud Nedim's conservatism went against the prevailing tide of reform sweeping eastern Europe and Asia. The grand vizier became so unpopular that theological students from the mosques and the remnants of the Young Turks—who had disbanded in 1871—took to the streets and rioted. The sultan dismissed Mahmud Nedim for good, but it was too late to save himself. When the Young Turks were fully revived, they forced the abdication of Abdülaziz shortly thereafter.

Manuel I the Fortunate (1469–1521)

After vastly improving Portugal's finances through overseas exploration, Manuel strengthened the power of the crown and helped form a colonial empire.

One of the reasons Manuel is known as "the Fortunate" is that he was the ninth child born to a father who was not in the direct line of royal succession—yet he ascended the Portuguese throne. He was born on May 31, 1469, the nephew of King Afonso V. When his father died, Afonso became Manuel's guardian. Manuel's sister was married to Afonso's heir, John II, who would later execute Manuel's only remaining brother on conspiracy charges. When John's own son died, he named Manuel his heir. Manuel therefore ascended to the Portuguese throne in 1495 on John's death.

As king, Manuel authorized the expeditions of Vasco da Gama—including his momentous voyage around Africa to open trade routes east—and the voyages of Pedro Alvares Cabral to Brazil and around the Cape of Good Hope to India. Cabral lost half his ships in the Indian expedition of 1500, but it was a profitable enterprise nevertheless. For his part, Vasco da Gama brought back much gold from East Africa in 1502. The wealth born of discovery allowed Portugal to lay claim to an expansive colonial empire, which was legitimated by the papacy and rival expansionist power Spain.

To gain Spanish concurrence in his colonial enterprise and to ward off Spanish incursions into Portuguese politics, Manuel married Isabella, the daughter of King FERDINAND and Queen ISABELLA. As a condition of the marriage, Manuel pledged to expel all Jews and Moors from Portugal. In December 1496, he grudgingly and half-heartedly ordered all Jews and Muslims to convert or to leave the country within 10 months. Unlike Ferdinand and Isabella, who vigorously promoted the Inquisition in Spain, Manuel was wary of the economic consequences of losing Jews with business skills. Accordingly, he offered not to inquire into the validity of the compelled conversions for 20 years.

At home, Manuel both promoted and suppressed the nobility. In hopes of raising the prestige of his court, he made thousands of nobles royal pensioners, creating a palace aristocracy. However, he also revised the law to consolidate royal power and rescinded any legislative power held by the parliament. He limited local authority, creating a highly centralized royal government regulated by ministries.

In the East, Manuel attempted to monopolize the spice market through his colonial possessions. He lacked the military resources to enforce the monopoly effectively. With the death of two of his most capable ministers by 1515 and the burdensome cost of long-distance voyages, the Portuguese spice monopoly, together with the wealth it would bring, failed to materialize. Manuel died on December 13, 1521.

Further Reading: Elaine Sanceau. *The Reign of the Fortunate King, 1495–1521* (Hamden, Conn.: Archon, 1969); H. V. Livermore. *A New History of Portugal* (New York: Macmillan, 1966).

Mao Tse-tung [Mao Zedong] (1893–1976)

One of the founders of the Chinese Communist Party (1921) and the founder of the People's Republic of China (1949), Mao Tse-tung—with Marx and LENIN—was one of the architects of Marxist political thought. He was also merciless in his efforts to bring about revolution on a massive scale in China.

Mao Tse-tung was born on December 26, 1893, the son of a land-owning and prosperous Hunan peasant family. At the local elementary school, he received a classical Chinese education, which included liberal exposure to Confucian philosophy and literature. He left school in October 1911, after forces under Sun Yat-sen overthrew the Ch'ing (or Manchu) dynasty. Mao served for six months during 1911–12 as an orderly in a militia unit, then, at the insistence of his stern and overbearing father, attended a commercial school during 1912–13. From 1913 to 1918, he lived in the provincial capital of Changsha, where he attended the First Normal School. Moving to Peking (Beijing) for one year—1918–19—he worked in the library of Peking University.

By the time he returned to Hunan in 1919, now as a teacher at the Changsha normal school, he had earned a reputation as an influential political intellectual. In 1920, he married Yang K'ai-hui, the daughter of one of his teachers, and the following year he served as Hunan's chief delegate to the founding congress of the Chinese Communist Party (CCP), held in Shanghai in July 1921. With the rest of the CCP, he joined the Nationalist Party—the Kuomintang (KMT)—in 1923 and was chosen as an alternate member of the KMT Shanghai Executive Committee in 1924.

Illness later that year forced his return to Hunan, but Mao was hardly idle there. He moved steadily to the left, organizing unions of laborers and peasants, which prompted an order for his arrest. In 1925, he fled to Canton, where he wrote for a radical weekly, then moved into CHIANG KAI-SHEK's inner circle, as head of the propaganda section of the KMT. Political differences with Chiang became evident almost immediately, and in May 1926 he was removed from the propaganda post.

Mao joined the Peasant Movement Training Institute, a far-left CCP cell. In April 1927, however, Chiang Kai-shek repudiated the KMT alliance with the CCP and attacked party members in his Northern Campaign. Mao retreated underground and, independently even of the CCP, organized a revolutionary army in August, which he led in the Autumn Harvest Uprising in Hunan during September 8–19. The uprising proved abortive, and Mao was drummed out of the CCP. He responded to this by gathering his remaining forces about him and retreating to the mountains, allying himself with another CCP outcast, Chu Teh, and forming in 1928 a peasant army called the Mass Line. Together, Mao and Chu established their own CCP republic, the Kiangsi Soviet, which by 1934 numbered some 15 million people. In doing this, they defied not only Chiang Kai-shek's KMT, but also the Russian-dominated international Communist party, which ordered would-be Communist revolutionaries to concentrate on capturing cities. Running counter to orthodox Marxist doctrine, Mao and Chu turned their attention not to the urban proletariat, but to the rural peasants. Between 1929 and 1934, using guerrilla tactics, they successfully resisted four KMT attempts to wipe out the soviet. In 1930, however, the KMT executed Mao's first wife, Yang K'ai-hui, and

after a fifth assault on the Kiangsi Soviet in 1934, Mao was forced to evacuate with some 86,000 men and women.

The mass evacuation of Mao's troops from Kiangsi resulted in the so-called Long March of some 6,000 miles to the province of Shensi. In October 1935, at Yenan, his followers now numbering a mere 4,000, Mao established a new party headquarters.

At this point, the Japanese invasion of China compelled the CCP and KMT to unite, and Mao made peace with Chiang Kai-shek in December 1936. Mao launched the Hundred Regiments offensive against the Japanese during August 20–November 30, 1940, but otherwise was less active in operations against the Japanese during the war years than he was in strengthening the CCP position in northern China and his own leadership of the party. Not only did Mao continue to organize peasants, he oversaw a program of purges during the war years that secured, in April 1945, his election as permanent chairman of the party's Central Committee. During this period, Mao also produced and published a series of essays in which he developed and promulgated the basis for Chinese communism. The CCP had begun the war years in 1937 with 40,000 members. It emerged in 1945 with 1,200,000.

The conclusion of the war also brought to an end the uneasy truce between the CCP and KMT. Despite efforts to create a coalition government, a bitter civil war erupted. Mao's forces steadily defeated the armies of Chiang Kai-shek during 1946 to 1949, and the Nationalists were forced at last to flee to the island of Taiwan. Late in 1949, Mao and his fellow Communists proclaimed the People's Republic of China on the vast mainland.

The United States, which remained committed to Chiang Kai-shek and Nationalist China, rejected Mao's attempts to establish diplomatic relations, thereby propelling him into a close alliance with Stalin's Soviet Union. Between 1949 and 1954, Mao relentlessly purged the party of opponents and moved against the nation's landlords in a program of enforced agricultural collectivization similar to Stalin's "five-year plans" during the 1930s. From November 1950 through July 1953, Mao ordered a massive intervention in the war between North and South Korea, which meant that the armies of Communist China and the United States contended on the battlefield.

During this period, Mao assumed greater and greater prominence in world communism, and with the death of Josef Stalin in 1953, he emerged as the preeminent Marxist leader. He professed dissatisfaction with the slowing pace of revolutionary change in the Chinese countryside, pointing out that senior party members often behaved like members of the old upper classes. Mao initiated the Hundred Flowers movement during 1956–57, under the slogan, "Let a hundred flowers bloom, let a thousand schools of thought contend." He began by encouraging intellectuals to criticize the party and its methods of government and administration. Whether by design or out of fear of the hostile tenor of the criticism that was quickly forthcoming, Mao soon turned the Hundred Flowers movement *against* the dissidents and worked to create a worshipful cult of personality about himself—much as Stalin had done. Simultaneously, he applied renewed pressure to achieve the complete transformation of rural ownership, calling for the total elimination of private property and the formation of people's communes. He promulgated a program called the Great Leap Forward, an attempt to accelerate industrialization on a grand scale.

The result of Mao's oppressive handling of the Hundred Flowers Movement, forced collectivization, and accelerated industrialization was massive administrative chaos and popular resistance compounded by bad weather conditions that resulted in widespread famine. Late in 1958, Mao stepped down as head of state and was replaced by LIU SHAO-CHI. He sought retirement and seclusion for the balance of the 1950s and early 1960s, returning to public life by the mid-1960s with a brilliantly orchestrated attack on Liu Shao-chi centered on what Mao proposed as a Great Proletarian Cultural Revolution. During roughly 1966 to 1969, Mao and his third wife, Chiang Ch'ing, engaged the nation in a frenzied national debate on its political future and, after Mao resumed his position as party chairman and head of state, propelled China into a state of perpetual revolution, the object of which was to transform the nation into a purely Marxist society, from which every vestige of traditional government and culture had been expunged.

The Cultural Revolution produced a mass army of radical Maoist students known as the Red Guards, who wrought anarchical havoc on China. To restore order, Mao turned to the military, led by Lin Piao, whose support he recruited by arranging to have him name his successor in the 1969 constitution of the Chinese Communist Party. The Red Guards had been considerably reined in by 1971, when Lin Piao was reported killed in a plane crash after having plotted to assassinate Mao.

Mao was again in control, but he had learned the value of moderation, giving dramatic evidence of this evolution in his thought when he made overtures to open diplomatic and economic relations with the United States, receiving President Richard M. Nixon in Peking in 1972. The aging chairman's health deteriorated during the early 1970s, and he died in Peking on September 9, 1976.

Despite Mao's late trend toward moderation, reaction against the would-be heirs of Mao's power came swiftly. Chiang Ch'ing and her closest associates, dubbed the Gang of Four, were arrested, and the chairman's handpicked successor, Hua Kuo-Feng, was ousted from the party's inner circle, as the government came under control of avowed moderates. The Cultural Revolution had been a remarkable amalgam of contradictions. Like the Hundred Flowers movement, its founding principles were constructive criticism and questioning of those in authority and the doctrine of "right to revolt," yet it produced an unquestioning mass personality cult devoted to the mind and person of Mao Tse-tung, whose image was ubiquitous in places public and private and whose "little red book"—a collection of *Quotations from Chairman Mao*—was in the hands of virtually every man, woman, and child in the nation. Within a few years after Mao's death, however, the Chinese Communist Party was willing to praise Mao as a pioneering revolutionary, but condemned the Cultural Revolution for its excesses, including the personal worship of Mao.

Further Reading: Alain Bouc. *Mao Tse-tung: A Guide to His Thought* (New York: St. Martin's, 1977); Eric Chou. *Mao Tse-tung: The Man and the Myth* (New York: Stein and Day, 1980); Stuart R. Schram. *Mao Tse-tung* (New York: Simon & Schuster, 1966); Stuart R. Schram, ed. *Quotations from Chairman Mao*, 2d ed. (New York: Simon & Schuster, 1967).

Marcos, Ferdinand Edralin   (1917–1989)

President and virtual dictator from 1966 to 1986, Ferdinand Edralin Marcos exercised absolute control over the Philippines, rewrote the country's constitution to give himself more power, and mercilessly persecuted his political enemies.

Marcos was born on September 11, 1917, in Sarrat, Philippine Islands. He attended school in Manila and in 1939 graduated first in his class from the law school of the University of the Philippines. During World War II, Marcos served with the Philippine armed forces. Captured by the Japanese, he was forced to take part in the Death March from Bataan to central Luzon and then miraculously escaped. By his own account, he then played a major role in the Filipino guerrilla resistance movement—though no record of this work exists in United States archives.

After the war, Marcos served as a technical assistant (1946–1947) to Manuel Roxas, the first president of the independent Philippine republic. Elected to the House of Representatives (1949–1959) and the Senate (1959–1965), he then cast his eye toward higher office, campaigning in the Liberal Party for the presidential nomination. Angered that he was passed over, he broke with the Liberals and ran as a Nationalist Party candidate against the Liberal president Diosdada Macapagal. After an expensive and bitterly fought campaign, Marcos won election and was inaugurated on December 30, 1965. Four years later he was reelected.

During his first and second terms in office Marcos instituted various agricultural, industrial, and educational reforms. Nevertheless, civil unrest increased nationwide, especially in urban areas. Marcos responded with increasingly repressive measures, finally declaring martial law on September 21, 1972, citing the increased activity of Communists and other "subversives." He summarily jailed his political opponents and used the armed forces as a kind of private police force. He suspended habeas corpus, dissolved the Congress, and set forth a new constitution that increased his powers. Although Marcos declared an end to martial law in January 1981, he continued, in fact, to rule the Philippines by decree.

Opposition to Marcos was organized chiefly around the Muslim secessionist movement of the Moro National Liberation Front and the Communist movement led by the New People's Army. Another threat to his power was embodied in a liberal political opponent, Benigno Aquino, Jr., whom Marcos had imprisoned after declaring martial law. The immensely popular Aquino had been released from prison after eight years' confinement and allowed to travel to the United States for a heart operation. On August 21, 1983, he returned to the Philippines. The moment he arrived at the Manila International Airport, he was assassinated, an event that set off massive anti-Marcos demonstrations. President Marcos appointed an investigation committee, which determined that the assassination was planned in part by the Philippines' highest-ranking general, Fabian Ver. A relative and a close confidant of the president, Ver was acquitted in a trial Marcos controlled.

In an effort to get a new purchase on his slipping power, Marcos called for presidential elections. Running against him was Aquino's widow, Corazon Aquino. In the February 1986 election, Marcos was certified the victor, but only after the walkout of 30 election-tabulating computer operators, who quit in protest of vote fraud. Marcos immediately arrested his opponents, notably Defense Minister Juan Enrile and General Fidel Ramos. This provoked a public revolt in Manila.

On February 25, 1986, both Aquino and Marcos were inaugurated in separate ceremonies, heightening the chaos and potential for violence. The evening following his inauguration, Marcos decided to accept an offer from the United States government to fly him and his wife, Imelda, to exile in Hawaii.

During his exile, evidence mounted that Marcos and his family had embezzled billions of dollars from the Philippine government. United States officials indicted him on racketeering charges, but Marcos, now ailing, was deemed too ill to stand trail. He died on September 28, 1989, in Honolulu, Hawaii.

Further Reading: John Bresnan. *Crisis in the Philippines: The Marcos Era and Beyond* (Princeton: Princeton University Press, 1986); Gary Hawes. *The Philippine State and the Marcos Regime: The Politics of Export* (Ithaca, N.Y.: Cornell University Press, 1987).

Maria Theresa   (1717–1780)

Maria Theresa was the only female ruler (1740–1780) of the Hapsburg dynasty in its 650-year history.

Born in Vienna on May 13, 1717, Maria Theresa inherited the Austrian throne when her father, Charles VI, died in 1740 without male heirs to succeed him. A capable monarch, she was admired by friend and foe alike. Even her arch-enemy FREDERICK II THE GREAT of Prussia called her "a credit to her throne and her sex."

Maria Theresa's reign was marred by three conflicts, the War of Austrian Succession (1740–1748), which began almost immediately upon her ascent to the throne; the Seven Years' War (1756–1764); and the War of the Bavarian Succession (1778–1779). Her experience in prosecuting these wars prompted her to undertake a sweeping modernization of her armies.

The bloody 1745 Battle of Fontenoy was one of many in the long War of the Austrian Succession, triggered by Maria Theresa's ascension to the Hapsburg throne. (From Charlotte M. Yonge, Pictorial History of the World's Great Nations, *1882*)

On the domestic scene, Maria restructured the tax system, started a universal school system that was separate from the church, and provided some relief to the beleaguered peasant class. A devout Catholic, she suppressed the Jesuits and was intolerant in her policies toward Jews.

Maria Theresa was the mother of 16 children, the most famous of whom were Joseph II, Holy Roman Emperor from 1765 to 1790, and Marie-Antoinette, the queen of France who fell victim with her husband, LOUIS XVI, to the French Revolution. Maria Theresa died in Vienna on November 29, 1780.

Further Reading: A. G. Dickens, ed. *The Courts of Europe: Politics, Patronage, and Royalty 1400–1800* (London and New York: Thames and Hudson, 1977); C. A. Macartney. *The Habsburg Empire, 1790–1918* (New York: Macmillan, 1969).

Mariam, Mengistu Haile (b. ca. 1937)

The fierce, Marxist military leader of Ethiopia who deposed Emperor HAILE SELASSIE, Mariam has ordered spontaneous purges and assassinations of political enemies.

A career military man, Mengistu Mariam joined the army at an early age and served as a palace baggage handler and logistics coordinator for Emperor Haile Selassie. He was trained as an officer at the Holeta Military College, where he formed friendships with many of the men with whom he would later rule the country. After further training by the United States Army at Fort Leavenworth, Kansas, Mariam attained the rank of major and was stationed on the Somali border with the Third Division.

In February 1974, discontent over the 40-year reign of Haile Selassie reached a fever pitch. Soldiers mutinied for higher wages and better conditions in the army, which led to demands from other sectors until a full-scale popular revolt was under way. Under direction from the military—with Mariam serving as chairman of the coordinating committee for all armed forces and police—some 200 advisers to the emperor were arrested for corruption, embezzlement, and maladministration. Selassie himself was deposed in September 1974, and Mariam, still a little-known backroom player, was appointed one of two vice-chairmen of the newly formed Provisional Military Administrative Committee—called the Dergue, meaning "shadow."

Ethiopians rejoiced in the overthrow of Selassie and the prospect of democracy, and the world praised the military for its bloodless, peaceful coup. This abruptly changed on November 23, 1974, when Mariam apparently ordered the execution of 59 members of the nobility who had supported Selas-

sie, including two former premiers, 12 provincial governors, 18 generals, and Selassie's grandson. That same night, forces loyal to Mariam moved on the home of Lt. General Aman Michael Andom, provisional chief of state, and executed him as well, with Mariam apparently taking part in the two-hour gun battle. It was said that "the old aristocracy was wiped out in a single stroke."

Although Aman Andom was replaced by General Tafari Banti as chief of state, Mariam became the real power as leader of the Dergue, and both the press and the military identified him as "the true moving force" behind the coup all along.

Mariam now turned to socialism to bring his country out of the morass of the Selassie regime, calling for the collectivization of agriculture and the seizure of foreign business interests. He also crushed all opposition, closing universities, high schools, and labor unions and arresting anyone he viewed as a threat. He took a very hard line in dealing with the independence movement in Eritrea, refusing to negotiate with the Eritreans on the grounds that any concessions would lead to dismemberment of Ethiopia. Whereas Aman Andom, three days before his death, had refused to send an additional 5,000 troops into Eritrea, in May 1978, Mariam ordered 20,000 Ethiopian troops into the region, capturing the capital of Asmara. By November, Keren, the principal rebel garrison, had been taken, but Mariam was unable to crush the rebels once and for all.

After a September 1976 assassination attempt in which he was wounded, Mariam ordered a crackdown on the Ethiopian People's Revolutionary Party, executing members on sight in the streets of the capital city of Addis Ababa. The Dergue, fearing a complete takeover by Mariam, limited his powers and promoted Banti in January 1975. In response, on February 3, Mariam had Banti and six others executed. Eight days later, what was left of the Dergue named Mariam head of state and commander-in-chief of the armed forces.

Mariam then launched a campaign of terror, in which hundreds were arrested, interrogated, tortured, and executed—their remains subjected to public display.

In February 1977, after U.S. president Jimmy Carter withdrew $6 million in foreign aid, Mariam ordered the expulsion of all Americans from Ethiopia and turned to the Soviet Union, from whom he received $100 million in aid.

Despite Mariam's cruelty, the Socialist programs brought positive results in increased agricultural production and a higher literacy rate. Ethiopia remains one of the poorest countries in the world, but, for those who have survived, life is better than it had been under the stagnant and corrupt Selassie regime.

Mary I   [Bloody Mary] (1516–1558)

Successor to Edward VI, Mary I ruled England from 1553 to 1558, earning the epithet Bloody Mary for the mass execution of some 300 Protestants that occured during her reign.

Born on February 18, 1516, Mary Tudor was the daughter of King HENRY VIII and his first wife, Catherine of Aragón. Concerned because Catherine had failed to bear him a male heir, Henry sought divorce from her so that he might marry Anne Boleyn. At first, Pope Clement VII was inclined to grant the divorce, but political considerations prompted him to change his mind, and in 1529, Henry began the process by which the Church of England was formed and its ties to the Roman Catholic Church severed. The divorce came in 1533, and the break with Rome the following year.

Mary now found herself, in effect, the unwanted "issue" of a union Henry had declared null, void, and illegal. She was treated harshly and compelled at last to proclaim her concurrence in the illegality of her parents' union and to renounce her Catholicism. The latter she did publicly, while secretly maintaining her Catholic faith through the balance of her father's reign and that of her sickly and short-lived half-brother, Edward VI (1547–53).

Although Henry VIII had declared Mary illegitimate, his will named her as second in succession to the throne, after her half-brother Edward. However, on the death of Edward VI, John Dudley, earl of Warwick and duke of Northumberland, staged an insurrection during July 6–19, 1553, in an effort to place his daughter-in-law, Lady Jane Grey, on the throne in place of the rightful heir, Mary. Although Jane Grey reigned for nine days, most of England rallied to Mary's cause, Northumberland was arrested, and Jane Grey was executed.

Soon after her coronation, Mary set about undoing the Protestant reformation her father had begun. She officially restored Catholicism, together with the traditional holy services and the authority of the pope. She made a marriage in 1554 to PHILIP II of Spain, son of Holy Roman Emperor CHARLES V. The marriage greatly increased English political and religious unrest, further alienating the nation's Protestants, but also dividing English Catholics, many of whom deeply distrusted the Catholics of Spain. Sir Thomas Wyatt, Sir Thomas Carew, and the duke of Suffolk organized a rebellion in Kent and marched on London. There the insurrection collapsed, and the leaders were executed. The union between Mary and Philip also embroiled England in Spain's ongoing wars with France. Not only were these conflicts wholly unpopular with the English people, a French siege of January 2–7, 1558, resulted in the fall of Calais, England's last possession on the European continent.

From roughly 1555 until the death of "Bloody Mary" ended her reign in 1558, some 300 Protestants were publicly executed—by burning at the stake—for heretical beliefs. Many hundreds of others fled or were sent into European exile.

Mary I died childless on November 17, 1558, and was succeeded by her half-sister, ELIZABETH I.

Further Reading: Carolly Erickson, *Bloody Mary* (Garden City, N.Y.: Doubleday, 1978); D. M. Loades. *The Reign of Mary Tudor* (Oxford and Cambridge, Mass.: Basil Blackwell, 1989).

Maximilian   (1832–1867)

Maximilian was installed by French emperor NAPOLÉON III as emperor of Mexico, only to be overthrown and executed by the resurgent republican forces of Benito JUÁREZ.

Born on July 6, 1832, in Vienna, Ferdinand Maximilian Joseph was the younger brother of Emperor FRANCIS JOSEPH I of Austria. Titled archduke, he was a rear admiral in the Austrian navy and served as governor-general of the empire's Lombardo-Venetian kingdom.

Napoleon III's France and other European powers had loaned Mexico large sums and had substantial business interests there. These nations became concerned about the soundness of the Mexican economy following the revolution that made Benito Juárez president. In 1863, Napoléon III schemed with conservative Mexican interests to oust the republican government and replace it with a monarchy. Maximilian accepted the offer of the throne, having been told—falsely—that the Mexican people had *elected* him emperor.

Maximilian journeyed to Mexico accompanied by his wife, Carlota, daughter of Leopold I of Belgium. He was crowned on June 10, 1864, and immediately shocked his European and conservative Mexican supporters by upholding and continuing the extensive social reforms Juárez had introduced. He even replenished the nation's barren treasury from his own inheritance.

Unfortunately for Maximilian, the United States invoked the Monroe Doctrine in 1865, demanding the removal from Mexican soil of the French troops whose presence was clearly necessary to maintain Maximilian's government. Carlota traveled to Europe, seeking support from Napoléon III and from Pope Pius IX, but she was rebuffed by aristocrats who wanted no part of Maximilian's liberalism. Carlota suffered a total nervous collapse.

In the meantime, in 1867, Napoléon III yielded to American pressure and removed his troops, whereupon Juárez and his army advanced on Mexico City, demanding that Maximilian step down. The emperor refused to abdicate, however, and led a small counterforce against Juárez.

There was no real battle. Instead, Maximilian and his small army were surrounded and starved into surrender on May 15, 1867, at Querétaro. Many of Europe's most distinguished liberals took pity on what they saw as the plight of a naive, misguided, but well-meaning emperor and petitioned Juárez to spare Maximilian's life. But, despite protests from the likes of Victor Hugo and Giuseppe Garibaldi, he was executed on June 19, 1867.

Maximilian I   (1459–1519)

Maximilian I added vast holdings to his family's Austrian realm, making the Hapsburgs the dominant family in 16th-century Europe. However, he fell far short of his major goal, which was to unite western Europe under himself as a kind of second Charlemagne.

An engraving of Maximilian I after a painting by Peter Paul Rubens. (From Charlotte M. Yonge, Pictorial History of the World's Great Nations, *1882)*

Maximilian I was born on March 22, 1459, in Wiener Neustadt, Austria, the son of Emperor Frederick III and his wife, Eleanor of Portugal. In 1477 he married Mary, the daughter of the duke of Burgundy, Charles the Bold, thereby acquiring Burgundy's possessions in the Netherlands along the border of France. When the French king LOUIS XI attempted to seize these domains, Maximilian defeated him at the Battle of Guinegate in 1479. However, following Mary's death in 1482, Maximilian had to concede the power of regency over the Netherlandish domains, which were inherited by his infant son Philip, to the States General of the Netherlands. In 1485, Maximilian prevailed against the States General and regained the regency for himself.

In 1486, Maximilian was elected king of the Romans, and from this position, in alliance with Spain, England, and Brittany, he prosecuted a war against France and rebellious elements in the Netherlands. In 1490, Maximilian married Anne of Brittany by proxy in a diplomatic attempt to surround France. However, Charles VIII of France, who had been betrothed to Maximilian's daughter Margaret of Austria, sent Margaret back to her father and ordered Anne to annul her marriage with Maximilian in order to return to France as queen. Thus thwarted in regard to France, Maximilian did obtain title to the Tyrol and made Innsbruck the center of his operations.

During this period, Maximilian also regained most of the Hapsburgs' Austrian possessions that had earlier been taken by Hungary, and by 1490 was a candidate for the Hungarian throne. However, Vladislav II of Bohemia won election to the throne instead, and Maximilian responded by waging war against him. Hostilities were ended in 1491 by the Treaty of Pressburg, which specified that the thrones of both Bohemia and Hungary would devolve upon the Hapsburgs if Vladislav failed to produce a male heir. Three years after this, in 1493, the Treaty of Senlis ended hostilities with France and the Netherlands, yielding to the Hapsburgs the duchy of Burgundy and the Low Countries.

Frederick II died in 1493, leaving Maximilian head of the Hapsburg family and sole ruler of its lands. He turned immediately to evicting the Turks from the southeastern frontier region, and in 1494 married Bianca Maria of the powerful Milanese Sforza family. Maximilian's son Philip was at last entrusted with the Netherlands, though Maximilian held the right of joint rule. The same year, CHARLES VIII invaded Italy. Maximilian responded in 1495 by forming the Holy League—consisting of Austria, Spain, Venice, Milan, and the Papal States—to evict France from Italy, which was accomplished in 1496. Maximilian also maneuvered on the diplomatic front during this time, marrying his son Philip to the daughter of FERDINAND and ISABELLA of Spain, Joan the Mad. He also arranged a marriage between his daughter Margaret and the Spanish crown prince. These unions resulted in Hapsburg succession in Spain as well as its dominions in Italy and the New World.

At home, Maximilian sought to create laws that would further strengthen his imperial authority. However, he was consistently blocked by the German princes, who did not want to cede so much of their power to a central government and sovereign. Maximilian responded to the opposition by establishing his own judicial and financial commissions outside of what the Reichstag had authorized.

In 1499, the emperor suffered another setback when his war against the Swiss Confederation failed. In the same year, the French returned to Italy, this time with the cooperation of Spain, and occupied Maximilian's imperial fief of Milan. In 1500, the Reichstag undermined Maximilian by investing the Reichsregiment, a council of 21 electors, princes, and other nobles, with some of the power that had been his prerogative. Indeed, Maximilian seemed on the verge of being deposed. However, he came to terms with France and prevailed in a dynastic conflict between Bavaria and the Rhenish Palatinate in 1504, thereby greatly raising his stock within the German empire. One of those most eager to see him go, Berthold of Mainz, died at this time, and Maximilian was also able to conclude favorable credit arrangements with powerful German business concerns that assured him of a dependable source of funds. In 1506 he successfully campaigned in Hungary, solidifying Hapsburg claims there.

Maximilian was frustrated, however, in 1508, when Venice refused him entry into Italy, thereby preventing his traveling to Rome, where he was to be crowned Holy Roman Emperor by Pope Julius II. Holding, then, only the title of Roman emperor elect, he formed the League of Cambrai among Austria, France, Spain, and the papacy in 1508 to oppose and ultimately partition Venice. The resulting war failed to achieve its purpose. At this point, Pope Julius fell ill, and the schismatic Council of Pisa offered Maximilian election as a rival pope. Tempted, Maximilian nevertheless declined.

In 1511 he formed a new Holy League among Austria, Spain, England, and the papacy. He prevailed with his English allies against the French in 1513 at the Battle of the Spurs, but was unsuccessful in recovering Milan. The 1515 Treaty of Brussels apportioned Milan to the French and Verona to the Venetians, leaving Maximilian with the Tyrol and lands immediately adjacent to it.

Undaunted, the emperor turned east, constructing complex alliances with Russia, Poland, Bohemia, and Hungary that enabled him to expand eastward. Despite various frustrations, by this time the Hapsburgs dominated central Europe and the Iberian Peninsula.

Maximilian died at Wels, Upper Austria, on January 12, 1519, while he was in the process of forming a coalition to oppose the Turks. A powerful monarch, skilled diplomat, and talented military commander, he had greatly expanded his family's sphere of influence, but he had fallen far short of his goal of uniting all of western Europe under the house of Hapsburg in a virtual revival of the Empire of the West under CHARLEMAGNE. Autocratic and ambitious, Maximilian was nevertheless progressive in his enthusiasm for science and literature. He also introduced military and administrative reforms, though his economic policies did little to help his empire.

Further Reading: Marian Andrews. *Maximilian the Dreamer, Holy Roman Emperor, 1459–1519* (New York: Scribner's, 1913).

Maximilian II Emanuel (1662–1726)

General and governor of the Spanish Netherlands, Maximilian thirsted for a kingdom of his own, but his opposition to the Hapsburgs cost him his opportunity.

The son of the elector of Bavaria, Ferdinand Maria, Maximilian Emanuel was born July 11, 1662, and succeeded his father as elector in 1679. From an early age, Maximilian had ambitions to ascend one of the European thrones, although he was not particular as to which one. In 1683, he joined Austria in its war with the Ottoman Empire and rescued Belgrade from the Turks, making his reputation as a general.

When the War of the League of Augsburg broke out in 1689, Maximilian aligned himself with the Austrian Hapsburgs and the rest of western and central Europe against LOUIS XIV of France. Upon his marriage to the Archduchess Maria Antonia, daughter of Leopold I of Austria, in 1685, it was hinted that a hereditary title might be arranged for Maximilian. As a reward for his support of the war effort against Louis, William III of Orange appointed Maximilian governor of the Spanish Netherlands in December 1691. It was a position that carried little absolute power and was not hereditary.

Because he was the son-in-law of the emperor, Maximilian had a small claim to the Austrian throne, which was somewhat enhanced when Maria bore him a son, Joseph Ferdinand. Maximilian's efforts to attain hereditary power were dashed, however, when Joseph Ferdinand, sole heir to the Spanish Hapsburg lands, died in February 1699. Now the Spanish crown was exclusively contended for by France and Austria. It was true that a clause in the Partition Treaty ending the War of the League of Augsburg named Maximilian successor to his son; however, Louis XIV contended that Maximilian could only succeed his son's accomplishments, not his unfulfilled expectations. In other words, since Joseph Ferdinand never assumed the throne, the clause was invalid.

The succession question remained unanswered by 1701, and the War of the Spanish Succession was forced when the contending parties could not agree on an acceptable candidate. Perhaps angry that the Hapsburgs did not support his claims in Spain, Maximilian aligned himself with Louis in March 1701, surrendering his position in the Spanish Netherlands in return for support of his candidacy for emperor.

Maximilian returned to Bavaria and gathered a force of 15,000 men. But the war did not go well for Louis, who was defeated at the decisive Battle of Blenheim in August 1704, a defeat that also drove Maximilian from Bavaria back to the Netherlands.

When the French were again defeated at Ramillies in May 1706, Maximilian was driven from the Netherlands and was, indeed, left with no place to go. He was officially banned from the empire and dispossessed of his lands. After a final stand at the siege of Lille in late 1709, Maximilian and the French were unable to hold off the Allies, and the citadel fell on December 9.

Maximilian became a refugee at the French court until 1713, when the Peace of Utrecht restored him to Bavaria. He never was able to obtain a throne, however, and died on February 26, 1726.

Maximinus [Gaius Julius Verus Maximinus] (r. 235–238)

The first Roman emperor to rise from the ranks of the common soldier, Maximinus and his reign inaugurated nearly a half century of civil war and crisis in the empire.

The son of a Goth peasant, Maximinus apparently was a shepherd before enlisting in the Roman army. Because of his immense size and strength, he moved up rapidly through the ranks, commanding a legion in Egypt in 232 and then receiving an appointment as governor of Mesopotamia. In 235, he was in command of a group of recruits who rose up and slew Emperor Severus Alexander, proclaiming Maximinus Roman emperor—the first emperor to come from the enlisted ranks of the Roman legions.

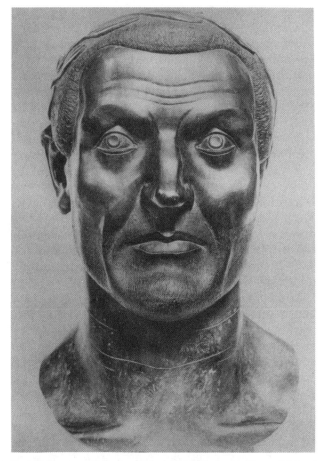

Portrait bust of Galerius Valerius Maximinus. (From Richard Delbruck, Antike Portrats, *1912)*

The Senate, perceiving that it had no other choice, reluctantly confirmed his elevation. Maximinus' first priority was to quell two internal revolts within the army, which threatened to install a new emperor. Maximinus proceeded ruthlessly and swiftly, crushing the incipient rebellions before they could come to fruition and summarily executing all parties involved. To forestall further plotting, the new emperor removed all officers who held senatorial rank and replaced them with professional soldiers, whom he personally promoted.

Assured of a loyal army, Maximinus began his conquest of the outlying frontier areas. Crossing the Rhine, he subdued Germany and then moved along the Danube, crushing the Sarmatians and the Dacians. When Gordianus, governor of Africa, and his son staged a revolt in the spring of 238, they received the support of most of the empire, including the Senate. Undaunted, Maximinus advanced on the Gordians and defeated them in 20 days. The Senate, likewise undaunted, defied Maximinus by naming Balbinus and Pupienus co-emperors.

At length, a relentless schedule of campaigning combined with senatorial sniping and a general lack of support from the empire began to take its toll on Maximinus. Army morale flagged as food shortages became commonplace and the discipline imposed by Maximinus became increasingly harsh. The army that had elevated him, sustained him in power, and on whom he relied absolutely rose up in mutiny. Maximinus was murdered in his sleep on May 10, 238. As emperor, he had never even had the opportunity to visit Rome.

Further Reading: Michael Grant. *Roman Emperors* (New York: Scribner's, 1985).

Maximinus [Galerius Valerius Maximinus] (r. 310–313)

A brutal persecutor of the Christians, Maximinus was one of two men to rule the Roman Empire following the dual abdication of Maximian and DI-OCLETIAN.

Apparently living as a shepherd early in his life, Maximinus joined the army and advanced rapidly with the help of his mother, who was GALERIUS' sister. Galerius adopted Maximinus as his own son and appointed him military tribune. When the co-emperors Maximian and Diocletian abdicated on May 1, 305, Galerius became emperor of the East and named Maximinus as caesar.

Maximinus zealously continued Diocletian's policy of ruthlessly persecuting the Christians. In 306, he issued his first edict, demanding that every man, woman, and child participate in a sacrifice of the Christians to the pagan gods. In 309, he ordered another mass sacrifice, claiming that all citizens should partake of the flesh of the sacrificed Christians.

In 308, Maximinus was disappointed to learn that Galerius had named Licinius as his heir rather than himself. But Maximinus' troops remained loyal, declaring Maximinus heir. Shortly before he died, Galerius bowed to military pressure and appointed both Maximinus and Licinius co-rulers. The two prepared for a fight. In the meantime, Constantine, caesar in the West, ordered Maximinus to halt his persecution of the Christians.

After a brutal march through the snows of Thrace, Maximinus met Licinius in battle. Maximinus enjoyed a two-to-one advantage, but was nevertheless defeated. He died in retreat in 313.

Further Reading: Michael Grant. *Roman Emperors* (New York: Scribner's, 1985).

Medici, Cosimo de' [Cosimo the Elder; Pater Patriae] (1389–1464)

Called Pater Patriae ("Father of His Country") by his fellow Florentines, Cosimo de' Medici was the patriarch of the most important branch of the powerful Medici family and established Medici rule in Florence from 1434 to 1537.

Cosimo de' Medici was born on December 27, 1389, in Florence, the son of Giovanni di Bicci. He was bred to the sophisticated world of Florentine high finance, becoming the representative of the Medici bank at the Council of Constance. As others commanded great armies of soldiers, Cosimo de' Medici marshaled vast sums of money and soon was called upon to manage the finances of the papacy. In 1462 Pope Pius II conferred upon him a monopoly on the Tolfa alum mines, the production of which was vital to the Florentine textile industry. Already rich, Cosimo quickly became the wealthiest man in Europe, controlling tremendous cash resources and holding notes of credit from the most prominent political and financial figures on the Continent.

Cosimo was the target of much fear and resentment, particularly among the aristocratic and oligarchic elements of the Florentine government. He made himself obnoxious to them on account of his advocacy of various "popular" policies. Finally, in 1431, the rival Albizzi family arranged to indict Cosimo on charges of having "sought to elevate himself higher than others"—a capital offense. Instead of fleeing, Cosimo decided to face the charges and was for a time imprisoned in the Palazzo Vecchio. Realizing that the Albizzi intended to assassinate him, Cosimo arranged for a lavish bribe to be given his jailer, who tasted all food served to Cosimo. Then Cosimo bribed the gonfalonier (chief magistrate) with a vast amount of gold to commute his death sentence to banishment. Released from the Palazzo Vecchio, Cosimo moved to Padua and then Venice, where he was fêted and hailed as royalty.

From his pleasant exile, Cosimo successfully manipulated the Florentine elections, fixing them so that the Signoria—the government council—was returned to Medici control. In 1434, Cosimo de' Medici journeyed back to Florence, which now received him joyously, and it was his enemies' turn to experience exile.

For the next century, from the year 1434 until 1537, Florence was ruled by the Medici. Popular history pictures Cosimo and the other Medici who succeeded him as absolute tyrants, who robbed Florentines of the liberties they had enjoyed under the Albizzi. It is true that Cosimo was a dictator, but, then, the Albizzi had been tyrannical as well—although they operated under the guise of a constitution. Cosimo de' Medici was simply more frank—perhaps more brazen—in the application of tyranny. Whereas, in the past, many official positions were filled by lottery, Cosimo arranged that only his handpicked men would be chosen. Dictatorial powers were always available to those who administered Florence, though it was understood that such powers were to be exercised only under extraordinary circumstances. Cosimo made the dictatorship routine, while still preserving the convention of a constitutional republic. Nor did he rely on manipulation of the law alone to secure his power. By paying the powerful Sforzas of Milan, he put at his disposal a substantial body of troops to provide the muscle necessary to scotch incipient rebellion. In August 1458 came the boldest step of all, the creation of a hundred-member senate composed entirely of retainers loyal to the Medici—the so-called Cento.

While Cosimo's rule was a study in government through self-interest and high-handed manipulation, it is undeniable that the Medici brought Florence to the height of political influence, economic power, and cultural sophistication. He and his family patronized some of the greatest artists of the Italian Renaissance, including Ghiberti, Donatello, Castagno, Fra Angelico, and others. He attracted great scholars to Florence and amassed one of Europe's most important libraries, today called the Laurentian after his grandson. An admirer of Plato, Cosimo actually recreated the philosopher's celebrated academy in his villa of Careggi, reviving the teaching of classical Greece for the first time in seven centuries. Paradoxically, then, this tyrant of finance and government fostered much that is most characteristic of Italian humanism and the Italian Renaissance.

Further Reading: K. Dorothea Ewart. *Cosimo de' Medici* (Port Washington, N.Y.: Kennikat, 1970); Janet Ann Ross. *Lives of the Early Medici* (London: Chatto & Windus, 1910).

Medici, Lorenzo de' [Lorenzo the Magnificent] (1449–1492)

The most celebrated of the Medici, Lorenzo the Magnificent was the very model of the benevolent despot, an absolute autocrat who had the welfare of his people at heart.

Lorenzo de' Medici was born on January 1, 1449, in Florence, the son of Piero de' Medici and the grandson of COSIMO DE' MEDICI, hailed by Florentines as the "father of his country." Beginning in 1469, Lorenzo ruled Florence with his brother Giuliano. Like the Medici before them, Lorenzo and Giuliano pledged allegiance to the Florentine constitution, but, also like them, ruled in fact as absolute autocrats. The tyranny of Lorenzo de' Medici was not, however, harsh, and he imposed upon Florentines anything but austerity. Under Lorenzo, Florence was a city of festivals, balls, ritual games, magnificent art, literature, and scholarship.

In 1478, the Pazzi family, rivals of the Medici, managed to take control of the papacy's finances away from the Medici. Moreover, the Pazzi conspired with Pope SIXTUS IV, his nephew Riario, and Francesco Salviati, archbishop of Pisa, to assassinate Lorenzo and Giuliano in the cathedral as they were attending Easter Mass on April 26. After the Medici were eliminated, Salviati planned to take over the Signoria, or council of government.

The assassination scheme was partly successful. Giuliano was slain, but Lorenzo escaped. Archbishop Salviati then attacked the Medici gonfalonier or city magistrate, who summarily caused him to be hanged from a window of the Palazzo Vecchio—still clad in his episcopal vestments. The people of Florence rallied to the Medici, seizing the remaining conspirators, whom they literally tore limb from limb.

Pope Sixtus IV responded not by publicly condemning the murder of Giuliano Medici, but by commanding the Florentines to deliver Lorenzo to him for having caused the death of the archbishop. Since the papacy was backed by the tyrannical king of Naples, Ferdinand I, who commanded a powerful army, Sixtus posed a grave threat to Florence. Still, the city and the Florentine clergy refused to hand Lorenzo over. Concerned for the safety of Florence and its citizens loyal to him, Lorenzo journeyed to Naples to call upon Ferdinand. In doing this, he certainly jeopardized his life, but the bold gamble paid off. Ferdinand was persuaded to come to terms with Florence, and the pope, therefore, had no choice but to back down.

The episode raised Lorenzo's popularity to unprecedented heights. Had he chosen to do so, Lorenzo de' Medici could have made himself a monarch, wielding over Florence a more traditional and absolute control. Instead, he moved merely to strengthen his hold upon Florence through quasi-constitutional means, including the dissolution of the old Cento—a kind of senate packed with pro-Medici representatives—and its replacement by the Council of Seventy, an even more pliable set of Medici partisans.

After the events of 1478, Lorenzo did adopt an increasingly regal style of life, marrying into the noble Orsini family and building the palatial villa at Poggio a Caiano. Like other Medici, Lorenzo gathered about him great poets and painters—though his coterie outshone even that of his grandfather. Pico della Mirandola, Botticelli, Verrocchio, Leonardo da Vinci, and Michelangelo all enjoyed Lorenzo's patronage. Lorenzo also sponsored another luminary, the Dominican friar Girolamo Savanarola, who ascended the pulpit of San Marco on August 1, 1490, and preached a doctrine of ascetic reform, condemning the papacy, modern Christianity—and, most vehemently, the Medici. Savonarola predicted the death of Lorenzo (who, in any case, was ailing at this time) and found a sympathetic ear in Florentines at last weary of ceaseless celebration, festivity, and general extravagance. Yet, when Lorenzo did die, on April 9, 1492, aged 43, the entire population of Florence turned out to attend his funeral.

Further Reading: Cecilia Mary. *Lorenzo de' Medici and Renaissance Italy* (New York: Macmillan, 1952).

Mehmed I   (r. 1413–21; d. 1421)

The fifth sultan of the Ottoman Empire, Mehmed I killed his brothers, took control of their territories, and reunited the empire after a long period of discord.

The son of BAYEZID I, Mehmed was one of three brothers among whom the Ottoman Empire was divided upon the death of their father. Suleyman ruled in Rumelia, while Mehmed had control of Amasya, and Isa ruled in Bursa. Mehmed first defeated and killed Isa and took control of Bursa (1404–1405). He then enlisted the aid of a fourth brother, Musa, and sent him to fight Suleyman. After defeating Suleyman in 1410, Musa declared himself sultan in Edirne, but his rule was short-lived. Aided by the Byzantine emperor Manuel II Palaeologus, Mehmed defeated Musa at Camurle, Serbia, in 1413, and claimed for himself the title of sultan of Anatolia and Rumelia, establishing his capital at Edirne.

Having regained control of the territory that had been divided at his father's death, Mehmed concentrated on expanding his holdings in the Balkans. He conquered most of Albania in 1415, made vassals of Wallachia in southern Romania in 1416 and the Byzantine state in 1417, then raided Hungary. In these conquered regions, Mehmed settled the nomadic Turkmen, thereby reducing the threat posed by their rebelliousness in Anatolia while strengthening his grip on the Balkans.

While Mehmed's military campaigns on land were generally successful, his navy failed him. In 1415 or 1416, the Venetian navy defeated the small Ottoman fleet, and Mehmed never gained control of the Venetian islands in the Aegean Sea.

In Anatolia, Mehmed defeated a coalition of Turkish princes who conspired to dethrone him in 1418. He also suppressed a religious revolt by a mystic order led by Sheik Bedruddin and neutralized the claims of Mustafa, who claimed to be a fifth son of Bayezid. When Mehmed died on May 26, 1421, in Edirne, he was succeeded by his son Murad II.

Further Reading: John W. Barker. *Manuel II Palaeologus, 1391–1425* (New Brunswick, N.J.: Rutgers University Press, 1969).

Meiji   [Mutsuhito] (1852–1912)

Meiji, one of the most beloved and successful emperors in Japanese history, brought Japan into the industrial age and opened it to Western culture.

Born into the imperial family on November 3, 1852, in Kyoto, Mutsuhito was the second son of the emperor Komei. Upon his designation as heir in July 1860, he took the name Meiji and in December 1866 ascended to the Japanese imperial throne, being formally crowned on January 9, 1867.

In January of 1868, the forces opposed to the Tokugawa military regime overthrew Yoshinobu Tokugawa, the last shogun of Japan. This restored supreme political authority to the emperor, ending almost a thousand years of feudal military control of Japan. In stark contrast to his father, Meiji favored introducing Western practices to Japan. He issued the Charter Oath on April 6, 1868, which underscored his commitment to modernization. He moved the court from the former capital of Kyoto to Edo, which was renamed Tokyo, "Eastern Capital."

Emperor Meiji's government replaced the autonomous provincial rulers in 1871 with centralized prefectural governments that reported directly to Tokyo. In 1872, the Meiji government revised the ancient feudal land policies, giving greater mobility to the peasants, and in 1873 it mandated national education and military conscription. It alleviated much of the social stress that accompanied Japan's rigorous social class system by banning the samurai class and lifting many restrictions, including job restrictions and caste regulations. The Meiji government consolidated its power by forcefully and effectively suppressing local rebellions over the next three years.

Japan's status in the international community was raised when the imperial government was changed to a constitutional monarchy—though it maintained the divine right and inviolability of the crown. The Meiji government also successfully prosecuted the Sino-Japanese War in 1894–95 and the Russo-Japanese War in 1904–05, annexed Korea and Taiwan and maintained tight control over Manchuria.

The Meiji government built much of the modern Japanese state. The emperor himself, although largely a figurehead, through his assent to the government's programs helped to insure their success. Well loved, he showed genuine concern for his subjects—a quality that served to minimize formal opposition to the many reforms of his government. When news of his illness was announced in 1912, thousands gathered outside the imperial palace to pray for him. He died on July 30 of that year.

Further Reading: Nobutaka Ike. *The Beginnings of Political Democracy in Japan* (Baltimore: Johns Hopkins University Press, 1950); Marius B. Jansen. *Sakatomo Ryoma and the Meiji Restoration* (Princeton: Princeton University Press, 1961).

Mejía Victores, Oscar Humberto (b. 1930–)

Like so many anti-Communist Central American military dictators, Guatemala's Mejía Victores seized power in a coup, backed financially and diplomatically by the United States.

After joining the army at the age of 18, Mejía Victores took special military courses in the U.S. Canal Zone in 1955. There he was influenced by the conservative foreign policies of the Eisenhower administration and his abilities were noted by his American instructors. In 1960, he attended the Superior Military School in Mexico City, where he fared equally well.

By June 1980, Mejía Victores had achieved the rank of brigadier general, but more importantly, he was now involved in the politics as well as the defense of Guatemala. After commanding the General Justo Rafino Barrios Military Zone in Guatemala City, he was subsequently appointed inspector general of the army and then vice-minister of defense. In March 1982, General Efrain José RÍOS MONTT led a group of young army officers, including Mejía Victores, in a coup against Guatemalan president Anibal Guevara.

Rios Montt named Mejía Victores minister of defense, essentially giving him complete control of a military that was totally loyal to him. When it appeared that Ríos Montt was not moving fast enough toward economic stability or cracking down hard enough on leftist guerrillas, Mejía Victores staged his own coup on August 8, 1983. Recognizing Mejía Victores as an anti-Communist ally, the Reagan administration in the United States sent millions of dollars in both economic and military support of the Guatemalan coup. With this aid, Mejía Victores made his coup a success.

Mejía Victores actively pursued the extermination of leftist guerrillas and was adamant in his opposition to the Communist tendencies of neighboring Nicaragua. The dictator's right-wing zeal led to serious human rights violations that undermined his regime's relationship with the United States. Unwilling to overlook the mounting violations of civil liberties in Guatemala, Congress cut off some $63 million in foreign aid.

Short of funds and facing mounting pressures from both inside and outside the country, Mejía Victores finally called for general elections in November 1985. After a runoff in December, the dictator was forced out of office, and Marco Vinicio Cerezo Arévalo became the first civilian Guatemalan president in two decades.

Further Reading: Georges A. Fauriol, and Eva Loser. *Guatemala's Political Puzzle* (New Brunswick, New Jersey: Transaction Publishers, 1988); James Painter. *Guatemala: False Hope, False Freedom* (London: Latin American Bureau, updated ed. 1989).

Menelik II (1844–1913)

Ethiopian Emperor Menelik II doubled the size of his country through territorial conquests and defeated a European army in one of the greatest battles in African history.

The son of Shewa king Haile Malakot, Menelik II was born on August 17, 1844, in Ankober, Shewa, a semiautonomous province of the Ethiopian empire, and was given the name Sahle Miriam. When his father was killed during the 1855 invasion of Shewa by imperial forces, Sahle Miriam was taken captive by Ethiopian emperor Tewodros II. In 1865, Sahle Miriam escaped and returned to Shewa. Only 21 years old, he ousted the Shewa ruler Bezebeh and declared himself *negus* (king) of the province.

Under the nominal control of two more emperors, Sahle Miriam increased his hold on Shewa and undertook territorial expansion on behalf of the crown. When Emperor Yohannes IV died in 1889, Sahle Miriam, the most powerful man in the country, assumed the imperial crown and took the name Menelik II.

In 1889, Menelik II signed the Treaty of Uccialli with Italy. The Italians drew up two versions of the treaty, one Italian and one Amharic. The former made Ethiopia an Italian protectorate. Menelik II vehemently opposed the duplicitous treaty and renounced the pact. In the Battle of Adowa on March 1, 1896, Menelik II's forces overpowered the Italian army in one of the greatest battles in African history. Subsequently, Ethiopia retained full sovereignty, and Menelik II's control over the country was never threatened.

In 1906 or 1907, Menelik II suffered a series of paralytic strokes. Power was held by his wife and a regent before devolving on his grandson, Lij Iyasu. Menelik II died on December 12, 1913, in the Ethiopian capital he founded, Addis Ababa.

Further Reading: Harold Marcus. *The Life and Times of Menelik II: Ethiopia 1844–1913* (Oxford: Clarendon Press, 1975).

Metaxas, Ioannis (1871–1941)

A strong monarchist and nationalist, Metaxas became premier of Greece and ruled as a dictator.

Born in Ithaca, Greece, on April 12, 1871, Ioannis Metaxas entered the Greek military and fought in the Greco-Turkish War of 1897. After the war, he went to Germany to receive a military education. He was named to the general staff during the Balkan Wars of 1912–13, becoming chief of staff in 1913. By 1916 he was made general.

At the outbreak of World War I, Metaxas was a close adviser to King Constantine I, but his open advocacy of Greek neutrality brought him into conflict with the premier, Eleutherios Venizelos. Metaxas was constantly at odds with Venizelos' military policies and resigned when Constantine abdicated in 1917. When Constantine was restored to the throne in 1920, Metaxas returned with him and again opposed Venizelos. He correctly predicted the disaster that befell the Greek offensive into Anatolia during 1921–22.

When Constantine's son George II was forced to abdicate in 1923, Metaxas again left the country, but returned shortly to become a ministry-level official in the new republic. He founded a small royalist party during this time and used it as a mouthpiece for opposition to the very government he was serving. When George II was restored in 1935, Metaxas was named minister of war and then, in April 1936, premier.

With royal authority, Metaxas imposed a dictatorship on August 4, 1936, initially on the Fascist model, though he maintained diplomatic ties with both Britain and France. Metaxas was successful in carrying out limited, though much-needed economic and social reform, but he brutally suppressed all opposition.

When Italy invaded Greece in 1940, Metaxas' ties to the West proved beneficial, as Greece received aid from England and was able to drive the Italians back to the Albanian border. Metaxas died on January 21, 1941, three months before the Nazi invasion of his country.

Milan IV   [Milan Obrenovic] (1854–1901)

Milan IV ruled Serbia as prince from 1868 until 1882, and as king from 1882 until 1889, when he abdicated.

On June 10, 1868, while strolling in a park near Belgrade, Michael Obrenovic, the prince of Serbia, was assassinated by a person or persons who have never been identified. Milan Obrenovic, a 13-year-old cousin of the deceased ruler, was chosen to succeed him. Born in Marasesti, Moldavia, on August 22, 1854, Milan was subject to a regency until he attained his majority. When he took control of the government in August 1872, however, Milan IV

showed little interest, desire, or ability to rule his people. He attempted to keep Serbia neutral when Bosnia-Hercegovina rose up against its Ottoman rulers in 1875, but, bowing to political pressure, he finally went to war with the Turks—and lost. The Russian victory in the Russo-Turkish War of 1877–78 is all that saved him and Serbia from total destruction at the hands of the Turks.

Milan IV declared Serbia a kingdom in 1882 and became its first king. He abdicated in favor of his son, Alexander, in March 1889, and left the country, returning briefly in 1897 as military commander in chief. Despite the beneficial reforms he instituted in the army, Milan was unpopular. After disputing with his son over the latter's choice of a wife, Milan IV went into permanent exile in 1900. He died in Vienna on February 11, 1901.

Further Reading: H. C. Darby, R. W. Seton-Watson, et al. *A Short History of Yugoslavia* (Cambridge: Cambridge University Press, 1966).

Minh Duong Van   *See* DUONG VAN MINH

Minh Mang   [Chi Dam] (1792–1841)

Minh Mang, emperor of Vietnam, became infamous for his persecution of Christian missionaries.

Born Chi Dam to Emperor Gia Long on May 24, 1792, Minh Mang was the fourth son of the emperor, but was chosen as his successor because of his demonstrated intense dislike for Europeans. He took the name Minh Mang on his accession in 1820.

Minh Mang was a strict Confucian, and that dominated his policies more than any other single factor. He believed that all other religions, including Buddhism and Taoism, but especially Christianity, undermined the basic principles of Vietnamese cultural, political, and theological life. More directly, he saw non-Confucian belief as a direct threat to the emperor's divinity and to the absolute necessity of obeying the emperor.

Minh Mang's contempt for foreigners was exhibited early when he sent a personal letter to Louis XVIII of France stating in no uncertain terms that he would allow no commerce between France and Vietnam. He also refused to establish an office in his government to deal with foreign affairs, calling Europeans "barbarians" and declaring them unworthy of the attention of his government. In an attempt to control the French Catholic missionaries that abounded in southern Vietnam, Mang called them to the capital city of Hue, claiming that he needed interpreters. When new missionaries continued to arrive, however, and refused to confine themselves to Hue, Minh Mang barred the entry of all missionaries in 1825. After a revolt led by Le Van Khoi in 1833, Minh Mang suspected Catholic complicity (which was later verified), and outlawed the teaching of Christianity in any form within the country. He imprisoned all priests, not just the French, but all Catholics. Several missionaries escaped, but one, Reverend François Gagelin, was captured and brought to Hue, shackled like an animal. He was tried for "preaching the religion of Jesus" and executed by strangulation in October 1833. Over the next seven years, Mang would execute 10 more missionaries with similar cruelty.

Minh Mang did little to improve the lot of his people. He undertook no public works programs and produced no social or land reform. His support began to erode as he continued to alienate foreigners, and by the time of his death in January 1841, he had good reason to doubt the loyalty of his own people. His persecution of the Christians was a direct cause of the French invasion of Vietnam in 1858, an occupation that would not end until the French defeat at Dien Bien Phu in 1954.

Miramón, Miguel   (1832–1867)

As president and, later, "grand marshal" of Mexico, Miramón helped establish MAXIMILIAN as emperor of Mexico and was executed along with him.

Born in Mexico City on September 29, 1832, Miguel Miramón entered the military at the age of 15 when he enrolled in the Mexican Military Academy. Near the end of 1847, he joined the Mexican army under General SANTA ANNA in the war with the United States. After the war, he returned to the academy as an instructor, and by 1855 he had attained the rank of colonel. He fought on the side of the conservatives in the Revolution of Ayutla in 1856 against the liberals, who removed Santa Anna from power and gave the presidency to Ignacio Comonfort and then to his successor, Benito JUÁREZ.

Disagreement over Comonfort's liberal Constitution of 1857 led to bitter civil war between the liberals and conservatives called the War of the Reform (1858–61). The conservatives named General Félix Zuluoga president in 1859. After Zuluoga's death, Miramón succeeded him in 1860 as president and head of the conservative forces. Juárez, whose supporters had named him president, continued the fight.

As a leading conservative general, President Miramón twice spearheaded assaults against the liberal stronghold of Veracruz but was unsuccessful. Moreover, his presidency was short-lived. When Juárez's forces stormed Mexico City in December 1860, Miramón was forced to flee to Cuba, then to Europe.

While in European exile, he negotiated with Napoleon III of France, who, to secure certain loans made to Mexico by France and other European powers and to further his own imperialist agenda, persuaded the archduke of Austria, Maximilian, to assume the Mexican throne. After Maximilian was established as emperor in 1863, Miramón was named grand marshal. In 1864, he was named ambassador to Germany, but returned in 1866 when the empire appeared on the verge of collapse. He returned to active military duty and assumed command of a division, but was wounded and taken prisoner by the liberals at the Battle of Querétaro in June 1867. He was executed with the emperor on a nearby hill on June 17, 1867.

Mithradates VI   (132 B.C.–d. 63 B.C.)

Mithradates expanded the kingdom of Pontus, established supremacy in Asia Minor, and, for a short time, presented a formidable challenge to Rome in that region.

At the age of 12 or 14, Mithradates succeeded his father, Mithradates Euergetes, to the Pontic throne in 120 B.C. His mother ruled as regent until 115 B.C. when Mithradates had her deposed and imprisoned, thereafter ruling on his own. He developed a taste for war and conquest early on and dispatched troops to the Crimea and lands along the Black Sea, adding them to Pontus. When Mithradates invaded the Greek regions of the Crimea, he was welcomed by a populace that readily gave up independence in exchange for security against the marauding Scythians.

The Pontic dominions in Anatolia were in a state of severe disorder at Mithradates' accession. Paphlagonia had declared its independence, and Phrygia was now linked to Rome. Hoping to take back Paphlagonia, Mithradates partitioned it, dividing it between himself and Nicomedes III of Bithynia. The two parted company over the question of Cappadocia, however, which Mithradates occupied. On two separate occasions, Mithradates attempted to assert his hegemony in the region, but Rome stepped in and forced him out. With the aid of his son Tigranes, king of Armenia, Mithradates again marched on Cappadocia, only to be ousted by Rome again in 92 B.C.

Mithradates vowed to expel the Romans from Asia Minor. He made attempts to depose the puppet Nicomedes IV, who had succeeded his father. Nicomedes in turn attacked Mithradates with the help of the Romans in 88 B.C. At first, Mithradates was successful in throwing the Romans back, and he came to occupy Roman Asia. Much of the Greek world—including Athens—supported Mithradates, but withdrew after the king suffered a string of defeats during 86 and 85 B.C. at the hands of the Roman generals Sulla and Fimbria. In 88, a desperate Mithradates ordered a general massacre of all Roman and Italian residents of his empire, killing as many as 80,000, hoping thereby irrevocably to commit the Greeks to the war. But the military disasters continued, and the war began to look hopeless. Mithradates now turned against the Greeks, ruthlessly deporting, imprisoning, and murdering all those who opposed him. These tactics failed to coerce their cooperation, and he was forced to conclude a peace with the Romans in 85 B.C.

By 83 B.C., the Roman general Lucius Licinius Murena invaded Pontus without provocation, thereby triggering the Second Mithradatic War. Murena was defeated in 82 B.C., but frequent flare-ups occurred, and in 74 B.C., war was declared on both sides. Mithradates again gained the upper hand early on, but after the Roman general Lucullus was succeeded by Pompey, Mithradates and Tigranes suffered a crushing defeat in 66 B.C.

In 63 B.C., Mithradates was planning a retaliatory invasion of Italy via the Danube when his own troops mutinied against him. Realizing the situation was hopeless, he ordered one of his soldiers to kill him.

Further Reading: D. Magie. *Roman Rule in Asia Minor* (Princeton: Princeton University Press, 1950)

Mobutu Sese Seko [Joseph-Désiré Mobutu] (1930–)

Dictator of Zaïre since 1965, Mobutu Sese Seko has brutally oppressed all political opposition, bankrupted his country, and refused to accept political reform called for by a national conference.

Born in October 1930, in Lisala, Belgian Congo, Joseph-Désiré Mobutu joined the Belgian Congolese Army—the Force Publique—in 1949. Rising to the rank of sergeant-major, the highest rank attainable by Africans (who were not permitted officer status), Mobutu resigned from the army in 1956 and began a career in journalism.

When the Belgian Congo won independence on June 30, 1960, President Joseph Kasavubu and Premier Patrice Lumumba named Mobutu secretary of state for national defense. Just eight days after independence, however, Mobutu was asked to assume absolute control of the army, whose enlisted men had mutinied against their Belgian officers.

Over the next few months, Kasavubu and Lumumba engaged in a power struggle, and in September, Mobutu stepped in to seize control of the government. In February 1961, he returned power to Kasavubu, who named him commander in chief of the armed forces. Lumumba, arrested, fled to Katanga, where he was killed—many believe by Mobutu's army.

Mobutu took control of the government again in 1965, ousting President Kasavubu and his new premier, Moise TSHOMBE. Assuming the presidency, Mobutu nationalized the Katanga copper mines, encouraged foreign investment, announced that he would rule by decree, and reduced the authority of the army by bringing civilians into the government. In addition, he Africanized names throughout the nation, renaming his nation the Republic of Zaïre in October 1971 and taking for himself the name Mobutu Sese Seko in January 1972.

While proclaiming his African nationalism—he is always seen wearing a traditional leopard-skin hat—Mobutu has pillaged Zaïre's coffers, amassing a huge personal fortune by siphoning off the resources of the national treasury. He put down a revolt of his unpaid army in September 1991, and in the face of 6,000 percent annual inflation, he issued five-million-zaire bank notes—valued at less than two dollars each—which he used to pay the army in February 1993. When shopkeepers refused to accept the all but worthless currency, the army went on a killing spree that resulted in 300 deaths.

Confronted with massive civil unrest, Mobutu has called for free elections and a transition to democratic government, declaring in March 1993 that "The political crisis which has plunged the country into grief and poverty has lasted too long." Nevertheless, he has repeatedly thwarted the efforts of the National Conference to form such a transitional government and to conduct the democratic elections that would most likely result in the end of his 27-year reign as head of Zaïre's government.

Moctezuma I (r. 1440–68)

Less famous than the ruler who lost the Aztec Empire to CORTÉS, MOCTEZUMA II, Moctezuma I was the greater of the two, creating a public works program almost as expansive as his conquests.

Before succeeding his uncle, Itzcoatl, to the Aztec throne in 1440, Moctezuma was a powerful general who had brought much wealth to the Aztecs. At his capital of Tenochtitlán (modern Mexico City), Moctezuma built an aqueduct to bring fresh spring water from Chapultepec, and in the center of the city, he enlarged the great pyramid to include temples to the gods of rain, sun, and war. South of Tenochtitlán in a tropical valley, he built a vast botanical garden to include plants and flowers from all over the kingdom.

The empire extended rapidly, thanks to Moctezuma's passion for conquest—a passion he shared with his half-brother, Tlacaelel. Under Moctezuma, the Aztec kingdom stretched east, to the Gulf of Mexico, southwest through Oaxaca to the Pacific, and due west to the Baja peninsula. These lands brought immense wealth and treasure, including tobacco, copper, and weapons. The conquests also brought prisoners of war who were offered in sacrifice to the Aztecs' bloodthirsty gods.

The growth of the empire was halted in 1450–51 by disastrous floods that ruined the crops and led to severe famine the following two years. As the food shortage continued, the people hoped to appease the gods by sacrificing larger numbers of prisoners, and thousands of them were killed by the time the famine ended.

When Moctezuma died in 1468, he was succeeded by Axayacatl.

Moctezuma II [Montezuma II] (d. 1520)

Moctezuma II lost the vast Aztec empire to the Spanish conquistador Hernán CORTÉS during 1519–20.

Little is known about this ruler of a Native American empire the Spanish conquistador Hernán Cortes invaded, usurped, pillaged, and ultimately annihilated. Regarded by his subjects as the incarnation of divinity, Moctezuma II presided as absolute monarch over an empire extending from the Gulf of Mexico to the Pacific and from the Valley of Mexico south into Guatemala. When Cortés reached the Aztec capital of Tenochtitlán—present-day Mexico City—he beheld a city rivaling anything in Europe, full of ornate public buildings, palaces, places of worship, markets, well-engineered streets, and an elaborate system of aqueducts. Moctezuma himself lived in great splendor, arrayed in fabulous garments (changed and discarded four times a day) and attended by some 400 youthful servants who saw to his every need.

The wealth of the Aztec empire was derived from conquest and from the enslavement of the conquered, who were also subject to religious blood sacrifice. The Aztecs worshiped a pantheon of deities, most potent of which was Huitzilopochtli, a birdlike god of war who demanded human sacrifice and, to that end, enjoined the Aztecs to conquer all about them. Though rich and magnificent, the empire of Moctezuma II was relatively new, having come into existence perhaps 200 years before Cortés encountered it. It seems that the Aztecs had been only one among various nomadic subsistence tribes wandering through Central America when (as the foundation myth has it) Huitzilopochtli inspired a program of warfare and conquest. Moctezuma II's ancestors were all great warriors, who quickly and readily effected the submission of other peoples.

A late 17th-century engraving of the Aztec emperor Moctezuma II, who lost his empire to Cortés and his conquistadores in 1521. (Library of Congress)

With Moctezuma II, this warrior tradition abruptly ended. In his encounter with Cortés, he seems to have acted not with military resolve, but with fatal indecision, unsure whether the Spaniards were gods or men. A man of thought and inclined to trust in prophecy, he studied omens and at last determined that Cortés and his army were, in fact, invincible gods. Apparently deciding that armed opposition would be fruitless, Moctezuma threw open his city and his empire to the conquistadores, seeking to beguile them through lavish offers of gifts. These served only to whet the appetite of Cortés and his men, who made Moctezuma their captive.

The Spanish conquest of this bloodthirsty empire might itself have been relatively bloodless had not some of Cortés' men provoked violent resistance by suddenly slaughtering the Aztec celebrants of a feast devoted to Huitzilopochtli. Independently of their emperor, the inhabitants of Tenochtitlán violently drove the Spaniards out of their city on June 30, 1520, in an action the Spanish chroniclers called the Noche Triste ("Sorrowful Night"). During this uprising, Moctezuma II was killed. Spanish accounts say that he was assassinated by his own subjects— stoned to death when the Spanish exhibited him to prove he was alive—while Aztec chroniclers attributed his death to the Spanish.

Cortés and his conquistadores returned to Tenochtitlán 10 months later and laid siege to the city for three months, cutting off all sources of food and water. An epidemic of smallpox broke out in the city during the siege, killing Moctezuma II's successor, Cuitlahuac, and it was a new king, Cuauhtémoc, who at last surrendered to Cortés. He was tortured to death by the Spanish in their efforts to learn the whereabouts of a hoard of silver and gold they had been forced to abandon when they fled the city the previous year.

Further Reading: Alan Axelrod. *Chronicle of the Indian Wars: From Colonial Times to Wounded Knee* (New York: Prentice Hall, 1992); C. A. Burland. *Montezuma, Lord of the Aztecs* (London: Weidenfeld and Nicholson, 1973); Maurice Collis. *Cortes and Montezuma* (New York: Harcourt, Brace, 1955).

Mohammed II the Conqueror   (1432–1481)

Sultan Mohammed II greatly expanded the Ottoman Empire into Europe, most notably conquering the city of Constantinople, which had long resisted Ottoman domination.

Mohammed II was born at Edirne on March 30, 1432. The eldest son of Murad II, he became sultan for a time when his father retired to Magnesia in 1444, and then assumed the throne permanently after his father died in 1451. Mohammed II ruled a

Medal depicting Mohammad II the Conqueror. (From Stanley Lane-Poole, The Story of the Nations: Turkey, *1888)*

vast empire that extended to the east and west of Constantinople. His father had been content to allow the city, remnant of the once-mighty Byzantine empire, to exist—independent—in the midst of his realm. The son, restless and ambitious, decided to begin his reign by taking Constantinople once and for all.

He began in 1451–52 by boldly building a fortress, Rumeli Hisar, just outside of the city, covering both sides of the Bosporus. When Byzantine emperor Constantine XI protested this outrage, Mohammed had just what he wanted: an excuse to declare war. Constantine XI commanded an army of fewer than 10,000 against an Ottoman force of 80,000, including the elite corps of Janissaries and, under the command of renegade Hungarian artilleryman Urban, a siege train of 70 heavy cannon. Nevertheless Constantinople was a formidable objective. It was virtually surrounded by water, and landward defenses were extremely strong. Mohammed attempted to push his Turkish fleet into the Golden Horn, but was prevented by a boom thrown across the entrance by the city's defenders. In a spectacular move, the sultan decided to transport his fleet *overland* from the Bosporus into the Golden Horn. He built a one-mile-long plank road between the Bosporus and the Golden Horn, greased it with vast quantities of animal fat, and slid 80 vessels across in a great *portage*. Beginning on April 2, 1453, these ships, combined with land-based artillery, set up a withering barrage. The city withstood siege and bombardment until May 29, 1453, when artillery had made a sufficient breach to allow a Janissary charge. Constantine XI was killed in the battle, and the Turks pillaged and sacked the city for three days. Despite the initial ruin, Mohammed II attempted to preserve as much of the city as possible, encouraging the learned and the cultured to remain. But the city rapidly fell into decay, and, while Mohammed had succeeded in conquering Constantinople, he was, in large measure, deprived of the real value of the prize he had coveted.

In 1456, the sultan, now known as El Fatih—the Conqueror—invaded Serbia and laid siege to Belgrade. John Hunyadi defeated him in a naval battle there on July 4, 1556, and on land during July 21–22. While the sultan withdrew from Belgrade, he overran Serbia during 1457–59. His forces also penetrated southern Greece during 1458–60, crushed the small empire of Trebizond in 1461, and successfully invaded Bosnia during 1463–64.

Always at odds with Venice—whose fleet had briefly aided Constantine XI in the defense of Constantinople—Mohammed II declared a long war against it in 1463. He raided Dalmatia and Croatia in

1468, then launched a spectacularly successful amphibious assault on the Venetian fortress of Negroponte in Euboea (Évvoia) from June 14 to July 12, 1470, capturing the city with few losses to himself. Venetian diplomacy prevailed on the Persians to attack at Erzinjan in 1473. Mohammad prevailed against this force and went on to capture the Crimean city of Kaffa (Feodosiya) from the Genoese.

In the meantime, in 1468, Mohammed reconquered Albania, which had been lost in the rebellion of the Janissary Skanderbeg (George Castricata) in 1443. The sultan went on to capture most of the Venetian ports along the Albanian coast. He then sent raiders from Croatia across the Alps into Venetia, bringing northeastern Italy to its knees. The Venetians made peace and agreed to recognize the Turks' conquests. Early in 1480, Mohammed's forces crossed the Adriatic and seized Otranto, going on to besiege the Knights of St. John on Rhodes during 1480–81. Here the sultan suffered a bad defeat. He withdrew to Tekfur Cauiri to plan a second assault on Rhodes, but fell ill and died there on May 3, 1481.

Best remembered as an expansionist and a conqueror, Mohammed II was no mere brute. Among the most cultivated of Turkish sultans, he was a patron of learning and the arts, and he left his people an important legal work, the Quanun-nmae, which codified government institutions and practices.

Montezuma I   See MOCTEZUMA I

Montezuma II   See MOCTEZUMA II

Montt, Manuel   (1809–1880)
Enlightened president of Chile who served two terms, Montt angered both liberals and conservatives by refusing to bend to either.

Born on September 8, 1809, Manuel Montt studied law at the Instituto Nacional, returning to his alma mater in 1835 to serve as its rector for five years. In 1840 he was elected to the Chilean congress, where he was instrumental in bringing to justice the assassins of the minister Diego Portales. Under President Manuel Bulnes, Montt served as minister of the interior and minister of justice. In 1851, he succeeded Bulnes in the presidency.

A confirmed conservative, Montt was unpopular with the liberals, who claimed election fraud and rose in armed revolt. Montt acted quickly to put down the rebellion. Unlike many South American leaders of the period, Montt refused to become a slave to popular opinion, liberal or conservative. Indeed, his policies often angered his conservative constituents. He offended religious leaders by as-

serting the state's right of patronage in the Catholic church, and he offended the landed aristocracy by removing restrictions on the sale and bequest of real property.

Montt reformed the civil service and embarked on an ambitious public works program financed by the reformed tax structure. He founded savings banks, totally reordered the educational system by establishing schools at all levels, and he brought industry to Chile. Industrial and economic output increased, in part due to the augmented labor force made available by Montt's policy of encouraging the immigration of many German dissidents.

For all its progressiveness, Montt's regime was still marked by violence and repression during the second revolt of the liberals. However, he came to terms with them, shifting support from a conservative successor to a liberal. After he stepped down as president in 1861, he continued to serve Chile as senator, envoy, and president of the Supreme Court. Manuel Montt died on September 20, 1880.

Further Reading: Luis Galdames. *History of Chile* (Chapel Hill: University of North Carolina Press, 1941).

Montt, Pedro   (1846–1910)
The son of Chilean president MANUEL MONTT, Pedro followed in his father's footsteps, but failed to improve the conditions of his people.

Pedro Montt graduated from the National Institute with a degree in law in 1870 and practiced for a short time before becoming interested in politics through the auspices of his father, a devoted public servant. In 1876, Pedro Montt successfully stood for election to the Chamber of Deputies and continued to serve that body, being elected its president in 1885. When José Balmaceda was elected president in 1876, Montt held two cabinet positions in Balmaceda's government, but resigned in 1891 and was active in helping to overthrow Balmaceda in that same year.

Under the authority of the new government, Montt journeyed to the United States, first as a supporter and representative of the military junta, then, following U.S. recognition of the new government, as minister from Chile. In 1901, Montt returned to Chile and ran unsuccessfully for the presidency. He ran again in 1906 under the banner of the conservative National Union Party and, this time, won by a large majority.

Pedro Montt's first act as president was to call out the army to suppress great labor strikes that were occurring throughout the country. He next attempted to undertake a public works program, which included a rail system spanning the length of the country and that was intended to support his program of expanded industrialization based on increased production of nitrates and copper. While the program was mildly successful, it did not benefit the people at large, and vast numbers remained hungry and out of work. Montt's health declined in 1910, and he left on a brief trip to Bremen, Germany, for medical treatment. He died in Bremen on August 16, 1910.

Further Reading: Luis Galdames. *History of Chile* (Chapel Hill: University of North Carolina Press, 1941).

Mpande (b. ca. 1800–1872)

The longest-reigning king of the Zulus, Mpande usurped power from his brother Dingane with the help of Afrikaners in Natal.

The third son of Zulu king Senzangakhona, Mpande was a soldier in the service of his half-brother SHAKA during the early years of Zulu unification (between 1816 and 1823). In 1828, another of his half-brothers, Dingane, seized power from Shaka and purged the royal family. Mpande escaped death during the purge by deliberately lying low.

After biding his time for a decade, Mpande led Zulu forces against the Afrikaners at Port Natal in 1838 and razed the settlement. Later, the Afrikaners retaliated and defeated the Zulus, and Dingane persuaded many of the Zulus to move with him to Swaziland. Mpande refused to follow, remaining in Zululand with about 17,000 tribal members. At this point, Mpande negotiated rather than fought with the Afrikaners. He promised that he and his followers would leave the Natal area if the white settlers would help him overthrown Dingane. At the battle of Magongo, during January 1840, Mpande's forces and his Afrikaner allies defeated the Zulu king. When Mpande was crowned, he honored his bargain with the Afrikaners and ceded land south of the Tugela to them.

As Mpande grew old, his two eldest sons, Mbulazi and Cetshwayo, fought each other for the crown. By the time of Mpande's death in 1872, Cetshwayo had won the civil war and was acknowledged ruler of the Zulus.

Further Reading: Alan Lloyd. *The Zulu War* (London: Hart-Davis, MacGibbon, 1974).

Mubarak, Mohamed Hosni (1928–   )

Succeeding Anwar Sadat after his assassination in 1981, Mubarak led Egypt in the same direction as Sadat while emerging as a foreign policy specialist.

Born in the fertile Nile Delta region on May 4, 1928, to an official of the Ministry of Justice, Hosni Mubarak attended local schools before enrolling in the Egyptian Military Academy, graduating in February 1949. He then attended the two-year Air Force Academy, where he stayed on as a flight instructor

until 1959. He served two stints in the Soviet Union in advanced bomber training and attended the elite Soviet Frunze General Staff Academy. In the 1960s, Mubarak commanded the Egyptian bomber force during the Yemeni civil war.

In 1967, President Gamal NASSER named Mubarak as director of the Air Force Academy and charged him with rebuilding the Air Force, which was destroyed on the ground by the Israelis in the Six Day War of June 1967. He was then promoted to Air Force Chief of Staff, and in 1972, President Anwar Sadat named him Commander in Chief of the Air Force. With the Air Force rebuilt, Sadat launched the Yom Kippur War on October 6, 1972, beginning with an air strike that had been proposed by Mubarak. Undermanned and equipped with inferior planes, Mubarak's forces nevertheless destroyed over 90 percent of the Israeli installations they had targeted, one of the greatest victories in Egyptian military history.

When radical Islamic fundamentalists assassinated Sadat on his reviewing stand during a parade in October 1981, Mubarak succeeded him as president. Immediately following his accession, he rounded up 2,500 radical Muslims, crushing an Islamic uprising. He ordered the execution of those directly implicated in the assassination and sentenced many others to prison terms. He vowed to carry on Sadat's programs, particularly the momentous strides Sadat had made toward bringing peace between Egypt and Israel. Mubarak's diplomatic savvy personally restored Egypt's standing in the Arab world without repudiating the Arab-Israeli treaty.

Muhammad Ali (1769–1849)

Viceroy and pasha of Egypt from 1805 to 1849, Muhammad Ali neutralized the Mamluk threat to his power and founded a dynasty that ruled until the mid-20th century.

Born in Kavala, Macedonia, in 1769, Muhammad Ali was orphaned at an early age and raised by the governor of Kavala. At the age of 18, he married one of the governor's relatives, who was the mother of five of Muhammad Ali's 95 children.

Muhammad Ali abandoned the tobacco trade in which he had been engaged and joined the Ottoman sultan's military expedition to Egypt, which had been occupied by the forces of Napoleon Bonaparte in 1798. Maneuvering himself into positions of increasing responsibility, he eventually was named viceroy of Egypt, with the rank of pasha. He immediately set about restoring order to the chaos left in the wake of the French, who withdrew in 1801. He nationalized most of the farmland, restricted the activities of the merchants and artisans, neutralized the Bedouins and peasant rebels, and eliminated all threats to his power posed by the Mamluks, a powerful military mercenary caste originally composed of Turkish slaves, whom the British had attempted to restore in 1807. Muhammad Ali thwarted these efforts, routing the British troops at Rosetta and forcing them to withdraw. In 1811 he solved the Mamluk problem once and for all by ordering their wholesale execution throughout Egypt.

In 1819, Muhammad Ali conquered Arabia and the next year invaded the Sudan. When the Greeks revolted against the Ottoman Empire, he sent a fleet of 60 ships to aid the sultan. European powers intervened, and at the naval battle of Navarino on October 20, 1827, his fleet as well as the Turkish naval force were destroyed. As compensation, Muhammad Ali demanded that the sultan give him Syria and Damascus. When the sultan refused, Muhammad Ali invaded Syria in 1831 and the next year captured Acre and Damascus, defeating the sultan's Turkish forces at Konya. Russia then came to the sultan's aid, and soon the British and French intervened as well. The result was the Convention of Kutahya, signed April 6, 1833, by which Muhammad Ali gained control of Syria, Damascus, Aleppo, and Itcheli. Later Adana was added to his realm.

Massive revolts broke out the following year in Muhammad Ali's holdings. The pasha brutally suppressed protests against high taxes, government monopolies, and conscription. The Turkish sultan, believing that Muhammad Ali's position was now threatened, took the opportunity to invade Syria, but was routed at Nezib in 1839. Once again, European nations entered the fray. Troops from Russia, Great Britain, Austria, and Prussia put an end to the hostilities and captured Acre in November 1840. The subsequent treaty, the London Convention, signed on February 13, 1841, formalized the division of territories between the Ottoman Empire and Egypt. Muhammad Ali was given hereditary rights to the Egyptian pashalik in return for his abandoning most of the territory he held outside Egypt. According to the convention, Egypt was to remain nominally a part of the Ottoman Empire.

In 1848, Muhammad Ali relinquished his authority to his son Ibrahim Pasha, who served as regent until his own death in November of that year. Muhammad Ali died on August 2, 1849, in Alexandria. His successors continued to rule Egypt until the installation of a republican government in 1952.

Further Reading: Henry Dodwell. *The Founder of Modern Egypt* (Cambridge: Cambridge University Press, 1931); Helen Anne B. Rivlin. *The Agricultural Policy of Muhammad Ali in Egypt* (Cambridge, Mass: Harvard University Press, 1961).

Muhammad ibn Falah (b. ca. 1400–1461)
The founder of the radical Mushasha sect of the Shiite Moslems, Muhammad developed an extremist state founded on his messianic zeal.

A descendant of a Shiite imam, Muhammad ibn Falah received the standard Islamic education at al-Hillah, a well-known Shiite center for Islamic study. During his education at al-Hillah, Muhammad developed extremist views so contrary to traditional Islamic thinking that many deemed them heretical. When he began to expound these views to others, he was excommunicated.

By 1436, Muhammad began preaching to his fellow tribesmen, wandering from clan to clan, broadcasting his extremist version of Islam. He hoped to found a coalition of discontented Muslims on what is now the border between Iran and Iraq. He claimed to be the Mahdi and the representative of Ali, the successor to the Prophet Muhammad.

Orthodox Islamic forces hoped to put an end to Muhammad's teachings and marched against his coalition in 1440, defeating him. However, he was able to regroup and capture Hoveyzeh in February 1441. Muhammad made the city the capital of his Mushasha sect.

Orthodox Islamic forces continued to resist the breakaway sect for 10 years, sporadically attacking Hoveyzeh, only to be repulsed each time. Muhammad extended his influence over the area and eventually controlled the region from Hoveyzeh to the Tigris River. He wrote the Mushasha Doctrine, which was similar to the Koran, naming himself not only as the religious leader but the military and temporal ruler as well. He was succeeded by his son on his death.

Muhammad ibn Tughluq (b. ca. 1290–1351)
Briefly extending the rule of the Delhi sultanate, Muhammad ruled with a combination of severity and incompetance that finally brought about the decline of the sultanate.

As a child, Muhammad possessed a sharp mind, becoming thoroughly versed in the Koran, Muslim jurisprudence, astronomy, logic, philosophy, medicine, and rhetoric. He was a military leader before his accession, his father having sent him to the Deccan to suppress the Hindu rajas, an exercise that prepared him for the future. After Muhammad succeeded his father to the throne in 1325, he would have to deal with 22 rebellions during his reign.

Hoping to legitimate his authority and consolidate power, Muhammad attempted to win over the Muslim divines and mystics. These groups, however, adamantly refused, and Muhammad succeeded only in dispersing them throughout northern India, an action that made him appear irreligious. In 1327, he attempted to move the capital 750 miles from Delhi to the Deccan, forcing a migration of much of the population. After realizing that the move was proving a failure, he ordered the capital returned to Delhi.

In 1328, hoping to offset the financial folly of the move, Muhammad levied higher taxes on the delta area between the Ganges and Jamuna rivers. The brutality his officials practiced in their efforts at collection bred insurrection that resulted in the ruin of much of the rich crop land, further damaging the kingdom's economy. In an effort to stabilize the faltering currency, Muhammad issued copper coinage, without, however, taking steps to safeguard the copper supply. The result was tremendous inflation and a high rate of counterfeiting.

In an attempt to expand his frontiers to the west, Muhammad planned an expedition into Khorazan, which, however, failed to materialize. Next, in an effort to stabilize the northern boundary in 1329, Muhammad was severely defeated by Chinese forces. Muhammad was killed in battle in 1351 while attempting to subdue one of the rebel leaders in Sind. His death marked the beginning of the end for the Delhi Empire.

Muizz, al- (b. ca. 930–975)

The founder of the city of Cairo, al-Muizz, one of the most powerful of the Fatimid caliphs, ultimately conquered Egypt.

Succeeding his father, al-Mansur, in 953 at the age of 22, al-Muizz became Fatimid caliph, reigning over Morocco, Algeria, and Tunisia. He soon added Sicily by conquest. Outraged over what he termed the insolence of the western regions of his realm, al-Muizz sent his most capable general, Jawhar, to re-impose the authority of the caliph, especially at the city of Fez. In 955, Jawhar moved toward the Atlantic and invaded Muslim Spain, plundering the coast and putting to the torch large numbers of ships.

The ultimate design of al-Muizz was to conquer Egypt, something no Fatimid caliph had ever accomplished. He began planning the invasion as early as 966, but it was delayed because his mother wished to make a pilgrimage to Mecca and had to travel through Egypt. On her return from Mecca, she pleaded with her son to wait because she had received such good treatment from the Egyptian ruler Kafur. Resignedly, al-Muizz waited until after Kafur's death in 968. When the invasion finally got under way, Jawhar routed the Egyptians within a year.

In an effort to maintain Fatimid control of Egypt, al-Muizz moved his capital from Morocco to Egypt, developing the city of Cairo around 972, just north of the old city of al-Fustat. Now in control of Egypt, al-Muizz next marched the Fatimid armies into Syria shortly before his death in October 975. He was succeeded by his son, al-Aziz, who consolidated Fatimid control over Syria that would last until the 11th century.

Murad I (b. ca. 1326–1389)

Sultan of the Ottoman Empire from about 1360 to 1389, Murad I expanded his empire to include the Balkans and central Anatolia, making vassals of the Balkan princes and the Byzantine emperor along the way.

The son of Orhan and Nilufer Hatun, Murad I was born about 1326. Early in his reign, he conquered Adrianople (1361), which he renamed Edirne and made his European capital. He also made Byzantine Emperor John V Palaeologus his vassal. Then he attacked Thrace in 1364 and invaded the Balkans.

The crusader Amadeus VI of Savoy occupied Gallipoli in 1366 only to be crushed by the Turks under Murad I's command the following year.

Beginning in 1366, Murad fought against the Serbs and Bulgarians and their occasional allies the Walachians, Albanians, and Bosnians. Sofia fell to Murad's army in 1385, followed by Nis in 1386, and the princes of northern Serbia and Bulgaria became vassals of the Ottoman Empire.

In central Anatolia, the Karamanids invaded Murad's territories after he had secured through marriage, purchase, or war Germiyan, Tekke, and Hamid for his empire. Victory was his in 1386, when he defeated a coalition of Turkmen at Konya, freeing him for a return to the Balkans.

In 1388, Murad fought the Serbs and Bosnians again, and his army was stopped at Plocnick. On June 15, 1389, he was preparing to fight the combined Serbian-Bosnian forces at Kosovo Polje when he was assassinated. His army, however, fought the battle, and its victory opened all of the Balkans to Ottoman domination.

One of the most important aspects of Murad's military legacy was his founding of the Janissary corps, an elite fighting force that served many Ottoman rulers as a formidable weapon against all foes and came to be a powerful political force in its own right.

Further Reading: Michael Doukas. *Decline and Fall of Byzantium to the Ottoman Turks* (Detroit: Wayne State University Press, 1975).

Murad IV (1612–1640)

The last Ottoman sultan to lead armies in combat personally, Murad was ruthless in dealing with those he vanquished and with his subjects.

Ascending to the sultanate of an empire on the brink of ruin, Murad IV faced a civil government rife with jealousies and conflicting personal agendas and a military staffed with malcontents and mercenaries. His strategy was to preserve his empire by being more ruthless than they.

Assuming the throne at the age of 11 in 1623, Murad ruled through the regency of his mother for several years, but the real power was held by the military and the civil aristocracy. To make matters worse, the treasury was virtually empty, containing only three bags of gold in 1623. In that year, too, the military—the *sipahis*—raided the palace and demanded that the sultan relinquish 17 high officials, including the sultan's close friend, the grand vizier. Murad had no choice but to give up his friend. Humiliated, he vowed never to find himself in that position again.

Gathering his loyal guard and all those faithful to him, Murad set about seeking vengeance, personally watching the decapitation of the *sipahis* ringleader and searching out all the others involved. He then gathered on the shores of the Bosporus all key members of the military, the aristocracy, and the leading magistrates. Having obtained oaths of allegiance on the Koran from all those willing, he summarily executed those who had failed to volunteer allegiance. Murad next dispatched a corps of henchmen to patrol Istanbul in search of spies and rebels. Anyone suspected was killed on sight, his body thrown into the Bosporus to wash ashore as a warning to others.

Murad brutally enforced an Islamic code of morality by outlawing all tobacco, alcohol, and coffee; offenders against the proscription were publicly hanged or impaled. Indeed, Murad's cruelty soon took on legendary status. Angered by the noise of several women dancing and singing in a meadow by the water, he had them all drowned. It is believed that in five years, he directed the murder of some 25,000 persons.

While Murad disported himself as a monster, he did regain control of his empire and pulled it back from anarchy and bankruptcy. In the spring of 1635, he began his first Asiatic campaign, an exercise in studied slaughter. Enforcing iron discipline, Murad easily took Erivan back from the Persians, and won respect by sharing the hardships with his men and showing superior generalship.

Early in the summer of 1638, Murad began what would be his most triumphant, and final, campaign. His objective was the reconquest of Baghdad from the Persians. A tradition, begun by Suleiman the Magnificent, held that Baghdad could be taken only by a sovereign in person. Accordingly, Murad rode at the front of his columns on the march. Arriving precisely on schedule, Murad's troops set about laying siege, Murad himself donning a soldier's uniform, digging trenches, and positioning cannon. Legend has it that a Persian giant challenged the boldest Turk to hand-to-hand combat and that it was Murad who stepped forth. The fall of Baghdad was followed by the wholesale massacre of soldiers and civilians.

In view of Murad's religious prohibition against strong drink, it is supremely ironic that his sudden death came in 1640—from alcohol poisoning.

Further reading: Nurhan Atasoy. *Splendors of the Ottoman Sultans* (Memphis, Tenn.: Lithograph Publishers, 1992).

Mursilis I [Murshilish] (r. ca. 1620 B.C.–ca. 1590 B.C.)

Mursilis was a Hittite ruler who consolidated Hittite sovereignty over northern Syria.

Mursilis succeeded his adoptive grandfather, Hattusilis, to the throne of the Hittite kingdom around 1620 B.C. Like his grandfather, Mursilis was active in campaigning against northern Syria. During one of these campaigns, he subdued and destroyed the city of Aleppo. After his victories in Syria, Mursilis turned his attention to Babylon and was responsible for ending the powerful Amorite dynasty there. Later, after defeating the Hurrians along the Euphrates River, he returned to the Hittite capital, Huttusas (located in modern Turkey). Shortly after his return, he was killed in a conspiracy launched against him by his brother-in-law, Hantilis.

Mursilis II (r. ca. 1346 B.C.–ca. 1320 B.C.)

Mursilis II is one of the few rulers of the ancient past who documented his own conquests.

Mursilis II succeeded to the throne his older brother, Arnuwandas III, who had in turn only recently succeeded their father, the great Hittite ruler SUPPILULIUMAS. Little was expected of the youngest son, but his 26-year reign belied these expectations. Mursilis II succeeded in maintaining his father's empire through aggressive campaigns against the ever-warring Kaska in the north and through renewed allegiances among the states to the north in Syria.

Perhaps it was because Mursilis was afflicted with a speech impediment—which eventually made him altogether mute—that he documented as much of his accomplishments as he did. In verses that sometimes rival even those in the Old Testament for beauty, Mursilis wrote entreaties to his gods, begging forgiveness and deliverance from punishment for various and sundry sins. His empire was marked by war and turmoil—pacification of the Kaska, for example, was virtually an annual military chore—and his writings are filled with references such as, "The following year I marched . . . I vanquished . . . I laid waste. Then I returned home." They are sufficiently detailed to provide valuable insight into Hittite military strategy.

Further Reading: Johannes Lehman. *Hittites, People of 1,000 Gods* (New York: Viking, 1977).

Mussolini, Benito   (1883–1945)

The founder of Italian fascism, Mussolini became premier and dictator of Italy. Seeking to restore his nation to its classical Roman greatness by allying himself with Adolf HITLER's Germany in World War II, he led his people to disaster.

Although he is closely associated in the popular mind with his wartime ally, Adolf Hitler, Benito Mussolini emerged from a very different background. He was born on July 29, 1883, the son of a blacksmith with strong Socialist and anti-church beliefs. Young Mussolini, a spirited and unruly boy, imbibed his father's beliefs, which he embellished with the romantic, even mystical tendencies of his mother, who convinced her son that he was destined for greatness. Mussolini was an avid reader, who voraciously consumed the works of such political philosophers as Louis-Auguste Blanqui, Friedrich Wilhelm Nietzsche, Georges Sorel, and, perhaps most significantly, Niccolo Machiavelli. Enamored of ideas, Mussolini attended the Salesian college of Faenza and the normal school, from which he obtained a teaching certificate. By the time he was 18, Mussolini received an appointment as a schoolteacher in the provinces. He then began to travel, spending a few years in Switzerland and the Austrian Trentino. As his experience broadened, he gave up teaching to pursue Socialist journalism.

In 1912, Mussolini became editor of the Milan Socialist Party newspaper *Avanti!* As a Socialist, he was strongly opposed to war and wrote articles arguing against Italy's entry into World War I. However, in perhaps the most momentous decision of his life, he suddenly abandoned the Socialist Party line and urged Italy's entry into the war on the side of the Allies. When the party responded to this change of heart by expelling him, Mussolini quickly started his own newspaper, *Il popolo d'Italia,* in Milan. It was in the pages of this paper that he evolved and broadcast the message of what became the Fascist movement. But first, Mussolini enlisted in the Italian army as a private in 1915, serving until he was wounded in the buttocks by trench mortar fragments early in 1917.

Following his convalescence, he resumed publication of his newspaper. On March 23, 1919, in part encouraged and inspired by the poet, novelist, romantic patriot, and glamorous adventurer Gabriele d'Annunzio, he and other war veterans founded in Milan a revolutionary nationalistic group they dubbed the Fasci di Combattimento. The Italian word *fascio,* "bundle" or "bunch," suggested union, and the *fasces,* a bundle of rods bound together around an ax with the blade protruding, was the ancient Roman symbol of power.

Mussolini's fascism quickly moved away from the Socialist left and became a radical right-wing nationalism—although, paradoxically, many of Mussolini's early pronouncements were more pro-labor and anti-church than anything even the Socialist left had yet advocated. But it was the nationalism, charged with visions of recreating ancient Roman imperial grandeur, that gained the enthusiastic support of the influential d'Annunzio, powerful landowners in the lower Po valley, important industrialists, and senior army officers. Mussolini also created squads of thugs, the Blackshirts, who waged a brutal street-level civil war against Socialists, Communists, Catholics, and liberals.

By 1922, Mussolini had moved very far from socialism and had gained the support of the moneyed and powerful, yet also commanded a vast following among the masses. On October 28, 1922, he led a Fascist march on Rome, obtaining a mandate from King Victor Emmanuel III to form a coalition government. Mussolini obtained dictatorial powers set to last one year. During this time, he reshaped Italy's economic structure, cutting government expenses for public services, reducing taxes on industry to encourage production, and centralizing and consolidating government bureaucracy. Such measures did indeed do much to boost Italy's lackluster economy. For many observers, the single most symbolic evidence of Mussolini's reforms was the fact that he introduced a new discipline into the notoriously undependable Italian railroad system, and "Mussolini made the trains run on time" became a kind of catch phrase used to characterize the early years of his regime.

During this period, Mussolini also replaced the king's guard with his own Fascist *squadisti* and secret police force, called the Ovra. He increased his prestige as a handler of foreign affairs when he responded to the murder of some Italian officials at the hands of bandits on the Greek-Albanian border by demanding a huge indemnity from the Greek government and bombarding and seizing the Greek island of Corfu. Mussolini also negotiated an agreement with Yugoslavia to obtain possession of the long-contested Fiume. In all of this, Mussolini at first avoided any direct attack on labor, though he was successful in brutally suppressing the strikes that traditionally plagued the country's industry.

In 1924, Mussolini ostensibly relinquished his dictatorial powers and called for new elections—after carefully securing legislation that would guarantee a two-thirds parliamentary majority for his party regardless of the popular vote. Among the handful of Socialists elected that year was Giacomo Matteotti, who embarked on a series of scathing speeches in opposition to Mussolini and the Fascists, exposing outrages ranging from acts of intimidation and violence, to misuse of public funds, to murder. When Matteotti's own murdered body was found shortly after these pronouncements, a lengthy parliamentary crisis developed, and the opposition press attacked Mussolini and his followers.

Mussolini responded by the outright imposition of a single-party dictatorship and a policy of strict censorship. His henchmen terrorized all opponents, even beating one liberal editor to death. In the meantime, Mussolini reinforced his power base among Italian capitalists by abolishing free trade unions. He also reached rapprochement with the Catholic church by the Lateran Treaty of 1929, by which the Vatican was established under the absolute temporal sovereignty of the pope.

Having secured his absolute dictatorship at home, Mussolini—now widely called Il Duce ("the Leader")—embarked on an aggressive foreign policy during the 1930s. Using as a pretext a clash over a disputed zone on the Italian Somaliland border, Mussolini invaded Ethiopia during 1935–36 without a declaration of war, brutally bombing and gassing the populace. On May 9, 1936, Italy annexed the African nation. During this period, Mussolini also assisted Generalissimo Francisco FRANCO in the Spanish Civil War, and developed an alliance with Adolf Hitler's Germany during 1936–39.

In April 1939, Mussolini sent his armies to occupy Albania, but stayed out of World War II until June 1940, when the fall of France was in the offing and Germany seemed unstoppable. Hitler welcomed his Italian partner, but soon had reason to regret the alliance, as Mussolini's military forces suffered disaster after disaster in Greece and North Africa.

By the middle of the war, the popular tide had turned against the dictator who had led the nation into an orgy of death and destruction, and the leaders of his own party abandoned him. King Victor Emmanuel dismissed Mussolini as premier on July 25, 1943, and ordered his arrest. But Hitler effected

his rescue on September 12 and installed him as a puppet in northern Italy, which had yet to be taken by the Allies.

By the spring of 1945, Allied forces were closing in on Mussolini. In April, he and his mistress, Clara Petacci, fled, only to be captured by Italian partisans at Lake Como. The couple was executed by firing squad on April 28, and their bodies were hung in a public square in Milan.

Further Reading: Richard Collier. *Duce!* (New York: Viking Press, 1971); Ivone Kirkpatrick. *Mussolini: A Study in Power* (New York: Hawthorn, 1964).

Mutesa I [Mutesa Walugembe Mukaabya] (b. ca. 1838–1884)

One of the greatest of the Ganda kings of Buganda (southeast Uganda), Mutesa brought military might and substantial wealth to his kingdom while exhibiting a virtuoso's skill in his handling of Western missionaries.

The son of the reigning *kabaka*—or ruler—Mutesa received the backing of many powerful members of Ganda society in his successful bid to succeed his father in 1856 as king of Buganda. The first six years of his reign were rocked by instability, and Mutesa brutally put down repeated insurrections that threatened his rule. He tolerated no opposition and ruthlessly suppressed any who dared cross him.

Mutesa built a navy of war canoes to prowl vast Lake Victoria in order to raid neighboring countries, bringing much wealth to his government.

Although a confirmed Muslim by the mid-1860s, Mutesa was not opposed to Christianity, and when Christian missionaries arrived in 1862, they were greatly impressed with Buganda, and sent word to other missionaries. Faced with a Sudanese threat from the north, Mutesa shrewdly welcomed the missionaries, hoping their presence would help stave off the advance. The missionaries brought much enlightenment to the country; most receptive were the youth of Buganda.

Although Mutesa himself never wholeheartedly embraced Western culture, he used imported Western technology and material goods to dominate East Africa. At his death in October 1884, the nation of Buganda dominated East Africa.

Further Reading: Sir Frederick Lugard. *The Rise of Our East African Empire* (London: Cass, 1968).

Mutesa II [Sir Edward Frederick William Walugembe Mutebi Luwangula Mutesa] (1924–1969)

The last ruler of independent Buganda, Mutesa II was twice forced into exile.

The son of King Daudi Chwa II, Mutesa was born November 19, 1924. He was educated by private tutors and at Cambridge University. Upon his father's death in 1939, Mutesa succeeded him as *kabaka*, ruling under a regency until 1942.

In 1953, the British secretary of state for colonies proposed a federation of the East African British colonies, similar to the British-mandated union of Rhodesia and Nyasaland. Many Africans were fearful that such a federation would further increase European control over Africa. Citing the original English agreement with Buganda, Mutesa demanded separate independence and, to gain bargaining leverage, refused to aid the British in developing Uganda as a separate state. Unable to sway Mutesa to their side or break his firm hold over the country, the British, under the direction of Governor Andrew Cohen, exiled him to England on October 30, 1953. This only rallied his people behind Mutesa, and the Bugandans were completely uncooperative with the regency imposed by the British. Twice, a state of emergency was declared. With the regency an utter failure, the British were forced to allow Mutesa to return in 1955 after less than two years' absence.

Mutesa continued calling for an independent Buganda in June 1960 when he announced that Buganda would not participate with Uganda in the proposed elections unless concessions were made to Buganda. The elections proceeded anyway and resulted in an independent Uganda. In 1961, a British commission recommended that Buganda become part of the new Uganda as a single federal entity. Following intense opposition, Mutesa agreed to the plan in October. After unifying his party with that of Milton Obote, Mutesa and Obote were able to control the 1962 elections—Obote being elected prime minister, and Uganda receiving formal independence from Britain.

Problems soon erupted between Obote and Mutesa. In 1963, Obote appointed Mutesa as president, a non-executive post, and Mutesa's influence began to fade. In 1966, the government was charged with aiding and abetting the illegal shipment of gold from the Congo. Obote promptly suspended the constitution, arresting five ministers and dismissing Mutesa, who retreated into his palace. Obote then abolished Buganda as a separate entity. Tensions increased until Obote's forces stormed Mutesa's palace on May 24, 1966, forcing him into exile again. Granted asylum in England, Mutesa died in London on November 21, 1969.

N

Nabis (d. 192 B.C.)

After killing the Spartan king Pelops, Nabis became the last ruler of independent Sparta.

In 207 B.C., Nabis succeeded Machanidas as regent to the Spartan king Pelops. He immediately killed his charge and seized the crown. He formed a mercenary guard, undertook revolutionary land reforms, emancipated slaves, and went to war with the Achaean League. Nabis was defeated by Flamininus and Philipoemen, and was killed by the Aetolians in 192 B.C.

The large following Nabis had attracted through his revolutionary reforms then massacred the Aetolian troops attempting to occupy Sparta. Independence for the city-state was not secured, however, and Sparta was soon included in the Achaean League.

Further Reading: Diana Bowder. *Who Was Who in the Greek World* (Ithaca, New York: Cornell University Press, 1982).

Nadir Shah (1688–1747)

Sometimes called the Persian Napoléon, Nadir Shah conquered India and preserved a united Persia.

The son of a sheepskin clothier, Nadir Shah was born on October 22, 1688. As a youth, he attracted the attention of a local chieftain, Ahmadlu Afshar, who made Nadir a protégé, and in whose service he rapidly advanced, eventually being named governor of Abivard. Eventually, however, he fell out of favor with Afshar and became a rebel, gathering a sizable army. In 1727, after allying himself with Tahmasp II, heir to the Safavid dynasty which had been effectively deposed by Afghan invaders five years earlier, Nadir began to retake Persia from the Afghans. By 1729, following the climactic Battle of Murchehkhor, he had pushed the Afghans out of Persia. Unfortunately, his ally Tahmasp, unsupported, moved against the Turks while Nadir Shah was putting down Khorazanian revolt. His forces crushed, Tahmasp was compelled to agree to a humiliating peace, forfeiting all of Georgia and Armenia.

Enraged, Nadir Shah summarily deposed his erstwhile ally and installed his infant son on the throne, naming himself as regent. He immediately made war on the Turks in 1733 and, within two years, not only recaptured the lost territory, but pushed the Turks all the way into Asia Minor. He then turned his troops toward Russia and demanded the Caspian provinces, which the czar relinquished in 1735 without a fight.

Nadir Shah now turned toward India and prepared his most ambitious campaign yet. After capturing Kabul, Nadir Shah marched his army through the Khyber Pass and into the Indus Valley. Reaching a point 60 miles north of Delhi, he met the Indian army at the Battle of Karnal in 1739, dealing it a severe defeat. He plundered Indian treasures, taking with him the famed jewel-encrusted Peacock throne and the Koh-i-Noor diamond, which still reside in an Iranian vault and, with the balance of the plunder, remain as the guarantor of Iranian currency.

His thirst for military conquest was never satiated, and the only thing that kept Nadir Shah from ruling more of the world was, it seemed, lack of transportation. He built a navy, captured Bahrain from the Arabs, conquered Oman, and was at constant war with the Turks. Once, when he was told that there was no war in paradise, Nadir Shah was reported to have said, "How can there be any delights there?"

Although ruthless, he was not a successful administer of his empire. The financial burden of constant war was more than his people could bear, and his sheer cruelty was insufferable. When he suspected his own son of plotting against him, he had the young man blinded. He was supposed to have ordered all his Persian officers executed, but before the command could be carried out, he was assassinated by members of the army on June 19, 1747.

At his death, Nadir Shah's empire extended to the expansive boundaries of ancient Persia—but it was an empire he left bleeding to death.

Further Reading: Laurence Lockhart. *Nadir Shah: A Critical Study Based Mainly upon Contemporary Sources* (London: Luzac, 1938).

Napoléon I [Napoléon Bonaparte] (1769–1821)

Perhaps the most brilliant figure in military history, Napoléon I reshaped Europe, commanding hatred and admiration in his own time and exerting a near mythic fascination that endures to this day. His name is simultaneously synonymous with conquest, unbounded ego, absolute power, and abject defeat.

Napoléon's early life gave little hint of the momentous role he was to play. He was born Napoleone Buonaparte on August 15, 1769, at Ajaccio,

211

Corsica, recently acquired by France, the second surviving son of Carlo and Maria Letizia Buonaparte. He attended the Royal Military College at Brienne-le-Château from April 1779 to October 1784, but was spurned as a provincial and a foreigner. Thus rejected, the young man grew aloof and threw himself into his studies. Nevertheless, he managed to graduate only near the bottom of his class, 42nd of 58 members. Abandoning naval for artillery training, Napoléon pursued further study at the École Militaire in Paris; he was commissioned a second lieutenant of artillery on September 1, 1785, and was assigned garrison duty with the La Fère artillery regiment.

During this period, Napoléon was influenced by the military theorist J. P. du Teil and also became involved in a Corsican nationalist movement beginning in 1789. He was transferred to the Grenoble artillery regiment in February 1791, securing promotion to first lieutenant. At this time, he became active in the Jacobin Club of Grenoble, traveled to Corsica, and engineered his election as lieutenant colonel of the Ajaccio Volunteers on April 1, 1792. After participating in an unsuccessful action in Sardinia during February 21–26, 1793, Napoléon fell into a dispute with the anti-French Corsican nationalist Pasquale Paoli. With his family, Napoléon fled to Marseille on June 10, 1793.

When the Revolt of the Midi (July) broke out, Napoléon joined on the side of the republicans and was appointed commander of artillery in the army of General Jean-Baptiste Carteaux. On September 16, 1793, he participated in the successful siege of Toulon, a royalist stronghold occupied by the British. By December 19, the British had been driven out, and Toulon fell to the republicans.

As a reward for his able command of the artillery, Napoléon was made a brigadier general, then designated artillery commander of the French Army of Italy in February 1794. With the overthrow of Maximilien ROBESPIERRE in July 1794, however, Napoléon was imprisoned from August 6 to September 14, 1794.

Following his release, Napoléon declined artillery command of the Army of the West and was assigned instead to the war office's Topographical Bureau. Appointed second in command of the Army of the Interior, he ended the Parisian uprising of 13 Vendémiaire (October 5, 1795), which protested the means of implementing the new constitution introduced by the National Convention. Napoléon dispersed the insurrectionists with a "whiff of grapeshot," thereby saving the Convention. The Directory, as the new government was called, rewarded him with full command of the Army of the Interior. It was at this

time—in March 1796—that Napoleon married Joséphine de Beauharnais, the rather notorious widow of a titled republican general, and changed his surname to Bonaparte.

Once in command of the Army of the Interior, Napoléon moved vigorously against Piedmontese (Sardinian) and Austrian forces, bringing about an armistice with the Piedmontese by the end of April after defeating them at Ceva and Mondovi in April, thereby securing the cession of Savoy and Nice to France. He next moved swiftly and brilliantly against the Austrians, defeating them at Lodi on May 10, then entering Milan on May 15. He drove the Austrian forces out of Lombardy during May and June. Mantua, the last Austrian stronghold in the region, fell to Napoleon in February 1797 following a lengthy siege. Napoleon next advanced toward Vienna itself, a move that sent the Austrians to the peace table. The commander himself negotiated the Treaty of Campo Formio on October 17, 1797, by which the war of the First Coalition—the first of the French revolutionary wars—was ended.

Napoléon reshaped Italian politics, creating the Cisalpine Republic, establishing what were in effect various puppet governments in Italy, and pillaging Italian art collections to help finance French military operations. Hailed as a hero by the Directory, that body proposed to send the conqueror of Italy to invade England. But Napoléon successfully promoted another grand strategy: the invasion of Egypt in order to secure a staging area for an invasion of British India. Accordingly, he sailed on May 19, 1798, with some 35,000 troops bound for Alexandria. He took Malta on the way to Egypt, handily evading the British fleet under the command of Horatio Nelson, then occupied Alexandria and Cairo. Wisely, Napoléon guaranteed the preservation of Islamic law, but set about modernizing the secular government during September 1798–February 1799.

On August 1, 1798, Admiral Nelson's fleet destroyed the French fleet at Aboukir Bay, cutting Napoléon off from France. This defeat notwithstanding, Napoléon continued Egyptian operations. When the Ottoman Turks declared war on France in February 1799, Napoléon sought to head off a Turkish invasion of Egypt by preemptively invading Syria. Turkish troops under British command halted his advance at Acre during March 15–May 17, and the French army was stricken with plague. Napoléon brought his army back to Cairo in June, then, on July 25, defeated an Anglo-Turkish invasion attempt at Aboukir.

At this point, the French situation in Europe had reached a crisis, as French forces were suffering defeat at the hands of the Second Coalition. Napoléon embarked for France on August 24, 1799, arriving in Paris on October 14. There he participated in the coup d'état of November 9 (18 Brumaire) against the Directory. Appointed commander of the Paris garrison, Napoléon secured appointment as one of three consuls in a new Consulate. Under the Constitution of the Year VIII, he was elected first consul, with power to appoint members of the council of state, government officials, and judges, and was installed in February 1800. As first consul, Napoléon consolidated what soon amounted to dictatorial power, radically centralizing government and bringing it under his personal control.

The mood of the nation favored him. Racked by years of revolutionary terror and lawlessness, still faced with a formidable royalist faction, the people were willing to hand over authority to one strong man. It was during this period that Napoléon participated in the creation of the Code Napoléon, which codified civil law. The first consul concluded the 1801 Concordat with Pope Pius VII, reestablishing Roman Catholicism as the state religion. Napoléon radically restructured the French national debt, setting the French economy on a sound footing. He encouraged the development of industry and the improvement of the educational system, and he initiated an ambitious program of construction inspired by the classical examples of imperial Rome.

In the meantime, Napoléon continued to establish France as a world power, defeating the Austrians at the Battle of Marengo on June 14, 1800, bringing about the Treaty of Lunéville (February 9, 1801) and initiating a brief interval of peace with all of Europe, including England, which signed the Treaty of Amiens (March 27, 1802). By virtue of plebiscite, a grateful France created Napoléon first consul for life on August 2, 1802.

Once again, Napoléon set about reshaping the face of Europe. In Holland he occupied the Batavian Republic and in Switzerland the Helvetic Republic. He annexed Savoy-Piedmont, then took the first step toward abolishing the Holy Roman Empire by means of the Imperial Recess of 1803, which consolidated free cities and minor states dominated by the Holy Roman Empire. (He also attempted to recover the Caribbean island nation of Haiti, which had rebelled against French colonial domination.) Napoléon's renewed aggression, coupled with his refusal to grant trade concessions to Britain, reignited war in May 1803.

As Napoléon prepared an army of 170,000 troops to invade England, an assassination scheme, financed by the British, was discovered. Alarmed by this, the French Senate petitioned Napoléon to establish a hereditary dynasty. The first consul eagerly

The emperor Napoléon in the plain uniform he wore while campaigning. (From Charlotte M. Yonge, Pictorial History of the World's Great Nations, *1882)*

seized the opportunity and, on December 2, 1804, as Pope Pius VII looked on, he crowned himself emperor. Abrogating the republic for which he had fought, Napoléon created a royal court populated by former republicans and royalists alike. Not content merely to create a dynasty for France, he eventually installed members of his family on the thrones of newly created kingdoms of Naples, Holland, Westphalia, and Spain. In 1809, he divorced Joséphine because she had failed to bear a male heir. On April 2, 1810, he married Marie-Louise, daughter of the Austrian emperor, and a son (the king of Rome) was born to the couple within a year.

In the meantime, Napoléon formulated a strategy to draw the mighty British fleets away from England in order to facilitate his planned invasion. This strategy collapsed, however, and Austria now prepared to renew war; Napoléon was compelled to table his invasion plans. On May 26, 1805, he was crowned king of Italy in Milan and during July through September maneuvered against the Austrians, led by General Karl von Mack von Leiberich, encircling and defeating him at Ulm during September 25–October 20, 1805. This triumph on land was offset, however, by the defeat of his fleet at sea when Admiral Nelson annihilated most of the French ships at the Battle of Trafalgar (off Spain) on October 21. Invasion of England was now out of the question.

Napoléon advanced and took Vienna on November 13, then continued into Moravia, where the Russian army under Marshal Mikhail Kutuzov offered battle at Austerlitz. Napoléon's complete victory here on December 2 was his greatest single military triumph. By the end of the month, Austria signed the Treaty of Pressburg, relinquishing Venice and Dalmatia to Napoléon's Kingdom of Italy. On July 12, 1806, Napoléon abolished the Holy Roman Empire, organizing in its stead the Confederation of the Rhine, a French protectorate of German states. In an attempt to ease hostilities with England, Napoléon offered to return Hanover to British control, which provoked war with Prussia in September.

Under Prussian direction, the Fourth Coalition against Napoléon was created, but its armies were decisively defeated at the battles of Jena and Auerstedt (both on October 14, 1806). Following this, Napoléon met the Russian army at Eylau on February 8, 1807, which resulted in a draw, and then at Friedland, on June 14, 1807, a clear victory for the emperor that enabled Napoléon to compel Czar Alexander I to sign the Treaties of Tilsit in July 1807. These created the French-controlled Grand Duchy of Warsaw, gained Russia recognition of other European entities created by Napoléon, and removed

Napoléon directing his armies in Spain. (From Charlotte M. Yonge, Pictorial History of the World's Great Nations, *1882)*

from Prussia all lands between the Rhine and Elbe rivers.

The emperor now enjoyed unparalleled sway over Europe, but he was not satisfied. Unable to defeat England by military means, he instituted in 1806–1807 the Continental System, a blockade of British trade intended to destroy the British economy. This measure created tremendous unrest throughout Europe, and Portugal immediately announced that it would not participate in the blockade. Napoléon launched the Peninsular War to compel Portugal's obedience. This provoked unrest in Spain and the abdication of King Charles IV and his son Ferdinand VII during May 5–6, 1808, as well as a popular revolution against Napoléon's chosen successor to the Spanish throne, his brother JOSEPH BONAPARTE.

While Napoléon was embroiled on the Iberian peninsula, Austria formed the Fifth Coalition, prosecuting a war that resulted in early coalition victories but that culminated in a decisive French victory at the Battle of Wagram on July 5–6, 1809. Napoléon married Marie-Louise following the July 12 armistice with Austria, which, by the Treaty of Schönbrunn (October 14, 1809), relinquished Illyria and Galicia.

Despite this major victory, Napoléon was losing his grasp on Spain and Portugal. Now Russia also refused to participate in the Continental System, and a militarily overextended Napoléon invaded that country on June 23–24, 1812. The Russian armies retreated before the emperor's advance, pulling him deeper and deeper into that vast land. Napoleon was victorious at Borodino on September 7, 1812, and arrived in Moscow within a week.

But Czar ALEXANDER I refused to surrender, and Russian partisans set fire to the city. Under attack by freshly reinforced Russian armies, and with the vicious Russian winter closing in, Napoléon began a painful retreat that soon became an unmitigated disaster. Although he managed to preserve himself and the core of his Grand Army, much of his forces were destroyed by December.

In the wake of this defeat, the Prussians abandoned their short-lived alliance with the French to form against Napoléon a Sixth Coalition, consisting of Prussia, Russia, Britain, and Sweden. In Paris, the emperor built a new army, with which he defeated coalition forces at Lützen on May 2, 1813, and at Bautzen on May 20–21, bringing about a brief armistice. In August, Austria joined the Sixth Coalition. Napoléon defeated Austrian troops at Dresden during August 26–27 but, badly outnumbered, the French were in turn defeated at the Battle of the Nations at Leipzig on October 16–19, 1813.

Napoléon retreated across the Rhine, but refused to surrender any conquered territory. The next year, coalition armies invaded France itself, but the emperor prevailed against each attempt to penetrate to Paris until repeated mauling of his dwindling forces prompted a mutiny of his marshals and the fall of the capital on March 31, 1814.

A few days after this, on April 4, Napoléon abdicated in favor of his son. The allies rejected this, and Napoléon abdicated unconditionally on April 6. He was exiled to the British-controlled island of Elba. In 1815, however, Napoléon returned to France, landing at Cannes on March 1. The Bourbon monarch, Louis XVIII fled, and Napoléon occupied Paris on March 20. The allies, meeting at the Congress of Vienna, spurned Napoléon's claim of peaceful intentions. Seeking to forestall combined attack by Russian and Austrian armies, Napoléon decided to strike first in order to divide and destroy Prussian and Anglo-Dutch armies in Belgium. Indeed, Napoléon prevailed against the Austrians at Ligny on June 16 and against the British at Quatre-Bras on the same day, but he was defeated at Waterloo by the Duke of Wellington reinforced by troops under Gebhard von Blücher on June 18, 1815.

Napoléon returned to Paris, abdicated for the second time on June 22, and surrendered to the captain of the *Bellerophon*, a British warship. He was exiled, this time to the island of Saint Helena. There he composed his memoirs and grew increasingly ill. Some authorities believe that he succumbed to cancer of the stomach on May 5, 1821; others have theorized that he died of gradual arsenic poisoning, which may have been the result of a deliberate assassination effort or due to overmedication with the arsenic-based drugs popular during the period.

Further reading: David G. Chandler. *The Campaigns of Napoleon* (New York: Macmillan, 1966); Chandler. *Napoleon* (New York: Saturday Review Press, 1973); Felix Markham. *Napoleon* (New York: New American Library, 1964).

Napoléon III   [Louis-Napoléon Bonaparte] (1808–1873)

A headstrong imperialist, Napoléon III brought France into the modern era, but saw his empire go down in defeat in the Franco-Prussian War of 1870–71.

Born in Paris on April 20, 1808, Louis-Napoléon was a nephew of Napoléon Bonaparte (NAPOLÉON I) and a son of Napoléon's brother, Louis Bonaparte, at one time the king of Holland. When his uncle fell from power in 1815, the young Louis-Napoléon was exiled with the rest of the Bonaparte family. Louis-Napoléon ended up in Switzerland with his mother, a step-daughter of Napoléon I.

When Louis' cousin, the duke of Reichstadt, who was Napoléon I's only child, died in 1832, Louis-Na-

poléon resolved that he would be acknowledged the Bonaparte heir to France. Accordingly, he set himself upon a rigorous training regime that would better prepare him for his duty when the day finally arrived that would see the Bonaparte name re-established in French politics. In 1836, he attempted to recruit troops to participate in a coup d'état against King LOUIS-PHILIPPE, but, unsuccessful, was exiled to the United States. Returning briefly to Switzerland the following year because of his mother's ill health, he soon moved to England.

Louis-Napoléon attempted another coup in 1840 and was again thwarted and imprisoned. He escaped in 1846 and fled to England, where he bided his time. Opportunity came with the revolution of 1848. Louis-Napoléon returned to France and managed to get himself elected to the Constituent Assembly. Trading on the popularity of his name, exploiting the uneasiness of the times, and disseminating a good deal of propaganda, Louis-Napoléon was elected president of France in December 1848, garnering almost 5.5 million votes. Aware that the republican constitution barred him from succeeding himself in office, Louis-Napoléon staged a successful coup de'état in 1852 and declared himself emperor.

As Emperor Napoléon III, Louis-Napoleon proved to be a farsighted imperialist statesman. He initiated a foreign policy that strengthened French influence in Africa and in Indochina. He lent his backing to the construction of the Suez Canal. He concluded an important commercial treaty with Great Britain, which secured for France an enviable economic situation. Far less successful was his high-handed imposition of the Austrian archduke Maximilian as emperor of an unwilling Mexico. Intended to secure Mexican debts to France and other nations, the scheme failed miserably—and with tragic consequences for the well-meaning Maximilian.

When Prussia tried to place a member of its royal family on the Spanish throne, Napoléon III declared war and plunged France into the 1870–71 Franco-Prussian conflict. The result was a ruinous and humiliating defeat for the French. Desperate, Napoléon III threw himself into the forefront of the decisive Battle of Sédan, deliberately exposing himself to death. He survived the battle, however, and surrendered on September 2, 1871. Two days later, he was deposed, as the Third Republic was declared. Ailing, Louis-Napoléon went to live in England, where he died, in Kent, on January 9, 1873, following bladder surgery.

Further reading: Albert Guerard. *Napoleon III* (Cambridge: Harvard University Press, 1943); J. M. Thompson. *Louis-Napoleon and the Second Empire* (New York: Norton, 1967).

Nasser, Gamal Abdel   (1918–1970)

President of Egypt from 1956 to 1970, Gamal Abdel Nasser led a revolution that instituted social and agrarian reform in the country, and attempted to forge a union of Arab states in the Middle East.

Born on January 15 or 16, 1918, in the village of Bani Morr in the Upper Egyptian province of Asyut to a middle-class family, Gamal Abdel Nasser rose to power over a period of 14 years, beginning in 1937, when he entered the military academy. Nasser graduated in 1938 as a second lieutenant, and served in the town of Mankabad, finding close friends in two other recent graduates, Zakaria Mohieddin and Anwar al-Sadat, who, with Nasser, would become prominent in the Free Officers movement that overthrew King Farouk in 1952. Nasser returned to the academy in 1941 as an instructor and forged many more close alliances with young officers. The cadet corps had begun to change dramatically beginning in 1936, when an official decree allowed lower- and middle-class Egyptian boys to be admitted. Nasser had much in common with this newly constituted corps, and over the next few years he recruited members for the Free Officers movement.

During the 1940s and early 1950s, deep social unrest spread through Egypt. One tenth of one percent of all landowners owned 20 percent of the land, 35 percent of the land was owned by 95 percent of the landowners, and most small landowners owned only an acre or less. Malnutrition and disease were rampant, and dismal conditions in rural areas sent many peasants to the cities, where prices and unemployment were driven steadily higher. The time was ripe for action by the Free Officers. Two thousand troops led by 200 officers stormed army headquarters in Cairo during the night of July 22–23, 1952. By morning, a new political order was in place, with Major General Mohammad Naguib as its head.

Nasser remained in the background as the Revolutionary Command Council took control, but in the spring of 1954, in a reaction against left-wing radicalism, Naguib was deposed, and it was Nasser who emerged as the self-proclaimed prime minister.

Land reform was the new government's first order of business. A 1952 law limited land ownership to 200 acres per person. That limit was subsequently lowered to 100 acres in 1961 and 50 acres in 1965. Middle-class farmers then came to dominate rural society, where once a small elite of wealthy landowners held sway. But Nasser knew that land reform was not enough to shake Egypt out of its downward economic spiral. A special stimulus was needed as well, and Nasser seized on the construction of the massive Aswan Dam on the Nile as a vehicle for economic recovery. He first negotiated with

Britain and the United States for financial backing for the project. Uneasy about Nasser's courting of Eastern bloc and Soviet support (he had signed an arms deal with Czechoslovakia in 1956), Britain, the United States, and the World Bank withdrew from the project. Undaunted, Nasser nationalized the Suez Canal, whose proceeds had previously gone to European bondholders, and stated that use fees would be dedicated to constructing the new dam. Israel, pursuant to agreements with Britain and France, then invaded Egypt and occupied the Canal Zone, but when the Soviet Union and the United States objected to the occupation, the troops withdrew.

Nasser's reputation soared after the Suez crisis. He had successfully met opposition from Western countries and had pushed Israel out of Arab territory. In addition, the nationalization of the canal brought much-needed funds to Egypt, and the construction of the Aswan Dam proceeded, with aid from the Soviet Union.

Nasser then set out to realize yet another goal—the unification of Arab countries. In 1958, the government of Syria merged with Egypt to form the United Arab Republic. It was Nasser's goal to recruit all of the other Arab countries into the fold. The republic was short-lived, however. Not only did the other nations fail to join, but Syria withdrew in 1961. Nevertheless, Egypt did become a haven for Arab radicals and anticolonial revolutionaries as Nasser welcomed political refugees from other Arab countries. Even as he embraced foreign radicals, he cracked down on civil freedom in his own country. Private mail was routinely opened, the media was censored, and newspapers were nationalized. Concentration camps were constructed to hold political prisoners, and a well-organized secret police fanned out through the country to ensure that Nasser's government would remain in complete control. Elections were held, but they were dominated by handpicked candidates who generally ran unopposed.

Despite the repressive measures he instituted, Nasser remained immensely popular, except during a crisis in 1962, brought on when he dispatched troops to North Yemen to fight a war sometimes called "Nasser's Vietnam."

The end seemed to come in 1967, when Nasser called for the withdrawal of United Nations Emergency Force troops from the Gaza Strip and instituted a blockade of Eilat, precipitating a brilliant preemptive war by Israel that destroyed Egypt's air force on the ground. On June 9, 1967, Gamal Abdel Nasser appeared on Egyptian television to announce his resignation. Hundreds of thousands of Egyptians took to the streets to demonstrate their demand that

Nasser remain in power. While some of the demonstrations may have been engineered by Nasser himself, it is undeniable that some were indeed spontaneous. A hard-liner against Israel and the West, supremely repressive at home, Nasser—from his assumption of power in 1954 until his death from a heart attack on September 28, 1970—was nevertheless the most popular Arab leader of his day.

Further reading: Jean Lacoutre. *Nasser: A Biography* (New York: Knopf, 1973); Robert Stephens. *Nasser: A Political Biography* (New York: Simon & Schuster, 1971).

Natusch Busch, Alberto (1936–   )

Military ruler of Bolivia for 16 days, Natusch Busch desperately attempted to hold power, only to be overthrown.

Little is known of Alberto Natusch Busch before his rule of Bolivia aside from the fact that he was an unexceptional career military man, reaching the rank of colonel by November 2, 1979. That is when, with the support of the military, he seized the presidential palace of Walter Guevara Arze and many government buildings, overthrowing the first civilian government to rule Bolivia in more than 10 years. When Natusch Busch's troops opened fire on crowds outside the palace, six were killed and 21 wounded.

President Arze denounced the coup and vowed to oppose Natusch Busch by calling a general worker's strike. The strike paralyzed the cities, and the Bolivian Congress met in support of Arze against Natusch Busch. The colonel responded by forcibly dissolving Congress and assuming dictatorial powers. In the meantime, the United States suspended its $27.5 million aid package to Bolivia. Natusch Busch responded with a pledge to improve the country's infrastructure and cooperate with labor, but after gunfire erupted in the capital of La Paz, many felt that Natusch Busch was losing support even from the military.

In a show of force, Natusch Busch ordered tanks and jet planes to move against demonstrators, and he authorized them to open fire on November 5. When the general strike continued unbroken, Natusch Busch ordered the machine gunning of labor headquarters by tanks and armored cars. In a third day of fighting with labor, troops again opened fire on demonstrators, killing at least two more.

Natusch Busch was finally forced to step down November 16 when the military deserted him, refusing to continue the battle against the strikers.

Nebuchadnezzar II (r. 605–562 B.C.)

Nebuchadnezzar II was the most important of the Chaldean, or Neo-Babylonian, kings and is remembered for having brought Babylonia to the pinnacle of its power and for subjugating the Jews after having destroyed Jerusalem.

The name of this monarch, who reigned from 605 to 562 B.C., is more accurately transcribed from the Babylonian original as Nabu-kudur-usur, and modern historians often refer to him as Nebuchadrezzar. However, he is most popularly known by the name supplied in the King James translation of the Old Testament, Nebuchadnezzar. He was the son of the powerful Nabopolassar, who founded the Chaldean dynasty in Babylonia, when, as Assyrian-appointed governor of the region, he revolted in 626, allying himself with the Medes. In 612, Nabopolassar destroyed the Assyrian capital of Nineveh and succeeded in driving the Assyrians into northwestern Mesopotamia. At this point, Nabopolassar entrusted further military operations to his son, Nebuchadnezzar.

Nebuchadnezzar not only continued the dispersal of the Assyrians, but, in 605 B.C., at the Battle of Carchemish, he defeated forces under the pharaoh Necho, thereby evicting from Syria the Egyptians, Assyria's principal ally. Nebuchadnezzar was mounting an invasion of Egypt proper when he learned of his father's death. Immediately, he returned to Babylon to assume the throne.

In the course of his long reign, Nebuchadnezzar campaigned vigorously and efficiently in Syria, Palestine, and Phoenicia to put down sporadic rebellions. By the standards of the ancient Middle East, however, his reign was relatively peaceful, and he propelled his nation into a major program of monumental building that included the great stepped pyramid or ziggurat known as the Hanging Gardens of Babylon, revered as one of the seven wonders of the ancient world. Under Nebuchadnezzar, Babylon reached a most impressive level of cultural sophistication.

In the Judeo-Christian tradition, the Babylonian monarch is remembered far less for his cultural achievements than as the cruel tyrant who twice besieged Jerusalem—in 597 and 586—and carried off the Jews into the long "Babylonian captivity" recounted in Scripture. This was in the course of Nebuchadnezzar's ongoing struggle with the Egyptians; for the Jewish kingdom of Judah had the misfortune of being located between the contending empires, and its political position, no less than its geographical position, was untenable. Neither power would allow Judah to remain independent or neutral, yet to side with one meant annihilation by the other.

The later years of Nebuchadnezzar's reign are clouded in obscurity. The Book of Daniel portrays him as an infirm and senile monarch and describes him eating grass and undergoing a transformation suggesting severe mental derangement and physical illness. Some biblical historians believe that he was overthrown by his son. However, some modern scholarship, based on material found in the Dead Sea Scrolls, suggests that Nabonidus, who reigned as the last Chaldean king from 556 to 539 B.C., was the afflicted old monarch of the Bible, not Nebuchadnezzar.

Further Reading: George S. Goodspeed. *A History of the Babylonians and the Assyrians* (New York: Scribner's, 1902).

Nero   [Nero Claudius Caesar] (37–68)

Nero, who reigned from A.D. 54 to 68, rivals only CALIGULA as Rome's most infamous emperor.

Born on December 15, A.D. 37, Nero was the son of Consul Domitius Ahenobarbus and Caligula's sister Agrippina II. After Ahenobarbus' death, Agrippina married her uncle, the emperor CLAUDIUS, whom she persuaded to adopt Nero. When Claudius died—quite possibly having been poisoned by Agrippina—both the Praetorian Guard and the Senate proclaimed Nero, who was not quite 17, as the new emperor.

Nero promised great things, paramountly his full cooperation with the Senate in creating for Rome, wearied by a series of bad emperors, a new golden age. But almost immediately, Agrippina schemed to achieve additional power, struggling with Burrus, former favorite of Agrippina and now prefect of the Praetorian Guard, as well as with Nero's tutor Seneca for access to and influence over the young emperor. In the first wave of these maneuvers, Agrippina—or, perhaps, Nero himself—eliminated one possible rival, poisoning in the year 55 13-year-old Britannicus, Claudius' son by his earlier marriage to Messalina.

There followed an interval of relative calm—and even decent administration—although the Senate was already feeling slighted by an emperor who, despite his initial pledge, rarely consulted that body. In 59, however, the court of Nero again turned ugly. The emperor, weary of his mother's interference in his affairs, had her murdered. Three years later, the two other dominant influences on Nero left power: Burrus died in 62, and, that same year, Seneca retired. Nero was thus unleashed upon Rome.

He fell under the influence of a new praetorian prefect, Tigellinus—of infamous reputation—and of one Poppaea Sabina, who ingratiated herself with Nero and engineered his divorce from Octavia, Claudius' daughter. After the divorce, Poppaea encouraged Nero to have Octavia murdered, and she herself wed the emperor in 62. Steeped in the blood of his family, Nero now reactivated a long-disused all-encompassing treason law and instituted a purge

In a long line of "wicked" Roman emperors, Nero stands out as one of the worst. (From Richard Delbruck, Antike Portrats, *1912)*

program in which persons were executed on the merest pretext of having committed an offense.

While Nero schemed and murdered, the administration of the empire suffered badly. The uprising of Boudicca, queen of the Iceni tribe of Britons, was sparked by Roman greed and was put down only at great cost. On the frontier with Asia Minor, the empire lost sway over Armenia, and an economic crisis followed, resulting in the depreciation of Roman coinage. Despite these problems, Nero lived in extravagant luxury. When a great fire swept Rome in 64, Nero not only rebuilt the monuments of the city, but constructed his lavish Golden House, a palace of unprecedented extravagance and expense. Soon rumors widely circulated that Nero had deliberately started the fire to clear space for his palace. Nero, who fancied himself a poet and songster, was said to have recited and sung as he watched the city burn.

The emperor took the rumors against him seriously and embarked on a program of rumor and propaganda of his own, accusing the city's emerging sect of Christians (whose spread Nero saw as a threat to himself in any case) of having started the fire. This touched off the first wave of Roman persecution of Christians.

The following year, A.D. 65, saw a sharp increase in executions for treason, as a plot to assassinate Nero was discovered. Among those who perished were respected senators and also luminaries of Roman letters and learning, including the poet Lucan and the philosopher Seneca, as well as the Stoics Thrasea Paetus and Barea Soranus, and the celebrated arbiter of taste, Gaius Petronius. The famed general Corbulo was also induced to take his own life.

Perhaps most horrifying was the detachment with which Nero, far more passionate about art and luxury than statecraft, dispatched his perceived enemies. With Rome in a crisis of his own making, Nero toured Greece in 67, claiming from the Greeks an array of prizes and honors for his triumphs in chariot races and musical performances. Inexorably, however, his political power eroded, and in 68 Julius Vindex, legate of Gallia Lugdunensis, persuaded Servius Supoicius Galba, legate in Spain, and Clodius Macer, legate in Africa, to open revolt. This bold move incited the Praetorian Guard against the emperor, who panicked and fled, committing suicide on June 9, 68.

Further Reading: John H. Bishop. *Nero: The Man and the Legend* (London: Robert Hale, 1964); Michael Grant. *Nero: Emperor in Revolt* (New York: American Heritage, 1970); Brian H. Warmington. *Nero: Reality and Legend* (New York: Norton, 1970).

Neto, Antonio Agostinho (1922–1979)

Neto used his background as a poet and physician to further the Angolan independence movement against Portuguese colonialism.

Agostinho Neto was born September 17, 1922, in Luanda, the capital of Angola, and was raised in the home of a Methodist minister. His mother was a teacher, and for that reason he was one of a privileged minority to receive a secondary education. Beginning work for the government health services in 1944, Neto also participated in the formation of nationalist cultural associations after political parties were outlawed by the Portuguese.

Neto won a scholarship to study medicine at the University of Lisbon and then at Coimbra. In Lisbon, he became an activist against the SALAZAR dictatorship and was arrested on several occasions. He wrote poetry as an expression of the nationalist movement and was arrested on account of that as well. But his poetry became widely known and greatly admired. Artists and politicians agitated for Neto's release, and, that secured, he finished medical school in 1958.

Back in Angola, Neto continued to write, but he also spurned the life of privilege which was now his

as a trained physician. He opened what amounted to a free clinic, available to all Angolans. His writings and poetry again provoked his arrest—this time in his own waiting room—and when his patients protested, Portuguese authorities opened fire on the crowd, killing and wounding hundreds. Neto was exiled to the Cape Verde Islands and subsequently sent to Portugal. In 1962, he managed his escape to Morocco, moving on to present-day Zaîre.

By the end of 1962, Neto was elected president of the Popular Movement for the Liberation of Angola (MPLA). The MPLA advocated armed resistance to the Portuguese authorities, and Neto organized the movement for 12 years. During this period, he traveled throughout Europe and Africa, gaining support for the movement. When Salazar was overthrown in Portugal by a coup, Neto opened negotiations for an independent Angola.

Angola was declared independent in 1975, but was divided among its three independence factions. Neto and the MPLA, with Cuban help, held the central territory containing the capital. On November 11, 1975, Neto, a confirmed Marxist, was sworn in as the first president of the People's Republic of Angola. He eventually gained control of the entire country and began instituting Socialist change in a nation with a literacy rate below 15 percent. His rule was cut short by cancer on September 10, 1979.

Further Reading: Lawrence W. Henderson. *Angola: Five Centuries of Conflict* (Ithaca, N.Y.: Cornell University Press, 1979).

Ngo Dinh Diem (1901–1963)

President of South Vietnam from 1954 until his assassination in 1963, Ngo Dinh Diem was a fervent anti-Communist and ardent Catholic, who governed through repression and intrigue.

Born to a noble family on January 3, 1901, in Quang Binh province, northern Vietnam, Ngo Dinh Diem attended Catholic school in the ancient Vietnamese capital of Hue and studied for the civil service at a college in Hanoi. Within a few years of his graduation, he was named minister of the interior (1933), but he soon resigned, in protest over the French refusal to grant Vietnam a greater degree of autonomous home rule.

For the next 20 years, Diem held no public office, but became an outspoken critic of the French colonial system on the one hand and of communism on the other. The latter doctrine began to spread in the northern part of the country after World War II under the leadership of HO CHI MINH. Indeed, in 1945, Diem was captured by forces under Ho Chi Minh, who invited Diem to join their ranks. Diem refused and fled the country, traveling to the United States in 1950, where he sought backing for an independent, Western-aligned government. Among those Diem met were the senator from Massachusetts, John F. Kennedy, on whom he would later call for support in his war with Ho Chi Minh's North Vietnam.

In 1954, Vietnam's emperor BAO DAI offered Diem the position of prime minister of what would later became the Republic of Vietnam (South Vietnam). Diem accepted, and over the next few years, consolidated his control over the southern portion of the now-divided country. He pushed aside the emperor in the fraudulent elections of 1955 and in the same year rejected the reunification elections called for in the Geneva Accords. Diem ruthlessly and violently neutralized powerful religious sects, and he installed members of his family in high government positions.

A 1960 coup attempt against him prompted even stronger acts of repression as Diem imprisoned hundreds of his political enemies and reneged on promised social and land reforms. Also in 1960, he attacked Buddhist dissidents, killing hundreds in a brutal confrontation, which he justified by claiming that they were aiding the North Vietnamese. This outrage at last alienated even Diem's supporters in the United States, which now indicated to South Vietnamese leaders a willingness to accept a change of government—in effect sanctioning another coup.

On November 1, 1963, the army moved, overthrowing Diem, who was executed with his brother Ngo Dinh Nhu on the following day at Cho Lon, South Vietnam.

Further Reading: Denis Warner. *The Last Confucian.* (New York: Macmillan, 1963).

Nicephorous I   (r. 802–811)
This Byzantine emperor heavily taxed his people in order to build the empire's military.

Under Empress Irene, Nicephorous became finance minister near the end of the eighth century. When Irene was overthrown in a palace coup in 802, Nicephorous was proclaimed emperor. In 803, Barcanes Turcus rose in rebellion, attempting to seize control of the empire, but Nicephorous crushed the uprising before it gained momentum. He was forced to suppress a similar revolt by Arsaber in 808.

Nicephorous followed the religious policies of Irene by outlawing iconoclasm and maintaining orthodoxy, which pleased the ecclesiastical establishment. The priesthood was not happy, however, when Nicephorous appointed a layman as patriarch. Worse, in 809, he convoked a synod and exempted himself from ecclesiastical laws. He further incurred wrath at home by imposing heavy taxes to pay for his military campaigns, often confiscating property to raise revenue.

In 805, Nicephorous withheld the tribute that was due to the Persian caliph HARUN AR-RASHID, which resulted in war. Nicephorous was defeated in Phrygia in 805, and the following year Harun ar-Rashid invaded Asia Minor, capturing much territory and forcing Nicephorous not only to pay the tribute he owed but also a heavy fine. In a struggle with CHARLEMAGNE over Byzantine territories, Nicephorous retained the territories in question in return for his recognizing Charlemagne's sovereignty.

In 811, Nicephorous again made an attempt at military conquest, hoping to contain the Bulgars, who had been raiding the northern Byzantine provinces. Accordingly, he invaded Bulgaria and rejected the peace offering of Krum, the Bulgar khan. Hoping to annihilate Krum and the khanate for good, Nicephorous was himself destroyed when he and his army were led into a mountain defile and killed. As a trophy of battle, Krum had Nicephorous beheaded and his skull lined with silver for use as a drinking cup.

Nicephorous II Phocas   (912–969)
Nicephorous employed his tactical skill to create a resurgence of Byzantine military might, especially at the expense of the Muslims.

The son of a general who successfully defended Byzantium's Anatolian border, Nicephorous Phocas followed his father into the military and soon demonstrated his courage and quick mind while fighting against the Hamdanid Arabs around 950. In 954, Emperor Constantine IV named him to replace his aging father as commander in chief in the East. Nicephorous immediately set about restructuring the army, enforcing strict discipline, avidly recruiting new troops, and writing treatises on tactics.

When Emperor Romanus II, Constantine IV's successor, ordered Nicephorous to march against the Arabs at Crete, Nicephorous mobilized the entire Byzantine fleet and 24,000 men. In a great battle on March 7, 961, Nicephorous emerged victorious, regaining Crete for the empire for the first time in 135 years. He then massacred all the Arabs there to break any future resistance.

When Romanus died in 963, his will named a eunuch to preside over affairs of state while the empress was to serve as regent for his two small children. The people of Constantinople revolted against the eunuch, and the army proclaimed Nicephorous emperor on July 3, 963. He continued his conquest of Arab territories by retaking Cilicia and Cyprus in 965 and marching on Antioch in 969. By the end of his reign, Nicephorous had recovered all the territory lost to the Arabs and established himself as one of the greatest rulers in Byzantine history.

Despite his military achievements, Nicephorus was a reclusive man, who progressively retreated into paranoia. By the end of his reign, he had dismissed, one by one, his best ministers for fear that they were plotting against him. Eventually, he retired to his personal bunker, abandoned by everyone. He was assassinated by three former friends in early December 969.

Nicholas I (1796–1855)

In an era of progressive reform in Europe, Czar Nicholas I maintained a stern reactionary hold over the Russia he governed.

Nicholas, who was born on July 6, 1796, never expected to assume the Russian throne, but his eldest brother, Czar ALEXANDER I, died childless in December 1825 and his next older brother, Constantine, secretly renounced the crown before Alexander's death to marry a Polish commoner. The resulting confusion over succession sparked the Decembrist Uprising, a revolutionary cabal, chiefly made up of young army officers, that proposed to overthrow the newly ascended Nicholas. On December 26, three regiments in Saint Petersburg assembled in the Senate Square and refused to pledge allegiance to Nicholas. The new czar ordered them fired upon, with the result that about 80 of the soldiers and civilian spectators were killed. Five leaders of the rebellion were hanged, others were imprisoned, and many more were sent into Siberian exile. This was the nation's first taste of Nicholas' commitment to a rigidly reactionary policy, which manifested itself in a reign of sustained repression.

Nicholas, who had been given an austere military education, held an absolutist world view in which he saw himself as the agent of God—and responsible to God and God alone—while his subjects were responsible to himself and owed to him their unquestioning allegiance. Through his minister of education, he articulated the absolutist policy he meant to inculcate in Russian children: "Orthodoxy, autocracy, and nationality."

Nicholas I accomplished little of a tangible nature, except rigorously to suppress liberalism. During his reign, the empire's laws were codified into a uniform system of justice, and, as he devoted himself to imposing order at home, so he intervened in the disputes of other European nations. He brutally suppressed a Polish rebellion in 1830–31, and he assisted Austrian forces in quelling the Hungarian revolution of 1848–49. Nicholas' most significant intervention was in the Crimea. The war there began in a dispute concerning jurisdiction over the Holy

Places of Turkish-held Jerusalem. France intervened as protector of Catholicism, while Nicholas, eager for an opportunity to dominate Turkey, committed Russian forces in the name of the Orthodox faith. Nicholas died during this most futile of wars on March 2, 1855.

Further Reading: W. Bruce Lincoln. *Nicholas I* (Bloomington: Indiana University Press, 1978).

Nicholas II (1868–1918)

The last czar of imperial Russia (1895 to 1917), Nicholas and his family were executed following the Russian revolution of 1917.

Nicholas II succeeded his father, Czar ALEXANDER III, on November 1, 1894, the same year he married Alexandra of Hesse. As czar, Nicholas was indecisive, noncommittal, and often simply thoughtless. He randomly bypassed accepted administrative channels, as when he concluded an alliance with German kaiser WILHELM II in 1905 at Bjorko, despite Russia's alliance with France, Germany's enemy. This cavalier attitude toward government left Russian policy in disarray.

Following Russia's humiliating defeat in the Russo-Japanese War (1904–05), discontent mounted, soon growing into a full-fledged revolutionary movement. The czar's secret police crushed this early revolt, but the seeds of discontent had been sown.

In the meantime, Nicholas grew increasingly autocratic and more and more out of touch with the Russian people. Nicholas was uxorious, repeatedly yielding to his strong-willed wife, who brought to court the spiritual leader RASPUTIN—the infamous "Mad Monk"—who soon acquired great power over both the czar and czarina. And Rasputin was merely the most notorious of a host of irresponsible advisers with whom Nicholas surrounded himself.

The assassination of Archduke Francis Ferdinand at Sarajevo in 1914 prompted Nicholas to diplomatic efforts aimed at averting war. When war did break out, the crisis temporarily enhanced his popular support. But, arbitrarily autocratic as ever, Nicholas soon alienated the people by ignoring the Duma (parliament) and discouraging the efforts of patriotic volunteers. Worse, Nicholas again bowed to Alexandra's advice in relieving the tremendously popular Grand Duke Nicholas as commander in chief of the armed forces and assuming direction of the army himself. Ministers and advisers who opposed this decision were summarily dismissed.

Not only was Nicholas totally inexperienced in matters of war, his departure for the front meant that the running of the country was left to Alexandra—and, worse, Rasputin, who immediately began appointing new members to the cabinet and the clergy. Rasputin was subsequently murdered by a conspiracy of nobles, but not before his scandalous and grotesque presence during Russia's greatest crisis fanned the flames of revolution. Predictably, too, the war was going badly, and Russian troops were falling by the thousands.

At last, on March 8, 1917, riots broke out throughout Russia. Seven days later, Nicholas abdicated in favor of his brother Michael, who, however, declined the crown. Had Nicholas shown sufficient flexibility to withhold his opposition to the revolution, he and his family might have suffered a fate no worse than exile to Great Britain. However, the royal family was instead imprisoned and then transported to Yekaterinburg (Sverdlovsk) in the Ural Mountains. When it looked as if anti-revolutionary White Russian forces might arrive to rescue the royal family, they were executed—slaughtered on the night of July 16/17, 1918, in the cellar of the house in which they were held.

Further Reading: Richard Charque. *The Twilight of Imperial Russia* (London: Phoenix House, 1958); Marc Ferro. *Nicholas II: Last of the Tsars* (New York: Oxford University Press, 1993); Marvin Lyons. *Nicholas II: The Last Tsar* (New York: St. Martin's, 1974). Robert K. Massie. *Nicholas and Alexandra* (New York: Atheneum, 1967).

Nkrumah, Kwame   (1909–1972)

The first president of Ghana, Kwame Nkrumah was an African revolutionary whose theories of pan-Africanism were eventually decried even by Africans he hoped to unite.

Originally named Francis Nwia, Nkrumah was born September 21, 1909, in a small village in the Gold Coast. After attending Catholic missionary schools for nine years, he attended Achimota College, graduating in 1931. After college, he began teaching at local Catholic schools and at a seminary, where he became seriously interested in the priesthood. But in 1934, Nkrumah was exposed to the pan-African movement by American-educated Nigerian Nationalist Nnamdi Azikwe, who persuaded Nkrumah to study in the United States.

Arriving at Lincoln University in Pennsylvania in 1935, Nkrumah studied the writings of such revolutionary leaders as LENIN, NAPOLÉON, and Gandhi. He also studied Marcus Garvey and his Back to Africa Movement. Nkrumah continued to immerse himself in revolutionary studies and writings in graduate school at the University of Pennsylvania. In 1945, he went to England for further study at the London School of Economics and stepped up his political activism, editing a pan-African journal, becoming vice president of the West African Students'

Union, and helping to organize the Fifth Pan-African Conference in Manchester.

At home, a moderate nationalist organization called the United Gold Coast Convention (UGCC) formed and invited Nkrumah to become general secretary, which he did in November 1947. The Gold Coast was suffering from the postwar depression and a British government more concerned with rebuilding Britain than attending to her colonies. Riots, which broke out in 1948 over economic conditions, were blamed on the UGCC, and members of its leadership, including Nkrumah, were jailed. Upon their release, a rift developed between the more radical Nkrumah and the conservative UGCC. Nkrumah broke with the organization and formed the Convention People's Party in 1949.

Nkrumah and his followers agitated for immediate self-government. Again Nkrumah was arrested, but the unrest he had caused prompted the first national elections to a new legislative assembly, held in 1951. Nkrumah's party dominated at the polls, and on his release, Nkrumah was named prime minister. An offshoot of the UGCC sprang out of tribal movements in opposition to Nkrumah, but this only intensified the radical leader's desire for absolute power.

The Gold Coast received total independence and was renamed Ghana on March 6, 1957, but British officials warned Nkrumah not to attempt to dictate a radical change in policy. Nevertheless, he continued to expound his theories of African unity and gained considerable power at home, arresting many members of parliament and leaders of the opposition. A 1960 plebiscite proclaimed Ghana a republic, and Nkrumah was elected president.

As Nkrumah's popularity grew, so did his authoritarian policies. He freely used the Preventive Detention Act, which allowed him to imprison anyone he felt was a security risk. He rigorously clamped down on any opposition, officially declaring Ghana a one-party state in 1964, and proclaiming himself president for life. Following two determined efforts to assassinate him, Nkrumah became even more authoritarian.

But even intimidation and force could not sustain Nkrumah in the face of his failing economic policies. When a food shortage crisis struck, Nkrumah seemed more interested in pursuing his now unpopular pan-Africanist theories. While Nkrumah was visiting China in 1966, the army seized the palace on February 24, deposing the president and outlawing his party. The coup was attended with general rejoicing, as mobs destroyed or renamed everything that bore Nkrumah's likeness or name. He was exiled to Guinea, where he died in solitude on April

27, 1972, claiming to the end the need for African unity. Despite his exile, his body was returned to his native village, where it was buried with full honors.

Further Reading: Yrui Smertin. *Kwane Nkrumah* (New York: International Publishers, 1987); Henry Bretton, *The Rise and Fall of Kwame Nkrumah* (New York: Praeger, 1967).

Noriega Morena, Manuel Antonio (1938–)

The only head of state ever convicted as a felon by the United States government, this former Panamanian dictator raised disturbing questions about the Reagan-Bush administration's handling of foreign policy during the 1980s.

Born in Panama City on February 11, 1938, to a poor family, Manuel Noriega joined the Panama Defense Forces at the age of 22. Gaining rapid promotion in the PDF after attending military schools in Panama, Peru, and the United States, Noriega was instrumental in suppressing a 1969 coup attempt against Panamanian President General Omar TOR-RIJOS. For his actions, Noriega was made chief of Torrijos' intelligence organization, a powerful position Noriega exploited to gather information on political enemies and thereby assure his ascendancy through the ranks of the Panamanian military and political hierarchy.

In 1981, Torrijos was killed in a plane crash that many believe had been engineered by Noriega. Within two years, Torrijos' successor, Ruben Paredes, retired, clearing the way for Noriega to head the PDF—and the Panamanian government—by 1983. Although Panama is ostensibly governed by civilian rule, the PDF long exercised de facto authority. As head of the PDF, Noriega controlled both the military and the civil government. Over the next six years, Noriega forced the removal of four civilian presidents, who had tried to implicate him in any number of illegal activities, including drug-trafficking, kidnapping, and murder. Noriega did not deal harshly only with opposition leaders. In general, human rights violations under the Noriega-controlled PDF abounded. Terror, intimidation, beatings, and murders were commonplace. At the very least, those who demonstrated their opposition to the Noriega regime were subject to imprisonment without trial.

Noriega was a distasteful but valuable asset to the United States intelligence community. Beginning in the mid-1970s, he had supplied reports on Central America to George Bush, who was at the time director of the Central Intelligence Agency. After Noriega assumed total control of Panama, President Ronald Reagan found him useful in carrying out a covert plan to aid the anti-Sandinista "Contra" rebels in Nicaragua. U.S. congressional investigations revealed that Noriega was instrumental in a scheme to launder drug money through the Bank of Credit and Commerce International (BCCI—popularly known as the Bank of Crooks and Criminals International) and deliver it to the Contra rebels, in exchange for U.S. aid to Panama. The testimony of White House aide Colonel Oliver North implicated President Reagan and Vice President Bush in this covert operation aimed at circumventing Congress, which had refused to vote funding to the Contras. (Neither Reagan nor Bush was ever formally charged with wrongdoing, though President Reagan embarrassed himself with a series of mutually contradictory statements on the matter, and the "Iran-Contra affair" became an issue in the 1988 presidential campaign of George Bush.) During this period, Noriega also continued to supply information to the United States concerning Fidel CASTRO—material so detailed and accurate that CIA director William Casey regularly flew to Panama to meet with Noriega.

Despite Noriega's value as a means of funneling funds to the Contras and as an intelligence "asset," the mounting record of human rights violations in Panama, the implication of Noriega's personal involvement in the murder of political opponent Hugo Spadafora, and blatant evidence of his large-scale trafficking in drugs resulted in the cessation of all U.S. aid to Panama in 1987 and the freezing of Panamanian assets in U.S. banks. With the 1988 presidential campaign of George Bush, Noriega had become a major embarrassment, and when President Bush took office, he went on the offensive against his former ally, calling on the Panamanian people to oust him. Following a failed coup against him, Noriega publicly declared early in December 1989 that a state of war existed between Panama and the United States. On December 16, a U.S. soldier was shot dead by PDF troops, and on December 20, 1989, the United States invaded Panama, primarily to arrest Manuel Noriega on charges of racketeering and drug-trafficking. After a military fiasco in which thousands of Panamanian citizens were killed, Noriega was finally captured by American troops on January 20, 1990.

The trial of Noriega began in Miami in the fall of 1991. Most of the prosecution witnesses were criminals on a par with Noriega or worse and were given immunity in return for testifying against him. According to testimony, Noriega laundered Colombian drug money in Panama, with the aid of the BCCI, and used Panama as a clearing house for cocaine on its way to the United States. In 1983, on an official visit to the United States to meet with then-Vice President George Bush, Noriega arrived in a plane loaded with cocaine for distribution in the United States. On April 10, 1992, Manuel Noriega was con-

victed on eight counts of cocaine trafficking, racketeering, and money laundering, and sentenced to 40
years in prison—the first time in American history
that a head of state was convicted of criminal
charges.

Further Reading: R. M. Koster. *In the Time of the Tyrants:
Panama, 1968–1990* (New York: Norton, 1990).

Novotný, Antonin   (1904–1975)
First secretary of the Czech Communist Party and
president of the country, Novotný was deposed in a
reform movement in 1968.

Antonin Novotný was born on December 10, 1904,
in Letnany, near Prague, the son of a bricklayer.
Trained as a locksmith, he joined the Communist
Party in 1921.

Imprisoned during the German occupation of
Czechoslovakia from 1941 to 1945, Novotný was
elected to the Central Committee of the Communist
Party in 1946 and played a major role in the Stalinist
takeover of the government. In 1951, he became a
member of the Politburo and was selected as first
secretary of the Communist Party two years later. At
the death of President Antonin Zapotocky on November 13, 1957, Novotný was named president and
was reelected in 1964.

Novotný kept Czechoslovakia thoroughly under
the domination of Moscow, despite a nationalist
movement that steadily gained ground during the
1960s. Finally, nationalist and reform factions within
the Czech Communist Party moved against Novotný
in January 1968. Although his presidential term was
not set to expire for another year, Novotný was
forced first to resign his position in the Communist
Party and, two months later, the presidency. He was
succeeded by Alexander Dubček as first secretary of
the Communist Party and by Ludvik Svoboda as
president.

Novotný died on January 28, 1975, in Prague.

O

Obando, José Maria   (1795–1861)
A lieutenant of Simón Bolívar, Obando helped create the Republic of New Granada and promulgated a liberal constitution before he was ousted.

José Obando served the Spanish crown in the Latin American war of independence in the 1820s. He changed sides and joined Simón Bolívar's forces in the newly formed union of New Granada, Ecuador, and Venezuela known as the Republic of Great Colombia in 1822. Obando broke with Bolívar over the latter's ideas for a strong central government and helped Francisco Santander and the liberals establish the Republic of New Granada (Colombia) in 1831.

To remove any potential opposition, many believe that Obando engineered the assassination of Bolívar's top aide, Antonio José de Sucre. Obando served as the first vice president for a year, then as secretary of war. When the liberals were defeated in 1838 by the conservatives, Obando led an uprising against President José Ignacio Marquez, but it failed, and he was exiled to Peru.

When the liberals returned to power in 1849, Obando returned as well and was elected to congress, becoming president of New Granada in 1853. As president, he immediately promulgated a liberal constitution and adopted reforms separating church and state. However, he faced strong opposition both from conservatives and radicals and was ousted the following year, again going into exile. When civil war broke out in 1860, Obando yet again returned to New Granada. He was killed leading troops at the Battle of Sobachoque on April 29, 1861.

Oda Nobunaga   [Kichihōshi, Saburō] (1534–1582)
Japanese warlord who overthrew the Ashikaga shogunate (military regime; 1335–1573) and brought half of Japan under his control.

Born in Owari Province, Japan, Oda Nobunaga was related to the imperial Fujiwara family. The son of a wealthy government official, he inherited his father's estate in 1549 and ruthlessly overpowered other family members, ultimately wresting control of Owari Province in 1560. Later in the year, he turned his attention to a neighboring province and destroyed the forces of the much-feared feudal lord Imagawa Yoshimoto, thereby taking the first steps toward the unification of Japan.

Controlling the fertile agricultural plains of Owari and the mercantile interests of Nagoya, its principal city, Nobunaga made an alliance with the feudal lord of Mikawa Province and then advanced toward the city of Gifu to the north. With the help of Ashikaga Yoshiaki, a member of the ruling military family, he secured Kyoto, the traditional center of Japanese power, and installed Yoshiaki as shogun. The two men soon disagreed, however, and Nobunaga handily deposed the shogun in 1573, effectively ending the powerful Ashikaga line of military leaders founded by ASHIKAGA TAKAUJI in 1335.

To consolidate his hold on Kyoto and the other regions, Nobunaga diminished the authority of the *daimyo* (feudal lords) by prohibiting them from collecting highway tolls and tribute money from the guilds. During this period, Nobunaga also took on the powerful Buddhist institutions that opposed his leadership, beginning in 1571 by destroying the monasteries of the Tendai sect, which had exerted a powerful hold on politics and religion since the eighth century. The fanatical Ikko ("Single-Minded" adherents of Pure Land Buddhism) sect was not so easily put down and yielded only after a decade of combat. Nobunaga finally secured the surrender of their fortress-monastery headquarters, Honganji, in 1580 through the mediation of the imperial court.

Having taken direct steps to suppress the political power of the Buddhists, Nobunaga aided the Jesuit missionaries in building a church and seminary in Azuchi. By helping the Jesuits secure a foothold in Japan, Nobunaga sought further to diminish the power of the Buddhist monasteries.

By the spring of 1582, Nobunaga had control of central Japan and was preparing to advance on the west. Gravely wounded by a rebellious vassal at this time, Nobunaga, though at the height of his power, committed suicide. At the time of his death, he held sway over half of Japan and had permanently reduced the power of the Buddhist religion as well as of the *daimyo*. TOYOTOMI HIDEYOSHI took up the reins of leadership, building on Nobunaga's gains to acquire control of all of Japan by 1590.

Ögödei   (1185–1241)
The son of Genghis Khan, Ögödei succeeded his father as khan in 1229, established a capital city at Karakorum, and defeated the Chin Empire in North

225

China and Russia, Iran, Iraq, Germany, Poland, and Hungary.

Ögödei was born in 1185 in Mongolia, the third son of Genghis Khan. As the hand-picked successor to the khan, who died in 1227, Ögödei took for himself the title of khagan ("great khan") and set out to expand the vast territories accumulated by Genghis.

Building a walled capital city at Karakorum on the Orhon River in central Mongolia in the 1230s, Ögödei then started his campaign to subdue the Chin Empire in northern China and Manchuria. Aided by the Sung dynasty of southern China, the Mongols conquered the Chin capital at K'ai-feng in 1234.

After subduing the Chin, Ögödei sent his warriors to Iran, Iraq and Russia. In 1240, Kiev was sacked, and for the next 200 years, the Russians were forced to pay tribute to the Ögödei's Golden Horde. In 1241, Ögödei defeated a combined force of Germans and Poles and marched through Hungary to the Adriatic Sea.

Ögödei died from excessive drinking in 1241 at his capital of Karakorum. He was succeeded first by his wife Toregene, who was regent, and then by their son Guyuk in 1246.

Olivares, Gaspar de Guzman y Pimental, count-duke of   (1587–1645)

Prime minister to King Philip IV of Spain, Olivares strove to centralize royal authority; his efforts provoked rebellion.

Gaspar de Guzman was born on January 16, 1587, the second son of a Spanish aristocratic family. As was traditional for noble second sons, he studied for the priesthood, attending the University of Salamanca in 1601, obtaining a degree in theology and an appointment from Pope Clement VIII as canon to Seville. Upon the death of his older brother, he resigned his appointment and returned home, where he joined his father at the royal court. When his father died in 1607, Olivares inherited one of the largest fortunes in Spain.

At court, Olivares met Crown Prince Philip in 1615 and quickly befriended the young heir, who was less than half his age. Olivares became one of Philip's six personal attendants, and by the time of Philip's accession to the Spanish throne in April 1621, Olivares was his most trusted friend and adviser. Philip named Olivares prime minister in 1623. Intensely loyal to the young king, Olivares saw as his primary objective the promotion of the crown's power and prestige—as well as his own.

Olivares also proposed economic reform to relieve the dependence on precious metals from the New World by recoining old copper alloys and introducing paper money; he abolished favoritism in the granting of licenses and charters and enacted legislation beneficial to industry. These economic reforms failed miserably, however, because the aristocracy refused to support them. Moreover, when it became clear that the motivation behind the reforms was in large part to centralize Spain, many in power feared the loss of regional autonomy. In 1640, the Catalans and the Portuguese revolted, and there was a movement to establish a separate Andalusian kingdom.

In an effort to bolster Spanish influence abroad, Olivares unwisely allied Spain with Austria in a Hapsburg coalition during the Thirty Years' War. This only exacerbated the strain on the Spanish economy and opened the way for French hegemony in Europe. Olivares also involved Spain in the Mantuan War of 1628, which led France's Cardinal Richelieu to invade in 1635, thereby provoking more internal rebellion.

At length, Philip was forced to remove his confidant in January 1643. This led to Olivares' exile in Toro, where he became insane and died on July 22, 1645.

Further Reading: J. H. Elliott. *The Revolt of the Catalans: A Study in the Decline of Spain, 1598–1640* (Cambridge: Cambridge University Press, 1963).

Ortega Saavedra, Daniel   (1945–)

Leader of the Sandinista movement that ousted Nicaraguan President Anastasio SOMOZA DEBAYLE in 1979, Daniel Ortega served on the military junta in control of the government and was elected president in November 1984.

Born on November 11, 1945, in La Libertad, Nicaragua, Daniel Ortega Saavedra was part of a politically active family; his father, mother, and two of his brothers were all engaged in revolutionary activity against the Somoza dynasty.

Ortega joined the rebellion against the Somozas as a high school student. Arrested and jailed several times for his role in the rebellion, he joined in 1963 the FSLN (Sandinista National Liberation Front), a Marxist-Leninist party working to overthrow the Somozas. During the mid-1970s, Anastasio Somoza Debayle stepped up the repression of political opposition, and three factions of the FSLN developed. Ortega and his brother Humberto were instrumental in setting the course of the Tercerista faction, which allied itself with the non-Marxist opposition. On March 26, 1979, the three factions of the FSLN coalesced, and Daniel and Humberto were selected to serve on the National Directorate. In June of that year, with the Somoza government in rapid retreat, Daniel Ortega was named to the junta of the National Reconstruction Government, which was charged with the administration of the government under the direction of the National Directorate. On July 17, 1979, Somoza and his retinue fled to Miami—though not before looting the Nicaraguan treasury—and the junta took formal control of the country on July 19.

Throughout the 1980s, first as part of the junta and then as president, Ortega sought to strengthen the economic position of his country. He was hampered in those efforts by an American-backed opposition force—the Contras—who perpetuated a bloody and economically ruinous civil war. With his country often near starvation, Ortega was forced to spend as much as 25 percent of his 1983 budget on defense.

In November 1983, Ortega announced that he would stop buying arms from abroad and would ask Cuban military advisers to leave Nicaragua. In February 1984, he announced that free elections would be held in November. Chosen as the Sandinista's official candidate, Ortega was elected with 63 percent of the popular vote. But the war with the Contras did not end with the elections. Inflation continued to skyrocket, and incomes dropped.

For Americans, aid to the Contras became a matter of increasing controversy, and as the Contras lost U.S. backing, the civil war wound down. But the economic damage had been severe. In an effort to secure some measure of relief, Ortega slashed the federal budget 44 percent and fired 35,000 government employees in January 1989. Faced with popular unrest, Ortega announced the following month that presidential elections would be held early. Daniel Ortega lost his bid for reelection in 1990 to Violeta Chamorro and since then has been active in Sandinista Party matters.

Further Reading: Thomas W. Walker, ed. *Nicaragua in Revolution* (New York: Praeger, 1982).

Orthagoras   (r. ca. 655–ca. 648 B.C.)

Orthagoras was the first of many tyrants who ruled Sicyon (a city located on the southern shore of the Corinthian Gulf).

It is assumed that Orthagoras was of royal parentage, since he was a division commander in the army. Legendary sources, however, relate that Orthagoras' father was a cook for noblemen, and that the Oracle at Delphi had predicted that whichever man in his group had a son born to him first after returning home would become tyrant of Sicyon. Orthagoras was the first child, but he, not his father, rose to become tyrant.

Orthagoras' reign was predominately benign, marked by respect for the law and a rare tolerance toward the citizenry as a whole.

Otto I the Great   (912–973)

One of the most significant monarchs of the European Middle Ages, Otto I essentially created the medieval German monarchy and reinvigorated—indeed, created—the Holy Roman Empire in the West.

The Germany into which Otto was born on October 23, 912, was a collection of fractious states. He was the son of Duke Henry, who later assumed the throne of Saxony as King HENRY I THE FOWLER. Otto married Eadgyth, the daughter of the English king Edgar the Elder in 929. Henry the Fowler nominated Otto as his heir, and the choice was confirmed by election among the German dukes convened at Aachen in August 7, 936, after the death of Henry.

Following his coronation by the bishops of Mainz and Cologne, Otto asserted his absolute authority over the ever-jostling German dukes, who included Otto's half-brother Thankmar and younger brother Henry. Allying himself with Dukes Eberhard of Bavaria and Eberhard of Franconia, Thankmar led a revolt against Otto in 939. Otto dealt with this threat swiftly and easily. A subsequent revolt, led by Henry with Eberhard of Franconia and Giselbert of Lorraine, received the support of Otto's brother-in-law King Louis IV of France and was much more formidable, lasting from 939 to 941. Nevertheless, Otto proved himself a skillful commander, achieving decisive victories at the battles of Xanten in 940 and Andernach in 941. Eberhard and Giselbert were killed, and brother Henry agreed to submit to Otto's authority. Otto not only pardoned Henry for his revolt, but also forgave him even after he discovered, in December 941, that Henry was plotting against his life. Both acts of clemency apparently won the younger brother's loyalty at last.

Otto was not inclined to show Louis IV similar forbearance and invaded France in 942. A peace was hastily concluded with Louis, but within two years Otto faced a revolt in Bavaria. In 944, Otto was defeated at the Battle of Wels by Duke Bertold, but during 946–47 he used a combination of military pressure and diplomacy to gain control over the rebellious region.

Otto invaded France for a second time in 948, this time to aid his brother-in-law Louis IV, who had been imprisoned by the rebellious Hugh the Great, count of Paris. After Otto defeated the forces of Hugh at Rheims, capturing that city, the count surrendered and restored Louis to the throne. In 950, Otto turned east to invade Bohemia, forcing Duke Boleslav to accept his suzerainty. Then, in answer to the plea of Princess Adelaide of Burgundy, who had been imprisoned by Berengar, margrave of Ivrea, Otto invaded Italy in 951, riding to the rescue of Adelaide, who was the widow of Italy's King Lothair. Defeating rival claimants to the throne of Lombardy in 952, he crowned himself king of the Lombards, freed Adelaide, and then took her as his second wife. Berengar now paid him homage.

Otto hardly had time to savor his Italian triumph before news reached him that his son Ludolf had staged a revolt with Duke Conrad the Red of Lorraine, Archbishop Frederick of Mainz, and others. Otto returned to Germany in 953, but was defeated and captured by the rebels. Managing to escape, he went on the offensive and attacked Mainz and Regensburg in 953–54, neither of which yielded. It was at this time, however, that some 50,000 to 100,000 Magyars mounted the Great Magyar Raid into Bavaria and Franconia. In 954, Conrad struck a treaty with the Magyars, helping them to cross the Rhine at Worms, then facilitating their entry into Lorraine. They crossed the Meuse River to ravage northeastern France, traveling through Rheims and Châlons into Burgundy, then to Italy, through Lombardy, and then into the valleys of the Danube and the Drava. From here, a Magyar force moved against Bavaria. Ludolf had little choice but to surrender Regensburg to Otto early in 955, so that his father could fight the invasion.

Leading an army of 10,000, Otto arrived at Augsburg, which was under siege by some 50,000 Magyars. On August 10, 955, the Magyars lifted the siege and offered battle (Battle of Lechfeld), at first outmaneuvering Otto, capturing his camp, and driving one-third of his forces from the field. Conrad, having been betrayed by the Magyars (who had overrun Lorraine), now sided with his former enemy Otto and helped him first to repel the enveloping Magyars, then to turn the tide of battle against them. By the end of the day, Otto had captured the Magyar camp, inflicting heavy losses. At the moment of victory, Conrad was slain, and Otto pursued the retreating Magyars for three days. Thus the Great Magyar Raid was brought to an end.

Directly after dealing with the Magyars, Otto marched to the north, where he joined forces with Gero, the margrave of Brandenburg, to drive the Slavic Wends out of Germany at the Battle of Recknitz in October 955. Five years later, in 960, Otto moved against Slavic tribes between the middle Elbe and the middle Oder. He embarked next for Italy, at the request of Pope John XII, to fight Berengar, who was now Berengar II, king of Italy. In the fall of 961, Otto subdued Berengar, who submitted to vassalage. Otto moved on to Rome, where Pope John XII crowned him Holy Roman Emperor on February 2, 962. To Otto's surprise and dismay, the pope began treating with Berengar, which provoked Otto to depose the pope and replace him with Leo VIII. Otto captured Berengar and sent him, as a prisoner, to Germany. Otto himself returned to Germany only after suppressing a Roman revolt against Leo, who was deposed by Benedict V. Since Leo died before the revolt had been put down, Otto appointed John XIII as his successor. This pontiff was driven out of Rome by yet another revolt in 965, which prompted Otto to invade Italy for a third time in 966.

Otto put down the Roman revolt, then marched to southern Italy, where he prevailed against the Saracens and Byzantines. Otto arranged a marriage between his son Otto II, his chosen successor, and the Byzantine princess Theophano on April 14, 972.

Otto returned to a Germany unified to a degree previously unknown. He had strengthened not only the German states, but the Holy Roman Empire, and the stability he brought to extraordinarily turbulent times fostered a brief period of artistic and intellectual productivity known as the Ottonian Renaissance. Unfortunately, Otto's death on May 7, 973, ushered in a five-year period of violent civil war, as Bavaria's Henry the Wrangler and Boleslav of Bohemia rebelled against Otto II.

P

Pahlavi, Muhammad Reza Shah (1919–1980)
Shahanshah ("king of kings") of Iran from 1941 to
1979, Pahlavi built a government closely supported
by the United States and finally toppled by an anti-
Western Islamic fundamentalist movement led by
the Ayatollah KHOMEINI.

Muhammad Reza Shah Pahlavi was born on October 26, 1919, the son of Reza Khan, who, as Reza
Shah Pahlavi, would become shah of Iran in 1925.
Young Muhammad Reza become shah after his father was deposed by a combination of British and
Soviet forces early in World War II. Muhammad
Reza cooperated with the Allies during the war, but
his prime minister, Muhammad Mosaddeq, gained
great power after the war. He spearheaded a successful effort to nationalize the Anglo-Iranian Oil
Company in 1951, then, in August 1953, engineered
the ouster of the shah himself. Secretly backed by
the United States, elements of the army loyal to the
shah reversed the coup, and Mosaddeq's brief government was brought to an end.

When the shah returned to power, he did so with
a vengeance, determined never to relinquish control
again. He oversaw all aspects of Iranian life and
sharply curbed the authority of the Majlis, the Iranian parliament. As he consolidated his own dictatorship, he forged a stronger alliance with the
United States, which helped back his so-called White
Revolution begun in 1963. This was essentially a
program of Westernization and reform that included
the forcible redistribution of land and a consequent
reduction in the wealth and authority of the *mullahs*,
the religious leaders. Muhammad Reza introduced
extensive educational reforms and made significant
strides in the emancipation of women, traditionally
subjugated in Islamic cultures.

The shah's program of Westernization and modernization was fueled by Iran's rich oil fields, which
made the nation a valuable ally of the Western powers. Encouraged by the United States and others, the
shah used his nation's growing wealth to accelerate
social change with a series of "development plans."
These not only succeeded in bringing Iran into the
20th century, they also provided ample opportunity
for profiteering and corruption on the one hand, and
political and cultural alienation on the other. In the
course of the fifth and most ambitious development
plan, executed throughout most of the 1970s, social

ferment, aggravated by runaway inflation, became
increasingly intense. The shah responded by deploying his brutal secret police force, the Savak, to
imprison or eliminate dissidents. But opposition
continued to grow, the most menacing developing
around the leadership of the exiled Islamic fundamentalist leader Ayatollah Ruhollah KOHMEINI. In
desperation, the shah belatedly made concessions to
the fundamentalist insurgents, but to no avail. Pahlavi was forced into exile by January 1979, as Khomeini returned to Iran from his own exile in Paris.

Terminally ill with cancer, the shah was admitted
into the United States for medical treatment in October 1979. This outraged the religious radicals who
controlled Iran, and the next month, on November
4, 1979, militants stormed the U. S. Embassy in Tehran, seizing 90 hostages, 63 of whom were American
nationals. The shah subsequently left the United
States, living briefly in Panama, then settling in
Egypt, where he died on July 27, 1980.

Further Reading: William Shawcross. *The Shah's Last
Ride* (New York: Simon & Schuster 1988); Marvin Zonis.
Majestic Failure (Chicago: University of Chicago Press,
1991).

Park, Chung Hee (1917–1979)
South Korean president Chung Hee Park seized
power in a military coup and ruled autocratically before he was shot and killed.

Chung Hee Park was born to a humble rural family on September 30, 1917, and was quickly recognized as a prodigy. After attending local schools, he
entered the Japanese-run Manchukuo Military Academy in 1940, graduating two years later at the head
of his class. During World War II, he served with
Japanese units in Manchuria, but returned to a liberated Korea in 1945 after Japan's defeat. Within a
year, he completed the course at the newly founded
Korean Military Academy and was commissioned a
captain in December 1946.

After being forced out of the military in 1948 over
questionable charges of Communist collaboration,
Park was recalled by the army when North Korea
invaded the south in June 1950. By war's end in
1953, he had earned numerous citations for meritori-
ous service and had reached the rank of brigadier
general. After the war, he became a leader within
the Korean army and moved from one prominent

assignment to the next until he was deputy commanding general of the Second Army. When Syngman Rhee was overthrown in March 1960 on charges of election fraud, he was replaced by John Chang as premier. Chang's government soon verged on collapse.

On May 16, 1961, Park led a military junta called the Supreme Council for National Reconstruction and seized power from the crumbling Chang government. Park was named chairman of the council in July and by November he was promoted to full general, serving as the nation's premier. He set about eliminating corruption in South Korea and reinvigorating the economy, accomplishing both in short order. He retired from the army in 1963 to run for president as the junta party's candidate in the first elections since the ouster of Rhee. Park won by a narrow margin, but in the assembly elections the following month, his party achieved a landslide. Under Park, the economy continued to improve and he was reelected in 1967.

Under the Korean constitution, Park could serve no more than two terms, but he threatened to resign in 1969 if he were not allowed to run again in 1971. After fierce debate in the assembly, a resolution was passed permitting Park another term, and he was reelected in 1971. The new term brought increasingly repressive and autocratic rule, which was challenged by numerous student demonstrations. In 1972, a new constitution was promulgated, giving Park dictatorial powers and sparking more violent unrest, which Park violently suppressed. In 1975, Park issued a decree outlawing criticism of the government and rigidly enforced it against his political enemies.

In one of history's more bizarre assassinations, Park was shot in November 1979 by the head of the Korean Central Intelligence Agency, Kim Kyu, at a private dinner. Reportedly, Kyu got into a violent argument with another man and shot him. When Park attempted to intervene, he was shot twice, one bullet piercing his spine. Park's bodyguards raced into the room, and Kyu then shot and killed all four of them. The question of how Kyu killed six men—hitting Park twice—with a six-round .45 semiautomatic handgun remains unanswered.

Pats, Konstantin   (1874–1956?)

One of the founders of Estonia, Pats served as its president before the Soviet sweep of eastern Europe following World War II.

The son of a farmer, Konstantin Pats was born on February 23, 1874, in the Parnu district of Estonia in the Russian Empire. He studied law, earning his degree in 1896, then traveled to Tallinn. In 1901, he founded the Socialist newspaper, *The Announcer*,

which was devoted to social and economic issues. In 1904, he became mayor of Tallinn. When the failed Russian revolution of 1905 sparked unrest in Estonia, Pats called for order and restraint, but, as an outspoken Socialist, he was singled out by authorities and sentenced to death. After fleeing the country, he returned in 1910 and was briefly imprisoned.

After his release, Pats began agitating for Estonian independence. With Moscow in an unstable position during the Bolshevik revolution of 1917, Estonia was able to break away as an independent republic on February 24, 1918. Pats was named head of the provisional government. The next day, however, the Germans invaded Estonia and arrested Pats, deporting him to Germany. With the German defeat in World War I later in the year, Pats returned and took up his position as head of the government.

After promulgating a constitution in 1920, Pats served as president three times in 12 years. He reformed the economy in an attempt to support the nation's large agrarian population. His economic plan gained him much support among the farming population. When a new constitution was adopted in October 1933, which called for a stronger executive, Pats learned that the sponsors, the Fascist "Vap" movement, planned a coup. He immediately declared a state of emergency, arrested the leaders, and assumed total control of the government himself. In March 1934, he suspended all political parties and ruled as an absolute dictator until a new constitution was adopted in 1937, when he was promptly elected to a six-year term as president.

At the outbreak of World War II, Soviet forces invaded Estonia and occupied Tallinn in June 1940. The Red Army arrested Pats and deported him to the Soviet Union.

Konstantin Pats was never seen again. It was later reported that he was imprisoned in the U.S.S.R. and died in 1956. In the postwar race for European supremacy, Estonia was swept up by the Soviet machine, not to become an independent republic again until the breakup of the U.S.S.R. 50 years later.

Paul I   (1754–1801)

Czar Paul I repealed PETER I THE GREAT's law of succession, which allowed czars to choose their successors, mandating primogeniture in its place. His reign was marked by general tyranny.

Officially the son of Peter III and CATHERINE THE GREAT, Paul may actually have been fathered by Sergei Saltykov, one of Catherine's many lovers. Born on September 20, 1754, he was consigned to his aunt, the empress Elizabeth, who raised him. It was she who arranged for Nikita Panin, later Catherine's chief diplomatic adviser, to be Paul's tutor.

Paul and Catherine had an acrimonious relationship. Following Peter's assassination in 1762, Catherine usurped the throne and became ruler in her own right, denying Paul the crown, but appeasing him with Gatchina, the estate of one of his father's assassins. There he set up his own small court, including a private army corps, which Paul drilled constantly in the Prussian style. As she advanced in age, Catherine became increasingly open in her dislike of Paul, and she attempted to name his son Alexander heir. This notwithstanding, Paul assumed the throne on November 6, 1796, following Catherine's death. His first order was to abolish the decree of Peter the Great giving each monarch the power to choose his own successor, mandating instead succession through the male line of the Romanov family.

Paul also hoped to establish greater control over the nobles. He increased bureaucratic control at the local level of government, imposed limits on aristocratic privilege, and expanded the rights of serfs. This alienated everyone from him, including the military, because he showed blatant favoritism toward the Gatchina units. In foreign policy, he embroiled Russia in a war with France, resulting in NAPOLÉON's invasion of Russia; he nearly brought on war with England as well over a planned invasion of British India; and he severed diplomatic relations with Austria.

Any criticism of Paul's policies was brutally suppressed. At all levels of Russian society, people lost faith in Paul, and it was generally believed that he was suffering from mental illness. At length, a group of civil and military officials planned to overthrow Paul, securing in this the consent of his son, Alexander, whom they intended to place on the throne. On March 23, 1801, they entered the royal palace. When the czar refused to abdicate, they executed him on the spot.

Further Reading: Roderick E. McGrew. *Paul I of Russia, 1754–1801* (Oxford: Clarendon Press, 1992); Kazimierz Waliszewski. *Paul the First of Russia, the Son of Catherine the Great* (Hamden, Conn.: Archon, 1969).

Pavia (y Rodriguez de Albuquerque), Manuel (1827–1895)

A high-ranking Spanish general, Pavia was instrumental in the overthrow of Isabella II and, subsequently, establishment of the first republic.

Born August 2, 1827, Manuel Pavia joined the military at a young age and quickly rose in rank, thanks in large part to his patronage of high-ranking officials in the government. In 1865, he joined the general staff of General Juan Prim, who was attempting to overthrow Queen Isabella II of Spain. After the

uprisings in 1866 were put down, Prim was exiled for two years but returned in 1868 and again agitated against the monarchy. With Pavia's help and manipulation of the army, Prim was able to effect Isabella's abdication that same year.

The Spanish throne was assumed by Amadeus, duke of Aosta, but he was forced to abdicate in February 1873, and the monarchy was abolished with the establishment of the first Spanish republic. In Catalonia, to the south, cantonalists, monarchical loyalists, rose up against the republic, and Pavia was sent near the end of July 1873 to restore order. Pavia quickly crushed any hopes still flickering after initial cantonalist victories. Within two days and with fewer than 3,000 men, Pavia took Seville; by August 7, he marched into Cádiz and Granada.

Pavia threw his support behind Prime Minister Emilio Castelar y Ripoll, who ruled from September 1873 to January 1874 when Ripoll was defeated in the Cortes, the national assembly, and forced to step down. Pavia, by this time captain general of Madrid, concerned that Ripoll would be replaced by more radical republicans and fearful of the consequent effect on the military, dissolved the Cortes on January 3 with the aid of the army. He then called on all parties, save the rebels and the restorationists, to form a national government and named General Francisco Serrano y Dominquez head of state. Pavia continued to run the government, however, and the remnants of the first republic were overthrown in December 1874 when the Bourbons were restored to the monarchy.

Pavia continued to serve in both the Cortes and the army until his death on January 4, 1895.

Pedro I   (1798–1834)

The first emperor of Brazil, Pedro declared Brazilian independence from Portugal and ruled as a constitutional monarch before abdicating in favor of his son.

Born in Portugal on October 12, 1798, Pedro was the only son of King John VI. When NAPOLÉON invaded Portugal in 1807, the royal family fled to Brazil, where it remained in exile until 1821. Before his return to Portugal, John named Pedro as regent of Brazil, which had been elevated from the status of colony to kingdom by the Portugese legislature in 1815. All of Pedro's ministers advised him to declare independence, and even his own father apparently suggested it, anxious to snare the independent empire for himself before it was lost to someone else. However, when the Cortes, Portugal's parliament, became suspicious of the independence movement afoot, that body recalled Pedro and demanded he complete his schooling. Instead, on September 7, 1822, Pedro declared Brazil an independent empire and within three months was crowned emperor.

The new legislature passed a liberal constitution in 1824, which Pedro promptly abrogated, then had one of his own written—also tending toward liberalism. It endured until the formation of the Brazilian republic in 1889. Despite his liberal leanings, Pedro created dissension by consistently appointing Portugese-born ministers rather than native Brazilians. This provoked a general popular distrust of the "foreigners" and of Pedro's regime in general.

When John died in 1826, Pedro inherited the Portuguese throne, but was pressed to abdicate by the Brazilians, who were wary of the consequences of joint rule. In deference to his Brazilian subjects, Pedro abdicated the Portugese throne in favor of his daughter, Maria. After losing modern-day Uruguay in a disastrous war with Argentina, Pedro faced strong opposition and a string of revolts. He was forced to abdicate the Brazilian throne in April 1831 in favor of his son, Pedro II.

Pedro I returned to Portugal to help his daughter rule. He died in Portugal on September 24, 1834.

Further Reading: Neill Macaulay. *Dom Pedro* (Durham, N.C.: Duke University Press, 1986); Sergio Correa da Costa. *Every Inch a King: A Biography of Dom Pedro I, First Emperor of Brazil* (New York: Macmillan, 1950)

Peisistratus   (ca. 605 B.C.–527 B.C.)

Using his bodyguards to seize the Acropolis, Peisistratus became tyrant of Athens, lost power to two competing factions, then regained control of the city-state twice more.

The son of Hippocrates and a relative of SOLON, Peisistratus was born about 605 B.C. He grew up in a time in which two factions—the Plain, led by Lycurgus, and the Coast, led by Megacles—vied for control of the archonship, the chief executive post of Athens. Gaining military fame in a war with the city of Megara (ca. 565 B.C.), Peisistratus organized his own faction—the Hillsmen—which included noble families from eastern Attica and a large number of Athenian urban dwellers as well. Herodotus recounts Peisistratus' rise to power: He gashed himself and his mules, drove his chariot into Athens, and displayed his wounds to all those at the marketplace. Reminding the Athenians of his victories against Megara, he persuaded them to provide an armed bodyguard. Then he ordered the guard thus provided to capture the Acropolis and thereby briefly established himself in power during 560 or 559. Later, he married a daughter of Megacles in order to assume office again (556–555), but was ousted by Lycurgus and Megacles.

Living in exile in northern Greece, Peisistratus conspired to regain power a third time. He exploited

the gold and silver mines of Mount Pangaeum and consolidated his support in Thebes, Argos, and Naxos. In 546, he moved his armed forces to the island of Euboea and from there launched an attack on Attica. He was victorious at Pallene near Mount Hymettus, where he attacked the Athenian army during the heat of midday when they were napping or gambling. This triumph propelled him to the head of the Athenian government.

As tyrant of Athens, Peisistratus maintained a mercenary bodyguard, composed in part of Scythian archers. He is thought to have disarmed the Athenian citizens and to have redistributed to peasants the land of exiled nobles. While he imposed a tax of perhaps 10 percent on agricultural products, he also is thought to have made loans to needy farmers. Peisistratus made numerous religious reforms, moving many of the Attican cults to the city and instituting branch shrines. He also promoted Athena as the major deity of the city.

The Panathenaea, an annual festival dedicated to Athena, was Peisistratus' special project. He added to the festival's fame by establishing athletic contests and literary prizes as part of a Great Panathenaea, held every four years. Celebrated as a patron of the arts and architecture, he invited poets and bards to attend his court, he commissioned many public buildings, including the Enneakrounos, or nine-spouted fountain house.

Peisistratus ruled until his death in 527 B.C. His reign was so successful that, according to Aristotle, the tyranny of Peisistratus became known as the age of Cronus—the Golden Age. He was succeeded by his sons Hippias and Hipparchus.

Further Reading: A. Andrewes. *The Greek Tyrants* (London: Hutchinson University Library, 1960); N. G. L. Hammond. *A History of Greece to 322 B.C.* 3d ed. (Oxford: Clarendon Press, 1986).

Periander   (r. 625–585 B.C.)

The second tyrant of Corinth, Periander encouraged trade and commerce, put the populace of Corinth to work, and killed the leading citizens to secure his control over the government.

Periander, the son of CYPSELUS, ruled Corinth from about 625 to 585 B.C. He recovered Corcyra for his kingdom and founded two trading colonies, Apollonia, which exported goods produced in southern Illyria, and Potidaea, which exported goods produced in Macedonia. To increase trade with his territories, he is believed to have constructed the *diolkos* (portage way) across the Isthmus of Corinth. Relying solely on import taxes for governmental revenue, he developed friendly relations with the tyrant of Miletus and the kings of Lydia and Egypt.

Periander was notorious for his ruthless treatment of the nobility. Herodotus wrote that Periander sent a messenger to Thrasybulus, tyrant of Miletus, to ask advice on how to secure absolute power over his subjects. When questioned by the messenger, Thrasybulus took the messenger into a field of wheat and then walked through the field knocking off the tallest shafts. Without replying to the question, he sent the messenger back to Periander. When the messenger told Periander about Thrasybulus' behavior, Periander interpreted the actions to mean that he should kill the leading citizens of Corinth—which he did with dispatch.

Herodotus also wrote about the tyrant's relationship with his sons. When his sons were 17 and 18 years old, they visited their maternal grandfather, Procles, who tried to turn them against their father. Procles led the younger boy, Lycophron, to an understanding that his father had killed his mother, Melissa. Lycophron severed all ties with his father and moved to Corcyra. At last Periander persuaded his son to return to Corinth, but before Lycophron departed, the Corcyreans captured him and killed him in retaliation for Periander's earlier abduction of 300 Corcyrean boys. These children had been sent to Lydia to become eunuchs.

Known for his hatred of idleness in any form, Periander put his subjects to work and forbade anything smacking of luxury. Despite Periander's severity and brutality, his rule brought Corinth a period of great prosperity, and for this he is considered one of the Seven Wise Men of Greece.

Pericles   (495?–429 B.C.)

Pericles was the statesman and *strategos* (general) under whose rule Athens won and enforced political and cultural dominance over other Greek city-states.

Pericles presents the modern historian with a set of tantalizing paradoxes. The most celebrated of Athenian statesmen, he is nevertheless an obscure figure who had no contemporary biographer. An ardent champion of democracy, he relentlessly employed the means of tyranny to force that form of government on city-states subordinate to Athens. While Pericles presided over the zenith of Hellas' greatness, opening Athenian democracy to the ordinary citizen, building the temples and statues of the Acropolis, and creating the Athenian empire, his unyielding drive to impose his nation's will on others stirred the discontent and rebellion that eventually led to the fall of Athens and, ultimately, the decline of Greece.

The son of Zanthippus, a prominent statesman, and Agariste, a member of the influential Alcmaeonid family, Pericles first came to public attention in 472, when he provided and trained the chorus for Aeschylus' play *The Persians*. He was elected *strategos* (general) in 458, a key policy-setting office that carried a one-year term, and Pericles was frequently re-elected over the next 30 years. Despite his noble lineage, Pericles was a supporter of democracy in a time of almost universal tyranny—though his personal political style was as haughty, reserved, and aristocratic as that of any tyrant.

The same may be said of his dealings with other city-states. The Delian League was a confederation

Pericles was a prototypical Greek tyrant: a high-minded benevolent despot. (From Richard Delbruck, Antike Portrats, *1912)*

of city-states formed to fight Xerxes and the Persians. Athens collected money from many of the member states to maintain an army and build a navy. These forces were soon dominated by Athenians, and the other states of the confederation grew to resent paying tribute to maintain forces that often served to impose the Athenian model of government on them. Moreover, a portion of the tribute money was diverted to finance Pericles' program of sculpture-raising and temple-building. Worse, under the system of *cleruchy*, Athenian colonists were granted lands abroad while retaining the rights and privileges of Athenian citizenship. It became clear that Athens was building an empire of tributary states.

In a celebrated speech recorded by the historian Thucydides, Pericles declared that all subjects of Athens "confess that she is worthy to rule them." This high-handed assertion finally proved untrue. While Pericles realized his ambition to make Athens preeminent among Greek states, and while the oppression Athens wrought upon those states did at least enforce peace, stability, and the rule of law, he also lived to see Sparta lead the powers of the Peloponnesus in a revolt against Athens (the Peloponnesian War). While Athens was under siege during the conflict, a plague swept the city. Amid the turmoil, Pericles and those associated with him were censured: his mistress Aspasia and his teacher Anaxagoras were accused of impiety; his protégé, the great sculptor Phidias, was charged with embezzlement; and Pericles himself was briefly deposed from office. A few weeks later, in a fit of repentence, the Athenian people restored Pericles to office, investing him with even greater power. However, weakened by a bout with the plague, he died within a year.

Further Reading: A. Andrews. *The Greek Tyrants* (London: Hutchinson University Library, 1960); Arthur James Grant. *Greece in the Age of Pericles* (New York: Scribner's, 1893); Donald Kagan. *Pericles of Athens and the Birth of Democracy* (New York: Free Press, 1991).

Perón, Juan   (1895–1974)

Rising to power with the aid of his mistress (subsequently his wife), Eva Duarte (Evita), Perón served as president of Argentina from 1946 to 1955 and from 1973 to 1974. He used Fascist-inspired methods to suppress political opposition even as he initially championed the cause of laborers and the poor. Returned to power in 1973 after living in exile in Spain, he turned his back on left-wing Perónistas and affiliated himself more strongly with union bureaucracies and the military.

Juan Perón was born on October 8, 1895, in Buenos Aires Province, Argentina, and entered military school at the age of 16. After graduation, he progressed fairly quickly through the ranks, securing a plum post as military attaché to Benito MUSSOLINI's Italy in the late 1930s, where he imbibed the elementary lessons of Fascism.

Returned to Argentina in 1943, Perón and other officers effected the overthrow of the nation's civilian government. For the next three years of military rule, Perón remained in the background—in positions such as secretary of labor and social welfare and by 1945 as minister of war. But it was from these positions that he consolidated his support from labor and the military.

The military regime lasted until October 1945, when a group of civilians, bent on restoring the constitutional government, ousted and arrested Perón and other army officers. Peron's mistress, the beautiful and extremely popular actress Eva Duarte, rallied workers, who demanded his release, which occurred two nights after his arrest. He addressed 300,000 people from the balcony of the presidential palace that night, promising that, with their support, he would win the upcoming presidential election and bring justice and better economic times to the nation. He and Eva—or Evita, as she was popularly called—were married a few days later.

Perón triumphed in the February 1946 election in part because of his strong appeal among the poor and the working classes and in part because of the Fascist-style street politics his thugs practiced against all opposition. He characterized his political ideology as *justicialismo*—or *perónismo*—a program of political, economic and social reforms somewhere between capitalism and communism and backed by military muscle. Pursuant to a five-year program aimed at improving the national economy, he brought under the government's control imports and exports, wage controls, railroads, utilities, and banks.

His efforts failed miserably. Bad weather resulted in agricultural disaster, which was exacerbated by the gross mismanagement of Perón's corrupt bureaucrats. When courageous voices of protest rose from the media and from academia, Perón responded by nationalizing some newspapers and closing others, limiting the activity of political opposition parties, and purging the university of professors who opposed his programs. These repressive measures secured Perón reelection in 1951—though by a smaller margin. Four years later, his administration was ousted by a group of army and navy officers who staged a coup on September 19, 1955.

Perón fled to Madrid, married his third wife (Evita having died from cancer in 1952), and remained, despite exile, very much in control of the Perónista movement in Argentina. To ensure that no strong personality would emerge back home to head the Perónistas, he encouraged factionalism within the party.

In 1973, General Alejandro Lanusse, who had come to power two years earlier, promised to restore democracy to Argentina and, as a step toward this goal, eased restrictions on political parties. That was all Perón needed. In the March 1973 elections, Perónistas captured the presidency (the candidate was Hector Campora) as well as majorities in the legislature. Three month later, they brought their leader home. Juan Perón was greeted with wild enthusiasm wherever he went. He was so popular that President Hector Campora stepped aside to make way for him. In a special election that October, Perón captured 60 percent of the popular vote.

The strong-arm tactics that had always served Perón were even more in evidence during his second regime. Working more closely than ever with the army and right-wing groups, he turned his back on the labor unions and leftist Perónists whom he had courted throughout his exile. During his first six months in office, the economy did markedly improve, but then leftist guerrillas resumed terrorist operations, and inflation became rampant again.

Juan Perón died of natural causes on July 1, 1974, and was succeeded in office by his fourth wife, Vice President Isabel Perón. She remained in power for only two years before a military junta deposed her on March 24, 1976. The Perónistas rose again to political power in 1989, when their candidate, Carlos Saul Menem, was elected president.

Further Reading: Joseph A. Page. *Peron: A Biography* (New York: Random House, 1983).

Pétain, Henri Philippe (1856–1951)

One of France's most skillful commanders in World War I, Pétain headed the Vichy government in collaboration with the Nazi occupiers of France during World War II.

Henri Philippe Pétain was born on April 24, 1856, in the town of Cauchy-à-la-Tour, Pas-de-Calais, France. He was the son of a peasant family, but showed great promise and excelled at the École de Saint-Cyr, the élite French military academy. He was commissioned in the *chasseurs alpins* in 1876 and slowly progressed up the ranks. It was 1900 before he was promoted to major, at which time he was given a battalion-level command. Six years later, his abilities as a theorist were recognized by an appointment to the École de guerre. However, Pétain's characteristically conservative, methodical, and essentially defense-oriented ideas concerning the destructive effect of firepower were at odds with the prevailing war policies of marshals Foch and Grandmaison, who advocated the all-out attack.

At the outbreak of World War I in August 1914, Pétain was a colonel in command of the 33rd Regiment and quickly distinguished himself, achieving promotion to brigadier general by the end of the month. Brilliant performance at the Battle of the Marne (September 4–10) earned him promotion to general of division, and by October 25 he was in command of XXXIII Corps in Artois. Again, Pétain performed superbly, this time during the Arras offensive of May 9–16, 1915, and was given command of the Second Army in June. In February 1916, when the all-important fortress of Verdun was menaced, Pétain was called into command and pronounced the phrase for which he became best known in the war: *Ils ne passeront pas!* ("They shall not pass!").

Calm and steady, Pétain successfully defended Verdun, until his superiors became concerned that he was too committed to a defensive posture. Pétain was promoted to command of Army Group Center, and his subordinate, the aggressive and flamboyant Robert Nivelle, was put in full command of the Verdun sector. Subsequently, Nivelle was promoted ahead of Pétain, but, in April 1917, failed miserably with his Chemin-des-Dames offensive. The following month, Pétain was called to relieve Nivelle and to assume supreme command of the French armies.

Upon his elevation to the top post, Pétain was immediately faced with a mass mutiny of the ranks. He responded swiftly and harshly—though not unfairly. While he aggressively prosecuted the ringleaders of the mutiny, he did seek to address the soldiers' grievances and instituted reforms to humanize the French army and the treatment of the common soldier.

Pétain conducted the closing months of the war with great skill, always stressing preparedness and achievable goals rather than the often debilitating, even suicidal policy of unconditional all-out attack. At war's end, he was made marshal of France in recognition of his service to his country, and in 1920 he was appointed vice president of the Supreme War Council. In 1922, he became inspector general of the army.

Pétain served as minister of war during the brief government of Gaston Doumergue in February–November 1934. Finding himself in civilian politics, he became an outspoken critic of civilian politicians, whom he accused of neither leading nor governing. During the 1930s, he made clear his disdain of liberalism and his advocacy of strong, even autocratic government. Appointed ambassador to Spain in March 1939, he was recalled to France in May 1940 as his nation faced defeat at the hands of the Nazis.

Although Pétain was showing his age—some have suggested that he was sinking into senility—a desperate French president Albert Lebrun called upon him to save France as he had during World War I. Lebrun asked Pétain to form a new government, and on June 22, 1940, as titular head of the French government, Pétain negotiated surrender to the Germans.

Pétain was accorded emergency dictatorial powers—and was forever afterward branded as a collaborationist and traitor. In fact, Pétain attempted to retain as much independence from German domination as possible, even dismissing, in December 1940, Pierre Laval, the frankly collaborationist foreign minister who had been instrumental in bringing Pétain to power. The Germans applied steady pressure, however, and Pétain, aged and often uncomprehending, steadily backed down, recalling Laval in 1942. In November 1942, the Germans occupied Vichy, the seat of the Pétain government, and in August 1943, they arrested Pétain, eventually imprisoning him in Germany. After the war, he was returned to France in April 1945, where he was tried for treason and sentenced to death. Charles de Gaulle, wartime leader of the Free French forces and now provisional president of the republic, remembered the Pétain under whom he had served during World War I. He commuted the sentence to life imprisonment.

Pétain was consigned to a fortress on Île d'Yeu, and when he fell ill there he was transferred to a villa at Port-Joinville, where he died on July 23, 1951.

The career of Marshal Henri Phillipe Pétain was a personal and national tragedy. There can be little doubt that he acted from patriotic motives and with the intention of sparing the French people the devastation the Germans had already visited upon nations in eastern Europe. But it is a fact that the Vichy government collaborated in the persecution of French citizens, including the deportation, forced labor, and death of thousands of French Jews. Pétain's government also sacrificed French national identity and honor. One of Pétain's aides put the marshal's position best when he criticized him for thinking "too much about the French and not enough about France."

Further Reading: Richard M. Griffiths. *Petain: A Biography of Marshal Philippe Petain of Vichy* (Garden City, N.Y.: Doubleday, 1972); Jean-Raymond Tournoux, trans. by Oliver Coburn. *Sons of France: Petain and de Gaulle* (New York: Viking, 1966).

Peter the Cruel [Peter the Just (of Castile)] (1334–1369)

Confronted by the treachery of his bastard half-brothers, Peter crushed rebellions with a vigor that earned him the contemporary epithet "the Cruel"; later writers bestowed on him the byname "Peter the Just" because of his strong administration of justice.

Peter came to the throne at the age of 15, following the death of his father, Alfonso XI. John II of France took advantage of the young man's inexperience to force a long-desired alliance between his nation and Castile against England in 1352, and, to seal the arrangement, Peter was compelled the next year to marry Blanche, daughter of the duke of Bourbon, although he was passionately in love with María de Padilla. Peter abandoned Blanche as soon as they were married, went to live with María (who would remain his mistress until her death in 1361), and thereby dissolved the alliance with France.

The rupture with France would cause Peter great grief. A collection of bastard half-brothers, led by Henry of Trastámara (subsequently HENRY II [1333–79], aligned themselves against Peter by supporting the authority of the Castilian magnates against the growing power of the crown. Peter squelched a series of revolts with unsparing vigor, and Henry fled to France in 1356, where he conspired with the disaffected French monarch in campaigns against Peter. Worse, Henry secured the support of Peter IV of Aragón, and for a decade, from 1356 to 1366, Castile was embroiled in a bitter and costly war with that kingdom. In the face of repeated military defeats, Henry of Trastámara launched a propaganda war against his half-brother (it was Henry who labeled Peter "the Cruel"), but, by and large, the effort failed to shake Peter's loyal following.

With Peter gaining ground against Aragón, King Charles V of France (who had succeeded John II), Pope Urban V, and Peter IV financed an expedition of French mercenary troops led by Bertrand du Guesclin to invade Castile, overthrow Peter, and place Henry of Trastámara on the throne. Peter fled to Gascony and enlisted the aid of English allies under Edward the Black Prince to fight the Trastámarans and their mercenary allies. Peter and the Black Prince were victorious at the Battle of Nájera on April 3, 1367, and Peter resumed the throne.

But Charles V was not through with Peter. He furnished Henry of Trastámara with a new French contingent and sent him back to Spain. Peter met the forces of his half-brother on the field at Moniel, France, and was defeated. He died, not in battle, but at the hands of Henry, who murdered him on March 23, 1369.

Peter I the Cruel [Peter the Just (of Portugal)] (1320–1357)

This Portuguese monarch's paradoxical bynames attest to the ambiguity of his reign: on the one hand, he is remembered for having cruelly avenged the death of his mistress Inés de Castro, and, on the other, he is revered for having introduced many reforms, particularly in the administration of justice.

Peter I, born in Coimbra, Portugal, on April 8, 1320, was the son of King Alfonso IV. After unsuccessfully putting forth a claim to the throne of Castile in 1354, he became king of Portugal in 1357.

In 1336, Peter married Constanza of Castile, who arrived in Portugal with her cousin, Inés de Castro. An intense passion developed between Peter and Inés, and the two lived together after Constanza's death in 1345, the union producing several children. In the meantime, friction developed between Peter and his father, Alfonso, who became fearful of the growing court influence of Inés and her two brothers. When Peter presented himself as a candidate for the Castilian throne, Alfonso resolved to get rid of Inés. On January 7, 1355, Alfonso delivered his son's beloved mistress into the hands of assassins.

Peter rebelled, but was apparently reconciled with his father. When Alfonso died two years later, Peter ascended the throne, ordered the deaths of all those who had been involved in the murder of Inés, and then had her body moved to a magnificent mausoleum in the church at Alcobaca. It is said that Peter ordered the corpse crowned and commanded his courtiers to kiss the long-dead hand of his mistress.

Peter made sweeping reforms in the administration of justice through an act of 1361 and elevated the Portuguese church to national status by claiming the right of *beneplácito régio*—royal approval of all papal bulls prior to publication in Portugal.

Peter I the Great (1672–1725)

Probably the greatest of the Russian czars, Peter I did much to bring Russia into the European mainstream and was a model of the enlightened despot.

Born on June 6, 1672, in Moscow, to Czar Feodor III Alakseevich and his second wife, Natalia Kirillovna Naryshkina, Peter was proclaimed czar when he was only 10 years old, in 1682, upon the death of his father. Later that year, however, the *streltsi*—militia musketeers—staged a revolt, forcing the boy to share the throne with his semi-imbecile brother Ivan V under the regency of their sister Sophia. During this early period, young Peter became interested in the world beyond Russia and developed a passion for European culture, learning, fashion, and military practices. Living outside Moscow in Prebrazhenskoye, he formed two élite regiments of guards and

plotted with his guardian, Prince Boris Golitsyn, the overthrow of Sophia. Golitsyn moved successfully against Sophia in August 1689, and Peter took control of the government.

The young man, whose stature, at a then remarkable six feet, six inches, was singularly commanding, moved with great energy to consolidate his newly won power during the period 1689–96. He undertook military expeditions to the White Sea during 1694–95 and wrested the Azov region from Turkish control during 1695–96. Following this conquest, he realized an ambition nurtured since childhood—to travel to western Europe. From March 1697 to August 1698, he toured Germany, Britain, and the Netherlands, hungrily observing examples of the most advanced technology and science then available as well as examples of western European fashion, style, and mores.

Peter was forced to cut short his tour when news reached him of another *streltsi* revolt, which he put down with savage fury during the course of the summer of 1698. Having crushed the *streltsi*, Peter set about a program of commensurately vigorous social reform. He commanded the court nobility—the boyars—to shave their traditional beards and to don European-style dress. He introduced European learning into Russia, and he even abandoned the traditional Julian calendar for the new Gregorian calendar, which was just then gaining currency in the nations of Europe (this latter transformation was not universally adopted until after the Russian revolution of 1917).

Peter also remodelled his army during this period by introducing conscription, drafting some 32,000 commoners. Thus prepared, he allied himself with Augustus II of Poland and Saxony in November 1699 and, with him, attacked the Swedes at Livonia in August 1700. Peter's military ambition outstripped his skill as a commander, and he was defeated by Swedish king CHARLES XII at the Battle of Narva on November 30, 1700.

The young monarch did not give up, however, and continued his transformation of Russia into a European-style industrial and military power. Peter established factories, arms manufactures, and military schools. He developed a system of internal transport, as well as encouraged the growth of a shipbuilding industry in order to open up commerce with the rest of the world. Having learned from his defeat at Narva to put his trust in good military advisers, he secured the leadership of Field Marshal Count Sheremetev in an invasion of Ingria, then held by the Swedes. On January 9, 1702, Peter and Shermetev defeated a Swedish army at Erestfer and then, on July 29, at Hummelshof in Livonia. Peter occupied the valley of the Neva River in December 1702, and he founded the city of Saint Petersburg on May 16, 1703. Built on a frozen marsh on the Gulf of Finland, Saint Petersburg became Peter's pride and joy, a monument designed according to the latest models of European neoclassicism, intended to attract the best of European culture and learning. Peter called the new city his "window on the West."

From June 12 to August 21, 1704, Peter besieged Narva, this time successfully. His ally, Augustus II, had surrendered to Charles XII of Sweden when Peter, now holding Narva, proposed a peace with the Swedish monarch. Charles angrily rejected the offer and invaded Russia during 1707–08, pushing an overextended Peter as far as the central Ukraine, where he holed up at Poltava during the winter and spring of 1708–09. But on July 8, 1709, Peter massed his forces against the Swedish army and defeated Charles at the Battle of Poltava, virtually destroying the opposing army.

Having disposed of the northern threat for the time being, Peter turned next to the south, moving against Turkish Moldavia in March of 1711. Outmaneuvered by Turkish forces, he was hemmed in at the River Pruth and was compelled to negotiate a settlement on July 21, 1711. Three years later, Peter again directed his efforts against the Swedes, planning with Admiral Feodor Apraskin a devastating attack on the Swedish fleet near Hangö in the Baltic on July 7, 1714. By this single, masterful stroke, Peter gained control of the Baltic Sea, including the prizes of Livonia, Estonia, Ingria and southern Karelia, which were ceded to Russia by treaty on August 30, 1721.

With his empire greatly expanded, his court modernized and the fractious nobility under control, Peter I took the title of emperor of all the Russias (rather than czar) in 1721. He spent the next two years campaigning against Persia on his empire's Asian frontier, occupying Derbent (in Dagestan), Rasht, and Baku during 1722–23.

Peter the Great died on February 8, 1725, in his beloved Saint Petersburg from complications arising from a cold he had caught while helping to rescue soldiers who had fallen into the frozen Neva River.

Further Reading: Aleksei Nikolaevich Tolstoi. *Peter the Great* (New York: Covici, Friede, 1932).

Peter II (1648–1706)

King of Portugal, Peter consolidated royal power at the expense of the parliament, and also helped win his nation's final independence from Spain.

When his father, John IV, died in 1656, Peter's brother Alfonso was crowned as Alfonso VI. However, Alfonso was mentally ill and impotent, so Peter and Alfonso's wife usurped power in 1687,

setting up a regency for the disabled monarch. Alfonso's wife secured an annulment on the grounds of her husband's impotence and married Peter, who did not officially become King Peter II until Alfonso's death in September 1683.

Peter's first act was to bring the war for independence from Spain to a close. Hoping to end the costly struggle as soon as possible, Peter, with the help of Charles II of England, received assurances of Portuguese independence, but, despite the string of Portuguese military victories, did not pursue further concessions.

Drained from the war with Spain, Portugal's overseas empire was devastated. Its possessions in Africa and Asia had either been overrun by the indigenous Muslims or taken over by the Dutch. However, when gold was discovered in Brazil, the Portuguese economy rallied, and the sting of losing other possessions was greatly reduced. This new source of revenue allowed Peter to rule on his own, without the financial consent of the Cortes, the Portuguese parliament.

Although he was weary of war, Peter entered the War of the Spanish Succession in 1703. However, he became gravely ill soon after, and rule passed to a regent. Peter died on December 9, 1706, before the war's conclusion.

Phan Thanh Gian [Phan Thang Giang] (1796–1867)

An ultraconservative adviser to a series of Vietnamese emperors, Phan Thanh Gian ceded much of his country to the forces of French imperialism.

Phan Thanh Gian was born in the Ben Tre province of Cochin China (present-day northern Vietnam), the son of a minor government worker. A brilliant scholar, he earned the first doctoral degree awarded in Vietnam and became a close adviser to Emperor MINH MANG. An extreme conservative, Phan Thanh Gian adhered absolutely to an esoteric and orthodox Confucianism. He repeatedly criticized the emperor on Confucian grounds, which finally incurred Minh Mang's wrath. The emperor stripped Phan Thanh Gian of all titles and sent him into Quang Nam, central Vietnam, to fight as a common soldier. To the surprise of his comrades, commanders, and Minh Mang himself, Phan Thanh Gian acquitted himself with remarkable gallantry in battle, and the emperor recalled him to court, where he was installed in the highest diplomatic and advisory positions and served Minh Mang and subsequent rulers.

Phan Thanh Gian's overweening conservatism caused him to distrust and fear all Western influence. Ironically, this conservatism motivated two treaties, which, aimed at containing French colonialism in Vietnam, actually opened the door to it.

In 1862, France responded to Vietnamese persecution of Christian missionaries by invading the southern portion of the country and capturing Saigon (present-day Ho Chi Minh City), Bien Hoa, and Vinh Long. Fearful that the French would take over the entire country, Phan Thanh Gian negotiated a treaty ceding to France the three easternmost provinces of the southern portion of Vietnam. In 1863, Phan Thanh Gian followed this with a second treaty, by which France would agree to halt colonization and return the three provinces in exchange for commercial settlements around major southern cities, the payment of tribute money, and the emperor's pledge to declare the southern region a French protectorate. The treaty was concluded in 1864, but in 1865 the French reneged and reverted to the terms of the first treaty. Realizing that his efforts to contain the French had, in fact, delivered his nation into their hands, Phan Thanh Gian committed suicide on August 4, 1867, in Vinh Long.

Phibunsongkhram, Luang   (1897–1964)

A Japanese collaborator in World War II, Phibunsongkhram helped assert the rise of military government in Thailand.

Born in a farming village on July 14, 1897, Luang Phibunsongkhram first attended Buddhist monastery schools but then entered the Siamese Royal Military Academy in Bangkok in 1909. After graduating in 1914, he entered the Siamese artillery corps and from there was sent to France in 1924 for advanced military training. In France, he became involved with several other Siamese students agitating against the government. When he returned to Bangkok in 1927, he began his rise in the military hierarchy, serving on the general staff and gaining promotion to major.

In June 1932, Phibunsongkhram took part in the coup that toppled the monarchy in Siam. He then served in the first constitutional government. The next year, he helped overthrow the civilian government to install a military directorate and quell the rebellion of Prince Boworadet. In 1934, he became minister of defense, strengthening not only the army, but the army's role in the government—and in society generally; he established a Fascist paramilitary youth organization.

After surviving three assassination attempts, Phibunsongkhram became prime minister in December 1938, as well as minister of defense and the interior. As prime minister, he changed the name of the country from Siam to Thailand.

After the fall of Paris to the Nazis in 1940, Phibunsongkhram provoked war with French Indochina—

modern day Vietnam—hoping to regain Cambodia and Laos. Having established close ties with Japan before the war, when that nation invaded Thailand in December 1941, Phibunsongkhram quickly arranged an alliance to avoid occupation. He declared war on the United States and Great Britain in January 1942.

The Japanese soon began to treat Thailand as an occupied territory, and there was much public resentment against them and against Phibunsongkhram. When the war began to swing against Japan, Phibunsongkhram was overthrown in a public insurrection and a civil government was installed. The new government quickly proved incompetent and unpopular. After King Anada was mysteriously killed in 1946, the army retook the government and installed Phibunsongkhram as prime minister in 1948.

Allying Thailand with the West, Phibunsongkhram opposed the Soviet bloc in the Cold War and helped establish the South East Asia Treaty Organization (SEATO), headquartered in Bangkok. However, rampant corruption and a faltering economy soured public opinion at home. Hoping to curry public favor, Phibunsongkhram announced free elections, the lifting of his ban on political parties, and the resumption of free speech in 1957.

With his popularity flagging, Phibunsongkhram resorted to flagrant electoral fraud—and, even then, barely won a majority. This victory, limited though it was, did not last long. A September 1957 coup overthrew Phibunsongkhram, who was exiled to Japan, where he died on June 11, 1964.

Further Reading: David A Wilson. *Politics in Thailand* (Ithaca, N.Y.: Cornell University Press, 1962).

Philip II   (382–336 B.C.)

King of Macedon and father of ALEXANDER III THE GREAT, Philip II conquered Greece, established the League of Corinth, built a formidable army, and began the Macedonian invasion of Persia, which was completed by his son.

The son of Macedonian king Amyntas III, Philip II was born in 382 B.C. At the age of 15, he was sent to Thebes as a hostage and remained there for three years, learning much about warfare from the Greek general Epaminondas. In 359, his brother Perdiccas was killed in battle, and Philip II assumed the Macedonian throne—perhaps as regent for Perdiccas' son, perhaps in his own right.

His rule over Macedon included the unification of the principalities of upper Macedonia and the formation of a professional army. The "Companions," members of the landed nobility, were bound to him in service as members of the cavalry, and Philip organized the free peasants and shepherds into an infantry corps. The army also benefited from Philip's innovation in tactics and battle equipment, including the *sarissa* (a pike nearly 50 percent longer than the Greek spear) and the torsion catapult.

In 358, Philip put his new army to the test. He invaded Paeonia and defeated the Illyrians and then, in 356, invaded Thrace, capturing the silver and gold mines of Mount Pangeios. The capture of the mines, which produced a thousand talents each year, was contested by the Athenians, who battled intermittently with Philip for 10 years. A year after the invasion of Thrace, Philip entered southern Thessaly and in 348 destroyed Chalcidian Olynthos. This victory brought to him election as head of the Thessalian League (about 352), a confederation that tied Thessaly to Macedonia for more than 150 years.

In 348, Philip annexed Chalcidice and enslaved the population of Olynthus and other people of the region. Peace with Athens came in 346, and over the next three years he consolidated his control over Greece, mainly through diplomatic means. Athens broke the peace in 340, but Philip ended the hostilities at Chaeronea.

Philip consolidated his hold on territory stretching from the Hellespont to Thermopylae, and in 337 he held a meeting of the Greek states, except Sparta, that resulted in the formation of the Corinthian League. Philip was named commander and president of the alliance. Through this political entity, Philip increased the size of his army by requiring the states to supply troops and ships according to a quota system. Philip abrogated the democratic constitution of Thebes and stationed a Macedonian garrison in the region. He was careful, however, not to provoke Athens; for he needed the support of the Athenians for his next great campaign—war against Persia.

During the last few years of his life, Philip prepared his army for war. The combined Greek and Macedonian forces crossed the Hellespont in 336, but Philip was deprived of the honor of leading his troops to victory in Persia by an assassination plotted by his wife and jealous Macedonian nobles. He was stabbed to death by Pausanias, a young Macedonian noble, during the wedding of his daughter Cleopatra to King Alexander of Epirus.

Further Reading: George Cawkwell. *Philip of Macedon* (London: Faber & Faber, 1978); Miltiades B. Hatzopoulos. *Philip of Macedon* (Athens: Ekdotike Athenon, 1980).

Philip II (1527–1598)

King of Spain from 1556 to 1598 and of Portugal from 1580 to 1598, Philip II propelled Spain to its greatest period of power and influence.

The son of Holy Roman Emperor CHARLES V and Isabella of Portugal, Philip was born on May 21, 1527, in Valladolid, Spain. As a young man, he was given increasingly responsible positions in his father's court, and when his father died in 1556, Philip inherited the larger portion of the Hapsburg possessions: the Low Countries, Franche-Comté, Sicily, southern Italy, Milan, and Spanish colonies in the New World. Other Hapsburg dominions passed to Ferdinand, Philip's uncle, who was also named Holy Roman Emperor.

Before ascending to the throne, Philip married Maria of Portugal in 1543. Their son Don Carlos was mentally and physically handicapped, but, as he grew into adulthood, he continually attempted to engage himself in matters of state. Believing that his son was unfit to inherit the crown, Philip II had him imprisoned. On July 25, 1568, Don Carlos died mysteriously while in custody, and no evidence has ever surfaced to explain the cause of his death.

During most of his reign, Philip II was intent on maintaining peace. In fact, his third marriage, to Elizabeth of Valois, daughter of Henry II of France, had been arranged as part of the peace negotiations between Spain and France. In 1571, however, he joined forces with Venice and the papacy to fight the Turkish navy. At the battle of Lepanto, the combined Catholic forces were victorious.

Philip was not so lucky in 1588, when he determined that the only way to put down a rebellion in the Netherlands was to conquer England and France, both of which had been sending aid to the rebels. He ordered his Invincible Armada and the Spanish Army in the Netherlands to invade England—a most unfortunate expedition. Nevertheless, Philip recovered from this crushing defeat and, following the murder of Henry III in 1589, laid claim to the French throne for his daughter by Elizabeth of Valois. He lost that bid, however, when Henry of Navarre converted to Catholicism and became HENRY IV of France.

Philip II died at the Escorial in 1598. While he had not enlarged the Spanish empire, and indeed had lost control of the northern Netherlands, he did bolster the cause of the Counter-Reformation and made Catholicism secure throughout the rest of his empire.

Further Reading: J. H. Elliott. *Imperial Spain, 1469–1716* (Cambridge: Cambridge University Press, 1963).

Philip II Augustus (1165–1223)

Philip II Augustus ruled France from 1179 until 1223 and is best known for the reestablishment of local sovereignty over French lands formerly held by England.

Philip II was born in Paris on August 21, 1165. His father, King Louis VII, installed him as king during his own lifetime and thus immediately set off a power struggle among several French provinces and England over control of the 14-year-old monarch. When HENRY II (1333–89) of England turned over all English territories in France (except Normandy) to his son John, his older son, RICHARD I THE LION-HEARTED, rebelled. With Philip's assistance, Richard acquired the contested lands for himself and appointed Philip as his feudal lord.

In the meantime, Jerusalem had fallen to the armies of Saladin in 1187, and Philip joined forces with FREDERICK BARBAROSSA and Richard to form the major thrust of the Third Crusade. After the combined forces captured the city of Acre, Philip returned home, leaving Richard to attempt to capture Jerusalem. Failing in this, Richard set out for England, but was captured in Austria and held for ransom, during which time Philip became an ally of John in an attempt to wrest Normandy from Richard.

Philip II Augustus emerged triumphant in the Battle of Bouvines, July 26, 1214, repelling a German invasion of France led by Otto IV. (From M. Guizot, A Popular History of France from the Earliest Times, *n.d.)*

Upon Richard's death in 1199, John became king of England, and again, Philip turned from ally to enemy. Finally, in 1202, Philip declared all English holdings in France to be void and returned to the French crown, thereby ending a conflict that had raged for years. King John's attempt to repossess his lost French real estate ended in a battle fought at Bouvines on July 27, 1214, at which Philip defeated Otto IV of Germany and his combined army of English, German, and Flemish knights.

Philip was also known for his internal reforms, most especially the awarding of high-ranking positions in the govenment to those who were qualified to hold them, rather than to those claiming them by hereditary right. His plans to make Paris a leader among European capitals culminated in the construction of a defensive wall around the city, the paving of its streets with stone to reduce dust and mud, and the improvement of the University of Paris.

The last years of Philip's reign were peaceful, and when the monarch died at Nantes, France, on July 14, 1223, he left behind a kingdom that was one of the most powerful in Europe.

Further Reading: Robert Fawner. *The Capetian Kings of France: Monarchy and Nation, 987–1328* (London: Macmillan, 1960).

Philip IV the Fair (1268–1314)

Philip IV was king of France from 1285 until his death in 1314, during which time he strengthened the French monarchy by overthrowing the pope's authority in France's internal affairs.

Born in Fontainebleau, France, 1268, Philip was dubbed "the Fair" because of his handsome features. He inherited the crown from his father, Philip the Bold, in 1285. Nine years into his reign, Philip went to war with England, a decade-long conflict that practically drained the French crown of all resources. Peace was finally brought about by the marriage of Philip's daughter Isabella to Edward II of England.

Philip's disagreements with the pope began in 1296, when Boniface VIII attempted to forbid clerics from being taxed without papal authority. Philip, along with Edward I of England, backed the prelate down, and Boniface retracted his edict. Tempers between Philip and the pope flared again in 1301, when Philip had the bishop of Pamiers, Bernard Saisset, arrested for treason. After a long dispute in which Boniface unsuccessfully attempted to bring Philip under his control once and for all, Philip again emerged triumphant.

Philip the Fair is also remembered for his expulsion of the Jews from France in 1306. In addition, shortly afterwards, he also expelled all members of the Knights Templar, and, finally, in 1311, banished the Italian bankers (the Lombards). In each case, Philip enriched the royal coffers with the confiscated property of these exiles and through a program of heavy taxation.

Philip died in 1314, leaving three sons—Louis X, Philip V, and Charles IV—each of whom succeeded him briefly as king of France. The last, Charles IV, outlived his father by only 14 years, leaving at his death an heir apparent in Philip's grandson, EDWARD III, who at the time was king of England. The French nobility, seeking to prevent the possibility of an English king, enacted the Salic Law, barring women and their heirs from ascending to the throne. Consequently, Philip VI of Valois, a nephew of Philip the Fair, became king of France in 1328, and the Hundred Years' War was ignited.

Further Reading: Joseph R. Strayer. *The Reign of Philip the Fair* (Princeton: Princeton University Press, 1980).

Phraates IV (r. ca. 37–2 B.C.)

Having murdered his father to gain the throne of Parthia, Phraates was continually at war with Rome during his reign.

The second son of the Parthian king Orodes II, Phraates was not in the line of succession for the throne. His older brother, Pacorus, was Orodes' heir, as well as favorite son, but he died around 36 B.C. under questionable circumstances (many historians believe Phraates was responsible for his death). Orodes was devastated by the loss of Pacorus, and became desperately ill after naming Phraates his heir. The ailing king refused to die, however, and Phraates, growing impatient, finally killed his father and seized the throne.

As king, Phraates tolerated no opposition. When his nobles spoke out against him, he executed some and exiled others. In 37, when Phraates learned of the planned Roman invasion of Parthia, he had one of his generals, Monaeses, pose as a traitor in order to·penetrate the camp of Marc Antony to discover the Roman commander's plans. This ruse apparently failed, however, and Monaeses returned to lead the Parthian armies in the field—something Phraates himself never did.

Marc Antony, driving through Armenia into Media Atropatene, attacked Parthia, but was repulsed, retreating with heavy casualties. In 34, however, the king of Media, Phraates' vassal, made an alliance with Marc Antony and allowed the Romans to occupy Media. After Marc Antony's forces withdrew, Phraates marched his army into Media and savagely exacted revenge on the supporters of his treacherous vassal.

Unrest in Parthia caused Tiridates, one of Phraates' generals in the war against Marc Antony, to revolt in late 32. By the summer of 31 B.C., he had expelled Phraates from Parthia, forcing him to flee to the Saka nomads. After receiving aid from the Scythians in 30, however, Phraates returned, in turn expelling Tiridates, who nevertheless escaped to Rome with Phraates' son as prisoner.

Hoping to redeem his son, Phraates made peace with AUGUSTUS and formally recognized Armenia and Osroene as Roman dependencies. Augustus pledged to return Phraates' son on condition that Roman prisoners and standards be released. Phraates agreed, secured the release of his son, but he did not comply, and the following year Augustus unleashed his army against Parthia once again. Thus pressured, Phraates released the prisoners and restored the standards. In return, Augustus sent him a slave girl, Thea Urania Musa, as a concubine. She persuaded Phraates to send four of his sons to Rome as hostages, thereby securing the succession of her own son. Musa then poisoned Phraates in 2 B.C.

Picado (Michalski) Teodoro (1900–1960)

President of Costa Rica from 1944 to 1948, Teodoro Picado Michalski headed the first Communist government in the Americas.

Teodoro Picado Michalski was born on January 10, 1900, in San José, Costa Rica, the son of a Costa Rican father and a Polish mother. He became a professor in the School of Agriculture during 1917–23, then professor of history in the Liceo of Costa Rica from 1918 to 1923. From 1923 to 1930, he served as lawyer and notary for the United Fruit Company and Northern Railway Company. In 1919–20, Picado was secretary of the Costa Rican legation to the Central American conferences, and in 1929 served as a delegate to the International Congress of Statistics in Warsaw. He returned briefly to academic life during 1930 and 1932, then entered Costa Rican government in that year as secretary of public education. Six years later, he was elected a deputy to the nation's congress and became president of Costa Rica in 1944.

Picado's administration was marked by widespread civil unrest, including street fighting and a series of attempted coups. Picado enlisted the aid of the Communist Party, which had come to play a dominant role in the nation's politics, to void the election of 1948, in which he could not succeed himself. This action prompted a revolt led by Colonel José Figueres, which sent Picado fleeing to Nicaragua, where he served as secretary to that nation's repressive strongman, General Anastasio SOMOZA

GARCIA. Picado died in Managua, Nicaragua, on June 1, 1960.

Pilsudski, Jozef (1867–1935)

This Polish revolutionary and military commander modernized his country's army prior to World War I, saved Poland from Soviet domination following the war, and settled in as absolute dictator of his nation.

Jozef Pilsudski was born on December 5, 1867, at his well-to-do family's country estate, Zulova, 40 miles northeast of Vilnius (Vilna), Lithuania. For generations, the families of his mother and father had been active in Polish politics, and Pilsudski's mother in particular was an ardent nationalist. She instilled in her son a hatred of the nations that had, over the years, dissected the old kingdom of Poland: Sweden, Austria, Germany, and especially Russia. At the time of Pilsudski's birth, Lithuania—rightfully, according to his mother, Polish—had long been annexed to Russia, and Poland itself was nothing more than that country's "Vistula province."

In 1874, when Pilsudski was seven years old, the sheltered world of his early childhood was consumed by a fire that destroyed Zulova, and the family moved to Vilnius. There young Pilsudski was subjected to the full force of Russian domination of his homeland. Although the Pilsudskis were Catholics, all education and religious instruction came at the hands of Russian Orthodox priests; children were compelled to pledge allegiance to the czar; and even the Polish language was forbidden—all instruction was in Russian. The Russian governor of Lithuania was a sadist who deliberately abused and alienated the population. At the age of 12, Pilsudski wrote and circulated a tract he titled *The Zulova Pigeon*, calling for the overthrow of Russia in Poland. He and his brother Bronislas created a secret league of like-minded youthful would-be revolutionaries. Later, when he was a medical student at the Ukranian University of Kharkov, he fell in with still more young rebels and expanded his secret league. In 1887, he and Bronislas became involved in a plot to assassinate Czar ALEXANDER III using a poison bomb. The conspirators were discovered by the Russian secret police, Bronislas was exiled to Siberia for eight years, and Jozef for three.

Jozef Pilsudski's experience in Siberian exile transformed him into a mature revolutionary. He returned to Poland, married, and settled in Lodz, from where he wrote and circulated a subversive paper called *Workman*. In 1900, police seized the press and imprisoned Pilsudski, who feigned insanity in order to be transferred to a hospital from which he could make an escape. He fled to London for a time, then secretly returned to Crackow. In 1905, during the Russo-Japanese War, he traveled to Tokyo in an abortive attempt to persuade the Japanese to bankroll his Polish Socialist Party in an uprising. When this failed, he organized a series of raids and robberies in Poland to raise needed funds. Originally committed to non-violence, Pilsudski now set about training a small army. In 1914, when World War I began, Pilsudski, acting on his own authority, used his force against the Russians, then offered the services of his "Polish Legion" to Russia's enemy Austria if the Axis would recognize Poland as a free and independent state. This was granted, but when Germany insisted that Polish soldiers swear allegiance to Kaiser Wilhelm II, Pilsudski abruptly disbanded the legion in 1917. He was arrested and imprisoned for 15 months in Germany.

On November 9, 1918, the kaiser abdicated, and partisans freed Pilsudski from prison in Magdeburg. He was transported back to Warsaw and, the armistice having ended the war on November 11, neither Germany nor Russia was in control of Poland. Pilsudski assumed leadership of a new government.

It was hardly a dream come true. Postwar Poland was torn by dissension; its economy was in shambles, and its military force was dispersed. Pilsudski pulled together the disparate fragments of his country through a combination of charisma and ruthless dictatorship that included the creation of the "Defensive," a powerful secret police force that quickly evolved into a body as feared and hated as the czar's secret police had been.

Pilsudski rebuilt the Polish army and, exploiting the chaos of the Russian civil war, used it against the Soviets in the Russo-Polish War (also called the War of Intervention) of 1920. His object was expansion. In May, Pilsudski led some 200,000 men against Kiev, but was defeated and driven back by Red Army forces under Marshal Mikhail N. Tukhachevski and Cossacks under General Semën M. Budënny. By August, Soviet forces were massed outside of Warsaw. It was then that Pilsudski mounted a brilliant counteroffensive that issued in the momentous Battle of Warsaw during August 16–25. Overshadowed by the mass destruction of the recently ended world war, the Battle of Warsaw was one of the 20th century's most decisive engagements. At a cost of some 50,000 Polish casualties, Pilsudski killed 150,000 Soviet troops out of a force of about 200,000, arresting communism's initial thrust into the West. Moreover, Pilsudski capitalized on the victory by advancing into the Russo-Polish frontier areas bordering White Russia and the Ukraine. Tukhachevski was badly beaten at the Battle of Niemen (September 26) and the Battle of the

Schara (September 27). An armistice was concluded on October 12, 1920, and, on March 18, 1921, by the Treaty of Riga, the Soviets conceded all of Poland's territorial claims in White Russia and the Ukraine.

Pilsudski had expanded Poland into territories of mixed Polish and Russian allegiance, and he instituted increasingly dictatorial measures to enforce stability and obedience. When he retired from leadership in 1924, the government rapidly disintegrated, factions fell into destructive dispute, and, in 1926, elements in the Polish Senate and Seym (House of Commons) circulated stories that Pilsudski had plundered the wealth of the Polish government, even stealing the crown jewels from the Belvedere Palace. The dictator quickly emerged from retirement, mustered three loyal army regiments, and marched on Warsaw. This military coup of May 12–14, 1926, was successful, and while Pilsudski declined to resume the presidency himself, he appointed a puppet, Ignace Moscicki, in his place. Through Moscicki, Pilsudski ruled Poland with an iron hand, increasingly relying on the secret police to enforce order. On January 26, 1934, Pilsudski concluded a non-aggression pact with Adolf HITLER's Germany, guaranteeing respect for existing territorial rights for 10 years. Despite this, Poland—like the rest of the world—was drifting toward World War II. Pilsudski was spared his long-suffering nation's greatest ordeal when he died on May 12, 1935.

Pinochet (Ugarte) Augusto   (b. 1915)

Riding in on a bloody military coup, General Augusto Pinochet ruled Chile for the better part of two decades, in the process perpetrating severe human rights violations.

Born on November 11, 1915, into Chile's upper-middle class, Pinochet was early destined for a military career. At the age of 18, he entered the Chilean military academy, Escuela Militar, and graduated with the rank of second lieutenant in 1936. After stints as an instructor at both Escuela Militar and Academia de Guerra (the Chilean war college), and numerous postings throughout Chile, Pinochet returned to the capital of Santiago. By 1968, he had attained the rank of brigadier general.

In 1970, Salvador Allende, a Marxist, was elected president in Chile—the first popularly elected Marxist president in the Western Hemisphere. Despite good intentions, Allende instituted programs and policies that resulted in skyrocketing inflation rates, a severe decline in production, and severe food shortages. Seizing the moment of crisis, Pinochet, now commander in chief of the army, enlisted the cooperation of the chiefs of the air force, navy, and

national police, creating a military junta aimed at the overthrow of Allende.

Beginning in the early daylight hours of September 11, 1973, the four began what would prove, even by Latin American standards, a very bloody coup. The navy seized the critical port of Valparaíso, and, at the presidential palace in Santiago, Pinochet gave Allende the ultimatum of either stepping down or being overrun. Allende refused, and the palace was taken several hours later. Infantrymen found Allende dead. Some maintain that he killed himself rather than face certain execution, while others claim he was killed in the revolt. Whatever the cause of Allende's demise, it was welcomed in official U.S. government circles. The United States had isolated the Marxist regime through stiff economic sanctions, and the CIA had invested millions of dollars, much of it in aid to Pinochet, to destabilize the Allende regime.

The junta took immediate and draconian measures to hold what they had seized. Martial law was declared and a curfew imposed, with violators shot on sight. On September 13, Pinochet was named president of the junta. After summarily breaking off relations with Cuba, Pinochet began proceedings against 14,000 leftists, who would be tried and executed or expelled from the country. Pinochet and the junta claimed that their only goal was "to restore institutional normality" to Chile, but the toll taken on human life was enormous. As many as 20,000 people were estimated to have been killed, and up to 14,000 political prisoners were reportedly still being held a year after the coup. Although Pinochet has always denied it, torture of leftist prisoners was widespread.

After being peacefully rejected in a 1988 plebescite, Pinochet finally relinquished the presidency in March 1990. He stayed on, however, as army chief of staff, and, from this position, continued to defend the actions and policies of the preceding two decades.

Further Reading: Robert J. Alexander. *The Tragedy of Chile* (Westport, Conn.: Greenwood Press, 1978); Gary MacEoin. *Chile Under Military Rule* (New York: IDOC/North America, 1974).

Pius V   [Saint Pius] (1504–1572)

One of the central figures of the Catholic Reformation, Pius V implemented the decrees of the Council of Trent and ruthlessly used the Inquisition as a means of weeding out heretics.

Pius was born Antonio Michele Ghislieri on January 17, 1504, and was a shepherd until he joined the Dominican order at the age of 14. He was ordained in 1528 and taught theology and philosophy. In 1551 he was made commissary general of the Inquisition, a position in which he gained notice for his zeal in identifying and persecuting heretics. He was made bishop in 1556, cardinal in 1557, and grand inquisitor for life in 1558.

When Pius IV died in 1565, Antonio was handily elected pope, taking the name Pius V at his coronation on January 7, 1566. The watchword for Pius was reform, and he immediately set about reforming all of Christendom. He cleaned up Rome, setting a new standard of morality for the city, banning bull fighting, prostitution, gambling, profanity, and desecration of the sabbath. He held officials of the church to a higher standard of morality and enforced compliance with harsh penalties.

Pius vigorously stepped up the pace and scope of the Inquisition. In March 1569, he expelled the Jews from the Papal States, except in Rome and Ancona, where, for reasons of commerce, they were allowed to remain (albeit under unfavorable conditions). In 1570, Pius excommunicated Queen ELIZABETH I of England and ordered all Catholics to renounce their allegiance to her. This only succeeded in heightening Elizabeth's power and increasing the persecution of Catholics in England.

Pius V's most enduring reform was his enforcement of the Council of Trent and the reforms instituted there. But in his brutal quest for reform and ascetic morality, Pius managed to alienate most of western Europe. This proved to be destructive when he was gathering forces to push back the Ottoman advances in the East. Only Spain and Venice joined Pius in his crusade against the Turks—but that proved to be sufficient, as the Turks were defeated at the great naval battle of Lepanto on October 7, 1571.

Shortly after returning from the crusade, Pius V died on May 1, 1572. He was subsequently canonized.

Further Reading: H. Daniel Rops. *The Catholic Reformation* (London: Dent, 1962); John P. Dolan. *Catholicism, An Historical Survey* (Woodbury, N.Y.: Barron's Educational Series, 1968).

Pizarro, Francisco   (b. ca. 1475–1541)

This Spanish conquistador conquered Peru for Spain, though he failed to subdue the native population entirely, and the region remained one of Spain's most troublesome New World possessions.

The bastard son of a Spanish hidalgo, Pizarro received no formal education and was forced as a youth to earn his living herding swine. When his relative Hernán CORTÉS voyaged to Hispaniola in the New World, Pizarro eagerly seized the opportunity to join him and make his fortune.

In 1510, Pizarro was a member of an expedition exploring the Gulf of Urabá in northern Colombia, and he served as Balboa's lieutenant on the 1513 expedition that sighted the Pacific Ocean. Spanish exploration and colonization depended in large measure on individual initiative and entrepreneurship, and in 1522, Pizarro struck a partnership with another conquistador, Diego de Almagro, and a priest, Hernán de Luque, to undertake a series of expeditions deep into South America. The first expedition took them as far as the San Juan River in Colombia before unrelenting hardship turned them back. The second, conducted in 1526–28, was even more harrowing than the first, plagued by starvation, disease, and mutiny, but it was also far more fruitful. Reaching the Santa River in Peru, Pizarro and his men returned to Panama laden with gold, cloth, and llamas.

Fearing Pizarro's growing power, the governor of Panama denied him permission for further exploration, whereupon the conquistador went to Spain in 1528 and presented his case directly to the king. The two hammered out an agreement giving the Spanish crown all of Peru, its people, and its treasure. For his part, Pizarro was created a knight of Santiago and named governor and captain-general of whatever lands he conquered. His partners received much less and justly believed they had been swindled.

In June 1530, Pizarro, several of his brothers, and 180 men sailed from Panama for the coast of the Gulf of Guayaquil. They devastated the settlement of Tumbes, Peru, then marched inland, meeting with ATAHUALPA, ruler of the Incas, at Cajamarca on November 15, 1532. Pizarro treacherously took Atahualpa captive and demanded a vast ransom for his release. Once the ransom was collected, the conquistador ordered Atahualpa's death by strangulation on August 29, 1533.

Within a year, Pizarro's expedition had taken Cuzco, the Inca capital. Manco Capac, the son of Atahualpa, launched a desperate campaign to recover Cuzco, but was defeated by Almagro during 1536–37. Subsequent to this, Almagro, bitter over the inequitable division of spoils, opened a dispute with Pizarro, which escalated into full battle. Pizarro triumphed, captured Almagro, and executed him.

The one-time swineherd was now elevated to the Spanish aristocracy and spent the rest of his life attempting to consolidate all that he had conquered. He apportioned lands as well as Indian serfs among his loyal men, created new settlements, and established agricultural operations. In 1535, Pizarro founded Lima, making it the capital of Peru. However, in eliminating Almagro, Pizarro had fallen short of neutralizing all opposition to himself, and, on June 26, 1541, partisans of Almagro assassinated the conquistador.

Further Reading: Frank Shay. *The Incredible Pizarro: Conqueror of Peru* (New York: Mohawk Press, 1932); Alpheus Hyatt Verrill. *Great Conquerors of South and Central America* (New York: D. Appleton, 1929).

Pol Pot   [Saloth Sar] (b. 1928–   )

As Communist dictator of Democratic Kampuchea (formerly Cambodia), Pol Pot caused the deaths of perhaps 1,000,000 Cambodians in a program meant to achieve the Maoist ideal of a purely agrarian Marxist society.

Pol Pot was born on May 19, 1928. He became a follower of HO CHI MINH and joined Ho's Indochinese Communist Party during the era of World War II. Pol Pot assumed leadership of the Khmer Rouge guerrilla movement, which overthrew the American-backed Cambodian government of Lon Nol in 1975. Pol Pot became prime minister of Democratic Kampuchea—the new regime's name for Cambodia—in April 1976.

Pol Pot and the Khmer Rouge believed in a radical form of MAO TSE-TUNG's ideal of agrarian communism. Pol Pot caused the death of perhaps a million Cambodians in an effort to reshape the nation's society in accordance with his extreme interpretation of Marxist theory. Pol Pot's regime was overthrown in January 1979 by Vietnamese forces, which invaded Kampuchea and sent the dictator fleeing to the hill country bordering Thailand. He returned to power in 1982, forming a coalition government of Democratic Kampuchea with non-Communist elements. He announced his retirement as head of the Khmer Rouge in 1985, but retained a so-called military advisory role.

Suggested Reading: David P. Chandler. *Brother Number One: A Political Biography of Pol Pot* (Boulder, Colo.: Westview Press, 1992).

Polycrates   (d. ca. 522 B.C.)

Polycrates was tyrant of Samos from about 540 B.C. until his death around 522 B.C.

Polycrates was born in Sardis about 522 B.C. After invading Samos, he ruled it jointly with his brothers, Pantagnotus and Syloson, but after a short time, he disposed of the two and established himself as sole ruler.

Polycrates made a treaty with Egypt, which he promptly broke when Persia advanced against the pharaoh in 525 B.C. Polycrates hoped to eliminate his political opponents by dispatching them with the fleet he sent to Persia. His intended victims soon re-turned, however, accompanied by a Spartan force bent on deposing the tyrant. Polycrates bought off the Spartans with specially made counterfeit coins, and the affair ended.

Although he was an outspoken advocate of military supremacy, so dramatically embodied in his magnificent fleet, Polycrates was also a man of learning and culture. Theodorus and the poet Anacreon lived at his court, and he also invited foreign craftsmen to his island. The two famous architectural landmarks of Samos, the Temple of Hera and the aqueduct, are often attributed to Polycrates, but in fact, their construction may have begun before his reign. Polycrates died when Oroetes, the Persian governor of Sardis, tricked him into visiting him on the mainland and ordered his crucifixion.

Pompey the Great   [Gnaeus Pompeius Magnus] (106–48 B.C.)

A member of the First Triumvirate of Rome, Pompey was one of the great figures of the Roman Republic.

Born into the senatorial nobility of Rome on September 29, 106 B.C., Pompey spent his early years developing his military and diplomatic skills under the tutelage of his father, a Roman consul. When civil war broke out between the followers of Lucius SULLA and Gaius Marius, Pompey's father sided with Marius' faction. Following his father's death, however, Pompey distanced himself from Marius and concentrated on developing his own power base. After gaining control of three legions through mutiny, Pompey joined Sulla in fighting Marius and driving him from Rome.

Pompey next secured the Senate's permission to campaign for the recovery of Sicily and Africa from Marius, completing the mission in two offensives during 81 B.C. Marius' troops called him Sulla's Butcher because he ruthlessly slaughtered any and all who surrendered themselves to him.

After defeating Marius' troops, Pompey marched on Rome and demanded that Sulla give him an independent command. Sulla complied, but soon abdicated, leaving Lepidus as consul in 78. Pompey supported Lepidus until he attempted to establish a brutal dictatorship. Thereupon, Pompey joined forces with those opposed to Lepidus and overthrew him.

Pompey's power increased after he defeated Lepidus. Again he refused to disband his army and demanded proconsular authority in Spain to help defeat the Marius factions there. After straining his resources to the maximum, Pompey was victorious in Spain and this time was more generous in his dealings with the vanquished. He again returned to Rome with his army, this time to put down a slave

Portrait bust of Pompey the Great. (From Richard Delbruck, Antike Portrats, 1912)

revolt led by Spartacus. With the aid of Marcus Crassus, he crushed the rebellion and now looked forward to a consulship. The Senate named both Pompey and Crassus consul in 70, and the pair quickly set about reversing many of Sulla's policies that had corrupted the Republic.

Pompey now stayed close to Rome in order to build a following and increase his popularity, which had been growing considerably ever since his first defeat of Marius' forces. When pirate raids off the Mediterranean coast became a menace in 67 B.C., Pompey received carte blanche to deal with the problem. Within three months, he defeated the pirates.

In the East, MITHRADATES VI EUPATOR, king of Pontus, waged war in Asia Minor. In 66, the Senate, though wary of Pompey's growing popularity, gave him even more power—command of the entire East—in order to deal with Mithradates. Within the year, Pompey had subjugated Mithradates and added most of Pontus to Rome's tributaries. For good measure, Pompey laid siege to Jerusalem in 62

B.C., taking it after three months. When he returned to Rome, he was the most celebrated general of the age.

The Senate, now extremely jealous of Pompey's power and popularity, refused him the traditional allotment of lands he requested for himself and his soldiers. The Senate was also wary of Crassus and of Julius CAESAR, each of whom had his own personal agenda for power. The three, realizing they needed each other if they were to gain anything, secretly formed the First Triumvirate in 59 B.C. The alliance proved successful almost immediately, with each of the three receiving the offices and rewards they sought.

They renewed the alliance in 56 B.C., but the situation soon deteriorated as each triumvir wanted more than the others. Pompey and Crassus were renamed consuls in 55 B.C., but Crassus died in battle two years later. With Caesar gaining personal wealth and fame in Gaul, Pompey essentially dominated Rome. He came to control the Senate and was able to get much of what he wanted through careful diplomacy or outright skullduggery. In 52 B.C. he was named sole consul, essentially the most powerful man in the Roman world.

Pompey now felt that a showdown between him and Caesar was imminent. He demanded that Caesar surrender his powers and his army, which Caesar refused to do. At this impasse, Pompey had the Senate issue the "last decree" on January 7, 49 B.C., effectively declaring war on Caesar. Caesar responded by crossing the Rubicon, his point of no return in his march against Pompey in southern Italy.

The two met in minor battles across southern Europe and eventually fought the climactic Battle of Pharsalus in Thessaly on August 9, 48 B.C. Caesar smashed Pompey's forces, and the consul fled to Egypt, hoping to secure refuge from King Ptolemy. Fearing the wrath of the victorious Caesar, Ptolemy had Pompey executed on September 28, 48 B.C.

Further Reading: Peter Greenhalgh. *Pompey: The Roman Alexander* (London: Weidenfeld & Nicholson, 1980); John D. Leach. *Pompey the Great* (London: Croom Helm, 1978).

Popé (ca. 1630–ca. 1690)

This Tewa medicine man successfully planned and executed a mass rebellion among the pueblos of the American southwest against the oppressive regime of the Spanish colonizers.

Popé was a respected medicine man of the Tewa pueblo at present-day San Juan, New Mexico (north of Santa Fe). By the 1670s, the pueblos had endured nearly a half-century of persecution, exploitation, and general cruelty at the hands of the Spanish colonial government. Desperate, the Indians of the pueblo made an alliance with their hereditary enemies, the Apache (whose very name was derived from a Zuni word for "enemy"), and terrorized the Spanish. Colonial governor Antonio de Otermín determined in 1675 to put a stop to the resistance by arresting the influential medicine men in 47 pueblos. The governor hanged three and imprisoned the rest, among them Popé.

After some years, Popé was released. Far from having been broken in spirit, he was determined to throw off the Spanish yoke once and for all. He decided to unite the far-flung pueblos in one great revolt. In doing this, he faced a formidable problem of politics as well as logistics. To begin with, decisions among the pueblos were customarily the result of debate, discussion, and mutual agreement. None of the pueblo towns was likely to act without securing the unanimous consent of its council, and the Tewa medicine man had first to persuade the council of each pueblo to commit that pueblo and to act in concert with the others. In this, Popé was remarkably successful. Not only did he persuade all but a few of the most remote settlements along the Rio Grande to participate, but he managed to do so while preserving absolute secrecy.

Next came the logistical problem of coordinating the moment of the attack. Popé devised an ingenious scheme whereby runners were dispatched to the various towns, each bearing a knotted cord designed so that the last knot would be untied in each pueblo on the day set for the revolt: August 13, 1680. Popé was ruthless in his enforcement of secrecy. He even killed his brother-in-law because he suspected him of treachery. Despite his vigilance, word did leak, and Popé was forced to launch the attack three days early, on the 10th.

Despite the sudden change in plan, the rebellion was devastatingly successful. The missions at Taos, Pecos, and Acoma were burned to the ground and the priests killed, their bodies heaped upon the hated altars. Lesser missions fell one by one, as did the surrounding haciendas, which were destroyed along with their inhabitants. By August 14 or 15, leading 500 warriors, Popé advanced against the colonial capital of Santa Fe. The settlement was defended by a small garrison of 50, but it harbored some 1,000 settlers. The garrison was also equipped with a brass cannon. After four days of fierce fighting, Santa Fe fell, and Popé installed himself in the palace Governor Otermín had evacuated at the last possible moment. In all, some 400–500 settlers had been killed, together with 21 out of 33 missionaries assigned to the region. About 2,500 Spaniards fled downriver in terror, many as far as present-day El Paso, Texas. They abandoned all that they had owned.

As the Spanish had sought to wipe out all manifestations of the Indians' "pagan" culture, so Popé now directed his followers in an orgy of destruction across a region extending from Taos to Isleta.

The pleasures of liberation and revenge were short-lived for the Indians. Popé set himself up as a tyrant oppressive as any Spaniard had been. Until his death about 1690, he taxed and plundered his people relentlessly. Against marauding Utes and Apaches he showed none of the military brilliance that had guided the rebellion. This raiding, combined with internal strife and general famine, reduced the population of the pueblos from some 30,000 at the outbreak of the revolt to about 9,000 in 1692, two years after the dictator's death, when Spanish governor Don Diego de Vargas exploited the dissension and weakness of the pueblos to lay siege to Santa Fe and retake it. Within four years, all of the pueblos were once again firmly under Spanish colonial domination.

Further Reading: Alan Axelrod. *Chronicle of the Indian Wars: From Colonial Times to Wounded Knee* (New York: Prentice Hall, 1992); C. W. Hackett and C. C. Shelby. *Revolt of the Pueblo Indians of New Mexico and Otermin's Attempted Reconquest, 1680–1682* (Albuquerque: University of New Mexico Press, 1970).

Portales, Diego (José Victor)   (1793–1837)

One of the founders of modern Chile, Portales became a symbol for Chilean unity and nationalism.

Diego Portales was the scion of a wealthy and influential family. He was awarded a monopoly from the government on tobacco, liquor and tea in 1824, from which he—and the government—reaped tremendous profits. The monopoly worked a stranglehold on Chilean laborers, creating unrest among them. When Portales left the monopolistic venture after two years, he went into the newspaper business, publishing two papers in which he gave voice to his extremely conservative, anti-labor policies.

When the Conservative Party gained power in 1830, Portales was named chief minister, a position from which he ruled Chile by decree. Opposed to democracy and all its works, he ruthlessly suppressed opposition wherever he found it, imprisoning his opponents and gaining control of the army. Portales was given an additional mandate for power by the conservative constitution of 1833, which created a centralized state dominated by a landed oligarchy and the Catholic church.

Portales briefly withdrew from political life, returning in 1835 as minister of war and interior as well as chief adviser to President Joaquin Prieto.

Problems with the nation's traditional trade rival, Peru, intensified when a combined Peru-Bolivia empire seemed imminent. After it was discovered that Peruvians were behind a failed coup attempt, Portales armed for war. He led his forces against Peru in 1836 and enjoyed success in his campaign, but, before the war was concluded, Portales was assassinated while reviewing his troops on June 6, 1837.

Porus (d. 317 b.c.)

Porus was an Indian prince who almost singlehandedly stood up to the onslaught of ALEXANDER III THE GREAT's army as it invaded the Punjab.

Little is known about the early life of Porus. In 326 b.c., when Alexander's armies approached the Hydaspes River, the border of Porus' domain, the prince met the Greeks head-on with an army of his own. The most intimidating element of the Indian army was its elephant corps, which terrified the soldiers of Alexander, who faced the mighty animals across the swollen river. After a long stalemate, Alexander finally ordered his men to cross the river several miles upstream in order to attack Porus from the rear. Even then, the Indian army fought long and valiantly, until the elephants panicked and turned on their handlers.

When Alexander met with the defeated Porus to discuss surrender terms, he was so impressed with the prince's valor on the field, as well as his eloquence at the bargaining table, that he allowed Porus to keep all of the conquered territory and to rule it as a Macedonian dependent. Shortly after Alexander's death, Porus was murdered by one of Alexander's generals, Eudemus.

Further Reading: Catherine B. Avery, ed. *The New Century Classical Handbook* (New York: Appleton-Century-Crofts, 1962).

Postumus, Marcus Cassianius Latinius (d. 268)

Postumus, most likely a Gaul, was a Roman military governor stationed in Germany, who broke away from the empire and declared himself, "The Restorer of the Gauls."

In about 259, the emperor GALLIENUS set off to crush a revolt by his own father, Ingenuus, and left his trusted governor, POSTUMUS, in control of the Rhine River frontier. A quarrel between Postumus and Silvanus, the praetorian prefect and guardian of Gallienus' son Saloninus, resulted in Postumus' ordering the deaths of both Silvanus and Saloninus. He then established himself as emperor in Gaul, with the provinces of Spain and Britain reporting to him.

Postumus ran his renegade empire as a completely separate entity from Rome. Its citizens elected their own senate and consuls and even minted their own coinage for the region. Gallienus, in the meantime, vowed not to tolerate Postumus' break-away empire and, in 263, marched into Gaul to reclaim it for Rome. After cinching a pair of victories but failing to follow up on them, Gallienus was wounded and had to be taken from the field. The effort to bring Gaul back into the imperial fold had failed, and Postumus was left to pursue his own destiny.

His end came in Germany at the hands of his own soldiers in 268, after he refused to allow his army to sack a recently conquered town.

Further Reading: Michael Grant. *The Roman Emperors* (New York: Viking, 1985).

Powhatan [Wahunsonacock, Wa-hun-sen-a-cawh] (d. 1618)

Chief of the Powhatan Confederacy of Indian tribes, Powhatan ruled over the Tidewater and alternately menaced and befriended the English settlers at Jamestown and surrounding areas.

Powhatan's father, a Pamunkey Algonkin chief, had managed to conquer neighboring Algonkin-speaking bands to form a loose confederacy in the Virginia Tidewater area. Upon his succession to power, Powhatan conquered several others, creating the 32-band Powhatan Confederacy, which controlled the southern end of Chesapeake Bay in Maryland down to Albemarle Sound in North Carolina and west to the headwaters of the Rappahanock and Rapidan Rivers, west of Fredericksburg and Richmond. In all, Powhatan dominated as many as 200 villages consisting of more than 9,000 inhabitants.

In dealing with his own people, Powhatan was intolerant of anything other than total subservience. He was vain and irascible. When the English established Jamestown in 1607, Powhatan initially offered no opposition. As the true character of the settlers became increasingly apparent through acts of exploitation and usurpation, Powhatan reacted decisively, refusing to sell corn to the often-starving colonists and periodically ambushing and murdering them as they attempted to scratch out sustenance in their poor fields.

A pattern of attack and reprisal continued until Powhatan's daughter, Pocahontas (who had earlier saved Captain John Smith from execution at the hands of her father), married the English planter John Rolfe. Out of respect for his daughter, Powhatan negotiated a peace agreement that promoted amity between the two groups that endured uneasily until Powhatan's death. At this time, his half-brother, Opechancanough began a war of extermination against the English. By this time, the colony was larger and more firmly established. Opechancanough's war resulted in the virtual extermination of his own people.

Further Reading: Alan Axelrod. *Chronicle of the Indian Wars* (New York: Prentice Hall, 1993); Jean Fritz. *The Double Life of Pocahontas* (New York: Putnam, 1983).

Primo de Rivera, José Antonio (1903–1936)

Son of the dictator Miguel PRIMO DE RIVERA, José Antonio Primo de Rivera founded the Spanish Fascist party, the Falange.

José Antonio Primo de Rivera was born in Madrid on April 24, 1903, the son of the strongman who was Spain's absolute dictator from 1923 to January 1930. Inheriting his father's right-wing authoritarian views, José Antonio entered military service, then became a lawyer in 1925. Eight years later, he founded the Falange Española—more widely known simply as the Falange—a Fascist movement dedicated to blocking Spanish Communists. He was elected to the Cortes (parliament) in 1933 and edited two Fascist periodicals, *F.E.* in 1934 and *Arriba* in 1935, both of which were suppressed by the left-wing Republican government.

In 1935, the parties of the left coalesced into the Popular Front and were thereby able to come to power with the elections of February 1936. Primo de Rivera lost his Cortes seat and was arrested. While imprisoned, he was reelected as representative from Cuenca, but the Popular Front annulled his candidacy and dissolved the Falange. At this juncture, the Spanish Civil War began in earnest, and on November 20, 1936, Primo de Rivera was hastily tried, convicted of treason, and executed.

Foolishly, the Republicans had given the Spanish political right just what it needed—a martyr. Falangists rallied around their fallen hero and merged their party with other right-wing groups to form the Nationalist movement.

Further Reading: Shlomo Ben-Ami. *Fascism from Above: The Dictatorship of Primo de Rivera in Spain* (Oxford: Clarendon Press, 1983).

Primo de Rivera, Miguel (1870–1930)

A Spanish dictator who came to power through a coup d'état, Primo de Rivera based his repressive regime on the motto "Country, Religion, Monarchy."

Born to a military family in Cádiz on January 8, 1870, Primo de Rivera graduated from the General Military Academy, Toledo, in 1888 and served in Morocco, Cuba, and the Philippines, places in which he saw firsthand the results of popular insurrection. He became military governor of his native Cádiz in

1915 and captain general of Valencia in 1920. Two years later, he was named captain general of Barcelona. He quickly gained a reputation for swift, decisive, and effective action in suppressing civil disorder.

Primo de Rivera let it be known that the discontent and disobedience rife in Spain during the 1920s was the result of a corrupt, weak, and inefficient parliamentary government. When a coup d'état propelled him to the head of the Spanish government in September 1923, he acted immediately to dissolve the Cortes (parliament) and suspend the Spanish constitution.

A proto-Fascist, Primo de Rivera did—in the short run—succeed in imposing order on Spain. He successfully ended the Moroccan War in 1927, he resolved a multitude of crippling labor disputes, and he set up a number of popular public works programs. But he made the fatal mistake of alienating the middle class and of relying on support from landlords, a move that blocked any serious effort at agrarian reform. Erosion of popular support by the end of the 1920s made his strident appeals to patriotism and Spanish traditions ring particularly hollow. Moreover, his program to suppress Catalonia's bid for greater autonomy strained military and civil resources, while further damaging Primo de Rivera's popularity.

By 1929, Spain was close to financial collapse—and so was the regime of Primo de Rivera. The final straw came when the army itself withdrew its support. At this, the dictator resigned, retired, and was quickly overtaken by ill health. He died in Paris on March 16, 1930.

Further Reading: Harold Livermore. *A History of Spain* (New York: Farrar, Straus and Cudahy, 1958).

Psamtik I (d. 610 B.C.)

With the aid of Greek mercenaries, Psamtik I reunited Egypt, expelled the Assyrians from its territories, and founded the 26th dynasty.

What little is known about this important ruler is found in the pages of the Greek historian Herodotus. Psamtik was apparently one of 12 co-rulers of Egypt, which was wholly under the domination of Assyria. He employed an army of Greek mercenaries to wrest power from his 11 peers and emerged for a time as Egypt's sole ruler. However, his vassals rebelled against the Assyrians in 663 B.C., an action that apparently proved abortive. Contrary to what might have been expected, the Assyrians reinstalled Psamtik as governor of Athribis, a city on the Nile Delta. Now it was Psamtik's turn to bridle under vassalage, and he forged an alliance with Gyges, king of Lydia, by which he was able to subdue his fellow vassals and the Assyrian princes throughout the Delta during 658–651 B.C.

After establishing a capital at Sais, the city of his birth, Psamtik set about remaking Egypt. The Cushites—who inhabited a kingdom south of Egypt—dominated Thebes. Psamtik persuaded the priestess of Amon, the god of Thebes, to adopt his daughter. Although the governor of Thebes remained a Cushite appointee, the adoption gave Psamtik access to the great wealth of the Theban temples. Moreover, Psamtik was able to install his own administrators elsewhere in the south and in middle Egypt.

Psamtik showed similar political acumen in dealing with the threat posed by the resident military classes throughout Egypt. He created a corps of Greek mercenaries, answerable directly to himself, as a permanent part of the Egyptian army. He also sought to head off feudal fragmentation by developing a policy of large property donations to temples. On a more directly cultural level, Psamtik counteracted the pressures of foreign influence by encouraging a revival of Old Kingdom notions of religion and art.

Psamtik I had managed to regain some of Egypt's former strength and cohesion, and the revived empire was maintained after his death by his son, Psamtik II, but succumbed to a Persian invasion in 535 B.C., which grandson Psamtik III failed to stop.

Ptolemy XI Alexander II   (ca. 115–80 B.C.)
Ptolemy XI Alexander II, the last fully legitimate Ptolemaic king of Egypt, married BERENICE III and ruled with her jointly for 19 days before murdering her.

Ptolemy XI Alexander II was the son of Ptolemy X Alexander I, king of Egypt and Cyprus. As a boy, Ptolemy XI was sent to the Aegean island of Cos during a war with the Seleucid Empire. However, he was captured in 88 B.C. (about the time of his father's death) by MITHRADATES VI EUPATOR, king of Pontus, who had captured Cos from Rome. In Ptolemy XI, Mithradates recognized a valuable political hostage and treated him well. However, at the first opportunity, Ptolemy XI escaped to the protection of Lucius Cornelius SULLA, dictator of Rome, during a battle between Sulla and Mithradates in 84 B.C.

Sulla also regarded Ptolemy XI Alexander II as a valuable hostage and kept him in Rome until 81 B.C. In that year, Ptolemy XI's uncle, Ptolemy IX Soter II, died, leaving his widow, Berenice III, as sole ruler of Egypt. Sulla, who had inculcated in Ptolemy XI Alexander II a measure of Roman loyalty and obedience to himself, sent the young man to Egypt to marry Berenice III and rule—presumably as his puppet—jointly with her. Not known for his sensitivity,

Sulla had bothered to consult neither Berenice nor the Egyptian people before making this decision. Ptolemy XI Alexander arrived in Egypt and married Berenice, who, however, insisted on ruling alone. After 19 days in the company of his wife, Ptolemy XI resorted to the expedient of murder. This act so enraged the people, who loved their queen, that a mob killed Ptolemy XI Alexander, thereby eliminating the last fully legitimate Ptolemaic king.

Pyrrhus   (ca. 319 B.C.– 272 B.C.)
Ruler of Epirus (northwestern Greece), Pyrrhus defeated a Roman army at Heraclea in 280 at ruinous cost to his own forces, thereby bequeathing to history the eponymous phrase "pyrrhic victory."

Pyrrus, king of Epirus, defeated Roman forces at the battles of Heraclea and Asculum in 280 and 279 B.C., but incurred losses so great himself that the term "Pyrrhic victory" was coined to describe such costly triumphs. (From Charlotte M. Yonge, Pictorial History of the World's Great Nations, *1882)*

A relative of ALEXANDER III THE GREAT of Macedon, Pyrrhus ascended the Epriote throne in 307 B.C., when he was only 12 years old. His early reign was tumultuous, and he quickly formed an alliance with Demetrius I Poliorcetes. However, Pyrrhus was nevertheless driven from power by a revolt, whereupon he fled into Asia to join Demetrius and the aged Antigonus I Doson in one of the many struggles that constituted the Wars of the "Diadochi"—the feuding successors of Alexander the Great. At the Battle of Ipsus, in Asia Minor, Pyrrhus' two allies were defeated by Seleucus and Lysimachus. Demetrius escaped, establishing control over western Asia Minor, Antigonus was killed, and Pyrrhus was sent as a hostage to the court of Ptolemy I as a result of a treaty between the ruler of Egypt and Demetrius. Within a short time, Pyrrhus and Ptolemy formed a friendship and an alliance, whereby Ptolemy helped him regain the Epriote throne in 297 B.C.

Pyrrhus was at first content to share power with his kinsman Neoptolemus II, but soon engineered his assassination in 296, assumed sole rule, and exploited the chaotic situation of Greece and Macedonia to expand his kingdom. His erstwhile ally, Demetrius, having seized Macedonia in 294, soon became the target of a decade of Pyrrhus' military operations. With the aid of Ptolemy and Lysimachus (another of the Diadochi), Pyrrhus succeeded in overthrowing Demetrius in 286. Deserted by his army, Demetrius fled to Asia Minor, surrendering at last to Seleucus, who imprisoned him. Demitrius died in captivity.

Pyrrhus left Greece for Italy in 280 in answer to a plea from the Greek colony of Tarentum (modern Taranto) for relief from Roman attack. Pyrrhus led some 25,000 men and 20 elephants, twice defeating the Romans, most famously at Heraclea in 280. Congratulated on the victory, which had nearly destroyed his own army, Pyrrhus reportedly replied, "One more such victory and I shall be lost."

Despite his triumph, the Romans refused to negotiate with Pyrrhus, and he pushed on toward Rome itself, but was compelled to retire to southern Italy, where he raised more troops. At Asculum in 279 he won another "pyrrhic victory," incurring a severe wound to himself as well. Turning away from Rome, he decided to advance on Sicily in order to relieve Syracuse from Carthaginian siege in 278. During 278–276, Pyrrhus enjoyed some successes, but failed to dislodge the Carthaginians from their strongholds. In the meantime, Carthage forged an alliance with Rome, and Pyrrhus rushed back to Italy in 276 to confront Roman forces once again. The Battle of Beneventum in 275 resulted in Pyrrhus' defeat when the Roman general M. Curius Dentatus was able to drive Pyrrhus' own elephants back upon his lines, creating havoc and panic.

The luckless Pyrrhus returned to Epirus, then met and defeated Antigonus II Gonatus at Thessalonica in 274. Having secured Macedonia, he failed to consolidate his gains there, but turned instead to Greece, launching an attack on Sparta in a bid to restore his ally Cleonymus to the Spartan throne. Pyrrhus was killed in a minor nighttime skirmish on the streets of Argos in 272 B.C.

Further Reading: N. G. L. Hammond. *Epirus* (Oxford: Clarendon Press, 1967); Geoffrey Neale Cross. *Epirus* (Cambridge: The University Press, 1932).

Q

Qaddafi, Muammar al- (1942–)

Muammar al-Qaddafi, Libya's revolutionary dictator since 1970, is one of the most independent and intractably anti-Western leaders in the Arab world.

Born in the Libyan desert near Sirte in 1942 of poor Berber stock, he attended school in Sirte, but because his family lived far from the town, the boy could only visit them on holidays. Qaddafi's schoolmates often made fun of him for being a poor shepherd boy. When his family moved four years later, Qaddafi enrolled in a preparatory school. The Suez Canal crisis in 1956, coupled with Egyptian prime minister Gamal Abdel NASSER's nationalization program, played significant roles in young Qaddafi's political development. He quickly adopted Nasser as his hero and role model. During his high school years, he was quick to criticize the colonial powers for their presence in Africa, and in 1961, he was expelled for demonstrating against the demise of the short-lived United Arab Republic, the president of which was his idol, Nasser.

In 1963, while attending the Military Academy, Qaddafi and some of his preparatory school friends formed an organization aimed at overthrowing the existing Libyan government. Following graduation in 1965, he attended an army signal school in England, and the next year, he was commissioned a signal officer in the Libyan Army. In the army, Qaddafi gathered about him a small circle of like-minded men calling themselves the Free Unionist Officers. In September 1969, Qaddafi led the group in a bloodless coup that overthrew the government.

Qaddafi favored dramatic changes in the structure of the government, and espoused the brand of socialism practiced by his neighbor, Nasser. Other participants in the coup desired to keep relations with the West on a more friendly basis and were wary of cooperative involvement with Nasser. Qaddafi asked Nasser to send Egyptian troops to Libya, and the issue was summarily decided in his favor.

The new dictator did not tarry in implementing his programs. In 1970, he removed all United States and British military bases. He expelled most Jews and Italians from the country and began a campaign to nationalize all foreign-owned petroleum operations. Public transportation facilities, electric and communication utilities, and insurance companies were all nationalized as well. Qaddafi's redistribu-

tion of his country's wealth resulted in the construction of new plants, schools, and housing, but a shortage of water, skilled workers, and raw material rendered these improvements ineffective, and Qaddafi's industrial program failed.

The drop in oil prices during the 1980s, coupled with economic sanctions imposed by the Western powers, further impaired Qaddafi's efforts to bring social and economic reforms to his country. In April 1986, American warplanes bombed Tripoli and Benghazi in retaliation for Libyan-sponsored terrorist activity. Faced with economic ruin and continued threats to his regime by internal disident factions, Qaddafi realized by 1988 that his policies had failed to bring about the desired changes, and he moderated his previously uncompromising position on such issues as the private ownership of businesses, the institution of free markets, and the repatriation of exiled citizens.

A critical assessment of Qaddafi, his goals, and his achievements in Libya reveals an individual who is at least as interested in world revolution as he is in improvement of the lives of his people. His moral and financial support for such radical movements as the Nation of Islam and the Black Panthers in the United States and the Irish Republican Army, along with his continued virulent attacks on the Western powers, clearly portray a man whose mission is the complete overthrow of democratic, capitalist government wherever it might exist.

Further Reading: Bernard Reich, ed. *Political Leaders of the Contemporary Middle East & North Africa: A Biographical Dictionary* (New York: Greenwood Press, 1990); Bruce St. John. *Qaddafi's World Design: Libya's Foreign Policy 1969–1987* (London: Sagi Books, 1987).

Qassim, Abdul Karim *See* KASSEM, ABDUL KARIM

Quisling, Vidkun (1887–1945)

Quisling betrayed his countrymen and aided the Nazi invasion of Norway in 1940, only to be tried for treason and executed at the close of the war. His name became a synonym for traitor.

Born on July 18, 1887, in Fryesdal, Vidkun Quisling began his training for a military and diplomatic career early in life. After completing his education in 1905, he became an officer, passed the War College exams in 1911, was named assistant to the general staff in 1916, and served as military attaché in Petrograd (later Leningrad and today, as originally, St. Petersburg) and later Helsinki from 1918–21. Quisling was commissioned a captain in 1917 and made major of field artillery in 1931. He also served on many international committees in the League of Nations.

Quisling became minister of defense in the Karlstad cabinet in 1931 because of his expertise in Russian affairs. His foray into high-level politics failed, however. An arch-conservative, he was rabidly opposed to communism and felt the labor wing in Norway was under the influence of the Bolsheviks and was plotting revolution. This position put him in diametrical opposition to that of the rest of the cabinet. Disgusted with his colleagues' liberalism, he founded his own political party, the National Union Party—essentially the Norwegian Nazis—on the platform of suppressing "revolutionary" parties and "freeing" labor from union control. The National Union Party lost badly in the 1933 elections, garnering only 2 percent of the vote. In the next two elections, the party's power base was successively halved, so that by 1939 it was virtually extinct.

In the face of public rebuke, Quisling became an associate of Alfred Rosenberg, the leading ideologue of National Socialism. Through this connection he attracted the attention of Adolf HITLER, who was especially interested in the defenses of Oslo Fjord and the inner harbor areas of the capital city. On the night of April 5, 1940, Quisling was in Berlin at the Reich Chancellery; three days later, German warships, led by U-boat wolfpacks, steamed into Oslo and, armed with the necessary intelligence concerning coastal and harbor defenses, easily penetrated and overran Norway.

Without the consent or support of the Nazis, Quisling proclaimed himself premier of Norway almost immediately, simply by announcing it over the air. The Nazis, in the meantime, were unsuccessfully trying to force the abdication of King Haakon, who also refused to recognize Quisling. Realizing that by forcing Quisling on Norway, the people would likely rally to the side of their king in opposition to the Nazis, the Germans likewise refused to support Quisling, who was compelled to resign after a week.

The Nazi invaders put him in charge of Norwegian demobilization, and he traveled to Berlin. When he returned to Norway on August 20, 1940, he made another attempt to build a following. This was failing miserably until the Norwegian parliament refused to oblige the Germans by setting up a puppet government. Nazi patience wore thin, and they at last installed Quisling as premier and outlawed all political parties except for his National Union Party.

When the Germans withdrew from Norway, Quisling was arrested on May 9, 1945. He was convicted of treason on September 10 and executed as a traitor on October 24, 1945.

R

Rahman, Ziaur [Zia] (1936–1981)
Leader of the Bangladesh independence movement, head of the country's military regime, and president of Bangladesh from 1977 until his assassination in 1981, Ziaur Rahman—Zia—outlawed political opposition and arrested thousands of opponents during his administration.

Ziaur Rahman was born in Shylhet, East Bengal, India, in 1936 and became an officer in the Pakistan Army in 1953, serving through 1971. On March 27, 1971, Zia led his unit in Chittagong—known as the "Z Force"—against the Pakistanis and proclaimed independence for Bangladesh. He remained in the newly formed Bangladesh army, becoming chief of staff in August 1975, following the assassination of Mujibur Rahman, the new nation's leader. Later that year he was named deputy chief martial law administrator and the following year, chief martial law administrator.

In 1977, he resigned from the army and succeeded Abu Sadat Mohammad Sayem as president. Promising governmental reform and free elections, he claimed that an attempted coup in November 1977 slowed the democratic process. Zia ordered the arrests of thousands of opponents, and Amnesty International reported in February 1978 that 130 military personnel had been executed and that the number of political prisoners held in Bangladesh jails exceeded 15,000. Eight months after the coup attempt, Zia finally authorized elections, which confirmed him in office. But on May 30, 1981, elements of the Bangladesh army led by Major General Mohammad Abdul Manzoor, a revolutionary comrade-at-arms, rose against the president and assassinated him in Chittagong, Bangladesh. Manzoor and 12 other army officer were executed for their part in the assassination and uprising.

Rais, Gilles de [Gilles de Retz] (1404–1440)
Rais was a Breton baron and soldier who was later tried and executed for satanism and the abduction and murder of children.

By fighting in the 15th-century wars of succession in France, Gilles de Rais gained wealth and prestige as a general. After fighting in Brittany in 1420, he served the duchess of Anjou in her efforts to secure the throne for the dauphin Charles against the claims of the English crown in 1427. Later he was assigned the command of Joan of Arc's divisions in the French victory over the English at Orléans in 1429.

After Charles' coronation at Reims in 1429, Rais was made marshal of France and continued serving under Joan of Arc when Paris was attacked. After Joan's capture and subsequent execution by the English, Rais returned to his lavish estate in Brittany.

The baron's wealth came not only from his illustrious military career, but also from lands inherited from both his wife and his father. Nevertheless, Rais kept a court so lavish—at least on par with that of the king himself—he soon began to live beyond his means. Rais began to sell off his dominions, but was halted in July 1435 when his family sought a decree from the king forbidding any further sale or mortgage of land.

Forced to find alternate means of making money, Rais turned to sorcery, alchemy, and satanism, hoping to gain power through the invocation of the devil. In September 1440, he was accused of the abduction and murder of more than 140 children used in sacrificial offerings to the devil. He was arrested and brought to trial at Nantes, where he refused to answer any of the charges. Threatened with excommunication, he entered a plea of not guilty.

Trial by an ecclesiastical court found him guilty of heresy, and subsequent trial by the civil court found him guilty of murder. Sentenced to death, he confessed to all the killings and the satanical practices shortly before his execution on October 26, 1440. Despite his confession, many scholars question the legitimacy of the trial proceedings. For example, the duke of Brittany, who was instrumental in the trial, stood to benefit from Rais' death. It is also a fact that the confession was exacted under threat of torture.

Ramses II the Great (ca. 1320–ca. 1225 B.C.)
Ramses II, or Ramses the Great, of the 19th Dynasty, ruled Egypt for 67 years, longer than any other pharaoh except Pepe II of the Sixth Dynasty, who reigned for 90 years.

Ramses II was one of the most powerful kings ever to rule Egypt. Raised in the royal house of his father, Pharaoh Seti, the young boy, as heir apparent, was virtually swaddled in governmental affairs. By the age of 10, Ramses had already attained the rank of captain in the army, and even this early in

Rameses II the Great. (From Richard Delbruck, Antike Portrats, *1912)*

his life, he had demonstrated the skill and understanding of military strategy that would characterize his mature career.

Seti made Ramses a co-ruler, and when Seti died around 1290, his son was fully prepared to govern. For years, Seti had tried to defeat the Hittite forces that occupied lands claimed by Egypt along the eastern Mediterranean coast. The Hittites were formidable warriors, however, and Seti made no headway against them. Ramses II inherited this longtime problem and, in his fourth year as pharaoh, he led a well-equipped army out of the Delta toward present-day Syria and eastern Turkey to attempt to defeat the Hittites once and for all. As Ramses and his

troops approached the Hittite town of Kadesh, two captured soldiers told him that most of the Hittite army was miles away at the city of Aleppo. Believing this to be true, Ramses attacked Kadesh, only to discover that the entire enemy army was actually behind the town. Since a large portion of Ramses' troops had not yet advanced to the battle area, the Hittites, with 2,500 chariots and 7,500 men, grossly outnumbered the Egyptian army. The pharaoh and his vanguard were quickly surrounded and on the verge of surrender when the bulk of the army arrived to save the day from total disaster. The battle was a tactical victory for Ramses, yet the Hittites still held the strategic town of Kadesh. A quick truce was declared, the Egyptians went home, and the Hittites maintained occupation of the land.

Some years later, after another unsuccessful foray into Hittite-held territory—and another unsuccessful attempt to add Hittite land to the Egyptian empire—Ramses and the Hittite ruler agreed to a permanent truce that left boundaries as they were and brought about a long-overdue peace.

His proclivity for combat notwithstanding, Ramses II was a prolific builder. On all of his military campaigns against the Hittites, he left monuments to his achievements, and on the home front, he is noted for building the temples at Abu Simbel, the largest of which depicts four statues of Ramses, each over 65 feet high. (When the Aswan Dam was completed in the 1960s, this massive temple, carved out of rock, was cut into sections and moved to the top of the cliff to protect it from the flood waters of the Nile River). Another, smaller temple memorializing Nefertari, Ramses' favorite wife, was built at the same time downstream.

Ramses II was the last pharaoh to maintain Egypt's imperial glory. After his reign, the kingdom continued to decline, as other, newer powers around the Mediterranean Sea attained political and economic dominance.

Reference: James Henry Breasted. *A History of Egypt From the Earliest Times to the Persian Conquest* (New York: Scribner's, 1942).

Ramses III (ca. 1219–ca. 1156 B.C.)

Ramses III has been called the last great pharaoh of the New Kingdom, and it was during his rule that the Egyptian Empire had to defend itself against three foreign invasions.

When Ramses inherited the throne from his father, Sethnakhte, the first king of the 20th Dynasty, Libyans from the west and "Sea People," most likely Phoenicians, from the north had been attempting for some time to invade Egypt. Years before, the son of

Ramses the Great, Merneptah, had waged wars with these peoples, and so far, the incursions had been checked. Now, shortly after Ramses III became pharaoh, the Libyans again tried to move into western Egypt.

Ramses had no sooner defeated the Libyans than the Sea People arrived to attempt another invasion. Ramses' armies lured the ships and sailors of the Sea People into the myriad of swampy channels that make up the Nile Delta. Superior Egyptian strategy and the puzzle of the Delta saved the day for Ramses, whose persistent adversaries were, once again, defeated.

Finally, Ramses had to face the Libyans a second time. Egypt emerged victorious from this affair as well, claiming three major military victories in six years.

On the home front, Ramses devoted his energies to creating lasting monuments to himself and his recent victories. His mortuary complex is at Thebes, and he built three shrines at Karnak, as well as a palace near present-day Cairo. However, before his reign was over, he had to deal with internal strife, labor strikes, and general social unrest.

Ramses III was not as dynamic a pharaoh as his earlier namesake, RAMSES II, but during his 31-year rule, he repeatedly checked foreign invasion and enjoyed some success in keeping an increasingly restless population satisfied as well.

Further Reading: James Henry Breasted. *A History of Egypt From the Earliest Times to the Persian Conquest* (New York: Scribner's, 1942).

Rasputin, Grigory Yefimovich [Grigory Novykh] (ca. 1865–1916)

Rasputin, Russian Orthodox monk and self-proclaimed mystic, wielded great and sinister influence over Russian czar NICHOLAS II and his wife, Alexandra.

Born Grigory Novykh to a Siberian peasant family, Rasputin earned the name by which he is far better known—it means "debaucher"—through the wild and generally demented behavior that characterized his youth. Somewhat later in life, apparently penitent, Rasputin entered the church and soon gained a wide reputation as a miracle-working faith healer. This renown spread beyond the peasant community until, about 1907, Rasputin was introduced at the imperial court.

Rasputin exercised his most powerful influence over Czarina Alexandra Fyodorovna, in large part because his quasi-hypnotic ministrations were effective in alleviating the pain and suffering of her hemophiliac son, Crown Prince Aleksei. For his part,

Nicholas II, a weak ruler easily swayed, saw Rasputin as a "true representative" of the Russian people—in contrast to the "aberrant" revolutionary masses, who would soon bring about his overthrow and death.

Despite the high regard in which the czar and czarina held Rasputin, he soon reverted to the crudely licentious ways of his youth—conduct he made little effort to hide from an increasingly shocked and disgusted Russian court and public.

The outrage at all levels of government and society was exacerbated when, during World War I, Nicholas assumed personal command of his forces at the front, leaving Alexandra—and Rasputin—in St. Petersburg to rule in his stead. The scandalous presence of the "Mad Monk," as Rasputin was popularly called, hastened the deterioration of the czar's prestige among the Russian people. Recognizing this and fearing the imminence of revolution, a cabal of old-line nobles plotted and carried out the assassination of Rasputin.

That turned out to be more difficult than any of the conspirators could have imagined. On the night of December 29–30, 1916, Prince Felix Yusupov, husband of the czar's niece, invited Rasputin to his house and feasted him on poisoned wine and tea cakes. When he did not die, a frantic Yusupov shot him. That succeeded only in sending the wounded monk running out into the courtyard, where he was shot again. Finding him still living, the conspirators beat and bound Rasputin, then forced him through a hole in the ice on the frozen Neva River, finally succeeding in drowning him.

Further Reading: Alex De Jonge. *Life and Times of Gregorii Rasputin* (New York: Coward McCann, 1982); Joseph T. Fuhrman. *Rasputin: A Life* (New York: Praeger, 1990).

Rhee, Syngman (1875–1965)

First president of the Republic of Korea—and reelected to that office three times—Rhee assumed dictatorial powers over South Korea until forced to resign in 1960.

Born in Whanghae, Korea, on March 26, 1875, Syngman Rhee was educated in the classical Confucian manner, then enrolled in a Methodist school. He became both a Christian and an ardent nationalist, helping to found the Independence Club in 1896, an organization that agitated for Korean independence. In 1898, right-wing forces destroyed the club, and Rhee was arrested and imprisoned until 1904. On his release, he traveled to the United States, earning a Ph.D. from Princeton University in 1910. That year he returned to Korea, which had just been annexed to Japan. Unable to disguise his hostility toward Japanese rule, he returned to the United States in 1912 and spent the next 30 years trying to win international support for Korean independence.

In 1919, following the independence uprising of March 1, Rhee was elected president of the Korean Provisional Government in Exile at Shanghai. Disagreements with other independence leaders led to his impeachment in 1925. Although he was officially replaced by Kim Ku, Rhee refused to recognize his authority and continued to work toward the goal of Korean independence. In 1940, he moved to Washington, D.C., where he spent the war years lobbying for U.S. recognition of an independent Korea. This was largely an uphill battle until Rhee convinced many in Washington that the Soviet Union opposed the provisional government. Seeing an anti-Communist ally, much of official Washington began to rally behind Rhee, so that, by the end of World War II, he had backing from conservative American politicians and the American occupation authorities.

Returning to Korea on October 16, 1945, he amassed great political influence and the muscle to enforce it. His strongarm squads—largely members of the police—intimidated or assassinated all opposition. When negotiations between the United States and the Soviet Union over the reunification of the north and south occupied zones failed, Rhee was elected president of the Republic of Korea (South Korea) in 1948. He was reelected in 1952, 1956, and 1960.

Rhee was president during the bitter and inconclusive war between North and South Korea, but even in the uneasy peace that preceded and followed the war, he tolerated no opposition to his programs. He outlawed the Progressive Party, which opposed him, and executed its leader. He assumed control of nearly every aspect of government, even on the local level, through his control over the appointment of village mayors and chiefs of police. He even attempted to wreck the United Nations peace talks during the Korean War by releasing prisoners of war in South Korea rather than returning them to North Korea as had been stipulated during the negotiations.

By 1960, South Koreans could no longer tolerate a leader who had sacrificed their freedom in a long campaign that was supposed to secure freedom and unification. Rhee's popular support rapidly decayed and, amid charges of election fraud, uprisings by students, and protests by the National Assembly, he resigned as president on April 27, 1960, and fled to Honolulu, where he lived in exile until his death on July 19, 1965.

Suggested Reading: Richard C. Allen. *Korea's Syngman Rhee: An Unauthorized Portrait* (Rutland, Vt.: Tuttle, 1960);

Robert T. Oliver. *Syngman Rhee: The Man Behind the Myth* (New York: Dodd, Mead, 1954).

Rhodes, Cecil John   (1853–1902)

Rhodes, the leading force in British colonial activity in southern Africa in the late 19th century, founded the British South Africa Company, acquiring Rhodesia and Zambia as British colonies.

The son of a vicar in England, Cecil John Rhodes was born July 5, 1853. A sickly boy, he suffered a weakness of the lungs for most of his life, and his poor health deterred his father from sending him to university to prepare for a professional career. Instead, he was sent to South Africa in 1870 to join his brother Herbert and work on a cotton farm. After attempting for a year without success to make the venture work, the brothers gave up on cotton and succumbed to diamond fever. They moved to Kimberley in 1871 and set up a diamond mine.

For the next 10 years, Rhodes divided his time between Kimberley and Oxford, where he began work on a degree. He graduated in 1881 and shortly thereafter formed the famous De Beers Consolidated Mines, Ltd., the largest and most productive diamond company in the world. By 1891, Rhodes controlled over 90 percent of the world's diamond production. He also formed the Gold Fields of South Africa Company in 1887, mining vast quantities of ore. His combined ventures made him one of the richest men in the world. His wealth also whetted his appetite for new adventures.

Rhodes was elected to the Cape Colony parliament in 1880, and his goal throughout his political life would be to expand British colonial interests "from the Cape to Cairo." He helped secure Bechuanaland for the British in 1885 and swindled the local chief out of what would later be Rhodesia. Rhodes founded the British South Africa Company in 1889 and received a royal charter to colonize these new areas. This blatant colonialism provoked local insurrection, but it was quickly crushed and the chief killed.

Rhodes soon controlled Cape politics. By July 1890 he was elected prime minister of the colony and envisioned himself at the head of a British-led South African federation. The only obstacle to this dream was the Dutch settlement called Transvaal, which would later become the country of South Africa. The president of Transvaal, Paul Kruger, had constantly been a thorn in Rhodes' side; however, the non-Dutch settlers in the region were very dissatisfied with Kruger's government, and he was losing much public support. The National Union, a political party of non-Dutch settlers founded by Rhodes' brother, agitated for reform, and a conspiracy against Kruger was born.

Seizing the main chance, Rhodes encouraged the Union, even going so far as to plan a raid into Transvaal in conjunction with an uprising by the National Union. At the last minute, however, the Unioners lost heart and cancelled their uprising. Rhodes' lieutenant, Leander Jameson, went ahead with the raid anyway and all were captured, save for the few who were killed in combat. It was an ignominious defeat for Rhodes, who was forced to resign as colonial premier and as president of the charter company. Worse, the botched raid consolidated Kruger's faltering support and thereby ruined any chance for the federation.

With his political career in ruin, Rhodes went into a steep decline, dying of a heart attack on March 26, 1902, at the age of 49. In his will, he decreed that the bulk of his considerable fortune be set aside for scholarships to his alma mater, Oxford University, available to students from Germany, the United States, and all British colonies.

Further Reading: Neil Bates. *Cecil Rhodes* (London: Wayland & Priory, 1976); H. Hensman. *Cecil Rhodes* (London: Verry, 1974).

Richard I the Lionhearted (1157–1199)

As king of England, Richard's only ambition was to liberate Jerusalem. His ardor in the crusade earned him the epithet "Lionhearted."

The son of HENRY II, king of England, and Eleanor of Aquitaine, Richard was born on September 8, 1157, in Oxford. As the third son, Richard was not in line to inherit his father's kingdom or lands, but he was destined to receive his mother's, Aquitaine, and was named duke of Aquitaine in 1172. He quickly proved himself adept at the military as well as the political arts as he worked to curb the power of the aristocracy in Aquitaine.

When his three brothers rose in rebellion against Henry, Richard joined, having learned that Henry intended to replace him in Aquitaine with his older brother John. What followed in 1173–74 was one of England's more bizarre struggles for power, as the four brothers and Henry continually shifted alliances among themselves. Finally, it was Henry who stood alone. He twice invaded Aquitaine before Richard submitted. The father pardoned the son in 1174.

Richard next occupied himself in the brutal suppression of revolts among the barons in his duchy. The barons, outraged, called upon Richard's brothers Henry III and Geoffrey of Brittany to drive Richard from Aquitaine. But that rebellion collapsed when Henry III died in 1183, leaving Richard as heir to the throne.

A poor ruler who showed little interest in England, Richard I the Lion-Hearted is nevertheless celebrated for his tenacity, skill, and courage in prosecuting the Third Crusade. (From M. Guizot, A Popular History of France from the Earliest Times, *n.d.)*

Now that Richard was in line to receive Normandy and Anjou as well as England, his father pressured Richard to yield Aquitaine to his youngest brother, John. Refusing to give up the lands with which he had been invested, Richard aligned himself with PHILIP II AUGUSTUS of France, and they marched against the elder Henry, forcing him to acknowledge Richard as heir and supreme power in the region. The war was concluded two days before Henry II's death on July 6, 1189.

As king, Richard cared little about domestic policy. His consuming goal was to "liberate" the Holy Land from the infidel, and he immediately set about gathering the forces of Christendom. To finance his crusade, he put literally everything up for sale: offices, clerical investiture—Richard even sold the king of Scotland his feudal obligation for 10,000 marks. Thus financed, Richard set out for Sicily in 1190.

Richard alienated his German allies by taking Messina, Sicily, on October 4; the Germans had their own designs on the town. After Messina, Richard

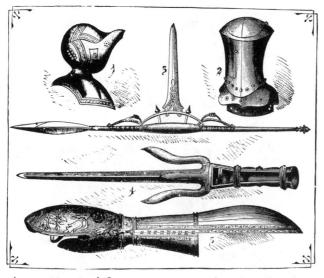

An assortment of Saracen weapons used against Crusaders. (From M. Guizot, A Popular History of France from the Earliest Times, *n.d.)*

conquered Cyprus and then Joppa, before reaching Acre in July 1191. The Christian coalition quickly took Acre and advanced to within a few miles of Jerusalem by December 1191. It was there that the coalition, weakened since the controversy at Messina, began to fall apart, and after two attempts to take the city, the coalition disintegrated altogether. As a result of his crusade, Richard was able to obtain nothing more than pilgrimage rights to the Holy Land.

On his return from the crusade late in 1192, Richard was taken prisoner by his enemy Duke Leopold of Austria, who handed him over to Henry IV, the Holy Roman Emperor. Henry, still angry over the Messina debacle, held Richard hostage, demanding an outrageous ransom of 150,000 marks that took two years to raise.

Immediately after his return to England, Richard moved to Normandy to save his lands from Philip II and a state of chronic warfare ensued. Although Richard made peace with Philip, he was fatally wounded on April 6, 1199, while besieging the castle of the viscount of Limoges in a dispute over the ownership of a treasure of gold discovered by a local peasant.

Further Reading: Christopher Gibb. *Richard the Lion Heart and the Crusades* (New York: Watts, 1985); Kate Norgate. *Richard the Lion Heart* (New York: Russell & Russell, 1969).

Richard II (1367–1400)

Richard's prolonged power struggle with the nobility of England led to his own abdication and did much to destabilize the monarchy.

Born during one of the bleakest periods of English history, Richard was the son of Edward the Black Prince and the grandson of King EDWARD III. He was born in Bordeaux, France, on January 6, 1367, while Europe was in the throes of the Black Plague, the devastating Hundred Years War, and, in the case of England, the general misgovernment of Edward.

When plague claimed his father in 1376, Richard became prince of Wales and assumed the throne on June 22, 1377, after his grandfather's death. Richard's uncle, John of Gaunt, duke of Lancaster, was named regent during Richard's minority. Gaunt was a holdover of the same misgovernment that dominated Edward's reign, and, under his regency, England fell into an economic depression, which sparked the Peasant's Revolt of 1381, led by Wat Tyler. At the age of 14, Richard showed great courage and diplomatic promise by meeting with the rebels personally in June 1381 and managing to pacify them without caving in to their demands.

In 1383, Richard attempted to wrest control of the government from Parliament and the nobles by appointing his own advisers and naming his own chancellor. After Richard raised several of these men to high noble status, the hereditary nobles who opposed Richard rose in anger, impeached his chancellor, and, in 1386, forced Richard to accept an 11-man commission to oversee his activities. When Richard declared these actions treasonable, the nobles convened the Merciless Parliament of 1387, which imprisoned many of the king's closest friends and advisers, of whom several were executed.

At length, Richard, who formally came of age in May 1389, bowed to the will of the five principal nobles who opposed him (called the appellants). He was only biding his time, however; by 1397 he had developed a loyal following and persuaded Parliament to pass death sentences on three of the five appellants (one was actually executed, another banished, and the third was apparently murdered before the formal execution could take place). When a quarrel broke out between the two remaining appellants in September 1398, Richard had them banished as well.

Having apparently solidified his position, Richard left for Ireland to attend to the tumultuous affairs of that country. Henry Bolingbroke, one of the banished appellants, seized upon Richard's absence and invaded England in 1399. On his return to England, it was apparent that Richard had lost all of his support and was forced to abdicate in September 1399. He was imprisoned by Henry Bolingbroke—now King Henry IV—and died in captivity on February 14, 1400.

Further Reading: Anthony Steel. *Richard II* (Cambridge: The University Press, 1941); Harold F. Hutchinson. *The Hollow Crown: A Life of Richard II* (New York: John Day, 1961).

Richard III   (1452–1485)

The last Yorkist king of England, Richard III bloodily suppressed all those who opposed him, but was defeated in the final battle of the Wars of the Roses.

Born in Northamptonshire on October 2, 1452, during the Wars of the Roses between the houses of York and Lancaster, Richard was the son of the duke of York, who was killed by Lancastrian forces at the Battle of Wakefield in December 1460. Richard's older brother Edward deposed King Henry VI in 1461, but was himself deposed by Richard Neville, earl of Warwick, nine years later. Richard commanded forces in two important Yorkist victories—Barnet and Tewksbury—which helped lead to Edward's restoration. Richard also had a hand in the murder of the deposed king, Henry VI, on May 21, 1471.

When Edward died in 1483, he left his 12-year-old son, Edward V, as heir, with Richard as regent. When his widow's family, the Woodvilles, at-tempted to bring the new king to London with an army in order to establish themselves in power, Richard gathered his own forces and that of the duke of Buckingham to oppose them. Richard and Buckingham intercepted Edward V and persuaded him to have the conspirators arrested. In the meantime, Richard also purged many of his closest advisers in 1483, suspecting that they had plotted against the protectorate.

In June 1483, London clerics were persuaded to declare Edward IV's marriage illegal and his children, therefore, illegitimate. It is unclear if Richard prompted this declaration or only exploited it. Regardless, he obtained the endorsement of an assembly of lords and commoners on June 25 and was crowned on July 6, 1483.

Richard promptly rounded up anyone he deemed a threat, particularly among the Woodvilles, and had them executed. During this period, Edward V and his nine-year-old brother remained in the Tower of London. In August, they disappeared, and it was later discovered that they had been murdered. It is unclear to what extent, if any, Richard was directly responsible for this.

When Henry Tudor rose in opposition to Richard in 1485, Richard's rivals flocked to him in hopes of a restoration of the house of Lancaster. Henry landed in Wales in early August and marched east, where he was met by the Yorkist forces under Richard at the Battle of Bosworth Field on August 22, 1485. In an attempt to defeat Henry quickly, Richard personally led a valiant charge, but was cut down. At this, the Yorkists fled the field, leaving Henry victorious, establishing the house of Tudor, and ending the Wars of the Roses.

Richard's corpse was stripped, tied to a horse, and paraded to ridicule. Richard III was, without doubt, a ruthless tyrant bent on achieving and maintaining power at any price. However, his reputation was further blackened throughout the Tudor epoch, especially by Shakespeare's portrayal of him in the play *Richard III*.

Further Reading: Charles D. Ross. *Richard III.* (Berkeley: University of California Press, 1981).

Vicious, degenerate, and probably deformed, Richard III is best remembered for Shakespeare's portrayal of him in Richard III. *(From J. N. Larned,* A History of England for the Use of Schools and Academies, *1900)*

Richelieu, Armand Jean du Plessis, cardinal and duke of   (1585–1642)

As principal minister to Louis XIII, Cardinal Richelieu in effect ruled France, establishing the basis of French royal absolutism and guiding his nation to a dominant place in European affairs.

Born Armand Jean du Plessis on September 9, 1585, in Paris, the future cardinal and duke of Richelieu was the youngest son of a poor but noble family

As chief minister to Louis XIII, Cardinal Richelieu was, in his day, certainly the most powerful man in France and probably even in all Europe. (From M. Guizot, A Popular History of France from the Earliest Times, *n.d.)*

from Poitou. He was groomed for a military career, but, after an older brother died, he hastily sought ordination in order to secure his family's traditional benefice, the bishopric of Luçon. Henry IV nominated him as bishop in 1606, and he was ordained in Rome the following year. The clergy of Poitou elected him to the Estates General, and he traveled to Paris in 1614 for its session. He remained afterward, becoming secretary of state for foreign affairs in 1616 through the favor of Marie de' Medici, the queen mother and regent. When King Louis XIII overthrew his mother's authority in 1617, Richelieu was removed as secretary, but remained in general favor with the court through his role as peacemaker between the king and his mother.

Richelieu became a cardinal in 1622 and was made chief of the royal council in 1624. His title was changed to first minister in 1628. As first minister, Richelieu developed a single-minded policy of developing the absolute authority of the crown and, with it, the preeminence of France in European affairs. To achieve these ends, he was willing to sacrifice whatever was necessary, including morality, religion, and ordinary law. When a program of warfare was called for, Richelieu was ruthless in his taxation of the lower classes—and it is this willingness to exploit the common folk that created his historical reputation as a crafty and heartless archvillain.

Richelieu was faced with treacherous choices in matters of foreign affairs and religion. It was essen-

tial to the rise of France that the European hegemony of Spain and the Austrian Hapsburgs be broken. Accordingly, he initially supported the Protestant cause in the Thirty Years' War (1618–48), desiring an alliance with the Protestant states joined against Spain and Austria. However, at home, the French Protestants, the Huguenots, were becoming increasingly powerful, and their independence posed a threat to the absolute rule of the monarchy. Richelieu temporarily reconciled France with Spain and directed his attention to the Huguenots, successfully campaigning against their forces at La Rochelle and Languedoc, resulting in the Peace of Alès, which deprived them of military and political privileges while guaranteeing toleration of their religion. The policy of toleration alienated the devout Catholic party and others among the nobility, including Marie de' Medici and the king's brother, Gaston d'Orléans. Richelieu found himself beset by numerous conspiracies to remove him from office, but, with consummate craft and the unwavering support of Louis XIII, he retained his power.

It was not the court and nobles alone who wished to see the overthrow of the first minister. In the tortuous course of the Thirty Years' War, Richelieu carefully engineered a series of complex alliances with Sweden, the Netherlands, Denmark, Saxe-Weimar, Saxony, and Brandenburg, so that, on May 21, 1635, he could declare war on Spain. Success against the Spanish was at first slow in coming, but Richelieu was prepared to expend whatever sums were necessary to prosecute the war. To finance the struggle, he levied extraordinarily heavy taxes against those least able to pay, the lower classes. The result was substantial French gains in the war against Spain, but also the perpetual alienation of the lower classes, which, in the provinces, settled into a chronic state of revolt. To cope with the disorder in the provinces, Richelieu appointed and ruthlessly employed commissioners—*intendants*—to oversee them.

Richelieu's interests did extend beyond politics and the amassing of power. A brilliant man, he had an intense interest in literature and theology and became founder of the Académie française in 1635. However, his overriding preoccupation was with foreign affairs, to the unfortunate exclusion of domestic reform. Richelieu must be regarded as one of the founders of modern France, but, in the process, he was also one of the architects of the social inequities that LOUIS XIV began to reform but that, in the course of the 18th century, intensified and made violent revolution inevitable. Cardinal Richelieu, exhausted by overwork, died in his Parisian palace on December 4, 1642.

Further Reading: Joseph Bergin. *Cardinal Richelieu* (New Haven: Yale University Press, 1985); Geoffrey Treasure. *Cardinal Richelieu and the Development of Absolutism.* (London: Adam & Charles Black, 1972).

Ríos Montt, José Efraín (1927–)

Proclaimed president of Guatemala following the March 1982 uprising against President Fernando Romeo Lucas García, José Efraín Ríos Montt was himself overthrown in a coup 17 months later following a regime characterized by widespread human rights violations.

Born in Huehuetenango, Guatemala, in 1927, José Efraín Ríos Montt entered the army in 1943 and rose steadily through the ranks, receiving specialized training under the auspices of the U.S. Army. In 1974, he retired from the Guatemalan army to run for president under the banner of the National Opposition Front (FNO), but was defeated by General Kjell Laugerud in a fraudulent election. He returned to the army and, from 1974 to 1978, was military attaché in Madrid. In 1978, he became a convert to the Protestant fundamentalist Church of the Word (which is based in California) and retired from the army to become an evangelical preacher.

When a coup of March 23, 1982, overthrew President Fernando Romeo Lucas García, Ríos Montt returned to the political arena as one of the three-man military junta and as minister of defense. In June 1982, three months after the coup, he proclaimed himself president and commander in chief of the army.

Ríos Montt instituted the death penalty for a wide range of offenses, replaced town mayors with his followers, and ruled by decree. He authorized brutal scorched-earth tactics in battles against guerrillas in rural areas. In addition, he instituted the "rifles and beans" *(frijoles y fusiles)* program, in which thousands of Indians were relocated to model villages and ordered to take part in civil defense patrols. These conditions endured until August 8, 1983, when, after three unsuccessful attempted coups, the army overthrew Ríos Montt and installed General Oscar Humberto MEJÍA VÍCTORES as president.

In 1989, several right-wing parties placed Ríos Montt's name in nomination for president, but the courts disqualified him from running on the basis of his participation in the 1982 coup.

Further Reading: Phil Gunson, Greg Chamberlain, Andrew Thompson. *Dictionary of Contemporary Politics of Central America and the Caribbean* (New York: Simon and Schuster, 1991).

Robert Guiscard (ca. 1015–1085)

A Norman adventurer who dominated Italy, Robert eventually ruled Naples, Calabria, and Sicily.

Arriving in southern Italy from Normandy around 1047, Robert Guiscard joined his half-brother Drogo to fight the Byzantines for control of southern Italy. Robert's brothers sent him to Calabria to pacify the region and take it from the Byzantine dukes. Robert promptly ransacked the countryside. In 1053, he led a force of Normans against the Byzantines, the Lombards, and the pope, defeating them all and thereby further enhancing Norman prestige and power. With three of his brothers dead by 1057, Robert now became count of Apulia.

He now set about consolidating Norman power in the region. He married the daughter of a Lombard prince to strengthen ties with that clan, and in exchange for an oath of fealty and defense rendered to Pope Nicholas II, Robert received papal lands in southern Italy and was virtually assured of papal non-interference in Norman affairs. Robert now stepped up his attacks on the Byzantines in Italy, finally driving them from all of Italy after the Battle of Bari in 1071.

The battle was a triumph, but, during this period, the careful diplomacy and coalitions that had helped secure his duchy began to unravel. After a period of peaceful relations with the Lombards following his marriage, Robert and the Lombards broke, and Robert's father-in-law, Gisulf II, allied himself with the Byzantines in hope of their return to the region. Robert advanced on papal lands to meet this threat when Pope Gregory VII, fearful of Robert's incursions, excommunicated him in 1074. Gregory then supplied military aid to Gisulf against Robert. The resulting war was short but decisive. Within two years, Robert smashed Gisulf's forces and captured Palermo in Sicily, making it his capital.

Hoping to unify his newly captured lands into a homogenous state, Robert crushed all rebellion with an iron fist, allowing no local lord to gather a following or stir up popular discontent. In a bid to enhance his own popularity, Robert sought reconciliation with the pope in 1080, reconfirming his earlier commitments to Nicholas II.

In the meantime, following the ouster of Byzantine emperor Michael VII in 1078, Robert conceived designs on the Byzantine throne while securing his possessions in southern Italy by capturing the Balkan ports on the Adriatic Sea. Accordingly, he landed at Epirus in 1083, easily defeated the Turkish army, and prepared to march east. At this point, the pope recalled him to Rome immediately to deal with Henry IV, Holy Roman Emperor, who was invading southern Italy. Robert returned, quickly turned back the invaders, and dealt mercilessly with any who opposed himself or Gregory. Having secured the region, Robert returned to his Byzantine plans, but he died of typhoid on July 17, 1085, while laying siege to Cephalonia.

Robespierre, Maximilien-François-Marie-Isidore de (1758–1794)

Lawyer and Jacobin member of the Committee of Public Safety during the French Revolution, Robespierre was a principal architect of the Reign of Terror in 1793.

The son of a prominent French lawyer, Robespierre became a lawyer in 1781. Like many young Frenchmen at the time, he aspired to the Enlightenment ideals of Jean-Jacques Rousseau, especially the concepts of natural rights and laws.

In 1789, Robespierre was chosen to represent the city of Arras at the convening of the Estates General in Versailles—the crisis assembly half-heartedly convened by LOUIS XVI. As a member of the Third Estate—the bourgeoisie (the other two estates were the nobility and the clergy)—Robespierre distinguished himself at Versailles. When the Estates General became the National Assembly, Robespierre served as a vocal leader of the body from 1789 to 1791. In June 1790, he was elected secretary of the National Assembly, and by April, the humble lawyer from Arras had become a leader of the Jacobin Club, the radical spearhead of the Revolution.

Instrumental in the creation of the new French constitution of 1791, which included the Enlightenment-inspired Declaration of the Rights of Man, Robespierre was a leading advocate of the destruction of the *ancien régime*, the old order. After the Parisian insurrection in 1792, which ended the reign of Louis XVI, Robespierre called for the trial and subsequent execution of Louis and his wife, Marie-Antoinette, on charges of treason. In 1793 he became head of the infamous Committee of Public Safety, which was set up to achieve the most radical goals of the Revolution and gave rise to the Reign of Terror, a fanatical and violent purging of both the left- and right-wing parties. During the Terror, two of Robespierre's closest associates, Jacques Hebert and Georges Danton, were guillotined.

In the end it was his own creation, the Terror, that turned against Robespierre as well. The radical left accused him of being a moderate, and the more moderate revolutionary faction accused him of radicalism. Robespierre's public support waned, and on July 27, 1794, he was arrested. The next day, he and 107 loyal supporters were guillotined before a cheering mob at the Place de la Révolution in Paris.

Further Reading: Norman Hampson. *The Life and Opinions of Maximilian Robespierre* (London: Duckworth, 1974); James M. Thompson. *Robespierre and the French Revolution* (New York: Macmillian, 1953).

Romanos IV Diogenes (r. 1068–1071)

Rising to become Byzantine emperor, Romanos IV Diogenes faced constant threats from his in-laws, who secretly conspired to gain the throne for themselves.

An Anatolian magnate, Romanos was also a competent general. He became the commanding general of the Danubian frontier forces under Emperor Constantine X. The emperor's wife, Eudokia, claimed Romanos had conspired with the Hungarians against her, but upon Constantine's death in 1068, she had a charge of heart, married Romanos, and made him emperor on January 1, 1068.

Technically part of the quartet of power, Romanos ruled with Constantine's three sons, Michael VII, Andronikos, and Konstantios; however, Romanos controlled the army and, therefore, held the real power. Relatives of the others—chiefly the caesar, John Doukas—feared that Constantine's sons would be disinherited. Romanos was obliged to be constantly on guard against Doukas' plots.

Romanos attempted to revive Byzantium's former greatness through military exploits, and he immediately began a campaign to reconstruct the Anatolian army through new recruits and foreign mercenaries. However, while Romanos was campaigning in eastern Anatolia, the Seljuk Turks sacked Ikonion and Chonai. In an attempt to retaliate, Romanos engaged Alp Arslan and the Turks at the Battle of Mantzikert in 1071. He was routed at Mantzikert following the defection of a large portion of his troops through the treachery of Andronikos. Romanos himself was captured, but released on the condition that he yield claims to Armenia, pay reparations, and support Arslan in the future.

Upon his return to the empire, Romanos was treated as a rebel by Doukas and his clan. He received no internal support, and a civil war ensued. The Doukas clan prevailed. Romanos surrendered, and the caesar blinded him, sending him to a monastery, where he died in August of 1072.

Further Reading: George Ostrogorsky. *History of the Byzantine State* (Oxford: B. Blackwell, 1968).

Rudradaman I (r. ca. 128–150)

A Saka satrap, Rudradaman I extended his rule over western India by waging war on his son-in-law.

Rudradaman was the son of Jaydaman and the grandson of Chastana, founder of the Saka dynasty in India. Coming to power in about 128, Rudradaman became the mightiest ruler of the dynasty. He defeated Pulamayi II, the Andhra king who had married his daughter Dakshamitra, and consolidated Pulamayi's holding with his own. His dominion came to include Surashtra, Malwa, Cutch, Sind, Konkon, and other districts of western India.

Rudradaman is remembered for repairing the embankments of Lake Sudarsana, originally constructed by CHANDRAGUPTA MAURYA. The story of the repairs—told in the "Junagarh inscription"—was found on a stone near the lake. Rudradaman's hand-iwork lasted for another three centuries before it needed to be repaired.

Further Reading: Sachchidanamda Bhattacharya. *A Dictionary of Indian History* (New York: Braziller, 1967); B. G. Gokhale. *Ancient India: History and Culture* (Bombay: Asia Publishing House, 1959).

S

Saladin [Salah Ad-din Yusuf Ibn Ayyub, "Righteous of the Faith"] (ca. 1138–1193)
Saladin was Muslim sultan of Egypt, Syria, Yemen, and Palestine from 1171 to 1193, and founded the Ayyubid dynasty.

Born in Takrit, Mesopotamia, Saladin was the son of an influential Kurdish general and, as a young man, accompanied his uncle Shirkuh on an expedition to keep Egypt from falling under Latin-Christian (Frankish) domination in the complex political circumstances that followed the First Crusade. He served briefly as the governor of Alexandria, and when his uncle died, about 1169, he became the vizier of Egypt and the commander of Syrian troops. Within two years, he had established himself as the sole ruler of Egypt.

For the next decade, Saladin's primary goal was to unite the various countries of the Middle East under the standard of Islam, a mission in which he had tremendous success. The Islamic Empire at the time spread over thousands of square miles—from Gibraltar in the west to beyond the Indus River in the east, and from Turkey in the north to the tip of the Arabian Peninsula in the south. Saladin's effort to reconcile the disparate factions of Islam made the empire stronger than it had ever been.

Saladin's success in the unification of the various Islamic entities, a victory attained only after much intense fighting with his Muslim brethren, was accompanied by tremendous cultural developments and a growth in learning. Motivated by the notion of *jihad*, or "holy war," Saladin made Islam a haven for religious scholars and teachers, to whom he assigned the responsibility for instilling in the masses the tenets of the faith.

By 1187, Saladin had made his sultanates sufficiently secure that he was ready to wage war on the Christian Crusader states in Syria and Palestine established since 1099. Jerusalem itself had been occupied for 88 years, and one of Saladin's top priorities was to reestablish Islamic influence there. In northern Palestine, on July 4, 1187, Saladin and his well-trained army met a poorly equipped Latin-Christian army near the city of Tiberius. Within hours, the Islamic forces had completed routing the army of the Latin-Christian Kingdom of Jerusalem and, within the span of three months, were able to capture the cities of Acre, Toron, Beirut, Sidon, Nazareth, Caesarea, Nabulus, Jaffa, Ascalon, and Jerusalem.

Saladin declined to persecute the defeated Christians as the Crusaders had persecuted those whom they had conquered years before. Instead, he treated the vanquished with fairness and courtesy. Nevertheless, when news of the fall of the Latin-Christian Kingdom of Jerusalem reached Europe, calls were issued for a new crusade—the third—and RICHARD I THE LIONHEARTED of England, Philip II of France and Frederick I of Germany took their armies to the Holy Land in this latest attempt to "free" it once and for all. However, Frederick was drowned on the journey east, and after reoccupying Acre, Philip returned home, followed by Richard, who concluded a peace with Saladin. The Third Crusade, then, ended as a victory for Saladin. Most of the Islamic Empire stayed intact, and Jerusalem remained in his hands.

Saladin exercised great diplomatic and military skill, greatly strengthening the culture and religion of the Muslim world.

Through his efforts, the influence of a century of crusader activity in the Holy Land, while not totally eliminated, was dramatically reduced. Finally, all of this was accomplished with a high degree of humanity, mercy toward enemies, and a spirit of fairness to all concerned.

Saladin died in Damascus on March 4, 1193, shortly after the end of the Third Crusade. He is revered as the most famous of Islamic heroes.

Further Reading: Stanley Lane-Poole. *Saladin and the Fall of the Kingdom of Jerusalem* (London: Putnam's, 1926).

Salazar, Antonio de Oliveira (1889–1970)
Under Salazar, Portugal stabilized, implemented a constitution, and became an important member of NATO.

Born in Portugal's Beira Province on April 28, 1889 to bright and ambitious parents, Antonio Salazar began his education in a seminary. After graduation in 1908, he took preliminary orders and spent two years as prefect of students at Via Sacra College; however, he soon realized that the priesthood was not his calling. After receiving a bachelor's degree from the University of Coimbra in 1914, he joined the faculty there and wrote two essays, one on the gold standard and another on agriculture, which established him as one of Portugal's preeminent young economists.

After the deposition of King Manuel II in 1911, the British parliamentary system was made the basis of Portuguese government, and Salazar became active by speaking on both political and social issues. Salazar formed the Portuguese Catholic Center Party and in 1921 was elected to the Cortes, the parliament. After attending one session, however, he determined that the body was worthless and returned to his university chair, where he remained until 1926, when a military coup placed generals Antonio Oscar de Fragoso Carmona and Gomes da Costa at the head of the government. With the country bankrupt, they called on Salazar to become minister of finance. After studying the problem for two days straight, he demanded a free hand in economic reform; the generals refused, and Salazar again returned to his university chair.

Carmona ousted da Costa in 1926, installing himself as acting president and premier. Carmona called on Salazar again, this time giving him the free hand he demanded. Salazar announced that he would tax everything he could get his hands on, but that each year, the taxes would be decreased. In one year, he balanced the budget for the first time since the fall of the monarchy. By 1932, Salazar had liquidated the last of Portugal's foreign debt and put the currency, the escudo, at a premium on the exchanges.

Antonio Salazar succeeded Carmona as premier in November 1932 and immediately drafted a constitution based on papal bulls from Popes Leo XIII and Pius XI. The most important part of the document established the parliament not on party lines but as a corporative assembly representing a national union. Although Salazar enforced a rigid censorship of the press and outlawed alternative political parties, he instituted some impressive social reforms, including workmen's compensation, social security, and various public works projects. He also engineered an apparently neutral course during World War II, while secretly helping the Allies.

Perhaps Salazar's greatest triumph was the inclusion of both Portugal and Spain in NATO in 1952 while simultaneously achieving a modicum of trust with longtime adversary Generalissimo Francisco FRANCO. The two leaders declared the Iberian Peninsula a unified strategic bloc.

Samori Touré   (ca. 1835–1900)
A despotic Dioula war chief, Samori Touré resisted French colonial domination of Guinea, Mali, and the Ivory Coast.

Samori Touré was the son of a merchant family near Sanakoro, Guinea. He became a soldier, and when he was in his thirties, in 1868, he took the title of *almani*, or prayer leader, then proclaimed himself chief of Bissandougou and organized the *sofa*, a well-equipped and well-trained army.

Into the 1870s, Samori Touré consolidated his power, expanding Bissandougou into a kingdom subject to his absolute rule, maintained by an army financed through an exorbitant tribute exacted from the numerous tribes under his control. By the start of the 1880s, he controlled an empire along the eastern side of the upper Niger and bounded by Burkina Faso (in Upper Volta) to Fouta Djallon (in northwestern Guinea).

When French colonial forces occupied Bamako (in present-day Mali) in 1883, Samori mounted an offensive, engaging the troops numerous times between 1884 and 1885. In 1886, he signed the Treaty of Bissandougou with the French, establishing the Niger River as the western limit of his domain and agreeing to French "protection"—characteristically a code word for the acceptance of colonial domination. Samori quickly violated the provisions of the protectorate, however, when he attacked Sikasso (in present-day Mali), seeking to expand his kingdom. When French forces aided the local tribes in repelling Samori's attacks during 1887–88, he repudiated the Treaty of Bissandougou and declared all-out war on the colonial forces, beginning about 1891. As the French forced Samori from position to position, he set up guerrilla bases near Dabakala (in the present-day Ivory Coast) by 1893. From here, he terrorized the countryside for the next three years.

Samori consolidated his guerrilla activities into full-scale invasion when he moved against Burkina Faso in 1896, invading the districts of Lobi and Sanufo (between the Léraba and Black Volta rivers). He established a stronghold at Darsalami during the early summer of 1897, then, in July and August, moved against Noumodara, to which he laid siege and subsequently destroyed. Retreating at the approach of French colonial forces, Samori terrorized and razed Kong (on the Ivory Coast) toward the end of 1897 and Bondoukou (on the border of the Ivory Coast and Ghana) during mid-1898.

French forces nevertheless closed in on Samori Touré, taking him captive at Guelemou, Ivory Coast. French authorities exiled him to Ndjole, an island in the Ogooué River in Gabon. He died on this island on June 2, 1900.

Samudragupta   (r. ca. 330–380)
Son of CHANDRAGUPTA I, Samudragupta prosecuted a series of wars that greatly expanded the territory left to him. Known as the "Exterminator of Kings,"

he ruled a vast portion of modern-day India from about 330 to 380.

When Chandragupta I died, his son Samudragupta inherited territory that extended from Magadha to Allahabab. He quickly determined to expand that territory and accordingly waged war on a host of lesser kings in the Upper Ganges Valley, killing them one after the other. From his base near present-day Delhi, he spared but reduced to vassalage the kings of Samatata (eastern Bengal), Davaka (Nowgong in Assam), Kamarupa (western Assam), Napal, Kartripura (Garhwal and Jalandhar), and numerous tribal states in the eastern and central Punjab, Malwa, and western India as well as the chiefs of the Kushans and Sakas. Following these conquests, he ventured into the Deccan, in which he defeated, captured, then reinstated (in return for heavy tribute) a veritable catalogue of rulers.

By means of his many campaigns, Samudragupta's holdings came to include vast tracts extending south from the Himalayas to Narmada, and west from the Brahmaputra to the Jumna and Chambal. In addition, kings in east Bengal, Assam, Nepal, the eastern portion of Punjab, and several tribes of Rajasthan paid tribute to him. During the course of his wars of expansion, he killed a total of nine kings and subjugated 12 others.

Called by modern scholars—though with unintentional condescension—the Indian NAPOLÉON, Samudragupta was more than a mere conqueror, since he brought a measure of benevolence and culture to the regions he conquered. It was most likely in these early days of the Gupta dynasty that Indian society adopted its long-enduring and characteristic Hindu theological system and code of social conduct.

Santa Anna, Antonio López de   (1794–1876)

Mexican general, president, and dictator, Antonio López de Santa Anna opportunistically changed allegiances and positions to enrich himself and gratify his own ambitions, thereby creating much of the political turbulence that plagued Mexico even into the 20th century.

Born on February 21, 1794, in Jalapa, Veracruz, to the family of a minor colonial official, Antonio López de Santa Anna entered the Spanish army in Mexico as a young man, achieving the rank of captain. From the beginning of his political career, he demonstrated the faculty of duplicitous agility that allowed him to fight on both sides of most issues. During a time of much political confusion and intrigue, he first supported Augustín de Iturbide in the war for Mexican independence during 1821; two years later, he help overthrow Iturbide. Next, in 1828, he helped

Vicente Guerrero in his bid for the presidency; later, he participated in his overthrow.

Santa Anna became well know to the Mexican people in 1829 when he fought Spanish forces in their attempt to regain Mexico. Hailed as the "Hero of Tampico," he rode to the presidency in 1833 on a wave of popularity and promises of a federalist government. Over the next three years, however, Santa Anna actually established a centralized absolutist state.

The end for Santa Anna seemed to come in 1836, when Texas declared independence from Mexico. In response, Santa Anna marched his army to the Alamo, attacked the garrison, and slaughtered it to a man. This, of course, galvanized the Texans' resolve, and when Santa Anna moved on to do battle at the San Jacinto River, he was defeated by forces under Sam Houston on April 21, 1836. Santa Anna successfully pleaded with Houston to spare his life, and the Texas commander sent him to Washington for a dressing-down at the hands of President Andrew Jackson. Following his defeat and subsequent humiliation, Santa Anna returned to Mexico, stepped down as president, and went into retirement.

He did not stay out of military and political affairs for long. In 1838, when French forces landed at Veracruz to claim reparation for injuries to French citizens in Mexico, Santa Anna led an expedition to Veracruz. By the time he arrived, the French fleet was already in the process of departing, but there was skirmishing and Santa Anna was wounded.

He lost a leg, but he regained his prestige, becoming dictator of Mexico from March to July 1839, while the duly elected president was away. Two years later, he led a revolt against the government and seized power again, but in 1845 he was driven into exile in Cuba.

When war broke out between the United States and Mexico following the U.S. annexation of California and Texas, Santa Anna craftily devised a way to get back into the fight. Promising to help restore peace, he arranged with U.S. president James K. Polk to send him back to Mexico on board an American ship. Once he arrived, however, he catapulted himself to the head of the Mexican army. The war as he prosecuted it was a disaster for Mexico, which suffered defeat after defeat, ultimately ceding to the United States New Mexico, Arizona, Nevada, Utah, and California. Santa Anna retired in 1847, even before the war was officially concluded by the Treaty of Guadalupe Hidalgo, and went to live first in Jamaica, then in New Granada (Colombia).

Recalled to Mexico as dictator between 1854 and 1855, he was again ousted and exiled to Nassau. He offered his old gambit yet again when Napoleon III installed Archduke MAXIMILIAN of Austria as emperor of Mexico in 1863. Incredibly, Santa Anna appealed to the United States to support him in an attempt to oust the emperor—even as he offered Maximilian his support against the Mexican nationalists. By this time, both sides knew full well that Santa Anna was untrustworthy and declined his proposals.

Santa Anna remained in exile until 1874, when, impoverished and blind, he was allowed to return to Mexico. He died in Mexico City on June 21, 1876.

Suggested Reading: Wilfred Hardy Calcott. *Santa Anna: The Story of an Enigma Who Once Was Mexico* (Hamden, Connecticut: Archon, 1964); Oakah Jones. *Santa Anna* (New York: Twayne, 1968); Santa Anna, ed. by Ann Fears Crawford. *The Eagle: The Autobiography of Santa Anna* (Austin: University of Texas Press, 1967).

Sargon of Akkad (r. ca. 2334–2279 B.C.)

The first Semitic king of Mesopotamia, Sargon of Akkad founded the Akkadian dynasty, conquered all of southern Mesopotamia and parts of Syria, Anatolia, and Elam, and ruled for 56 years.

Little is known about how Sargon of Akkad became king of Mesopotamia. Legend holds that he was born about 2350 B.C. to a Semitic nomad father and a temple votary mother. His mother is said to have put him in a basket in the river, where he was found by a gardener who then raised him. As a young man, Sargon became a cup-bearer to the Sumerian king of Kish, Ur-Zababa. Somehow, he managed to overthrow the king and claim his throne.

Once in power, probably around 2334 B.C., Sargon set out on a series of military campaigns. Defeating Lugalzaggesi of Uruk, who had dominated the city-states of Sumer, Sargon became ruler of all of southern Mesopotamia. Wanting to increase trade for his empire, Sargon then defeated the cities along the middle Euphrates. In addition, he stretched his control to the silver region of southern Anatolia and captured Susa, the capital of the Elamites in the Zagros Mountains of present-day western Iran. He may even have reached Egypt, Ethiopia, and India.

Following these conquests, Sargon had access to the cedar of Lebanon and the lapis lazuli mines of Badakhshantrade. He built Agade into a magnificent capital (somewhere along the Euphrates in Akkad; its precise location has never been determined). His trade flourished throughout the Indus Valley, the coast of Oman, the islands and coastal towns of the Persian Gulf, the Taurus Mountains, Cappadocia, Crete, and possibly Greece.

Further Reading: C. F. Gadd. "The Dynasty of Agade and the Gutian Invasion" in *Cambridge Ancient History*, rev. ed., vol. 1, ch. 19 (New York: Macmillan, 1924–53).

Sargon II (r. ca. 721–705 B.C.)

As king of Assyria from ca. 721 to 705 B.C., Sargon II extended the empire of his father through many new conquests.

A younger son of TIGLATH-PILESER III, Sargon II came to the Assyrian throne in about 721 B.C., following the reign of his brother Shalmaneser V. His brother's reign was so short that many believe Sargon usurped the throne; in any case, his name in Assyrian is *Sharru-kin*, meaning "the king is legitimate."

Immediately after being crowned, Sargon was faced with three threats: from Chaldean and Aramaean chieftains in southern Babylonia, from the Urartians and the Armenians of the northern highlands, and from the Syrians and Palestinians. His father had conquered most of these people in a military sense, but it was left to Sargon to integrate them fully into the Assyrian empire.

During his many military campaigns, Sargon captured Samaria, capital of the Israelites, and deported its inhabitants. He then turned against the Syrian vassals at Qarqar. He crushed a revolt of Iranian tribes, which had been instigated by the kingdom of Urartu. In 717, Sargon suppressed a revolt by King Midas of Phrygia, so that by 710, he had control of all of Syria and Palestine, except for Judah. In 708, he was crowned king of Babylon, only to be killed in battle against the Cimmerians three years later.

Further Reading: Albert Ten Eyck Olmstead. *History of Assyria* (New York: Scribner's, 1923).

Saul (r. ca. 1020–1000 B.C.)

Saul was the first king of Israel, unifying the disparate Hebrew tribes into a nation and defending it against the military might of the Philistines.

The son of Kish from the tribe of Benjamin, Saul gained renown for his military prowess. All that is known of him is contained in the Old Testament, 1 Samuel 9–12, which provides no single, unambiguous history of how he came to power. It is clear, however, that Samuel, an influential leader of what was a loosely constituted league of Hebrew tribes, supported the elevation of Saul to ruler of the tribes—though he also sought to avoid a dictatorship or absolute monarchy. It must have been clear to Samuel and others that, in a state of disunity, the tribes stood little chance against the well-organized Philistines, and Saul, well known as a brave and able warrior, was a promising candidate to govern the tribes and lead them to military success.

Gustave Doré depicts the moment at which Saul turns against his former favorite, David. (From Gustave Doré, The Doré Bible Gallery, *1879)*

Saul did succeed in unifying the Hebrew nation and in pushing the Philistines out of the central hill country. He extended his rule into Judah and the northern Transjordan region. Saul also earned a reputation as a just and wise ruler. However, as Samuel relates the history, Saul grew increasingly jealous of his charismatic protégé, the young warrior DAVID. This jealousy grew into obsession, which clouded the king's vaunted judgment, causing him to turn his back on the renewed threat posed by the Philistines. As a result, he was ill-prepared for battle against the Philistines at Mount Gilboa. Facing defeat and desperate to avoid capture, he committed suicide. David succeeded Saul as king of Israel.

Selim I [Yavuz] (1470–1520)

Selim I, sometime called Yavuz, meaning the Grim, was the ninth Ottoman sultan; he extended his empire to include Syria, the Hejaz region of Arabia and Egypt.

Selim was born in 1470 at Amasya. An extraordinarily ambitious ruler, Selim once declared that his wish was to be the conqueror of both the East and the West, in the manner of Alexander the Great some 1800 years earlier. Selim assumed the Ottoman throne by forcing his father, BAYEZID II, to abdicate.

Then, before Ahmet and Korkud, his two brothers, both of whom were favored to succeed their father, could react, he seized the helm. Subsequently, to secure his sovereignty, Selim had his brothers murdered.

Upon ascending the throne in 1512, Selim organized a large army and marched against Shiite supporters of the Iranian ruler, Shah Isma'il, who was threatening Ottoman interests in eastern Anatolia. Before embarking for battle, however, he put to death some 40,000 officials, envoys, and others loyal to the shah, thereby spreading terror throughout the countryside. Defeating Isma'il's followers in Caldiran in August 1514, Selim failed to follow up on his victory, but instead turned his attention to the Egyptian and Syrian Mamluk rulers with whom he had been disputing for some time. In August 1516, Selim led his Ottoman army against the Mamluks and, after defeating them, brought into the empire's fold the valuable states of Egypt, Syria, and the Hejaz, as well as the holy cities of Medina and Mecca.

Selim is remembered as one of the mightiest and most terrible of the Ottoman sultans, who added vast territory to the Ottoman holdings. However, it was left to his son, SULEYMAN I THE MAGIFICENT, to consolidate these acquisitions and fashion them into an integral part of the Ottoman Empire.

Further Reading: Peter M. Holt. *Egypt and the Fertile Crescent, 1516–1922* (London: Longmans, 1966).

Sennacherib (r. 704–681 B.C.)

One of the greatest kings of the late Assyrian Empire, Sennacherib expanded his realm, ruthlessly destroying Babylon in the process.

After succeeding his father, SARGON II, Sennacherib was faced almost immediately with rebellion in Babylonia and Palestine, which were always unstable. The Chaldeans, with Iranian help, took over Babylonia in 703 B.C., but Sennacherib was able to recover the northern section of the region, while destroying the southern section, where the insurrection had originated.

Sennacherib next put down an Egyptian-backed revolt in Palestine, retaking loyal sections, razing rebel cities, and laying siege to Jerusalem. Although he was unable to capture Jerusalem, Sennacherib did exact a heavy tribute from the city in return for lifting the siege. Further rebellion in Babylonia, again instigated by the Chaldeans, moved Sennacherib to install his son on the Babylonian throne in a bid to increase stability there. This, however, failed to quell the rebellions, and Sennacherib was again forced to invade and ravage Babylon.

In 691 B.C., yet another Chaldean monarch took control of Babylon, looting the treasuries of the city with which he bought support from the Elamites. A joint Chaldean-Elamite army met Sennacherib at Halule (Khalule). Sennacherib emerged victorious, but suffered crippling losses that put him out of action for two years. However, in 689, he returned to Babylon with a vengeance, utterly sacking the region, burning all walls and structures, secular and holy, obliterating all of the religious images, and flooding the towns. The magnitude of the destruction and desecration shocked the ancient world, but did not bring a halt to further revolts.

The most lasting of Sennacherib's accomplishments was the building of Nineveh. A destroyer of cities, Sennacherib also proved an able builder, who laid out beautiful streets for his capital, enhanced its aqueduct system to bring water from as far off as 50 miles, and built inner and outer defensive walls that stand to this day.

Sennacherib was killed by one or two of his sons in an attempted coup on January 681 as he worshiped in the temple of Nineveh. His loyal son,

Sennacherib put down revolts in Palestine, Syria, and Babylon by laying waste the cities and populations who rebelled. His army was repulsed at Jerusalem in 701 or 684 B.C., most likely because it had been greatly weakened and reduced by pestilence. In the Old Testament, 2 Kings xviii and xix, this is related as the "Destruction of Sennacherib's host," which Gustave Doré depicted in this 1879 engraving. (From Gustave Doré, The Doré Bible Gallery, *1879)*

ESARHADDON, defeated the rebels and ascended the throne as his father's successor.

Further Reading: Albert Ten Eyck Olmstead. *History of Assyria* (New York: Scribner's, 1923).

Sergius III (d. 911)

An opportunistic pope during a most tumultuous period of church history, Sergius III strangled his two chief rivals for power, the antipope Christopher and Pope Leo V.

Although he had been made bishop of Caere by Pope Formosus, Sergius became a supporter of Formosus' rival Pope Stephen VI (VII), who caused the exhumation of Formosus' corpse and put it on trial in a grotesque display that became know as the Cadaver Synod. The result of the trial was the nullification of Formosus' acts and pontificate, which triggered a bloody eight-year struggle over the papacy during which seven popes and one antipope—alternate supporters and denigrators of Formosus' memory—passed in succession.

In 898, Formosus' detractors elected Sergius pope, while the supporters of Formosus elected their own candidate, who was recognized as Pope John IX. Sergius attempted to seize the papacy, but was expelled from Rome.

John IX's papacy ended in 900. After the brief pontificate of Benedict IV, Leo V ascended the throne, but was driven out of Rome by the antipope Christopher in 903. The next year, Sergius, having secured military aid from Alberic I of Spoleto, marched on Rome and deposed Christopher, whom he ordered strangled along with Leo V. Sergius was consecrated pope on January 29, 904.

Sergius installed the powerful Count Theophylactus—like Alberic I, a Tusculani—as virtual dictator of his administration. Theophylactus used the resources of the papacy to expand his territorial holdings. The connection between Theophylactus and Sergius ran more deeply than politics, since Sergius was the lover of the count's daughter Marozia, by whom he had a child, the future Pope John XI.

In the course of his pontificate, Sergius plunged the church into deep dissension by yet again nullifying all of Formosus' acts and ordinations. He declared John IX, Benedict IV, Leo V, and Christopher all to have been antipopes.

Seti I (ca. 1339–1279 B.C.)

Seti I, the son of Ramses I and Queen Sitre and the father of RAMSES II THE GREAT, was the second pharaoh of the 19th Dynasty who ruled Egypt from 1290 to 1279 B.C.

Seti is generally accepted as the real founder of the Ramessid pharaonic line. Early in his career, he recovered much of the territory lost by pharaohs of the previous dynasty, and he fought at least one battle with the Hittites, a powerful nation in Asia Minor.

Seti I did much to restore Egypt's lost prosperity, and he was prolific as a supporter of mine and well development, frontier fortification, and monument construction and repair. He continued the work on the temple at Karnak begun by Ramses I, and he build his own mortuary temple at Abydos. His grave site is the most impressive in the Valley of the Kings.

Seti I allowed his son Ramses the Great to rule alongside him during the latter part of his reign. It was perhaps the close association with his father during this formative period that gave Ramses the strong foundation of statesmanship and diplomacy that were his when he ascended the throne as sole ruler after his father's death.

Further Reading: Margaret Bunson. *Encyclopedia of Ancient Egypt* (New York: Facts On File, 1991).

Severus [Lucius Septimius Severus Pertinax] (146–211)

An absolute despot, Severus founded a dynasty that was to remain in power until 235.

Entering the Roman Senate about 173, Septimius Severus became consul in 190, and by the time the Emperor COMMODUS was assassinated on December 31, 192, he was governor of Upper Pannonia, in command of the largest army on the Danube. When Pertinax, the successor of Emperor Commodus, was murdered in March 193, the title was auctioned off to Marcus Didius Julianus. Declaring himself the avenger of Pertinax, Severus proclaimed himself emperor with the support of his troops on April 13. As Severus led legionnaires on Rome, the Senate sentenced Didius Julianus to death, and he was assassinated on June 1 in his now-deserted palace.

Severus immediately set about reorganizing the military. He disbanded the Praetorian Guard, replacing it with troops from the legions and doubling it in strength. He also expanded the size of the regular army, including those units assigned to defend Rome, both from external invasion and internal plotting. He raised the number of men permanently under arms to over 30,000, including 33 legions. He improved the lot of the common soldier by raising his pay and allowing him, for the first time in the history of the empire, to marry.

After improving his ability to make war, he promptly made it, advancing on Gaius Pescennius Niger, governor of Syria, who had proclaimed himself emperor in the East. At the Battle of Issus in 194, Severus' legions crushed Niger, and Severus acted swiftly to pacify the region, splitting it in two to discourage further rebellion.

He turned next to Britain, where he was now strong enough to battle with Clodius Albinus, the governor whom Severus had previously designated as heir in a vain effort to secure his loyalty. Severus now openly rebuked Albinus by naming his own eldest son heir. In response, Albinus' troops proclaimed their leader emperor, and he advanced with them into Gaul, preparing to march on Rome. Severus met him at the Battle of Lugdunum (present-day Lyons, France) in 197 and easily defeated the usurper.

Upon his return to Rome, Severus began rooting out those who had supported Albinus, executing 29 senators and countless knights. He next set about punishing those on the frontier who had failed to support him. He made war on the Parthians and captured their capital in 198; he also annexed Mesopotamia to the empire, the second such annexation in 30 years. His further exploits ended in defeat when he attempted to push into what is now southern Iraq. Twice he was turned back.

After falling ill in 211, during a military campaign in Britain, Severus called his two sons to his deathbed and urged them to favor the military. "Be good to the soldiers," he advised, "and take heed of no one else!"

Further Reading: Maurice Platnauer. *The Life and Reign of the Emperor Lucius Septimius Severus* (Westport, Conn.: Greenwood, 1970); Gerard J. Murphy. *The Reign of the Emperor L. Septimius Severus* (Philadelphia: Privately printed, 1945).

Sforza, Francesco (1401–1466)

Duke of Milan from 1450 to 1466, Francesco Sforza was the patriarch of the powerful Sforza family, which ruled Milan and wielded tremendous influence throughout Europe for more than a century.

Francesco Sforza, who was born in San Miniato, Tuscany, on July 23, 1401, was the illegitimate child of Muzio Attendolo Sforza, a mercenary commander. Educated at Ferrara, Sforza was sent by his father to Naples as a hostage to King LADISLAS. He returned a year later to join his father in military service. When the elder Sforza drowned in battle in 1424, Francesco succeeded him as commander. His military prowess quickly won him a reputation as one of the leading condottieri of the time, and the duke of Milan, Fillipo Maria Visconti, enlisted Sforza in his Venetian campaigns of 1425. For the next 20 years, Sforza would fight both for and against the duke.

In 1435, Sforza visited Florence, where he developed a friendship with COSIMO DE' MEDICI, which was key to Sforza's rise to power. In 1443, Sforza married Fillipo's only child, Bianca Maria, thereby becoming the heir to the Milanese dukedom.

Fillipo, however, always distrusted Sforza and, despite the marriage, tried to block the possibility of his ascension to the throne. Thus, in 1447, while fighting for the Venetians, Sforza rushed to Milan upon learning of Fillipo's death. The Milanese, however, had set up an Ambrosian Republic, which denied him the dukedom. Sforza responded by laying siege to the city, starving the population into insurrection against the republic. On February 26, 1450, carrying loaves of bread and other provisions, Francesco Sforza entered the city as duke of Milan.

Sforza's rule in Milan was that of an enlightened despot. In 1454, he capitalized on his friendship with Cosimo de' Medici to conclude an alliance between Milan and Florence, which led to the momentous Peace of Lodi, legitimating Sforza's ascendency and bringing an unprecedented degree of stability to a customarily tumultuous Italy. Sforza's reign was not only diplomatically successful, but popular with the Milanese people. Moreover, he was a great patron of the arts and a promoter of Italian humanism. Despite his military skills and inclinations, Francesco Sforza ruled a peaceful Milan until his death there on March 8, 1466.

Sforza, Ludovico [il Moro, "the Moor"] (1452–1508)
Duke of Milan from 1494 to 1498, Ludovico Sforza reigned during one of the most culturally significant periods of the Italian Renaissance.

The second son of Sforza patriarch Francesco SFORZA, young Ludovico was brought up in the court of Milan where his dark complexion and black hair earned him the nickname "the Moor." His brother Gian Galeazzo succeeded Francesco on his death in 1466, but his harsh rule and inability to reconcile internal disputes ended 10 years later with his murder. By 1479, Ludovico had secured the regency for himself and held it from 1480 to 1494. In 1491, he married Beatrice d'Este, who bore him the two future dukes, Massimiliano and Francesco.

As regent and then duke, Ludovico exhibited a dual nature. On the one hand, this cultivated despot patronized such artists as Leonardo da Vinci and the great architect Donato Bramante. On the other hand, his elaborate court placed heavy tax burdens on his people, and his alliances with MAXIMILIAN I—who bestowed upon Ludovico the title of duke of Milan in 1494—and King CHARLES VIII of France alienated him from the other Italian states. It was Machiavelli who complained that Ludovico encouraged his

French ally to invade Italy, which badly tarnished Ludovico's reputation among Italians.

It was Ludovico's unwise alliances that eventually brought about the end of his reign. In April 1500, the new French king, Louis XII, related through his grandmother to the last Visconti duke of Milan, decided to "reclaim" the state as his own. Ludovico turned to the Milanese for help, but the people, disgusted with his rule, refused. He hired German and Swiss mercenaries, who, however, failed to fight for him in a critical battle. Louis captured Ludovico, reclaimed the Milanese dukedom, and imprisoned Ludovico at Louches, in Touraine. In Milan, rejoicing at Ludovico's fall was universal. Although he unsuccessfully attempted to escape, "the Moor" died in captivity on May 27, 1508.

Shaka [Chaka, Tshaka] (ca. 1787–1828)
Shaka ruled the Zulu empire from 1816 until his death in 1828, transforming in the course of his reign a minor African tribe into one of the most formidable body of warriors on the African continent.

Shaka was the son of a Zulu chieftain and a princess who belonged to the same clan, the Langeni. This close relationship between husband and wife being foreign to Zulu custom, Shaka's parents separated after a few years of marriage. Shaka grew up fatherless; when he was about 15 years old, he and his mother, Nandi, were driven out of the Langeni village and found a home among the Dietsheni, a subclan of the Mtetwa. A few years later, Shaka was called to render military service to his adopted clan and performed his duties with brilliance.

In 1816, Shaka's natural father died, and his adoptive father, Dingiswayo, a chief among the Mtetwa, returned the young man to become chief of the Zulu, at the time still a small and relatively unimportant clan that counted no more that 1,500 members. One of the first feats Shaka performed as chief was to transform the Zulu army from a poorly armed and inadequately trained mob into a disciplined, polished, and well-equipped professional fighting machine that, over the next few years, struck fear in everyone with whom it came into contact.

Traditionally, the warriors of southern Africa were armed with a rather small shield and a long spear made for throwing. Shaka adopted a large shield that covered the entire front of the body and reduced the size of the spear so that it could be used for jabbing in hand-to-hand combat. Traditionally as well, native troops faced each other from a distance, threw their spears, jeered at each other, and called the fight off, usually with no clear-cut winner. When Shaka had completed his overhaul of the Zulu army, his men were trained to get in close, protect themselves with the large shield, and slash with the short, powerful spear.

Shaka also instituted a regimental concept in his army, with men domiciled, according to regiment, in separate *kraals,* or villages, distributed across the countryside. He developed a tactic of offense in which his army was divided into four elements, shaped like a bull. The central element, or "chest," would engage the enemy, while the "horns" enveloped the foe and attacked from behind. The "loins," a reserve element, backed up the "chest," if needed.

The results of Shaka's military innovations were overwhelming. His army conquered sub-clans and clans, and as battle after battle was won, the ranks of the Zulu army grew until over the next few years he had multiplied his fighting forces manyfold. Shaka killed anyone who stood in his way. In 1817, when Zwide, head of the Ndwandwe, murdered Dingiswayo, Shaka's overlord, Shaka was positioned for the complete takeover of the Zulu nation.

Over the next decade, Shaka and his now vast armies annihilated tribe after tribe, so that by the 1820s more than two million people had been killed or displaced, leaving much of southern Africa depopulated when the Boers made their "Great Trek" in the 1830s.

Shaka's mother, Nandi, died in 1827, an event that sent her son on a redoubled rampage of killing that lasted for a year. More than 7,000 Zulus perished to appease Shaka's grief. Shaka ordered no crops to be planted, and he forbade the drinking of milk, a staple food among the Zulus. Pregnant women were killed along with their husbands.

In 1828, Shaka committed his exhausted army to several campaigns with no interval of rest between them. In September, his two half-brothers, Dingane and Mhlangana, weary of Shaka's relentless drive and the violent reprisals that had followed his mother's death, assassinated him on September 22, 1828.

Further Reading: D. R. Morris. *The Washing of the Spears: A History of the Rise of the Zulu Nation Under Shaka and Its Fall in the Zulu War of 1879.* (New York: Simon & Schuster, 1965).

Shalmaneser III   (r. 858–824 B.C.)

King of Assyria, Shalmaneser III spent his nearly 35-year reign in a state of constant warfare aimed at increasing the size of his domain.

King of Assyria from 858 to 824 B.C., Shalmaneser III was the son of ASHURNASIRPAL. Like his father, Shalmaneser conducted many military expeditions to replenish his treasury and increase his territory. His battlefields ranged from the mountains of Arme-

nia to the head of the Persian Gulf, and from the Zagros ranges west to Cilicia in Asia Minor. He exacted tribute from the Israelite King Jehu and from the Phoenician princes.

During the last years of his reign, a civil rebellion broke out in his empire. When he died, his son Shamshi-Adad V enlisted the aid of Marduk-zakir-shumi, the king of Babylon, to put down the rebels. Despite this, Assyria entered a period of decline, and Shalmaneser's successors lost control of the territories he had acquired.

Further Reading: Joan Oates. *Babylon* (London: Thames and Hudson, 1979).

Shapur I   (d. 270 or 273)

Ruler of the Sasanian Empire from 243 until his death, Shapur I expanded the holdings of ancient Iran and built great cities in his empire, using the forced labor of prisoners of war.

Shapur I inherited an expanding empire from his father, ARDASHIR I. Continuing the empire's wars with Rome, he defeated the Roman emperor Gordian in 244 and extracted a huge ransom from Philip the Arab, Gordian's successor. Twelve years later,

An ancient relief depicting Shapur I. (From Richard Delbruck, Antike Portrats, 1912)

the Roman Empire still cast a covetous eye on Armenia and Syria, but Shapur I successfully repelled all Roman advances.

After conquering Dura-Europos, on the Euphrates River, and Antioch, the capital of Syria, Shapur I relocated the defeated population of these towns—many of them Christians—to Iran. There he forced them to work on massive construction projects, including palaces, bridges, dams, and entire cities.

The Roman emperor VALERIAN moved to lift Shapur's sieges of Carrhae and Edessa beginning in 258, but Shapur's forces captured the emperor of Edessa in 260, imprisoning him for life at Gundeshapur, a city built expressly to house prisoners of war.

Having made such sweeping conquests, Shapur I took the title king of Iran and Aniran, meaning "non-Iran." At the time of his death, his Sasanian Empire comprised Mesopotamia, the Transcaucasus, Oman, and the Kushan territory. Through his shahrabs, Shapur I ruled over 15 royal cities, and his sons reigned over Mesene, Armenia, and Gilan. With many former Roman outposts now in the hands of the Sasanians, the patterns of trade in the Euphrates region were disrupted and the spread of Roman Christianity was slowed. Ruthless in conquest, Shapur was nevertheless tolerant of Christianity, Judaism, and other religions, but he actively promoted Zoroastrianism within his empire.

Further Reading: Ehsan Yarshater, ed. *Cambridge History of Iran*, vol. 3, *The Seleucid, Parthian, and Sasanian Periods* (Cambridge: Cambridge University Press, 1983).

Shapur II the Great   (309–379)

Tenth ruler of the Sasanian Empire, Shapur II (known as Shapur the Great) expanded the holdings of the empire and began the official persecution of Christians and ordered the massacre of messianic Jews. Enthroned as an infant, Shapur II ruled from 309 until his death in 379, the longest reign of any of the Sasanian emperors.

Shapur II, son of Hormizd II, was named heir to the Sasanian Empire as an infant, taking control of the empire from his regents in 325. Much of the empire, consolidated by SHAPUR I, who reigned until 273, had dwindled under the rule of Shapur I's successors. Shapur II was determined to regain the lost territories, and in 337 marched his forces across the Tigris River to Armenia and Mesopotamia, waging inconclusive warfare until 350. Attacked by the Chionites, now allied with Rome, Shapur II was compelled to turn from the Mesopotamian campaign in order to drive these invaders out of eastern Iran.

During this period, Shapur II became suspicious that a Christian fifth column was developing within his empire. He decided to destroy the religion, which had been allowed to flourish under his predecessors and which had become the official religion of the Roman Empire with the conversion of Constantine the Great. Shapur II imposed heavy taxation, general persecution, and forced conversion to Zoroastrianism on his Christian subjects from 339 until the end of his reign. In addition, he began an official persecution of the Manicheans, whose property he confiscated, and the messianic Jews, whom he killed by the thousands in 360.

Securing peace with the Chionites in 358, Shapur decided to take on the Romans again. He invaded Mesopotamia with great success until the Roman emperor Julian met him in battle in 363. The Romans advanced as far as Ctesiphon, scoring a stunning victory against Shapur II at this Sasanian city on the Tigris. But the legions were stopped when Julian fell in battle, whereupon his successor, Jovian, concluded a 30-year truce with Shapur II and ceded to him five Roman provinces, including all of Armenia. Shapur II pillaged Armenia in 365, deporting vast numbers of its population, including many Jews.

Further Reading: Ehsan Yarshater, ed. *Cambridge History of Iran*, vol. 3, *The Seleucid, Parthian, and Sasanian Periods* (Cambridge: Cambridge University Press, 1983).

Simeon I   (ca. 864–927)

Greatest of Bulgar rulers, Simeon challenged the Byzantine Empire and dominated the Balkans.

Although born and raised in Constantinople, Simeon I became an enthusiastic supporter of Greek culture and came to dislike everything Byzantine. When Simeon's father, Boris I, abdicated in 889 in favor of his eldest son Vladimir, Bulgaria suffered under the ruthless cruelty of the new emperor, who imposed paganism on the Bulgars. Boris returned from monastic retirement and overthrew his own son in 893. He quickly installed Simeon as Bulgar emperor.

Simeon extended the Bulgar Empire, raising it to its zenith. To the west, he conquered territory on the Adriatic Sea, defeating the Serbs and taking possession of the southern regions of Macedonia and Albania. His overriding ambition, however, was to conquer the Byzantine Empire. Beginning in 894, he led at least five separate campaigns against the Magyars and the Byzantines, more than once defeating them, but always failing to subjugate the Byzantines outright. He never captured his home city of Constantinople.

His military efforts in Byzantium were not his only unsuccessful endeavors. Bulgaria lost the prosperous lands north of the Danube River. After expending huge sums of money, men, and material on his Byzantine campaigns, Simeon realized their fruitlessness and relented. In 924, after again enjoying a moderate measure of success against them, Simeon made peace with the Turks and was able to gain some territory to the east.

After saving face in Anatolia, Simeon declared himself czar (emperor) of all the Bulgarians and Greeks. As czar, he raised the archbishop of Bulgaria to the rank of patriarch. He continued his support of Greek culture by encouraging the translation of Greek works into Slavonic. He also helped establish an independent Bulgarian literature and culture.

Simeon died on May 27, 927 and was succeeded by his second son, Peter I.

Shuysky, Vasily (1552–1612)

A Russian boyar whose actions contributed to the Time of Troubles, Vasily murdered Czar Dmitry and then assumed the throne himself.

Vasily Shuysky, a direct descendant of the Rurik dynasty, was born into the Russian nobility in 1552. Vasily first came to public attention when he was instructed to conduct an autopsy on Dmitry Ivanovich, the brother of Czar Fyodor I, the mental incompetent who ruled at the end of the 16th century. Vasily determined that the boy had killed himself with a knife while in the throes of an epileptic seizure.

When Fyodor's regent, Boris GODUNOV, succeeded him as czar in 1598, staunch opposition arose from many who considered Godunov a usurper. A pretender to the throne claiming to be Dmitry presented himself, and Vasily, joining the number of boyars arrayed against Boris, reversed his earlier statements and claimed that the body he examined was not that of Dmitry. When Boris died in 1605, Vasily had Boris' son killed and swore allegiance to the false Dmitry.

After Dmitry had been named czar, however, Vasily again changed his story and denounced Dmitry as an impostor. Vasily was banished, but he relied on the support of the boyars to organize a plot to overthrow Dmitry. After instigating a popular riot, Vasily returned and had the czar murdered in May 1606. The same month, Vasily was crowned czar. Hoping to avoid further claims from Dmitry, Vasily put the pretender's body on exhibition and had the czarevitch canonized in June.

Next, in an effort to gain the continued support of the boyars, Vasily announced he would rule in accordance with the Duma, a council of boyars. Owing to conditions in Moscow that precipitated the Time of Troubles, mainly a horrendous crop failure that caused thousands to starve to death, opposition grew against Vasily, and his administration came under fire from all classes. He was forced to put down an open revolt of Cossacks, peasants, and nobles in October 1607.

Despite his precautions, however, another pretender arose in the spring of 1608, gaining support from all who opposed Vasily, including the defeated rebels and the Poles. Desperate, Vasily enlisted the aid of Sweden in suppressing the advances of the latest false Dmitry. With Swedish help, Vasily was able to push the pretender back to his base at Tushino in January 1610 and restore order to northern Russia. The Poles, angry at Swedish intervention, declared war on Vasily and threatened an advance on Moscow. This led to a renewed offensive by the pretender and the collapse of order in Moscow as riots broke out in the city. Vasily again called for Swedish aid, but the Poles routed Vasily's forces at Tushino, and Vasily himself was deposed in July. He was forced to "retire" to a monastery, where he died on September 12, 1612.

Sixtus IV (1414–1484)

Like a number of Renaissance popes, Sixtus used his office not primarily for spiritual purposes but chiefly for the aggrandizement and enrichment of himself and his family.

Born Francesco della Rovere on July 21, 1414, near Savona, the future pope became a Franciscan friar and was chosen minister general of the order in 1464. Pope Paul II elevated him to cardinal, and it was that pontiff whom he succeeded as Sixtus IV on August 9, 1471.

Pope Sixtus IV did make some abortive attempts to act in the interest of the church. He sent a fleet to participate in an assault against the Muslims at Smyrna in 1472, but a second expedition the next year failed, and Sixtus turned away from crusading. He made gestures toward reuniting the churches of Rome and Russia, but these came to nothing. Of far greater interest to Sixtus IV was Italian politics, which he manipulated to his advantage and that of his family, on whom he lavished an abundance of church offices and material rewards.

On April 26, 1478, Sixtus brought scandal on himself and the papacy by his limited complicity in the infamous assault on LORENZO DE' MEDICI (Lorenzo the Magnificent) and his brother Giuliano. Under the direction of Sixtus' nephew Girolamo Riario, assassins set upon the two Medici, wounding Lorenzo and killing his brother. Sixtus did his best to make Lorenzo himself look like the guilty party in this plot. He excommunicated him and put the city of Florence, which stood behind their leaders, under interdict. Sixtus prevailed upon King Ferdinand I of Naples to declare war on Florence, but Lorenzo scored a diplomatic coup by making a separate peace with Ferdinand in defiance of Sixtus.

Sixtus IV also incited Venice to attack Ferrara in 1482, only to place Venice under an interdict the following year when that city refused to break off hostilities.

For all his political meddling and abuses of power, Sixtus IV did build or restore some of Rome's greatest churches, of which the Sistine Chapel is the most famous, and he commissioned work from such artists as Botticelli and Antonio del Pollaiuolo. In 1471, he became the benefactor of the great Vatican Library, which he opened to scholars as a center of learning. However, even these magnificent cultural achievements were financed with money derived from burdensome taxation and rampant simony.

Smith, Ian (Douglas)   (1919–   )

Appointed first prime minister of the former British colony of Southern Rhodesia in 1964, Ian Smith led his oppressive white minority government until 1977.

Ian Smith was born in 1919, in Selukwe, Rhodesia (now Zimbabwe), then part of the British colony of Southern Rhodesia. He enrolled in Rhodes University in Grahamstown, South Africa, but in 1939 withdrew to join the British Royal Air Force (RAF). Becoming a fighter pilot, Smith was shot down twice during World War II. After the war, Smith returned to Rhodes University and by 1948 had graduated, becoming a member of the colonial legislative assembly in Rhodesia.

In 1961, Smith founded the Rhodesian Front Party with a platform that included white minority rule and independence from Britain. In a surprise victory, Smith emerged as prime minister in 1964 and embarked on a brutal program of suppressing black resistance. As a result, Britain severed ties with Smith's government. In retaliation, the prime minister declared independence from the Commonwealth on November 11, 1965.

Smith's intolerance and arrogance, especially his absolute refusal to empower any part of the black majority, led to tough economic sanctions leveled against Rhodesia by the United Nations Security Council. Nevertheless, on March 2, 1970, Rhodesia officially proclaimed itself a republic.

The proclamation hardly put an end to escalating civil strife. An anti-Smith opposition party, the Patriotic Front, led by black nationalist Robert Mugabe, began a guerrilla campaign against the Smith regime. In 1977, following a massive white exodus from the republic and the economic consequences of his oppressive military rule, Smith relinquished much of his power. He remained nominal prime minister until 1979, but he was, in effect, no more than acting head of the transitional government charged with overseeing the installation of the new black majority-led regime of what would now be called Zimbabwe. Smith continued to serve in the nation's Parliament until 1987.

Solomon   (r. ca. 965–ca. 925 B.C.)

Solomon, son of King DAVID and Bathsheba, has been called the greatest king of Israel.

While still king himself, Solomon's father, David, turned over the throne to his youngest son amid a great deal of palace intrigue in which the monarch's older children jockeyed for the throne. Once he became king, Solomon plunged into enlarging his already vast empire. Most of the expansion was achieved through marital arrangements with the daughters of kings and leaders of other nations. Solomon is said to have had 700 wives and 300 concubines, and, as was the custom of the day, he used marriage freely to enhance his power. For example, through his alliance with the daughter of the Egyptian pharaoh, Solomon was able to acquire the seaport of Ezion-geber on the Gulf of Aqaba, which gave him direct access to the Red Sea and the Indian Ocean beyond. Among the great powers of the day, only one other, Egypt, could boast access to both the

King Solomon by Doré. (From Gustave Doré, The Doré Bible Gallery, *1879)*

Indian Ocean and the Mediterranean Sea. This advantageous trade position and strategic location, connecting Africa with Asia, placed Israel at the forefront of the world's leading nations.

Solomon's rapidly growing empire necessitated strong defenses, and the king embarked on a massive building program that, in time, severely taxed his resources. He had built a new wall around the capital city of Jerusalem; he built fortified cities at Hazor, Megiddo, and Gazer; and he enlarged the armed forces to unprecedented strength. Solomon's building program also included non-military projects, including the magnificent Temple at Jerusalem, a structure that would become a central shrine in both Judaism and, centuries later, early Christianity. Some years earlier, Solomon's father, King David had made peace with King Hiram of Tyre, and the friendly relationship between the two nations continued into Solomon's reign. Hiram's friendship was vital to Solomon's building campaign. With Hiram's cooperation, strong cedar logs, for use in the Temple, as well as hundreds of craftsmen and artisans were shipped to Israel in exchange for grain and other foodstuffs.

In matters of politics and administration Solomon also took a firm lead. He divided his empire into 12 districts (which bore no relation to the historic "twelve tribes" of Israel); for one month per year, each of these districts was expected to finance the cost of running the government. While this arrangement brought administrative order to the empire, the financial burden placed on some of the less affluent districts served only to strain further the empire's already diminishing resources.

In addition to his military, political, and architectural legacy, Solomon is also remembered for his poetry and songs. Some Biblical scholars believe that he was the author of nearly 4,500 poems and parables, among them the Book of Proverbs and the Book of Ecclesiastes in the Old Testament.

Even as Solomon extended and consolidated his kingdom, discontent spread among the people, who were oppressed by a heavy tax burden. Upon the death of Solomon, his son and successor, Rehoboam, was unable to hold the kingdom together. A Northern Kingdom of Israel was organized by the dissatisfied elements, leaving the Southern Kingdom, henceforth called Judah, to Solomon's descendants.

Further Reading: Cyrus H. Gordon. *The Ancient Near East* (New York: Norton, 1965).

Solon (ca. 638–ca. 559 B.C.)

Solon, Athenian lawgiver, political reformer, and poet, has been described as the father of democracy.

Although his ancestors were nobles and he claimed descent from the last king of Athens, Solon was of modest parentage and grew up in middle-class surroundings. He first came to public attention around 600 B.C. when Athens was in combat against Megara over rule of Salamis. Although the majority of his countrymen was prepared to give up the fight, Solon convinced them, through patriotic poetry, to persevere, and Athens eventually prevailed. Throughout his political career, Solon used his poems to persuade and to guide. Long after his death and even after the demise of some of his political innovations, Solon's poetry survived, and Greek schoolchildren often memorized the more popular verses.

After the Salamis issue, Solon was thrust into the position of archon, or chief magistrate, of Athens. He immediately made it his responsibility to reform the constitution and devise a system of equitable participation in government for the poorer classes. At the time, all of Greece was comprised of either rich landowners or poor peasants, many of whom had sold themselves into slavery. Debt among these peasants was rampant, and few, if any, of the poor were ever able to work themselves out of their predicament. Solon attacked this problem by first canceling all debts based on potential enslavement for failure to pay. He set limits on the amount of land that any one owner could possess, thereby allowing the poorer classes a better opportunity of acquiring land for themselves. Since the wealthy landowners had participated in the massive exportation of grain, to the extent that the people were faced with a food shortage, Solon implemented a ban on the exportation of all Athenian products, except olive oil, which was produced in abundance. He divided all Athenian citizens into four classes according to wealth and directed that members of each group were thenceforth allowed to serve the government in specific roles and to pay taxes based on their ability to contribute.

Many of Solon's constitutional changes were revolutionary. He gave political rights to peasants, allowed representatives of all four classes to serve in the judiciary system, reduced the power of the council of former rulers, and instituted a method of selection of officials by election and by lot.

Unfortunately, Solon's new regulations and constitutional changes were not well received. Realizing that he could not please all of his subjects, he took a leave of absence to allow his citizens time to get used to his innovations. He visited Egypt, Cyprus, and many countries in Asia Minor. He returned after 10 years to a more or less tranquil public, but in 561 B.C., at an advanced age, he took up politics again in an unsuccessful effort to forestall a new tyranny instituted by his friend Peisistratus.

After his death, Solon was remembered as one of the Seven Sages of Greece, and his ashes were scattered over Salamis.

Somoza Debayle, Anastasio (1925–1980)
The second son of General Anastasio SOMOZA GARCIA of Nicaragua, Anastasio Somoza Debayle took office as president in 1967 and effectively ran the country until forced into exile by the Sandinistas in 1979.

Anastasio (Tachito) Somoza Debayle was the second of three sons born to General Anastasio Somoza Garcia, president and ruler of Nicaragua from 1936 until 1956. Tachito Somoza was educated in a New York military school and then attended and graduated from West Point, already holding the rank of captain in the Nicaraguan National Guard.

Returning to Nicaragua, he became a major in the Guard and was appointed head of the Nicaraguan military academy. Upon the assassination of his father in 1956, he was named commander of the National Guard, while his older brother Luis became president. Luis died in 1967 of a heart attack and was succeeded by Rene Schick, whom Tachito deposed that same year.

During his first term as president, Tachito Somoza modernized the National Guard, making it, in the process, a palace guard under his personal control. Somoza also negotiated with the opposition Conservative Party a pact that allowed him to succeed himself as president in 1971 in return for giving the Conservatives 40 percent of the legislature. (His father had negotiated similarly with the Conservatives in order to quell opposition.)

After a devastating 1972 earthquake, which destroyed a large part of the capital city of Managua, Somoza managed to seize control of much of the relief money flowing into the country. He used these funds to finance his family's many business interests, which included real estate, construction, finance and insurance companies, food processing, fisheries, retail outlets, recording firms, ports, the state airline and merchant shipping line, hotel chains, newspapers, radio and television stations, banks, and plastics and chemical factories. In addition, he and his family held half of the nation's land deeds and owned a quarter of the best arable land. Through all of these concerns, Tachito had increased his father's estate from some $150 million to an estimated $900 million by 1979.

Throughout the 1970s, opposition to Somoza's political and business dealings mounted. After his election to a third term in office in 1974, the Sandinistas,

a leftist guerrilla force named in honor of revolutionary Augusto Cesar Sandino (1893–1934), stepped up their attacks. Somoza responded by declaring a state of siege, which lasted until September 1977. Opposition and fighting continued, however, until Somoza was at last forced to resign. He fled first to Miami and then, in 1979, to Paraguay, where he was assassinated in a September 1980 bazooka attack in Asuncion.

Suggested Reading: Richard Miller. *Guardians of the Dynasty: A History of the U.S.–Created Guardia Nacional and the Somoza Family* (Maryknoll, New York: Orbis, 1977).

Somoza Garcia, Anastasio (1896–1956)
President of Nicaragua and commander of the National Guard, Anastasio Somoza established a repressive and largely self-serving dynasty that controlled the country from 1937 until 1979.

Born in San Marcos, Nicaragua, to the family of a wealthy coffee planter, Anastasio Somoza was educated in Nicaragua and then in the United States at the Pierce Business School in Philadelphia. Returning to his homeland, he married into the wealthy Debayle family, who were active in the Nicaraguan Liberal Party (PLN). In 1926, he and other PLN members were successful in the ouster of President Adolfo Diaz, and Somoza assumed the title of general. He served President José Maria Moncada as under secretary for foreign affairs while acting as a translator for United States Marines serving as an intervention force in Nicaragua. He so ingratiated himself with the Americans that when the U.S. troops pulled out of the country, they left him as their chosen commander of the newly created National Guard.

Somoza used his position in the National Guard to build a strong power base. Rallying his supporters, he was able to oust President Juan Bautista Sacasa (who was his wife's uncle) in 1936, after which he was elected president. After taking office, he extended the presidential term from four to six years and served two terms before allowing his 1936 political opponent, Leonard Arguello, to be elected in 1947. Arguello's tenure was short. Somoza declared him "incapacitated" less than a month after his inauguration and assumed the reins of government, officially returning to the presidency in 1950 and serving until 1956.

Having taken absolute control of the Liberal Party, Somoza allowed no other parties to operate until the Conservatives signed pacts that provided them with a specified percentage of seats in the legislature in return for decreased opposition to Somoza's rule. Throughout his presidency and during the administrations of his puppets, Somoza shrewdly maneuvered governmental policy to aid him in amassing a fortune of many millions and huge landholdings.

On September 21, 1956, Somoza was shot by nationalist poet Rigoberto Lopez Perez. Flown to an American military hospital in the Panama Canal Zone, he died a week later. His elder son, Luis Somoza Debayle took over the presidency, and his younger son, ANASTASIO SOMOZA DEBAYLE, became head of the National Guard.

Further Reading: Richard Miller, *Guardians of the Dynasty: A History of the U.S.–Created Guardia Nacional and the Somoza Family* (Maryknoll, New York: Orbis, 1977).

Soulouque, Faustin-Élie [Faustin I] (1788–1873)

A former slave, Soulouque became president and then emperor of Haiti.

Born a slave while Haiti was a colonial possession of France, Faustin-Élie Soulouque participated in the 1803 rebellion that expelled the French, and he served for the next 44 years in the Haitian army, becoming chief of the presidential palace guard.

In 1847, a group of mulatto leaders seized on Soulouque as a likely puppet who would molify the black majority while taking orders from the mulatto elite. Installed as president, Soulouque turned against the mulatto faction that had put him in office, ousted or killed them, and, in 1849, created himself Emperor Faustin I.

Faustin did nothing to help the impoverished black majority that had supported his rise to emperor. Instead, he occupied himself in unsuccessful schemes to conquer the neighboring Dominican Republic, which resulted in the intervention of the United States, France, and Great Britain. Like such later Haitian leaders as "Papa Doc" and "Baby Doc" DUVALIER, Faustin used voodoo to influence and intimidate the rural population. He also created the *zinglin*, a private police force that foreshadowed the Tonton Macoutes of the 20th century.

With his support even among blacks eroding, Emperor Faustin was deposed in 1859 by forces of the mulatto minority, which rallied behind the chief of the army's general staff. Faustin fled into exile, dying in 1873.

Ssu-ma Yen [Wu Ti] (236–290)

The founder and first emperor of the Western Chin dynasty, Wu Ti briefly reunited China after the fall of the Han dynasty.

A member of the great Ssu-ma family, Yen became the chief minister of Wei, one of three states known as the Three Kingdoms that arose in China after the dissolution of the Han dynasty. Powerful warlords ruled each state. By 263, Yen was able to attack the central kingdom of Shu Han and conquer it, incorporating it as part of Wei. In 265, with the support of the army, Yen was able to overthrow the Wei emperor, proclaiming the Chin dynasty. By 280, Yen had conquered the southern kingdom of Wu and reunited China for the first time since the fall of the Han. Working to reform government and at the same time consolidate his own power, Yen disbanded the army to cut expenses but also to keep a rival from gaining control of it. He attempted to reform the unfair taxation of the peasants and the gouging practices of the powerful landholders who charged exorbitant rent. Disbanding of the army left him defenseless and prey to nomadic invasion. He was also unable to break the power of the landed families, and, when he died, his son and heir was unable to prevent his brothers from tearing the dynasty apart in the war known as the Revolt of the Eight Kings. Upon his death, Yen was given the name Wu Ti, by which he is known to history.

Stalin, Josef [Josef Vissarionovich Dzhugashvili] (1879–1953)

Absolute dictator of the Union of Soviet Socialist Republics from 1929 until his death in 1953, Stalin made his country a world superpower even as he forged one of the most destructive and ruthless political regimes in history.

Born Josef Vissarionovich Dzhugashvili on December 21, 1879, in Gori, a hill town in czarist Georgia, Stalin was subjected to a brutal childhood at the hands of his alcoholic and abusive father, an impoverished shoemaker. After his father's death in a brawl, 11-year-old Josef was indulged by his doting mother, who groomed him for the Orthodox priesthood. By the time he entered the Tiflis Theological Seminary at age 14, the youth's rebelliousness had earned him the nickname Koba, after a legendary Georgian bandit and rebel. He soon bridled under the harsh corporal discipline of the seminary and became involved in radical anti-czarist political activity in 1898. In 1899, he abruptly left the seminary to become a full-time revolutionary organizer. Within three years, he was a member of the Georgian branch of the Social Democratic Party, touring the Caucasus, stirring up laborers, and organizing strikes. Like his German contemporary, Adolf HITLER, young "Koba" came from a squalid and brutal family background and showed remarkably little early promise. Unlike Hitler, the aspiring Georgian revolutionary possessed neither personal magnetism nor appreciable rhetorical skills, but he was fearless, ruthless, and a brilliant organizer.

In 1903, the Social Democrats split into two groups, V. I. LENIN's radical Bolshevik ("majority") faction and the more moderate faction Lenin called the Mensheviks—the "minority"—which actually outnumbered the Bolsheviks. Stalin fell in with the radicals and grew close to Lenin. For the next decade, from 1903 until he was exiled to Siberia in 1913, Stalin worked to expand the party's power, organizing cell after cell across the nation, and financing the party's work by planning and executing daring robberies. His activities caused him to be arrested many times, but he always managed to escape. In 1912, Lenin elevated him to the Bolshevik Central Committee, the party's inner circle. Though taciturn and even inarticulate, Stalin became the first editor of *Pravda* ("Truth"), the Bolsheviks' official newspaper. It was during this period that he took the name Stalin—"Man of Steel."

In 1913, Stalin's ability to escape capture and punishment at last failed him, and he was sentenced to Siberian exile. He endured four fateful years, returning to Russia only after the overthrow of Czar NICHOLAS II in March 1917. In the wake of the failure of the first Bolshevik attempt to seize power during the summer of 1917—and in the absence of Leon Trotsky, who had been arrested, and Lenin, who had gone into hiding—Stalin worked to reorganize the party, thereby playing a major role in its successful acquisition of power during the November Revolution. With Lenin's return from self-imposed exile, Stalin was given a succession of commissar posts, all the while working quietly to consolidate greater power. By 1922, he was named general secretary of the party's Central Committee, a position of tremendous influence from which Stalin controlled the apparatus and official personnel of most of the party. When Lenin died in 1924, Stalin promoted himself as the Communist leader's handpicked successor and ruthlessly exploited his position as general secretary to eliminate all who opposed him.

Stalin quickly demonstrated his ability and willingness to manipulate ideology in order to ensure his personal supremacy. He began by announcing a retreat from Lenin's ideal of world Communist revolution by advocating "socialism in one country." He also proposed an economic program far more moderate than what others who had been close to Lenin envisioned. Trotsky, Lev Kamenev, and Grigory Zinoviev, party leftists, went on the offensive against Stalin and his moderate policies, but by 1928, Stalin consolidated the party's right wing in opposition to the left and managed to oust that faction's leadership. Having accomplished this, he performed an abrupt about face and summarily adopted radical leftist economic programs, including the wholesale collectivization of agriculture and greatly accelerated industrialization. Now he successfully attacked the party's right wing, led by Nikolai Bukharin. Within a year, opposition on the left *and* the right had been quashed, and Stalin emerged as absolute dictator of the Soviet Union.

Stalin sought to transform the Soviet Union from a primarily agricultural nation into a modern industrial power. To do this, he was willing to sacrifice human life on an unprecedented scale. Late in 1928 he expropriated the lands of the middle-class farmers ("kulaks"), "deporting" or killing those who offered resistance. Stalin's regime proposed a series of "five-year plans" by which collectivization and industrialization were to be achieved. His administration adhered rigorously to the plans, raising capital to finance industrialization by exporting grain and other produce despite a devastating famine that swept the Soviet Union in 1932. Millions who resisted were executed, and millions more starved to death. A 1988 estimate put the number of deaths that directly resulted from the forced collectivization of 1928–33 at 25 million.

During the period of the first five-year plan, opposition to Stalin mounted, and there was a short-lived peasant revolt, which the dictator easily crushed. When the 17th Party Congress showed support for Sergei Kirov, a moderate and a potential rival, Stalin engineered his assassination in December 1934. Having disposed of Kirov, Stalin then used his murder as a pretext for arresting most of the party's highest-ranking officials as counterrevolutionary conspirators. From 1936 to 1938 Stalin conducted a long series of public trials in which party officials and many in the senior officer corps of the Red Army were convicted of outrageous crimes or acts of treason. The results of the purge were devastating. By 1939, 98 of the 139 Central committee members elected in 1934 had been executed, and 1,108 of the 1,966 delegates to the 17th Congress arrested. Worse, under KGB chief Lavrenti Beria, the secret police arrested, executed, exiled, or imprisoned millions of individuals in the general population. By the eve of World War II, Stalin had destroyed all serious opposition and had terrorized his nation into submission even as he built it into an industrial giant and created about himself a cult of personal worship.

As Adolf Hitler came to dominate more and more of Europe in the late 1930s, Stalin had no desire to oppose this ideological antithesis of communism. He did make attempts to reach agreements with the Western democratic powers, but was rebuffed. So he turned instead to Hitler himself, concluding a Nazi-

Soviet non-aggression pact on August 23, 1939. With the German invasion of Poland, Stalin moved to increase Soviet influence in the West by invading Finland on November 30, 1939. A short but costly war secured Finland's surrender on March 12, 1940. Then, on June 22, 1941, Hitler abrogated the non-aggression pact by invading the Soviet Union.

Early resistance to the invasion was poorly coordinated because Stalin's purges had stripped the Red Army of thousands in its senior officer corps. After an initial period of panic and disorganization, Stalin took personal command of the Red Army and organized an increasingly effective counter force. He acted swiftly to move vital war industries east, into Siberia and central Asia, just ahead of the advancing German armies. He rallied the Soviet people by appealing to patriotism and even disbanded the Communist International and officially rehabilitated the Orthodox church. Despite the damage he himself had inflicted on his officer corps, Stalin identified dependable—even brilliant—commanders in Marshals Georgi Zhukov and Ivan Konev, supporting them in extremely costly but ultimately successful campaigns against the invaders.

By the middle of the war, Stalin had earned great prestige as a military leader and was in a strong negotiating position at the major Allied conferences conducted in Tehran, Yalta, and Potsdam. By the end of the war, many Russians—and others—were willing to overlook the enormities of Stalin's regime, regarding him now as the savior of his nation.

Having triumphed over Hitler, however, Stalin quickly instituted a new regime of terror and repression at home, imposing more taxes on peasants, and announcing fresh discoveries of sabotage and conspiracy. Hard on the heels of victory in World War II, Stalin aggressively expanded the Soviet sphere of influence into neighboring regions, setting up puppet regimes and client states among the nations of the Balkans and eastern Europe, creating what Winston Churchill called an Iron Curtain separating the Communist realm from the rest of the world, and touching off nearly four decades of "cold war" between Soviet-aligned nations and the West.

In 1953, Stalin declared that he had discovered a plot among the Kremlin's corps of physicians, and the Soviet people trembled on the brink of what seemed an imminent and inevitable new round of blood purges. But the aging dictator was ailing by this time, and on March 5, 1953, he died of a cerebral hemorrhage.

Further Reading: Alan Bullock. *Hitler and Stalin: Parallel Lives* (New York: Knopf, 1992); Isaac Deutscher. *Stalin: A Political Biography*, 2d ed. (New York: Oxford University Press, 1967); Robert H. McNeal. *Stalin: Man and Ruler* (New York: New York University Press, 1988).

Stambolov, Stefan Nikolov (1854–1895)

Sometimes called the "Bulgarian Bismarck," Stambolov used the tactics of terror to preserve a reactionary Bulgarian government against popular uprisings.

Stambolov was born in Turnovo, Rumelia (now Bulgaria) on January 31, 1854, to a family of innkeepers. He became active in the Bulgarian underground, which sought to overthrow Turkish rule, and was leader of minor uprisings against the Turks in 1875 and 1876. He fought against Turkey in the Russo-Turkish War of 1877–78, and, after Bulgaria secured independence from Turkey in 1878, he was elected to the Sobranye, the Bulgarian general assembly. Stambolov became president of that body in 1884, a position from which he persuaded Bulgaria's Prince Alexander I to form a union with Eastern Rumelia in 1885.

Russia supported a revolution that ousted Prince Alexander in 1886, to which Stambolov responded by establishing a counterrevolutionary regime based in his native Turnovo. After the prince formally abdicated, Stambolov was placed at the head of a regency council, maneuvering so skillfully that he avoided Russian intervention and brought to the Bulgarian throne a most compliant Prince Ferdinand of Saxe-Coburg-Gotha on July 7, 1887.

As Ferdinand's prime minister, Stambolov distanced his nation from Russia, while pulling closer to Bulgaria's old enemy, Turkey. Stambolov also made overtures to Macedonia in an effort to extend the Bulgarian sphere of influence there. Domestically, however, Stambolov was occupied with ferreting out and brutally suppressing a host of conspiracies and armed uprisings epidemic throughout Bulgaria. Stambolov's use of violence, torture, and intimidation repelled not only the Bulgarian people, but, finally, Prince Ferdinand, who rose up against the minister who had long dominated him. Ferdinand forced Stambolov into resigning on May 31, 1894. Subject to no end of harassment and threats after he left office, Stambolov was ambushed on the streets of Sofia and fatally beaten on July 18, 1895.

Stroessner, Alfredo (1912–)

Alfredo Stroessner, the president and dictator of Paraguay for 35 years before his ouster in 1989, continues to exert influence on his former nation's political affairs.

Alfredo Stroessner was born on November 3, 1912, the son of a German beer maker. He received a local education and at the age of 16 entered the national military school, where his abilities brought him to the attention of his superiors. By 1940, he had attained the rank of major and was appointed to the Paraguayan army's general staff in 1946.

Stroessner remained loyal to President Higinio Morínigo during the 1947 civil war in Paraguay, but later threw his support to Felipe Molas Lopez in his successful coup against Morínigo. Later betraying Lopez as well, Stroessner backed Federico Chaves for the presidency and became commander-in-chief of all Paraguayan armed forces under Chaves. He maintained this position until he, in turn, engineered the ouster of Chaves on May 5, 1954, at which time he assumed the presidency.

Stroessner was supported not only by the ruling Colorado Party, but by such factions as women's, labor, veterans' and youth groups. As commander in chief of the military, the new president had its support as well, and during his long tenure as president, Stroessner kept close control of Paraguay's military.

Stroessner was a staunch anti-Communist and maintained good relations with the United States and its allies. Although he tolerated political parties other than his own, his government brutally suppressed any faction that might seriously challenge Stroessner's administration.

In 1988, President Stroessner was elected to an unprecedented eighth term in office, polling (according to official government figures) 90 to 98 percent of the registered vote. However, in that same year, Stroessner evoked international controversy when he refused to allow Pope John Paul II to meet with civic leaders. Later, in private discussions with the pope, the president declared Paraguay to be a peaceful democracy. Reiterating his claim before the United Nations in New York, Stroessner returned home to find widespread dissension among the masses. In February 1989, Stroessner was deposed in a coup led by strongman General Andres Rodriguez.

Further Reading: Paul H. Lewis. *Paraguay Under Stroessner* (Chapel Hill: University of North Carolina Press, 1980).

Stuyvesant, Peter (ca. 1592–1672)

Stuyvesant was the last and most important governor of New Netherland before it was seized by the British.

The son of a Calvinist minister, Peter Stuyvesant was born in Holland and was educated there, entering the University of Franeker in 1629. For reasons unknown, he was expelled after only a year. An adventurer, Stuyvesant joined the Dutch West India Company in 1635 and traveled to the New World. In 1638, he became the chief commercial officer for Curaçao and was made governor by 1643. It was at this time that he lost his leg in an ill-fated attack against the Portuguese-held St. Martin. Popular accounts often picture Stuyvesant stumping about on his wooden leg, which contributed to the probably accurate image of him as a quick-tempered and irascible autocrat.

In 1645, Stuyvesant volunteered to serve as governor of New Netherland, arriving in what would later become New York on Christmas Day. Stuyvesant, a devout Calvinist, immediately set restrictions on the sale of alcohol and mandated strict observance of the sabbath. He vigorously persecuted non-Calvinists, particularly Quakers and Lutherans, fearing that they would be most likely to instigate revolt.

Stuyvesant did attempt to provide an honest and efficient administration, including a limited public works campaign of improving roads, repairing fences, constructing a wharf on the East River, and building a defensive wall on the northern edge of New Amsterdam along what would later be known as Wall Street. His greatest loyalty, however, was to the Dutch West India Company, and this, combined with his despotism, elicited general protest. Colonists, particularly the burghers of New Amsterdam (later New York), clamored for more self-government. To appease them, Stuyvesant instituted the Board of Nine Men in September 1647 as an advisory council—but he reserved the right to appoint the members. His high-handed and autocratic ways untempered by the Board, the citizens of New Amsterdam appealed directly to the West India Company. In February 1653, the company directed Stuyvesant to grant independent municipal control to New Amsterdam.

Beyond the confines of New Netherland, Stuyvesant had mixed success in dealing with the colonies of other European powers. In 1655, he invaded the Delaware Valley and forced the surrender of New Sweden. He was not as fortunate in dealing with New England, however. In 1650, he was compelled, by the Treaty of Hartford, to cede the entire Connecticut Valley to English control.

Although, of all the colonial powers, the Dutch often enjoyed the most peaceful and profitable relations with the Indians, Stuyvesant could be ruthless toward them. In 1655, the so-called Peach War broke out when a Dutch farmer killed a Delaware Indian woman for picking peaches in his orchard. This act brought reprisals, and Stuyvesant called out the militia in a punitive campaign. Three years after this, Stuyvesant sought to end chronic violence between the Esopus Indians and Dutch settlers by enlisting Mohawks to terrorize the tribe. Violence escalated, and in 1659 the Dutch settlement of Wiltwyck (modern Kingston, New York) was attacked. Stuyvesant called for a parley, whereupon a delegation of Esopus chiefs entered the town for a conference. Stuyvesant ordered the chiefs killed as they slept following the first day of talks. Predictably, this brought Indian reprisals, to which Stuyvesant responded by taking as hostages the children of the Esopus and other tribes. When the Esopus refused to yield all of their children as directed, Stuyvesant sold those hostages he held into the West Indian slave trade.

Continued strife between Stuyvesant and the British climaxed on September 8, 1664, when British warships sailed against the colony and the Dutch residents simply refused to defend themselves. Stuyvesant had no choice but to surrender, having at least secured trading rights for the West India Company. He retired to his farm—the Bouwerie (through which Bowery Street now passes)—on Manhattan Island. He died there in February 1672.

Further Reading: Alan Axelrod. *Chronicle of the Indian Wars: From Colonial Times to Wounded Knee* (New York: Prentice Hall, 1993); Henry Kessler, and Eugene Rachlis. *Peter Stuyvesant and His New York* (New York: Random House, 1959).

Suárez Flamerich, Germán   (1907–   )

Suárez was provisional president of the 1950–52 Venezuelan junta following the assassination of President Delgado Chalbaud.

Born in Caracas on October 4, 1907, Suárez received a doctorate in political science and became a lawyer and educator, specializing in civil law at Venezuela's Central University from 1936 to 1940. Suárez served as chief council to the military junta that took over the democratically elected government of Romulo Gallegos following a coup in 1948. Colonel Carlos Delgado Chalbaud, leader of the coup, appointed Suárez his foreign minister in 1949. When Chalbaud was assassinated the following year, Suárez was chosen to replace him.

Suárez took steps to establish a civil government, but was unable to dislodge the already established military junta. Colonel Marcos Pérez Jiménez, the most powerful member of the junta, mandated elections in 1952, compelling the Venezuelan public to register and vote or face severe legal penalties. With the election of Pérez Jiménez, Suárez left Venezuela for Europe until 1954, when he returned to Venezuela as an educator.

Suharto   (1921–   )

After ruthlessly suppressing a Communist coup d'etat, Suharto became head of the military government in Indonesia and ruled virtually unopposed into the 1990s.

Born in Central Java on June 8, 1921, Suharto finished high school and worked for a small bank in the Dutch colony of Indonesia shortly before the outbreak of World War II. When hostilities commenced, the Dutch hastily put together a local defense force, which Suharto joined, rising to the rank of sergeant. With the German invasion of the Netherlands, the Dutch were forced to abandon the colony to the Japanese, and Suharto joined the local volunteer defense force sponsored by the Japanese, eventually rising to company commander.

When the Japanese surrendered to the Allies in 1945, the Dutch attempted to reestablish control of the colony, but the local volunteer units the Japanese had developed now turned against the Dutch imperial interests, which they defeated, and Indonesian independence was declared in August 1945.

Suharto, who continued to serve in the military, rose steadily through the ranks, but showed no inclination toward politics—although he was a virulent anti-communist. In 1963, Suharto was promoted to major general and was named to a short stint as commander in chief of the army's strategic command. During this brief period, Communist factions attempted to seize power on the night of September 30, 1965. The rebels assassinated six senior generals, but Suharto was able to mobilize the army and put down the rebellion.

In the days following the revolt, it was discovered that President SUKARNO had had some complicity in the affair. Suharto, with the backing of the senior military leadership, now took over the government and ruthlessly purged Communist elements and other political opponents. The army and vigilante groups massacred an estimated 500,000 people. In March 1968, the Consultative Congress elected Suharto to a five-year term as president.

Once installed in office, Suharto instituted his "New Order" Regime, in which he attempted to revitalize the Indonesian economy with the help of American-educated economists and industrialists. He was able to interest foreign investors and procured over $200 million in foreign aid. He also ended his nation's costly war with Malaysia and clamped down on runaway inflation by following strict Keynesian economic policies. By the mid-1970s, the Indonesian economy had rebounded, and Suharto was reelected in 1973, 1978, 1983, 1988, and 1993.

Further Reading: William Lidster. *Suharto Finds the Divine Vision: A Political Biography* (Honolulu: Semangat, 1990).

Sukarno   [Kusnasosro] (1901–1970)

First president of independent Indonesia, Sukarno became increasingly dictatorial, abolishing parliament, and declaring himself Indonesia's president for life.

Born on June 6, 1901, Sukarno was originally named Kusnasosro. While studying civil engineering at Bandung Technical College, he became active in—and finally chairman of—the General Study Club, a student political group that advocated systematic "noncooperation" with Indonesia's Dutch colonial regime. By 1928, under Sukarno's leadership, the club evolved into a full-fledged radical party, the Indonesian Nationalist Party, and the would-be civil engineer discovered that he was an electrifying speaker and an able political organizer.

Throughout the 1930s, Sukarno and his party worked to undermine the Dutch grip on the nation. Periodically, authorities arrested and imprisoned or even exiled the political leader. With the advent of World War II and the Japanese invasion of the Netherlands East Indies in 1942, Sukarno saw a chance to deal a severe blow to the Dutch colonial government by cooperating with the invaders. During this period of collaboration, however, he secretly coordinated an Indonesian nationalist underground. At the end of World War II, Sukarno moved swiftly. With the Dutch as well as the Japanese out of the way, the underground emerged, and Sukarno proclaimed Indonesia's independence.

Sukarno easily won election as the republic's first president and carefully carved out a policy of neutrality with regard to the great foreign powers. In the late 1940s and early 1950s, he presided over a relatively democratic, non-aligned government, but as the decade progressed, he became increasingly autocratic and leaned toward alliance with the Communist regimes. In 1959, he summarily dissolved parliament, and four years later proclaimed himself president for life.

Sukarno came to distrust his own military, and on September 30, 1965, he approved a Communist-inspired assault on his top commanders. The attack provoked a decisive response from the military, led by General SUHARTO, who led a coalition of anti-Communists to counter Sukarno's attack. Over the next three years, Suharto pressured Sukarno into retirement. Sukarno died on June 21, 1970, two years after stepping down as Indonesia's president.

Further Reading: J. D. Legge. *Sukarno: A Political Biography* (New York: Praeger, 1972); C. L. M. Penders. *The Life and Times of Sukarno* (Rutherford, N.J.: Fairleigh Dickinson University Press, 1974).

Suleyman I the Magnificent (ca. 1494–1566)

Suleyman, Ottoman sultan from 1520 until his death in 1566, enlarged his empire while fostering its art and architecture.

Suleyman was the only son of Sultan SELIM I. As such, the young man was given an administrative role early on. While his grandfather, Sultan BAYEZID II, ruled the Ottoman Empire, Suleyman was appointed governor of Kaffa, in the Crimea. Later, during his father's reign, young Suleyman became governor of Manisa in Asia Minor.

Suleyman became sultan in 1520 and almost immediately began a series of campaigns against the Christian nations that bordered the Mediterranean Sea. He took Belgrade in 1521 and Rhodes in 1522. Suleyman defeated the Hungarian king Louis II at Mohacs in August 1526 and installed a vassal, John, in his place. When John died in 1540, Suleyman committed vast resources to the final conquest of the country. By 1562, after years of fighting, no progress had been made, and Suleyman agreed to a peace.

In the meantime, as early as 1534, Suleyman had turned his eyes eastward and begun a series of wars against Persia. Following up on his father's earlier efforts, Suleyman captured eastern Asia Minor and Iraq. However, two additional protracted eastern

Suleyman I the Magnificent—perhaps the most powerful of the Ottoman rulers. (From Stanley Lane-Poole, The Story of the Nations: Turkey, *1888)*

campaigns failed to gain for Suleyman all of the territory that he wanted.

In addition to his considerable skills as commander of land forces, Suleyman also became famous for amassing a considerable navy. In 1538, the sultan's ships defeated a combined force sent by Venice and Spain, and in 1551, his navy attacked and took the city of Tripoli. The Ottoman navy sailed far and wide, even reaching India.

In the course of his military operations in Europe, Suleyman demonstrated great cunning in pitting Protestant factions against the pope and his followers. Although he was not particularly interested in Western religion, Suleyman realized that it was to his benefit to keep Europe divided in matters of religion, with the Protestant nations in direct conflict with the rulers of the Ottoman's arch-rival Hapsburg Empire. In Hungary, for example, Suleyman allowed Calvinism to flourish, and so liberal was his treatment of Protestantism—when it served his purposes—that some churchmen looked upon the sultan as their protector.

Suleyman strengthened the Ottoman Empire, raising it to a position of leadership in eastern Europe, the Mediterranean basin, and the Near East. He also brought Ottoman culture to a height that surpassed anything in Europe of the day. In addition to Suleyman's massive building programs, which produced scores of mosques, bridges, fortresses, and other public works, his administrative efforts included the transformation of Constantinople into Istanbul, making it the center of Ottoman government. However, as Suleyman grew older, his empire was shaken by disputes between his two sons. Neither of them had inherited his father's zeal for conquest, nor his diplomatic acumen. Accordingly, after Suleyman fell in battle during a September 1566 assault against a Hungarian fortress, the Ottoman Empire fell into a long period of decline under a series of weak and even degenerate sultans.

Further Reading: Roger B. Merriman. *Suleiman the Magnificent, 1520–66* (New York: Cooper Square Publishers, 1966).

Sulla, Lucius Cornelius (ca. 138–78 B.C.)

Lucius Cornelius Sulla rose to the dictatorship of Rome, instituting a harsh regime of largely self-serving reforms.

Sulla was born into a patrician family of little distinction and, as a foppish and effete young man, exhibited nothing to foretell his rise. The military tribune Gaius Marius put Sulla on his staff as quaestor in 107 B.C., and Sulla gained an immediate reputation by engineering the capture of the Numidian king Jugurtha in 105, thereby bringing the Jugur-

thine Wars to a successful conclusion. Although Marius retained Sulla's services in his campaigns against the Cimbri and the Teutons during 105–101, he became increasingly jealous of the young man's triumphs.

In 93 Sulla became praetor—and, the following year, governor—of Cilicia (the southern portion of modern Turkey). In this post he installed Ariobarzanes as king of Cappadocia. From 91 to 88, Sulla was called back to Italy to take command of forces prosecuting the Social War (war against the Allies or Socii) and successfully laid siege to Pompeii in 89. His growing reputation earned him election as consul for 88, and he obtained the command against the powerful MITHRIDATES VI of Pontus, the conqueror of Anatolia. M. Sulpicius Rufus, a partisan of Marius, attempted to replace Sulla with Marius, an action that prompted Sulla to march on Rome with six legions. He took the city and drove Marius into exile, then continued his program of military triumph unimpeded. In 86, Sulla invaded Greece and captured Athens. He performed brilliantly against the superior number of a Pontic army led by Archelaus at Chaeronea in the summer of 86.

The successor to Marius, Lucius Cornelius Cinna, made an attempt to prosecute Sulla for treason, but Sulla sailed east, defeated Archelaus again at Orchomenus in 85, then invaded Asia, taking it upon himself to conclude a hasty treaty with Mithridates—notwithstanding the presence of another Roman legion under G. Flavius Fimbria. Flushed with victory, Sulla returned to Italy, landing at Brundisium (modern Brindisi) in 83, where he joined forces with Marcus Licinius Crassus and Pompey the Great for a full-scale advance on Rome. In the spring of 82, he and his allies defeated the Marians and their allies at the Battle of the Colline Gate and captured Rome. Much as Marius had done before him in 87 B.C., Sulla and his allies embarked on an orgy of massacres and proscriptions in order to purge the capital of their enemies. Soon afterward, Sulla was made dictator (82–81), then dictator and consul (80).

Sulla introduced a number of sweeping reforms, strengthening the Senate—and making it impossible for outsiders to challenge the powerful families who controlled that body—and revamping the criminal courts. In an effort to thwart incipient opposition, he greatly reduced the power and authority of the tribunes. He also secured, by force, the settlement of his many veterans in Italy.

Soon after achieving his ends, Sulla retired from public life, retreating to his estate in Campania in 79, where he died a year later.

For all the bloodshed associated with them, Sulla's reforms did not appreciably outlive him. His personal example, more than his reforms, determined the shape of the Rome to come. He failed to inject new life into the traditional oligarchic republic. Instead, he provided a model of absolute personal leadership that inspired the likes of the egocentric and ambitious Pompey and Julius CAESAR to overturn republicanism altogether in favor of autocratic dictatorship.

Further Reading: Plutarch. *Plutarch's Life of Lucius Cornelius Sulla* (Cambridge: The University Press, 1886).

Suppiluliumas I (r. ca. 1380–ca. 1346 B.C.)
Suppiluliumas was the most powerful ruler ever to ascend the Hittite throne.

As the Hittite kingdom gained ascendancy, thanks to the continued conflict between the Egyptians and the Hyksos, Suppiluliumas, called by some scholars the "CHARLEMAGNE of the Near East," emerged as the region's dominant figure, spreading his kingdom's influence over much of Syria and the Euphrates River Valley. He and his armies were in constant conflict with the Mitanni in the east, and he was obsessed with establishing the permanent occupation of Syria. He rebuilt the Hittite capital at Hattusas and extended his kingdom to the proportions of a great empire.

Suppiluliumas was feared and respected by most of his neighbors. Even the powerful Egyptians cultivated his friendship, as evidenced by the fact that Tutankhamon's widow proposed that he send one of his sons to be her new husband. Suppiluliumas, suspecting that this request was part of a nefarious Egyptian plot, sent an envoy to investigate. When the minister returned with the report that the proposal was legitimate, Suppiluliumas did, indeed, send one of his sons to become the new pharaoh. By the time the young man arrived in Egypt, however, an anti-Hittite movement had been organized, and the hapless son was murdered. Suppiluliumas himself died soon after this of the plague, introduced into his homeland by Egyptian prisoners of war.

Further Reading: Kurt W. Marek. *The Secret of the Hittites* (New York: Knopf, 1967); Johannes Lehmann. *Hittites: People of 1000 Gods* (New York: Viking, 1977).

T

Takeda Shingen   [Harunobu] (1521–1573)

Takeda was perhaps the most violent of the many warlords who contended for power during Japan's "Warring States" period.

Takeda's given name was Harunobu, and he was the oldest son of Takeda Katsuyori, whom he deposed in 1541 to preempt his younger brother's bid to inherit his father's domains. Takeda took up where his father had left off, aggressively expanding his territory in the provinces of Shinano and Hida. By 1547, he engaged Uesugi Kenshin, warlord of Echigo province, in battle for the first time. The struggle between Takeda and Uesugi would consume the next 30 years, ending only with Takeda's death in 1573. The warfare involved annual battles fought in the vicinity of Kawanakajima from 1553 to 1564. Characteristically, the outcome of each of these contests was a futile draw in a mutual blood bath. In one, some 8,000 samurai perished, and Takeda himself was severely wounded in the 1561 engagement.

In 1567, Takeda forged an alliance with the powerful general and statesman Tokugawa Ieyasu to attack Imagawa Ujizama, who held sway over Suraga province. The house of Imagawa, which had been weakening, fell to Takeda. But even he proved unable to hold the province, which was subject to unrelenting attack from the Hojo clan.

Following his experience in Suraga, Takeda became a Buddhist priest, taking the name of Shingen. He did not, however, renounce his holdings or his warlike ways. In 1572, he turned on his recent ally, who had joined forces with ODA NOBUNAGA, a powerful warrior well on his way to consolidating enough power to make him warlord of a unified Japan. Takeda attacked Tokugawa Ieyasu at Mikatagahara in 1572, soundly defeating him. For some reason, however, Takeda failed to capitalize on his victory. It is possible that he had taken a musketball in the head during the siege of Tokugawa's stronghold and lost heart for the fight. He died—perhaps from this wound—the next year.

Tamerlane   [Timur, Timur the Lane] (1336–1405)

As the spectacularly aggressive amir of Samarkand, Tamerlane invaded and overran Mesopotamia, Persia, Afghanistan, and much of India with the object not of building an empire but of gaining plunder.

Born at Kesh, near Samarkand, in 1336, most likely the son of a Tatar chieftain, Tamerlane became vizier to Khan Tughlak Timor of Kashgar in 1361, but left this post to join his brother Amir Hussain in an expedition to conquer Transoxiana. The brothers raided in this area from 1364 to 1370. In 1369, Tamerlane succeeded his father as amir of Samarkand, then campaigned against the khans of Khwarizm and Jatah for the next 10 years. In 1381, Tamerlane invaded Persia, capturing Herat, then in the course of 1382–85, raiding Khurasan and eastern Persia. During 1386–87, Fars, Armenia, Azerbaijan, and Iraq fell to him in succession. His former ally TOKTAMYSH invaded Samarkand in 1385–86 and again in 1388 and 1389. All three times, Tamerlane defeated Toktamysh, and in 1390–91 pushed him back into Russia. He was unable to capitalize on this advance, however, since he was called back to Persia to put down a rebellion mounted there by Shah Mansur at Shiraz in 1392. Tamerlane defeated the shah and went on to reconquer Armenia, Azerbaijan, and Fars during 1393–94. In 1393, Tamerlane captured Baghdad, and within two years held Mesopotamia and Georgia.

At this point, in 1395, Toktamysh invaded yet again, unleashing all of Tamerlane's wrath in response. Tamerlane defeated the upstart at the Battle of Terek late in the year, then went on to ravage southern Russia and the Ukraine, visiting great destruction and misery in a relentless punitive raid. Taking no prisoners, he slaughtered all of the Mongols he encountered.

Tamerlane interrupted this orgy of killing when he returned again to Persia to suppress rebellion there in 1396–97, then launched a massive invasion of India with a large force of cavalry in 1398. As he had in Russia, Tamerlane cut a broad swath of destruction on his way to Delhi. At the outskirts of that city, he met and routed the army of Sultan Mahmud Tughluq and entered Delhi proper on December 18, 1398. He turned his troops loose upon the city for little more than two weeks, killing tens of thousands, looting all that was worth taking, then began a march back toward Samarkand. While he did not seek to occupy India or add it to his empire he did pillage it mercilessly, thereby undermining the Delhi sultanate, which soon decayed and fell.

Following the Indian expedition, Tamerlane invaded Syria, annihilating the Mamluk army at the Battle of Aleppo on October 30, 1400. After sacking Aleppo and Damascus, he returned to rebellious Baghdad, which he utterly destroyed in 1401 as retribution for revolt. Though awash in blood, Tamerlane was unsated and moved on in 1402 to invade Anatolia, smashing the army of Sultan Bayazid I at Ankara on July 20, 1402. When he captured Smyrna from the Knights of Rhodes, he collected tribute from the Sultan of Egypt as well as from Byzantine emperor John I.

Undefeated, Tamerlane returned to Samarkand in 1404 and set about planning a large-scale invasion of China. He was stricken with illness and died on January 19, 1405, before putting his plans into operation.

Further Reading: Harold Lamb. *Tamerlane: The Earth Shaker* (Garden City, N.Y.: Garden City Publishing, 1932); Edward D. Sokol. *Tamerlane* (Lawrence, Kansas: Coronado Press, 1977).

Taraki, Noor Mohammed (1917–1979)

President of Afghanistan from April 1978 to September 1979, Noor Mohammed Taraki continued the widespread human rights abuses against Muslim rebels begun under his predecessor Mohammad Daud Khan and continued under his successor HAFIZOLLAH AMIN.

Noor Mohammed Taraki was born in Afghanistan's Ghazna Province in 1917 and began his political career in 1963 when King Mohammad Zahir announced a more flexible home and foreign policy. Taraki and others founded the Khalq ("Masses") Party. Later that year, Mohammad Daud led the overthrow of the monarchy, and the Khalq Party split in two factions—one under Taraki, the other under Daud. The party was reunited in 1977 as the People's Democratic Party with Taraki as secretary-general.

In 1978, backed by the Soviet-trained Afghan army, Taraki overthrew the Daud government and killed Daud, his family, and dozens of supporters. Orthodox Muslims were hostile to Taraki's government, and rebellion spread through the country: in August 1978, at the fort of Bala Hissar; the following month, near Kabul; and later on the border with Pakistan. Each of these uprisings was crushed by Taraki's massive Soviet-supplied army.

In December 1978, Taraki signed a 20-year pact of friendship with the Soviet Union even while he insisted that Afghanistan was not a Communist country and would remain unaffiliated with the Soviets.

Taraki's reign of terror against the Muslim rebels was short. Soviet premier Leonid Brezhnev advised Taraki to get rid of his prime minister Hafizullah Amin, but it was Amin who forced Taraki out in September 1979. Taraki's death was officially announced on October 9, 1979, and was attributed to "a severe and prolonged illness." Apparently, Taraki had actually died on September 16 of wounds sustained in a presidential palace gun battle that broke out after Amin dismissed two members of Taraki's cabinet.

Further Reading: Ainslee T. Embree, ed. *Encyclopedia of Asian History* (New York: Scribner's/Asia Society, 1988).

Thani, Shaykh Khalifa ibn Hamad al- (1932–)

This autocratic emir of Qatar was arrested in the United States on charges of illegal insider trading in the stock market.

A lifelong civil servant, Shaykh Kahlifa Thani held a number of government jobs in the 1950s and 1960s, ranging from chief of security forces, to director of education, to minister of finance and petroleum affairs. In February 1972, Thani overthrew his cousin, Shaykh Ahmad, whose extravagant habits had raised among the people grave questions of corruption and graft.

Thani freely practiced nepotism in staffing his new government, finding official positions for his sons and brothers, who ran Qatar like a family business.

A boom in oil production in petroleum-rich Qatar brought tremendous wealth to the nation, but also wrought social changes that outpaced the ability of the nation to adapt to them. Thani attempted to enforce control of modernization through a strongly centralized and high-handed economic policy. He attempted to expand other industries, such as agriculture, by building fertilizer plants intended to grow with and prosper from the oil economy.

In 1976, Thani banned all political parties and labor unions and ruled by decree—although he did not in practice violate the constitution nor did he exceed Islamic law and traditions. After stepping down as president in 1980, Thani became minister of the interior, but in 1984 he was arrested by the United States Securities and Exchange Commission on charges of insider trading in the merger of the Santa Fe International Corp and the Kuwait Petroleum Corp. It was estimated that Thani illegally made a $6 million personal profit from the merger.

Tharawaddy (r. 1837–46)

King of Burma in the 19th century, Tharawaddy repeatedly clashed with the British and nearly brought on full-scale war between the two governments.

In 1937, Tharawaddy overthrew his brother, King Bagyidaw, who, suffering from mental illness, had become unfit to rule. Tharawaddy's first efforts were to curb the corruption and abuses rampant in government, particularly in the Burmese legal system. He ruthlessly purged former officials and court figures responsible for previous injustices and summarily executed them, including Bagyidaw's son, the former crown prince, and his mother, the queen. When revolts broke out in Lower Burma in 1838, Tharawaddy violently clamped down on the insurgents and succeeded in putting down the revolt, although this left him in a politically unstable position.

In 1837, Tharawaddy repudiated his brother's Treaty of Yandabo with the British, which had imposed humiliating terms on Burma, including the cession of the provinces of Arakan and Tenasserim to the British. Tharawaddy declared the treaty invalid and refused to deal with the British political resident from India, demanding to negotiate directly with the crown. Indeed, Tharawaddy ejected the resident, Harvey Burney, from the capital of Amarapura in June 1837. When Burney was replaced, Tharawaddy again refused to deal with his successor, contending he was merely an instrument of the *Indian* administration.

In 1840, Lord Auckland, the Indian governor general, suspended the residency and severed British diplomatic ties with Burma, a condition that would last for over 10 years. In 1841, Tharawaddy further provoked the British by taking a large military escort with him to Rangoon on religious pilgrimage. The British interpreted this as an act of war, and many called for a British declaration in response to it. Only Britain's entanglement in Afghanistan kept troops from marching on Tharawaddy.

Near the end of his life, Tharawaddy suffered from mental illness similar to what had plagued his brother. His condition deteriorated, and he was deposed shortly before his death in October 1846. He was succeeded by his son Pagan.

Themistocles (ca. 528–ca. 462 B.C.)

Themistocles was the architect of the Greek naval victory over the Persians at Salamis in 480 B.C.

Themistocles was born into a wealthy Greek family, but traditional sources say that his mother was not a Greek. Nevertheless, he was a citizen of Athens, and in 493 B.C. was elected archon. In 490, he participated in the Battle of Marathon, in which Athenian spearmen fought off an attempted Persian occupation of their city. Although most of his colleagues thought that the Persian menace had been ended by this victory, Themistocles knew that the Persians would be back. Accordingly, he urged Ath-

ens to build a large naval force and dispatch it into the Mediterranean Sea to fend off all would-be invaders. After persuading the assembly to dedicate the entire proceeds of a new state-owned silver mine to strengthening the navy, Themistocles pushed his proposed reforms through, and by 480 B.C., when Persia threatened Greece again, the Athenian navy consisted of 200 warships. In 480 B.C., Themistocles lured the Persian navy into the narrow straits of Salamis. The enemy ships, designed for sailing in open water, emerged clumsily from the straits and were readily destroyed by the Athenian navy.

On his return to Athens, Themistocles was denied the hero's welcome he deserved and was not reelected as archon. Dispirited he retired to Asia Minor, where he died, possibly by suicide.

Further reading: R. J. Lenardon. *The Saga of Themistocles* (London: Thames and Hudson, 1978).

Theodora (ca. 500–548)

Perhaps the most powerful woman in the history of the Byzantine Empire, Theodora used her influence to gain rights for women and religious tolerance for her faith.

Theodora was raised on the margin of society. She was the daughter of a bear keeper in the Constantinople Hippodrome and became an actress at an early age. She gave birth to at least one child out of wedlock, and she made her own living as a wool spinner. When Emperor JUSTINIAN met her, he was attracted to her immediately and made her his mistress. After elevating her to the rank of patrician, he married her in 525. When Justinian was crowned in 527, she was named queen.

As queen, Theodora was Justinian's most trusted adviser. Indeed, many believed that she was the power behind the throne. Her name appears in nearly all important legislation of the time, and she corresponded with and received foreign officials. When the two political parties of Byzantium rose against Justinian and attempted to overthrow him in the Nika Rebellion of January 532, Justinian's ministers advised him to abdicate. It was Theodora who convinced him not to yield, and it was she who ordered the military to round up the rebels and confine them in the arena, where they were executed en masse for treason.

Theodora was decisive and autocratic, but she also emerged as a champion of women's rights in an age when females were generally regarded as little more than chattel. She oversaw the revision of the divorce laws, giving women greater legal protection. She promoted legislation outlawing the employment of girls as prostitutes. She was less successful in her efforts to temper her husband's persecution of the

Monophysites, a religious sect to which Theodora belonged. She did finally halt outright persecution in 533, but the Monophysites were never truly accorded religious freedom and the protection of the law.

When Theodora died of cancer in June 548, Justinian was devastated, and the empire lost a determined leader and an advocate for the rights of the unenfranchised.

Theodoric I the Great (ca. 454–526)

A ruler of contradictory nature, Theodoric was often cruel, yet he fostered learning on the eve of the Dark Ages, promoted religious tolerance, and came close to reestablishing the old Western Roman Empire.

Born in Panonia (western Hungary and northern Serbia), Theodoric was the son of Theodemer, a triumvir ruling the Ostrogoths. As a child and youth, from 461 to 471, he lived in Constantinople as a hostage of the Byzantines to ensure the good behavior of the Ostrogoths. In Constantinople, Theodoric was exposed to the highest level of learning then available in Europe.

Shortly after being reunited with his father, he led a secret attack on the Sarmatians, capturing the city of Singidunum (modern Belgrade). The death of Theodemer in 474 thrust Theodoric into a power struggle with his rival and namesake, Theodoric Strabo, for succession to the Ostrogoth throne. The contest, which lasted until Strabo's death in 481, often involved open fighting and led to conflict with the Byzantine emperor Zeno. Upon the death of Strabo, Theodoric planned and commissioned the murder of Strabo's successor in 484, which enabled him to assume the kingship of the Ostrogoths at long last unopposed.

Settling his people in Yugoslavia and Bulgaria, Theodoric did not yet find peace. His dispute with Zeno escalated into war, and Theodoric successfully invaded Thrace during 485–86. Zeno sought to appease the Ostrogoth by commissioning him the invasion of Italy. Theodoric moved his entire people—some 150,000 Ostrogoths, a large percentage of whom were warriors (some 50,000)—from the Balkans to Italy. He met with resistance from the Gepidae at Sirmium in the spring of 489, but easily overcame it, crossing the Julian Alps into Italy in August 489. Confronting Odoacer, the Germanic king of Italy, he engaged him in battle at the Sontius on August 28. Odoacer fell back on Verona, where Theodoric, continuing his advance into Italy, again defeated him, on September 30. This time Odoacer consolidated his forces and withdrew into the fortress city of Ravenna. Mustering reinforcements, Odoacer took the offensive in the spring of 490, at-

tacking Theodoric at Faenza. Theodoric repelled the attack and drove Odoacer back into Ravenna, to which Theodoric now laid siege. The city fell on February 26, 493, and, three weeks later, on March 15, Theodoric executed his rival.

Having established himself ruthlessly, Theodoric settled in as a capable, high-minded ruler of Italy. He did much to revive classical learning, exerting his powerful influence in the control and suppression of a factitious petty urban bureaucracy on the one hand and over his own less cultivated Ostrogoth noblemen on the other. Energetic, diplomatic, and strong, Theodoric brought years of stability to the hitherto unsettled Italian political landscape. In 508, he fought a brief war with the Byzantine Empire, after which he expanded his influence beyond Italy and into Provence. Soon, the Visigoths of Spain acknowledge him as overlord as well.

Theodoric demonstrated his respect for learning when he named the philosopher Boethius a Roman consul in 510. He also showed, however, that he had not left his Ostrogothic ruthlessness entirely behind him when, accusing Boethius of participating in a conspiracy against him, he imprisoned the philosopher and caused him to be executed in 524. During his imprisonment, Boethius wrote *The Consolation of Philosophy (De Consolatione Philosophiae)*, destined to be one of the most popular intellectual works of the Middle Ages.

Unfortunately, the rebirth of classicism and the new stability it brought to the territory corresponding to the former Western Roman Empire proved to be largely dependent on the powerful presence of Theodoric himself. When the ruler died on August 30, 526, his kingdom quickly buckled and was invaded by JUSTINIAN I in 535.

Further Reading: Thomas Hodgkin. *Theodoric* (New York: AMS, 1980).

Theodosius I the Great [Flavius Theodosius] (347–395)

As the last emperor of a united Roman Empire, Theodosius vigorously suppressed paganism and promoted universal Christianity.

Theodosius served in the Roman army under his father, also called Theodosius, in the Moorish rebellion. When his father was unjustly tried and executed for treason in 376, Theodosius retired to his family's estate.

His retirement was brief. Following the death of the eastern emperor Valens at the hands of the Goths in August 378, Gratian, emperor of the West, recalled Theodosius—who had, after all, proven himself an able general under his father—and proclaimed him co-emperor, with dominion over the East, on January 19, 379.

Immediately, Theodosius was forced into battle against the Visigoths, who had killed the emperor Valens. Realizing the empire was not strong enough to expel the invaders and that he was in command of badly demoralized troops, Theodosius concluded a treaty, offering the Goths the unprecedented right to live within the empire as an autonomous people in exchange for their military assistance whenever required.

In 383, Gratian was murdered in the West, and Maximus was proclaimed emperor and became a direct threat to Theodosius, who nevertheless realized that he lacked the regional security and military might to challenge Maximus. Theodosius allowed the usurper to take Britain and Gaul, but when Maximus invaded Italy in 387, Theodosius felt prepared to offer opposition. Theodosius moved against Maximus in the Balkans during the spring of 388 and succeeded in defeating him by July. This victory secured the West for Valentinian II, and Theodosius was able to install his own most trusted ally, the Frankish general Arbogast, as an adviser to Valentinian.

As early as 380, Theodosius moved to unify Christian practice within the empire by issuing an edict declaring that the Nicene Creed was binding on all of his subjects. The creed promulgated the consubstantiality of God the Father, Son, and Holy Spirit, and may be taken as the founding document of Catholicism. Within a decade, Theodosius actively moved to stamp out the pagan cults that had dominated Roman life for centuries. In 391, he officially closed all pagan temples and forbade all pagan practices. This measure heightened political tension in the empire, which became sharply divided into pagan and Christian camps, and when Valentinian died in 392, Arbogast treacherously appointed Eugenius, a pagan, as emperor in the West. Theodosius was not pleased, but he did not wish to risk a war, and he allowed Eugenius to occupy Italy in 393. However, he did strengthen his anti-pagan edicts of 391, and he elevated his son Honorius to augustus, in effect proclaiming that he would tolerate no emperor other than himself and his heir.

At last, in 394, Theodosius realized that civil war was inevitable and that it would decide the spiritual future of the empire. He set out from Constantinople in May, and, after suffering an initial defeat at the Frigidus River on September 5, Theodosius counterattacked the following day, crushing the paganist forces. With the defeat of Arbogast and Eugenius, Theodosius ruled both East and West. The exertion of the campaign had weakened him, how-

ever, and, feeling that the end was near, he provided for the continued unification of the empire under his two sons. He appointed Stilicho, the trusted commander who had achieved victory at the Frigidus, as adviser to his boys, one of whom would rule in the East and the other in the West. Theodosius died in January 395. Although Stilicho tried earnestly to guide the sons, other advisers precipitated discord, and the union of East and West dissolved.

Further Reading: Averil Cameron. *The Later Roman Empire* (Cambridge: Harvard University Press, 1993).

Thutmose I   (r. 1504–1492 B.C.)

Thutmose I, pharaoh of the 18th Dynasty, pushed the borders of the Egyptian Empire to its farthest limits.

Thutmose I, who may have co-ruled Egypt for a time with his predecessor, AMENHOTEP I, was the son of a non-royal mother, but his marriage to Amenhotep's daughter assured him of the succession. Upon ascending the throne, Thutmose embarked on a well-planned invasion of Nubia. Rich gold deposits had been found far upriver on the Nile, and a desire to profit from them, plus a need to subdue hostile forces on Egypt's southern frontiers, motivated this foray beyond the Fourth Cataract. It was farther than any Egyptian army had ever before penetrated.

Soon after the Nubian expedition had been successfully concluded, Thutmose set off to the north to evict the barbarian Hyksos from the Delta. Completing this mission, he marched his army as far as the Euphrates River, commemorating this feat with a stele that still survives to tell the story.

The achievements of Thutmose I were not confined to conquest. He added significantly to the temple of Amon at Karnak and built a hypostyle hall of cedar wood, decorated with copper, gold, and electrum to commemorate his own victories.

Further Reading: A. H. Gardiner. *Egypt of the Pharaohs* (Oxford: Clarendon Press, 1961).

Thutmose II   (r. 1492–1479 B.C.)

Unlike the reigns of either his father, THUTMOSE I, or his son, THUTMOSE III, the 13 years Thutmose II occupied the Egyptian throne were largely uneventful.

Other than that he led a campaign to Nubia to suppress hostile elements there and possibly sent an expedition to Palestine, little is known about the reign and achievements of Thutmose II. He married his half-sister, HATSHEPSUT, who held more power during the royal service of her nephew, Thutmose III, than during her own husband's rule. Indeed, perhaps the most important aspect of Thutmose II's career is that he appointed Hatshepsut regent over his young son.

Further Reading: A. H. Gardiner. *Egypt of the Pharaohs* (Oxford: Clarendon Press, 1961).

Thutmose III (r. 1479–1425 B.C.)

Thutmose III, pharaoh of the 18th Dynasty, has been called the greatest of all ancient Egyptian rulers.

Thutmose III, the son of THUTMOSE II and a lesser wife named Isis, shared the throne with his aunt and regent, HATSHEPSUT, for several years during his minority. During much of this period, Hatshepsut actually took on the role of pharaoh, and, under her, Egypt lost control of many of its foreign dependencies, the empire shrinking from the extent achieved in the days of Thutmose I, who had expanded Egypt's borders far south into Nubia and eastward as far as the Euphrates River.

When Thutmose became sole ruler upon his aunt's death, he spent the next 20 years attempting to reclaim Egypt's lost territories in Syria and Palestine. Later in his reign, he also marched his army southward to Nubia and established a provincial capital near the Fourth Cataract.

Thutmose enlarged Egypt's army and, even more importantly, organized it into an effective fighting force without equal or precedent. Separate divisions of bowmen, spearmen, and axmen, along with an armored corps of chariots, instilled fear in any enemy it faced. A complex communications system was developed using a series of forts and garrisons distributed throughout the Levant.

Although Thutmose III appears to have accepted Hatshepsut's guiding hand during his early years as pharaoh, he eventually turned against her memory and ordered the destruction of all images of her in public places. This, however, was common practice among pharaohs and may therefore have indicated no extraordinary condemnation or repudiation of her policies.

In turn, Thutmose actively boasted of his own achievements, and records of his feats are recorded at the Temple of Amon at Karnak and other places. The two obelisks known today as Cleopatra's Needles were erected by him, as well as many other obelisks testifying to his fame.

As Thutmose sensed his death was near, he appointed his son, AMENHOTEP II, to rule with him as co-regent. The following year, Thutmose died and was buried in an elaborate tomb in the Valley of the Kings. His remains were discovered in 1889 and today lie in the Egyptian Museum in Cairo. The Egyptologist James Henry Breasted characterized Thutmose III as a "genius" who "rose from an obscure priestly office." Calling to mind "an Alexander

or a Napoleon," Breasted observed, Thutmose "built his first empire, and is thus the first character possessed of universal aspects, the first world-hero. From the fastnesses of Asia Minor, the marshes of the upper Euphrates, the islands of the sea, the swamps of Babylonia, the distant shores of Libya, the oases of the Sahara, the terraces of the Somali coast and the upper cataracts of the Nile, the princes of his time rendered their tribute to his greatness."

Further Reading: A. H. Gardiner. *Egypt of the Pharaohs* (Oxford: Clarendon Press, 1961).

Tiberius [Tiberius Caesar Augustus] (42 B.C.–A.D. 37)

Beginning as a competent and successful military commander and ruler, Tiberius ended his reign a paranoid and reclusive tyrant.

The son of a prominent Roman who had supported Marc Antony in the civil wars following the death of Julius CAESAR, Tiberius was born on November 16, 42 B.C. When AUGUSTUS finally defeated Marc Antony, Tiberius' family was forced to flee to Sicily until an amnesty was declared in 45 B.C. Augustus, infatuated with the beauty of Tiberius' mother, Livia, ordered the boy's father to divorce her so that he could marry her himself. Tiberius remained with his father until he died, and then was sent with his brother to live with their mother and the emperor.

With no clear law designating succession, Tiberius and his brother were both trained as potential heirs. Tiberius soon began to assume more responsibility simply because he was older. He received his first military command at the age of 22 and he was sent to Parthia, where he recovered several Roman standards that had been lost 33 years earlier in battle. This earned him much acclaim and popularity. Next, he was dispatched to Pannonia to pacify the region, a task he accomplished with such efficiency and regard for the welfare of his troops that he became a popular hero.

Tiberius' years of happiness came to an end when his younger, much-beloved brother, Drusus, died while campaigning in Germany. A heartbroken Tiberius escorted the body back to Rome, making the entire journey on foot. The next blow fell when Augustus compelled Tiberius to divorce Vipsania to become the third husband of his daughter Julia. Not only was Tiberius forced to leave the love of his life to marry a woman for whom he had no feelings, Julia came to him freighted with a reputation as a harlot. Tiberius requested a posting on the far frontier, away from Rome and his undesired wife.

Despite personal despair, Tiberius was at the height of popularity and power in Rome. Nevertheless, Augustus passed him over in naming his successor, choosing his three grandchildren instead. Distressed by this and everything else that had befallen him, Tiberius retired to the island of Rhodes, shutting himself off from Roman society. During this period of self-imposed exile, he became very bitter, reclusive, and wrathful—a perverse and unpleasant old man at the age of 36.

After all of Augustus' grandchildren had died or had been exiled, Tiberius was recalled to Rome in A.D. 4 and restored to his former place in Roman society, being named heir to the throne. In A.D. 9, he led a campaign against the Cheruscans along the Rhine frontier, avenging their destruction of three Roman legions. On August 19, A.D. 14, Augustus died, and Tiberius was named Roman emperor.

Tiberius consolidated his power immediately by executing the only possible remaining claimant from Augustus' family and holding the Praetorian Guard massed around Rome to intimidate the Senate. His greatest accomplishment was the stabilization of the treasury, cutting waste and poor spending and increasing revenues. In the course of his reign, Tiberius swelled Roman coffers by a factor of twenty. He was, however, as savage and repressive as any of the harshest emperors. In Rome, when it was alleged that four Jews had been involved in a robbery, Tiberius responded by deporting the entire Jewish population. The emperor also prided himself in responding to provincial insurrection with deliberate cruelty in order to deter further unrest.

His return to Rome and elevation to power had gained Tiberius brief respite from the depression and emotional instability to which he had succumbed on Rhodes. But he soon began to revert to his former bitter and reclusive behavior. In A.D. 15, he named Sejanus to head the Praetorian Guard, increasingly yielding the control of the government to him. By A.D. 23 Tiberius was emperor in name only.

Sejanus knew how to nurture Tiberius' mental illness—his paranoid fear of plots and revolts—in order to maintain himself in power. Prompted by Sejanus, Tiberius ordered executions for treason on a virtually daily basis. The bloodletting failed to quell Tiberius' delusions. Pursued by his private demons, he fled Rome in A.D. 27, taking refuge on the island of Capri, never to return. At this time, he was also afflicted with a grotesque disease, possibly a form of leprosy, that caused him to break out in pus-filled, malodorous, and excruciating lesions.

Afflicted in spirit and body, Tiberius nevertheless came to realize that he had created a monster in Sejanus. From Capri, he dispatched a letter to the Senate denouncing Sejanus and calling for his immediate execution. Backed by the Praetorian Guard and

the undiminished reputation of Tiberius, the order was carried out about A.D. 33. Indeed, in its zeal, the Senate did away not only with Sejanus, but with all suspected of having plotted with him.

As for Tiberius, his health continued to deteriorate. He cast about for an heir among the few who had managed to survive Sejanus' reign of terror. Gaius Julius Caesar Germanicus, better known as CALIGULA, was Augustus' great grandson through Julia, Tiberius' unfaithful wife. Tiberius regarded the young man as the least offensive among an unsavory lot, though, in naming Caligula his successor, he declared, "I am nursing a viper in Rome's bosom."

Tiberius, periodically insane, injured himself in a ceremonial game in A.D. 37. He lapsed into a coma, Caligula was summoned, and the Praetorian Guard declared their support for him. Caligula's succession was no sooner proclaimed than Tiberius rallied from his coma. Macro, commander of the Praetorian Guard, smothered the ailing emperor with his deathbed linen on March 16.

Further Reading: Robert Seager. *Tiberius* (Berkeley: University of California Press, 1972); Frank B. Marsh. *The Reign of Tiberius* (Cambridge: Heffer, 1959); Barbara M. Levick. *Tiberius the Politician* (London: Croom Helm, 1976).

Tiglath-pileser I   (r. ca. 1115–1077 B.C.)

Tiglath-pileser I, king of Assyria, conquered most of his kingdom's enemies—the nomadic Mushki, the tribes around Lake Van in Armenia, the mountaineers of the Zagros ranges, and the Aramaeans—and established a brutal and bloody pattern of Assyrian war making.

When Tiglath-pileser I came to power as king of Assyria in about 1115 B.C., his kingdom was surrounded by enemies. He first conquered an Anatolian horde, the Mushki, who were threatening the city of Nineveh and Assyria's trade routes with Asia Minor. Next, he repelled the tribes ravaging the region around Lake Van in Armenia and the mountain nomads in the Zagros ranges. Marching across Syria to the Mediterranean coast, Tiglath-pileser I secured tribute from several Phoenician cities, pushed the Aramaeans, Semitic nomads, back across the Euphrates River, and captured Babylon.

Tiglath-pileser I controlled territory vaster than that of any of his Assyrian predecessors, and he ruled his far-flung domain through terror, rather than by establishing a strong bureaucracy. His army's brutality and reliance on torture, recorded in Assyrian inscriptions of the period, came to be the standard style of battle and conquest for all future Assyrian kings. The shortcoming of this method became apparent when Tiglath-pileser I died about

1077 B.C. The peoples he had conquered rose in revolt, dismantling the great realm he had created.

Further Reading: Samuel Noah Kramer and the editors of Time-Life Books. *Cradle of civilization* (New York: Time, Inc., 1967); Joan Oates. *Babylon* (London: Thames and Hudson, 1979).

Tiglath-pileser III   (r. 744–727 B.C.)

Assyrian king Tiglath-pileser III returned Assyria to its former pre-eminence in the Middle East, established an imperial government that would last a hundred years, and made far-reaching conquests, including Babylonia, Syria, and Palestine.

In 745 B.C., two sons of Adad-nirari III were locked in a power struggle that resulted in Tiglath-pileser III's assuming the Assyrian throne. The former governor of Calah, Tiglath-pileser was a masterful administrator who knew how to use governors effectively. He divided among strong and loyal governors the larger Assyrian provinces, which had been vying for independence. In outlying regions, he installed Assyrian officials directly accountable to him. By 738 B.C., Assyrian government had come to include some 80 provinces.

During Tiglath-pileser's reign, the Assyrian army drastically changed in character. Previously, it had been composed of Assyrian peasants called to military service during time of crisis and released once the crisis abated. Tiglath-pileser now created a standing army composed primarily of Assyrians, but significantly supplemented by foreign mercenaries and troops of vassal states.

With his empire thus reorganized and a strong standing army in place, Tiglath-pileser then set out to conquer his surrounding enemies. First he struck against Zamua, then the Medes and the Puqudu, northeast of Baghdad. These regions he annexed to Assyrian provinces. To maintain control, Tiglath-pileser instituted a policy of mass relocation. In cases where the king had reason to doubt their loyalty, the residents of defeated regions were resettled elsewhere. Between 742 and 741, tens of thousands of conquered people were relocated.

In 743, Tiglath-pileser attacked and defeated Urartu and its allies, the neo-Hittites and Aramaeans. For three years, he laid siege to the city of Arpad, which ultimately fell in 741. With the defeat of Arpad, Tiglath-pileser was able to command tribute from Damascus, Tyre, Cilicia, and other important cities.

During the 730s, the Assyrian king conquered Syria and Palestine, and ousted the Chaldean chief Ukin-zer, who had seized the Babylonian throne in 734. In 729 or 728, Tiglath-pileser claimed the throne himself, becoming King Pulu, or Pul, of Babylon. He died shortly afterwards.

Further Reading: J. D. Hawkins. "The Neo-Hittite States in Syria and Anatolia," in John Boardman et al., eds. *The Cambridge Ancient History*, 2nd ed., vol. 3, part 1 (New York: Macmillan, 1924–53).

Tigranes   (ca. 140–55 B.C.)

This long-lived and very able tyrant built Armenia into the most powerful kingdom of western Asia.

Tigranes' origins are somewhat obscure. Through Artavasdes, who was either his uncle or his father, he was part of the Artaxiad dynastic line founded by Artaxias I. In his youth, he was taken hostage by the Parthian monarch Mithridates II, to whom he was forced to cede territories corresponding to present-day central Iran in exchange for his freedom. After assuming the throne in 95 or 94 B.C., Tigranes set about augmenting his kingdom.

He began by attacking and deposing the ruler of Sophene (Diyarbakir region), annexing his kingdom in 93. He allied himself with the Pontine monarch MITHRIDATES VI EUPATOR by marrying his daughter Cleopatra (not to be confused with her far more famous namesake, who lived 69–30 B.C.). Thus allied, he invaded Cappadocia (modern-day central Turkey), but was driven out by the forces of the Roman governor SULLA during 93–92. Although he next voiced his support for his Pontine ally's first war against Rome during 89–84, he did not send troops, but instead waged his own war against Parthia, which was reeling after the death of Tigranes' former captor, Mithridates II.

From 88 to 84 B.C., Tigranes conquered much of Media, northern Mesopotamia, and Atropatene (modern Azerbaijan, Iran). He also dominated Gordyene, Adiabene, and Osroene. In 83, he invaded Syria, defeating the Seleucids.

With the death of the Roman governor Sulla, Tigranes again moved against Cappadocia, this time successfully, occupying much of it by 78. He staged a second Syrian invasion, then raided Cilicia (in modern southern Turkey), destroying Soli, a city near Tarsus. Emboldened by success after success, Tigranes moved against Cleopatra Selene of Egypt.

In conjunction with his military triumphs, Tigranes set about reshaping the realms he now dominated. He began by building a new capital city, Tigranocerta, east of the Tigris River. He transplanted a large Greek population to Armenia and moved Arabs into Mesopotamia in an effort to stabilize his conquests and consolidate his power. This did not go unnoticed by Rome, which feared an erosion of its influence. With a small army, Lucius Licinius Lucullus invaded Tigranes' kingdom and attacked the new capital. The Battle of Tigranocerta, fought on October 6, 69, resulted in the defeat of

Tigranes, whose forces, effective against any number of semibarbarian peoples, were no match for Roman soldiers. Lucullus attacked next at Artaxata in September of 68, defeating Tigranes again, but then was recalled to Rome.

Tigranes and his ally Mithridates VI, duly chastened, welcomed the respite. But Tigranes' hotheaded son, also called Tigranes, rebelled against his father. The son fled to Parthia, then returned with an army of Parthians in 67, intending to resist the Romans. Tigranes the elder offered a bounty for the death or capture of his own son, then surrendered to the forces of Gnaeus POMPEY when he invaded Armenia in 66.

Having secured control of Armenia, Pompey acted with great moderation, permitting the now-aged Tigranes senior to remain on the throne. Pompey sent the younger Tigranes to Rome, where he was out of harm's way and could do no harm himself. When Tigranes senior died 10 years later, another son, Artavasdes, was permitted to inherit the Armenian throne.

Timoleon   (d. ca. 337 B.C.)

Timoleon was a Corinthian Greek who liberated Syracuse from military dictatorship.

Timoleon's first recorded deed is his assassination, around 365 B.C., of a favorite brother who would not support his despotism. His activities for the next 20 years are obscure, but in 345 B.C., the citizens of Syracuse called upon him to rescue them from a reign of terror under the administration of Dionysius the Younger. Compounding the Syracusans' plight was the fact that a Carthaginian fleet was sailing to Sicily, intent on exploiting the city's weakness under Dionysius.

Timoleon slyly maneuvered his ships around the Carthaginians, who were lying in the harbor awaiting him. In a decisive offensive—the details of which are not recorded—the Corinthians defeated both the Carthaginians and Dionysius.

After his triumph, Timoleon began a campaign to purge Sicily of its tyrants. Next, he opened the country to immigrants from mainland Greece and Italy. Timoleon fought a second battle against the Carthagian army in about 341 B.C., which resulted in another overwhelming victory and an enduring peace with Carthage.

As Timoleon grew older, his eyesight failed, but he lived out his years in retirement in Syracuse, where he died.

Further Reading: R. J. A. Talbert. *Timoleon and the Revival of Greek Sicily* (London: Cambridge University Press, 1974).

Tisza, István   (1861–1918)

As prime minister of Hungary before World War I, Tisza was a supporter of Austria-Hungary's dual monarchy and promoted alliance with Germany.

The son of a Magyar minister president, István Tisza was born in Budapest on April 22, 1861, and, like his father, embarked on a career in politics. Tisza entered the Hungarian Parliament in 1886 as a member of the Liberal Party, shortly becoming head of the party, which supported the dual monarchy of Austria-Hungary. When liberals gained majority power in 1903, Tisza was named prime minister, but was severely defeated, with the rest of his party, in the subsequent 1905 elections.

Following the defeat of the Liberals, Tisza dissolved that party and formed the Party of Work in 1910. Despite the name, which suggests a party of the laboring man, Tisza's platform was one of Magyar chauvinism and staunch defense of the landed gentry. He was elected president of the lower house in 1912 and returned as prime minister in June 1913.

When Serbian radicals assassinated the Austro-Hungarian archduke Francis Ferdinand in July 1914, Tisza opposed declaring war on Serbia because he believed that, by annexing the country, the resulting influx of Serbian Slavs would endanger the dualist system. He supported Austria-Hungary's entry into the war only after securing guarantees that Serbia would not be annexed.

Tisza ruled Hungary sternly during World War I, virulently opposing any attempts at federalizing Austria-Hungary, which, he believed, would diminish Hungary's importance. When Austro-Hungarian emperor FRANCIS JOSEPH died in 1916, Tisza refused to approve the attempt of the new emperor, Charles I, to broaden voting rights and resigned in protest in June 1917. He was then commissioned in the military and took a command on the Italian front, only to return to Hungary at war's end to try to establish a new union with Austria to replace dualism, which was now hopelessly defeated.

The Peace of Paris—sometimes called the "Peace to end all peace"—which ended the war, was exceedingly harsh on Hungary. The public blamed Tisza for Hungary's suffering during and after the war. During the rioting that accompanied Hungary's declaration of independence, István Tisza was murdered by a mob on October 31, 1918.

Tito   [Josip Broz] (1892–1980)

The first Communist national leader openly to defy the Soviet Union, Tito brought Yugoslavia out of the ashes of World War II and led it as absolute dictator for five decades.

Born Josip Broz on May 7, 1892 in Kumrovec, near Zagreb, Tito was one of 15 children of a peasant family. At the age of 13, he moved to the town of Sisak to become a locksmith's apprentice, after which he traveled about central Europe as a metalworker. Broz joined the metalworkers trade union, which led him to membership in the Social Democratic Party of Croatia.

The outbreak of World War I in 1914 interrupted his Socialist activism, and he enlisted in the 25th Regiment of Zagreb, which marched against the Serbs in August 1914. Broz was accused of disseminating antiwar propaganda and was imprisoned, only to be released in January 1915 after the charges were dropped. He was sent back to his regiment on the Carpathian front and was decorated for bravery. The 25th was then transferred to the Bukovina front, where it saw heavy action. Broz was severely wounded in hand-to-hand combat and taken prisoner by the Russians.

Broz was laboring as a prisoner of war in the Ural Mountains when the Bolshevik Revolution took place in 1917. He made his way to Siberia, where he sided with the Bolsheviks and fought in the Red Guard during the Russian Civil War. Finally returning home again in 1920, Tito now considered himself a Communist—albeit a moderate in the degree of his convictions.

He joined the Communist Party of Yugoslavia (CPY) and was promptly arrested in 1923, tried, and acquitted. He began working in a shipyard in Croatia, but was arrested again in 1925 and sentenced to seven months' probation. Government harassment only strengthened his resolve, and he now began a climb in the Communist hierarchy, gaining membership in the Zagreb Committee of the CPY in 1927, and in 1928 becoming deputy of the Politburo of the Central Committee of the CPY, as well as secretary general of the Croatian and Slavonian committees. In August 1928, he was again arrested. Declaring that the tribunal had no right to judge him, Broz was sentenced to five years' imprisonment.

After his release in 1934, Broz traveled throughout Europe on behalf of the party. For reasons of security on these trips, he adopted the codename Tito, which he would use thereafter. Returning to Moscow in 1935, Tito worked in the Balkan section of the Comintern, the organization of international communism. In August 1936, Tito was named organizational secretary of the CPY Politburo.

In 1937, JOSEF STALIN began his infamous purges, and prominent Yugoslav Communists were among the first to be "liquidated." Some 800 Yugoslavs disappeared in the Soviet Union, and only a high-rank-ing Comintern official saved the CPY from total dissolution. Tito not only escaped the purge, but by the end of 1937, he was named secretary general by the Executive Council of the Comintern. He returned to Yugoslavia to reorganize the Communist Party and was formally named secretary general of the CPY in October 1940.

The international Communist movement was stunned when Stalin concluded a nonaggression pact with Adolf Hitler's Germany, betraying communism's unshakable opposition to fascism. Yugoslavia itself was officially neutral in the war that had just begun. But when the pro-Axis leader Prince Paul was overthrown in a coup, Hitler promptly invaded Yugoslavia in reprisal. Even under German occupation, the Yugoslavs at first remained passive. This changed dramatically in June 1941, after Hitler launched Operation Barbarossa and, in violation of the nonaggression pact, invaded the Soviet Union.

Tito now led his followers in a well-coordinated campaign of sabotage and resistance against the occupying Germans. His movement was so successful that, in the summer of 1942, he was able to organize an offensive into Bosnia and Croatia, forcing the Germans to commit substantial numbers of troops to stop the partisans. Despite the counteroffensive, the partisans held their own, and by December 1943, Tito announced a provisional government in Yugoslavia, with himself as president, secretary of defense, and marshal of the armed forces.

With the defeat of Nazi Germany in May 1945, Tito went about the business of establishing his government on a permanent basis. He formed a party oligarchy, the Politburo, and held Soviet-style elections in November. In the manner of Lenin and Stalin, he promulgated a five-year plan for economic recovery and development, and was greatly aided in these efforts by his universal popularity as a war hero and patriot.

It was these very qualities that Stalin feared and resented, especially as it became clear that Tito would not allow Yugoslavia to become a Soviet puppet. Tito's stance as a Yugoslav first and a Communist second—in bold defiance of Stalin—further enhanced the dictator's popularity. Indeed, the word *Titoism* was coined to describe the opposition by Communist satellites to Soviet domination.

Tito was a 20th-century example of what the 18th and 19th centuries would have called an "enlightened despot." His grip on Yugoslavia was absolute, yet, within a framework of totalitarianism, he granted considerable constitutional leeway. He was a Communist, yet he refused to align his nation with the Soviet bloc, and he permitted a substantial degree of free enterprise that made Yugoslavia one of the richest of eastern European nations. Moreover, he brought three decades of stability to a country traditionally racked by violence, dissension and civil war.

When Tito died on May 4, 1980, three days shy of his 88th birthday, he was a living legend in Yugoslavia and around the world. His opposition to Stalin and the mother Soviet state made him more appealing to the democratic West. His longevity allowed him to travel throughout eastern Europe and Asia speaking on communism and Titoism to nonaligned countries and his firsthand observations of some of the most important events in the history of the world.

Further Reading: Phyllis Auty. *Tito* (New York: McGraw Hill, 1970); Henry M. Christian, ed. *The Essential Tito*, (New York: St. Martin's, 1970); Ernst Halperin. *The Triumphant Heretic* (London: Heinemann, 1958).

Titus [Titus Flavius Vespasianus] (39–81)

Titus, an early emperor of Rome, brutally suppressed the revolt of the Jews in Judaea and was responsible for the construction of the Colosseum in Rome.

Titus, born on September 30, 39, was the son of the emperor VESPASIAN. As a young man, he served with the legions in Britain and Germany, and then as legion commander in Judaea, where he brutally put down the Jewish revolt begun in 69. The following year, after a siege of four months, his legionnaires occupied Jerusalem and destroyed the temple there.

The victory over the Jews made Titus an extremely popular figure, who was practically idolized by his father's constituents. Vespasian showed no jealousy and declared, "Either my son shall be my successor, or no one at all." By 70, the year of Titus' victory in Judaea, Vespasian made his son joint consul, and in 71, Titus was declared emperor-designate.

When Titus ascended the throne in 79, on the death of Vespasian, he set about liberalizing his image in an attempt to mitigate his reputation for ruthlessness. Fate gave him very little time to accomplish this rehabilitation, however, since he died after serving as emperor for only two years.

Titus' brief administration was marked by three momentous events. First, only one month after he had become emperor, the towns of Pompeii, Herculaneum, Stabiae, and Oplontis were devastated by the volcanic eruptions of Mount Vesuvius. Titus mobilized the empire's resources to assist the residents of these villages. Shortly after the eruption of Vesuvius, Rome itself was swept by a three-day conflagration that destroyed a great number of public buildings and private residences. Again, Titus was quick to render aid to the afflicted. Finally, a massive epidemic of plague broke out, killing thousands of Romans, and again Titus responded with aid.

Brief though his reign was, Titus showed himself to be an ambitious, progressive, and well-respected emperor.

Further Reading: Michael Grant. *The Roman Emperors: A Biographical Guide to the Rulers of Imperial Rome 31 B.C–A.D. 476* (New York: Viking, 1985).

Tojo Hideki (1884–1948)

Tojo was Japan's prime minister and military leader during World War II.

It is safe to say that, during the period of World War II, the only man the people of the Allied nations hated as much as Adolf HITLER was Tojo Hideki. Yet Hitler was a genuine—if evil—political leader, while Tojo was little more than the bureaucratic head of a military regime that dominated Japanese government. Tojo was not famed among his countrymen as a popular leader, but was celebrated by his fellow bureaucrats as "The Razor"—a hyper-efficient administrator who knew how to get things done.

Tojo was born on December 30, 1884, in Iwate prefecture. His was a traditional military (samurai) family—his father, Tojo Eikyo, was a general—and it was a foregone conclusion that Hideki would attend the military academy (graduated 1905) and pursue a career in the army.

Most of Tojo's career was distinguished, but hardly glorious. His only combat experience came in August 1937, when he directed operations against the Chinese in Chahar (vicinity of Ch'ang-chia-Kou [Kalgan]). Prior to this, he held regimental staff assignments from 1905 to 1909. He graduated from the Army Staff College in 1915 and served in Berlin as assistant military attaché from 1919 to 1921. During this period he attained the rank of major, becoming a resident officer in Germany from 1921 to 1922. Tojo's diplomatic service brought him into the inner circles of government, and he soon became involved with military efforts to take control of national policy and administration. Promoted to lieutenant colonel in 1924, Tojo became chief of the army ministry's important Mobilization Plans Bureau, a position that put him at the heart of Japan's war preparations.

After being promoted to full colonel in 1929, Tojo was given regimental command, then made chief of the Organization and Mobilization Section of the Army General Staff. He served in this capacity from 1931 to 1933, when he was promoted to major general and made deputy commandant of the military academy.

Tojo continued his orderly rise in the military hierarchy when he was given command of an infantry brigade in 1934–35, then of the Kwantung (Guandong) Army Gendarmerie, a post in which military leaders of the highest rank were traditionally groomed. He held this position until 1937, gaining promotion to lieutenant general in 1936. From 1937 to 1938, he was chief of staff of the Kwantung Army.

Following his experience in China, Tojo became vice minister of the army and chief of Army Air Headquarters on the eve of World War II (1938–41). During this period, Tojo emerged as a leading spokesman for the most aggressive, pro-Axis faction of the army, which was coming increasingly to dominate the government. Promoted to general in 1941, he was named prime minister. Even members of the government who objected to military domination approved Tojo's selection because they felt that failure to give him the post would result in an outright military coup.

Tojo established a hard line in international and military affairs, propelling his nation into war and steadily expanding the scope of that war. During 1941 to 1944, he was often given wide-ranging dictatorial powers in foreign as well as domestic affairs. For most of the war, Prime Minister Tojo was also chief of the Army General Staff. In this capacity, he directed military operations with ruthless but indifferent skill, failing to develop a long-term strategy. After Saipan fell to Allied forces on July 12, 1944, a coalition of Japanese statesmen exerted their influence to force Tojo's removal as military head. Shaken by his country's rapidly deteriorating military situation, Tojo bowed to the coalition's wishes without a struggle. He attempted suicide after the surrender of Japan in 1945, but failed, and was taken into custody by Allied forces. A tribunal convicted him as a war criminal, and he was hanged in 1948.

Tokhtamysh   (r. ca. 1376–ca. 1395)

Tokhtamysh, was the last great ruler of the Golden Horde, the Mongol khanate that dominated eastern Russia and Europe, before its gradual demise and partition into the separate khanates of Crimea and Kazan.

Tokhtamysh, a vassal and protégé of the great Mongol ruler TAMERLANE, was khan of the Golden Horde when it was defeated by the Muscovites at Kulikovo Polye in 1380. Two years later, the Mongols defeated the Muscovites, but by this time, the power of the Golden Horde was in rapid decline, and its people were gradually being assimilated into the modern state of Russia.

Tokhtamysh then invaded Caucasia and set about ravaging Transoxiana. In 1391, his mentor Tamerlane turned his attention from campaigning in Iran to defeat Tokhtamysh on the Kandurcha near the Ural Mountains. Tokhtamysh forged alliances with Vytautas of Lithuania and Vassili of Moscow against Tamerlane, who, however, utterly crushed his army when Tokhtamysh again attacked Caucasia in 1394–95. These military operations drained the resources of the Golden Horde, and a rival ruler, Edigü, proclaiming himself Tamerlane's vassal, displaced Tokhtamysh. The once-defiant khan was killed as a fugitive by a local ruler named Shadibeg.

Tokugawa Ieyasu [Tokugawa Takechiyo] (1543–1616)

Founder of the last shogunate (military dictatorship) of Japan, Tokugawa Ieyasu brought a new measure of unity to the warlord-ravaged country.

Born in Okazaki to a family of the feudal warrior class on January 31, 1543, Tokugawa Ieyasu spent much of his early life as a hostage in service to the Imagawa family in Sumpu. Trained in the military and governmental arts, he led his first military expedition in the late 1550s.

When Imagawa was killed in battle in 1560, Ieyasu returned to his father's lands, took control of the family castle and vassals, and allied himself with the powerful ODA NOBUNAGA. As the Imagawa domain disintegrated under weak leadership, Ieyasu moved toward the east, taking land bit by bit. By the early 1580s, he had become a powerful *daimyo* (feudal lord), with holdings stretching from Okazaki to the mountains at Hakone (the western region of Honshu island).

When Oda Nobunaga committed suicide after having been wounded by a rebellious vassal, TOYOTOMI HIDEYOSHI took control of the slain leader's holdings. Ieyasu became his primary rival, but, after a few minor battles, Ieyasu wisely allied himself with Hideyoshi. In 1589 the two joined forces in a successful battle against Hojo Ujimasa, a powerful warlord of eastern Honshu island. Hideyoshi then forced Ieyasu to abandon his holdings west of the Hakone mountains and take instead the old Hojo domain. Ieyasu spent the next several months moving thousands of vassals, together with their equipment and households, to Edo (modern-day Tokyo).

Over the next several years, Ieyasu organized his holdings carefully. Trusted vassals were placed on lands closest to Edo; those whom Ieyasu suspected might cause trouble were placed on outlying lands. A large parcel of land near the town was put under the administration of Ieyasu's officials. The crops from this land were meant to support the town in times of siege. Ieyasu disarmed the surrounding villagers to forestall any future rebellion and spent much time attracting artisans and businessmen to Edo. By the end of the 16th century, he had under his command the largest army and the most productive lands in all of Japan.

Hideyoshi's death brought about an intense struggle among the *daimyo*. As the recognized head of one of the principal warring factions, Ieyasu led his army to battle at Sekigahara in 1600. His forces won, and Ieyasu became the undisputed leader of Japan. He reorganized the *daimyo* at large, much as he had reorganized his vassals in his own domain, with the object of neutralizing threats to his power. He placed allies in strategic positions near his enemies, and then adopted administrative procedures to keep the *daimyo* under control.

The imperial court was forced to confer on Ieyasu the title of shogun, or supreme military commander, in 1603. Two years later he retired, having secured the title for his third son Hidetada. Ieyasu spent his retirement years engaged in foreign affairs for the imperial court. Portuguese, Dutch, and English traders and Portuguese and Spanish missionaries sought his permission to operate in Japan. At first, he granted all such requests. By 1612, however, he decided that Western culture was becoming too influential and took steps to restrict Christian missionary activity and even foreign trade. Within a few years, most Western influence had vanished.

Ieyasu's "retirement" years were also a period of great construction activity. He directed the building of what was then the largest castle in the world. The Edo fortress included broad moats, huge stone walls and gatehouses, wooden parapets, and fireproof warehouses. Financed by his vassals, the castle was the center of a bustling mercantile city.

Despite his having secured the title of shogun for his successor, he still worried about threats to his family's power. Toyotomi Hideyoshi had left one son, headquartered at Osaka Castle. Gradually the young man gathered a contingent of warrior supporters, and in him Ieyasu recognized a potential adversary. In 1615, he decided to eliminate the threat, mobilizing his forces against the castle and destroying it with its inhabitants.

A year later, the founder of the Tokugawa Shogunate died, aged 73, in Sumpu. The period of Japanese history in which his shogunate prevailed is known as "The Great Peace." Scholars have attributed Ieyasu's success in establishing a shogunate not only to his military and administrative ability, but also to luck. He outlived his chief rivals—Oda Nobunaga and Toyotomi Hideyoshi—and was survived by more sons than they.

Further Reading: A. L. Sadler. *The Maker of Modern Japan: The Life of Tokugawa Ieyasu* (New York: AMS, 1977).

Torquemada, Tomás de (1420–1498)

The grand inquisitor of the Spanish Inquisition, Torquemada became known for his ruthless zeal in persecuting anyone suspected of being a non-Catholic.

Entering the Dominican order of friars at an early age, Tomás de Torquemada quickly earned a reputation for piety. In 1452, he was appointed prior of the Dominican monastery at Santa Cruz in Segovia, where he served until 1474. At Santa Cruz, he developed the belief that all Jews and Muslims, even those of both groups who had converted to Catholicism, threatened the political and spiritual integrity of Spain and its hopes for unification.

Torquemada's extreme religious beliefs and his great piety brought him to the attention of King FERDINAND V of Aragon and Queen ISABELLA I of Castile, who made him their chief adviser and confessor. It is unclear who influenced whom, but what is indisputable is that religious uniformity was seen as absolutely necessary to the effective unification of Spain. Torquemada was named grand inquisitor general of Spain in 1483 and quickly set up the bureaucracy needed for a nationwide persecution of all those whose faith was suspect.

Torquemada's most sweeping action was his administration of the expulsion of the Jews—160,000 to 170,000 people—from Spain in 1492. Ironically, Torquemada was of Jewish descent himself. He set up local tribunals to exact confessions and root out heresy. He created a set of 28 articles as a guide to help inquisitors root out blasphemy, heresy, adultery, apostasy, bigamy, and so on. He authorized torture—to and beyond the point of death—to exact such evidence. More than 2,000 people were burned at the stake in Torquemada's tenure as grand inquisitor.

His extreme methods, however, soon drew harsh criticism from all circles, including the Vatican. Pope ALEXANDER VI appointed four assistant inquisitors in June 1494 to restrain Torquemada. By the end of 1494, ill health forced him to retire from active duty, although he remained a leading figure in the Inquisition from his monastery at Avila, continuing to oversee the persecution until his death on September 16, 1498.

Torrijos (Herrera), Omar (1929–1981)

Panamanian dictator who negotiated the 1977 Panama Canal treaties with the United States, leading to Panama's assumption of control over the canal in 2000.

Omar Torrijos was born on February 13, 1929, in Santiago de Veragua, Panama, and was educated in military schools in El Salvador, the United States, and Venezuela. He was commissioned second lieutenant in 1952 in Panama's National Guard and quickly rose in the officer corps, becoming a colonel in 1968, the year in which he participated in the coup that overthrew President Anulfo Arias.

Within six months of the coup, Torrijos emerged as the real leader of the country, claiming for himself the title of "Maximum Leader of the Revolution" and, after promoting himself to the rank of brigadier general in 1969, commander of the National Guard. Subsequently, he officially became Chief of Government and Supreme Leader of the Panamanian Revolution, hand-picking puppets to serve him in the nominal office of president. Torrijos outlawed political parties, suspended constitutional rights, usurped the power traditionally held by urban elites, and strengthened the political position of provincial leaders. Opponents of his regime were imprisoned without trial, and the press was put under government control. Politically influential priests were forced into exile, and the University of Panama was closed while 3,000 students of questionable loyalty were purged.

Having gained absolute control of the government, Torrijos turned his attention to wresting control of the Panama Canal and the Canal Zone from the United States. Following extensive negotiations, American president Jimmy Carter and Torrijos signed treaties on September 7, 1977, calling for the gradual transfer of the canal and surrounding region to Panama to be completed by 2000.

Torrijos was killed on July 31, 1981, in an airplane crash near Penonomé while he was on a military tour of inspection. Some supporters suspected CIA involvement in the "accident," while others have ascribed it to the work of General Manuel NORIEGA, Torrijos' successor.

Further Reading: American University Foreign Area Studies. *Panama: A Country Study* (Washington, D.C.: American University Press, 1980).

Touré, Sekou [Ahmed] (1922–1984)

First president of the Republic of Guinea, Sekou Touré helped gain his nation's independence from French colonial rule in 1958 and governed until 1984.

A Muslim, born in Faranah, French Guinea, the grandson of SAMORI TOURÉ, 15-year-old Touré was expelled from the colonial trade school after organizing a food strike. Touré went to work for the post office in 1941 and, as general secretary of the postal workers' union, promptly organized the first successful strike in Guinea, which lasted 76 days. Touré's ability as a speaker and his skill at organization made him a natural leader.

In 1946, Touré joined the Rassemblement Démocratique Africain (RDA), a movement seeking independence for the colonies of French Africa. On two different occasions during 1951–54, he was elected—only to be denied—to a seat on the French National Assembly. In 1956, Touré was allowed his seat and the following year was elected vice president of the Executive Council of Guinea. A referendum on colonial self-rule initiated by French president Charles de Gaulle in 1958 inspired Touré to seek independence for Guinea, and he founded the Parti Démocratique de Guinée. His campaign was successful, and on October 2, 1958, Guinea became the first independent French-speaking state in Africa, with Touré as president.

Achieving independence was one thing, but maintaining the nation in the absence of the colonial dole and in the teeth of punitive diplomatic and economic isolation was another. Touré's Guinea was on the verge of economic collapse. He resorted to a series of Communist-bloc alliances and to a brutal domestic policy based on intimidation and the continual presence of terror. In 1971, Touré violently purged leading dissenters, securing his reelection and consolidating his power base. In subsequent elections, he ran unopposed.

Internationally, Touré was a member of the Organization of African Unity (OAU), and he also played a significant role in the Franco-African summit in Vitrell, France. He died on March 26, 1984, the unchallenged leader of Guinea.

Toussaint L'Ouverture [Toussaint-Louverture], François Dominique (ca. 1743–1803)

Born a slave in the French colony of Saint-Domingue, François Dominique Toussaint L'Ouverture led the only successful slave revolt in modern history and became governor-general for life of Haiti.

François Dominique Toussaint L'Ouverture was born François Dominique Toussaint Breda on the Breda plantation in northern Saint-Domingue (Haiti), the son of an educated slave. His intelligence and resourcefulness won him the favor of the manager of the plantation on which he worked, and he rose to the post of cattle steward, after which he was legally emancipated in 1777.

Having achieved a measure of success, Toussaint was uncommitted in August 1791, when a slave rebellion erupted in the northern province of the French island colony. Torn between loyalty to his former master and the cause of the slaves, he helped the plantation manager to escape, then joined the rebellion, which grew increasingly violent. Toussaint quickly realized that the indiscriminate killing, burning, and looting would only bring further repression. He gathered and trained a guerrilla slave army of his own in 1793, took the name L'Ouverture ("the Opening," signifying the opening of freedom for Haiti's slaves), then brilliantly capitalized on a war that had begun between France and Spain. He put his army in the service of Spain, and, after winning substantial victories against the French, was made a general and knighted.

The French Legislative Assembly had, meanwhile, sent Léger-Félicité Sonthonax (September 1792) to St.-Domingue as its commissioner. A product of the worst excesses of the French Revolution, Sonthonax was an atheist, who advocated extermination of all Europeans in St.-Domingue, believing they were all royalists or separatists. Sonthonax was ejected within a year, however, and replaced by Étienne Laveaux.

L'Ouverture's efforts, together with those of the Spanish forces and the British, who now occupied the main ports of the South and West provinces of St.-Domingue, brought the French to the verge of absolute defeat. But, suddenly, in May 1794, L'Ouverture threw in his allegiance to the French, citing France's decision in February to abolish slavery. His forces now turned brutally against his former Spanish allies, slaughtering them in large numbers. Following this, the Spanish evacuated Haiti, ceding their portion of the island (Santo Domingo) to France, and the British suffered severe reverses. Étienne Laveaux, the French commander, nominally stepped aside to make Toussaint governor. In truth, the two worked together until 1796, when Toussaint, who had systematically defied French authority all along, eased him out of office entirely. During the next two years, 1798–99, the former slave negotiated with British officials for their complete withdrawal from the island.

For a time, Toussaint L'Ouverture's Haiti enjoyed profitable trade with Britain and the United States, and the British even offered to recognize the leader as king. This Toussaint L'Ouverture scornfully declined, in part fearful that the British would return to the island and reinstitute slavery.

While Toussaint enjoyed much support and even adoration from his followers, the French persisted in efforts to oust him. The revolutionary Directory sent Gabriel Hédouville in 1798 to support an opposing leader, André Rigaud. Although Toussaint L'Ouverture drove Hédouville out of the country, brutal warfare resulted between Rigaud's mulatto supporters and forces led by Toussant L'Ouverture's second-in-command, Jean-Jacques Dessalines, resulting in the massacre of large numbers of mulattos and forever alienating that large faction from Toussaint L'Ouverture's government.

After gaining control of Saint-Domingue, Toussaint L'Ouverture turned against the slaveholding Spanish at Santo Domingo, overrunning that part of the island in January 1801. With this, he assumed authority over all of the island and promulgated a constitution that named him governor-general for life. Appropriating land abandoned by former colonial officials, he provided decent wages, medical care, and housing for agricultural workers, but he did not allow them to move about the island freely, reimposing forced labor.

By seizing control, Toussaint L'Ouverture had defied NAPOLÉON Bonaparte, at the time first consul of France. Yet the leader wavered in his stance toward Napoleon. He believed that the first consul would attempt to retake the colony and would reinstitute slavery in an effort to restore this French possession to profit France. Alternately defiant and almost worshipful of Napoléon, Toussaint L'Ouverture alienated many who had supported him. Worse, as his leadership faltered, the island was subjected to acts of atrocity perpetrated by one faction against another.

Napoléon exploited this atmosphere of disunity and unrest by sending forces under General Charles Leclerc to invade Haiti in November 1801. Toussaint L'Ouverture surrendered on May 5, 1802, and was taken to France where he was imprisoned at Fort-de-Joux. There he died on April 7, 1803.

Further Reading: John R. Beard. *The Life of Toussaint L'Ouverture* (Westport, Conn.: Greenwood Press, 1970).

Toyotomi Hideyoshi (1536/37–1598)

Imperial regent (1585) and chief minister of Japan from 1585 to 1598, Toyotomi Hideyoshi completed the unification of Japan begun by ODA NOBUNAGA.

Born in Nakamura, Owari Province (now part of Aichi Prefecture), to a peasant family, Hideyoshi became a masterful military strategist best known for his success in unifying the competing warlords of late medieval Japan, where civil war had raged for more than a hundred years. Early in his military career, he aligned himself with ODA NOBUNAGA, a *daimyo* (feudal lord) from Owari who captured one-third of Japan before his death in 1582. Following this, Hideyoshi continued his rise by consolidating his control of Nobunaga's followers and by undertaking military campaigns in various provinces. In 1586, in recognition of his power, the Japanese emperor awarded him the family name Toyotomi and appointed him chief minister.

Once Toyotomi Hideyoshi gained dominion of nearly all of Japan in 1590, he became head of an alliance of feudal lords.

Under his absolute rule were the *daimyo*, who numbered some 200 by the time of his death. Hideyoshi oversaw their ownership of land, regulated marriages among them, and dispensed discipline through their ranks. He exacted from the *daimyo* homage and military service. Lest they become too powerful, Hideyoshi promulgated *shiro wari* ("destruction of castles," a program to dismantle some of the *daimyo* fortifications). Hideyoshi's absolute control extended beyond the *daimyo* to the farmers, the merchants, and the monks, classes he effectively disarmed through the *katana kari* ("sword hunting," a law prohibiting such persons the use of arms). Likewise, his power over the military classes was very great. Instituting a monumentally repressive caste system (*shi-nō-kō-shō*) that forbade warriors, farmers, artisans and tradesmen from changing station or residence, Hideyoshi attempted to eliminate once and for all every possible source of disorder in Japanese society. He also outlawed piracy and instituted a policy of persecuting Japan's Christian minority for fear that foreign influence would lead to disunity.

During his later years, Hideyoshi turned his attention abroad, to Korea, which he invaded twice in preparation for a planned attack on China. At his death in 1598, he was deified and given the title Hokoku Daimyojim, meaning "Most Bright God of the Bountiful Country."

Further Reading: Walter Dening. *The Life of Toyotomi Hideyoshi*, 3d. ed. (Kobe, Japan: J. L. Thompson, 1930).

Trajan   [Marcus Ulpius Traianus] (53–117)

Under Trajan, the Roman Empire reached its greatest extent, and, after his death, began its 1,300-year decline.

One of the greatest martial emperors of Rome, Trajan was born not in Italy, but in Spain, in Italica, a town near present-day Seville. His father was an able general in the Roman army, and Trajan served as a military tribune from 78 to 88, sometimes under the command of his father in Syria. In 88, Emperor DOMITIAN gave him a legion to command in Spain, then quickly summoned him with it to Germany to fight Antonius Saturninus during 88–89. His success earned him a consulship in 91, and in 96 he was made governor of Upper Germany by the emperor Nerva, who had succeeded to the throne after the assassination of Domitian.

Nerva, as ineffectual a ruler as Domitian had been tyrannical, was despised by his own Praetorian Guard, who mutinied against him in 97. On October 27, to stave off outright revolt, the emperor named as his successor Trajan, by now enormously popular

Portrait bust of the emperor Trajan (From Richard Delbruck, Antike Portrats, 1912)

with the military. Nerva died late in January 98, but Trajan delayed coming to Rome to assume the purple until he had completed an inspection tour of the Rhine and Danube frontiers.

Trajan's first major military expedition was against Decabulus, ruler of the Dacians, a warlike tribe who lived in the area corresponding to modern Hungary and Romania. The Dacians had long terrorized their neighbors by extorting tribute payments, and in 101–102 Trajan defeated them, but, shortly afterward, Decabulus rebelled, sending raiding parties into Moesia (northern Bulgaria). Trajan pushed these forces out of Moesia and, after a difficult campaign spanning 105–106, took the Dacian capital of Sarmizgetusa. He annexed Dacia to the empire in 107, and Decabulus committed suicide.

Even while he was prosecuting the Dacian campaigns, Trajan moved his forces into Arabia Petraea—the Sinai, Negev, and part of Jordan—in 106, taking the capital city of Petra and annexing the region to the empire. Chosroes of Parthia, a region roughly corresponding to modern Iran, put a puppet ruler on the throne of Armenia in 113. Trajan responded by invading Armenia as well as Mesopotamia during 113–114, then captured the Parthian capital city of Ctesiphon, whence he sailed down the

Tigris River to the Persian Gulf during 114–115. Having lost much of his territory, Chosroes raised a new army and staged a vigorous counterattack that drove Roman occupying forces out of northern Mesopotamia. Trajan responded with equal vigor in 116, pushing Chosroes out of the region.

At this triumphal juncture, however, the emperor fell ill. Early in 117, he designated Publius Aelius Hadrianus—HADRIAN—as his successor, and he embarked on a desperate journey back to Rome. His condition worsened, however, and Trajan died at Selinus in Cilicia (part of modern Turkey) on August 8, 117. Almost immediately, the greatly enlarged empire began to shrink, as Hadrian relinquished the hard-won Mesopotamian and Assyrian conquests to Parthia. Whereas Trajan had begun his reign by subduing the barbarian tribes that demanded tribute, Hadrian initiated a policy of appeasement, which resulted in further reductions of the empire. The 20-year reign of Trajan was indeed the highwater mark of the Roman Empire.

Trujillo Molina, Rafael Leónidas (1891–1961)

Rafael Trujillo was dictator of the Dominican Republic from 1930 until his assassination in 1961.

Born on October 24, 1891, to a lower middle-class family in San Cristóbal, Dominican Republic, Rafael Trujillo received little formal education and made his living as a small-time thief and telegraph operator before he entered the army of the Dominican Republic in 1918 during the U.S. occupation of the country (1916–1924). He received training from the U.S. Marines, and by 1925 was commanding colonel of the national police and by 1927 was promoted to commanding general of the army.

In 1930, General Trujillo overthrew the government of President Horacio Vasquez. From this point until his assassination in 1961, Trujillo was in absolute control of the country. He commanded the army, placed family members in key political office, and did not scruple to kill many of his political opponents. He held the title of president himself from 1930 to 1938 and from 1942 to 1952, but even when he was not formally in office, his puppets were. One title he never relinquished was "The Benefactor"—meant, of course, to define his role with regard to the nation, but in actuality a far more accurate description of the service he performed for his family, who soon had a stranglehold on the economy of the Dominican Republic.

While the Dominican people did enjoy a measure of increased prosperity and stability under "The Benefactor's" rule, they also suffered a loss of civil rights and liberties. Haitian migrants became the tar-

get of a 1937 massacre that killed some 20,000 agricultural laborers who had drifted across the border into the Dominican Republic looking for work in the sugar cane fields.

During the Trujillo years, only one political party, the Partido Dominicano, was allowed to exist, and Trujillo himself handpicked the legislators in congress. Several secret police units, reporting directly to the dictator, were dispatched throughout the country to suppress dissident political activity. The press was also completely under government control.

On May 31, 1961, Trujillo was assassinated by a cabal of soldiers and civilians who were backed by the American Central Intelligence Agency. Ramfis, Trujillo's eldest son, took control of the country for a brief period before fleeing into exile along with other family members, who took with them a collective fortune of some $500 million.

Further Reading: Robert D. Crassweiler. *Trujillo: The Life and Times of a Caribbean Dictator* (New York: Macmillan, 1966).

Ts'ao Ts'ao (155–220)

Chief minister to the last ruler of the Han dynasty and, in effect, founder of the Wei dynasty, Ts'ao was a military and political master who saved North China during the fall of the Han dynasty.

Ts'ao Ts'ao, son of the adopted son of a eunuch in the imperial court, came of age amid the disintegration of the Han dynasty. In 184, Ts'ao, a successful general, suppressed the Yellow Turban Rebellion that would serve as a prototype for Chinese revolt for the next two centuries. Ts'ao now rose rapidly in the imperial court. When Tung Cho seized the emperor and burned the capital around 190, Ts'ao fled to the countryside to raise an army and save the Han dynasty from extinction.

For the next 20 years, Ts'ao was engaged in one of the bloodiest civil wars in Chinese history. In 200, he met Yuan Shao at the Battle of Kuan-tu, defeating him and the Yuan family. All of China now was awash in blood, with the country divided in three sections under three competing generals. After defeating another powerful general in the region, Ts'ao came to control the most strategic region, the north.

Failing to expand his control beyond the north, Ts'ao spent the rest of his life consolidating his power in that region. He was named prime minister in 208 and Prince of Wei in 216, but he never actually took the imperial title. When he died on March 15, 220, it was his son Ts'ao P'i who officially proclaimed the Wei dynasty and took the title of emperor.

Further Reading: Rafe de Crespigny. *The Last of the Han* (Canberra, Australia: Australian National University, 1969).

Tshombe(-Kapenda), Moise   (1919–1969)

Tshombe led the secession of Katanga from the Congo, was exiled, then brought back as prime minister of the Congo Republic (present-day Zaire), only to be exiled again.

Born into a wealthy family on November 10, 1919, Moise Tshombe was educated by American Methodists before he went into business with his father. He proved a most inept manager and had to be bailed out repeatedly after his father's death in 1951. Because of his family's wealth, Tshombe was appointed to the advisory Katanga Provincial Council, but his term there was undistinguished.

In 1958, however, he became chairman of the Lunda tribal association, which helped form CONAKAT, the Confederation of Tribal Associations of Katanga. Many African nationalists withdrew from CONAKAT after it accepted a political program heavily influenced by Belgian mining interests, and Tshombe assumed the leadership. Tshombe now sought to utilize CONAKAT as a tool to achieve Katangan independence while still maintaining close ties to economically powerful Belgium. This put Tshombe and CONAKAT in opposition to other African nationalist forces, most notably the nationalist movement led by Patrice Lumumba.

In 1960, the Belgians called a conference to discuss independence for the Congo. There, Tshombe presented his plan for a loose federation of semi-autonomous provinces, such as Katanga. This plan was rejected in favor of a strong centralized Congolese state. In the May 1960 elections, CONAKAT won only 8 of the 137 seats in the parliament, but the party received a plurality in the Katanga Provincial Assembly, and Tshombe became president of the province. Two weeks after Congolese independence, the national militia mutinied, and Tshombe used this as a pretext to declare Katanga independent of the Congo on July 11, 1960.

When the Congolese prime minister, Patrice Lumumba, tried to end the secession by force, he was ousted by President Joseph Kasavubu. Lumumba was later abducted and murdered in Katanga; the extent of Tshombe's complicity in this action has never been determined. Negotiations to rejoin Katanga to the Congolese republic failed, it was only through the intervention of the United Nations, led by the United States, that the province was brought back into the Congo in January 1963. Following this, in June, Tshombe fled the Congo for Spain.

Kasavubu recalled Tshombe in 1964 to put down a revolt in the eastern Congo, and named him prime minister of the republic. Tshombe, heavily criticized for using white mercenaries in his suppression of the rebellion, was dismissed in 1965. He again returned to Spain, living there until 1967 when rumors circulated that he was about to return to the Congo to seize power. He was kidnapped and taken to Algeria. The new Congolese president, Joseph Mobutu, demanded his extradition to stand trial for treason. Algerian officials refused, and, on June 29, 1969, Tshombe, still under house arrest, died, reportedly of either a heart attack or a stroke.

Further Reading: Anthony T. Bouscaren. *Tshombe* (New York: Twin Circle, 1967); Ian Colvin. *The Rise and Fall of Moise Tshombe: A Biography* (London: Frewin, 1968).

Tz'u-hsi   [Yehonala] (1835–1908)

Tz'u-hsi was one of the most powerful women in the history of China, serving as regent for two emperors and thereby essentially controlling the nation for over 60 years.

A low-ranking concubine to emperor Hsien-feng, Tz'u-hsi bore the emperor his only surviving son, who succeeded to the throne in 1835 upon the emperor's death. The boy, T'ung-chih, was only five at the time of the emperor's death, and Tz'u-hsi managed to get control of the regency with the help of T'zu-an, consort of Hsien-feng, and Prince Kung, Hsien-feng's brother.

With the conservative Tz'u-hsi at the helm, the government was mildly revitalized. Tz'u-hsi harshly suppressed the Taiping Rebellion in 1864 and the Nien Rebellion in 1868. Schools were created, customs services were instituted, and an effort was made to end the rampant corruption in the government. The young T'ung-chih was never consulted about any of these decisions until he reached his majority in 1873. Even then, Tz'u-hsi continued to exercise great influence over the government. In any case, T'ung died only two years after coming of age, and Tz'u once again assumed full control of the government.

Tz'u-hsi flagrantly violated the succession laws by having her three-year-old nephew, who was of the same generation as T'ung, named emperor. This would allow her to continue as regent for many more years. When Tz'u-an died in 1881, Tz'u was the sole regent, and within three years she had forced out Prince Kung as well, effectively coming to rule all of China in her own right.

In 1889, Tz'u-hsi relinquished a degree of her power and retired to a summer palace she had built with funds intended for the modernization of the Chinese navy. Her retirement ended when the Chinese were severely defeated in the Sino-Japanese War of 1894–95, and, in the wake of defeat, radical reforms were being pushed through the government by emperor Kuang-hsu in an effort to modernize— and Westernize—China. Tz'u gathered the conservative elements and engineered a coup with the help of the military. The emperor was placed under house arrest in his palace, and Tz'u-hsi again became sole regent of China.

When foreign troops arrived in 1900 to crush the Boxer Rebellion, Tz'u-hsi, who had encouraged the rebellion by her efforts to eradicate foreign influences in China, fled Beijing and ultimately agreed to the humiliating peace treaty of 1902. The day before her death on November 15, 1908, the emperor was killed according to Tz'u-hsi's deathbed wishes.

U

Ulbricht, Walter   (1893–1973)

East German Stalinist dictator from 1950 to 1971, most infamous for having supervised the construction of the Berlin Wall in 1961 and for his other iron-fist policies.

Born in Leipzig, Saxony, on June 30, 1893, Walter Ulbricht grew up in a small working-class family. His father was a tailor, and young Ulbricht was apprenticed to a cabinetmaker. Early in his life, Ulbricht fell under the influence of Marxist ideology, and at age 19 joined the SPD, Germany's Socialist party. He broke with the SPD in 1912 to join the more radically Marxist Sparticus Society. Unable to achieve political power, the Sparticus Society dissolved, reconstituting itself in 1919 as the German Communist Party (KPD).

Ulbricht served on the Eastern Front in World War I, deserting twice, and after the war joined the new KPD. Elected to the party's central committee in 1923, he worked to bring the party closer to the Bolshevism of Stalin, and in 1928 was elected to the Reichstag of the Weimar Republic, serving until 1933. Beginning in 1929, he also led party organization in Berlin.

KDP strategy during the years of the Weimar Republic was to aid the Nazi Party in its battle with the Socialists toward the goal of defeating Germany's weak democracy. This strategy backfired on the Communists after the Nazi political victory of 1933, and Ulbricht fled abroad, serving as a KPD agent, and as a member of the Cominterns of Paris, Moscow, and, during the Spanish Civil War (1936–39), in Spain, working in all these places to establish Communist cells according to Stalinist principles while opposing and persecuting Trotskyites.

Commissioned a colonel in the Red Army, Ulbricht was handpicked by Josef STALIN to return to Germany in 1945, following World War II, to reestablish the KDP, which he merged with the SDP to form the Social Unity Party (SED).

Ulbricht and other hard-line Communist members of the SED quickly gained control of the party. Running on a platform that promoted a national front—the reunification of Germany—and opposed the United States and its democratic allies, Ulbricht secured his eventual leadership of the German Democratic Republic (East Germany), which was created from the postwar Soviet Occupation Zone. On October 11, 1949, Ulbricht became deputy prime minister and, in 1950, general secretary of the SED as well. This effectively gave him control of the government of the German Democratic Republic.

Ulbricht wasted no time in carrying out a massive purge of his party. Along Stalinist lines, he instituted forced collectivization of industry and agriculture while continuing his efforts to unify Germany under Communist rule. In 1951, he issued an appeal to West Germans to resist United States aid through sabotage and general strikes. When East Germany's nominal president, Wilhelm Pieck, died in 1960, Ulbricht abolished the office of presidency and assumed chairmanship of the council of state, thereby formally assuming supreme authority over the GDR.

Crushing all opposition, Ulbricht also sought to block a Western-backed military buildup in West Germany while he continued to strengthen his ties with Moscow. In 1961, partly in an effort to stem the exodus from East to West in the divided city of Berlin, Ulbricht ordered the construction of the Berlin Wall. For the United States and its allies, the wall became a terrifying and ugly symbol of what totalitarian communism meant: forced obedience and an utter loss of freedom. While the Berlin Wall did much to regulate passage from East to West, it was a disastrous public relations error, serving to galvanize Western opposition against communism.

Under Ulbricht, East Germany became one of the most industrialized nations of eastern Europe and one of the most repressive. He retired as first secretary of the SED in 1971, but remained technically head of state until his death in East Berlin on August 1, 1973. He was succeeded in office by Erich Honecker.

Further Reading: Gregory W. Standford. *From Hitler to Ulbricht* (Princeton: Princeton University Press, 1983); Carola Stern. *Ulbricht: A Political Biography* (New York: Praeger, 1965).

V

Valerian [Publius Licinius Valerianus] (d. 260) One of the more obscure of Roman emperors, Valerian reigned from 253 to 260 and was a vigorous persecutor of Christians.

Valerian first appears in the records of Roman history as consul under Emperor Severus Alexander, who reigned from 222 to 235, and was instrumental in obtaining senatorial support for the rebellion of Gordian I against Emperor MAXIMINUS in 238. His name does not surface again until the reign of Decius in 249–51. Next, he appears as commander of a legion on the Upper Rhine in the service of Emperor Gallus (reigned 251–53). Summoned to aid in the suppression of Gallus' rival, Aemilian, Valerian arrived too late to save the emperor, but he did avenge him and was therefore named Gallus' successor.

Valerian resumed, with redoubled vigor, Emperor DECIUS' practice of persecuting Christians, and he ordered the execution of—among others—Bishop Cyprian of Carthage and Bishop Xystus (Sixtus II) of Rome. Valerian was also the first Roman emperor to divide the realm into two empires, that of the East and that of the West, naming his son GALLIENUS to govern the West while he marched with an army to the east in order to meet a Persian invasion under SHAPUR I. That monarch, however, took Valerian captive in June 260, and the Roman emperor died a prisoner soon after.

Velasco Ibarra, José María   (1893–1979)

Five times the president of Ecuador, Velasco Ibarra was nevertheless unable to maintain a permanent political organization, typifying the instability of Latin American politics.

Born into a wealthy family on March 19, 1893, José Velasco Ibarra received a thorough and advanced education, including postdoctoral work at the Sorbone in Paris. An avowed liberal, he was more concerned with ethical reform and the elimination of fraud from politics than party loyalty. In 1933, he was elected to congress and became speaker of the Chamber of Deputies. In the Chamber, he led the fight against president Juan Mera, who had been elected fraudulently. Congress declared the office vacant in 1934, and Velasco Ibarra carried a coalition of both liberals and conservatives, winning the presidency.

The coalition quickly dissolved, however, and Velasco Ibarra was ousted after only 11 months in office. He then went into exile in Colombia, but the people soon clamored for his return. The then-current president, Carlos Arroyo, attempted violently to suppress the pro-Velasco Ibarra demonstrations, but it was Arroyo who was overthrown, and Velasco Ibarra was acclaimed president in May 1994. Again he was backed by a coalition, this time without the liberals. After calling for general elections in 1946, Velasco Ibarra was rightfully elected, but then promptly ousted by his minister of defense. He then went into exile in Argentina.

Velasco Ibarra returned in 1952 to stand for election yet again and, yet again, won—this time with the backing of the liberals as well as the conservatives. He managed to complete his four-year term and was finally able to effect some lasting reforms. He reorganized the diplomatic corps and pared down the civil service, he instituted price controls to stabilize the economy and gave aid to both agriculture and industry in hopes of generating greater domestic production. Velasco Ibarra also instituted a modest public works program.

Ecuadorian law prohibited consecutive terms, but Velasco Ibarra returned in 1960, winning reelection by a landslide. He retained the support of the liberals, but when he backed away from Castro and Cuba, the liberals and the conservatives allied against him and the army deposed him, then deposed his successor, finally installing a military junta to run the country.

Velasco Ibarra returned in 1968 for his final term as president. When Congress opposed him, he disbanded it in June 1970 and replaced the then-current constitution with that of 1946. The army backed him for eight months of this term, then became increasingly strident in their demands for special concessions. Rather than serve as a puppet of the military, Velasco Ibarra resigned in February 1972, six months before the end of his term. He died on March 30, 1979.

Further Reading: George I. Blanksten. *Ecuador: Constitutions and Caudillos* (Berkeley: University of California Press, 1951).

Vercingetorix   (ca. 45 B.C.)

Vercingetorix was a Gallic chieftain famed for opposing Julius CAESAR in Gaul.

Little is known about the origin of Vercingetorix other than that he was the son of a king of the Arverni tribe in central Gaul. Early in the winter of 53 B.C., the Roman army was distributed throughout northern Gaul and Julius Caesar himself was in Italy. Vercingetorix seized the opportunity to rebel, rallying followers to his cause at Cenabum (modern Orléans) and gathering a large army. The rebellious chieftain set about training his army in the tactics of the Roman legion, so that, when Caesar returned to Gaul from Italy, he found himself confronted by a very formidable force. Caesar's first task was to break through Gallic opposition in order to join the main body of his legions in the north. He managed to do this and, with his united forces, retook Cenabum.

At this point, Vercingetorix transformed himself into a guerrilla leader, eschewing the Roman battle tactics he had instilled into his troops in favor of methods of harassment and an unsparing scorched earth policy, which worked hardship on the legions and the Gallic people alike.

Despite these measures, Caesar laid siege to the rebel stronghold of Avaricum (modern Bourges) beginning in February 52 B.C. Vercingetorix unsuccessfully attempted to relieve the fortress, but it fell to Caesar's forces in March. The Roman leader did not prevail against his next objective, however. The Arverni capital of Gergovia held out against a siege, and the legions could not long support themselves in a country ravaged by Vercingetorix's scorched earth measures. During April and May of 52 B.C., Caesar withdrew his forces from central Gaul.

Encouraged by this triumph, Vercingetorix once again assembled a large army, numbering some 80,000 infantrymen and 15,000 cavalry troops, in an attempt to keep the legions from leaving the valley of the Saone for the valley of the Seine. Roman cavalry, however, handily defeated Vercingetorix's mounted troops at the Vingeanne River, prompting Vercingetorix to pull back rather than engage in a major battle. In July, he was holed up in Alesia, a commanding hilltop fortress. Caesar led 50,000 troops in siege, forcing the Gallic leader and his army to take refuge within the walls of Alesia. As Caesar settled in for a protracted siege, Vercingetorix appealed to allied tribes for relief. They obliged, but lacked strong leadership, and Caesar was able to drive off the relief forces.

Throughout the summer and into early autumn, Caesar patiently maintained the siege, cutting off Vercingetorix from food and supplies. Each attempt to break out failed, and each new attempt was weaker than the last. His troops facing certain starvation, Vercingetorix surrendered and was taken into captivity, in which he was held for more than a decade before he was at last put to death about 45 B.C.

Vespasian   [Titus Flavius Vespasianus] (9–79)

Reigning as emperor of Rome from 69 to 79, Vespasian brought peace and prosperity to an empire racked and wearied by wars external and internal.

Vespasian was born on November 17 or 18, A.D. 9, near Reate (modern Rieti), Italy. He embarked on a military career at a young age, serving first in Thrace, then as quaestor in Crete and Cyrenaica. Popular and able, he became aedile and then praetor. He served with distinction in the German provinces during the 30s, then commanded a legion in Britain under Aulus Plautius. During 43–44, he conquered the Isle of Wight and advanced with his Second Legion to the region of modern-day Somersetshire. After serving a brief term as consul in 51, he became governor of the African provinces in 63. Vespasian accompanied Nero on his Greek tour, then, late in 66, was dispatched to Palestine to put down the Jewish rebellion in Judaea. There he confronted determined, even fanatical resistance, but by 69 had opened the siege of Jerusalem.

Portrait bust of Vespasian. (From Richard Delbruck, Antike Portrats, *1912)*

While Vespasian was occupied in the Middle East, NERO died by his own hand in 68, and Servius Sulpicius Galba was proclaimed emperor and recognized as such by most of the empire. The Praetorian Guard, always a volatile force, turned on Servius, however, and murdered him in order to bring to the throne early in 69 their favored candidate, Aulus Vitellius, who had served as commander of Roman forces in Germany. In July 69, the army in Egypt and his own forces in Judaea proclaimed Vespasian emperor. Vitellius, in Rome, had the support of the German legions, but Vespasian garnered the backing not only of the Middle Eastern troops, but those in the Balkans and in Illyria. With loyalties thus aligned, Vespasian entrusted command of the Middle Eastern forces to his son Titus and made his way back to Italy while another ally, Antonius Primus, used the legions of the Danube region to invade Italy and engage Vitellius, whom he defeated at the second Battle of Bedriacum in October 69. When Vespasian arrived in Rome in December 69, his rival emperor was dead and the city itself was held by Primus' troops.

Vespasian assumed the throne just as his son Titus effected the capture of Jerusalem in 70. This same year, Vespasian's forces put down the Rhineland revolt of Claudius Civilis. With these matters successfully resolved, Vespasian turned to a program of sorely needed domestic reform. Nero's extravagance had created a dangerous treasury deficit, which Vespasian quickly reduced and eliminated through a combination of economy measures and increased taxation. He broadened Rome's tax base in part by granting Roman citizenship to selected towns and provinces. After annexing portions of Anatolia and Germany, he reinforced garrisons in Great Britain, especially Wales and Scotland. Although he practiced prudent economies, Vespasian embarked on an ambitious program of construction, the grandest product of which was the Roman Colosseum.

Vespasian reintroduced Rome to something it had lacked for many years: good government conducted for the public benefit. Concerned about bringing lasting stability to Rome, Vespasian established the Flavian dynasty by naming his son TITUS as his successor. He gave him the strategic appointment of prefect of the notoriously dangerous Praetorian Guard. The strategy worked. When Vespasian died —of natural causes—on June 4, 79, having brought prosperity and peace to the empire, Titus succeeded him with the full support of the Praetorians and the acclamation of the Senate. Titus and, after him, DOMITIAN had learned well from their father. Like him, they ruled wisely, honestly, and equitably.

Visconti, Gian Galeazzo (1351–1402)

Gian Galeazzo Visconti, viscount, then duke of Milan, extended his domain by usurping power from his uncle, marrying his daughter to the French king's brother, purchasing a princedom from the German emperor Wenceslas, and building a strong administration for northern Italian cities.

The son of Galeazzo II Visconti, Gian Galeazzo Visconti was born in 1351 in Milan. In 1360, he married Isabella of Valois, the daughter of the king of France. In 1378, following the death of his father, who had ruled Milan with his brother Bernabo, Gian Galeazzo inherited the rule of the western half of Milan and its dependent territories, establishing his headquarters in Pavia. Bernabo retained control of the eastern half.

In 1382, Bernabo allied himself with the French prince Louis of Anjou and planned the marriage of his daughter to Louis' son. Afraid that Bernabo's position would be greatly enhanced by the alliance and marriage, Gian Galeazzo ambushed his uncle in 1385 and imprisoned him. Bernabo died while in captivity, possibly the victim of poisoning. In 1387, Gian Galeazzo undertook much the same plan that Bernabo had concocted: he offered the hand of his own daughter to the French king's brother Louis, duke of Orléans.

With his uncle removed from power, Gian Galeazzo united the two parts of Milan under his rule. In 1387, he overthrew the della Scala dynasty of Verona and took control of a large part of the March of Treviso, north of Venice. He paid the German emperor Wenceslas 100,000 florins for hereditary titles to parts of the Holy Roman Empire, becoming duke of Milan in 1395 and count of Pavia in 1396.

As his power increased and his bureaucracy became more efficient, more cities yielded to Gian Galeazzo's rule: Pisa and Siena in 1399, Perugia and other Umbrian towns in 1400, Bologna in 1402. With the annexation of Bologna, Gian Galeazzo came to control all of northern Italy—except Florence. As he was preparing to attack that city-state, he died of the plague on September 3, 1402, in Melegnano, near Milan. His vast domain was divided between two sons: Giovanni Maria and Filippo Maria.

Further Reading: Hans Baron. *The Crisis of the Early Italian Renaissance* (Princeton: Princeton University Press, 1955).

Vlad the Impaler [Vlad III Dracula] (ca. 1431–1476)

Vlad the Impaler, whose life was the inspiration for novelist Bram Stoker's Count Dracula, was prince of Wallachia in 1448, from 1456 until 1462, and again for a short period in 1476.

Vlad was born of noble parentage, and when he was only about 17 years old, he appointed himself prince of Wallachia for the first time, after he led a Turkish army to the city of Tirgoviste and occupied it. His reign was brief, however, and later in the year he was forced to flee into exile. For eight years, he wandered from place to place, spending most of his time in Adrianople, Moldavia, and Transylvania.

In 1453, the Turks conquered Constantinople, and from that point on posed a tremendous threat to the Balkans. Although Vlad's principality of Wallachia paid allegiance to the Catholic kings of Hungary, its people were also obliged to pay tribute to their recently arrived Turkish masters. Vlad quickly developed an intense hatred for the Turks, a trait that was to have dire consequences for his enemy for years to come.

In 1456, aided by Hungarian supporters, Vlad assumed the reins of government in Wallachia for the second time. Although his administration was decidedly anti-Turkish, it was not necessarily pro-Hungarian. Relations worsened between Vlad and the Hungarian king, Matthias Corvinus, and Vlad embarked on a campaign of torturing and killing Transylvanian merchants and their entire families—women and children included—by impaling them on wooden stakes.

When Vlad refused to pay the Turks the annual tribute of 10,000 ducats and 500 youths, the Turks sent a negotiator to lure Vlad into a trap so he could be killed once and for all. Vlad, however, learned of the plot and put the man, along with thousands of Turkish and Bulgar captives, to death by impaling them. When MOHAMMED II THE CONQUEROR personally marched into Wallachia and saw for himself the carnage, he reportedly cried and remarked that, "A man who could inspire such fear in his subjects might have performed wonders at the head of a great army."

Fleeing before Mohammed and his Turkish army, Vlad took refuge in Hungary for the next 12 years, where he lived under house arrest. He was converted to Catholicism and, in 1476, he was once again installed as prince of Wallachia. He volunteered his services as part of a Hungarian campaign against the Turks and was killed, either in combat, or by treachery.

Vlad's importance in history lies not in his military prowess, nor in his ability to rule, nor in the conquests he made. Rather, he is remembered for his obscene ruthlessness, his boundless brutality toward prisoners, and the sadistic abandon with which he tortured and killed so many, irrespective of sex or age. Vlad's character was the perfect inspiration for Bram Stoker's bloodthirsty vampire, Dracula, a figure that has entered legend and popular culture.

Further Reading: Radu Florescu and Raymond T. McNally. *Dracula: A Biography of Vlad the Impaler, 1431–1476* (New York: Hawthorn Books, 1973).

Vladimir II Monomakh   (1053–1125)

One of the last grand princes of Kiev before that state's decline, Vladimir was constantly at war, mostly with the nomadic inhabitants of the steppe.

The son of Grand Prince Vsevolod I, Vladimir Monomakh became immersed in Kievan politics early. Vladimir succeeded his father as crown prince of Chernigov in 1054 when Vsevolod became grand prince. Vladimir ruled Chernigov for 16 years, earning a place of prominence among the ruling princes. He gained a reputation for fairness and diplomacy in his efforts to avoid war among the princes.

When Vsevolod died in 1093, the people of Kiev implored Vladimir to succeed his father, but he deferred to his cousin Svyatopolk, whose claim to the throne was more legitimate. When Svyatopolk died the following year, again the Kievans offered the throne to Vladimir and, this time, he accepted, becoming grand prince in 1113. Kiev prospered under Vladimir's reign, although he was almost constantly at war. In his memoirs, he recounts at least 83 separate military campaigns in his 12-year role. These campaigns were generally directed against the Polovtsy, a nomadic Turkic people who had settled in the steppe regions south of Kiev and who had been raiding the region for years.

Although he fought the Polovtsy, Vladimir, an adept administrator and diplomat, deftly avoided the internecine warfare that would ultimately bring about the decline of the Kievan state. The renaissance Vladimir brought to Kiev was short-lived and did not endure after the death of the grand prince.

Before Vladimir died on May 19, 1125, he founded the city of Vladimir, which replaced Kiev as the seat of the grand prince.

W

Walker, William (1824–1860)

Called the "gray-eyed man of destiny," William Walker became the foremost filibuster during the 1850s, when he was elected president of Nicaragua.

William Walker was born on May 8, 1824, into a well-to-do Nashville family. His father, James, was a successful insurance executive, and his mother was a recently converted member of the newly formed denomination called the Church of Christ. At the age of 14, Walker became one of the youngest men ever to graduate from the University of Nashville. His parents hoped he would follow a ministerial career, but an early interest in medicine and a friendship with a local doctor convinced the young man that his future lay in Nashville as a physician. In 1843, after graduating from the University of Pennsylvania Medical School, he returned to his hometown, no doubt one of the youngest medical doctors in the United States.

Walker quickly became bored with his fledgling medical practice, however, and enrolled in the University of Edinburgh, following this with a journey across much of western Europe. He returned to Nashville, but was soon off again, this time to New Orleans, where he studied law and was admitted to the Louisiana bar. In 1848, he embraced a third occupation, journalism, and eventually moved to California, where he became the editor of a San Francisco newspaper.

During his California days, the restless Walker became obsessed with the idea of liberating the Mexican state of Sonora. Accordingly, in November 1853, accompanied by a rag-tag army of 45 men, Walker invaded Mexico. Six months later, after establishing his own "republic" of Sonora and getting himself elected its president, Walker and his men surrendered to American authorities at the international border. Public approval and acceptance of his filibustering activities, plus a "not guilty" verdict on the charge of violation of neutrality laws, whetted Walker's appetite for an even more grandiose venture—the invasion of Nicaragua.

The Nicaragua of the time was ripe for revolution. Internal strife and a power struggle among several leaders there had torn the country apart. Walker was quick to take advantage of the situation. In late 1854, he obtained a contract from the de facto government of Nicaragua, allowing him to bring to that country some 300 colonists to settle a land grant of 50,000 acres. In return, Walker and his American colonists would be liable for military service, for which they would receive monthly compensation. Walker legitimated his operation by subjecting the papers concerning it to review by the U.S. Attorney at San Francisco and by the commander of the Pacific Division of the U.S. Army.

Walker and 56 companions arrived at Realejo on June 1, 1855, and were immediately absorbed into the Nicaraguan army. After he led his small contingent to several victories against anti-government insurgents, Walker was proclaimed a national hero and elected to the presidency of Nicaragua in June 1856. Conflicts with American business leaders who were interested in building a canal across his country, as well as difficulties with the U.S. government over neutrality laws combined with ceaseless internal strife in Nicaragua to prompt Walker to resign the presidency in May 1857.

William Walker attempted to recapture Nicaragua several times during the late 1850s. In 1860, in a last attempt, Walker was captured by British authorities who turned him over to the Honduran army. He was executed at Trujillo, Honduras, at age 36.

Further Reading: Albert Z. Carr. *The World and William Walker* (Westport, Conn.: Greenwood, 1975).

Wei Chung-hsien (1568–1627)

The most powerful eunuch in Chinese history, Wei ruthlessly dominated the government for three years.

Originally a butler serving the chief concubine of Emperor Ming T'ai Chang, Wei Chung-hsien became close to Prince T'ien-chi's nurse and, through her, gained the trust of the young prince. When T'ien-chi assumed the throne at the age of 15 in 1620, he was more interested in carpentry than diplomacy and was too weak to provide effective leadership. Wei was able quietly to usurp power and, ultimately, to run the government.

In 1624, Wei persuaded T'ien-chi to grant him what was essentially a power of attorney, and he now ruled the government openly. Wei formed a division of eunuch troops to guard the palace, and he established a spy network to keep himself informed of the activities of enemies and potential enemies. Wei levied heavy taxes on the provinces and greatly increased the wealth of the state as well as himself. Under his rule, the government became rife with corruption and opportunists.

When a group of reform-minded Confucianists from the Tung-lin party objected to Wei's practices, he savagely crushed them, imprisoning and torturing many and killing hundreds. Government officials learned to practice abject toadyism in order to survive, and they vied for his approval.

Wei's run as a tyrant proved brief, however, ending when the emperor died in 1627. Rather than face trial and certain execution, Wei committed suicide.

Wen Ti [Yang Chien] (c. 541–604)

A wily and ruthless man, Emperor Wen Ti unified China, proclaiming the Sui dynasty, creating a powerful and well-administered central government, extending construction of the Great Wall, and commencing the Grand Canal.

Originally called Yang Chien, little is known of Wen Ti's early life beyond the fact that he was of mixed Chinese and Hsien-pi (Turko-Mongol) heritage and served the Hsien-pi Northern Chou dynasty as a military leader in North China. Yang distinguished himself as a commander and was named duke of Sui. He went on to lead Chou forces against the Northern Ch'i dynasty, effectively reuniting northern China under the Northern Chou in 577. Having consolidated Chou dominion over northern China, Yang seized on the death of the Chou emperor to place on the throne a 17-year-old youth in 580, securing for himself appointment as regent. Barely a year later, Yang compelled the boy to abdicate, whereupon Yang assumed the throne and established the Sui dynasty. To secure his power, the new emperor subsequently arranged for the death of the teenager he had displaced.

Wen Ti mobilized forces against Turkic tribes west of his realm, campaigning against them from 582 to 603. While he did not succeed in utterly subjugating these people, he did extend Chinese influence deep into central Asia. He moved, at first unsuccessfully, against Korea, managing by 589 to dominate that country's northern region. His greatest campaign, however, was conducted against the Ch'en dynasty of southern China. Massing a vast army—Chinese historical tradition puts its number at half a million—he defeated the Ch'en in 589, thereby unifying northern and southern China for the first time since the end of the Han dynasty three centuries earlier.

Yang Chien was not only a military genius, but an extraordinarily skilled administrator. He reintro-duced Han governmental policies and ushered in a return to Confucianism. To combat the deadly cycle of harvest and famine that ravaged the country, he caused large, centralized granaries to be built and he introduced a just and productive system of taxes based on harvest yield. Remorseless in his grasping for power, he was himself killed under obscure circumstances. Historians suspect that he was murdered by his own son, Yang Ti, in 604.

Weyler y Nicolau, Valeriano (1838–1930)

A Spanish general whose harsh measures against Cuban rebels brought an onslaught of criticism from the United States, Weyler later returned to Spain in an attempt to overthrow the government.

After joining the Spanish military in his youth, Valeriano Weyler y Nicolau first fought against the Cuban rebels in 1868, remaining in that country for four years. After his tour of duty in Cuba, Weyler returned to Spain to fight against the Carlists, the conservative Spanish royalists, who were attempting a Bourbon restoration. Following his success in helping to put down the Carlist uprising, Weyler was sent to the Canary Islands in 1878, where he was named captain-general (military governor), serving until 1883, when he was sent to the Balearic Islands, and then to the Philippines in order to suppress rebel uprisings there.

In January 1896, Weyler was sent back to Cuba to put down yet another Cuban revolt. He replaced the ineffective Martinez Campos as commander in chief and was determined to handle the rebellion as a straightforward war in which force was to be met with overwhelming force. The Cuban rebels had achieved a fearsome reputation for savagery, and Weyler intended to meet this threat with savagery of his own, including the institution of concentration camps to imprison captured rebels.

Weyler had badly misjudged the Cuban rebellion as a "simple" military operation. His uncompromising harshness might have made military inroads, but it also incited tremendous popular outrage in the United States and sparked sensational accounts of Spanish brutality in the "yellow" press of William Randolph Hearst and Joseph Pulitzer. Finally, in 1898, the United States effectively maneuvered Spain into a declaration of war.

By that time, however, Weyler, having largely defeated the rebels and killed their leader, Maceo, in December 1896, had been recalled to Spain in October 1897 because of the criticism leveled against him concerning his policies. Back in Spain, Weyler held a number of government appointments and became army commander in chief in 1921. In 1926, he participated in an abortive attempt to overthrow the regime of MIGUEL PRIMO DE RIVERA. Weyler died on October 20, 1930.

William I the Conqueror (ca. 1028–1087)

Called the Conqueror after his momentous victory over the Anglo-Saxon forces at the Battle of Hastings in 1066, this Norman monarch brought a semblance of centralized order to feudal England by establishing the tradition of primacy in determining royal succession.

Born the bastard son of the duke of Normandy, Robert I, in the city of Falaise, William would have had no claim to his father's title except Robert I died without legitimate issue in 1035. Although Robert had designated William as heir, his illegitimacy did lead to several attempts to murder him or to replace him with other members of his father's family. Although the young duke remained unscathed, four of his guardians were murdered in the course of nine years.

A determined effort by William's cousin Guy of Burgundy to oust him in 1046 would certainly have succeeded if William's feudal overlord, HENRY I (1008–1060), king of France, had not come to his aid at the Battle of Val-es-Dunes the following year.

An engraving, after the Bayeux Tapestry, depicting William I the Conqueror. (From J. N. Larned, A History of England for the Use of Schools and Academies, *1900)*

With Guy's defeat, William had secured his rule over Normandy. Indeed, his firm handling of potential usurpers left a strong impression on the aristocracy, and he maintained a very good relationship with them that was virtually unique for the time and that enabled him to make full use of all available resources.

The force of William's rule and personality soon prompted King Henry I of France to look upon him as a potential rival, and he abrogated his previously amicable ties with the Norman ruler. Henry found further excuse for making war against William on account of his consanguinous marriage to Mathilda, daughter of the Count of Flanders. Accordingly, Henry allied himself with GEOFFREY II MARTEL, count of Anjou, and attacked. William twice defeated the allies, at the Battle of Mortemer in 1054 and again at the Battle of Varaville in 1058. With these victories behind him, William had gained the feudal independence that allowed him to turn his attention to more distant matters.

Affairs in England had reached a state of chaos, and in return for Norman support, King Edward the Confessor named William heir to the English throne. William's aspirations to the English throne were further bolstered when Harold Godwin, brother of Edward's wife, was shipwrecked in Normandy. In exchange for his freedom, Harold pledged to support William's bid for the throne. In 1060, both Henry I and Geoffrey II Martel died, leaving William dominant in northern Europe. William quickly marched into Anjou and conquered Maine before the Angevin succession could be determined. William now felt that he could make his move on England.

In the meantime, however, Edward, on his deathbed at the beginning of 1066, designated HAROLD II GODWINESON as heir to the throne. Harold abrogated his oath to William and assumed the throne in 1066. William raised an army and landed at the southern tip of England in September 1066, at the town of Pevensey. William advanced on Hastings, where he met and defeated the army of Harold on October 15.

William now moved northward, terrorized the English countryside, and finally took London in December with little opposition. He was crowned William I, king of England, in Westminster Abbey on Christmas Day, 1066. There were many uprisings in the wake of William's accession. These he put down swiftly, effectively, and brutally. By 1071, the seeds of rebellion had been trampled under.

William ruled England and Normandy concurrently, frequently journeying back and forth between the two, managing the effective administra-

The Battle of Hastings in 1066 marked the end of the Anglo-Saxon hegemony in England and the introduction of Norman rule under William I the Conqueror. (From Charlotte M. Yonge, Pictorial History of the World's Great Nations, 1882)

tion of both. Shortly before his death in 1087, William designated his first son, Robert, as the heir to the duchy of Normandy, and his third—and favorite—Rufus, as heir to the English throne. Rufus reigned as William II and established the law of primacy henceforth to govern the succession of English monarchs.

Further Reading: Jacob Abbot. *William the Conqueror* (New York: Harper, 1900); David Bates. *William the Conqueror* (London: Philip, 1989); Hillaire Belloc. *William, the Conqueror* (London: Davies, 1933); Edward Freeman. *William, the Conqueror* (New York: Macmillan, 1888).

William I of Sicily   [William the Bad] (1120–1166)

William I, sometimes called William the Bad, ruled his Norman kingdom of Sicily, from 1154 until his death in 1166.

William was the son of Roger of Sicily, one of the Norman kings who had ruled Sicily since its occupation during the early days of the Crusades. William often seems to have been more interested in promoting the arts than in ruling his country. During his reign, his court was filled with scholars from all over the Mediterranean. William was influenced by the eastern culture of some of his scholarly and artistic visitors, and although Sicily was still a Lombard kingdom, it more resembled a Byzantine state than it did a western European one.

In 1154, at the beginning of his reign, William sent a fleet to subdue rebellion in Sicily's North African possessions. The next year, William successfully repelled a Byzantine invasion of his southern possessions. Despite these military successes, by 1159 most of the foreign lands his father once controlled had

gained their independence from Sicily. Toward the end of his reign, William I was intimidated by a consortium consisting of FREDERICK BARBAROSSA and Genoese and Pisan merchants. In the uprising that followed, William was captured, but later freed by loyal constituents. William exacted harsh revenge on those responsible for the uprising. He died in Palermo on May 15, 1166, leaving to his son, William II, a smaller kingdom than he himself had inherited.

William II Rufus   (ca. 1056–1100)

The son of WILLIAM I THE CONQUEROR, William II Rufus was king of England and later de facto ruler of Normandy.

The second surviving—and favorite—son of William I the Conqueror, William II was crowned king of England on September 26, 1087. As was customary, William I gave his inherited lands, Normandy, to his firstborn son, Robert, but reserved his conquered kingdom for William. Many Normans, however, did not wish to see the two kingdoms split, and they attempted to depose William and place Robert on the English throne. Led by the boys' uncle, Odo of Bayeaux, earl of Kent, the Norman nobles revolted in 1088. The English rallied to their new king, who pledged tax relief and milder forest laws (promises he broke), and, aided by loyalists, William savagely suppressed the rebellion.

In 1091, William marched against his brother and the nobles, gaining much of Normandy in return for a pledge of aid from Robert in retaining the county of Maine (William did not completely honor this promise, either). In 1095, led by Robert de Mowbray, earl of Northumberland, the Norman nobility again sought to overthrow William. Once again, the king crushed the revolt with brutality sufficient to discourage further rebellions by the nobles.

William was given to violence and greed, constantly seeking the ends of both, conquest and wealth. He marched on Scotland in 1091, and when the Scottish king Malcolm rose against him, William executed him in 1093. Thereafter, William held Scotland as a fiefdom, and by 1097 he had subjugated Wales as well. Not a very religious man, William realized that if he kept the church offices vacant, he could collect the church revenue for himself, which is what he did, leaving the bishopric of Canterbury vacant for over nine years.

When Robert needed financing to go on a Crusade, he offered to mortgage Normandy in return for 10,000 marks. William quickly accepted and, shortly after Robert's departure, marched into Maine, adding that county to his domains. He now completely controlled almost all of Normandy without officially ruling it.

While hunting with his youngest brother Henry, William took an arrow in the back and died on August 2, 1100. Henry almost certainly planned this assassination, and he may have employed Walter Tirel, lord of Poix in Ponthieu, to let fly the shot. In any event, Henry abandoned his brother's body in the forest and hurried to seize the treasury and crown for himself.

Further Reading: James Chambers. *The Norman Kings* (London: Weidenfold & Nicholson, 1981); Edward A. Freeman. *Reign of William Rufus* (New York: AMS Press, 1980).

William [Wilhelm] II   (1859–1941)

The last kaiser of Germany, William was hardly as capable as he thought himself to be; his actions had led to the escalation of World War I.

A member of the reigning Hohenzollern family that had ruled Prussia for centuries, William II was born on January 27, 1859, the son of Crown Prince Frederick William, later Kaiser Frederick III, and grandson of Kaiser William I. The predominant influence in his youth was his mother, Victoria, daughter of Queen Victoria of England. Victoria tried to raise William as an English gentlemen and a liberal, contrary to the prototype of the traditional Prussian ruler, who was militant, firm, frugal, and conservative. Caught between his mother and his heritage, William became neither a true liberal nor conservative.

When William I died in March 1888, Frederick William was already dying of cancer. He reigned for a mere 99 days before succumbing, and William II became kaiser on June 15, 1888. Chancellor Otto von Bismarck looked favorably on his accession, feeling that William was a more apt successor to his conservative grandfather than his liberal father. Yet William and Bismarck soon clashed as the kaiser assumed prerogatives that had been the chancellor's. At length, William, whose ambition was to restore the monarchy to the degree of absolute authority Frederick the Great had enjoyed, dismissed Bismarck in March 1890 and attempted to rule through hand-picked puppet chancellors.

Yet William II proved unable to dominate men the way Bismarck had done, and he was further unable to institute lasting and meaningful policy. He wanted the world and Germany to believe he ran the country, but, in fact, he was quite incapable of doing so. William fancied himself adept at foreign policy, feeling that central European politics still revolved around Germany as it had a century before around Brandenburg-Prussia. In 1896, he sent a telegram to South African President Paul Kruger, congratulating him on his suppression of the British-led Jameson raid. He further insulted the British by secretly challenging their supremacy on the seas. William let his ministers talk him into not renewing Bismarck's 1887 Reinsurance Treaty with Russia. In consequence, Russia promptly aligned itself with France, Germany's bitterest enemy. Finally, the kaiser added insult to injury by giving a tactless interview to *The Daily Telegram*—on British soil no less—declaring the majority of German citizens were adamantly anti-English.

As kaiser, William had the power to appoint the chancellor, who ran the civil government, but the military was not under the civil government. It was run at the discretion of the kaiser and his general staff. William effectively relinquished control of the military to his generals, who began to plan and arm for global conflict, developing the famed Schlieffen Plan, first developed in 1904. Germany was not the only country to have large-scale war contingency plans—France, for example, developed Plan 17—but William, essentially a non-belligerent, failed to curtail a military bloodlust that soon got out of hand.

When Austro-Hungarian Archduke Francis Ferdinand was assassinated in June 1914, William pushed for the punishment of Serbia by Austria-Hungary in the hope of solidifying that unstable ally. He failed to realize that, because of the Triple Entente and the Triple Alliance, any conflict would quickly escalate to engulf all of Europe. When the interlocking treaties were activated, the kaiser backed away, even as World War I began, and the Schlieffen Plan was being put into effect with Germany's advance toward Paris.

Yielding before the juggernaut of world war, William increasingly relinquished control of the country to his two senior generals. By early 1918, after four ruinous years of slaughter, it was apparent that Germany could not win the war. The chancellor, Prince Max of Baden, announced William's abdication without even consulting him, and General von HINDENBURG informed the kaiser that the army would no longer support him. Accordingly, William fled to the Netherlands.

Thus the kaiser left Germany to a humiliating peace. His own life was spared because the Dutch government declined to extradite the kaiser to the Allies, who intended to try him as the author of the war. William remained in Dutch exile until his death at the threshold of the Second World War, on June 4, 1941.

Further Reading: Virginia Cowles. *The Kaiser* (New York: Harper & Row, 1963); Joachim von Kurenberg. *The Kaiser: A Life of Wilhelm II, Last Emperor of Germany* (London: Cassell, 1954) Alan W. Palmer. *The Kaiser: Warlord of the Second Reich* (New York: Scribner's, 1978).

Wu P'ei-fu (1873–1939)

This Chinese warlord, who controlled much of northern China, was defeated when he opposed CHIANG KAI-SHEK.

The son of a tradesman, Wu P'ei-fu was born April 22, 1873. He became interested in poetry and philosophy early in his childhood and remained interested in them for the rest of his life, but he chose to pursue a military career and entered the Tientsin military academy in 1898. Upon graduation shortly after the turn of the century, Wu joined the Peiyang Army led by Yüan Shih-k'ai, the Ch'ing dynasty's most able general, and gained nominal recognition in minor campaigns. When the Ch'ing was overthrown and the Chinese Republic declared in 1912, Wu quickly established himself as a dominant figure in the northern region.

The republic did not offer a strong centralized government, and regional warlords soon assumed great local autonomy. Wu rapidly built a power base in the north from among the middle classes, who were tired of the Ch'ing wars. Soon, he controlled five major provinces, becoming the most powerful warlord of the north. Yüan became the second provisional president of the republic and later proclaimed himself emperor, and when he died in 1916, Wu, as the dominant warlord, emerged as the single most powerful leader in China.

Wu's opponents, the monarchists, Sun Yat-sen in the south, and Chang Tso-lin in Manchuria, sought either to seize the republic for themselves or to crush it altogether. When Chang began advancing into the north in 1922, Wu swiftly moved against him, defeating him in a series of battles and pushing him all the way back to Manchuria. Now Wu hoped to unify all of China under the republic and prepared for a massive campaign.

Wu treated his military as well as civilian associates coolly and even harshly. This manner, combined with his savage suppression of a railroad strike in 1923, cost him much-needed popularity in his upcoming campaign. It may have moved his leading ally, Feng Yu-hsiang, to defect to Chang shortly before the campaign got under way.

Chang defeated Wu at a tremendous battle at Tientsin in 1924. Wu made one last attempt to achieve dominance over all China in 1926, when he opposed Chiang Kai-shek and his Kuomintang Army as they advanced northward toward Peking. Wu was heavily defeated, however, and he retired to a Buddhist monastery, where he died on December 4, 1939.

Wu Ti (154 B.C. ca. 87 B.C.)

Wu Ti, the fifth Han emperor, spread his empire across much of Asia and is regarded as one of China's greatest rulers.

A son of Emperor Ching Ti, Wu Ti was designated heir by his father from his deathbed, even though he was not the oldest son. Wu Ti succeeded his father around 141 B.C. and ruled with his relatives serving as advisers because of his youth. He began to rule in his own right around 135 B.C. and decided that the defensive nature of the dynasty's foreign policy meant that other rulers would always dominate the Han. Accordingly, in 133, Wu Ti made war on the roaming Hsiung-nu bands, the Han's principal enemy to the north.

After defeating the Hsiung-nu and driving them into the Gobi desert, Wu-Ti believed that the expansion of the empire was necessary for its survival. By the turn of the century, his forces had expanded the Han south all the way into south-central Vietnam and north into north-central Korea. He also moved into Fergana in the west, in an effort to gain horses. The first invasion in 104 B.C. was a failure, but by 101, Wu Ti was victorious and brought back horses—as well as the ruler of Fergana's head.

His costly war drained the state treasury, and Wu Ti looked to creative taxation as a way to raise more revenue. He instituted state monopolies on salt, iron, and wine as well as the practice of selling favors to the nobility and even selling criminal amnesty.

Wu Ti's last years were not peaceful. His heir was accused of witchcraft, and a rebellion broke out in which hundreds were killed and his son committed suicide. His other son, only eight years old, became heir, and to avoid his domination by relatives, Wu Ti had his wife imprisoned and murdered before his own death in 87 B.C.

Further Reading: Hans Bielenstien. *The Bureaucracy of Han Times* (Cambridge: Cambridge University Press, 1980); Ku Park. *The History of the Former Han Dynasty* vol 2, (Baltimore: Waverly Press, 1938).

Wu Wang (r. ca. 1111–1104 B.C.)

The founder of the Chou dynasty, Wu Wang overthrew the Shang dynasty, but his generosity in victory helped solidify his new regime.

The son of a minister to the Chou dynasty, Wu Wang succeeded his father as head of the Chou state. Wu continued to build on the power base his father had established in the Wei Valley. He opposed the cruel and despotic Shang ruler, Chou Hsin, waging guerrilla warfare against him, but resisting calls for all-out war as, aided by his brother, the Duke of Chou, he assembled an army of abused and disenchanted nobles.

As Wu's forces grew, they clamored more loudly for an attack on Chou Hsin, but Wu resisted until he felt that they were strong enough. Wu bided his time for some two years, as hatred of Chou Hsin mounted steadily. At last, he assembled his army at Meng ford, marched on the Mu plain, just south of the Shang capital, then completely annihilated the Shang forces, prompting Chou Hsin to commit suicide.

Wu declared the Shang dynasty over and proclaimed the Chou dynasty, about 1122 B.C. (some historians place it as late as 1027 B.C.).

In an effort to maintain control over his new empire, Wu established a feudalist system, apportioning land to all who had supported him. He also gave land to the defeated Shang, hoping thereby to win their loyalty.

Wu died several years after establishing the dynasty, sometime before the turn of the 11th century B.C.

Further Reading: Friedrich Hirth. *The Ancient History of China to the End of the Chou Dynasty* (New York: Columbia University Press, 1923).

X

Xerxes I   (ca. 519–465 B.C.)

Successor to Darius I, Xerxes I, king of Persia, is best known for his unsuccessful invasion of Greece. His defeat at a naval battle at Salamis marked the beginning of the decline of the Achaemenid dynasty.

In 486 B.C., at the age of 35, Xerxes I inherited the throne of the Persian Empire upon the death of his father, Darius I. Xerxes' first significant act was to regain control of Egypt, which, for two years, had been in the hands of a usurper. In 484 B.C., Xerxes attacked the Nile Delta and swiftly suppressed the Egyptian rebellion. Almost immediately afterward, he learned of another revolt, this time in Babylon. Xerxes sent his son-in-law to the region to quell the rebellion. Persian forces tore down Babylon's fortresses, pillaged temples, and destroyed the statue of Marduk, the Babylonian god.

Once firmly in control of his empire, Xerxes was persuaded by his brother-in-law Mardonius to attack the Greeks in retaliation for the humiliating defeat they had dealt Darius I at Marathon in 490 B.C. For three years, Xerxes prepared for war. He gathered some 360,000 troops from across the realm, built a navy of 700 to 800 ships, dug a channel across the Isthmus of Actium, and built boat bridges to be used at the Hellespont.

Xerxes himself led his army from Sardis in 481 B.C. Tolerating no deviation from his battle plans, he became enraged when storms destroyed his carefully constructed boat bridges. He ordered his troops to punish the sea by whipping it with lashes.

Despite the mishap at the Hellespont, Xerxes triumphed at Thermopylae in August 480, and moved on to occupy Attica and Athens. By the end of September, however, his navy suffered a stunning defeat at Salamis, and he was forced to retreat, leaving Mardonius in Thessaly. When Mardonius was killed the following year at Plataea, the entire Persian army withdrew.

For the remainder of his life, Xerxes turned his attention to monumental construction projects. In his capital city of Persepolis, he built a huge terrace of the Apadana, completed his father's palace, and then built one of his own, including a building called the Harem, which may have served as his treasury. Construction was also begun on the Hall of a Hundred Columns—the throne room.

During the last years of his life, Xerxes was drawn into various palace intrigues. Persuaded by the queen that his brother's family meant to do him in, he had them killed preemptively. Nevertheless, in 465, he and his eldest son were apparently murdered by a court cabal that included Xerxes' trusted minister Atabanus. Another of the king's sons, Artaxerxes I, succeeded Xerxes to the throne.

319

Y

Yang Chien *See* WEN TI

Yazdegerd II (r. 438–457)

This Sasanian emperor of Persia savagely persecuted Jews and Christians.

The son of Bahram V, Yazdegerd succeeded his father as ruler of the Sasanian empire around 435. A fervent follower of Zoroaster, Yazdegerd nevertheless was at first tolerant of other religions in his domains. During this period, while Rome was busy with uprisings in the West, Yazdegerd took advantage of the chaotic situation to wreak havoc in the East. In 441, he set out from Nisibis and raided and sacked several towns on his way to Roman Armenia, which he intended to ravage. He was hampered by bad weather, however, and the Ephthalites were able to cross the Caspian Sea to oppose him. Yazdegerd was persuaded to agree to a year-long truce in return for money and the surrender of some Christian refugees held by Roman forces. Yazdegard and the Romans further sought to demilitarize the empire's frontier by agreeing that no more fortifications would be built within a certain distance of it. This did not bring peace to the area for long, however, as the Huns moved west out of Asia and into occupied lands. The Huns first invaded the Roman Empire in 448, during the Persian War, and continued raiding for many years. Yazdegerd again profited from this diversion of Rome's forces by waging war against the Kushans and Kidarites of the East.

While he menaced the Roman Empire from the beginning of his reign, it was later during his rule that Yazdegerd's zealous adherence to Zoroastrianism persuaded him to abandon his former tolerance of Christians and Jews and to embark on a program of savage persecution.

Yazdegerd was succeeded by his son Hormizd III.

Yen Hsi-shan (1882–1960)

Yen Hsi-shan was among the more notable of the many warlords contending for power during turbulent early 20th-century China.

Yen Hsi-shan was born in Shansi province and was educated at the Taiyuan Military Academy, which trained him for a career in the Taiyuan New Model Army, which he entered in 1904. Four years later, he was sent to Japan, to study at its advanced military academy. There, during 1908–10, he met the young military leaders of China's growing nationalist movement, which was bent on overthrowing the Ch'ing (Manchu) dynasty. Yen was installed as a regimental commander of the Taiyuan garrison in October 1911, when the Chinese Revolution broke out. He led his troops in support of the revolutionaries, eventually casting his lot with the faction of Yüan Shih-k'ai.

Yen's genius lay in his ability to navigate the treacherous waters of revolutionary China. His allegiance to Yüan gained him the military governorship of Shansi, which he ruled with an autocratic hand—though he also instituted a far-reaching program of modernization and industrialization unknown under the emperors. By 1915, it was clear to Yen that Yüan was losing his power base, and he quickly shifted allegiance to the Anhwei faction led by Premier Tuan Ch'i-jui. This move gained him the civil governership of Shansi, a strong foundation on which to consolidate and build additional power. When, in his turn, Tuan faltered and fell in 1918, Yen skillfully shifted his apparent allegiance between WU P'EI-FU and Feng Yü-hsiang. Finally, in 1925, he joined Chang Tso-lin, military governor of Fengtien, to drive Wu out of north-central China. Then, with Wu disposed of, he quickly shifted alliance to the KMT (Kuomintang, or Nationalist Party) and was put in command of the Nationalist Third Army Group. From September 1927 to June 1928, he joined in a successful assault against Peking.

The nationalists rewarded his services to the cause by making him interior minister and commander of the Peking-Tientsin garrison. With even more than his usual agility, however, Yen turned his back on the KMT, took neither post, and joined in the revolt of Feng Yü-hsiang and Wang Ching-wei in 1930. When this proved abortive, Yen suffered exile to Dairen (Luda), but returned to Shansi a scant six months later, in 1931, and contented himself with governing the province. This was no small accomplishment, since the overwhelming majority of Chinese warlords failed to command sustained loyalty and were subjected to almost continual revolt. Yen, though stern and dictatorial, did exhibit concern for the people he governed. He also commanded great loyalty from his military subordinates. But he did not depend on progressive programs and personal loyalty alone. He was among the first of the Chinese revolutionary leaders to develop and employ the methods of political indoctrination that Mao Tse-tung would later bring to a high state of evolution in forging the People's Republic of China.

When the Japanese invaded China during July 1937, Yen put up a stout resistance that resulted in an uneasy stalemate, during which he maneuvered among the sharply contending forces of the Japanese, the KMT, and the CCP (Chinese Communist Party), pitting one against the other in a sustained and highly successful effort to retain his own power. Remarkably, after the Japanese defeat in World War II, Yen retained the military services of four divisions of the Japanese army to keep the CCP out of Taiyuan from 1945 to 1949. When it fell at last in April 1949, Yen quietly relinquished power, retired, and died of natural causes in 1960.

Yung Lo   [Chu Ti] (1360–1424)

Third emperor of China's Ming dynasty, Yung Lo (born Chu Ti) usurped the throne from his nephew, purged the court of the deposed emperor's family, friends, and advisers, and ruled China from 1402 to 1424.

The fourth son of the Emperor Hung Wu, founder of the Ming dynasty, Yung Lo was born on May 2, 1360, in Nanking. Modern scholars believe that he was the son of a secondary consort of Korean origin—though, in order to support his later claims to the throne, Chu Ti himself maintained that he was the son of his father's principal consort.

Hung Wu gave each of his 26 sons territories to govern. The ten-year-old Chu Ti was named prince of Yen (the Peking region) in 1370. Completing his education in Nanking, Chu Ti moved to Peking in 1380. Over the next 12 years, he was engaged in patrolling the northern frontier and learned military tactics from leading generals of the day.

In 1392, the eldest son of Hung Wu died. Although Chu Ti was his father's favorite son, the emperor held to the traditional laws of succession and named Chu Yun-wen (reign title: Chien Wen), the son of the dead crown prince, heir to the throne. When the emperor died in 1398, Chu Yun-wen was named emperor. Advised by Confucian scholars and officials, the young emperor realized the threat to his power posed by his uncles. He instituted a series of reforms to strip them of their power, and during the first few years of his reign, several of the princes were imprisoned, exiled, or committed suicide.

In August 1399, Chu Ti rebelled against the emperor, claiming that the young ruler had been ill-advised by the court. From 1399 to 1402, civil war spread through the western Shantung Province and the northern part of the Huai River Basin. In 1402, Chu Ti's army broke through the imperial forces, sped south along the Grand Canal, forced the imperial fleet to surrender, and was let into the walled city of Nanking by court defectors. Chu Ti burned the palace, and the emperor presumably died—although some contemporary accounts hold that he fled the city and became a recluse somewhere in the south. In any case, Chu Ti claimed the throne on July 18, 1402, and took the name Yung Lo.

The capital city was filled with officials who remained loyal to the deposed emperor. Chu Yun-wen's advisers and friends, along with all their families, were executed in a purge that left thousands dead. The new emperor, eager to wipe out all resistance, even ordered history to be rewritten to eradicate all mention of Chu Yun-wen.

Although as the Prince of Yen, Yung Lo had suffered under Chu Yun-wen's decision to strip the princes of power, he perpetuated the policy, realizing how perilous his own position was. Over the next few years, he removed his brothers from their strategic locations throughout the kingdom, placed them in central and southern China, and stripped them of all governmental authority.

During his reign, Yung Lo engaged in several military campaigns: against Annam, China's southern neighbor, and against the Mongols to the north. In addition, he sent emissaries far beyond China's borders to claim tribute money.

In 1407, Yung Lo ordered his capital moved from Nanking to Peking, where a new palace was constructed. Other improvements to China's infrastructure included the rebuilding of the Grand Canal that linked the Yangtze and Yellow River valleys.

Yung Lo fell ill after a campaign into Mongolia and died en route to Peking on August 5, 1424. His son Chu Kao-chih (Hung Hsi) was named emperor.

Further Reading: Paul Pelliot. *Notes on Marco Polo,* vol. 2 (Paris: Impr. Nationale, 1963); D. Pokotilov. "History of the Eastern Mongols During the Ming Dynasty from 1368–1634," *Studia Serica,* ser. A, no. 1 (Chengtu, 1947); Wang Yi-t'ung. *Official Relations between China and Japan, 1368–1549* (Cambridge: Harvard University Press, 1953).

Z

Zelaya, José Santos (1853–1919)

As president of Nicaragua, Zelaya attempted to dominate Central America but was thwarted by the United States.

Born to a wealthy coffee planter in Managua on October 31, 1853, José Zelaya attended school in Granada but traveled to France for further study. Returning from France in 1876, Zelaya became active in politics and in the conspiracies against the conservative administrations that dominated Nicaragua during the late 19th century.

The Conservative Party began to disintegrate in the 1890s, however, and the internal dissension that resulted toppled the regime of Roberto Sacasa. After much confusion and a succession of leaders jockeying for the presidency, Zelaya was elected in July 1893. He set out an ambitious and successful public works program, building new schools and providing furniture and instructional materials for them, as well as securing a pay increase for teachers. He also built roads and extended the railway system, made numerous agricultural improvements, and began the transformation of Managua from a village to a real capital city.

Zelaya was also a ruthless politician, who was as corrupt as he was repressive. He managed to stay in power through repeated election fraud, and he sold government concessions as well as demanded kickbacks from anyone doing business with Nicaragua. Refusing to send delegates to the Central American conference in San José in 1906, he instead invaded Honduras and overthrew the government there, occupying Tegucigalpa. Next, he invaded El Salvador, where he attempted to incite a revolution. When war appeared imminent, the United States intervened, convening the Central American Conference in Washington in 1907, which pledged all the countries to end hostilities toward each other. Zelaya quickly broke the treaty, however, and the United States supported the Conservative bid to retake control of the government and oust Zelaya.

In 1909, when two American soldiers of fortune were executed on Zelaya's orders, the U.S. broke diplomatic relations with Nicaragua. Facing the combined opposition of the rest of Central America backed by the U.S., Zelaya was forced to resign in December 1909. After spending some time in Mexico, Zelaya moved to the United States and died in New York City on May 17, 1919.

Further Reading: Dana G. Munro. *The Five Republics of Central America* (New York: Oxford University Press, 1918).

Zhivkov, Todor (b. 1911–)

Zhivkov was first secretary of the Bulgarian Communist Party's Central Committee from 1954 to 1989, and president of Bulgaria from 1971 to 1989.

Zhivkov was born in Pravets outside Botevgrad to an indigent peasant family. In his teens, Zhivkov joined the Komsomol, an outlawed Soviet cell in Bulgaria. During World War II he became a leader of the Bulgarian resistance party known as the People's Liberation Insurgent Party.

When a Soviet-backed regime came into power in Bulgaria after the war, Zhivkov rapidly advanced through the Communist Party hierarchy, becoming a member of the Politburo in 1951 and its president in 1954. At 43, Zhivkov was the youngest Soviet bloc leader at that time.

Zhivkov was a hard-line Communist, who adhered closely to direction from the Soviet Union. His personal friendship with Soviet premier Nikita KHRUSHCHEV survived the latter's expulsion. By 1971, Zhivkov had consolidated his power by becoming both first secretary of the Bulgarian Communist Party and president of the Bulgarian state. It took the disintegration of Soviet communism itself to dislodge Zhivkov, who stepped down in 1989 after the dismantling of the Communist Party in the U.S.S.R. Zhivkov was subsequently arrested by officials of the new Bulgarian regime in 1990.

Zia [Zia-ul-Haq], Mohammad (1924–1988)

Zia assumed power in a bloodless coup and tightened his grip on Pakistan by refusing to grant free elections and by stringently limiting civil liberties.

Born on August 12, 1924, in East Punjab, now part of the Republic of India, Mohammad Zia-ul-Haq began his military career early in life. After attending the Royal Indian Military Academy, Zia was commissioned in 1945 and served with British armored forces in Burma, Malaysia, and Indonesia near the end of World War II. He began military life under British rule and continued to serve in the army of the Republic of Pakistan, which was created when British India was partitioned into India and Pakistan in 1947.

After graduating from the Command and Staff College in Quetta in 1955, Zia took two of his three trips to the United States, including a course at the Command and General Staff College in Fort Leavanworth, Kansas. In 1965, as a lieutenant colonel, Zia led troops in Pakistan's war with India over Kashmir. By 1968, he had reached the rank of brigadier general and commanded an armored brigade. Continuing warfare resulted in further promotion, and Zia became a major general by 1972, commanding an entire armored division and also presiding over the military tribunals that tried army and air force officers charged with plotting against the regime of Zulfikar Ali bhutto.

On March 1, 1976, Zia was promoted to full general, and President Bhutto appointed him army chief of staff. While Zia was a competent soldier, this move surprised some and outraged others. Zia had been promoted over generals with seniority who were in line for the position. Bhutto, however, believed that Zia had no political aspirations of his own and could be depended on to deliver the allegiance of the military as needed. For Bhutto, this judgment would prove a fatal mistake.

Social and economic conditions in Pakistan were in crisis and failed to improve under Bhutto. A coalition of nine parties united against the regime had a spirited run in the March 1977 elections. However, Bhutto still received 155 of the 200 seats in the assembly. When the coalition claimed fraud and called for a strike, Bhutto quickly arrested the opposition leaders and called for military rule in the most populous cities.

The next four months brought widespread riots followed on July 5, 1977, by a bloodless coup led by Bhutto's trusted Zia, who detained Bhutto and his cabinet—*and* the opposition leaders. Zia imposed martial law throughout Pakistan, banned all political activity, installed a ruling military council, and dissolved the National Assembly, though he maintained the constitution and permitted the prime minister, Fazal Elahi Chaudhry, to continue in office.

While insisting that martial law would last only as long as it took to stabilize the country in order to conduct free elections, Zia revived traditional Islamic principles of law, imposing harsh punishment even for minor infractions, but also launching an investigation of Bhutto's secret police, lifting some press censorship, confiscating illegal weapons, and instituting some measures to stimulate the Pakistani economy, including a 5 percent cut in military spending.

Zia intended to allow Bhutto to reenter the political fray and run in the upcoming free elections, but he concluded that Bhutto had been running the country along what he called "more or less Gestapo lines" and, pursuant to a decision of a civil court, ordered his arrest in 1977. An outcry from Bhutto supporters led Zia to postpone the promised elections, and Zia ordered the widespread arrest of Bhutto partisans. Martial law was not only extended, but made more severe.

In January 1978, Zia yielded to public demands for civilian government, eventually (by August) setting up an all-civilian cabinet—while retaining for himself the most important and influential positions. When Bhutto was convicted and executed on April 4, 1978, massive rioting broke out, and Zia responded by banning all political parties and meetings, outlawing labor strikes, restricting the press, and generally subjecting to arrest anyone who differed with him. He also postponed free elections indefinitely. In September 1978, Zia replaced Chaudhry as president of Pakistan and embarked on a hard-line "Islamization" of Pakistan by instituting harsh fiscal and penal laws from the Koran.

Zia enjoyed the support of the United States Central Intelligence Agency, which pumped $400 million into Pakistan, which was seen as a buffer against the Soviets, who had invaded neighboring Afghanistan in 1979. Bolstered by the United States, Zia continued in power, finally holding a form of free elections in 1985, in which his policies were rebuked. Zia nominally lifted martial law, but in 1988 dismissed the elected government and announced new nonparty elections. However, on August 17, 1988, Zia was killed, along with the U.S. ambassador to Pakistan, when his airplane exploded in midair over Pakistan.

Index

The index is alphabetized letter by letter. **Boldface** headings and locators indicate main essays.

A

Abbad I 1
Abbadid al-Mu'tadid 1
Abbasid dynasty 123–124
Abbas I the Great 1–2
ABC Society 183
Abd Allah 2
Abd al-Mu'min 2–3
Abd ar-Rahman III 3
abdication
  of Bayezid II 32, 270
  of Maximinus predecessors 194
  of Napoléon I 215
  of Pedro I 232
  of Richard II 260
  of Wen Ti predecessor 313
  of William (Wilhelm) II 316
abduction 223–224, 255, 305
Abdul-Aziz 3, 184–185
Abdul-Hamid II 3–4
Absalom 81
Abu Bakr Muhammad 5
Abun, al-Djarad 5
Abydos, Battle of 31
Abyssinia 5 *see also* Ethiopia
Achaean League 211
Achaemenid dynasty 79
Achilleus 85
Actium, Battle of 26, 68
Adalbert, Archbishop of Bremen 122
Adbulmalik-al-Mozaffar 1
Adil Shah 5
Adowa, Battle of 197
Adrets, François de Beaumont, baron des 4
Adrianople 311
Aegospotami 80
Aetius 25
Afghanistan
  invaders
    Genghis Khan 112
    Tamerlane 288
  rulers
    Ahmad Shah Durrani 6
    Amin, Hafizollah 16
    Kanishka 156
    Karmal, Babrak 157–158
    Taraki, Noor Mohammed 289
  Soviet military intervention
    Brezhnev and 40
    Hoxha and 144
    Zia and 323
Aflaq, Michel 145
Afonso I 4–5
Afonso V 147
Afrikaners 51–52, 204
Afshar, Ahmadlu 211
Agathocles 5
Agesilaus II 181
Aggrippina the Younger 67
Agha Mohammad Khan 5

Agincourt, Battle of 131
Agis II 10
Agrippina 218
Ahmad Gran 5
Ahmad ibn Tulun 5–6
Ahmad Shah Durrani 6
Ahmed, Khandakar Mushtaque 6
Ahmose I 6–7
Ahmose Sitayet 7
Ahuitzotl 7
Akbar 7
Akhenaton 7–8, 15, 142
Akkadian dynasty 269
Alamanni 69
Alamo, Battle of the 268
Alamut, Battle of 124
Alaric 8–9
Albania 143–144
Albert the Bear 102
Albinus, Clodius 272
Albizzi family 194
Alboin 9
alchemy 255
Alcibiades 9–10
alcoholism 226
Alcuin 53
Alemanni 153
Alès, Peace of 262
Alexander, Severus 308
Alexander I (Russia) **10–11,** 214, 221
Alexander I (Yugoslavia) **11–12**
Alexander II (Russia) 4, **12,** 13
Alexander II, Pope 122
Alexander III the Great 12–13, 13
  opponents of
    Chandragupta Maurya 52
    Darius 80
    Porus 249
  relatives of
    Philip II 239
    Pyrrhus 252
  rulers inspired by
    Caesar 43
    Caracalla 45
    Selim I 270
  rulers likened to
    Cyrus II the Great 77–78
    Genghis Khan 111
Alexander III (Russia) **13–14,** 221, 243
Alexander IV, Pope 14, 96
Alexander V, Antipope 163
Alexander VI, Pope 14–15, 38, 300
Alexandria (Egypt) 85
Alfonso XII 42
Alfonso XIII 102
Alfred the Aetheling 122
Algeria 50–51, 206, 305
Allende, Salvador 244
Almagro, Diego de 245

Almohad dynasty 2–3
Almoravid dynasty 2
Alnwick, Battle of 128
Altmark, Truce of 118
Altranstädt, Treaty of 59
Alvarado, Pedro do 74
Alvares Cabral, Pedro 185
Amadeus VI 206
Amarna Letters 15
Amboise, Edict of 50
Ambrose, Edict of 4
Amenhotep I 292
Amenhotep II 15, 293
Amenhotep III the Magnificent 7–8, **15–16**
Amenhotep IV 8
American Revolution 49, 113–114
Amiens, Battle of 130
Amiens, Treaty of 213
Amin, Hafizollah 16, 157, 289
Amin, Idi 16
Amnesty International 255
Amnon 81
Amon (Egyptian god) 8, 142, 251
Amorite dynasty 207
Amphictyonic League 67
Anacreon 246
Anastasius I 154, 167–168
Anatolia 31, 32, 43, 74, 220, 269, 270, 276, 294, 310
Anaxagoras 234
Anchimolius 137
An Chinghsu 17
ancien régime 58, 264
Andernach, Battle of 227
Andom, Aman Michael 17, 189
Androcles 10
Anfao, Battle of 20
Angelos, Isaac 146
Angevin Empire 127
Anglo-Dutch War (1672-78) 178
Angola 219
An Lushan 16–17
Anne of Cleves 134
Announcer, The (newspaper) 230
Antigonus I Doson 252
Antigonus II Gonatus 252
Antiochus IV 82
Antiochus V 82
Antonescu, Ion 17–18
Antoninus, T. Aurelius 119
Antonius Saturninus, Lucius 26, 87
Apache Indians 248
A-pao-chi 18
Aper 85
Apollo 75
appeasement 139, 304
Apraskin, Feodor 238
"April Theses" 166
aqueducts 200, 246, 271
Aquino, Corazon 188
Aquino Jr., Benigno 188
Arafat, Yasir 18, 21

Aragón 32, 98
Arbenz Guzman, Jacobo 46
Arboga, Articles of 94
Arbogast 292
Archaemenid Empire 80
archery 20
Ardashir I 18–19, 274
Arévalo Bermejo, Juan José 46
Argentina 46, 109–110, 234–235
Arguello, Leonard 279
Arias, Anulfo 301
Aristotle 232
Ark of the Covenant 81
Armada, Spanish *see* Spanish Armada
Armenia 108, 199, 218, 242, 275, 295–296, 303
Arminians 163
Arnold of Brescia 102
Arnulf of Carinthia 33
Arriba (periodical) 250
Arroyo, Carlos 308
Arslan, Alp 264
Arslan, Kilidsh 103
Artabanus V 19
Artavasdos 167–168
Artaxerxes I 80, 319
arts
  patrons
    Abbadid al-Mu'tadid 1
    Alexander VI 15
    Augustus 26
    Chandragupta II 52
    Elizabeth of Russia 92
    Harsha 123
    Hippias 137–138
    Louis (Ludwig) II 180
    Louis XIV 177
    Mahmud of Ghazna 184
    Cosimo de' Medici 195
    Lorenzo de' Medici 195–196
    Mohammed II the Conqueror 203
    Otto I the Great 228
    Peisistratus 232
    Polycrates 246
    Psamtik I 251
    Francesco Sforza 273
    Ludovico Sforza 273
    Sixtus IV 277
    Solon 278–279
    Suleyman I the Magnificent 285–286
    William I of Sicily 315
  students/practitioners
    Frederick the Great 92
    Hitler 138
    Leopold I 169
Ashikaga Takauji 19, 225
Ashikaga Yoshiaki 225
Ashurbanipal 19–20
Ashurnasirpal II 20, 274
Asia Minor
  Bayezid II and 32
  Darius I and 79

Darius II Ochus and 80
Demetrius I Soter and 82
Leo III the Isaurian and 167
Mithradtes VI and 199–200
Nero and 218
Set I and 272
Themistocles and 290
Tiglath-pileser I and 294
Askia Muhammad 20–21
Askian dynasty 20–21
Asoka 21
Aspasia 234
asphyxiation 1, 50, 294
Assad, Hafiz al- 21–22
assassination
  perpetrators/plotters
    Ahmed 6
    Idi Amin 16
    Attila the Hun 24
    Baybars I 32
    Christophe 65
    Coard 69
    Darius III 80
    Gómez Castro 115
    Hasan-e-Sabbah 124–125
    Hussein 145
    Kassem 158
    Marcos 188
    Mariam 189–190
    Nero 219
    Obando 225
    Pyrrhus 252
    Severus 272
    Stalin 281
    Timoleon 296
  survivors of plots/attempts
    Claudius 66
    Commodus 69
    Hitler 140
    Cosimo de' Medici 194
    Lorenzo de' Medici 195
    Napoléon I 213
    Phibunsongkhram 239
  victims
    Albion 9
    Alcibiades 10
    Alexander I 11–12
    Alexander II 12
    Hafizollah Amin 16
    An Lushan 17
    Caesar 43
    Canalejas 44
    Canute IV 44
    Caracalla 45
    Castillo Armas 47
    Catherine the Great's
      husband 48
    Charles of Portugal 54
    Charles I of France adviser
      55
    Chilperic I 63
    Doe 85–86
    Dollfuss 86
    Domitian 87
    Duong Van Minh 88
    Ferdinand II general 99
    Gallienus 109
    García Moreno 111
    Harsha's elder brother 123
    Henry II dissident
      churchman 127
    Henry III 129
    Henry IV predecessors 130
    Heureaux 137

Hippias brother 137
Hojo Masako's eldest son
  141
Julianus 154
Leo V 168
Nadir Shah 211
Ngo Dinh Diem 219–220
Nicephorous II Phocas 221
Philip II of Macedon 240
Pizarro 246
Portales 249
Rahman 255
Shaka 274
Anastasio Somoza Debayle
  279
Anastasio Somoza Garcia
  280
Suárez Flamerich
  predecessor 284
Suharto military colleagues
  284
Trujillo Molina 304
William II Rufus 316
Assassins (sect) 32, 124–125
Assyria 19–20, 94–95, 217,
  250–251, 269, 270–271, 274,
  294–295, 304
astronomy 34
Aswan Dam (Egypt) 216
Atabanus 319
Atahualpa 22–23, 245–246
Atatürk, Mustafa Kemal 23–24
Athens (city-state) 9–10, 65–66,
  79–80, 87, 137–138, 232,
  233–234, 278–279, 290, 319
Aton (sun god) 7–8, 142
Atossa 78
Attalus II 82
Attila the Hun 24, 24–25
Auckland, Lord 290
Audencia 129
Audoin 9
Auerstedt, Battle of 214
Augsburg, League of 178
Augsburg, War of the League of
  170, 192–193
"Augustan age" 26
**Augustus, Gaius Julius Caesar
Octavianus 25,** 25–26, 136, 242,
  293
Augustus II 58
Aurelius, Marcus see Marcus
  Aurelius
Austerlitz, Battle of 11, 214
Austin, Hudson 69
Austria 86, 92, 100–101, 139,
  169–170, 214
Austria-Hungary 97, 100–101,
  296, 316
Austrian Succession, War of the
  (1740–48) 105, 188
Austro-Prussian War (1866) 180
Autumn Harvest Uprising 186
Avanti! (newspaper) 208
Avars 9, 28–29, 53, 135
Awami League 6
Ayub Khan, Muhammad 34
Ayyubid dynasty 32, 266
Azikwe, Nnamdi 222
Aztec Empire 7, 73–74, 200–202

B

Baal (god) 91

Ba'ath Party 21, 145
Babur 27
Babylon/Babylonia 13, 33, 74,
  78, 82, 94, 120–121, 207,
  217–218, 269, 270–271, 294, 295,
  319
"Babylonian Captivity" 217
Bacchylides 75
Bacon, Nathaniel 27–28
Bacon, Sir Francis 27
"Bacon's Rebellion" 27–28
Bactria 81–82
Bairam Khan 7
Baja California 74
Bajan 28–29
Bakr, Ahmed Hassan 145
Balbinus 193
Balkan League 97
Balkans 3, 4, 32, 275–276, 311
Balkan War, Second (1913) 97
Balkan Wars of 1912-13 11, 97,
  198
Balkh, Battle of 1
Ballivián, José 29
Balmaceda, José 203
Bana 123
Bandit Suppression Campaigns
  62
Bangladesh 6, 35, 255
Bank of Credit and Commerce
  Internaional (BCCI) 223
Banti, Tafari 189
Bao Dai 220
Barbarossa 29–30
Barbarossa, Operation see
  Operation Barbarossa
Bardiya 78
Barebones Parliament 76
Bari, Battle of 263–264
Bar Kochba, Simon 119
Barrientos Ortuño, René 30
Basil II Bulgaroctonos 30–31
Basiliscus 108
Basques 53
Bastille (French prison) 57, 179
Bataan Death March 187
Bathsheba 81
**Batista (y Zaldívar), Fulgencio
31–32,** 47–48
Bavaria 103, 174, 180, 227
Bavarian Succession, War of the
  (1778-79) 188
Baybars I 32
Bayezid I 32, 196
Bayezid II 32, 270, 285
Bay of Pigs Invasion 47–48
Beatrice of Burgundy 102
Beauharnais, Joséphine de 212
Becket, Thomas à 127
Bedriacum, Battle of 310
Beer Hall Putsch 138
beheading
  of Abd ar-Rahman III foe 3
  by Charlemagne, of 4000
    Saxons 53
  of Clement IV foe 67
  of Harun ar-Rashid adviser
    124
  by Herod Antipas, of John the
    Baptist 135
  of Laud 164
  of Murad IV political
    opponent 207

of Nicephorous I 220
Bekbulatovich, Simeon 149
Bela III 33
Bela IV 33
Belgium 170–171, 305
Bellerophon (British warship) 215
Belshazzar 33
Belzu, Isidro 29
Benedict IV, Pope 34
Benedict V, Pope 228
Benedict XIII, Antipope 163
Beneventum, Battle of 252
Berbers 2–3, 29–30
Berchtold, Leopold 101
Berengar 33–34, 227–228
Berenice II 34, 34
Berenice III 34, 251
Beria, Lavrenti 281
Berkeley, William 27–28
Berlin, Treaty of 4
Berlin Wall 307
Bestuzhev-Ryumin, Aleksei 92
Béthencourt, Jean de 130
Bethlen, István 143
Bhutto, Benazir 35
Bhutto, Zulfikar Ali 34–35, 323
Biblical figures
  Belshazzar 33
  David 80–81
  Herod Antipas 135
  Nebuchadnezzar II and
    217–218
  Saul 269–270
  Solomon 277–278
Bicci, Giovanni di 194
Bignone, Reynaldo 110
Bindusara 53
**Birendra Bir Bikram Shah Dev
35**
Bishop, Maurice 35–36, 69
Bismarck, Otto von 40, 100–101,
  180, 282, 316
Bissandougou, Treaty of 267
Black Panthers 253
Blanqui, Louis-Auguste 208
Blenheim, Battle of 170, 193
blinding
  by Basill II, of 15,000
    Bulgarians 31
  of Berengar foe 34
  of Boleslav III the Blind 37
  of Boleslav III the
    Wry-Mouthed's brother 37
  of Harald IV Gille foe 122
  of Nadir Shah's son 211
blockade
  of Agathocles' Syracuse 5
  by Bayezid I, of
    Constantinople 32
  of Castro's Cuba 48
  by Christian III allies, of the
    Baltic 64
  by John I Zimisces, of the
    Danube 152
  by Lysander, of Athens 180
  by Napoléon I, of British
    trade 214
  by Nasser, of Eilat 216
Blood River, Battle of 84
Blücher, Gebhard von 215
Boabdil, Muhammad XI 36
Boers 84, 274
Boethius 291

Bohemia 37, 46, 113
Bohemian Diet 99
Bokassa, Eddine Ahmed 36–37
Boleslav I the Cruel 37
Boleslav I the Brave 37
Boleslav II the Bold 37
Boleslav II the Pious 37
Boleslav III the Blind 37
Boleslav III the Wry-Mouthed 37
Boleyn, Anne 92, 133, 134, 190
Bolingbroke, Henry *see* Henry IV
Bolívar, Simon 29, 225
Bolivia 29, 30, 110, 217
Bologna, Concordat of 169
Bolsheviks and Bolshevik Revolution 14, 142, 162, 165–167, 230, 254, 281, 298, 307
Bonaparte, Joseph 37–38, 214
Bonaparte, Napoléon *see* Napoléon I
Boniface VIII, Pope 114, 176, 241
Boniface IX, Pope 163
Book of Common Prayer 163
Borgia, Alonso de 14
Borgia, Cesare 15, **38**
Borgia, Lucrezia 38
Boris III 38–39
Bose, Subhas Chandra 39
Bosnia-Hercegovina 97, 198, 202, 206
Bosworth Field, Battle of 132, 261
Botticelli, Sandro 195, 277
Boudicca 218
Boulanger, Georges Ernest 40
Bourbon Compact 55
Bouvines, Battle of 103
Boxer Rebellion 306
boxing 16
Boyars 115, 148–149, 237
Brahmanism 156
Bramante, Donato 273
Braun, Eva 140
Brazil 99–100, 231–232, 238
Breasted, James Henry 293
Brest-Litovsk, Treaty of 167
Brezhnev, Leonid Ilich 40–41, 289
Britain, Battle of 139
Broz, Josip *see* Tito
Brundisium, Treaty of 26
Brussels, Treaty of 192
Brutus, Marcus Junius 26, 43
bubonic plague 155, 298
Buckingham, Duke of 54–55, 261
Buddhism
    adherents to
        Ashikaga Takauji 19
        Asoka 21
        Hojo Masako's wife 141
        Kanishka 156–157
    foes of
        Minh Mang 198
        Ngo Dinh Diem 220
        Oda Nobunaga 225
    friends of
        Kublai Khan 162
    students of
        Phibunsongkhram 239
Budenny, Semen M. 243
Buganda 209–210
Bukharin, Nikolai 281

Bulgaria 31, 38–39, 61, 97, 185, 282, 322
Bulgars 168, 206, 220, 275–276, 311
Bulge, Battle of the 140
bull fighting 245
Bulnes, Manuel 203
Burma 289–290
Burney, Harvey 290
Burrus 218
Busch, Germán 30
Bush, George 223–224
"Butcher of June" *see* Cavaignac, Louis-Eugène
Byzantine Empire
    allies
        Bajan 28
        Baybars I 32
        Bela III 33
        Frederick I Barbarossa 103
    foes
        Charlemagne 53
        Harun ar-Rashid 124
        Mohammed II the Conqueror 202
        Simeon I 275–276
        Theodoric I the Great 291
    overlords
        Murad I 206
    rulers
        Basil II Bulgaroctonos 30–31
        Heraclius 135
        John I Zimisces 151–152
        Justinian I 154–155
        Leo III the Isaurian 168
        Leo V 168
        Nicephorous I 220
        Nicephorous II Phocas 220–221
        Romanos IV Diogenes 264
        Theodora 290–291
    soldiers in army of
        Harald III Sigurdson 122

C

Cabrera y Grinó, Ramón 42
Cadaver Synod 271
Caesar, Gaius Julius 25, **42–43,** 67–68, 136, 247, 287, 293, 308–309
Caesar, L. Aelius 119
Calais (France) 190
calendar 237
California 268
Caligula 43–44, 66–67, 135, 218, 294
Calixtus III, Pope *see* Borgia, Alonso de
Calonne, Charles-Alexandre de 179
Calvinism 170, 283, 286
Camargo, Alberto 115
Cambodia 246
Cambon, Pierre-Paul 40
Cambrai, League of 192
Cambyses 78
Camillus, Marcus Furius 44
Campo Formio, Treaty of 212
Campora, Hector 235
Canalejas y Méndez, José 44
canals 79
Canary Islands 130, 313
cannibalism 36–37

Canute IV 44
Capetian-Angevin War 146
Capetian dynasty 125–126
Cappadocia 82
Caracalla 45, 45, 91
Carchemish, Battle of 217
Carew, Sir Thomas 190
Carinus 85
Carlist Party 42
Carmona, Antonio Oscar de Fragoso 267
Carol II 45–46
Carolingian Empire 33
Carranza, Venustiano 144
Carrera, José Miguel 46
Carteaux, Jean-Baptiste 212
Carter, Jimmy 40, 189, 301
Carthage 5, 66, 85, 108, 111, 120, 252, 296
Casey, William 223
Casimir IV 46, 113, 148
Cassius Longinus, Gaius 26, 43
Castelar y Ripoll, Emilio 231
Castile, Kingdom of 32, 128, 129–130, 147, 236
Castillo Armas, Carlos 46–47
castration 5
Castro Ruz, Fidel 32, **47–48,** 223, 308
Catalonian Wars 98
Cateau-Cambrésis, Peace of 128
Catherine II the Great 48–49, 92, 230–231
Catherine de' Medici 49–50, 128–129
Catherine of Aragón 98, 132–133, 190
Catherine of Lancaster 130
Catholic League 129
Cavaignac, Louis-Eugène 50–51
Ceausescu, Elena 51
Ceausescu, Nicolae 51
Celestine III, Pope 146
censorship
    by Chin Shih Huang-ti 63
    by Cleisthenes of Sicyon 67
    by Gómez Castro 115
    by Husák 145
    lifted by Frederick the Great 105
    by Zia 323
Cento (Florentine senate) 195
Central African Republic 36–37
Central Intelligence Agency (CIA) 46, 47, 88, 157, 223, 244, 304, 323
Cerezo Arévalo, Marco Vinicio 197
Cespedes, Carlos Manuel de 31
Cetshwayo 51–52, 204
Châlons, Battle of 25
Chamorro, Violeta 227
Chandragupta I 52, 267–268
Chandragupta II 52
Chandragupta Maurya 21, **52–53,** 265
Chang, John 230
Chang Tsol-lin 317
chariots 10, 67, 232, 256, 293
Charlemagne 33–34, **53–54,** 102–103, 174, 191, 192, 220, 287
Charles I (England) 54, **54–55,** 75–77, 164

Charles I (Holy Roman Empire) 296
Charles I (Portugal) 54
Charles II (England) 76–77, 164, 238
Charles II (Spain) 170
Charles III the Fat 33–34, **55–56**
Charles IV (Spain) 214
Charles V (Holy Roman Empire) 30, *56,* **56–57,** 64, 128–129, 133, 190, 240
Charles VI (France) 131
Charles VIII (France) 15, **57,** *57,* 98, 191, 273
Charles IX (France) 50, 130
Charles IX (Sweden) 94
Charles X (France) 57–58, 180
Charles X Gustav (Sweden) 105
Charles XI (Sweden) 58
Charles XII (Sweden) 58–59, 237–238
Charles the Bold 59–60
Charter Oath 196
Chaudhry, Fazal Elahi 323
Chaves, Federico 283
Cheka (secret police) 167
Ch'en Chiung-ming 61
Ch'en dynasty 313
Cheng Ch'eng-kung 60
Cheng Chi-lung 60
Cheng-te 60–61
Chervenkov, Vulko 61
Chiang Ch'ing 187
Chiang Kai-shek 61–62, 63, 186–187, 317
Chile 29, 46, 203–204, 244, 248–249
Chilperic I 62–63
China
    communist leaders
        Chou En-lai 63–64
        Deng Xiaoping 82–83
        Liu Shaoqi 172
        Mao Tse-tung 185–187
    conquerors of
        Genghis Khan 112
    emperors
        An Lushan 16–17
        A-pao-chi 18
        Cheng Ch'eng-kung 60
        Cheng Chi-lung 60
        Cheng-te 60–61
        Chin Shih Huang-ti 63
        Hung Hsiu-ch'uan 144
        Kao Tsu, T'ang 157
        Kuang Wu Ti 161
        Liu Pang 172
        Su-ma Yen 280
        Ts'ao Ts'ao 304–305
        Tz'u-hsi 305–306
        Wei Chung-hsien 312–313
        Wen Ti 313
        Wu P'ie-fu 317
        Wu Ti 317
        Wu Wang 317–318
        Yen Hsi-shan 320–321
        Yung Lo 321
    foreign leaders and
        Castro 48
        Hoxha 143–144
        Kim Il Sung 160
        Kittikachorn 161
        Tojo Hideki 298
    nationalist leaders

Chiang Kai-shek 61–62
Chin dynasty 18, 63, 112
Ching Ti 317
Chin Shih Huang-ti 63, 172
Chosroes I 155
Chou dynasty 317–318
Chou En-lai 63–64
Chou Hsin 317
Christian III 64
Christian IV 64, 105
Christianity *see also* Christians,
   persecutors of; Church of
   England; Roman Catholic
   Church
      Afonso I and 4–5
      Atahualpa and 22–23
      Basil II and 31
      Boleslav III the Wry-Mouthed
         and 37
      Constantine I the Great and
         70–72
      Harald II Eiriksson and 121
      Heraclius and 135
      Herod Antipas and 135
      Hung Hsiu-ch'uan and 144
      Justinian I and 154–155
      Mutesa I and 209
      Shapur I and 275
      Suleyman I the Magnificent
         and 285
      Theodosius I the Great and
         291–292
      Toyotomi Hideyoshi and 303
      Yazdegerd II and 320
Christians, persecutors of
      Decius 81
      Diocletian 85
      Galerius 108–109
      Julian the Apostate 153–154
      Maximinus 194
      Minh Mang 198–199
      Nero 218
      Phan Thanh Gian 239
      Saladin 266
      Shapur II the Great 275
      Valerian 308
Christophe, Henri 64–65
Chronicles (book by Holinshed)
   182
Chrysopolis, Battle of 31
Chu Kao-chih 321
Churchill, Sir Winston 132, 282
Church of England 93, 133–134,
   190
Chu Ti 321
Chu Yun-wen 321
Cicero 26
Cilicia 220
Cimmerians 95
Cimon 65–66
**Cincinnatus, Lucius Quinctius
   66**
circumcision 119
civil liberties *see* human rights
civil wars *see* English civil wars;
   Spanish Civil War
Clarendon, Council of 127
Claudius 66–67, 218
Cleisthenes of Sicyon 67, 137
Clemenceau, Georges 40
Clement II, Pope 129
Clement III, Pope 103
Clement IV, Pope 67

Clement VII, Pope 49–50, 133,
   190
Clement VIII, Pope 226
Clement, Jacques 129
Cleomenes I 137
Cleonymus 252
Cleopatra VII 26, 43, **67–68,** 136
Cleveland, Grover 171
Clovis I 68–69
Coard, Bernard 36, **69**
codes
   of Hammurabi 121
   of Solon 87
Cognac, League of 56
Cohen, Andrew 210
coinage
   Darius I and 79
   Kao Tsu and 157
   Muhammad ibn Tughluq and
      206
   Nero and 218
   Postumus and 249
Colbert, Jean-Baptiste 177
Cold War 40–41, 101, 282
Coleridge, Samuel Taylor 161
collectivization 281, 307
Colombia 115
colonialism
   imposers/upholders of
      Afonso I 4–5
      Cortés 73–74
      Elizabeth I 93
      Ferdinand II 98
      Frontenac 106–107
      George III 113–114
      Henry III the Sufferer 130
      Isabella I 147
      Kieft 159–160
      Leopold II 170–171
      Louis XIV 177
      Manuel I the Fortunate 185
      Pizarro 245–246
      Rhodes 258–259
      Smith 277
      Stuyvesant 283–284
   opponents of
      Bose 39
      Cetshwayo 52
      Ho Chi Minh 140
      Mutesa II 210
      Neto 219
      Ngo Dinh Diem 219–220
      Nkrumah 222
      Phan Thanh Gian 238–239
      Popé 247–248
      Powhatan 249–250
      Samori Touré 267
      Suharto 284
      Sukarno 285
      Tharawaddy 290
      Touré 301
      Toussaint L'Ouverture
         301–302
      Tshombe 305
Colosseum (Rome, Italy) 298, 310
Columbus, Christopher 98, 147
Comentiolus 29
Comintern 140, 162, 167, 298, 307
Committee of Public Safety 264
Commodus 69, **69–70,** 119, 154,
   272
communism
   opponents of
      Boris III 38–39

Chiang Kai-shek 61–62
   Horthy 142–143
   Kassem 158
   Kittikachorn 161
   Marcos 188
   Ngo Dinh Diem 219–220
proponents of
   Bishop 36
   Brezhnev 40–41
   Castro Ruz 47–48
   Ceausescu 51
   Chervenkov 61
   Chou En-lai 63–64
   Coard 69
   Deng Xiaoping 82–83
   Ho Chi Minh 140
   Hoxha 143–144
   Husák 145
   Jaruzelski 150
   Karmal 157–158
   Kim Il Sung 160
   Kun 162
   Lenin 165–167
   Mao Tse-tung 185–187
   Neto 219
   Novotny 224
   Picado 242–243
   Pol Pot 246
   Stalin 280–282
   Tito 296–298
   Ulbricht 307
   Zhivkov 322
Como Berenices (constellation) 34
Comonfort, Ignacio 152, 199
Companions (nobles who served
   Philip II) 239
Conan IV 112–113
concentration camps 139, 216
Conflans, Treaty of 59–60
Confucianism 62, 63, 162, 185,
   198–199, 238, 257, 313, 321
Congo 170–171, 200, 305
Conley incident 164–165
Conrad I 126–127
Conrad II 129
Conrad III 70
Consolation of Philosophy, The
   (book) 291
Constantine I the Great 70–72,
   71, 72, 183
Constantine IV 220
Constantine V 168
Constantine X 264
Constantine XI 202
Constantinople 4, 8–9, 24, 28, 32,
   70–72, 134–135, 146, 154–155,
   168, 175, 220, 275–276, 286, 292,
   311
Constantinople, Second Council
   of 155
Constantius I 108
Constantius II 72–73, 153–154
Constituent Assembly 215
Continental System 214
Contras 223, 227
Copenhagen, Treaty of 105
copper 204
Córdoba, Pact of 36
Corfu 30
Corinth 77, 232–233
Corinth, League of 80, 239
Corinthian War 181
Cortenuova, Battle of 96, 104

Cortés, Hernán *73,* **73–74,**
   200–202, 245
Cossacks 276
Costa Rica 242–243
Council of Clarendon 127
Council of Five Hundred 38
Council of Forty 100
Council of Nicaea 71
Council of Pisa 163, 192
Council of Seventy 195
Council of Ten 100
Council of Trent 244–245
"Count Dracula" 310–311
counterfeiting 206
Counter-Reformation 99, 118,
   170, 240
coups d'état
   participants in
      Mejía Victores 197
      Torrijos 301
   stagers of
      Agathocles 5
      Ahmed 6
      Hafizollah Amin 16
      Idi Amin 16
      Andom 17
      Barrientos Ortuño 30
      Batista 31
      Bishop 35–36
      Bokassa 36–37
      Carrera 46
      Coard 69
      Elizabeth of Russia 92
      Garcia Meza 110
      Gowon 115–116
      Khanh 158
      López Arellano 173–174
      Natusch Busch 217
      Nkrumah and 222
      Noriega 223
      Pilsudski 244
      Pinochet 244
      Qaddafi 253
      Salazar 267
      Stroessner 283
      Tz'u-hsi 306
      Zia 322–323
   survivors of
      Portales 249
      Rahman 255
      Suharto 284
   victims of
      Antonescu 18
      Bhutto 34–35
      Boris III 38–39
      Castillo Armas 46–47
      Haile Selassie 120
      Leguía y Salcedo 165
      Mariam 189
      Napoléon I 213
      Napoléon III 215
      Nicephorous I 220
      Nkrumah 222
      Pahlavi 229
      Péron 234
      Phibunsongkhram 239
      Picado 242
      Primo de Rivera 250
      Ríos Montt 263
Crabb, Henry Alexander 74
Crassus, Marcus Licinius 42, 247
Crépy, Peace of 30
Crete 220
Crimea 12, 199, 221

Crispius 72
Croatia 202
Croesus 74–75, 78
Cromwell, Oliver 55, *75,* **75–77,** 164
Cromwell, Richard 77
Cromwell, Thomas 133–134
crucifixion 246
Crusades
    Baybars I and 32
    Bayezid I and 32
    Conrad III and 70
    Edward I Longshanks and 90
    Frederick I Barbarossa and 102, 103
    Frederick II and 103–104
    Henry V and 132
    Heraclius and 135
    Innocent III and 146
    John and 150
    Louis IX and 176
    Louis VII and 175
    Philip II Augustus and 241
    Richard I the Lionhearted and 259–260
    Saladin and 266
    William II Rufus and 315
    William I of Sicily and 315
Cruz, Ramón Ernesto 173
Ctesias 75
Cuauhtémoc 202
Cuba 31–32, 36, 47–48, 73, 182–183, 219, 227, 244, 308, 313–314
Cuitlahuac 202
Cultural Revolution 187
Cunimund 28
currency 162
Cushites 251
Cyaxares 77
Cyprus 220
Cypselus 77, 232
Cyrus II the Great 77–78, 79
Cyrus the Younger 80, 180
Czechoslovakia 40–41, 139, 145, 162, 224

D

Dacian Wars 119, 193
Dacko, David 36–37
da Costa, Gomes 267
da Gama, Vasco 185
d'Albret, Constable Charles 131
Dalmatia 29, 33, 202
Danilo I 79
d'Annunzio, Gabriele 208
Danton, Georges 264
Darius I 79, 319
Darius II Ochus 79–80
Darius III 13, **80**
Darius the Mede 33
Das, C. R. 39
Datis of Media 79
Daudi Chwa II 210
David 80–81, 87, 270, 277–278
da Vinci, Leonardo 195, 273
D-Day 140
De Beers Consolidated Mines, Ltd. 258
Decabulus 303
decapitation *see* beheading
Decembrist Uprising 221

Decius 81
"Defender of the Faith" 134
de Gaulle, Charles 236, 301
Delgado Chalbaud, Carlos 284
Delian League 65, 233
Delium, Battle of 9
della Vigna, Pietro 104
Delphi, Oracle at *see* Oracle at Delphi
del Pollaiuolo, Antonio 277
Demetrius 81–82
Demetrius I Poliorcetes 252
Demetrius I Soter 82, *82*
de Narváez, Panfilo 74
Deng Xiaoping 82–83
Denmark 44, 58, 64, 94, 105, 117–118, 122, 126
Dentatus, M. Curius 252
Dessalines, Jean-Jacques 65, 302
détente 41
diamonds 211, 258–259
Diaz, Adolfo 279
Díaz, Porfirio 83–84, 144
Dimitry (II) Donskoy 84
Din, Khair ed- 29
Dingane 84, 204
Diocletian 71, **84–85,** 108, 194
Dionysius I 85
Directory (French legislative body) 38, 212, 302
Djidjelli 29–30
Dobrudja, Battle of 81
Doe, Samuel K. 85–86
Dolabella, Gnaeus Cornelius 42
Dole, Sanford 171
Dollfuss, Engelbert 86
Dominican Republic 137, 304
Domitian 87, 303, 310
Domitianus, Domitius *see* Achilleus
Domitilla, Flavia 87
Domna, Julia 45
Dom Pedro II 99–100
Donatello 195
Dönitz, Karl 140
Doria, Andrea 30
d'Orléans, Gaston 262
Doumergue, Robert 235
Dover, Treaty of 164
Draco 87
Drake, Sir Francis 93
Dresden, Battle of 11
drug trafficking 110, 223–224
Drusus 293
Duarte, Eva (Evita) 234–235
Dubcek, Alexander 145, 224
Dukas, Alexis 146
Duncan I 182
Duong Van Minh 87–88, 158
Dutch War of 1672-78 58
Dutch West India Company 283–284
Duvalier, François "Papa Doc" 88, 280
Duvalier, Jean-Claude "Baby Doc" 88–89, 280

E

Eadred of England 94
earthquakes 279
East Germany 307
East India Company 64

Ecloga (Roman legal code) 168
Ecuador 110–111, 308
Edict of Amboise 50
Edict of January (1562) 50
Edict of Nantes 130, 178
Edict of Restitution (1629) 99
Edmund II Ironside 95
educational reformers
    Abdul-Aziz 3
    Elizabeth (Russia) 92
    Frederick II 103
    Godunov 115
    Machado y Morales 182
    Maria Theresa 189
    Manuel Montt 203
    Napoléon I 213
    Nicholas I 221
    Philip II Augustus 241
    Zelaya 322
Edward I Longshanks 90, 241
Edward III (of Windsor) 90–91, *91,* 242, 260
Edward IV 132
Edward V 261
Edward VI 92–93, 134
Edward the Confessor 314
Edward the Martyr 95
Egypt, ancient
    foreign rulers and
        Alexander the Great 13
        Ashurbanipal 19
        Augustus 26
        Caesar 42
        Darius III 80
        Demetrius I Soter 82
        Diocletian 85
        Esarhaddon 95
        Solomon 277–278
        Xerxes I 319
    rulers
        Ahmose I 6–7
        Akhenaton 7–8
        Amenhotep the Magnificent 15–16
        Baybars I 32
        Berenice II 34
        Berenice III 34
        Cleopatra VII 67–68
        Hatshepsut 125
        Horemhab 142
        Maximinus and 193–194
        Psamtik I 250–251
        Ptolemy XI Alexander II 251
        Ramses II the Great 255–256
        Ramses III 256–257
        Seti I 271–272
        Thutmose I 292
        Thutmose II 292–293
        Thutmose III 293
Egypt, medieval 5–6, 266
Egypt, modern 2, 204–205, 206, 212, 216–217
Eisenhower, Dwight D. 32, 47, 197
Elagabalus 91–92
Elam 269
Eleanor of Aquitaine 112–113, 127, 175, 259
elephants 53, 249, 252
Eleusinian Mysteries 10
Elizabeth (Russia) **92**
Elizabeth I (England) **92–93,** *92–93,* 134, 190, 245
El Salvador 322

empire builders
    Abd al-Mu'min 2–3
    Abd ar-Rahman III 3
    Alexander the Great 12–13
    Ardashir I 18–19
    Ashurnasirpal II 20
    Basil II Bulgaroctonos 30–31
    Bayezid I 32
    Bayezid II 32
    Clovis I 68–69
    Cyrus II the Great 77–78
    Darius I 79
    Erik VII 94
    Genghis Khan 111–112
    Harsha 123
    Isabella I 147
    Kanishka 156–157
    Mahmud of Ghazna 184
    Manuel I the Fortunate 185
    Menelik II 197
    Mithradates VI 199–200
    Moctezuma I 200–201
    Mohammed II the Conqueror 202–203
    Nadir Shah 211
    Napoléon I 211–215
    Ogödei 225–226
    Peter I the Great 237–238
    Pilsudski, Jozef 244
    Pyrrhus 252
    Samudragupta 267–268
    Sargon of Akkad 269
    Selim I 270
    Sennacherib 270–271
    Shapur II the Great 275
    Simeon I 275–276
    Solomon 277–278
    Suleyman I the Magnificent 285–286
    Tamerlane 288–289
    Tiglath-pileser I 294–295
    Tiglath-pileser III 295
    Xerxes I 319
Enabling Act (1933) 139
England
    foreign rulers and
        Frederick I Barbarossa 103
        Philip II 240
    monarchs
        Charles I 54–55
        Edward I Longshanks 90
        Edward III 90–91
        Elizabeth I 92–93
        Ethelred II the Unready 95
        Geoffrey IV Plantagenet 112–113
        Harold I Barefoot 122
        Harold II Godwineson 122–123
        Henry I 126
        Henry II 127–128
        Henry V 131–132
        Henry VII 132–133
        Henry VIII 133–134
        John 150–151
        Mary I 190
        Richard I the Lionhearted 259–260
        Richard II 260–261
        William I the Conqueror 314–315
        William II Rufus 315
    nonmonarchical rulers/leaders

Cromwell 75–77
Laud 163–164
Lauderdale 164
England, Church of *see* Church of England
English civil wars 55, 75–77
Enlightenment
    Catherine the Great and 48–49
    Charlemagne and 53
    Frederick the Great and 105
    Leopold II and 170
    Louis XVI and 178–179
    Robespierre and 264
Enrile, Juan 188
Enzio of Sardinia 104
Ephialtes 66
Epirus 251–252
Eretria 79
Eric of Sweden 93
Erik I Bloodax 93–94, 121
Erik VII 94
Erik XIV 94
Eritrea 17, 189
Ermaneric 94
Esarhaddon 19, **94–95**, 271
Estimé, Dumarsais 88
Estonia 230
Ethelred II the Unready 95, 95, 122
Ethiopia 2, 17, 119–120, 189–190, 197, 209
Etruscans 44, 66
Eucratides 82
Eudemus 249
Eudoxia 108
Eugenius III, Pope 102, 175, 292
Eusebius 71
excommunication
    imposers of
        Alexander VI 15
        Gregory VII 117
        Innocent III 146
        Leo X 168–169
        Pius V 245
        Sixtus IV 276
    targets of
        Elizabeth I 93
        Ezzelino III da Romano 96
        Frederick I Barbarossa 102
        Frederick II 104
        George of Podebrady 113
        Henry IV 130
        John 151
        Louis IV the Bavarian 174
        Muhammad ibn Falah 205
        Rais 255
executioners
    Abd ar-Rahman III 3
    Ahmed 6
    Alaric 9
    Alexander VI 15
    Andom 17
    Assad 22
    Boleslav II the Bold 37
    Boris III 38–39
    Caligula 43–44
    Charles XII 59
    Cheng-te 60–61
    Chin Shih Huang-ti 63
    Claudius 66
    Commodus 69–70
    Cromwell 76
    Doe 86

Domitian 87
Edward III 90–91
Ferdinand I 97–98
Franco 101
Frederick I Barbarossa 102
Garcia Meza 110
Harun ar-Rashid 124
Henry VII 132
Henry VIII 134
Heureaux 137
Hojo Yoshitoki 142
Hoxha 143
Ivan IV the Terrible 148–149
Juárez 153
Khomeini 159
Leopold I 170
Leo X 169
Mariam 189
Mary I 190
Mubarak 204
Muhammad Ali 205
Murad IV 207
Nero 218
Phraates IV 242
Pinochet 244
Rahman 255
Rhee 258
Richard III 261
Robespierre 264
Stalin 281
Theodora 290
Theodoric I the Great 291
Tiberius 294
Valerian 308
William II Rufus 315
Yung Lo 321
Zia 323
execution victims
    Abbadid al-Mu'tadid 1
    Antonescu 18
    Atahualpa 23
    Bishop 36
    Carrera 46
    Ceausescu 51
    Charles I 54–55
    Cheng Chi-lung 60
    Crabb 74
    Demetrius I Soter cousin 82
    Julianus 154
    Kassem 158
    Laud 163–164
    Louis XVI 179
    Lysander 181
    Maximilian 190–191
    Miramón 199
    Mussolini 209
    Ngo Dinh Diem 220
    Nicholas II 221–222
    Paul I 231
    Pompey the Great 247
    Primo de Rivera 250
    Quisling 253–254
    Rais, Gilles de 255
    Vercingetorix 309
    Walker 312
exiled rulers
    Amin, Idi 16
    Batista 32
    Bayezid II 32
    Boabdil 36
    Bokassa 36–37
    Boleslav II the Bold 37
    Bonaparte, Joseph 38
    Boulanger 40

Cabrera 42
Caesar, Julius 42
Carol II 46
Charles X 57–58
Cleopatra 67
Díaz 84
Erik VII 94
Ethelred I the Unready 95
García Moreno 111
Gómez Castro 115
Haile Selassie 120
Henry II 128
Henry VII 132
Herod Archelaus 136
Hussein 145
Juárez 152
Khanh 159
Lenin 166
López 173
Louis-Philippe 180
Machado y Morales 183
Marcos 188
Medici, Cosimo de' 194
Milan IV 198
Miramón 199
Mutesa II 209–210
Napoléon I 215
Napoléon III 215
Neto 219
Nkrumah 222
Obando 225
Olivares 226
Pahlavi, Muhammad Reza Shah 229
Péron 234–235
Phibunsongkhram 239
Pilsudski 243–244
Rhee 258
Samori Touré 267
Santa Anna 268–269
Somoza Debayle, Anastasio 279
Souloque 280
Stalin 281
Tiberius 294
Tshombe 305
Velasco Ibarra 308
Vlad the Impaler 311
William (Wilhelm) II 316
Yen Hsi-shan 320
Yung Lo 321
exploration 73–74, 245–246
Ezzelino III da Romano 95–96

F

Fabianism 97
Fabianus, Pope 81
Fabius Maximus Cunctator Quintus 97
Fairfax, Sir Thomas 75
Faisal II 158
Falange Party 101, 250
Falkland Islands (Malvinas) War 109–110
famine 2, 51, 115, 167, 187, 201, 248, 281, 313
fascism 39
    Antonescu and 17–18
    Boris III and 38–39
    Carol II and 46
    Franco and 101–102
    Gómez Castro and 115
    Hayashi Senjuro and 125

Hitler and 138–140
Metaxas and 198
Mussolini and 208–209
Péron and 234–235
Primo de Rivera and 250
Fatah, al- 18
Fath Ali Shah 5
Fatimids 31
F.E. (periodical) 250
Feng Yu-hsiang 317
Feng Yun-shan 144
Ferdinand I (Bulgaria) 97
Ferdinand I (Castile) 1
Ferdinand I (Naples) 97–98, 195
Ferdinand II the Catholic (Ferdinand V of Castile and Aragón) 36, 56, **98–99**, 132–133, 147, 169, 185, 192, 300
Ferdinand II (Holy Roman Empire) 99
Ferdinand III (Holy Roman Empire) 99
Ferdinand VII (Spain) 214
Ferrara, Peace of 100
Fifth Coalition 214
Figueres, José 242
filibuster 74, 312
Fimbria 200
Finland 92, 282
First Coalition 212
Flamininus 211
Fleetwood, Charles 76
Flodden, Battle of 134
Florence, Republic of 98, 169, 194–196
Flores, Juan José 110
Florida 56
Foix, Germaine de 99
Fonseca, Manuel Deodoro da 99–100
Fontenoy, Battle of 174, *188*
Ford, Gerald 40
Foreign Legion 101
Foscari, Francesco 100
Fouquet, Nicholas 177
Fra Angelico 195
France
    as colonial power
        Bokassa and 36–37
        Ho Chi Minh and 140
        Nasser and 216–217
        Ngo Dinh Diem and 219–220
        Phan Thanh Gian and 238–239
        Samori Touré and 267
        Touré and 301
        Toussaint L'Ouverture and 302
    foreign rulers and
        Abdul-Aziz 3
        Bela III 33
        Edward III 90–91
        Frederick I Barbarossa 103
        Geoffrey IV Plantagenet 112–113
        Hitler 139
        Muhammad Ali 205
    monarchs
        Catherine de' Medici 49–50
        Charles VIII 57
        Charles X 57–58
        Henry I 125–126

Henry II 128–129
Henry III 129
Henry IV 130–131
Louis IX 175–176
Louis-Philippe 179–180
Louis VII 175
Louis XI 176–177
Louis XIV 177–178
Louis XVI 178–179
Napoléon I 211–215
Napoléon III 215
Philip II Augustus 240–241
Philip IV the Fair 241–242
nonmonarchical
  rulers/leaders
  Adrets 4
  Bonaparte, Joseph 37–38
  Boulanger, Georges Ernest
    40
  Cavaignac 50–51
  Frontenac 106–107
  Pétain 235–236
  Rais 255
  Richelieu 261–263
  Robespierre 264
Francis I (France) 50, 56, 134
Francis I (of the Two Sicilies)
  100
Francis II (France) 50
Francis Ferdinand, Archduke
  101, 142, 221, 296, 316
Francis Joseph 100–101, 190, 296
Franco, Francisco 32, **101–102,**
  115, 209, 267
Franco, Joao 54
Franco-Prussian War of 1870-71
  40, 171, 180
Franks 28, 53–54, 68–69, 153, 174
Franz Josef *see* Francis Joseph
Frederick I Barbarossa 70,
  102–103, 241, 315
Frederick II (Holy Roman
  Empire) 14, 95–96, **103–104**
Frederick II the Great (Prussia)
  104, **104–105,** 188–189, 316
Frederick III (Denmark) **105**
Frederick V (Bohemia) 99
Frederick William I 104, **105–106**
Frederick William III 170
Free Economic Society 49
Free Officers movement 216
French and Indian War 105
French Revolution 49, 50–51,
  57–58, 113–114, 170, 178–179,
  264, 302
Freycinet, Charles-Louis de
  Saulses de 40
Frontenac, Louis de Buade de
  106–107
Fuero de los Espanoles 101
fur trade 106–107
Fyodor I 276
Fyrileif, Battle of 122

G

Gagelin, François 199
Gairy, Eric 35–36
Gaiseric 25, **108,** *108*
Gaitán, Jorge 115
Galba, Servius Supoicius 219
Galerius 85, **108–109,** 194
Gallegos, Romulo 284
Gallienus 109, *109,* 249, 308

Galtieri, Leopoldo Fortunato
  109–110
Gamarra, Agustin 29
Gambara, Battle of 96
Gammelsdorf, Battle of 174
Gandhi, Mohandas 6, 39, 222
Gang of Four 83, 187
García Menocal, Mario 183
Garcia Meza Tejada, Luis 110
García Moreno, Gabriel 110–111
Garibaldi, Giuseppe 153, 191
Garter, Order of the 91
Garvey, Marcus 222
Gaspard, Nicholas 60
Gauls 25, 42–43, 44, 68, 153, 247,
  249, 308–309
Gaza Strip 216
Gelon 111
Genghis Khan 7, 27, **111–112,**
  161, 225–226
genocide 77, 138–140
Geoffrey II Martel 112, 314
Geoffrey IV Plantagenet
  112–113, 127
George II (Greece) 198
George III (England) **113–114,**
  114
George of Podebrady 113
Gepidae 25, 28
Germany 70, 104–105, 316 *see
  also* East Germany; Nazi
  Germany
Gestapo 139
Ghana 222–223
Ghazan, Mahmud 114
Ghazna 184
Gheorghiu-Dej, Gheorghe 51
Ghiberti, Lorenzo 195
Gibraltar 56
Gilboa, Battle of Mount 81
Goblet, René 40
Go-Daigo 19
Godunov, Boris 115, 276
God Worshippers, Society of 144
Goebbels, Josef 138, 139
Goering, Hermann 138
gold 238, 258–259, 292
Golden Horde 84, 148, 299
Gómez, José Miguel 182
Gómez Castro, Laureano
  Eleuterio 115
Gordian I 308
Gordianus 193
Gordon, Charles George 2,
  183–184
Gorga, Battle of 27
Goths 45, 81, 291
Go-Toba 142
Gowon, Yakubu 115–116
Granada 36, 98, 147
Grand Alliance, War of the *see*
  Augsburg, War of the League of
Grand Canal (China) 313, 321
Grand Progenitor 18
Grand Remonstrance of the King
  55
Grant, Ulysses S. 153
Gratian 291
Great Britain *see also* England;
  Ireland; Scotland; Wales
  as colonial power
    Abd Allah and 2
    Abdul-Aziz and 3

Ahmed and 6
    Amin and 16
    Bose and 39
    Cetshwayo and 52
    Mutesa II and 210
    Nasser and 216–217
    Nkrumah and 222
    Smith and 277
  foreign rulers/leaders and
    Elizabeth of Russia 92
    Galtieri 110
    Hitler 139
    Muhammad Ali 205
    Napoléon I 212–215
    Napoléon III 215
  monarchs
    George III 113–114
Great Depression 165
Great Leap Forward 187
Great Panathenaic Festival 137
Great Peace 300
Great Proletarian Cultural
  Revolution 172
Great Wall of China 313
Great Yen dynasty 17
Greco-Turkish War of 1897 198
Greece 31, 97, 139, 197–198
Greece, Seven Sages of 233, 279
Green Gang 61
Gregory VII, Pope *116,* **116–117**
Gregory IX, Pope 14, 104
Gregory XII, Pope 163
Grenada 35–36, 69
Grey, Lady Jane 190
Griots 88
Guadalupe Hidalgo, Treaty of
  268
Guagamela, Battle of 13
Guatemala 46–47, 197, 263
Gudden, Bernhard von 180
Gueiler Tejada, Lydia 110
Guerrero, Vicente 268
guerrilla warfare 2, 18, 47,
  106–107, 140, 246, 263, 267, 309,
  317–318
Guevara, Anibal 197
Guevara, Ernesto "Che" 30, 47
Guevara Arze, Walter 217
guillotine 179, 264
Guinea, Republic of 301
Guinegate, Battle of 191
Guiscard, Robert *see* Robert
  Guiscard
Gulf War *see* Persian Gulf War
Guntram 62
Gupta dynasty 52
Gustav II Adolf *117,* **117–118**
Gyges 74, **118,** 250

H

Haakon the Great 121, 254
Hadrian 102, **119,** 304
Hadrian's Wall (England) 119
Hafrsfjord, Battle of 121
Hafsun 3
Hague, Peace of the (1790) 170
Haile Selassie 17, **119–120,**
  189–190
Haiti 64–65, 88–89, 213, 280,
  301–302
Halley's Comet 156

Hall of a Hundred Columns
  (Persepolis, Persia) 319
Hamilcar Barca 120
Hammurabi 120–121
Hammurabi, Code of 121
Han dynasty 161, 172, 280,
  304–305, 313, 317
hanging 35, 207, 299
Hanging Gardens of Babylon 217
Hannibal 97
Hantilis 207
Hapsburg dynasty 100–101, 118,
  169–170, 188–189, 191–192
Harald I Fairhair 93, **121**
Harald II Eiriksson 121
Harald III Sigurdson 122, 123
Harald IV Gille 122
Harold I Barefoot 122
Harold II Godwineson 122,
  122–123, 314
Harsha 123
Harshacharita (book) 123
Hartford, Treaty of 283
Harun ar-Rashid 123–124, 220
Hasan-e-Sabbah 124–125
Hastings, Battle of 123, 314, *315*
Hatshepsut 125, 292–293
Hawaii 156, 171–172
Hayashi Senjuro 125
Hearst, William Randolph 313
Hébert, Jacques 264
Hédouville, Gabriel 302
Heimskringla (poem) 121
Helena, Saint 215
Helsinki Agreement (1975) 41
Helvius Pertinax, Publius 70
Hemayun 7
Henry I (France) 112, **125–126,**
  314
Henry I Beauclerc (England)
  126, 127
Henry I the Fowler 126–127, 227
Henry II (England) 112–113,
  127–128, 175, 259
Henry II (Castile) **128**
Henry II (France) 4, 50, 126,
  128–129, 236, 241
Henry III (England) 67, 90, 176
Henry III (France) 50, **129**
Henry III (Holy Roman Empire)
  116, **129**
Henry III the Sufferer 129–130
Henry IV (England) 260
Henry IV (Holy Roman Empire)
  116–117, 260
Henry IV of Bourbon-Navarre
  129, *130,* **130–131,** 147, 240
Henry V (England) **131–132**
Henry VI (England) 261
Henry VII (England) *132,*
  132–133, 134
Henry VIII (England) 92–93, 98,
  133, **133–134,** 169, 190
Henry of Navarre *see* Henry IV
  of Bourbon-Navarre
Henry the Wrangler 37, 228
Heraclius 134–135
Herat, Battle of 1
Hercules 70
Herod Antipas 135, 136
Herod Archelaus 135–136
Herod I the Great 135, **136–137**

Herodotus 74–75, 78, 79, 118, 138, 233, 250
"Hero of Tampico" 268
Heureaux, Ulíses 137
Hibrida, Gaius Antonius 42
hijacking 16
Himera, Battle of 111
Himmler, Heinrich 138, 139
Hinduism 35
Hipparchus 137
Hippias 137–138
Hippocrates 111, 232
Hiram of Tyre 278
Hitler, Adolf 138–140
　allies/supporters of
　　Antonescu 17–18
　　Gómez Castro 115
　　Horthy 143
　　Mussolini 208–209
　　Pétain 235–236
　　Pilsudski 244
　　Quisling 253–254
　　Tojo Hideki 298–299
　foes of
　　Dollfuss 86
　　Stalin 280–282
　　Tito 298
　inspirations for
　　Frederick the Great 105
　leaders contrasted with
　　Lenin 165
　observers of
　　Bose 39
Hittites 207–208, 255–256, 272, 287
Ho Chi Minh 140, 219–220, 246
Hohenstaufen dynasty 67, 70, 102
Hojo Masako 140–141
Hojo Tokimasa 141
Hojo Tokimune 141
Hojo Ujimasa 299
Hojo Yasutoki 141–142
Hojo Yoshitoki 142
Holinshed, Raphael 182
Holocaust 139–140
Holstein 94
Holy Alliance 11
Holy League 15, 130, 191
Holy Roman Empire
　emperors
　　Berengar 33–34
　　Charles V 56
　　Ferdinand II 99
　　Frederick I Barbarossa 103
　　Frederick II 103–104
　　Henry III 129
　　Leopold I 169–170
　　Leopold II 170
　　Louis IV the Bavarian 174
　　Otto I the Great 227–228
　foreign rulers and
　　Ezzelino III da Romano 95–96
　　Gregory VII 116–117
　　Henry II 128–129
　　Leo X 169
　　Napoléon I 213
homosexuality 91, 124, 180
Honduras 74, 173–174, 322
Honecker, Erich 307
Honorius III, Pope 103
Hood, Robin 80
Horace 26

Horemhab 142
Hormizd III 320
Horthy de Nagybányai, Miklós 142–143
hospitals 52, 165
Houston, Sam 268
Howard, Catherine 134
Howard, Thomas 134
How to Be a Good Communist (book) 172
Hoxha, Enver 143–144
Hsiang River Review (magazine) 172
Hsien-feng 305–306
Hsuang-tsang 123
Hua Guofeng (Hua Kuo-Feng) 83, 187
Huerta, Victoriano 144
Hugenberg, Alfred 138
Hugo, Victor 153, 191
Huguenots 4, 50, 129, 130–131, 178, 262
Huitzilopochtli (Aztec god) 201
human rights
　Abdul-Hamid II and 4
　Doe and 86
　Duvalier and 88–89
　Galtieri and 110
　Mejía Victores and 197
　Nasser and 216
　Noriega and 223
　Pinochet and 244
　Rios Montt and 263
　Taraki and 289
human sacrifice 7, 156, 194, 201, 255
Hundred Flowers Movement 187
Hundred Years' War 90–91, 128, 176–177, 260
Huneric 108
Hungary 33, 46, 99, 126, 142–143, 162, 169–170, 286, 296, 311
Hung Hsiu-ch'uan 144
Huns 24–25, 28, 94, 320
Hunyadi, John 202
Husák, Gustav 145
Hussein, Saddam (Takriti) 22, 145, 159
Hu Yaobang 83
Hyksos 6, 292
Hyperbolus 10
Hyrcania 80

I

Ibn Tumart 2
Iconoclasm 168
Iconoclastic Period, Second 168
Ides of March 43
Ignatyev, Nicolai 185
Il popolo d'Italia (newspaper) 208
Imagawa Yoshimoto 225
immolation 184
impaling 207, 311
impeachment 54–55
Imperialism: The Highest Stage of Capitalism (book) 166
Imphal, Battle of 39
Inca Empire 22–23, 245–246
India
　foreign rulers and
　　Ahmad Shah Durrani 6
　　Akbar 7

Alexander the Great 13
Birendra Bir Bikram Shah Dev 35
Demetrius 81–82
Genghis Khan 112
Mahmud of Ghazna 184
rulers/leaders
　Ahmed, Khandakar Mushtaque 6
　Babur 27
　Bose, Subhas Chandra 39
　Chandragupta I 52
　Chandragupta II 52
　Chandragupta Maurya 52–53
　Harsha 123
　Kanishka 156–157
　Muhammad ibn Tughluq 205–206
　Nadir Shah 211
　Porus 249
　Rudradaman I 264–265
　Samudragupta 267–268
Indian Wars (1675-76) 27–28
Indonesia 284–285
Ingavi, Battle of 29
Innocent III, Pope 14, 103, 146–147, 151
Innocent IV, Pope 14, 96, 104
Innocent VII, Pope 163
Innocent VIII, Pope 168
Inquisition 14, 98–99, 147, 185, 244–245, 300
insomnia 124
Ionia 80
Ipsus, Battle of 252
Iran 5, 114, 145, 159, 229
Iran-Contra Affair 223
Iran hostage crisis 159
Iraq 145, 158
Ireland 55, 76, 260
Ireton, Henry 76
Irish Republican Army (IRA) 253
Iron Curtain 282
Iron Guard (Romania) 17–18
Iroquois Confederacy 106
Isaac II Angelus 103
Isabella I 36, 56, 98–99, 132–133, 147, 185, 192, 300
Isabella II 42, 231
Ishbaal 81
Iskra (newspaper) 166
Islam
　adherents to
　　Abbad I 1
　　Abd al-Mu'min 2–3
　　Abd ar-Rahman III 3
　　Abdul-Aziz 3
　　Abdul-Hamid II 3–4
　　Ahmad Gran 5
　　Ahmad ibn Tulun 5–6
　　Ahmad Shah Durrani 6
　　Akbar 7
　　Askia Muhammad 20
　　Assad, Hafiz al- 21
　　Bayezid I 32
　　Bhutto, Zulfikar Ali 34–35
　　Boabdil, Muhammad XI 36
　　Ghazan, Mahmud 114
　　Hasan-e-Sabbah 124–125
　　Khomeini, Ayatollah Ruhollah 159
　　Mahdi, al- 183–184
　　Mahmud of Ghazna 184

Muhammad ibn Falah 205
Muhammad ibn Tughluq 205–206
Muizz, al- 206
Murad IV 207
Mutesa I 209
Qaddafi 253
Saladin 266
Taraki, Noor Mohammed 289
Thani, Shaykh Khalifa ibn Hamad al- 289
Zia 323
　foes of
　　Atatürk, Mustafa Kemal 24
　　Danilo 79
　　Haile Selassie 120
　　Isabella I 147
　　Louis IX 176
　　Nicephorous II Phocas 220–221
　　Torquemada 300
　foes of fundamentalism
　　Mubarak 204
　　Pahlavi, Muhammad Reza Shah 229
　friends of
　　Napoléon I 212
Israel, ancient 16, 18, 80–81, 269–270, 277–278
Israel, modern 21–22, 216–217
Issus, Battle of 272
Italian Renaissance 195
Italy 208–209, 214
Iturbide, Augustin de 268
Ivan III the Great 148
Ivan IV the Terrible 115, 148–149
Ivan VI 92
Ivory Coast 267
Iyasu, Lij 197

J

Jackson, Andrew 268
Jacobins 179–180, 212
Jamaica 77
James I 163
James IV 132–133
Jameson, Leander 259
Jameson raid 316
Jamestown (Va.) 249
Jamestown (Virginia) 27
Jamuka 111–112
Janissaries 32
Jansen, Cornelis 178
Japan
　foreign leaders and
　　Chiang Kai-shek 62
　　Hitler 139
　　Ho Chi Minh 140
　　Laurel 164–165
　　Phibunsongkhram 239
　　Yen Hsi-shan 321
　rulers/dictators
　　Ashikaga Takauji 19
　　Hayashi Senjuro 125
　　Hojo Masako 140–141
　　Hojo Tokimasa 141
　　Hojo Tokimune 141
　　Hojo Yasutoki 141–142
　　Hojo Yoshitoki 142
　　Meiji 196–197
　　Oda Nobunaga 225

Takeda Shingen 288
Tojo Hideki 298–299
Tokugawa Ieyasu 299–300
Toyotomi Hideyoshi
302–303
Jaruzelski, Wojciech 150
Jellaluddin 112
Jena, Battle of 214
Jerusalem
David and 81
Frederick II and 104
Hadrian and 119
Harald III Sigurdson and 122
Heraclius and 135
Louis IX and 176
Nebuchadnezzar II and
217–218
Nicholas I and 221
Philip II Augustus and 241
Pompey the Great and 247
Richard I the Lionhearted and
259–260
Saladin and 266
Sennacherib and 270–271
Solomon and 278
Titus and 298
Vespasian and 309–310
Jesuits 56, 99, 225
Jews *see also* Biblical figures
Alexander III and 14
Idi Amin and 16
Caligula and 44
Carol II and 45
Cromwell and 77
Cyrus II the Great and 78
Demetrius I Soter and 82
Domitian and 87
Ferdinand II and 98
Hadrian and 119
Henry III the Sufferer and
129–130
Herod Antipas and 135
Herod Archelaus and 135–136
Hitler and 138–140
John and 151
Leo III the Isaurian and 168
Manuel I the Fortunate and
185
Maria Theresa and 189
Nebuchadnezzar II and
217–218
Pétain and 236
Philip IV the Fair and 241
Pius V and 245
Qaddafi and 253
Shapur I and 275
Shapur II the Great and 275
Tiberius and 294
Titus and 298
Torquemada and 300
Yazdegerd II and 320
Joab 81
Joan of Arc 255
John (England) 128, 146,
150–151, *151*, 259
John I Zimisces 30–31, **151–152**
John II (Aragón) 147
John III (Sweden) 94
John V Palaeologus 206
John X, Pope 34
John XII, Pope 228
John XIII, Pope 228
John XXII, Pope 174
John of Gaunt 91, 128, 260

John Paul II, Pope 150, 283
Johnson, Andrew 153
Johnson, Lyndon B. 158
Johnson, Prince Yormie 86
John the Baptist 135
Jonathan 80–81
Jones, Michael 76
*Journey from St. Petersburg to
Moscow* (book) 49
Juan Carlos de Bourbon 101–102
Juárez, Benito (Pablo) 83–84,
152–153, 190–191, 199
Judea 135, 136–137, 298
judicial reformers
Charlemagne 53
Christian IV 64
Frederick II 104
Godunov 115
Hammurabi 121
Henry II 127
Hojo Yasutoki 142
Juárez 152
Justinian 155
Kamehameha 156
Leo III the Isaurian 168
Louis XIV 177
Mohammed II the Conqueror
203
Napoléon I 213
Tharawaddy 289–290
Julian the Apostate *153*, **153–154**
Julianus 154
Julius II, Pope 38, 169, 192
justicialismo (Perón ideology) 234
Justinian I 28, **154–155**, 290–291,
291
Justinian II 28, 167

K
Kadambari (book) 123
Kahnua, Battle of 27
Kalakaua 171
Kalaniopuu 156
Kamehameha I the Great 156
Kamenev, Lev 281
Kanishka 156–157
Kao Tsu, T'ang 157
Karari, Battle of 2
Karlowitz, Treaty of 170
Karmal, Babrak 157–158
Karnal, Battle of 211
Károlyi, Mihaly 162
Kasavubu, Joseph 200, 305
Kassem (Qassim), Abdul Karim
145, **158**
Katanga 305
Kennedy, John F. 47–48, 158, 220
Kerensky, Aleksandr 167
Khan, Shaibani 27
Khanh, Nguyen 158–159
Khartoum, Battle of 2
Khmer Rouge 246
Khomeini, Ayatollah Ruhollah
159, 229
Khosrow II 135
Khrushchev, Nikita 40–41, 47,
61, 143, 322
Khwarezm 112
kidnapping *see* abduction
Kieft, Willem 159–160
Kiev 311
Kim Chong Il 160

Kim Il Sung 160
Kim Ku (Rhee political
opponent) 258
Kim Kyu (Park assassin) 230
Kirov, Sergei 281
Kittikachorn, Thanom 160–161
Knared, Peace of 117
Koh-i-Noor (diamond) 211
Kolingba, André 37
Komyo 19
Konev, Ivan 282
Korea *see* North Korea; South
Korea
Korean War 186, 258
Kruger, Paul 258, 316
Kuang-hsu 305–306
Kuang Wu Ti 161
Kuan-tu, Battle of 304
Kublai Khan 141, **161–162**
Kulikovo Pole, Battle of 84
Kun, Béla 142–143, **162**
Kurds 145, 158
Kutahya, Convention of 205
Kutuzov, Mikhail 214
Kuwait 145
Ky, Nguyen Cao *See* Nguyen
Cao Ky

L
Ladislas 163, 272
lagtings (Harald I administrative
system) 121
Lambrino, Zizi 45
Lanusse, Alejandro 235
Lasus of Hermione 137
Lateran Council, Fifth 169
Lateran Treaty 209
Laud, William 163–164
**Lauderdale, John Maitland,
duke of 164**
Laugerud, Kjell 263
Laurel, José Paciano 164–165
Laval, Pierre 236
Laveaux, Etienne 302
League of Augsburg 178
League of Cambrai 192
League of Cognac 56
League of Corinth 80, 239
League of Mechlin 169
League of Nations 86, 120, 254
League of Princes 113
League of Public Weal 176
League of the Three Emperors
100
Lebensraum (one of Hitler's goals)
138
Lebrun, Albert 236
Lechfeld, Battle of 228
Leclerc, Charles 302
**Leguía y Salcedo, Augusto
Bernardino 165**
Leiberich, Karl von Mack von
213
Leleiohoku 171
Le Mans, Battle of 128
Lenin, Aleksandr 166
Lenin, Vladimir Ilich 162,
165–167, 185–187, 222, 281–282,
298
Leo I, Pope 25
Leo III the Isaurian 167–168
Leo V (Byzantine Empire) **168**

Leo VIII, Pope 228
Leo IX, Pope 116, 126, 129
Leo X, Pope 134, **168–169**, *169*
Leo XIII, Pope 267
Leopold I (Holy Roman Empire)
169–170
Leopold II (Belgium) **170–171**,
171
Leopold II (Holy Roman
Empire) **170**
Lepanto, Battle of 240, 245
Lepidus, Marcus Aemilius 26
Le Prestre de Vauban, Sébastien
178
leprosy 294
Lerdo de Tejada, Sebastian 84
Leszczynski, Stanislas 58
Le Van Khoi 199
Lewes, Battle of 90
L'Humanité (newspaper) 143
Liao dynasty 18
Liber augustalis 104
Liberia 85–86
libraries 19–20, 169, 195, 277
Libya 16, 253, 257
Liliuokalani 171–172
Lincoln, Abraham 153
Lin Piao 187
Li Shih-min 157
Lithuania 46, 58–59, 243–244
Liu Chin 61
Liu Hsiu 161
Liu Pang 172
Liu Shaoqi (Liu Shao-Chi) 83,
172, 187
Livonian War 149
Livy (Titus Livius) 26
Lodge, Henry Cabot 158
Lodi, Daulat Khan 27
Lodi, Ibrahim 27
Lodi, Peace of 273
Lollards 131
Lombard League 96, 103
Lombards 9, 28, 53, 155
London (England), Tower of 93
London Convention 205
Long March 82–83, 186
Long Parliament 55, 75–77
López, Carlos Antonio 172–173
López, Francisco Solano 173
**López Arellano, Oswaldo
173–174**
López Perez, Rigoberto 280
Loredan, Piero 100
Lothair I 174
Lothair II 37
Louis (Ludwig) II (Bavaria) **180**
Louis IV the Bavarian 174, 227
Louis VII (France) 127, **175**, 241
Louis IX (France) 32, 67, 90, *175*,
175–176
Louis XI (France) 59–60,
176–177, 191
Louis XII (France) 15, 169
Louis XIII (France) 261–263
Louis XIV (France) 58, 106–107,
170, *177*, **177–178**, 192–193, 262
Louis XV (France) 57
Louis XVI (France) 57, 170,
178–179, *179*, 189, 264
Louis XVIII (France) 57–58, 198,
215
Louis-Philippe 179–180, 215

Louvre (Paris, France) 178
Lovell, Lord 132
Lozano Díaz, Julio 173
Lucas García, Fernando Romeo 263
Lucullus, Lucius Licinius 295
Ludlow, Edmond 76
Lugalzaggesi of Uruk 269
Lugdunum, Battle of 272
Lully, Jean-Baptiste 177
Lumphanan, Battle of 182
Lumumba, Patrice 200, 305
Lund, Battle of 58
Lunéville, Treaty of 213
Lupescu, Magda 45
Luque, Hernán de 245
Luther, Martin 134, 168–169
Lutherans 64, 283
Lycophron 233
Lydia 74–75, 77, 118
Lysander 180–181

M

Macapagal, Diosdada 188
Macbeth 182
Macedonia 8, 12–13, 31, 66, 79, 232, 239–240, 252
Machado y Morales, Gerardo 31, **182–183**
Machiavelli, Niccolo 15, 38, 208
Macrinus 45, 91
Macro 44
Madero, Francisco 84, 144
Madrid, Treaty of 56
Maghrib 29–30
Magloire, Paul E. 88
Magna Carta 146, 150, *151*
Magnentius 72, 183
Magongo, Battle of 204
Magyars 33, 228, 275, 296
maharajadhiraja ("king of kings") 52
Mahdi, al- 2, **183–184**
Mahmud of Ghazna 184
Mahmud Nedim Pasha 184–185
Majorianus 108
Malaysia 284
Malcolm III 182
Malta 30
mamalahoe kanawai (Hawaiian judicial reform) 156
Mamluks 32, 114, 204–205
Manchu dynasty 60
Manchuria 62, 125, 196, 317
Manco Capac 245–246
Mansdotter, Karin 94
Mantineia, Battle of 10
Mantzikert, Battle of 264
Manuel I the Fortunate 4, 33, **185**
Manuel II 196, 267
Manzoor, Mohammad Abdul 255
Mao Tse-tung 63, 82–83, 144, 172, **185–187**, 246, 321
Marathon, Battle of 65, 79, 290, 319
Marc Anthony 26, 67–68, 136, 242, 293
Marcos, Ferdinand Edralin 187–188
Marcos, Imelda 188
Marcus Aurelius 69, 72, 154
Mardonius 79, 319

Margaret of Hungary, Saint 33
Margus River, battle on the 85
Maria, Jacques 50
Mariam, Mengistu Haile 17, **189–190**
Maria Theresa 170, 177, 178, **188–189**
Marie Antoinette 170, 178–179, *179*, 189, 264
Marius, Gaius 246–247
Marne, Battle of the 235
Marquez, José Ignacio 225
martial law
    Ahmed and 6
    Alexander III and 14
    Bhutto and 34–35
    Jaruzelski and 150
    Marcos and 188
    Pinochet and 244
    Zia and 323
Martinez de Campos, Arsenio 313
Marx, Karl 166, 185
Mary, Queen of Scots 93
Mary I (England) 92–93, 134, **190**
Massacre of the Innocents *136*, 137
massacres, perpetrators of
    Akbar 7
    Bokassa 36–37
    Boris III 39
    Catherine de' Medici 50
    Danilo 79
    Deng Xiaoping 82–83
    Ethelred II the Unready 95
    Gowon 116
    Herod Archelaus 136
    Herod I the Great *136*, 137
    Huerta 144
    Hussein 145
    Kieft 159
    al-Mahdi 183–184
    Mithradates VI 200
    Murad IV 207
    Nabis 211
    Nicephorous II Phocas 220
    Pol Pot 246
    Pompey the Great 246–247
    Shaka 274
    Shapur II the Great 275
    Suharto 284
    Toussaint L'Ouverture 302
    Trujillo Molina 304
Matteotti, Giacomo 209
Mau Mau revolt 16
Mauryan Empire 21, 52, 81–82
Maximilian (Mexico) 83–84, 153, **190–191**, 199, 215, 269
Maximilian (Holy Roman Empire) 169, *191*, **191–192**, 273
Maximilian II Emanuel 192–193
Maximinus (Gaius Julius Verus Maximinus) *193*, **193–194**
Maximinus (Galerius Valerius Maximinus) 194
Maximus, Lappius 87
Max of Baden 316
May Fourth Movement 63
Mazarin, Giulio 177
Mazeppa, Ivan 59
Mbemba, Nzinga *see* Afonso I
Mbulazi 204
Mecca 20, 206, 270

Mechlin, League of 169
Media 24, 77, 80, 242, 295
Medici, Catherine de' *see* Catherine de' Medici
Medici, Cosimo de' 194–195, 272
Medici, Giuliano de' 195
Medici, Lorenzo de' 98, **195–196**, 276
Medici, Marie de' 262
Medina 270
Mehmed I 196
Meiji 196–197
Mein Kampf (book) 138
Mejía Víctores, Oscar Humberto 197, 263
Memel strip 139
Menelik II 120, **197**
Menem, Carlos Saul 110, 235
Mensheviks 14, 166, 281
mental illness
    of Commodus 69
    of Elagabalus 91–92
    of George III 113–114
    of Louis (Ludwig) II 180
    of Nebuchadnezzar II 218
    of Olivares 226
    of Peter II's brother 238
    of Tharawaddy's brother 290
    of Tiberius 294
Mera, Juan 308
Merkit clan 111
Mermnad dynasty 74, 118
Mesopotamia
    Alexander the Great and 13
    Nebuchadnezzar's father and 217
    Roman Empire and 45, 108, 109, 193–194, 272, 303
    Sargon of Akkad as ruler of 269
    Tamerlane and 288–289
    Tigranes and 295
Metaxas, Ioannis 197–198
Mexico 83–84, 144, 152–153, 190–191, 199, 215, 268–269
Michael I 18, 168
Michael IV 122
Michael Obrenovic, Prince 198
Michal 80–81
Michelangelo 15, 195
Midhat Pasha 4, 185
Milan, Duchy of 9, 56, 100, 272–273, 310
Milan, Edict of 71
Milan IV 198
Military-Peasant Pact (1966) 30
Miliutin, Dmitri 12
Ming dynasty 60–61, 321
Ming T'ai Chang 312
Minh Mang 198–199, 238
mining 30, 258–259, 305
Minorca 56
Miramón, Miguel 199
Missionary Party 171
Mithradates VI 42, **199–200**, 247, 251, 295–296
Mithradatic War, Second 200
Mobutu, Joseph 305
Mobutu Sese Seko 200
Moctezuma I 200–201
Moctezuma II 73–74, 200, *201*, **201–202**

Moesia 81
Mohammed II the Conqueror 202, **202–203**, 311
Mohammed V 4
Mohawks 159, 283
Mohieddin, Zakaria 216
Molas Lopez, Felipe 283
Moldavia 59, 311
Molière, Jean Baptiste 177
Moncada, José Maria 279
Mongols 2, 18, 33, 84, 111–112, 114, 161–162, 225–226, 288, 299
Mongoose Gang 35
Monophysites 155, 291
Monroe Doctrine 153, 190
Montbrison, Battle of 4
Montenegrin Vespers 79
Montenegro 79
Montfort, Simon de 90
Montt, Manuel 203
Montt, Pedro 203–204
Moors 1, 53, 98, 130, 185
More, Sir Thomas 134
Morinigo, Higinio 283
Morocco 2, 206
Moro National Liberation Front 188
Mortemer, Battle of 314
Mortimer, Edmund 131
Mosaddeq, Muhammad 229
Moscicki, Ignace 244
Moscow University (Russia) 92
Movimiento Nacionalista Revolucionario (MNR) 30
Mpande 52, 84, **204**
MPLA (Popular Movement for the Liberation of Angola) 219
Mubarak, Mohamed Hosni 204
Mugabe, Robert 277
Mughals 7, 27
Muhammad Ali 204–205
Muhammad ibn Falah 205
Muhammad ibn Tughluq **205–206**
Muhammad Zahir Shah 157
Muhldorf, Battle of 174
Muizz, al- 206
Murad I 206
Murad II 202
Murad IV 206–207
Murad V 3–4
Murchehkhor, Battle of 211
murderers
    Asoka 21
    Caligula 44
    Caracalla 45
    Cheng-te 61
    Cleopatra 68
    Constantine I the Great 72
    Constantius II 72–73
    Darius I 79
    Dingane 84
    Erik XIV 94
    Ezzelino III da Romano 96
    Gyges 118
    Harold I Barefoot 122
    Henry III 129
    Herod I the Great 136
    Hitler 139
    Hussein 145
    Ivan IV the Terrible 149
    Julian the Apostate 154
    Maximinus 194

Mithradates VI 200
Murad IV 207
Nero 218
Noriega 223–224
Phraates IV 242
Ptolemy XI Alexander II 251
Richard III 261
Shuysky 276
Theodoric I the Great 291
Wu Ti 317
murder victims
  Berengar 34
  Berenice III 34
  Darius III 80
  Demetrius 82
  Elagabalus 92
  Catherine de' Medici son 50
  Park 230
  Peter the Cruel 236
  Porus 249
  Rais 255
  Rasputin 257
  Sennacherib 271
  Tisza 296
  Xerxes I 319
Murena, Lucius Licinius 200
Mursa, Battle of 183
Mursilis I 207
Mursilis II 207–208
Musa, Thea Urania 242
Mushki 294–295
Muslims see Islam
Mussolini, Benito 17, 39, 46, 86,
  119–120, 139, 165, **208–209**, 234
Mutesa I 209
Mutesa II 209–210

N

Nabis 211
Nabonidus 33
Nabopolassar 217–218
Nadir Shah 211
Nagananda (Sanskrit poem) 123
Naguib, Mohammad 216
Nájera, Battle of 236
Nakaz 49
Nanda dynasty 52
Nantes, Edict of 130, 178
Naples, Kingdom of 37–38,
  55–56, 97–98, 163, 213
Napoléon I 10–11, 37–38, 40,
  105, 204–205, **211–215**, 213, 214,
  222, 231, 302
Napoléon III 40, 51, 83, 152, 180,
  190–191, 199, **215**, 269
narcotics see drug trafficking
narodnost (Russian nationalism)
  14
Narva, Battle of 237
Naseby, Battle of 75
Nasser, Gamal Abdel 158, 204,
  216–217, 253
Nation of Islam 253
Nations, Battle of the 214
NATO (North Atlantic Treaty
  Organization) 267
Natusch Busch, Alberto 110, **217**
Navarino, Battle of 205
Nazi Germany 17–18, 86,
  101–102, 138–140, 198, 235–236,
  253–254, 307
Nebuchadnezzar II 33, **217–218**
Necho 217

Nefertiti 8, 256
Neile, Richard 163
Nelson, Horatio 212, 213–214
Neoptolemus II 252
Nepal 35, 52
Nero *218*, **218–219**, 309–310
nerve gas 145
Netherlands 56–57, 64, 76, 93,
  192–193
Neto, Antonio Agostinho 219
Neville, Richard 261
Newbury, Battle of 75
New Granada 225
New Jewel movement 69
"New Model Army" 75, 76
Ngo Dinh Diem 87–88, 158,
  219–220
Ngo Dinh Nhu 220
Nguyen Cao Ky 158
Nguyen Van Thieu 88, 158
Nicaea, Council of 71
Nicaragua 197, 223, 226–227,
  242, 279–280, 312, 322
Nicator, Seleucus 52–53
Nicene Creed 292
Nicephorous I 168, **220**
Nicephorous II Phocas 151,
  220–221
Nicholas I 12, **221**
Nicholas II 166, **221–222**, 257,
  281
Nicomedes III 199
Nicomedes IV 199
Niemen, Battle of 243
Nien Rebellion 305
Nietzsche, Friedrich Wilhelm 208
Nigeria 115–116
Night of the Long Knives 139
Nika Rebellion 290
Nineteen Proposals 55
Nineveh (Assyria) 19–20, 77, 95,
  135, 217, 271, 294
Nivelle, Robert 235
Niz, Battle of 122
Nkrumah, Kwame 222–223
Noche Triste (Sorrowful Night)
  201
Nonaligned Nations movement
  48
**Noriega Morena, Manuel
  Antonio 223–224**, 301
Normandy 314–315
North, Oliver 223
North Atlantic Treaty
  Organization (NATO) 267
North Korea 160, 229–230
North Yemen 216
Norway 59, 93–94, 121, 122,
  253–254
Novotny, Antonin 224
Nubia 6, 292, 293
Numerian 84–85
Nuremberg Racial Laws 139

O

OAS (Organization of American
  States) 48
Obando, José Maria 225
Obote, Milton 16, 210
Obregón, Alvaro 144
Occaneechi Indians 27

Octavia 218
Octavian 68
Octavius, Gaius 25
October Revolution see
  Bolshevik Revolution
Oda Nobunaga 225, 288,
  299–300, 302–303
Odoacer 291
Ogodei 225–226
O'Higgins, Bernardo 46
oil industry 253, 289
Ojukwu, Odumegwu 116
Olaf III 44
Oldcastle, Sir John 131
**Olivares, Gaspar de Guzman y
  Pimental, count-duke of 226**
Omdurman, Battle of 184
On the Miserable Condition of Man
  (essay) 146
On the Mysteries of Mass (essay)
  146
Opechancanough 249–250
Operation Barbarossa 139, 298
Oracle at Delphi 67, 74, 77, 118,
  137, 227
Ordono II 3
ordos (Mongol fighting units) 18
Organization for Revolutionary
  Education and Liberation 69
Organization of American States
  (OAS) 48
Orlov, Aleksei 48
Orlov, Gregori 48
**Ortega Saavedra, Daniel
  226–227**
Ortega Saavedra, Humberto 226
Orthagoras 227
Osroene 242
Ostrogoths 25, 94, 155, 291
Otermín, Antonio de 248
Otto I the Great 37, 127, **227–228**
Otto II 37
Otto III 37
Otto IV 146
Otto of Wittelsbach 103
Ottoman Empire
  foreign rulers and
    Abbas I the Great 1
    Abdul-Aziz 3
    Abdul-Hamid II 3–4
    Ahmad Gran 5
    Alexander VI 15
    Danilo I 79
    Ferdinand I (Bulgaria) 97
    Ferdinand I (Naples) 98
    Mahmud Nedim Pasha
      184–185
    Maximilian II Emanuel
      192–193
    Muhammad Ali 205
  sultans
    Bayezid I 32
    Bayezid II 32
    Mehmed I 196
    Mohammed II the
      Conqueror 202–203
    Murad I 206
    Murad IV 206–207
    Selim I 270
    Suleyman I the Magnificent
      285–286
  Ovando Candia, Alfredo 30
  Ovra (secret police) 208

P

Pacific, War of the (1879-84) 165
"Padlock Law" 44
Pahlavi, Muhammad Reza Shah
  159, **229**
Pakistan 6, 34–35, 255, 322–323
Palestine 13, 18, 32, 70, 78, 119,
  217, 266, 269, 292, 293, 295
Palestine Liberation
  Organization (PLO) 16, 18,
  21–22
Pamukey Indians 28
Panama 223–224, 300–301
Panama Canal 300–301
Panin, Nikita 48, 230
Panipat, Battle of 27
Paoli, Pasquale 212
Paphlagonia 199
Paraguay 172–173, 282–283
Pardiñas, Manuel 44
Paredes, Ruben 223
Paris, Peace of 296
Park, Chung Hee 229–230
Parr, Catherine 134
Parthia 43, 45, 242, 272, 293, 303
Parysatis 80
Paschal I, Pope 174
Passau, Treaty of 57
Pats, Konstantin 230
Paul I (Russia) 10–11, **230–231**
Paul II, Pope 113
Pavia, Battle of 56
**Pavia (y Rodriguez de
  Albuquerque), Manuel 231**
Paz Estenssoro, Victor 30
Pazzi family 195
Pearl Harbor attack 139, 165
Peasant's Revolt (1381) 260
Pedro I 231–232
Peisistratus 137, **232**, 279
Peloponnesian War 9–10, 180,
  234
Pelops 211
Peninsular War 214
People's Will Party 12
Pepe II 255
Pepin the Short 53
Periander 77, **232–233**
Pericles 9, 65–66, 233, **233–234**
Péron, Isabel Martinez de 109,
  235
Péron, Juan 234–235
Perrers, Alice 91
Persia 1–2, 11, 13, 18–19, 24, 28,
  33, 65, 68, 77–80, 109, 135, 154,
  211, 285, 290, 319, 320
Persian Gulf War 18, 21, 145
Persson, Joran 94
Peru 29, 165, 225, 245–246, 249
Pesqueira, Ignacio 74
Petacci, Clara 209
Pétain, Henri Philippe 235–236
Peter the Cruel (Castile) **236**
Peter I the Cruel (Portugal) 128,
  237
Peter I the Great (Russia) 12, 24,
  48–49, 58–59, 79, 92, 230–231,
  237–238
Peter II (Portugal) **238**
Peter III (Russia) 48

Pétion, Alexandre 65
Petition of Right 54
Phan Thanh Gian 238–239
Pharnabazus 80
Pharsalus, Battle of 67, 247
Phibunsongkhram, Luang 239
Phidias 234
Philip II (Macedon) 80, **239–240**
Philip II (Spain) 93, **240**
Philip II Augustus (France) 13, 33, 128, 130–131, 146, 150–151, 190, **240–241**, *241*, 259–260, 266
Philip IV the Fair (France) 226, **241–242**
Philip the Arab 274
Philip of Hohenstaufen 146
Philip of Ravenna 96
Philipoemen 211
Philippi, Battle of 26, 68
Philippines 164–165, 187–188, 313
Philistines 81, 269–270
Phocas, Bardas 31
Phoenicia 65, 217, 256–257
Phraates IV 242
Picado (Michalski), Teodoro 242–243
Pico della Mirandola, Giovanni 195
Pieck, Wilhelm 307
Pilate, Pontius 135
Pillnitz, Declaration of 170
Pilsudski, Jozef 243–244
Pinochet (Ugarte), Augusto 110, **244**
pirates and piracy 29–30, 42, 60, 247
Pisa, Council of 163, 192
Pitt the Younger, William 114
Pius, Antoninus 119
Pius II, Pope 14, 113, 194
Pius V, Pope 93, **244–245**
Pius VII, Pope 213
Pius IX, Pope 190
Pius XI, Pope 267
Pizarro, Francisco 22–23, **245–246**
plague *see* bubonic plague
Plato 118, 195
Plekhanov, Georgy Valentinovich 166
PLO *see* Palestine Liberation Organization (PLO)
Plutarch 9
Pocahontas 249–250
poison
  users of
    Ashikaga Takauji 19
  victims of
    Baybars I 32
    Berenice II 34
    Claudius 67
    Murad IV 207
    Napoléon I 215
    Nero 218
    Phraates IV 242
    Rasputin 257
    Visconti 310
Poland 37, 46, 58–59, 94, 118, 139, 148, 150, 243–244, 282
police
  under Díaz 84
  under Hussein 145
  under Ivan IV the Terrible 149

Karmal abolition of 157
  under Lenin 167
  under Mussolini 208
  under Nasser 216
  under Pahlavi 229
  under Pilsudski 243
  under Trujillo Molina 304
  Zia probe of 323
political purges
  conductors of
    Abd al-Mu'min 2
    Andom 17
    Ezzelino III da Romano 96
    Hayashi Senjuro 125
    Hitler 139
    Hoxha 143
    Husák 145
    Karmal 157
    Kassem 158
    Mao 186
    Mariam 189–190
    Mpande 204
    Nero 218
    Richard III 261
    Robespierre 264
    Stalin 281–282
    Suharto 284
    Tharawaddy 290
    Timoleon 296
    Touré 301
    Ulbricht 307
    Yung Lo 321
  victims of
    Caligula kin 43
    Kun 162
    Liu Shaoqi 172
Polk, James K. 268
Polo, Marco 161–162
Pol Pot 246
Poltava, Battle of 238
Polycrates 246
Pompeius, Sextus 26
Pompey the Great 42–43, **246–247**, *247*, 296
Popé 247–248
popes
  Alexander IV 14
  Alexander VI 14–15
  Clement IV 67
  Gregory VII 116–117
  Innocent III 146–147
  Leo X 168–169
  Pius V 244–245
  Sixtus IV 276–277
Popular Movement for the Liberation of Angola (MPLA) 219
portage 202
Portales, Diego (José Victor) 203, **248–249**
Portugal 2, 4–5, 54, 98, 185, 214, 219, 237, 238, 240, 266–267
Porus 249
Postumus, Marcus Cassianius Latinius 249
Potemkin, Gregori 48
Potsdam Conference 282
Potsdam Guard 106
Powhatan 249–250
Powhatan Confederacy 249–250
Praetorian Guard 43, 45, 66, 92, 154, 218, 272, 294, 303, 310
Prague, Defenestration of (1618) 99

Pravda (newspaper) 166, 281
Premyslid dynasty 37
Presbyterians 76, 163, 164
Pressburg, Treaty of 191, 214
Preston, Battle of 55, 76
Pretorius, Andries 84
Préveza, Battle of 30
Prieto, Joaquin 248
Prim, Juan 231
Primo de Rivera, José Antonio 101, **250**
Primo de Rivera, Miguel 250, 314
Prince, The (book) 15, 38
Priscus 28–29
Priyadarsika (Sanskrit poem) 123
Procles 233
prostitution 245, 290
Protestant Reformation *see* Reformation
Prussia 46, 58, 92, 100–101, 104–106, 118, 214, 215, 316
Psamtik I 250–251
Psamtik II 251
Psamtik III 251
Pteria, Battle of 74
Ptolemy III 34
Ptolemy IV Philopater 34
Ptolemy XI Alexander II 34, **251**
Ptolemy XII 67–68
Ptolemy XIII 43, 67–68
Pugachev, Yemelian 49
Pulitzer, Joseph 313
Pupienus 193
purges *see* political purges
Puritans 54–55, 75–77, 163–164
pyramids 200
"Pyrrhic victory" 252
Pyrrhus *251*, **251–252**

Q

Qaddafi, Muammar al- 16, **253**
Qajar dynasty 5
Qatar 289
Quakers 283
Quanun-nmae 203
Querétaro, Battle of 199
Quetzalcoatl 73
Quezon, Manuel 165
Quisling, Vidkun 253–254
"Quit India" movement 6
Quiwonkpa, Thomas 86
Quotations from Chairman Mao (book) 187
Qutuz 32

R

Radishchev, Aleksandr 49
Rahman, Mujibur 255
Rahman, Ziaur 255
railroads 137, 165, 203, 208, 322
Rais, Gilles de 255
Raleigh, Sir Walter 93
Ramiro I 1
Ramiro II 3
Ramos, Fidel 188
Ramses I 142
Ramses II the Great 255–256, *256*, 271–272
Ramses III 256–257
ransom 28, 42

Rasputin, Grigory Yefimovich 221, **257**
Rathmines, Battle of 76
Ratnavali (Sanskrit poem) 123
Ravaillac, François 131
Raymond of Toulouse 146
Reagan, Ronald 36, 150, 197, 223
Reciprocity, Treaty of 171
Recknitz, Battle of 228
Red Eyebrows 161
"Red Sultan" *see* Abdul-Hamid II
Reformation
  Adrets and 4
  Alexander VI and 15
  Charles V and 56–57
  Elizabeth I and 93
  Ferdinand II and 99
  Gómez and 115
  Henry VIII and 133–134
  Leo X and 168–169
  Mary I and 190
  Pius V and 244–245
Regalianus 109
Regimento 4
Reichstag fire 139
Reign of Terror 264
Reinsurance Treaty 316
Renaissance 195
René of Anjou 98
René II of Lorraine 98
Restoration 164
Retief, Piet 84
Revolt of the Midi 212
Rhee, Syngman 230, **257–258**
Rhine, Confederation of the 214
Rhodes, Cecil John 258–259
Rhodes, Herbert 258–259
Rhodesia 258–259, 277
Riario, Girolamo 276
Richard I the Lionhearted 112–113, 128, 150, 241, *259*, **259–260**, 266
Richard II 131, **260–261**
Richard III 132, **261**, *261*
Richard III (play) 261
Richelieu, Armand Jean du Plessis, Cardinal and Duke of 177, 226, **261–263**, *262*
Riff Rebellion 101
rifles and beans program 263
Riga, Treaty of 244
Rigaud, André 302
Rim-Sin 120–121
Ríos Montt, José Efraín 197, **263**
roads 79, 165, 182, 322
Robert Guiscard 117, **263–264**
Robespierre, Maximilien-Francois-Marie-Isidore de 212, **264**
Roccasecca, Battle of 163
Rodriguez de Francia, José Gaspar 173
Rodriquez, Andres 283
Roehm, Ernst 138, 139
Rojas Pinilla, Gustavo 115
Rolfe, John 249
Roman Catholic Church *see also* popes
  Adrets and 4
  Bela III and 33
  Catherine de' Medici and 50
  Christian III and 64
  Clovis I and 68–69

Ferdinand II the Catholic and 98
Ferdinand II of the Holy Roman Empire and 99
George of Podebrady and 113
Gustav II Adolf and 118
Henry III and 129
Henry VIII and 133–134
Isabella I and 147
Lauderdale and 164
Mary I and 190
Montt and 203
Mussolini and 209
Napoléon I and 213
Ngo Dinh Diem and 219–220
Nicholas I and 221
Philip II and 240
Richelieu and 262
Theodosius I the Great and 292
Vlad the Impaler and 311
Roman Empire
  colonial rulers
    Herod Antipa 135
    Herod Archelaus 135–136
    Herod I the Great and 136–137
  emperors
    Augustus 25–26
    Caesar, Gaius Julius 42–43
    Caligula 43–44
    Caracalla 45
    Cincinnatus, Lucius Quinctius 66
    Claudius 66–67
    Commodus 69–70
    Constantine I the Great 70–72
    Constantius II 72–73
    Decius 81
    Diocletian 84–85
    Domitian 87
    Elagabalus 91–92
    Fabius Maximus Cunctator Quintus 97
    Galerius 108–109
    Gallienus 109
    Hadrian 119
    Heraclius 134–135
    Julian the Apostate 153
    Julianus 154
    Magnentius 183
    Maximinus (Gaius Julius Verus Maximinus) 193–194
    Maximinus (Galerius Valerius Maximinus) 194
    Nero 218–219
    Postumus, Marcus Cassianius Latinius 249
    Severus 272
    Sulla, Lucius Cornelius 286–287
    Theodosius I the Great 291–292
    Tiberius 293–294
    Titus 298
    Trajan 303–304
    Valerian 308
    Vespasian 309–310
  foes
    Alaric 8–9
    Gaiseric 108
    Shapur I 274–275

Yazdegerd II 320
Romania 17–18, 45–46, 51, 162
Romanos IV Diogenes 264
Romanus II 151, 220
Roncaglia, Diet of 102
Roosevelt, Franklin D. 183
Rosenberg, Alfred 254
Rousseau, Jean-Jacques 264
Roxas, Manuel 165, 187
rubber atrocities 171
Rudolph II 34
Rudradaman I 264–265
Rufinus 8
Rullus, Publius Servilius 42
Rump Parliament 76
Russia, czarist
  foreign rulers and
    Abdul-Aziz 3
    Abdul-Hamid II 4
    Charles XII 58–59
    Ferdinand I 97
    Gustav II Adolf 117–118
    Muhammad Ali 205
    Nadir Shah 211
    Napoléon I 214–215
    Stambolov 282
  powers behind the throne
    Rasputin 257
  rulers
    Alexander I 10–11
    Alexander II 12
    Alexander III 13–14
    Catherine II the Great 48–49
    Dimitry (II) Donskoy 84
    Elizabeth 92
    Godunov, Boris 115
    Ivan III the Great 148
    Ivan IV the Terrible 148–149
    Nicholas I 221
    Nicholas II 221–222
    Paul I 230–231
    Peter I the Great 237–238
    Shuysky 276
Russian Revolution (1917) 166, 221–222
Russo-Japanese War (1904–05) 196, 221
Russo-Polish War (1920) 243
Russo-Turkish War (1877–78) 198, 282
Ryswick, Peace of 170

S
SA (Sturmabteilung) 139
Sabina, Poppaea 218
Sacasa, Juan Bautista 279
Sacasa, Roberto 322
Sacred War (595-596) 67
sacrifice *see* human sacrifice
Sadao, Araki 125
Sadat, Anwar al- 204, 216
Sadowa, Battle of 180
Safavid dynasty 211
St. Bartholomew's Day Massacre 50, 130
St. Peter's Basilica (Rome, Italy) 169
Saint-Germain, Treaty of (1570) 50
Saint Petersburg (Russia) 238
saints
  Helena 215
  Margaret of Hungary 33

Stanislav 37
Wenceslas 37
Saisset, Bernard 241
Saladin 266
Salamis, Battle at 65, 290, 319
Salazar, Antonio de Oliveira 219, **266–267**
Salome 135
Saloninus 249
SALT II (1979 treaty) 41
Saltykov, Sergei 230
Salviati, Francesco 195
Samori Touré 267, 301
Samos 246
Samosata, Battle of 151
Samudragupta 52, **267–268**
Sandinistas 279
Sandino, Augusto Cesar 279
San Domingo Improvement Company of New York 137
Sanetomo 141
Sanga, Rana 27
San Stefano, Treaty of 4
Santa Anna, Antonio López de 83–84, 152–153, 199, **268–269**
Santa Cruz, Andrés 29
Santander, Francisco 225
Santo Domingo 73
Saracens 228
Sargon II 94, **269**
Sargon of Akkad 269
Sar-i-pul, Battle of 27
Sarmatians 193, 291
Sasanian Empire 18–19, 274, 275, 320
satanism 255
Saturninus, Antonius 303
Saudi Arabia 16
Saul 80–81, **269–270,** *270*
Savanarola, Girolamo 15, 195
"Savior of Istanbul" 23
Saxony 126–127
Sayem, Abu Sadat Mohammad 255
Schara, Battle of 243–244
Schick, Rene 279
Schleswig 94
Schlieffen Plan 316
Schönbrunn, Treaty of 214
Schweitzer, Albert 88
Scipio, Publius Cornelius 97
Scotland 76, 90, 134, 182, 310, 315
"Scourge of God" *see* Attila the Hun
Scythia 24, 79, 199, 242
Second Coalition 212
secret police *see* police
Sédan, Battle of 3, 215
Sejanus 294
Seleucid dynasty 82, 295
Seleucus IV 82
Selim I 29, **270,** 285
Seljuk Turks 124, 264
Seneca 218, 219
Senlis, Treaty of 191
Sennacherib 94–95, **270–271,** *271*
Senzangakhona 204
Serbia 4, 33, 97, 100–101, 198, 206, 316
serfs 12, 49, 66, 106, 245
Sergius III 271
Serrano y Dominquez, Francisco 231

Serverus, Septimus 154
Sessanians 108
Seti I 271–272
Seven Sages of Greece 233, 279
Seven Years' War (1756-64) 92, 105, 113–114, 188
Seven Years' War of the North (1563-70) 94
Severus 45, 193, **272**
Seville, Kingdom of 1
sewage systems 165
Seymour, Jane 92, 134
Sforza, Francesco 272–273
Sforza, Ludovico 98, **273**
Sforza, Duke Maximilian 56
Sforza, Muzio 163
Shaka 204, **273–274**
Shakespeare, William 182, 261
Shalmaneser III 274
Shanghai Communiqué 64
Shapur I 274, **274–275,** 308
Shapur II the Great 275
Sheremetev, Count 237
Sher Shah Sur 7
shield money 127
Shiites 159, 205
Shuysky, Vasily 276
Sian Incident 62
Siberia 221
sibling rivalry
  Asoka and 21
  Atahualpa and 22
  Cetshwayo and 52
  Chandragupta II and 52
  Chilperic I and 62–63
  Cleopatra and 68
  Conrad III and 70
  Constantius II and 72–73
  Dingane and 84
  Diocletian and 85
  Erik I Bloodax and 93–94
  Ivan III the Great and 148
  Lothair I and 174
  Mehmed I and 196
  Mpande and 204
  Polycrates and 246
  Richard I the Lionhearted and 259–260
  Selim I and 270
  Sforza, Ludovico and 273
  Takeda Shingen and 288
  Tiglath-pileser III and 295
  Timoleon and 296
  William II Rufus and 315
  William I the Conqueror and 315
Sicily, Kingdom of 5, 55, 100, 111, 315
Sicyon 227
Siegebert I 28
sieges
  conductors of
    Abbas I the Great 1
    Bajan 29
    Charles the Bold 60
    Charles XII 59
    Genghis Khan 112
    Ivan III the Great 148
    Nebuchadnezzar II 217
    Peter I the Great 238
    Pompey the Great 247
    Sennacherib 270–271
    Sforza 273

Shapur I 275
Takeda Shingen 288
by Tokugawa Ieyasu 299
Vespasian 309–310
participants in
Caesar 42
Napoléon I 212
victims of
Boabdil 36
Mahdi, al- 183
Samori Touré 267
Vercingetorix 309
Sigebert 62–63
Sigismund 163
Sikhs 6
Silesia 105
Silvanus 249
Simancas, Battle of 3
Simeon I 275–276
Simnel, Lambert 132
simony 15, 116, 129, 277
Sino-Japanese War, First
(1894-95) 196, 306
Sino-Japanese War, Second
(1937-45) 62, 63
Sis, Battle of 1
Six Day War (1967) 204
Sixtus IV, Pope 195, 276–277
Skleros, Bardas 31
Skopje, Battle of 31
"Slaughters of the Innocents"
160
slavery 4–5, 20, 64–65, 120, 173,
246–247, 278–279, 280, 301–302
Slembi, Sigurd 122
Sluys Harbor, Battle of 91
smallpox 202
Smenkhkare 8
Smith, Ian (Douglas) 277
Smith, Capt. John 249
Sobachoque, Battle of 225
Socrates 9, 10
Sofia, Battle of 31
Soissons, Battle of 68
Solemn League and Covenant
164
Solidarity 150
Solomon 81, 277, 277–278
Solon 74, 87, 232, 278–279
Solon, Code of 87
Solway Moss, Battle of 134
Somoza Debayle, Anastasio
226–227, **279**
Somoza Garcia, Anastasio 242,
279–280
Songhai Empire 20–21
Song of Roland, The (chanson) 53
Sonthonax, Léger-Félicité 302
Soong Mei-ling 62
sorcery 255
Sorel, Georges 208
Soseki, Muso 19
Soulouque, Faustin-Elie 280
South Africa 52, 258
South Korea 229–230, 257–258
Soviet Union *see* Union of Soviet
Socialist Republics (USSR)
Spadafora, Hugo 223
Spain
as colonial power
Atahualpa and 22
Cortés and 73–74
Pizarro 245–246

foreign rulers and
Barbarossa 29–30
Charlemagne 53
Elizabeth I 93
Heureaux 137
Napoléon I 213
Popé 247–248
Salazar 267
monarchs (Christian)
Bonaparte, Joseph 37–38
Charles III 55–56
Charles V 56–57
Ferdinand II 98–99
Isabella I 147
Philip II 240
monarchs (Muslim)
Abbad I 1
Abd ar-Rahman III 3
nonmonarchical
rulers/leaders
Cabrera y Grinó 42
Canalejas y Méndez 44
Franco 101–102
Olivares 226
Pavia 231
Primo de Rivera 250
Torquemada 300
Weyler y Nicolau 313–314
Spanish Armada 93, 240
Spanish Civil War (1936-39)
101–102, 209, 250, 307
Spanish Inquisition *see*
Inquisition
Spanish Succession, War of the
(1703) 193, 238
Sparta (city-state) 8, 9–10, 66, 80,
137, 180–181, 211, 246, 252
Spartacus 42, 247
Spercheios, Battle of 31
Speyer, Peace of 64
Spurs, Battle of the 134, 192
SS (Schutzstaffel) 139
Ssu-ma Yen 280
Stainmore, Battle of 94
Stalin, Josef 280–282
Brezhnev and 40–41
Ceausescu and 51
Chervenkov and 61
Hitler and 139
Hoxha and 143
Kun and 162
Lenin and 165–167
Mao and 186
Tito and 298
Ulbricht and 307
Stambolov, Stefan Nikolov 97,
282
Stamford Bridge, Battle of 122,
123
Stanislav, Saint 37
Stanley, Sir Henry 171
Stanley, Sir William 132
state police *see* police
Stephen III, Pope 53
Stephen V, Pope 33
Stephen of Blois 126, 127
Stiklestad, Battle of 122
Stilicho, Flavius 8–9, 292
Stoker, Bram 310–311
Stolbova, Peace of 118
Strafford, Earl of 55
strangulation 23, 199, 271
Strauss, Richard 135
Streicher, Julius 138

Stroessner, Alfredo 282–283
Sturlison, Snorri 121
Stuyvesant, Peter 160, **283–284**
Suárez Flamerich, Germán 284
Sucre, Antonio José de 29, 225
Sudan 2, 183–184
Sudetenland 139
Suez Canal 18, 215, 216–217, 253
sugar 137, 182
Suharto 284
suicides
Abdul-Aziz 3
Boulanger 40
Christophe 65
Cleopatra 68
Constantius foe 73
Cyrus foe's son 78
Ermaneric 94
Hitler 140
Magnentius 183
Nero 219
Oda Nobunaga 225
Phan Thanh Gian 239
Saul 270
Themistocles 290
Wei Chung-hsien 313
Wu Ti's son 317
Wu Wang foe 318
Yung Lo's uncles 321
Sui dynasty 157, 313
Sukarno 284–285
Suleyman I the Magnificent 56,
207, **270**, *285*, **285–286**
Suleyman II 30
Sulla, Lucius Cornelius 34, 42,
200, 246–247, 251, **286–287**,
295–296
Sulpicianus, Titus Flavius 154
Sultania, Battle of 1
Sun King *see* Louis XIV
Sun Yat-sen 61, 185, 317
Suppiluliumas I 207, **287**
Supremacy, Second Act of (1559)
93
Susquehannock Indians 27
Suvorov, Aleksandr 48–49
Svoboda, Ludvik 224
Swaziland 84
Sweden 58–59, 64, 92, 94, 105,
117–118
Sweyn I 95
Sweyn II 122
Swiss Confederation 192
Syracuse (city state) 5, 10, 80, 85,
111, 252, 296
Syria
Ahmad ibn Tulun and 5–6
Assad as leader of 21–22
Baybars I as ruler of 32
Cyrus II the Great and 78
Demetrius I Soter as ruler of
82
Ghazan and 114
Leo III the Isaurian as ruler of
167–168
Muhammad Ali and 205
al-Muizz and 206
Mursilis I and 207
Napoléon I and 212
Nasser and 216–217
Nebuchadnezzar II and 217
Saladin as ruler of 266
Sargon II and 269

Sargon of Akkad and 269
Tamerlane and 289
Thutmose III and 293
Tiglath-pileser III and 295
Tigranes and 295

T

Tahmasp II 211
Taillebourg, Battle of the Bridge
of 176
Taiping Rebellion 144, 305
Taiwan 61–62
Takeda Shingen 288
Talfah, Khairallah 145
Tamar 81
Tamerlane 27, 32, **288–289**, 299
T'ang dynasty 16–17, 18, 157
Taoism 144, 198
Taraki, Noor Mohammed 16,
157, **289**
Tartars 32, 111–112, 115, 148, 149
taxation
under Akbar 7–8
under Canute IV 44
under Caracalla 45
under Charles I 54–55
under Charles III 56
under Cheng-te 61
under Christophe 65
under Erik VII 94
under Frederick William I 106
under George III 113–114
under Herod Archelaus 136
under John 151
under Justinian 155
under Kao Tsu 157
under Liu Pang 172
under Louis XI 176
under Louis XIV 177
under Mahdi 183
under Maria Theresa 189
under Manuel Montt 203
under Mussolini 208
under Nicephorous I 220
under Periander 232
under Philip IV the Fair 242
under Popé 248
under Richelieu 262
under Salazar 267
under Sforza 273
under Shapur II the Great 275
under Sixtus IV 277
under Solomon 278
under Solon 278–279
under Ssu-Ma Yen 280
under Stalin 282
under Vespasian 310
under Wei Chung-hsien 313
under Wen Ti 313
under William II Rufus 315
under Wu Ti 317
Taylor, Charles 86
tea 248
Tehran Conference 282
Teng Ying-ch'ao 63
Terek, Battle of 288
Teutonic Knights 46
Tewkesbury, Battle of 132
Tewodros II 197
Texas 268
Thailand 160–161, 239
Thanarat, Sarit 160–161

Thani, Shaykh Khalifa ibn Hamad al- 289
Tharawaddy 289–290
Thebes 6, 137, 251, 257
Themistocles 290
Theodora 290–291
Theodoric I the Great 25, **291**
Theodorus 246
Theodosius I the Great 8, **291–292**
Theodosius II 24
Theodosius III 167
Theodulf 53
Thermopylae (Greek city) 24
Theron 111
Theseus 65
Thessalian League 240
Thessalonica 252
Thieu, Nguyen Van see Nguyen Van Thieu
Third Coalition 11
Third Republic 215
Third Revolution 61
Thirty, Tyranny of 180
Thirty Years' War (1618–48) 64, 106, 117, 177, 262
Thousand and One Nights, The (book) 124
Thrace (city-state) 8, 10, 28, 31, 71, 79, 81, 167–168, 194, 206, 240, 291, 309–310
Thrasybulus 233
Three Emperors, League of the 100
Thucydides 234
Thuringia 69, 126
Thutmose I 125, **292**
Thutmose II 125, **292–293**, 293
Thutmose III 7, 125, 292, **293**
Tiananmen Square Massacre 82–83
Tiberius 26, 43, 136, **293–294**
Tiberius II 28
T'ien-chi 312
Tientsin, Battle of 317
Tigellinus 218
Tiglath-pileser I 294–295
Tiglath-pileser III 269, **295**
Tigranes 199, **295–296**
Tigranocerta, Battle of 295
Tilly, Johann 118
Tilsit, Treaty of 214
Time of Troubles 115, 276
Timoleon 296
Tinchebrai, Battle of 126
Tirel, Walter 316
Tissaphernes 80
Tisza, István 296
Tito 143, **296–298**
Titus 87, 298, 310
Tizoc (Aztec King) 7
Tlacaelel 201
tobacco 248
Tojo Hideki 298–299
Tokhtamysh 84, **299**
Tokimasa 141
Tokugawa Ieyasu 299–300
Tolbert Jr., William R. 85–86
Tontons Macoutes 88–89, 280
Tordesillas, Treaty of 15
Toros de Guisando, Accord of 147
Torquemada, Tomás de 300

Torrijos (Herrera), Omar 223, **300–301**
torture
    under Agha Mohammad Khan 5
    under Idi Amin 16
    under Assad 22
    under Cheng-te 61
    under Harald IV Gille 122
    under Ivan IV the Terrible 148–149
    under Julian the Apostate 154
    under Kieft 160
    under Carlos Antonio López 173
    under Mariam 189
    under Pinochet 244
    under Stambolov 282
    under Torquemada 300
    under Vlad the Impaler 311
    under Wei Chung-hsien 313
Tossila III 53
Touré, Sekou 301
Toussaint L'Ouverture, François Dominique 64–65, **301–302**
Toyotomi Hideyoshi 225, 299–300, **302–303**
Trafalgar, Battle of 214
Trajan 119, *303*, **303–304**
Transoxiana 299
Transylvania 311
Travendal, Treaty of 58
treason 87, 104, 219, 253–254, 281, 290, 294
Trebizond 202
Trent, Council of 244–245
Triennial Act 55
Triple Alliance 316
Triple Entente 316
Triumvirate, First 42
Trotsky, Leon 166–167, 281, 307
Troyes, Treaty of 131
Trujillo Molina, Rafael Léonidas 304
Tsankov, Alexander 38–39
Ts'ao P'i 304
Ts'ao Ts'ao 304–305
Tshombe, Moise (-Kapenda) 200, **305**
Tuan Ch'i-jui 320
Tughluq, Sultan Mahmud 288
Tukhachevski, Mikhail N. 243
Tulunid dynasty 5–6
T'ung-chih 305
Tunis 30
Tunisia 206
Turcus, Barcanes 168, 220
Turgot, Jacques 178
Turkey 23–24, 221
Turks see also Ottoman Empire
    Barbarossa and 29–30
    Charles XII and 59
    Leopold I and 170
    Nadir Shah and 211
    Vlad the Impaler and 311
Tutankhamon 8, 142
26th of July Movement 47
Tyler, Wat 260
Tyranny of Thirty 180
Tzarevlatz, Battle of 79
Tz'u-hsi 305–306

U
Uccialli, Treaty of 197
Uganda 16
Ukraine 94, 243
Ulbricht, Walter 307
Union of Soviet Socialist Republics (USSR)
    foreign leaders and
        Ahmed 6
        Amin 16
        Antonescu 17–18
        Assad 21–22
        Bishop 36
        Bose 39
        Castro 47–48
        Ceausescu 51
        Chervenkov 61
        Chiang Kai-shek 61
        Chou En-lai 63
        Coard 69
        Deng Xiaoping 82–83
        Hitler 139
        Ho Chi Minh 140
        Hoxha 143–144
        Husák 145
        Jaruzelski 150
        Karmal 157–158
        Kim Il Sung 160
        Kun 162
        Mao 186
        Mariam and 189–190
        Nasser 216–217
        Pats 230
        Taraki 289
        Tito 296–298
        Ulbricht 307
        Zhivkov 322
    leaders
        Brezhnev 40–41
        Lenin 165–167
        Stalin, Josef 280–282
United Arab Republic 216–217
United Fruit Company 46
United Gold Coast Convention (UGCC) 222
United Nations 18, 34–35, 101, 145, 160, 216, 258, 277, 283, 305
United Nations resolution 242 18
United States of America
    and Africa 16, 86
    and Asia 62, 64, 140, 158, 164–165, 187, 188, 219–220, 257–258
    and Bolivia 217
    as Bonaparte asylum 38
    and Chile 244
    in colonial times 27–28
    and Cuba 32, 47–48, 183
    and the Dominican Republic 137
    and Grenada 36, 69
    and Guatemala 46–47, 197
    and Haiti 88–89
    and Hawaii 171
    and Mexico 74, 144, 268
    and the Middle East 216–217, 229
    and Nicaragua 226–227, 312
    and Panama 223–224, 300–301
    and Paraguay 283
    and the Soviet Union 40–41
    and Spain 101
Unstrut River, Battle of the 127

Urban IV, Pope 67
Ursus Servianus, L. Julius 119
Utes 248
Utraquist Party 113
Utrecht, Peace of 193
Utus, Battle of 24
Uxbridge, Treaty of 75
Uzbeks 1

V
Vaillant-Couturier, Paul 143
Val-aux-Dunes, Battle of 125, 314
Valdejunquera, Battle of 3
Valens 291–292
Valentinian II 292
Valentinian III 25, 108
Valerian 109, 275, **308**
Valverde, Friar Vicente de 22–23
Vandals 9, 25, 108, 155
Van Twiller, Wouter 159
Varaville, Battle of 126, 314
Vasquez, Horacio 304
Vassili of Moscow 299
Velasco, José Miguel 29
Velasco Ibarra, José Maria 308
Velázquez de Cuellar, Diego de 73
Venezuela 284
Venice 202
Venizelos, Eleutherios 198
Ver, Fabian 188
Vercingetorix 308–309
Verdun, Treaty of 174
Verona 95–96
Verona, Battle of 34, 81
Verrocchio 195
Versailles, Palace of 178
Versailles, Treaty of 138
Versinikia, Battle of 168
Vervins, Treaty of 130
Vespasian 87, 298, *309*, **309–310**
Vesuvius, Mount 298
Vichy government 235–236
Victor Emmanuel III 208
Victoria I 52, 171, 316
Vienna, Congress of 11, 215
Viet Cong 140, 158
Viet Minh 140, 158
Vietnam 87–88, 140, 158–159, 198–199, 219–220, 238–239, 246
Villa, Pancho 84, 144
Villarroel López, Gualberto 30
Villeda Morales, Ramón 173
Viminacium, Battle of 29
Vindex, Julius 219
Viola, Roberto 109
Virgil 26
Visconti, Filippo Maria 100, 272
Visconti, Gian Galeazzo 310
Vishnu 35
Visigoths 8–9, 25, 69, 291, 292
Vladimir II Monomakh 311
Vladislav II 191
Vlad the Impaler 310–311
volcanoes 298
Von Hindenberg, Paul 139, 316
voodoo 88–89, 280
Vytautas of Lithuania 299

W
Wagner, Richard 180

Wagram, Battle of 214
Wakefield, Battle of 261
Walachians 206
Wales 90, 131, 310, 315
Walesa, Lech 150
Walker, William 74, **312**
Wallachia 310–311
Wallenstein, Albrecht von 99, 118
Wallingford, Battle of 127
Wang Mang 161
Warbeck, Perkin 132
War of Devolution (1667-68) 178
War of the Reform (1858-61) 83, 199
Warsaw, Battle of 243
Warsaw Pact 51, 144
Wars of Religion 4, 129
Wars of the Fronde 177
Wars of the Roses 91, 132, 261
Washington, George 66
Waterloo, Battle of 215
Wei Chung-hsien 312–313
Wei dynasty 304–305
Welfs 102
Welles, Sumner 183
Wellington, Duke of 215
Wels, Battle of 227
Wenceslas, Saint 37, 127
Wen Ti 313
Wentworth, Thomas 164
West India Company 64
Westphalia 213
Weyler y Nicolau, Valeriano 313–314
What Is To Be Done? (pamphlet) 166
White Mountain, Battle of 99
Widukind 53
Wilcox, Robert 171
Wilde, Oscar 135

William I the Conqueror 44, 112, 123, 125–126, *314*, **314–315**
William I of Sicily 315
William II Rufus (England) 126, **315–316**
William (Wilhelm) II (Germany) 101, 221, 243, **316**
Wilson, Woodrow 144
Windsor Castle (England) 91
witchcraft 317
Wittelsbach family 174
Wolsey, Cardinal 133
women
 Berenice II 34
 Berenice III 34
 Catherine de' Medici 49–50
 Catherine II the Great 48–49
 Cleopatra VII 67–68
 Elizabeth (Russia) 92
 Elizabeth I 92–93
 Hatshepsut 125
 Hojo Masako 140–141
 Isabella I 147
 Liliuokalani and 171–172
 Maria Theresa 188–189
 Mary I 190
 Theodora 290–291
 Tz'u-hsi 305–306
Wood, Leonard 164–165
Worcester, Battle of 164
Workman (newspaper) 243
World War I 11, 23–24, 97, 100–101, 138, 142, 162, 166, 198, 208, 243–244, 298, 316
World War II
 in Asia and the Pacific
  Chiang Kai-shek and 62
  Chou En-lai and 63
  Deng Xiaoping and 82–83
  Kim Il Sung and 160
  Laurel and 164–165
  Marcos and 187

Park and 229
 Phibunsongkhram and 239
 Suharto and 284
 Sukarno and 285
 Tojo and 298–299
 in Europe
  Antonescu and 17–18
  Boris III and 38–39
  Franco and 101
  Hitler and 139–140
  Horthy and 143
  Mussolini and 208–209
  Pétain and 235–236
  Quisling and 253–254
  Stalin and 280–282
  Tito and 297
  Ulbricht and 307
  Zhivkov and 322
Wu P'ie-fu 317, 320
Wu Ti 317
Wu Wang 317–318
Wyatt, Sir Thomas 190

X

Xanadu 161
Xanten, Battle of 227
Xenophon 78
Xerxes I 319
Xoxe, Koci 143

Y

Yalta Conference 282
Yang K'ai-hui 186
Yang Ti 313
Yarmuk, Battle of 135
Yaroslav I the Wise 122
Yazdegerd II 320
Yellow River, Battle of 112
Yellow Turban Rebellion 304
Yen dynasty *see* Great Yen dynasty

Yen Hsi-shan 320–321
Yesukai the Strong 111
Yohannes IV 197
Yom Kippur War 21, 204
Yorktown (Virginia) 28
Yoshinobu Tokugawa 196
Young Turk Movement 3, 4, 23–24, 184–185
Yuan Shao 304
Yuan Shih-k'ai 61, 320
Yugoslavia 11–12, 139, 143–144, 296–298
Yung Lo 321
Yusupov, Prince Felix 257

Z

Zaire 200
Zambia 258–259
Zapata, Emiliano 144
Zapotocky, Antonin 224
Zelaya, José Santos 322
Zemstvo Law 12
Zeno 291
Z Force 255
Zhao Ziyang 83
Zhivkov, Todor 322
Zhou Enlai 83
Zhukov, Georgi 282
Zia (Zia-ul-Haq), Mohammad 35, **322–323**
ziggurat 217
Zimbabwe 277
Zimrilim of Mari 121
Zinoviev, Grigory 281
Zoroastrianism 18–19, 156, 275, 320
Zulova Pigeon, The (tract) 243
Zulpich, Battle of 68
Zululand 51–52
Zuluoga, Félix 199
Zulus 84, 204, 273–274